COMMUNICATION ACTIVISM

Volume 3
Struggling for Social Justice Amidst Difference

Edited by

Lawrence R. Frey
University of Colorado Boulder

Kevin M. Carragee
Suffolk University

**HAMPTON PRESS, INC.
NEW YORK, NEW YORK**

Copyright © 2012 by Hampton Press, Inc.

All rights reserved. No part of this publication may be reproduced, stored in a retrieval system, or transmitted in any form or by any means, electronic, mechanical, photocopying, microfilming, recording, or otherwise, without permission of the publisher.

Printed in the United States of America

Library of Congress Cataloging-in-Publication Data

The Library of Congress has catalogued the combined volumes as follows:

Communication activism / edited by Lawrence R. Frey, Kevin M. Carragee/
   v. cm.
  Includes bibliographical references and index.
1. Communication in social action. 2. Communication--Social aspects. 3. Communication--political aspects. I. Frey, Lawrence R. II. Carragee, Kevin M.
  HM1206.C6475 2007
  361.201'4--dc22

                      2006035764

Cover photo by Ken Martin

Hampton Press, Inc.
307 Seventh Avenue
New York, NY 10001

CONTENTS

Introduction: Communication Activism for Social Justice Scholarship ... 1
   Kevin M. Carragee & Lawrence R. Frey

1 Opening Communication Pathways in Protracted Conflict: From Tragedy to Dialogue in Cyprus ... 69
   Benjamin J. Broome, Harry Anastasiou, Maria Hajipavlou & Bülent Kanol

2 Negotiating Dialectical Tensions in Communication Activism: A Decade of Working in the Countertrafficking Field ... 105
   Christopher Carey

3 Staging Sudanese Refugee Narratives and the Legacy of Genocide: A Performance-Based Intervention Strategy ... 139
   Linda Welker

4 Challenging Domestic Violence: Trickle-Up Theorizing About Participation and Power in Communication Activism ... 179
   Charlotte Ryan & Karen Jeffreys

5 Food Fights: Reclaiming Public Relations and Reframing a Runaway Food System through a Grassroots Movement ... 223
   Jeanette L. Drake

6 Saving Kenneth Foster: Speaking *with* Others in the Belly of the Beast of Capital Punishment ... 263
   Jennifer Asenas, Bryan J. McCann, Kathleen Feyh & Dana Cloud

7	Disrupting Whiteness at a Firehouse: Promoting Organizational Change through Relational Praxis *Chris Groscurth*	291
8	Activating Ethical Engagement through Communication in Organizations: Negotiating Ethical Tensions and Practices in a Business Ethics Initiative *Steve K. May*	325
9	Organizing for Social Change: Communicative Empowerment for Small Business Development and Job Training for People Who Are Poor *Wendy H. Papa, Michael J. Papa & Rick A. Buerkel*	367
10	Using Participatory Research to Address Substance Abuse in an American-Indian Community *Lorenda Belone, John G. Oetzel, Nina Wallerstein, Greg Tafoya, Rebecca Rae, Alvin Rafelito, Lula Kelhoyouma, Ira Burbank, Carolyn Finster, Jennifer Henio-Charley, Phoebe G. Maria, Yin-Mae Lee & Anderson Thomas*	401

About the Editors and Authors	433
Index	443

INTRODUCTION

Communication Activism for Social Justice Scholarship[1]

Kevin M. Carragee
Suffolk University
Lawrence R. Frey
University of Colorado Boulder

There certainly is no shortage of controversial issues confronting contemporary U.S. society. Consider, the following, for instance:

- the wars in Afghanistan and Iraq, with, as of May 10, 2011, 1,571 U.S. soldiers killed in Afghanistan (Iraq Coalition Casualty Count, 2011a) and 4,452 in Iraq (Iraq Coalition Casualty Count, 2011b), 32,049 U.S. soldiers wounded in Iraq (Iraq Coalition Casualty Count, 2011c), and 100,497 to 109,794 civilian deaths from the violence in Iraq (Iraq body Count, 2011);

- the number of people in the United States (46.3 million, 14.3%) living in poverty, the largest number in the 51 years of estimating poverty rates (DeNavas-Walt, Proctor, & Smith, 2010)
- the concerns raised about the continued use of capital punishment, with, since 1973, 138 people from 26 states being released from death row because of evidence of factual innocence (Death Penalty Information Center, n.d.), with each execution costing taxpayers (once all factors are considered) $30 million, and in some states, such as California, as high as $250 million (Dieter, 2009);
- the contested issue of gay marriage, with a federal discriminatory law, the Defense of Marriage Act, that defines marriage as a legal union exclusively between a man and a woman, and 40 states prohibiting same-sex marriage via state statutes or constitutions; and
- the heated debates about immigration, with a recent law voted on in Arizona (but as of April 11, 2011, a federal appeals court refusing to lift a stay blocking major parts of it) that makes it a crime not to carry immigration documents and gives police broad power to detain anyone suspected of being in the country illegally, a law that is an "open invitation for harassment and discrimination against Hispanics regardless of their citizenship status" and that President Barak Obama said threatened "to undermine basic notions of fairness that we cherish as Americans" (Archibald, 2010, para. 6, 5).

As this short list demonstrates (and, unfortunately, this is just the beginning of a very long list), there is no shortage of social issues and problems that confront us and that desperately need attention.

One might think that members of the academy would be at the forefront of confronting these and other important social issues. After all, many U.S. colleges and universities were established with, as part of their mission, generating knowledge to better their communities (see, e.g., C. W. Anderson, 1993; Barber, 1992; Checkoway, 2001; Kennedy, 1997). Unfortunately, over the years, higher educational institutions tended to abandon this civic mission (see, e.g., Boyer, 1990; Butler, 2000; Sandmann & Gillespie, 1991; Sirianni & Friedland, 1997) in favor of research directed toward a relatively small, insular group of fellow scholars, with an estimated 50,000 active scholarly journals (Tenopir, 2004a) that have a low number of readers (e.g., social scientists read an average of 191 articles per year; Tenopir, 2004b). This focus on research directed toward other scholars rather than toward helping communities to solve social problems probably was related to the privileging of "theory" over "application" in the academy, for if one follows the etymology of the word *theory*, derived from the Greek words *theoria* ("contemplation, speculation, a looking at, things looked at"), *theorein* ("to consider, speculate, look at"), *theoros* ("spectator"), and *thea* ("a view"; Online Etymology Dictionary, 2011), scholars are supposed to be spectators whose work is best done by looking at and contemplating what occurs without trying to affect it.

One might think that communication scholars, in particular, would be confronting societal issues. After all, communication inherently is a "practical discipline" (Craig, 1989, 1995) concerned with cultivating communicative *praxis* that yields useful knowledge. The historical roots of the formal discipline of communication (with the study of communication dating back at least to antiquity) were grounded in producing useful knowledge, such as teaching people to be better speakers in their everyday interactions and in the public sphere (e.g., W. H. Davis, 1915, on debating as related to nonacademic life), and to use effective communicative practices (e.g., Dewey's, 1910, reflective thinking process) for democratic group decision making (see, e.g., A. C. Baird, 1927; Elliott, 1927; Sheffield, 1926), as well as mass communication research directed toward understanding and improving media practices and people's ability to process mediated messages (e.g., not being easily persuaded by propaganda; for historical overviews of such research, see, e.g., Delia, 1987; Rogers, 1994; Schramm, 1997). Unfortunately, over time, communication scholars, like their counterparts in the social sciences and humanities, and perhaps, in part, because of their desire to obtain disciplinary legitimacy from those colleagues, all too frequently shied away from addressing important societal issues to focus, instead, on disciplinary concerns.

This failure to confront salient social issues is unfortunate, for given the sheer volume and significance of the issues and the potential contributions that communication knowledge can make to managing them, the exigency for communication scholars to engage in direct vigorous action in support of needed social change has never been more apparent and important. In short, communication scholars need to engage in "communication activism scholarship."

ACTIVISM AND SCHOLARSHIP

> Ac·tiv·ism: A doctrine or practice that emphasizes direct vigorous action especially in support of or opposition to one side of a controversial issue
> —Merriam-Webster Online (2011)

"Activism" has a long and distinguished history (see, e.g., Downs & Manion, 2004; Eno, 1920; T. V. Reed, 2005; Santiago, 1972; Valocchi, 2009;

Wigginton, 1991).[2] Literally thousands of books have been written about activism theory and practice (e.g., G. L. Anderson & Hess, 2007; Boggs, 2011; W. Clark, 2000; Falconer, 2001; S. Kahn, 2010; Maddison & Scalmer, 2006; McEvoy & McGregor, 2008; Shah, 2005; Shragge, 2003; Weissberg, 2005); activism art and performance (e.g., Afary, 2009; da Costa & Philip, 2008; Gómez-Peña, 2005; O. O. J. L. Jones, Moore, & Bridgforth, 2010; Moreno, 2007; Platt, 2011; Raunig, 2007; Rimmerman, 2010); and activist individuals (e.g., Avakian, 2000; DeLeon, 1994), groups/communities (e.g., Zake, 2009), governments (e.g., Newman & Jacobs, 2010), and networks (e.g., Ferree & Tripp, 2006; M. E. Keck & Sikkink, 1998; Still, 2008). Activism has been studied on every continent in the world, with the exception of Antarctica,[3] as well as across countries and/or global/transnational activism (e.g., Chandler, Wang, & Fuller, 2009; Davies, 2007; de Jong, Shaw, & Stammers, 2005; Graubart, 2008; Icaza, 2010; Joachim & Locher, 2008; Okafor, 2007; T. Olesen, 2011; Piper & Uhlin, 2004; Reitan, 2007; Reydams, 2011; Roces & Edwards, 2010; Seidman, 2007; Singh, 2009). Many specific contexts and forms of activism also have been studied,[4] as have particular times and places where activism flourished and was especially important (e.g., L. M. Alexander, 2008; Brodkin, 2007; Clavel, 2010; Donovan, 2006; J. M. Johnson, 2008; Klimke & Scharloth, 2008; Patterson, 2008; Pulido, 2006; Rael, 2008; Riser, 2010; M. C. Sanchez, 2009; Senker, 2011; Stole, 2006; Thompson, 2010).

Only recently, however, has the concept of "activism" been associated with "scholarship" or "research" (or "academic," "the academy," and "higher education," more generally), with a critical mass of scholars from virtually every discipline in the humanities, physical sciences, and social sciences now putting those terms together (see, e.g., Adler, 2002; Apple, 2009, 2010; Askins, 2009; Authers, Groeneveld, Jackson, Mündel, & Stewart, 2007; The Autonomous Geographies Collective, 2010; Barrett, 2007; Bart et al., 1999; Bérubé, 1997; Blomley, 1994; Boris, 1998; Cancian, 1993, 1996; S. J. Carroll, 2005; Chatterton, 2008; D. E. Collins, 2005; Crosby, Todd, & Worrell, 1996; Croteau, Hoynes, & Ryan, 2005; E. Cushman, 1999; Divinski, Hubbard, Kendrick, & Noll, 2009; Dolan, 1997; Dozier & Lauzen, 2000; D'Souza, 2009; Fine, 1989; Fine, & Vanderslice, 1992; Formwalt, 2007; Gates & Marable, 2000; George, 2005; Goodley & Moore, 2000; Grabill, 2000; Grewall, 2008; Hale, 2001, 2006, 2008; Hammett & Newsham, 2006; Harper, Jamil, & Wilson, 2007; Hay, 2001; Herman, 2005–2006; Herring, 2006, 2008; Hondagneu-Sotelo, 1993; Kershaw, 2003; M. G. Knight, 2000; Ladson-Billings & Donner, 2005; Ladwig & Gore, 1994; Lemisch, 2003; Lempert, 2001; Maigushca & Thornton, 2006; R. Martin, 2009; Martinez-Saenz, 2009; Maxey, 1999; McIntyre, 2006; Messer-Davidow, 2002; Muller, 1969; Munger, 2001; Nagengast & Vélez-Ibáñez, 2004; Naples, 2003; Naples & Steck, 2004; Napoli & Aslama, 2011; Nelson, 2009; Nelson & Watt, 2004; Nichter, 2006;

Nygreen, 2006; Ollman, 1993; Orta, 2008; R. Reed, 2009; Reidner & O'Conner, 1999; Rodriguez, 1996; Sanford, 2009; Schneider, 2003; Seliktar, 2005; Senn, 2005; Silliman & Bhattacharjee, 1999; A. Smith, 2007; Spalter-Roth & Hartmann, 1996; Speed, 2008; Storey, 2005; Strossen, 2005–2006; Sudbury & Okazawa-Rey, 2009; Townes, 2009; Turbin, 1996; Urrieta & Méndez Benavídez, 2007; VanderPlaat, 1999; S. Ward, 2001; Warwick & Auchmuty, 1995; Weber, 2006; Woodhouse, Hess, Breyman, & Martin, 2002; Zamarrón, 2009; Zerai, 2002; Zine, 2004; there even is a listserv devoted to it: https://lists.riseup.net/www/info/activistscholarship). Such scholarship emerges from the recent emphasis on "engaged (civic, community-based, or public) scholarship" (see, e.g., Barker, 2004; Boyer, 1990, 1996; Diener, & Liese, 2009; Fitzgerald, Burack, & Seifer, 2010; Gebissa, 2009; Kecskes, 2006; Van de Ven, 2007; Van de Ven & Zlotkowski, 2005), in which researchers collaborate with community partners to address pressing problems, which is an outgrowth of "applied scholarship" directed toward studying real-world issues. (The U.S. Library of Congress lists the first book published on "applied" as Braddock, 1833; contemporary views of such scholarship can be traced to Lazarsfeld's sociological research during the 1940s and his creation in 1944 of the Bureau of Applied Social Research at Columbia University; see, e.g., Delia, 1987; Rogers, 1994; Schramm, 1997.)

COMMUNICATION ACTIVISM FOR SOCIAL JUSTICE SCHOLARSHIP

To that growing literature on activism scholarship, we (Frey & Carragee, 2007) added the concept of "communication activism scholarship" (see also the communication activism approaches advanced by Broome, Carey, De La Garza, Martin, & Morris, 2005; Frey, 2006; essays in S. Kahn & Lee, 2011; Yep, 2008). That concept has a number of historical roots and important characteristics.

One historical root of communication activism scholarship is rhetorical studies, especially during the turbulent decade of the 1960s, that examined the communicative practices of social protest by activist individuals, groups, organizations, and movements (see, e.g., Andrews, 1969; J. E. Baird, 1970; Benson & Johnson, 1968; Bowen, 1963a, 1963b, 1967; Fernandez, 1968; Gregg, 1971; Haiman, 1967; Kerr, 1959; Kosokoff & Carlmichael, 1970; Lawton, 1968; Lomas, 1960, 1963; H. H. Martin, 1966; McEdwards, 1968; Rude, 1969; Scott & Smith, 1969; D. H. Smith, 1967; Toch, Deutsch, & Wilkins, 1960; Yoder, 1969). Such historical and contemporary analyses of activist communicative practices are alive and well today (e.g., Chvasta, 2006; DeLuca & Peeples, 2002; Endres, 2011; Grano, 2002; Hung, 2003; Kim

& Dutta, 2009; G. Knight & Greenberg, 2002; Kowal, 2000; McChesney, 2004; McGee, 2003; McHale, 2004; Napoli, 2009; Peeples, 2003; Pezzullo, 2001, 2003; Reber & Berger, 2005; J. Sanchez & Stuckey, 2000; Sender, 2001; Shi, 2005; Sowards & Renegar, 2004, 2006; Stevens, 2006; Stevens & Malesh, 2009; Stokes & Rubin, 2010; Theodore, 2002; Tracy, 2007; Weaver, 2010; West & Gastil, 2004). Many contemporary studies focus on media activism (see Huesca, 2008), such as activists' use of media (including "cyberactivism" on the internet) and efforts by social movement groups and organizations to influence news media coverage of societal issues (e.g., Atkinson, 2008, 2009; Atkinson & Dougherty, 2006; Banks, 2010; Bennett, 2003; Bob, 2005; Bradley, 2006; Bresnahan, 2007; Bullert, 2000; W. K. Carroll & Hackett, 2006; J. M. Chan & Lee, 2007; Coopman, 2000; de Jong et al., 2005; Diani, 2000; Diasio, 2010; Dichter, 2004; Dunbar-Hester, 2009, 2010; Earl & Kimport, 2011; Eaton, 2010; Francesco, 2010; Gan, Gomez, & Johannen, 2004; Garrett, 2006; D. C. Gibson, 2003; Gillan, 2009; Gillett, 2003; Gray, 2009; Greenberg & Knight, 2004; Gregory, Caldwell, Avni, & Harding, 2005; Hájek & Kabele, 2010; Harold, 2004; Joyce, 2010; R. Kahn & Kellner, 2004; Lee, 2008; Lievrouw, 2011; Mahrouse, 2009; McCaughey & Ayers, 2003; Meikle, 2002; Murray, Parry, Robinson, & Goddard, 2008; Nah, Veenstra, & Shah, 2006; Norman, 2009; Opel, 2004; Palczewski, 2001; Palmeri, 2006; P. Phillips & Project Censored, 2003; Pickerill, 2003; Pini, Brown, & Previte, 2004; Ryan, 1991; Ryan, Carragee, & Meinhofer, 2001; Ryan, Carragee, & Schwerner, 1998; Seo, Kim, & Yang, 2009; Slaughter, 2008; Stengrim, 2005; Thorson, Ekdale, Borah, Namkoong, & Shah, 2010; Van Alest & Walgrave, 2002; Van de Donk, Loader, Nixon, & Rucht, 2004; Zoch, Collins, Sisco, & Supa, 2008).

These studies of activists' communicative practices are part of a second historical root of communication activism scholarship in *applied communication scholarship*, "the development of knowledge regarding a real human communication problem or question" (Cissna, 1982, p. ii). An applied view of communication scholarship grew out of the 1968 New Orleans Conference on Research and Instructional Development, which encouraged research on the communication dimensions of current social problems (see Kibler & Barker, 1969, especially the essay in that text by Cronkhite, 1969). Five years later, in 1973, the *Journal of Applied Communications Research* was created (see Hickson, 1973), which subsequently became the *Journal of Applied Communication Research*, and now is sponsored (along with an Applied Communication Division) by the National Communication Association (for a historical overview of applied communication scholarship, see Cissna, Eadie, & Hickson, 2009). Although applied communication research, as compared with *basic communication research* (designed to test communication theory), certainly was a hotly contested issue for many years (for an overview of intellectual debates about applied communication scholarship, see Frey & SunWolf, 2009), today, applied scholarship is an integral part of the communication discipline (see, e.g., Frey & Cissna, 2009; Seibold, 2008).

Although rhetorical and applied communication studies have contributed substantially to understanding communicative practices of activist individuals, groups, and organizations, most of that scholarship constitutes *third-person-perspective studies*, in which researchers study individuals, groups, and organizations engaging in activism. Third-person-perspective researchers, thus, stand outside the stream of human events and observe, describe, interpret, explain, and, in some approaches (e.g., rhetorical criticism and cultural studies), critique what occurs, as well as (in applied communication scholarship) offer suggestions for what could or should occur. These studies stand in sharp contrast to *first-person-perspective studies*, where researchers get in the stream and affect it in significantly positive ways. Communication activism scholars, thus, intervene into discourses and study the processes and outcomes of their interventions. In so doing, they strive to make a difference *through* research rather than *from* research by hoping that someone else will use the research to make a difference (see Frey, 2009).

The impetus for first-person-perspective studies came primarily from applied communication scholars. Frey (2000), for instance, argued that given the common dictionary definition of the term *applied* as meaning "to put into practice," the most pressing question facing applied communication scholars was not whether to put communication into practice (which is what is done in a "practical discipline" such as communication) or what to put into practice (communication knowledge and skills), but *who* should put communication into practice. As Frey (2000) argued:

> We should start from the premise that in research, "to put into practice" applies to researchers, as opposed to simply anyone who puts communication into practice (e.g., the research participants studied). Accordingly *applied communication scholarship* might be defined as "the study of researchers putting their communication knowledge and skills into practice." (p. 179; for a critique of this position, see Seibold, 2000)

That position is fundamental to *engaged* communication scholarship (see, e.g., Applegate, 2002; Barge, Simpson, & Shockley-Zalaback, 2008; Cheney, Wilhelmsson, & Zorn, 2002; Harter, Dutta, & Cole, 2009; Krone & Harter, 2007; Simpson & Shockley-Zalabak, 2005).

Communication researchers, however, could intervene into discourses to accomplish a wide variety of goals, including making companies, such as BP (which posted profits of $26 billion in 2009; Monbiot, 2010), even wealthier. Indeed, an argument easily could be made that instead of there being too little engaged communication research, there is a significant amount, but that it serves powerful interests at the expense of those lacking power (see Frey, Pearce, Pollock, Artz, & Murphy, 1996), and, in so doing, this work perpetuates political and economic systems characterized by stark inequalities. For example, much of the research conducted in advertising, marketing, mediated communication, organizational communication, and public relations serves corporate and managerial interests. Carey (2002) placed this research in a historical context by noting the connections forged between universities and the political and economic establishment during World War II, connections that continue to endure. Consequently, considerable engaged communication scholarship comforts the comfortable and afflicts the afflicted.

Intervention, thus, is a necessary but not sufficient condition for communication activism scholarship; it must be coupled with the premise that researchers intervene into discourses to promote "social justice." Although social justice has a long and contested history (see, e.g., Mohapatra, 1999), from a communication perspective, *social justice* has been defined as "the engagement with and advocacy for those ... who are economically, socially, politically, and/or culturally underresourced" (Frey et al., 1996, p. 110; see also Hartnett, 2010; Kirby et al., 2009; Pearce, 1998; M. A. Pollock, Artz, Frey, Pearce, & Murphy, 1996; Swan, 2002; essays in Swartz, 2006; for critiques of this perspective, see Makau, 1996; Olson & Olson, 2003; Wood, 1996).

Communication activism for social justice scholars draw on the work of communication colleagues, especially in media studies, organizational communication, and rhetoric, who employ critical theory to not just understand or explain society but to critique and change it (see, e.g., the essays in Artz, Macek, & Cloud, 2006; Carey, 1982; Farrell & Aune, 1979; Hardt, 1986, 1989, 1992, 1993; Held, 1982; Huspek, 1991; D. Pollock & Cox, 1991; Real, 1984; Strine, 1991), and/or who have engaged cultural studies to analyze cultural practices in relation to social and political issues, such as gender, ideology, power, race, and social class (see, e.g., Artz & Murphy, 2000; Carey, 1983, 1989; Carlone & Taylor, 1998; Carragee, 1990; Carragee & Roefs, 2004; Davis, 1989; Grossberg, 1993a, 1993b, 1997; Grossberg, Nelson, & Treichler, 1992; Schwichtenberg & Davis, 1989). Rhetoricians working from these perspectives argued for "ideological criticism" (see, e.g., Rushing & Frentz, 1991; Wander, 1983, 1984; Wander & Jenkins, 1972), "critical rhetoric" (see, e.g., N. Clark, 1996; McGuire & Slembeck, 1987; McKerrow, 1989, 1991, 1993; Murphy, 1995; Ono & Sloop, 1992; Zompetti, 1997), and "partisan criticism" (Swartz, 2004, 2005)—forms of rhetorical theory and criticism that certainly represent an "activist" turn (see Andersen, 1993; see also E. Cushman, 1996; for critical responses to this rhetorical turn, see, e.g., Charland, 1991; Condit, 1993; S. Crowley, 1992; Hariman, 1991; Hill, 1983; Kuypers, 2000; McKerrow & St. John, 2006; Rosenfield, 1983). Organizational communication scholars who advocated these perspectives questioned the traditional privileging of management's interests and argued that research should root out normative systems of control and represent all stakeholders' voices, and, thereby, promote democracy in the workplace (see, e.g., Carlone & Taylor, 1998; Cheney, 1995; Deetz, 1982, 1988, 1992; Deetz & Mumby, 1990; Mumby, 1993).

Although critical theory and cultural studies communication perspectives have been very helpful, for the most part, that work has remained theoretical and abstract, with scholars writing about discourse rather than intervening into discourses (see, e.g., Cloud, 1994; Frey, 2006; Rakow, 2005). Communication activism for social justice scholarship, in contrast, goes beyond critique to conduct research that "identifies and foregrounds the grammars that oppress or underwrite relationships of domination and then *reconstructs* [emphasis added] those grammars" (Frey et al., 1996, p. 112). Frey et al. maintained that a "social justice sensibility" meant adopting, among other things, an activist orientation, claiming:

> It is not enough merely to demonstrate or bemoan the fact that some people lack the minimal necessities of life, that others are used regularly against their will and against their interest by others for their pleasure or profit, and that some are defined as "outside" the economic, political, or social system because of race, creed, lifestyle, or medical condition, or simply because they are in the way of someone else's project. A social justice sensibility entails a moral imperative to *act* as effectively as we can to do something about structurally sustained inequalities. To continue to pursue justice, it is perhaps necessary that we who act be personally ethical, but that is not sufficient. Our actions must engage and transform social structures. (p. 111)

Frey (1998a) subsequently edited a special issue of the *Journal of Applied Communication Research* on "Communication and Social Justice Research" that featured "original, empirically grounded case studies [by Artz, 1998; Crabtree, 1998; Hartnett, 1998; Ryan et al., 1998; Varallo, Ray, & Ellis, 1998] that demonstrated ways in which applied communication researchers have made a difference in the lives of those who are disadvantaged by prevalent social structures" (Frey, 1998b, p. 158). Subsequent communication studies by T. S. Jones and Bodtker (1998), Novek (2005), and Palmeri (2006) adopted this social justice perspective as well.

Finally, communication activism scholars have been aided in their social justice interventions by the articulation of research methods that promote "research as an empowering act, as a way of uniting people working for social change, disrupting restrictive ways of thinking, and transforming the social world" (Ristock & Pennell, 1996, p. 113; see also M. Fine, 2006; Sanford & Angel-Ajani, 2006; Swartz, 1997). Such methods include, among others, action (collaborative/community/participatory) research, critical ethnography, feminist methods, and performance ethnography.[5]

Communication activism for social justice scholarship, thus, emerges from a confluence of scholarly streams. Such scholarship is grounded in communication researchers taking direct vigorous action in support of or opposition to a controversial issue for the purpose of promoting social justice. This volume, along with the first two in this series, explores this significant form of scholarship by showcasing original studies of communication activism for social justice.

OVERVIEW OF THE BOOKS

For the first two volumes, designed originally as a single book, and for this volume, an open call was issued through various print and online sources seeking chapter proposals for original research studies that documented communication activism. All domains of communication scholarship (e.g., interpersonal, group, organizational, and media studies), theoretical perspectives (e.g., critical, interpretive, and positivistic/postpositivistic), and methodological approaches (e.g., qualitative, quantitative, and rhetorical) were welcome, as long as the proposed chapter focused on an intervention conducted by the *researcher* (as opposed to someone else) to assist people in securing social reform. Thus, we sought to showcase original studies of how communication scholars have employed their resources (e.g., theories, methods, pedagogies, and other practices) to promote social change, especially in assisting marginalized individuals, groups, organizations, and communities to secure social justice.

Because of the large number of high-quality proposals we received in response to the first call, we asked Barbara Bernstein at Hampton Press to produce a two-volume set, and she immediately agreed. Moreover, because of the excellent response to the first two volumes (see, e.g., Artz, 2007; Harold, 2008; Jansen, 2008; Pezullo, 2009; Wagstaff, 2009), Barbara encouraged us to pursue this third volume (as well as a book on communication activism pedagogy; Frey & Palmer, in press). We thank Barbara for her tremendous support for what now has become a de facto series. We also thank Ken Martin for allowing his photographs to be used for the book covers, as well as Jane Callahan and Fran Penner for their initial subject index to the second volume.

We especially thank the contributors to these books for their excellent chapters (and for their receptivity to our seemingly endless editing suggestions). In constructing chapters, we asked authors to address the following four important areas:

Introduction

1. Thoroughly explain the situation, problem/issue, and activities comprising their communication activism.
2. To the extent possible, situate the analysis of their communication activism within relevant theory, research, and practice.
3. Reflect on dialectical tensions and paradoxes they experienced in their communication activism scholarship.
4. Share salient lessons learned about communication activism scholarship that might benefit others who either are engaged in or wish to engage in this type of research.

In what follows, we provide a brief overview of the first two volumes and then focus on the chapters in this volume.

Volume 1, subtitled *Communication for Social Change*, focused on two broad types of communication activism: (a) promoting public dialogue, debate, and discussion; and (b) communication consulting for social change. Volume 2, subtitled *Media and Performance Activism*, focused on those two forms of activism. The studies in those volumes explored activism related to a wide range of important issues and concerns, including activism against capital punishment, domestic violence, globalization, racism, sexism, and sexual assault.

This third volume continues to showcase original studies of communication activism. In addition to meeting the goals of the previous volumes (e.g., describing the situation, and situating the analysis within relevant theory, research, and practice), because of the salience of *difference* (e.g., between researchers and community members, researchers and activists, and among community members) as a central component of these communication activism endeavors, authors also reflect on how they and their community partners struggled to promote social justice amidst important differences.

The first three chapters have an international focus, although they differ in the issues that the communication scholar-activists involved examine and in the conceptual and theoretical perspectives employed. Chapter 1 documents communication peacebuilding efforts in Cyprus; Chapter 2 explores the fight against human trafficking in South Asia, and Chapter 3, although based in the United States, explores the use of performance activism to highlight the genocide occurring in South Sudan.

In Chapter 1, Benjamin J. Broome, Harry Anasasiou, Maria Hadjipavlou, and Bülent Kanol discuss their long-term and ongoing communication initiatives to overcome historical tensions between Greek and Turkish Cypriots through bicommunal dialogue. The particular intervention described took place after a violent confrontation in 1996 between Greek and Turkish Cypriots in the United Nation's (UN's) buffer zone that divides the island. The violence inflamed divisions between the two communities, produced harsh ethnocentric rhetoric from both sides, and threatened to reverse earlier gains obtained through bicommunal dialogue facilitated previously by this team of scholars. Within this deeply troubled context, Broome et al. successfully reestablished common ground between Greek and Turkish Cypriots by conducting meetings that brought together representatives from the two communities, with dozens of dialogue and project groups formed in 1996 and 1997. In facilitating these groups and in connecting Greek and Turkish Cypriot students, many of them for the first time, the authors enlisted the support of the international diplomatic community, including representatives from the UN, Great Britain, the European Union, and the United States. In analyzing this communication activism, Broome et al. explain how two central theoretical approaches—perspectives on dialogue and Lederarch's (1995, 1997) theory of transformative peacebuilding—shaped their work in Cyprus. They conclude the chapter by underscoring the significance of peacebuilding groups within civil society and by highlighting how communication scholar-activists can contribute to building peace in areas affected by protracted conflicts.

Christopher Carey begins Chapter 2 by explaining the scope and severity of human trafficking, with an estimated 12.3 million people living in forced labor around the world (U.S. Department of State, 2010), including millions of children. Carey then carefully documents his work with The Daywalka Foundation, which he helped to form in 2002 and served as its executive director until 2007, to foster collaboration among multiple stakeholders in South Asia's countertrafficking efforts. Much of the chapter examines difficulties and tensions in forging connections between people and groups with diverse ethnic and cultural experiences and values. On a conceptual level, Carey provides a compelling critique of various approaches to international development, especially their failure to focus on local knowledge, empowerment, and capacity building. Similar to Broome et al.'s work in Cyprus, Carey employs perspectives on dialogue to inform the range of effective antitrafficking initiatives begun and sustained by The Daywalka Foundation, including scholarships awarded to at-risk youth in Nepal, a poetry program for trafficking victims, and multinational seminars bringing together representatives of antitrafficking groups and organizations from Bangladesh, Nepal, India, Thailand, and the United States. Carey concludes the chapter by emphasizing that starting and sustaining successful antitrafficking campaigns depends considerably on an awareness of, and respect for, local knowledge and cultures.

In Chapter 3, Linda Welker discusses a community-based theatre/performance project, *A Prayer for Sudan*, designed to increase awareness of, and encourage action to end, the genocide in South Sudan. Welker first reviews the origin and character of community-based theatre, a form of performance-based activism that frequently focuses on significant issues confronting marginalized and oppressed groups, and that employs community members from those groups as performers. In this case, because of the limited English-speaking skills of Sudanese refugees in the United States where Welker lived and taught, Welker's U.S. university students (the majority of whom were white and Christian) in a community-based performance course engaged in a cross-gender and cross-ethnic performance focusing on those refugees' experiences with violence in South Sudan, displacement from their native country, and their adjustment to life in the United States. Student interviews conducted with the Sudanese refugees shaped the performance, as did their research on the conflict in Sudan. Welker reflectively discusses opportunities and challenges confronting students as they *performed* difference. She also focuses on the different reactions of two audiences to the performances: the Sudanese refugees and a university audience comprised largely of students and faculty. Welker shows how this project produced forms of activist engagement by students in the course and by audience members who attended the play. In her discussion of lessons learned from the intervention, Welker stresses that forms of activism that cross significant cultural or social difference demand a difficult search for common ground through mindful listening, mutual self-disclosure, and empathic engagement.

The next three chapters (Chapters 4–6) share a common focus on collective action and, in part, examine how groups and organizations seeking meaningful social and political change attempt to influence the news media as a means to secure needed reform. The interventions discussed in these chapters are designed to influence three significant issues: domestic violence, factory farming, and capital punishment.

In Chapter 4, Charlotte Ryan and Karen Jeffreys explain their long-term collaboration to build the communication capacity of the Rhode Island Coalition Against Domestic Violence (RICADV) and enhance its ability to frame domestic violence as a public policy issue. In particular, they examine RICADV's successful campaign to force the resignation of a Rhode Island state legislator, Michael Farrell, who was arrested for battering his girlfriend. Ryan, a media sociologist and activist, and Jeffreys, RICADV's communication coordinator at that time, begin the chapter by reviewing research on structural obstacles confronting social movements' efforts to influence mainstream U.S. news organizations. Despite these obstacles and the difficulty in establishing and sustaining a collective actor, some movements, with sufficient organizational capacity and knowledge of news media practices, do influence news media definitions of political and social issues. Ryan and Jeffreys richly integrate multiple theoretical and conceptual perspectives, including social movement theory, framing theory, and Lukes's (2005) perspective on power, which they extend and apply to RICADV's campaign to force Farrell's resignation. Significantly, the authors explain how Global South models of participatory communication, which stress the significance of community dialogue and empowerment, and grassroots participation to produce democratic change, can inform organizing campaigns by social movements in the Global North. They also underscore that social movements should treat communication as a central component of all their activities, including grassroots organizing, lobbying, and news media outreach. The chapter concludes by discussing difficulties involved in bridging divides between scholars and activists, with Ryan and Jeffreys noting, for instance, that researchers need to maintain a close connection to activist groups but, simultaneously, retain sufficient distance from those groups to engage in critical reflection that informs activists' efforts.

Jeanette L. Drake, in Chapter 5, focuses on the struggle between a grassroots group, Concerned Citizens of Central Ohio (CCCO), and a factory farm, Buckeye Egg Farm, that CCCO sought to close because of the farm's negative environmental impact. Drake first situates this struggle in a broader context of the significant growth of concentrated animal feeding operations in U.S. agriculture and how the untreated waste from those factory farms sharply increases air and water pollution. Drawing on her experience in public relations, Drake assisted CCCO by developing the organization's communication strategies to generate news coverage of the controversy and to craft key organizational messages, simultaneously conducting a longitudinal frame analysis of news media coverage of the controversy. Although the grassroots group failed to close the factory farm, it did succeed in multiple ways, such as by transforming the situation into a problem; attracting considerable news coverage to the issue, including reporting by local news organizations, *The New York Times* and *The Wall Street Journal*, and the NBC television news program *Dateline*; and helping to increase government regulations of Ohio factory farms. In explaining this endeavor, Drake charts her evolution from a public relations practitioner and scholar to a scholar-activist. After criticizing public relations for sustaining corporate power and abuses, Drake reclaims those practices to promote social justice. She ends the chapter by discussing her efforts to negotiate tensions in the emerging and heterogeneous coalition opposing factory farms in Ohio, a coalition that includes rural and urban residents, animal rights activists, advocates for sustainable agriculture, environmentalists, progressives, and conservative Christians.

In Chapter 6, Jennifer Asenas, Bryan S. McCann, Kathleen Feyh, and Dana Cloud report on their participation in a diverse grassroots coalition that saved Kenneth Foster, Jr. from execution by convincing Rick Perry, Texas governor and an ardent proponent of capital punishment, to commute Foster's execution. Asenas et al. first locate their intervention within communication activism scholarship on the death penalty (see the contributions by Sunwolf and by McHale in Volumes 1 and 2, respectively) and within research showing how capital punishment is disproportionately applied to people of color and to those who are poor. Asenas et al. then discuss challenges and opportunities of interracial organizing, explaining how they navigated tensions between relatively privileged white activists and blacks, and between proponents of a public grassroots campaign that sought to link Foster's case to a broader campaign opposing the death penalty and advocates, including Foster's family, of a narrower campaign focused exclusively on legal issues relevant to Foster's commutation. The chapter documents their success in managing those tensions and in producing a grassroots campaign that attracted considerable news coverage and gained public support for the commutation. The authors highlight the need to *speak with* rather than *speaking for* marginalized individuals and groups, contending that scholar-activists need to forge partnerships with individuals, groups, and organizations that lack power; and respect the ability of people suffering injustices to define those injustices and to devise means to overcome them. In advancing this view, they criticize some engaged research for its patronizing view that researchers "give" voice to alleged "voiceless" victims of oppression.

Chapters 7 and 8 focus attention on communication activism interventions within organizations, both of which are located in the southeastern United States. The first intervention attempted to heighten awareness of racial and cultural issues in a fire department serving a diverse community; the second project sought to increase ethical awareness and practices in a media organization.

Chris Groscurth, in Chapter 7, reports on his effort to change organizational discourses concerning race in an overwhelmingly white fire department serving a multiethnic and multiracial community. Groscurth first explains how his intervention was informed by the dialogic perspectives of Bakhtin and Foucault, as well as critical whiteness studies (although he points to the lack of engaged research within that tradition to disrupt discourses of white privilege to create greater equality). A discourse analysis of selected documents within the fire department studied revealed a lack of communication about issues related to diversity, despite a professed organizational commitment to "equal opportunity." His interviews with firefighters also indicated a general reluctance to discuss race, given the perceived sensitivity of the subject, although some firefighters were willing to speak about it and admitted the need to know more about the diverse communities they serve. Groscurth's efforts to obtain organizational changes from senior members of the fire department, however, met with only limited success, with senior management authorizing a seminar for officers on the diverse nature of the community being served, but not including Groscurth, and rebuffing broader programs to promote multicultural knowledge and communication skills training.

Chapter 8, by Steven K. May, examines his intervention to enhance the ethical culture of a diversified media corporation with more than 500 employees. May first notes that communication activism research has devoted little attention to business ethics. In his "Ethics at Work Initiative," he proposes five practices of ethical engagement within an organization: dialogic communication, transparency, employee participation, ethical courage, and accountability. Using pre- and postintervention questionnaires assessing employees' perceptions of these five ethical practices, May documents increases in employees' perceptions of the company's commitment to these practices. Working with employees in focus groups, May helped to develop an organizational values statement and ethics code; other organizational changes linked to the initiative included an ethics-oriented performance appraisal and ethics training for new and continuing employees. Finally, May explores three major dialectical tensions characterizing organizational engagement: (a) a foundational–situational ethics tension (focusing, in part, on whether ethical behaviors are universal or need to be context-specific); (b) an individual–organizational ethical tension (focusing, in part, on whether the source of ethical decision making exists at the individual or organizational level); and (c) an ethics–performance ethics tension (focusing, in part, on whether priority should be given to ethical decision making or to organizations' need for profit). May explains how he managed these tensions and, simultaneously, strengthened the ethical culture at the media company.

The final two chapters of this volume examine communication activism scholarship relating to the consequences of poverty, albeit in very different contexts. The first example is set in an Ohio county where more than one in four residents live in poverty; the second is conducted on an American-Indian reservation in New Mexico.

In Chapter 9, Wendy H. Papa, Michael J. Papa, and Rick A. Buerkel discuss their creation—in collaboration with Ohio University (OU) students and Good Works, a local nonprofit organization that aids individuals suffering from poverty and homelessness—of a small business in Athens, Ohio, called "Good Gifts," to provide a living wage and job training to people who are poor. After reviewing communication scholarship on poverty, Papa et al. explain how multiple theoretical perspectives—including feminist perspectives on organizing, critical pedagogy, and social learning theory—informed their project. Interestingly, the project combined a local and global initiative to combat poverty, with merchandise sold by Good Gifts obtained from Ten Thousand Villages, an organization that purchases handcrafted products from Third World workers who receive a living wage. The authors carefully distinguish this type of social justice intervention from a traditional charity model, with social justice interventions both critiquing social problems and providing opportunities for those who are marginalized and oppressed to empower themselves. Since its founding in 1999, Good Works has provided job training to 35 people and has involved OU students in courses and independent studies that reflect on how community organizing and service-learning can produce social change. This project also demonstrates the power of collaboration between people who are disadvantaged and those who are relatively advantaged.

The final chapter of this volume by Lorenda Belone, John G. Oetzel, Nina Wallerstein, Greg Tafoya, and Rebecca Rae of the University of New Mexico (UNM), at the time, and Alvin Rafelito, Lula Kelhoyouma, Ira Burbank, Carolyn Finster, Jennifer Henio-Charley, Yin-Mae Lee, and Anderson Thomas of the Ramah Navajo Core Advisory Council, documents an ongoing public health intervention to prevent drinking in late elementary and early adolescent youth in New Mexico's Ramah Navajo community. After reviewing both the scope and causes of alcohol and illegal substance abuse among American Indians (the authors' preferred term), they discuss how a community-based participatory approach (CBPR) to public health campaigns shapes their Ramah Navajo Family Listening Project. In keeping with this approach, the intervention represents a collaboration between the researchers and the Ramah Navajo community that involves the community in the design, implementation, and evaluation of the public health campaign. This culturally sensitive approach is vitally needed given the widespread distrust of white researchers by many American Indians because of past top-down and culturally insensitive research projects. Belone et al. explain how the Advisory Council played a significant role in all aspects of this project, including developing curriculum focused on strengthening families, planning the health intervention, and designing how the campaign would be evaluated, as well as analyzing preliminary evaluation data. A pilot pretest and posttest of the campaign, involving 11 Ramah Navajo families, and combining quantitative and qualitative data, found that the project effectively enhances participants' understanding of Ramah Navajo culture, strengthens their family communication, and improves their general health. The authors conclude the chapter by highlighting benefits of CBPR in their ongoing culturally appropriate public health intervention, and how their culturally diverse research team, which included three Americans Indians, forged a connection to the Ramah Navajo community.

LESSONS LEARNED ABOUT COMMUNICATION ACTIVISM FOR SOCIAL JUSTICE SCHOLARSHIP

The chapters in this volume, and the previous two volumes, as a set, shed significant light on the nature and practice of communication activism for social justice scholarship. Here, we discuss some lessons learned about engaging in such scholarship (citing relevant chapters in this volume in alphabetical order with respect to authors or points made).

Lesson 1: *Communication activism for social justice scholarship* should not be confused with *communication activism for social justice* per se. We employ the term scholar-activists (rather than "activist scholars" or "activist-scholars") throughout these volumes to foreground the research nature of these communication activism endeavors. In that light, first and foremost, the majority of the contributors, and especially the lead authors, are scholars who conduct research to accomplish the goals of communication activism for social justice. If they wanted, primarily or solely, to be activists, they probably would not have the time to write chapters in these scholarly books.

Lesson 2: Communication activism for social justice research, like all scholarship, reflects a choice that scholars make about what communication phenomena they study, how they study those phenomena, and to what ends they put their research findings. The scholars who contributed to these volumes chose to conduct research that potentially could make an important difference for marginalized, oppressed, and underresourced individuals, groups, organizations, and communities struggling for social justice. In that sense, there is a significant difference between, for instance, research that springs from serving as a pro bono consultant to a struggling nonprofit organization confronting domestic violence (Ryan & Jeffreys) or factory farms (Drake), and that which emerges from being a paid consultant to the management of BP or IBM. Although the latter might be characterized as "engaged scholarship" because it connects academics, the academy, and community members, the question is whose agendas and interests are being served by the research and what end results are being promoted. As Becker (1995) pointed out, "The major question most of us face in our lives as scholars is not whether our research should be useful; it is, rather, what it should be useful for and for whom it should be useful" (p. 102). As noted previously, communication scholars have far too many partnerships that have served the interests of the powerful and far too few with marginalized, oppressed, and underresourced individuals, groups, organizations, and communities that challenge powerful interests and promote social justice.

Although we certainly respect scholars' right to choose how to devote their resources, scholars also are embedded within cultural, economic, political, and social systems, meaning that their research has important implications for maintaining or challenging those systems; consequently, their research choices must be open to being called into question. Conquergood (1995) forcefully explained the choice confronting "engaged" researchers:

> The choice is no longer between pure and applied research. Instead, we must choose between research that is "engaged" or "complicit." By engaged I mean a clear-eyed, self-critical awareness that research does not proceed in epistemological purity or moral innocence. There is no immac-

ulate perception. Engaged individuals take responsibility for how the knowledge that they produce is used instead of hiding behind pretenses and protestations of innocence. ... As communication scholars who traffic in symbols, images, representations, rhetorical strategies, signifying practices, the media, and the social work of talk, we should understand better than anyone else that our disciplinary practice is in the world. As engaged intellectuals we understand that we are entangled within world systems of oppression and exploitation. ... Our choice is to stand alongside or against domination, but not outside, above, or beyond it. (p. 85)

The communication scholars in these volumes chose to stand against domination, oppression, and other social injustices by using their theories, methods, pedagogies, and other practices to fight against alcohol abuse stemming, in large measure, from cultural marginalization and oppression (Belone et al.), capital punishment (Asenas et al.), domestic violence (Ryan & Jeffreys), ethnic conflict (Broome et al.), factory farming (Drake), genocide (Welker), human trafficking (Carey), poverty (Papa et al.), racism (Groscurth), and unethical treatment of employees (May). Their reasons for choosing these issues undoubtedly differ. Drake, for instance, first experienced the consequences of factory farming when visiting her parents in rural Ohio, and Carey became aware of the pressing issue of human trafficking as a tourist in South Asia; in contrast, Belone and Wallerstein had conducted previous research projects with the Ramah Navajo, and Ryan and Jeffreys had a long-term collaboration that focused on domestic violence. Ultimately, however, their choice to work for social justice with and for those who have been marginalized and oppressed springs from who they are as people and what they value. As Solomon (1980) contended, "Justice is neither in the heavens nor is it merely in the mud of self-deception. It is ultimately, as Socrates argued, in ourselves, a virtuous state of character with the appropriate emotions, attitudes, and actions" (p. 355). Other scholars, of course, will make other choices, but they must be willing to own those choices and the values that those choices represent.

Lesson 3: Communication activism for social justice scholarship transforms researchers into scholar-citizens (see, e.g., Ackerman & Coogan, 2010; Cherwitz, 2005; Grund, Cherwitz, & Darwin, 2001; Mitchell, 2007; Pestello, Saxton, Miller, & Donnelly, 1996; Rakow, 2005; Rosaen, Foster-Fishman, & Fear, 2001; Saxton, 1993; Trent, 2000; Valentine, 1936; Walsh, 2009) connected with communities and significant social justice issues confronting community members. Most of the projects featured in these volumes involve scholars promoting social justice with/in their local communities. Rakow (2005), in talking about the need for community research in the communication discipline, asserted, in both a joking and serious manner:

> According to the timeworn joke, the chicken crossed the road to get to the other side. So why did the scholar cross the road? To do research on the other side, presumably. Why do scholars go elsewhere to do research, like the proverbial wandering chicken, instead of staying right where we are? Is there nothing of significance in our own communities that is worthy of study? Is there no role for our research in the daily struggles of local citizens to create healthy and just communities? Is a scholar also a citizen? (p. 6)

The scholars who contributed to these volumes did not, for the most part, cross the road but, instead, stayed in their local communities. They engaged in communication activism with/for students in their courses and/or the universities where these scholars taught (Papa et al.; Welker), and for people in the neighborhoods, towns, and states where these scholars lived (Asenas et al.; Broome et al., with three of the authors living in Cyprus; Belone et al.; Drake; Papa et al.; Ryan & Jeffreys; Welker).

Opportunities for communication activism research, therefore, abound in the communities in which scholars live and work. However, local communities should be viewed as opportunities for engagement, not simply as opportunities for engaged research; hence, scholars, first and foremost, should be citizens involved in the civic life of their communities. Such an involvement might even be a precondition for superior engaged research because an activist orientation immerses scholar-citizens in patterns of both domination and subordination, and in the social networks of those who suffer from marginalization and oppression, and who challenge such inequalities, invariably offering a rich ground for communication activism for social justice scholarship.

However, even as communication scholars engage their local communities, they need to reflect on the often promoted claim that engaged scholarship should work with "the community." Advocates for engaged scholarship too often urge researchers to take an active role in "the community," as if, in any town or city, there is a single community sharing common goals, meanings, and values. Communication scholars need to remember that defining a community always is a political and contestable act, and that multiple interests define community in different ways and advance strikingly different agendas.

Engaged communication scholars, therefore, need to make difficult and reflective choices about using their communication expertise to serve particular community interests at the expense of others; consequently, they frequently need to enter the fray and pick sides in disputes (see Goodall, 2010). As these volumes show, we privilege engaged communication research that challenges powerful interests and institutions, exposes pressing inequalities and other systemic oppressive practices and problems, and works with and for marginalized individuals, groups, organizations, and communities to secure social justice.

Lesson 4: These studies also reveal that even as broader (e.g., national or global) communication activism needs to be expressed via local activism, the efficacy of local activism is linked to, and animated by, its engagement with broader social movements seeking to secure social and political change. For example, Asenas et al.'s local activism in Austin, Texas to save the life of Kenneth Foster, Jr. was aided by their connection to the national and international antideath penalty movement, and Ryan and Jeffreys's intervention not only improved the effectiveness of the organization with which they worked but that intervention also served as the basis for workshops they offered to aid the practices of groups and organizations in other states to combat domestic violence. The chapters, thus, show that communication activism for social justice scholarship truly is both local and global.

This combination of local activism coupled with broader social movements shows that communication activism for social justice research mobilizes collective action. An examination of U.S. history reveals that meaningful progressive change occurs through the mobilization and organization of collective actors, such as demonstrated in the civil rights, environmental, feminist, and labor movements. The reforms and changes secured by the interventions in these books resulted from the collective work of researchers, community groups, activists, and social movement organizations. Asenas et al., for instance, worked with the Save Kenneth Foster Campaign; Drake collaborated with the grassroots group Concerned Citizens of Ohio to oppose factory farms; Carey established The Daywalka Foundation to combat human trafficking; and Belone et al. partnered with Ramah Navajo activists to design and implement their health communication intervention. These and the other interventions included in these volumes demonstrate that collective action, and not simply the raising of individual consciousness, matters.

Lesson 5: Communication activism for social justice research necessitates scholar-citizens intervening in some way, for this type of scholarship, as explained earlier, involves first-person-perspective rather than third-person-perspective research. The interventions may differ slightly with respect to the degree to which scholars are positioned and participate in the group, organization, or community with which they are connected (e.g., Jeffreys serving as a staff member in the organization), but all of the interventions that scholars employ revolve, of course, around some form of communicative practice that they facilitate. The interventions documented in these chapters include: (a) conducting a grassroots public health communication campaign (Belone et al.); (b) facilitating public and stakeholder dialogue (Broome et al.; Carey); (c) influencing news coverage of controversial issues (Asenas et al.; Drake; Ryan & Jeffreys); (d) performing (Welker); (e) serving as an organizational communication consultant to secure progressive change (Groscurth; May); and (f) teaching interpersonal communication skills to those living in poverty to be successful in a small business (Papa at al.). These interventions and the issues they address span the communication discipline, from, for instance, interpersonal and group communication to organizational communication to media studies, demonstrating that all communication scholars can engage in communication activism for social justice research if they choose to do so.

Communication activism for social justice, thus, is a unique form of scholarship that uses the very essence of the discipline—communication theory and practice—to promote the goal of social justice, meaning that activism, fundamentally, is a communication process and practice. Whether there are forms of activism that are unique to other disciplines (e.g., political science or sociology) remains to be seen.

Lesson 6: These interventions are informed by and, in turn, inform theory. Wood (1996) cautioned communication scholars interested in pursuing social justice to

> bear in mind that passion alone is no guarantee of positive results, nor does the intent to empower oppressed peoples necessarily cohabit with genuine understanding of and respect for others and their interpretations of their lives. Such passion and intents are most effective when they are infused by theoretical understandings. (p. 165)

The chapters in these books demonstrate how theoretical understandings infuse communication activism for social justice scholarship. Not surprisingly, given their focus on describing and explaining systems of domination and subordination, and their interest in forms and practices of cultural and political resistance, critical theories shaped many of the interventions. For example, Groscurth's intervention to affect communication about race in a fire department relied on critical whiteness theory and research, Ryan and Jeffreys consulted Global South perspectives on participatory communication to enhance the organization's capacity to combat domestic violence, and feminist theory informed Papa et al.'s intervention to combat poverty. These chapters extend scholarship in a significant way by using these theories to inform practical interventions designed to assist individuals, groups, organizations, and communities to achieve social justice.

Interpretive theories also informed many of these studies. Drake, for example, used social constructionism and framing theory to affect media coverage of factory farms, Broome et al. employed transformative peacebuilding theory to structure bicommunal events that brought Greek Cypriots and Turkish Cypriots together, and perspectives on dialogue shaped the organizational communication interventions conducted by Groscurth and by May. These chapters highlight the need for communication activism research to examine the complex processes of meaning-making that are involved in promoting social change. Together with the chapters employing critical perspectives, these studies underscore that people live in both symbolic and material worlds, and that they are purposive social actors who define, interpret, critique, and can change oppressive structures and practices. Moreover, they reveal the tension or clash that so often occurs between the construction and expression of meaning by those who are marginalized and oppressed and broader hegemonic meanings produced, disseminated, and enforced by elite actors and institutions.

Positivistic (and/or postpositivistic) theories also shaped some of these intervention projects. Belone et al., for instance, employed intercultural workgroup communication theory to interpret the success of the community-based participatory research that they conducted with the Ramah Navajo; Drake extended the diffusion of innovation perspective by showing not only how sources use communication to raise people's awareness, acceptance, and adoption of innovations, such as factory farms, but also how the livestock industry engaged in subterfusion to effectively hide the rapid diffusion of this innovation from public scrutiny; and Papa et al. used social learning theory to influence interactions between university students and people suffering from poverty in their intervention.

Using theory to inform and make sense of communication interventions has the important consequence of contributing back to those theories by testing and fleshing them out in practice. Consequently, communication activism for social justice research, as Wood (1995) contended about applied communication research, "is practicing theory and theorizing practice" (p. 157). Moreover, an important lesson learned from the theoretical pluralism and integration demonstrated within and across these studies is that the distinctions often drawn between the three major social-scientific paradigms—critical, interpretive, and positivistic/postpositivistic—are facile when it comes to communication activism scholarship, for these paradigms can be employed individually or in combination to promote social justice.

Lesson 7: These studies also demonstrate that any research method and technique can be used to guide and document communication activism for social justice scholarship. Frey, Botan, and Kreps (2000) identified four major methods employed by communication scholars: experimental, survey, textual analysis (e.g., rhetorical criticism, content analysis, and performance studies), and naturalistic inquiry (e.g., autoethnography, critical ethnography, discourse analysis, ethnography, and performance ethnography). All of these studies, because they were first-person-perspective research case studies that employed participant observation, and, in many cases, in-depth interviewing, are a form of naturalistic inquiry. Some of the studies also employed survey methods (Belone et al.; Carey; May; Papa et al.) and textual analysis (Asenas et al.; Drake; Ryan & Jeffreys). (For an example using the experimental method, see Rich and Rodríguez, Volume 2). The methodological pluralism demonstrated in these and the studies in the other volumes as a set, like the theoretical pluralism, deconstructs the problematic traditional divide that supposedly separates qualitative, quantitative, and rhetorical methods, by demonstrating that all of the various research methods and techniques available can be employed, most typically in a multimethodological manner, in communication activism for social justice scholarship. Moreover, by grounding interventions in and contributing back to theoretical perspectives, and by using research methods and techniques as part of those interventions and/or to document intervention efforts, the chapters realize the elusive goal of *praxis*—no small accomplishment.

Lesson 8: The praxis of communication activism is based, in large measure, on the creation of a trusting, collaborative partnership that produces a reflexive research process shaped by both researchers and social actors seeking systemic change. Asenas et al., for instance, showed how the solidarity that developed among supporters of the Save Kenneth Foster Campaign resulted from the ethical and strategic position of speaking *with* rather than speaking *for* others; Belone et al.'s community-based participatory research project produced a culturally sensitive public health intervention for the Ramah Navajo; and Ryan and Jeffrey's long-term collaboration, and relationships they had developed with other organizations, enabled them to put enough pressure to force Michael Farrell to resign after battering his girlfriend. By recognizing that those who are marginalized and oppressed are purposive social actors, and by involving them in the research process, these projects democratize research (Greenwood & Levin, 2000) and, thereby, deconstruct the traditional divide drawn between researchers and the impoverished and patronizing view of social actors as "research subjects." Communication activism for social justice scholarship, thus, is grounded in "researchers' involvement in the life of 'another,' as opposed to studying 'an other'" (Frey, 1988b, p. 162).

Adopting a collaborative approach demands humility on the part of researchers, who are partners with social actors, not leaders who, because of their "enlightenment," direct the "intellectually unwashed." In that light, communication activism for social justice scholars need to avoid the too-often patronizing view that researchers "give voice to the voiceless" or "empower the powerless." No one gives another person a voice or empowers that person; people, including marginalized individuals, groups, organizations, and communities, have voices (an important exception is the case of animals; see Drake) and what researchers, especially communication researchers, can do is to create (more) opportunities to hear and listen to those voices.

Lesson 9: Attempting to enact these and other principles and practices of communication activism for social justice scholarship presents significant challenges. Some of these challenges are experienced in other forms of communication scholarship (e.g., gaining access to community groups, obtaining informed consent, and collecting data), but many of them spring from the unique nature of this type of scholarship.

One particularly significant challenge, as captured in the subtitle to this volume, involves the struggle for social justice amidst the "differences" of those involved. Important differences between researchers and social actors, for instance, potentially affect the quest for social justice. Belone et al. had to confront and overcome, through collaboration in every phase of their project, American Indians' historical mistrust of white researchers who have intervened without improving tribal communities; and Papa et al. had to alter through their actions the mistrust and suspicion that individuals living in poverty had toward those from the university community, and vice versa, in Athens, Ohio. In some instances, such differences cannot be managed, as demonstrated in Groscurth's case, where the powers that be at the fire department did not allow him to contribute to the diversity seminar that was planned as a result of his research, despite his repeated attempts to volunteer to design and facilitate the seminar. Differences between researchers and activists also can complicate the social change process, with both Asenas et al. and Ryan and Jeffreys talking about that potential conflict because of different agendas, backgrounds, interests, and needs. Further complications can arise when university researchers involve students in their projects, with Welker talking about the profound differences between student performers and the Sudanese refugees they sought to depict. Finally, differences between and among social actors/activists can have significant effects, with both Broome et al. and Carey noting the difficulties of facilitating dialogue respectively, between Greek and Turkish Cypriots, given historical tensions between these communities, and among the numerous stakeholders combating human trafficking in South Asia; Drake confronting problems in forging a coalition to oppose factory farming, given the diversity of groups, from animal rights activists to conservative Christians, challenging that agricultural practice; and May navigating between employees and management of the organization in which he intervened.

Although such differences can complicate the struggle for social justice, on one level, it is precisely because of material (and symbolic) differences that the need for social justice exists. Certain types of difference also bring a wealth of benefits, including multiple perspectives, experiences, and skills, in the struggle for social justice, as well as contribute to more civic-oriented, democratic structures and practices. Although achieving those benefits demands persistence by everyone involved, because of their educational background and the work they do, communication activism for social justice scholars should be ideally positioned to facilitate that accomplishment. Such a view does not mean that scholars should avoid conflict with activists and other social actors. As "outsiders-within" (P. H. Collins, 2000), scholar-activists need to identify and engage with those who seek social justice, but identification and engagement should not blind scholar-activists to weaknesses that hinder people from securing that goal.

Challenges also result from conducting communication activism research within the university context and academia, more generally, as well as within the communication discipline. Most of the scholars in this volume, in one way or another, are embedded within and subject to the constraints of the university context, and they and others who conduct such research are affected by that context. For instance, communication activism for social justice scholarship can take a much longer period of time than some other forms of scholarship (e.g., handing out questionnaires in a large lecture class and analyzing the data), making such scholarship vulnerable to the "quantity" argument that often surfaces in tenure and promotion considerations (for a narrative of balancing activism with the demands of tenure, see Few, Piercy, & Stremmel, 2007).

There are, unfortunately, those in the academy who argue against the engaged research reflected in communication activism for social justice scholarship. Fish (2004), for example, on leaving his position as dean of the College of Liberal Arts and Sciences at the University of Illinois at Chicago, offered the following advice to academics in an op-ed piece, titled "Why We Built the Ivory Tower," published in *The New York Times*:

> Don't confuse your academic obligations with the obligation to save the world; that's not your job as an academic. ... In short, don't cross the boundary between academic work and partisan advocacy, whether the advocacy is yours or someone else's.
>
> Marx famously said that our job is not to interpret the world, but to change it. In the academy, however, it is exactly the reverse: our job is not the change the world, but to interpret it. (p. A23; see also Fish, 2008)

Although the communication discipline probably is one of the better disciplines with respect to supporting activism scholarship (in part, because of having long ago dismissed the "debate" about quantitative vs. qualitative research and recognizing the centrality of applied communication scholarship, including the value of a social justice communication approach), some members of the discipline do share the anti-activism position preached by Fish (2004, 2008). Kuypers (2000), for instance, asked the question, "Must we all be political activists?" and then answered it by arguing that "the leaders of our discipline have gone too far in their attempt to foster social change, both within the discipline and society" and suggesting that "if critics in our discipline wish to engage in such [political partisanship] they should leave the academy. ... We should be professors, not social activists" ("Conclusion," para. 1, 16).

We certainly are not suggesting that all communication scholars should engage in communication activism for social justice scholarship. We do, however, advocate creating a space for activism in communication scholarship, contest the notion that communication scholars can remain politically neutral in what they study (and how they study and report it), and call on communication scholars to own their choice and be explicit about whose interests they privilege.

Finally, despite the pragmatic and systemic challenges involved, this scholarship can have tremendously important effects. Among the many effects documented in the chapters, Kenneth Foster, Jr. was spared from execution (Asenas et al.); a public health campaign benefitted a historically impoverished community (Belone et al.); a newly established foundation created programs and initiatives to stem human trafficking in South Asia, although, unfortunately, it recently closed its doors (Carey); a media corporation became more ethical in its treatment of employees (May); people living in poverty received job training (Papa et al.); an organization forced the resignation of a state legislator who had battered his girlfriend and enhanced its capacities to prevent domestic violence (Ryan & Jeffreys); and performers and audiences learned about, and hopefully will engage in action to prevent, genocide in Sudan (Welker).

Communication activism also has important implications for a person's scholarship and teaching. Many of the authors talked about how their activism deepened their understanding of the research topic, the theories on which they relied, and the research methods they employed, and how their research inspired them to continue wanting to engage in scholarship that promotes social justice. In two cases, the research projects stemmed directly from teaching (Papa et al.; Welker); in another, faculty members engaged graduate students in the intervention (Belone et al.); with the activism performed by Groscurth and by May resulting from being communication graduate students (regarding communication activism pedagogy, see Frey & Palmer, in press).

Communication activism, however, is not done simply to achieve the end products, for in many cases, the changes being advocated may take a long time to occur or never happen at all. Asenas et al. stopped the execution of Kenneth Foster, Jr., but Texas continues to execute people; Belone et al. have not redressed all the significant social inequalities confronting the Ramah Navajo; Broome et al. have not resolved the conflict between Greek and Turkish Cypriots; Carey did not end human trafficking in South Asia; Drake did not shut down the factory farm in Ohio; Groscurth does not know what long-term effects, if any, his research had on preventing racism at the fire department; and Papa et al. did not end poverty in Athens, Ohio. Scholars engaging in communication activism to promote social justice, thus, have to manage tensions between processes and outcomes, learning, among many other things, to be patient, persistent, sustain passion in the face of significant opposition, tolerate imperfect planning and execution, operate within contextual constraints, develop contingency plans, and cope with unsuccessful interventions. Hopefully, the expertise of communication scholar-activists in being able to talk about such issues will help to manage the inevitable tensions and challenges that they will experience, and will renew their joyful commitment to such scholarship, for as Hartnett (2010) contended:

> Working from such spaces of joyful commitment makes us better persuaders by enabling us to turn away from scholarship as critique and rejection toward scholarship as affirmation and empowerment; it protects us against burnout by enabling us to turn away from activism as anger and confrontation to activism as fulfillment and solidarity.... What I am calling joyful commitment amounts, then, to turning the tools of intellectual inquiry and the practices of social justice scholarship and activism into occasions for seeking solidarity and fulfillment with others. (pp. 86, 87)

CONCLUSION

Communication activism is a significant form of scholarship that can be engaged in by scholars from across the communication discipline using a wide range of interventions, theories, methods, and pedagogical practices to promote social justice with and for marginalized, oppressed, and underresourced individuals, groups, organizations, and communities. In the final analysis, although there are many potential rewards, scholars engage in such research because they are engaged citizens, using their knowledge and skills to promote social justice. They do it because, in so many ways, it is the right thing to do.

NOTES

1. Portions of this introduction are taken verbatim from the introduction to the first two volumes of *Communication Activism*.
2. We provide numerous sources about activism, privileging recent post-2000 published work that includes the word "activism" in the title, to make this introduction a valuable resource. Chapter authors provide additional sources relevant to the particular type of activism in which they engaged.
3. Activism has been studied in Africa (Britton, Fish, & Meintjes, 2009; Chibango & Kajau, 2010; Disney, 2008; Jeske, 2010; Mbazira, 2009; White & Perelman,

2011), Asia (Carapico, 1998; Faier, 2004; Gellner, 2009, 2010; Hedda, 2008; Hemment, 2007; Henry, 2010; Ho & Edmonds, 2007; Hsing & Lee, 2010; Kerns, 2011; Nawab & Ali, 2009; Offord, 2003; Ralston & Keeble, 2009; Reimann, 2009; Rho, 2007; Roces & Edwards, 2010; Saunders, 2006; Vijayalakshmi, 2005; Xie, 2009; Yang, 2009), Australia (J. Clark, 2008; Maynard, 2007; Offord, 2003), Europe (Bugajski & Pollack, 1989; Maloney & van Deth, 2010; S. Phillips, 2008; Vassallo, 2010), North America (in addition to the United States, M. Anderson, 2009; Canel, 2010; Couso, Huneeus, & Sieder, 2010; Disney, 2008; James et al., 2009; Li, 2007; Maier & Lebon, 2010; Staudt, 2008), and South America (Drogus & Stewart-Gambino, 2005; Hochstetler & Keck, 2007; Mische, 2008; Smale, 2010; Tate, 2007; Thayer, 2010).

4. Contexts and forms of activism that have been studied include (in alphabetical order) abortion/choice (e.g., Munson, 2008; Seaton, 1996; Staggenborg, 1991), African American/black (e.g., Alleyne, 2002; Bandele, 2008; Ginwright, 2010; F. C. Harris, Sinclair-Chapman, & McKenzie, 2006; Jennings, 1997; G. L. Knight, 2009; Moore, 2010; Shaw, 2009); AIDS (e.g., Hallett, 1997; Silversides, 2003; R. A. Smith & Siplon, 2006; Stockdill, 2003); American Indian/Native American (e.g., Cobb, 2008; Cobb & Fowler, 2007; Hauptman, 2011; T. Johnson, Nagel, & Champagne, 1997; T. R. Johnson, 1996; Krouse & Howard, 2009); animal rights/food (e.g., Ball & Friedrich, 2009; Beers, 2006; Donald, 2009; Gaarder, 2011; Gleason, 2010; Guither, 1998; Hawthorne, 2008; Joy, 2008; Lovitz, 2010; S. Miller, 2008; Schurman & Munro; 2010; W. Wright & Middendorf, 2009); apartheid (e.g., Culverson, 1999; Hostetter, 2006; Love, 1985); architecture/design (e.g., Bell & Wakeford, 2008; Faud-Luke, 2009); Asian American (e.g., Habal, 2007; Liu, Geron, & Lai, 2008); business/corporate (e.g., Burke, 2005; Cory, 2005; Holzer, 2010; John & Thompson, 2003; Monks, 1999; Rao, 2009; Tonello, 2008); Chicana/o/Latina/o (e.g., Ochoa & Ochoa, 2005; Urrieta, 2009); civil/human rights (e.g., Bernstein, 2011; Doak, 2008; Greenhaw, 2011; Madison, 2010; Rodger & Field, 2010; Stammers, 2009; Strain, 2005; M. R. Warren, 2010; Whitt, 2010); communism (e.g., Goldstein, 1994; Zake, 2009); conservatism (e.g., T. M. Keck, 2004; Lewis, 1999; Pierson & Skocpol, 2007); consumer/stakeholder (e.g., Chiu, 2010; Eisenhofer & Barry, 2006; Glickman, 2009; Hilton, 2009; R. E. Wright, Barber, Crafton, & Jain, 2004); disability (e.g., Panitch, 2007; L. Newman & Kurs, 2009; Sandell, Dodd, & Garland-Thompson, 2010); domestic violence (e.g., Fábián, 2010; Hopkins & McGregor, 1991; Rambo, 2009); education/teacher (e.g., N. S. Anderson & Kharem, 2009; Blackburn, Clark, Kenney, & Smith, 2010; Lea & Sims, 2008; Marshall & Anderson, 2009; Peterman, 2008); environmental (e.g., Bevington, 2009; Blum, 2008; Brodkin, 2009; N. Carter, 2007; Crowe, 2008; David, 2008; Dell, 2009; DeLuca, 1999; Gardner, 2009; Hess, 2007; Mauch, Stolzfus, & Weiner, 2006; Sandler & Pezzullo, 2007; Switzer, 2003); family/mothers and fathers (e.g., Collier & Sheldon, 2006; J. E. Crowley, 2008; Vargas, 2008); health (e.g., K. L. Baird, 2009; Cwikel, 2006; Gill, 2010; Kedrowski & Sarow, 2007; Klawiter, 2008; Nickitas, Middaugh, & Aries, 2009); homelessness/hunger/poverty (e.g., Hurwitz & Hurwitz, 1994; Kamberg, 2009; Stearman, 2010; Tompkins, 2009; Young, Boyd, Brodsky, & Day, 2008); immigration (e.g., Varsanyi, 2010); judicial/legal (e.g., Bolick, 2007; Dickson, 2007; Dow, 2009; Fisher, 1997; Lindquist

& Cross, 2009; Wolfe, 1997; Yackle, 2007); labor/worker (e.g., de Witte, 2005; Doak, 2008; Markowitz, 2000; Oliver, 2007); gay, lesbian, bisexual, and transgender (e.g., Barclay, Bernstein, & Marshall, 2009; Fetner, 2008; Glassgold & Drescher, 2007; Leyland, 2002; Quinn & Meiners, 2009; Rudacille, 2006; Shepard, 2010; Stevenson & Cogan, 2003; J. Ward, 2008); Mexican American (e.g., Espinosa & García, 2008; Nabhan-Warren, 2005); nuclear (e.g., Dawson, 1996; Holsworth, 1989; B. A. Miller, 2000); prison (e.g., Hartnett, 2011; Lawston, 2009; Lawston & Lucas, 2011; Marlow, 2009); public relations (e.g., Holtzhousen, 2010); religious/spiritual/faith/contemplative (e.g., Espinosa, Elizondo, & Miranda, 2005; Espinosa & García, 2008; Friend, 2008; Gould, 2006; Lampert, 2005; MacDonald, 2008; McGregory, 2010; Palacios, 2007; Smart, 2011; Timmerman, Hutsebaut, Mels, Nonneman, & Van Herck, 2007; Weiss, 2002, 2008; Wuthnow & Evans, 2002); science (e.g., da Costa & Philip, 2008; Rudacille, 2006); student/youth (e.g., Ardizzone, 2007; Arthur, 2011; Berta-Avila, Revilla, & Figueroa, 2011; Ginwright, 2010; Ginwright, Noguera, & Cammarota, 2006; Gordon, 2010; Rhoads, 1998; Sherrod, 2006; Taft, 2011); women/feminism/gender (e.g., Baumgadner & Richards, 2005; Caiazza, 2007; Cockburn, 2007; Dever, 2004; Dolhinow, 2010; Enke, 2007; Finley & Stringer, 2010; A. Harris, 2008; Hawkesworth, 2006b; Kilmartin & Allison, 2007; Mayock & Radulescu, 2010; Mikula, 2008; Pinsky, 2010; Sheridan-Rabideau, 2008; Shreve, 2011; Trigg, 2009; Whisenhunt, 2011)
5. Relevant sources include: action (collaborative/community/participatory) research (the journal *Action Research*; Alber, 2010; Costello, 2003, 2011; Greenwood & Levin, 2000, 2007; Hinchey, 2008; Jason, Keys, Suarez-Balcazar, Taylor, & Davis, 2003; A. P. Johnson, 2008; Kapoor & Jordan, 2009; Kemmis & McTaggart, 2005; Kindon, Pain, & Kesby, 2007; Lassiter, 2005; Liamputtong & Rumbold, 2008; McIntyre, 2008; McNiff & Whitehead, 2002, 2006, 2009, 2010; Minkler & Wallerstein, 2008; Mukherjee, 2009; Noffke & Somekh, 2009; Reason & Bradbury, 2008; Sagor, 2010; Stringer, 1999; in communication scholarship, Anyaegbunam, Karnell, Cheah, & Youngblood, 2005; Clift & Freimuth, 1997; Gaternby & Humphries, 1996; Jensen, 1990; Pilotta et al., 2001; Quigley, Sanchez, Handy, Goble, & George, 2000; Schoening & Anderson, 1995); critical ethnography (Foley & Valenzula, 2005; Thomas, 1993; in communication, Artz, 2001; Carbaugh, 1989; Carragee, 1996; Conquergood, 1991; D. P. Cushman, 1989; T. A. Gibson, 2000; Madison, 2005a, 2005b, 2006); feminist methods (Gaternby & Humphries, 1996; Hawkesworth, 2006a; Hesse-Biber, 2006; Jagger, 2008; Lykke, 2010; Nielsen, 1990; Oleson, 2005; Reinharz, 1992; Sprague, 2005; in communication, Bizzell, 2000; K. Carter & Spitzack, 1989; Dallimore, 2000; M. G. Fine, 1990; Lazar, 2007; Lemish, 2002; Lengel, 1998; McKinnon, Chávez, & Way, 2007; Schell & Rawson, 2010; Self, 1988; Speer, 2002; Sutherland, 2002; Tasker & Holt-Underwood, 2008; Tretheway, 1999); and performance ethnography (Denzin, 2003; Hamera, 2011; McCall, 2000; Mienczakowski, 1995; Turner & Turner, 1982, 1988; in communication, B. Alexander, 2005; Conquergood, 1985, 1991, 1992, 2002; Esquibel & Mejia, 2008; J. L. Jones, 2002; Olomo, 2006; Spry, 2011; J. T. Warren, 2006).

REFERENCES

Ackerman, J. M., & Coogan, D. J. (Eds.). (2010). *The public work of rhetoric: Citizen-scholars and civic engagement*. Columbia: University of South Carolina Press.

Adler, F. P. (2002). Activism in academia: A social action writing program. *Social Justice, 29*(4), 136–149.

Afary, K. (2009). *Performance and activism: Grassroots discourse after the Los Angeles rebellion of 1992*. Lanham, MD: Lexington Books.

Alber, S. M. (2010). *A toolkit for action research*. Lanham, MD: Rowman & Littlefield.

Alexander, B. (2005). Performance ethnography: The reenacting and inciting of culture. In N. K. Denzin & Y. S. Lincoln (Eds.), *Handbook of qualitative research* (3rd ed., pp. 411–442). Thousand Oaks, CA: Sage.

Alexander, L. M. (2008). *African or American? Black identity and political activism in New York City, 1784–1861*. Urbana: University of Illinois Press.

Alleyne, B. W. (2002). *Radicals against race: Black activism and cultural politics*. New York, NY: Berg.

Andersen, P. A. (1993). Beyond criticism: The activist turn in the ideological debate. *Western Journal of Communication, 57*, 247–256. doi:10.1080/10570319309374447

Anderson, C. W. (1993). *Prescribing the life of the mind: An essay on the purpose of the university, the aims of liberal education, the competence of citizens, and the cultivation of practical reason*. Madison: University of Wisconsin Press.

Anderson, G. L., & Herr, K. G. (Eds.). (2007). *Encyclopedia of activism and social justice*. Thousand Oaks, CA: Sage.

Anderson, M. (2009). *Black and indigenous: Garifuna activism and consumer culture in Honduras*. Minneapolis: University of Minnesota Press.

Anderson, N. S., & Kharem, H. (2009). *Education as freedom: African American educational thought and activism*. Lanham, MD: Lexington Books.

Andrews, J. R. (1969). Confrontation at Columbia: A case study in coercive rhetoric. *Quarterly Journal of Speech, 55*, 9–16. doi:10.1080/00335636909382923

Anyaegbunam, C., Karnell, A. P., Cheah, W. H., & Youngblood, J. D. (2005). Designing communication research for empowering marginalized populations: A participatory method. In S. H. Priest (Ed.), *Communication impact: Designing research that matters* (pp. 49–65). Lanham, MD: Rowman & Littlefield.

Apple, M. W. (2009). On being a scholar/activist in education. In E. C. Short & L. J. Waks (Eds.), *Leaders in curriculum studies: Intellectual self-portraits* (pp. 1–13). Rotterdam, The Netherlands: Sense.

Apple, M. W. (2010). Theory, research, and the critical scholar/activist. *Educational Researcher, 39*, 152–162. doi:10.3102/0013189X10362591

Applegate, J. L. (2002). Skating to where the puck will be: Engaged research as a funding activity. *Journal of Applied Communication Research, 30*, 402–410. doi:10.1080/00909880216597

Archibald, R. C. (2010, April 23). Arizona enacts stringent law on immigration. *The New York Times*. Retrieved from http://www.nytimes.com

Ardizzone, L. (2007). *Gettin' my word out: Voices of urban youth activists.* Albany: State University of New York Press.
Arthur, M. L. (2011). *Student activism and curricular change in higher education.* Burlington, VT: Ashgate.
Artz, L. (1998). African-Americans and higher education: An exigence in need of applied communication. *Journal of Applied Communication Research, 26,* 210–231. doi:10.1080/00909889809365502
Artz, L. (2001). Critical ethnography for communication studies: Dialogue and social justice in service-learning. *Southern Communication Journal, 66,* 239–250. doi:10.1080/10417940109373202
Artz, L. (2007). Re-defining activism, re-constructing change [Review of the books *Communication activism* (2 Vols.), by Lawrence R. Frey & K. M. Carragee, Eds.]. *Communication Research Trends, 26*(4), 33–36.
Artz, L., Macek, S., & Cloud, D. (Eds.). (2006). *Marxism and communication studies: The point is to change it.* New York, NY: Peter Lang.
Artz, L., & Murphy, B. O. (2000). *Cultural hegemony in the United States.* Thousand Oaks, CA: Sage.
Askins, K. (2009). "That's just what I do": Placing emotion in academic activism. *Emotion, Space and Society, 2,* 4–13. doi:10.1016/j.emospa.2009.03.005
Atkinson, J. D. (2008). Toward a model of interactivity in alternative media: A multilevel analysis of audiences and producers in a new social movement network. *Mass Communication & Society, 11,* 227–247. doi:10.1080/15205430801919705
Atkinson, J. D. (2009). Networked activism and the broken multiplex: Exploring fractures in the resistance performance paradigm. *Communication Studies, 60,* 49–65. doi:10.1080/10510970802623609
Atkinson, J., & Dougherty, D. S. (2006). Alternative media and social justice movements: The development of a resistance performance paradigm of audience analysis. *Western Journal of Communication, 70,* 64–88. doi:10.1080/10570310500506953
Authers, B., Groeneveld, E., Jackson, E., Mündel, I., & Stewart, J. (Eds.). (2007). Engaging academic activism [Special issue]. *Review of Education, Pedagogy, and Cultural Studies, 29*(4).
The Autonomous Geographies Collective. (2010). Beyond scholar activism: Making strategic interventions inside and outside the neoliberal university. *ACME: An International E-Journal for Critical Geographies, 9,* 245–275. Retrieved from http://www.acme-journal.org
Avakian, M. (2000). *Reformers: Activists, educators, religious leaders.* Austin, TX: Raintree Steck-Vaughn.
Baird, A. C. (1927). *Public discussion and debate.* Boston, MA: Guinn.
Baird, J. E. (1970). The rhetoric of youth in controversy against the religious establishment. *Western Speech, 34,* 53–61. doi:10.1080/10570317009373637
Baird, K. L. (with Davis, D.-A., & Christensen, K.). (2009). *Beyond reproduction: Women's health, activism, and public policy.* Madison, WI: Fairleigh Dickinson University Press.
Ball, M., & Friedrich, B. (2009). *The animal activists' handbook: Maximizing our positive impact in today's world.* New York, NY: Lantern Books.

Bandele, R. M. (2008). *Black star: African American activism in the international political economy*. Urbana: University of Illinois Press.

Banks, M. J. (2010). The picket line online: Creative labor, digital activism, and the 2007–2008 Writers Guild of America strike. *Popular Communication, 8*, 20–33. doi:10.1080/15405700903502387

Barber, B. R. (1992). *An aristocracy of everyone: The politics of education and the future of America*. New York, NY: Ballantine Books.

Barclay, S., Bernstein, M., & Marshall, A.-M. (Eds.). (2009). *Queer mobilizations: LGBT activists confront the law*. New York: New York University Press.

Barge, J. K., Simpson, J. L., & Shockley-Zalabak, P. (Eds.). (2008). Toward purposive and practical models of engaged scholarship [Forum]. *Journal of Applied Communication Research, 36*, 243–297.

Barker, D. (2004). The scholarship of engagement: A taxonomy of five emerging practices. *Journal of Higher Education Outreach and Engagement, 9*(2), 123–137.

Barrett, D. C. (2007). Gay activism and scholarship from the front lines: Contributions of Eric Rofes—A memoriam. *Journal of Homosexuality, 53*(3), 1–7. doi:10.1300/j082v53n03_01

Bart, P. B., Bentz, L., Clausen, J., Costa, L., Froines, A., Golan, G., . . . Sarker, S (1999). In sisterhood? Women's studies and activism. *Women's Studies Quarterly, 27*, 257–267. Retrieved from http://www.jstor.org/action/ShowPublication?journalcode=womestudquar

Baumgadner, J., & Richards, A. (2005). *Grassroots: A field guide for feminist activism*. New York, NY: Farrar, Strauss & Giroux.

Becker, S. L. (1995). Response to Conquergood: Don Quixotes in the academy—Are we tilting at windmills? In K. N. Cissna (Ed.), *Applied communication in the 21st century* (pp. 1–19). Mahwah, NJ: Lawrence Erlbaum.

Beers, D. L. (2006). *For the prevention of cruelty: The history and legacy of animal rights activism in the United States*. Athens: Swallow Press/Ohio University Press.

Bell, B., & Wakeford, K. (Eds.). (2008). *Expanding architecture: Design as activism*. New York, NY: Metropolis Books.

Bennett, W. L. (2003). Communicating global activism: Strengths and vulnerabilities of networked politics. *Information, Communication & Society, 6*, 143–168. doi:10.1080/1369118032000093860

Benson, T. W., & Johnson, B. (1968). The rhetoric of resistance: Confrontation with the warmakers, Washington, D.C., October, 1967. *Today's Speech, 16*(3), 35–42. doi:10.1080/01463376809385494

Bernstein, S. (2011). *Bridges of reform: Interracial civil rights activism in twentieth-century Los Angeles*. New York, NY: Oxford University Press.

Berta-Avila, Revilla, A. T., & Figueroa, J. L. (Eds.). (2011). *Marching students: Chicana and Chicano activism in education, 1968 to the present*. Reno: University of Nevada Press.

Bérubé, M. (1997). Intellectual inquiry and academic activism. *Asking Questions, 10*(4), 18–21. doi:10.1007/s12129-997-1111-3

Bevington, D. (2009). *The rebirth of environmentalism: Grassroots biodiversity activism from the spotted owl to the polar bear*. Washington, DC: Island Press.

Bizzell, P. (2000). Feminist methods of research in the history of rhetoric: What difference do they make? *Rhetoric Society Quarterly, 30*(4), 5–17. doi: 10.1080/02773940009391186

Blackburn, M. V., Clark, C. T., Kenney, l. M., & Smith, J. M. (Eds.). (2010). *Acting out! Combating homophobia through teacher activism.* New York, NY: Teachers College Press.

Blomley, N. K. (1994). Activism and the academy. *Environment and Planning D: Society and Space, 12*, 383–385.

Blum, E. D. (2008). *Love Canal revisited: Race, class, and gender in environmental activism.* Lawrence: University Press of Kansas.

Bob, C. (2005). *The marketing of rebellion: Insurgents, media, and international activism.* New York, NY: Cambridge University Press.

Boggs, G. L. (with Kurashige, S.). (2011). *The next American revolution: Sustainable activism for the twenty-first century.* Berkeley: University of California Press.

Bolick, C. (2007). *David's hammer: The case for an activist judiciary.* Washington, DC: Cato Institute.

Boris, E. (1998). Scholarship and activism: The case of welfare justice. *Feminist Studies, 24*, 27–31. Retrieved from http://www.jstor.org/action/showPublication?journalCode=feministstudies

Bowen, H. W. (1963a). Does non-violence persuade? *Today's Speech, 11*(1), 10–11. doi:10.1080/01463376309385325

Bowen, H. W. (1963b). The future of non-violence. *Today's Speech, 11*(3), 3–4. doi:10.1080/01463376309385342

Bowen, H. W. (1967). A realistic view of non-violent assumptions. *Today's Speech, 15*(3), 9–10. doi:10.1080/10463376709368832

Boyer, E. L. (1990). *Scholarship reconsidered: Priorities of the professorate.* Princeton, NJ: Carnegie Foundation for the Advancement of Teaching.

Boyer, E. L. (1996). The scholarship of engagement. *Bulletin of the American Academy of Arts and Sciences, 49*(7), 18–33.

Bradley, M. (2006). Reframing the Montreal massacre: Strategies for feminist media activism. *Canadian Journal of Communication, 31*, 929–936. Retrieved from http://www.cjc-online.ca

Braddock, A. P. (1833). *Applied psychology for advertisers.* London, England: Butterworth.

Bresnahan, R. (2007). Community radio and social activism in Chile 1990–2007: Challenges for grass roots voices during the transition to democracy. *Journal of Radio Studies, 14*, 212–233. doi:10.1080/10955040701583320

Britton, H., Fish, J., & Meintjes, S. (Eds.). (2009). *Women's activism in South Africa: Working across divides.* Scottsville: South Africa: University of KwaZulu-Natal Press.

Brodkin, K. (2007). *Making democracy matter: Identity and activism in Los Angeles.* New Brunswick, NJ: Rutgers University Press.

Brodkin, K. (2009). *Power politics: Environmental activism in South Los Angeles.* New Brunswick, NJ: Rutgers University Press.

Broome, B. J., Carey, C., De La Garza, S. A., Martin, J. & Morris, R. (2005). In the thick of things: A dialogue about the activist turn in intercultural communication. In W. J. Starosta & G.-M. Chen (Eds.), *Taking stock in intercultural com-*

munication: Where to now? (pp. 145–175). Washington, DC: National Communication Association.

Bugajski, J., & Pollack, M. (1989). *East European fault lines: Dissent, opposition, and social activism.* Boulder, CO: Westview Press.

Bullert, B. J. (2000). Progressive public relations, sweatshops, and the net. *Political Communication, 17,* 403–407. doi:10.1080/10584600050179022

Burke, E. M. (2005). *Managing a company in an activist world: The leadership challenge of corporate citizenship.* Westport, CT: Praeger.

Butler, J. E. (2000). Democracy, diversity, and civic engagement. *Academe: Bulletin of the AAUP, 86*(4), 52–55. Retrieved from http://www.aaup.org/AAUP/pubsres/academe

Caiazza, A. (2007). *I knew I could do this work: Seven strategies that encourage women's political activism.* Washington, DC: Institute for Women's Policy Research.

Cancian, F. M. (1993). Conflicts between activist research and academic success: Participatory research and alternative strategies. *American Sociologist, 24,* 92–106. doi:10.1007/bf02691947

Cancian, F. M. (1996). Participatory research and alternative strategies for activist sociology. In H. Gottfried (Ed.), *Feminism and social change: Bridging theory and practice* (pp. 187–205). Champaign: University of Illinois Press.

Canel, E. (2010). *Barrio democracy in Latin America: Participatory decentralization and community activism in Montevideo.* University Park: Pennsylvania State University Press.

Carapico, S. (1998). *Civil society in Yemen: The political economy of activism in modern Arabia.* New York, NY: Cambridge University Press.

Carbaugh, D. (1989). The critical voice in ethnography of communication research. *Research on Language and Social Interaction, 23,* 261–282. doi:10.1080/08351818909389324

Carey, J. W. (1982). The mass media and critical theory: An American view. In M. Burgoon (Ed.), *Communication yearbook* (Vol. 6, pp. 18–33). Beverly Hills, CA: Sage.

Carey, J. W. (1983). The origins of the radical discourse on cultural studies in the United States. *Journal of Communication, 33*(3), 311–313. doi:10.1111/j.1460-2466.1983.tb02431.x

Carey, J. W. (1989). *Communication as culture: Essays on media and society.* Boston, MA: Unwin Hyman.

Carey, J. W. (2002). *The engaged discipline.* Boston, MA: National Communication Association and Allyn & Bacon.

Carlone, D., & Taylor, B. (1998). Organizational communication and cultural studies: A review essay. *Communication Theory, 8,* 337–367. doi:10.1111/j.1468-2885.1998.tb00224.x

Carragee, K. M. (1990). Interpretive media study and interpretive social science. *Critical Studies in Mass Communication, 7,* 81–96. doi:10.1080/15295039009360166

Carragee, K. M. (1996). Critical ethnographies and the concept of resistance. In M. Morgan & S. Leggett (Eds.), *Mainstream(s) and margins: Cultural politics in the 90s* (pp. 126–142). Westport, CT: Greenwood Press.

Carragee, K. M., & Roefs, W. (2004). The neglect of power in recent framing research. *Journal of Communication, 54*, 214–233. doi:10.1111/j.1460-2466.2004.tb02625.x

Carroll, S. J. (2005). Reflections on activism and social change for scholars of women and politics. *Politics & Gender, 1*, 326–336. doi:10.1017/S1743923X05221074

Carroll, W. K., & Hackett, R. A. (2006). Democratic media activism through the lens of social movement theory. *Media, Culture & Society, 28*, 83–104. doi:10.1177/0163443706059289

Carter, K., & Spitzack, C. (Eds.). (1989). *Doing research on women's communication: Perspectives on theory and method.* Norwood, NJ: Ablex.

Carter, N. (2007). *The politics of the environment: Ideas, activism, policy* (2nd ed.). New York, NY: Cambridge University Press.

Chan, J. M. (2007). Media and large-scale demonstrations: The pro-democracy movement in post-handover Hong Kong. *Asian Journal of Communication, 17*, 215–228. doi:10.1080/01292980701306639

Chan, J. M., & Lee, F. L. (2007). Media and politics in post-handover Hong Kong: An introduction. *Asian Journal of Communication, 17*, 127–133. doi: 10.1080/01292980701306456

Chandler, R. M., Wang, L., & Fuller, L. K. (2009). *Women, war, and violence: Personal perspectives and global activism.* New York, NY: Palgrave Macmillan.

Charland, M. (1991). Finding a horizon and telos: The challenge to critical rhetoric. *Quarterly Journal of Speech, 77*, 71–74. doi:10.1080/00335639109383944

Chatterton, P. (2008). Demand the possible: Journeys in changing our world as a public activist-scholar. *Antipode, 40*, 421–427. doi:10.1111/j.1467-8330.2008.00609.x

Checkoway, B. (2001). Renewing the civic mission of the American research university. *Journal of Higher Education, 72*, 125–147. Retrieved from http://www.jstor.org/action/showPublication?journalCode=jhighereducation

Cheney, G. (1995). Democracy in the workplace: Theory and practice from the perspective of communication. *Journal of Applied Communication Research, 23*, 167–200. doi:10.1080/00909889509365424

Cheney, G., Wilhelmsson, M., & Zorn, T., Jr. (2002). 10 strategies for engaged scholarship. *Management Communication Quarterly, 16*, 92–100. doi:10.1177/0893318902161006

Cherwitz, R. A. (2005, January 17). Citizen scholars: Research universities must strive for academic engagement. *Scientist*, p. 10. Retrieved from http://www.the-scientist.com

Chibango, C., & Kajau, G. (2010). *Voice of the voiceless: Student activism in Zimbabwe.* Harare, Zimbabwe: Silveira House.

Chiu, I. (2010). *The foundations and anatomy of stakeholder activism.* Portland, OR: Hart.

Chvasta, M. (2006). Anger, irony, and protest: Confronting the issues of efficacy, again. *Text and Performance Quarterly, 26*, 5–16. doi:10.1080/10462930500382278

Cissna, K. N. (1982). Editor's note: What is applied communication research? *Journal of Applied Communication Research, 10*, i–iii. doi:10.1080/00909888209365216

Cissna, K. N., Eadie, W. F., & Hickson, M., III. (2009). The development of applied communication research. In L. R. Frey & K. N. Cissna (Eds.), *Routledge handbook of applied communication research* (pp. 3–25). New York, NY: Routledge.

Clark, J. (2008). *Aborigines & activism: Race and the coming of the sixties to Australia*. Crawley: University of Western Australia Press.
Clark, N. (1996). The critical servant: An Isocratean contribution to critical rhetoric. *Quarterly Journal of Speech, 82,* 111–124. doi:10.1080/00335639609384145
Clark, W. (2000). *Activism in the public sphere: Exploring the discourse of political participation*. Burlington, VT: Ashgate.
Clavel, P. (2010). *Activists in city hall: The progressive response to the Reagan era in Boston and Chicago*. Ithaca, NY: Cornell University Press.
Clift, E., & Freimuth, V. (1997). Changing women's lives: A communication perspective on participatory qualitative research techniques for gender equality. *Journal of Gender Studies, 6,* 289–296. doi:10.1080/09589236.1997.9960689
Cloud, D. L. (1994). The materiality of discourse as oxymoron: A challenge to critical rhetoric. *Western Journal of Communication, 58,* 141–163. doi:10.1080/10570319409374493
Cobb, D. M. (2008). *Native activism in Cold War America: The struggle for sovereignty*. Lawrence: University Press of Kansas.
Cobb, D. M., & Fowler, L. (Eds.). (2007). *Beyond red power: American Indian politics and activism since 1900*. Santa Fe, NM: School for Advanced Research.
Cockburn, C. (2007). *From where we stand: War, women's activism, and feminist analysis*. New York, NY: Zed Books.
Collier, R., & Sheldon, S. (Eds.). (2006). *Fathers' rights activism and law reform in comparative perspective*. Portland, OR: Hart.
Collins, D. E. (2005). Faculty activism: The ivory tower and scholar-activism. *Academe: Bulletin of the AAUP, 91*(5), Article 5. Retrieved from http://www.aaup.org/ AAUP/pubsres/academe
Collins, P. H. (2000). *Black feminist thought: Knowledge, consciousness, and the politics of empowerment* (Rev. ed.). New York, NY: Routledge.
Condit, C. M. (1993). The critic as empath: Moving away from totalizing theory. *Western Journal of Communication, 57,* 178–190. doi:10.1080/10570319309374441
Conquergood, D. (1985). Performing as a moral act: Ethical dimensions of the ethnography of performance. *Literature in Performance, 5*(2), 1–13. doi:10.1080/10462938509391578
Conquergood, D. (1992). Ethnography, rhetoric, and performance. *Quarterly Journal of Speech, 78,* 80–97. doi:10.1080/00335639209383982
Conquergood, D. (1995). Between rigor and relevance: Rethinking applied communication. In K. N. Cissna (Ed.), *Applied communication for the 21st century* (pp. 79–96). Mahwah, NJ: Lawrence Erlbaum.
Conquergood, D. (2002). Performance studies: Interventions and radical research. *TDR: The Drama Review, 46,* 145–156. doi:10.1162/105420402320980550
Coopman, T. M. (2000). High speed access: Micro radio, action, and activism on the internet. *American Communication Journal, 3*(3). Retrieved from http://www.acjournal.org
Cory, J. (2005). *Activist business ethics*. New York, NY: Spring.
Costello, P. J. M. (2003). *Action research*. New York, NY: Continuum.
Costello, P. (2011). *Effective action research: Developing reflective thinking and practice*. New York, NY: Continuum International.

Couso, J., Huneeus, A., & Sieder, R. (Eds.). (2010). *Cultures of legality: Judicialization and political activism in Latin America*. New York, NY: Cambridge University Press.

Crabtree, R. D. (1998). Mutual empowerment in cross-cultural participatory development and service learning: Lessons in communication and social justice from projects in El Salvador and Nicaragua. *Journal of Applied Communication Research, 26*, 182–209. doi:10.1080/00909889809365501

Craig, R. T. (1989). Communication as a practical discipline. In B. Dervin, L. Grossberg, B. J. O'Keefe, & E. Wartella (Eds.), *Rethinking communication: Vol. 1. Paradigm issues* (pp. 97–122). Newbury Park, CA: Sage.

Craig, R. T. (1995). Applied communication research in a practical discipline. In K. N. Cissna (Ed.), *Applied communication in the 21st century* (pp. 147–155). Mahwah, NJ: Lawrence Erlbaum.

Cronkhite, G. L. (1969). Out of the ivory tower: A proposal for useful research in communication and decision. In R. J. Kibler & L. L. Barker (Eds.), *Conceptual frontiers in speech-communication: Report of the New Orleans Conference on Research and Instructional Development* (pp. 113–135). New York, NY: Speech Association of America.

Crosby, F. J., Todd, J., & Worrell, J. (1996). Have feminists abandoned social activism? Voices from the academy. In L. Montada & M. J. Lerner (Eds.), *Current societal concerns about social justice* (pp. 85–102). New York, NY: Plenum Press.

Croteau, D., Hoynes, W., & Ryan, C. (Eds.). (2005). *Rhyming hope and history: Activists, academics, and social movement scholarship*. Minneapolis: University of Minnesota Press.

Crowe, T. R. (2008). *The end of Eden: Writings of an environmental activist*. Nicholasville, KY: Wind.

Crowley, J. E. (2008). *Defiant dads: Fathers' rights activists in America*. Ithaca, NY: Cornell University Press.

Crowley, S. (1992). Reflections on the argument that won't go away: Or, a turn of the ideological screw. *Quarterly Journal of Speech, 78*, 450–465. doi:10.1080/00335639209384010

Culverson, D. R. (1999). *Contesting apartheid: U.S. activism, 1960–1987*. Boulder, CO: Westview Press.

Cushman, D. P. (1989). The role of critique in the ethnographic study of human communication practices. *Research on Language and Social Interaction, 23*, 243–250. doi:10.1080/08351818909389322

Cushman, E. (1996). The rhetorician as agent of social change. *College Composition and Communication, 47*, 7–28. Retrieved from http://www.jstor.org/action/showPublication?journalCode=collcompcomm

Cushman, E. (1999). The public intellectual, service learning, and activist research. *College English, 61*, 328–336. Retrieved from http://www.jstor.org/action/showPublication?journalCode=collegeenglish

Cwikel, J. G. (2006). *Social epidemiology: Strategies for public health activism*. New York, NY: Columbia University Press.

da Costa, B., & Philip, K. (Eds.). (2008). *Tactical biopolitics: Art, activism, and technoscience*. Cambridge, MA: MIT Press.

Dallimore, E. J. (2000). A feminist response to issues of validity in research. *Women's Studies in Communication, 23,* 157–171. doi:10.1080/07491409.2000.10162567
David, L. (2008). *Stop global warming: The solution is you!: An activist's guide* (2nd ed.). Golden, CO: Fulcrum.
Davies, T. R. (2007). *The possibilities of transnational activism: The campaign for disarmament between the two world wars.* Boston, MA: Martinus Nijhoff.
Davis, D. K. (Ed.). (1989). Cultural studies [Special section]. *Critical Studies in Mass Communication, 6,* 404–461.
Davis, W. H. (1915). Debating as related to non-academic life. *Quarterly Journal of Public Speaking, 1,* 105–113. doi:10.1080/00335631509360471
Dawson, J. I. (1996). *Eco-nationalism: Anti-nuclear activism and national identity in Russia, Lithuania, and Ukraine.* Durham, NC: Duke University Press.
Death Penalty Information Center. (n.d.). *Innocence and the death penalty.* Retrieved from http://www.deathpenaltyinfo.org/innocence-and-death-penalty
Deetz, S. A. (1982). Critical interpretive research in organizational communication. *Western Journal of Speech Communication, 46,* 131–149. doi:10.1080/10570318209374073
Deetz, S. (1988). Cultural studies: Studying meaning and action in organizations. In J. A. Anderson (Ed.) *Communication yearbook* (Vol. 11, pp. 335–345). Thousand Oaks, CA: Sage.
Deetz, S. A. (1992). *Democracy in an age of corporate colonization: Developments in communication and the politics of everyday life.* Albany: State University of New York Press.
Deetz, S., & Mumby, D. (1990). Power, discourse, and the workplace: Reclaiming the critical tradition in communication studies in organizations. In J. A. Anderson (Ed.), *Communication yearbook* (Vol. 13, pp. 18–47). Thousand Oaks, CA: Sage.
de Jong, W., Shaw, M., & Stammers, N. (2005). *Global activism, global media.* Ann Arbor, MI: Pluto Press.
DeLeon, D. (Ed.). (1994). *Leaders from the 1960s: A biographic sourcebook of American activism.* Westport, CT: Greenwood Press.
Delia, J. G. (1987). Communication research: A history. In C. R. Berger & S. H. Chaffee (Eds.), *Handbook of communication science* (pp. 20–98). Newbury Park, CA: Sage.
Dell, P. (2009). *Protecting the planet: Environmental activism.* Minneapolis, MN: Compass Point Books.
DeLuca, K. M. (1999). *Image politics: The new rhetoric of environmental activism.* New York, NY: Guilford Press.
DeLuca, K. M., & Peeples, J. (2002). From public sphere to public screen: Democracy, activism, and the "violence" of Seattle. *Critical Studies in Media Communication, 19,* 125–151. doi:10.1080/07393180216559
DeNavas-Walt, C., Proctor, D., & Smith, J. C. (2010, September). *Income, poverty, and health insurance coverage in the United States: 2009.* Washington, DC: U.S. Government Printing Office. Retrieved from http://www.census.gov/prod/2010pubs/p60-238.pdf
Denzin, N. K. (2003). *Performance ethnography: Critical pedagogy and the politics of culture.* Thousand Oaks, CA: Sage.

Dever, C. (2004). *Skeptical feminism: Activist theory, activist practice*. Minneapolis: University of Minnesota Press.
Dewey, J. (1910). *How we think*. Boston, MA: D. C. Heath.
de Witte, H. (Ed.). (2005). *Job insecurity, union involvement, and union activism*. Burlington, VT: Ashgate.
Diani, M. (2000). Social movement networks virtual and real. *Information, Communication & Society, 3*, 386–401. doi:10.1080/13691180051033333
Diasio, F. (2010). AMARC and more than 25 years of community media activism. *Telematics & Informatics, 27*, 193–195. doi:10.1016/j.tele.2009.06.010
Dichter, D. (2004). U.S. media activism and the search for constituency. *Media Development, 51*(1), 8–13.
Dickson, B. (Ed.). (2007). *Judicial activism in common law supreme courts*. New York, NY: Oxford University Press.
Diener, M. L., & Liese, H. (2009). *Finding meaning in civically engaged scholarship: Personal journeys, professional experiences*. Charlotte, NC: Information Age.
Dieter, R. C. (2009, October). *Smart on crime: Reconsidering the death penalty in a time of economic crisis*. Washington, DC: Death Penalty Information Center. Retrieved from http://www.deathpenaltyinfo.org/documents/CostsRptFinal.pdf
Disney, J. L. (2008). *Women's activism and feminist agency in Mozambique and Nicaragua*. Philadelphia, PA: Temple University Press.
Divinski, R., Hubbard, A., Kendrick, J. R., Jr., & Noll, J. (2009). Social change as applied social science: Obstacles to integrating the roles of activist and academic. *Peace & Change, 19*, 3–24. doi:10.1111/j.1468-0130.1994.tb00596.x
Doak, R. S. (2008). *Dolores Huerta: Labor leader and civil rights activist*. Minneapolis, MN: Compass Point Books.
Dolan, J. (1997). Advocacy and activism: Identity, curriculum, and theatre studies in the twenty-first century. *Theatre Topics, 7*, 1–10. doi:10.1353/tt.1997.0003
Dolhinow, R. (2010). *A jumble of needs: Women's activism and neoliberalism in the colonias of the Southwest*. Minneapolis: University of Minnesota Press.
Donald, R. (2009). *Animal rights: How you can make a difference*. Mankato, MN: Capstone Press.
Donovan, B. (2006). *White slave crusades: Race, gender, and anti-vice activism 1887–1917*. Urbana: University of Illinois Press.
Dow, D. R. (2009). *America's prophets: How judicial activism makes America great*. Westport, CT: Praeger.
Downs, J., & Manion, J. (Eds.). (2004). *Taking back the academy!: History of activism, history as activism*. New York, NY: Routledge.
Dozier, D. M., & Lauzen, M. M. (2000). Liberating the intellectual domain from the practice: Public relations, activism, and the role of the scholar. *Journal of Public Relations Research, 12*, 3–22. doi:10.1207/S1532754XJPRR1201_2
Drogus, C. A., & Stewart-Gambino, H. (2005). *Activist faith: Grassroots women in democratic Brazil and Chile*. University Park: Pennsylvania State University Press.
D'Souza, R. (2009). Prison houses of knowledge: Activist scholarship and revolution in the era of "globalization." *McGill Journal of Education, 44*, 19–38. Retrieved from http://mje.mcgill.ca

Dunbar-Hester, C. (2009). "Free the spectrum!" Activist encounters with old and new media technology. *New Media & Society, 11*, 221-240. doi:10.1177/1461444808100160

Dunbar-Hester, C. (2010). Beyond "dudecore"? Challenging gendered and "raced" technologies through media activism. *Journal of Broadcasting & Electronic Media, 54*, 121-135. doi:10.1080/08838150903550451

Earl, J., & Kimport, K. (2011). *Digitally enabled social change: Online and offline activism in the age of the internet.* Cambridge, MA: MIT Press.

Eaton, M. (2010). Manufacturing community in an online activist organization. *Information, Communication & Society, 13*, 174-192. doi:10.1080/13691180902890125

Eisenhofer, J. W., & Barry, M. J. (2006). *Shareholder activism handbook.* New York, NY: Aspen.

Elliott, H. S. (1927). *The why and how of group discussion.* New York, NY: Association Press.

Endres, D. (2011). American Indian activism and audience: Rhetorical analysis of Leonard Peltier's response to denial of clemency. *Communication Reports, 24*, 1-11. doi: 10.10801/08934215.2011.554624

Enke, A. (2007). *Finding the movement: Sexuality, contested space, and feminist activism.* Durham, NC: Duke University Press.

Eno, H. L. (1920). *Activism.* Princeton: NJ: Princeton University Press.

Esquibel, E., & Mejia, R. (2008). Bridging the gap: Performance ethnography as a form of community building. *Rocky Mountain Communication Review, 4*(1), 41-46. Retrieved from http://www.rmcr.utah.edu

Espinosa, G., Elizondo, B., & Miranda, J. (Eds.). (2005). *Latino religions and civic activism in the United States.* New York, NY: Oxford University Press.

Espinosa, G., & García, M. T. (Eds.). (2008). *Mexican American religions: Spirituality, activism, and culture.* Durham, NC: Duke University Press.

Fábián, K. (Ed.). (2010). *Domestic violence in postcommunist states: Local activism, national policies, and global forces.* Bloomington: Indiana University Press.

Faier, E. (2004). *Organizations, gender and the culture of Palestinian activism in Haifa, Israel.* New York, NY: Routledge.

Falconer, T. (2001). *Watchdogs and gadflies: Activism from marginal to mainstream.* Toronto, Canada: Penguin Books.

Farrell, T. B., & Aune, J. A. (1979). Critical theory and communication: A selective literature review. *Quarterly Journal of Speech, 65*, 93-107. doi:10.1080/00335637909383461

Faud-Luke, A. (2009). *Design activism: Beautiful strategies for a sustainable world.* Sterling, VA: Earthscan.

Fernandez, T. L. (1968). Jonathan Baldwin Turner at Illinois College: Era of protest. *Today's Speech, 16*(3), 9-14. doi:10.1080/01463376809385489

Ferree, M. M., & Tripp, A. M. (Eds.). (2006). *Global feminism: Transnational women's activism, organizing, and human rights.* New York: New York University Press.

Fetner, T. (2008). *How the religious right shaped lesbian and gay activism.* Minneapolis: University of Minnesota Press.

Few, A. L., Piercy, F. P., & Stremmel, A. (2007). Balancing the passion for activism with the demands of tenure: One professional's story from three perspectives. *NWSA Journal, 19*(3), 47–66. Retrieved from http://muse.jhu.edu/journals/nwsa

Fine, M. (1989). The politics of research and activism: Violence against women. *Gender and Society, 3*, 549–558. Retrieved from http://www.jstor.org/action/showPublication?journalCode=gendersociety

Fine, M. G. (1990). Epistemological and methodological commitments of a feminist perspective. *Women and Language, 13*(2), 35–36.

Fine, M. (2006). Bearing witness: Methods for researching oppression and resistance—A textbook for critical research. *Social Justice Research, 19*, 83–108. doi:10.1007/s11211-006-0001-0

Fine, M., & Vanderslice, V. (1992). Qualitative activist research: Reflections on methods and politics. In F. B. Bryant, J. Edwards, R. S. Tindale, E. J. Posacav, L. Heath, E. Henderson-King, & Y. Suarez-Balcazar (Eds.), *Methodological issues in applied psychology: Social psychological applications to social issues* (Vol. 2, pp. 199–218). New York, NY: Plenum Press.

Finley, L. L., & Stringer, E. R. (2010). *Beyond burning bras: Feminist activism for everyone*. Westport, CT: Praeger.

Fish, S. (2004, May 21). Why we built the ivory tower. *The New York Times*, p. A23. Retrieved from http://www.nytimes.com

Fish, S. (2008). *Save the world on your own time*. New York, NY: Oxford University Press.

Fisher, R. E. (1997). *The concept of judicial activism: Its nature and function in United States constitutional law*. Sherman Oaks, CA: Banner Books International.

Fitzgerald, H. E., Burack, C., & Seifer, S. (Eds.). (2010). *Handbook of engaged scholarship: Contemporary landscapes, future directions*. East Lansing: Michigan State University Press.

Foley, D., & Valenzula, A. (2005). Critical ethnography: The politics of collaboration. In N. K. Denzin & Y. S. Lincoln (Eds.), *The Sage handbook of qualitative methods* (3rd ed., pp. 217–234). Thousand Oaks, CA: Sage.

Formwalt, L. W. (2007, February). Balancing scholarship and activism: An interview with Lawrence J. Friedman. *OAH Newsletter*. Retrieved from http://www.oah.org/pubs/nl/2007feb/friedman.html

Francesco, D. (2010). AMARC and more than 25 years of community media activism. *Telematics & Informatics, 27*, 193–195. doi:10.1016/j.tele.2009.06.010

Frey, L. R. (Ed.). (1998a). Communication and social justice research [Special issue]. *Journal of Applied Communication Research, 26*(2).

Frey, L. R. (1998b). Communication and social justice research: Truth, justice, and the applied communication way. *Journal of Applied Communication Research, 26*, 155–164. doi:10.1080/00909889809365499

Frey, L. R. (2000). To be applied or not to be applied, that isn't even the question; but wherefore art thou, applied communication researcher? Reclaiming applied communication research and redefining the role of the researcher. *Journal of Applied Communication Research, 28*, 178–182. doi:10.1080/00909880009365565

Frey, L. R. (2006). Across the great divides: From nonpartisan criticism to partisan criticism to applied communication activism for promoting social change and social justice. In O. Swartz (Ed.), *Social justice and communication scholarship* (pp. 35–51). Mahwah, NJ: Lawrence Erlbaum.

Frey, L. R. (2009). What a difference more difference-making communication scholarship might make: Making a difference from and through communication research. *Journal of Applied Communication Research, 37*, 205–214. doi:10.1080/00909880902792321

Frey, L. R., Botan, C. H., & Kreps, G. L. (2000). *Investigating communication: An introduction to research methods* (2nd ed.). Boston, MA: Allyn and Bacon.

Frey, L. R., & Carragee, K. M. (2007). *Communication activism* (2 Vols.). Cresskill, NJ: Hampton Press.

Frey, L. R., & Cissna, K. N. (Eds.). (2009). *Routledge handbook of applied communication research*. New York, NY: Routledge.

Frey, L. R., & Palmer, D. L. (Eds.). (in press). *Communication activism pedagogy*. Cresskill, NJ: Hampton Press.

Frey, L. R., Pearce, W. B., Pollock, M. A., Artz, L., & Murphy, B. A. O. (1996). Looking for justice in all the wrong places: On a communication approach to social justice. *Communication Studies, 47*, 110–127. doi:10.1080/10510979609368467

Frey, L. R., & SunWolf. (2009). Across applied divides: Great debates of applied communication scholarship. In L. R. Frey & K. N. Cissna (Eds.), *Routledge handbook of applied communication research* (pp. 26–54). New York, NY: Routledge.

Friend, H. E., Jr. (2008). *Gifts of an uncommon life: The practice of contemplative activism*. Herndon, VA: Alban Institute.

Gaarder, E. (2011). *Women and the animal rights movement*. New Brunswick, NJ: Rutgers University Press.

Gan, S., Gomez, J., & Johannen, U. (Eds.). (2004). *Asian cyberactivism: Freedom of expression and media censorship*. Bangkok, Thailand: Friedrich Naumann Foundation, East and Southeast Asia Regional Office.

Gardner, M. (2009). *Linking activism: Ecology, social justice, and education for social change*. New York, NY: Routledge.

Garrett, K. R. (2006). Protest in an information society: A review of literature on social movements and new ICTs. *Information, Communication & Society, 9*, 202–224. doi:10.1080/13691180600630773

Gaternby, B., & Humphries, M. (1996). Feminist commitments in organizational communication: Participatory action research as feminist praxis. *Australian Journal of Communication, 23*(2), 73–88.

Gates, H. L., Jr., & Marable, M. (2000). A debate on activism in black studies. In M. Marable (Ed.), *Dispatches from the ebony tower: Intellectuals confront the African American experience* (pp. 186–194). New York, NY: Columbia University Press.

Gebissa, E. (Ed.). (2009). *Contested terrain: Essays on Oromo studies, Ethipianist discourses, and politically engaged scholarship*. Trenton, NJ: Red Sea Press.

Gellner, D. N. (2009). *Ethnic activism and civil social in South Asia*. Thousand Oaks, CA: Sage.

Gellner, D. N. (Ed.). (2010). *Varieties of activist experience: Civil society in South Asia*. Thousand Oaks, CA: Sage.

George, S. (2005). If you want to be relevant: Advice to the academic from a scholar-activist. In R. P. Appelbaum & W. I. Robinson (Eds.), *Critical globalization studies* (pp. 3–10). New York, NY: Routledge.

Gibson, D. C. (2003). Use of staged event in successful community activism. *Public Relations Quarterly, 48*, 35–40.

Gibson, T. A. (2000). Beyond cultural populism: Notes toward the critical ethnography of media audiences. *Journal of Communication Inquiry, 24*, 253–274. doi:10.1177/0196859900024003002

Gill, T. M. (2010). *Beauty shop politics: African American women's activism in the beauty industry*. Urbana: University of Illinois Press.

Gillan, K. (2009). The UK anti-war movement online: Uses and limitations of internet technologies for contemporary activism. *Information, Communication & Society, 12*, 25–43. doi:10.1080/13691180802158532

Gillett, J. (2003). The challenges of institutionalization for AIDS media activism. *Media, Culture & Society, 25*, 607–624. doi:10.1177/01634437030255003

Ginwright, S. A. (2010). *Black youth rising: Activism and radical healing in urban America*. New York, NY: Teachers College Press.

Ginwright, S., Noguera, P., & Cammarota, J. (Eds.). (2006). *Beyond resistance! Youth activism and community change: New democratic possibilities for practice and policy for America's youth*. New York, NY: Routledge.

Glassgold, J. M., & Drescher, J. (Eds.). (2007). *Activism and LGBT psychology*. Binghamton, NY: Haworth Medical.

Gleason, C. (2010). *Animal rights activist*. New York, NY: Crabtree.

Glickman, L. B. (2009). *Buying power: A history of consumer activism in America*. Chicago, IL: University of Chicago Press.

Goldstein, P. (Ed.). (1994). *Styles of cultural activism: From theory and pedagogy to women, Indians, and communism*. Newark: University of Delaware Press.

Gómez-Peña, G. (2005). *Ethno-techno: Writing on performance, activism, and pedagogy* (E. Peña, Ed.). New York, NY: Routledge.

Goodall, H. L., Jr. (2010). *Counter-narrative: How progressive academics can challenge extremists and promote social justice*. Walnut Creek, CA: Left Coast Press.

Goodley, D., & Moore, M. (2000). Doing disability research: Activist lives and the academy. *Disability & Society, 15*, 861–882. doi:10.1080/713662013

Gordon, H. R. (2010). *We fight to win: Inequality and the politics of youth activism*. New Brunswick, NJ: Rutgers University Press.

Gould, K. (2006). *Catholic activism in south-west France, 1540–1570*. Burlington, VT: Ashgate.

Grabill, J. T. (2000). Shaping local HIV/AIDS services policy through activist research: The problem of client involvement. *Technical Communication Quarterly, 9*, 29–50. doi:10.1080/10572250009364684

Grano, D. A. (2002). Spiritual–material identification in the deep ecology movement. *Southern Communication Journal, 68*, 27–39. doi:10.1080/10417940209373249

Graubart, J. (2008). *Legalizing transnational activism: The struggle to gain social change from NAFTA's citizen petitions*. University Park: Pennsylvania State University Press.

Gray, M. L. (2009). "Queer nation is dead/long live queer nation": The politics and poetics of social movement and media representation. *Critical Studies in Media Communication, 26*, 212–236. doi:10.1080/15295030903015062

Greenberg, J., & Knight, G. (2004). Framing sweatshops: Nike, global production, and the American news media. *Communication & Critical/Cultural Studies, 1,* 151–175. doi:10.1080/14791420410001685368

Greenhaw, W. (2011). *Fighting the devil in Dixie: How civil rights activists took on the Klu Klux Klan in Alabama.* Chicago, IL: Lawrence Hill Books.

Greenwood, D. J., & Levin, M. (2000). Introduction to action research: Social research for social change. In N. K. Denzin & Y. S. Lincoln (Eds.), *Handbook of qualitative research* (2nd ed., pp. 85–106). Thousand Oaks, CA: Sage.

Greenwood, D. J., & Levin, M. (2007). *Introduction to action research: Social research for social change* (2nd ed.). Thousand Oaks, CA: Sage.

Gregg, R. B. (1971). The ego-function of the rhetoric of protest. *Philosophy and Rhetoric, 4,* 71–91. Retrieved from http://www.jstor.org/action/show Publication?journalcode=philrhet

Gregory, S., Caldwell, G., Avni, R., & Harding, T. (2005). *Video for change: A guide for advocacy and activism.* Ann Arbor, MI: Pluto Press.

Grewall, J. (2008). Theorizing activism, activizing theory: Feminist academics in Indian Pubjabi society. *NWSA Journal, 20,* 161–183. doi: 10.1353/nwsa.0.0000

Grossberg, L. (1993a). Can cultural studies find true happiness in communication? *Journal of Communication, 43*(4), 89–97. doi:10.1111/j.1460-2466.1993.tb01308.x

Grossberg, L. (1993b). Cultural studies and/in new worlds. *Critical Studies in Mass Communication, 10,* 1–22. doi:10.1080/15295039309366846

Grossberg, L. (1997). *Bringing it all back home: Essays on cultural studies.* Durham, NC: Duke University Press.

Grossberg, L., Nelson, C., & Treichler, P. A. (Eds.). (1992). *Cultural studies.* New York, NY: Routledge.

Grund, L., Cherwitz, R., & Darwin, T. (2001, December 3). Learning to be a citizen-scholar. *Chronicle of Higher Education.* Retrieved from http:// chronicle.com

Guither, H. D. (1998). *Animal rights: History and scope of a radical social movement.* Carbondale: Southern Illinois University Press.

Habal, E. (2007). *San Francisco's International Hotel: Mobilizing the Filipino American community in the anti-eviction movement.* Philadelphia, PA: Temple University Press.

Haiman, F. S. (1967). The rhetoric of the streets: Some legal and ethical considerations. *Quarterly Journal of Speech, 53,* 99–114. doi:10.1080/00335636709382822

Hájek, M., & Kabele, J. (2010). Dual discursive patterns in Czech activists' internet media communication. *European Journal of Communication, 25,* 43–58. doi:10.1177/0267323109354228

Hale, C. R. (2001). What is activist research? *Items and Issues: Social Science Research Council, 2*(1–2), 13–15.

Hale, C. R. (2006). Activist research v. cultural critique: Indigenous land rights and the contradictions of politically engaged anthropology. *Cultural Anthropology, 21,* 96–120. doi:10.1525/can.2006.21.1.96

Hale, C. R. (Ed.). (2008). *Engaging contradictions: Theory, politics, and methods of activist scholarship.* Berkeley: University of California Press.

Hall, M. C. (2009). *Martin Luther King, Jr.: Civil rights leader.* Edina, MN: Magic Wagon.

Hallett, M. A. (Ed.). (1997). *Activism and marginalization in the AIDS crisis*. New York, NY: Haworth Press.
Hamera, J. (2011). Performance ethnography. In N. K. Denzin & Y. S. Lincoln (Eds.), *The Sage handbook of qualitative research* (4th ed., pp. 317–329). Thousand Oaks, CA: Sage.
Hammett, D., & Newsham, A. (2006). Intervention: Widening the ethical debate— Academia, activism, and the arms trade. *Political Geography, 26*, 10–12. doi: 10.1016/j.polgeo.2006.10.012
Hardt, H. (1986). Critical theory in historical perspective. *Journal of Communication, 36*(3), 144–154. doi:10.1111/j.1460-2466.1986.tb01443.x
Hardt, H. (1989). The return of the "critical" and the challenge of radical dissent: Critical theory, cultural studies, and American mass communications research. In J. A. Anderson (Ed.), *Communication yearbook* (Vol. 12, pp. 558–600). Thousand Oaks, CA: Sage.
Hardt, H. (1992). *Critical communication studies: Communication, history and theory in America*. New York, NY: Routledge.
Hardt, H. (1993). Authenticity, communication, and critical theory. *Critical Studies in Mass Communication, 10*, 49–69. doi:10.1080/15295039309366848
Hariman, R. (1991). Critical rhetoric and postmodern theory. *Quarterly Journal of Speech, 77*, 67–70. doi:10.1080/00335639109383943
Harold, C. (2004). Pranking rhetoric: "Culture jamming" as media activism. *Critical Studies in Media Communication, 21*, 189–211. doi:10.1080/0739318042000212693
Harold, C. (2008). [Review of the books *Communication activism* (2 Vols.), by Lawrence R. Frey & K. M. Carragee, Eds.]. *Quarterly Journal of Speech, 94*, 365–370. doi:10.1080/00335630802210393
Harper, G. W., Jamil, O. B., & Wilson, B. D. M. (2007). Collaborative community-based research as activism: Giving voice and hope to lesbian, gay, and bisexual youth. *Journal of Gay & Lesbian Psychotherapy, 11*, 99–119. doi:10.1300/J236v11n03_06
Harris, A. (Ed.). (2008). *Next wave cultures: Feminism, subcultures, activism*. New York, NY: Routledge.
Harris, F. C., Sinclair-Chapman, V., & McKenzie, B. D. (2006). *Countervailing forces in African-American civic activism, 1973–1994*. New York, NY: Cambridge University Press.
Harter, L. M., Dutta, M. J., & Cole, C. (Eds.). (2009). *Communicating for social impact: Engaging communication theory, research, and pedagogy*. Cresskill, NJ: Hampton Press.
Harter, L. M., Hamel-Lambert, J., & Millesen, J. L. (Eds.). (2011). *Participatory partnerships for social action research*. Dubuque, IA: Kendall Hunt.
Hartnett, S. (1998). Lincoln and Douglas meet the abolitionist David Walker as prisoners debate slavery: Empowering education, applied communication, and social justice. *Journal of Applied Communication Research, 26*, 232–253. doi: 10.1080/00909889809365503
Hartnett, S. J. (2010). Communication, social justice, and joyful commitment. *Western Journal of Communication, 74*, 68–93. doi:10.1080/10570310903463778
Hartnett, S. J. (2011). *Challenging the prison-industrial complex: Arts, activism, and educational alternatives*. Urbana: University of Illinois Press.

Hauptman, L. M. (2011). *The Tonawanda Senecas' heroic battle against removal: Conservative activist Indians.* Albany: State University of New York Press.

Hawkesworth, M. E. (2006a). *Feminist inquiry: From political conviction to methodological innovation.* New Brunswick, NJ: Rutgers University Press.

Hawkesworth, M. E. (2006b). *Globalization and feminist activism.* Lanham, MD: Rowman & Littlefield.

Hawthorne, M. (2008). *Striking at the roots: A practical guide to animal activism.* Ropley, Hants, United Kingdom: O Books.

Hay, I. (2001). Critical geography and activism in higher education. *Journal of Geography in Higher Education, 25,* 141–146. doi:10.1080/03098260120067592

Hedda, J. (2008). *His kingdom come: Orthodox pastorship and social activism in revolutionary Russia.* DeKalb: Northern Illinois University.

Held, D. (1982). Critical theory and political transformation. *Media, Culture and Society, 4,* 153–160. doi:10.1177/016344378200400205

Hemment, J. (2007). *Empowering women in Russia: Activism, aid, and NGOs.* Bloomington: Indiana University Press.

Henry, L. A. (2010). *Red to green: Environmental activism in post-Soviet Russia.* Ithaca, NY: Cornell University Press.

Herman, S. N. (2005–2006). Balancing the five hundred hats: On being a legal educator/scholar/activist. *Tulsa Law Review, 41,* 637–659. Retrieved from http://heinonline.org/HOL/Index?collection=journals&index=journals/tlj

Herring, E. (2006). Remaking the mainstream: The case for activist IR scholarship. *Millennium: Journal of International Studies, 35,* 105–119. doi:10.1177/03058298060350011001

Herring, E. (2008). Critical terrorism studies: An activist scholar perspective. *Critical Studies on Terrorism, 1,* 197–211. doi:10.1080/17539150802187507

Hess, D. J. (2007). *Alternative pathways in science and industry: Activism, innovation, and the environment in an era of globalization.* Cambridge, MA: MIT Press.

Hesse-Biber, S. N. (Ed.). (2006). *Handbook of feminist research: Theory and praxis.* Thousand Oaks, CA: Sage.

Hickson, M., III. (1973). Applied communications research: A beginning point for social relevance. *Journal of Applied Communications Research, 1,* 1–5. doi:10.1080/00909887309365170

Hill, F. (1983). A turn against ideology: Reply to Professor Wander. *Central States Speech Journal, 34,* 121–126. doi:10.1080/10510978309368129

Hilton, M. (2009). *Prosperity for all: Consumer activism in an era of globalization.* Ithaca, NY: Cornell University Press.

Hinchey, P. H. (2008). *Action research primer.* New York, NY: Peter Lang.

Ho, P., & Edmonds, R. L. (2007). *China's embedded activism: Opportunities and constraints of a social movement.* New York, NY: Routledge.

Hochstetler, K., & Keck, M. E. (2007). *Greening Brazil: Environmental activism in state and society.* Durham, NC: Duke University Press.

Holsworth, R. D. (1989). *Let your life speak: A study of politics, religion, and antinuclear weapons activism.* Madison: University of Wisconsin Press.

Holtzhousen, D. (2010). *Public relations as activism: Postmodern approaches to theory and practice.* New York, NY: Routledge.

Holzer, B. (2010). *Moralizing the corporation: Transnational activism and corporate accountability*. Northampton, MA: Edward Elgar.

Hopkins, A., & McGregor, H. (1991). *Working for change: The movement against domestic violence*. North Sydney, New South Wales, Australia: Allen & Unwin.

Hondagneu-Sotelo, P. (1993). Why advocacy research? Reflections on research and activism with immigrant women. *American Sociologist, 24*, 56–68. doi:10.1007/bf02691945

Hostetter, D. L. (2006). *Movement matters: American antiapartheid activism and the rise of multicultural politics*. New York, NY: Routledge.

Hsing, Y.-t., & Lee, C. K. (Eds.). (2010). *Reclaiming Chinese society: The new social activism*. New York, NY: Routledge.

Huesca, R. (2008). Activist media. In W. Donsbach (Ed.), *The international encyclopedia of communication* (Vol. 1, pp. 31–33). Malden, MA: Wiley-Blackwell.

Hung, C.-j. F. (2003). Relationship building, activism, and conflict resolution: A case study on the termination of licensed prostitution in Taiwan. *Asian Journal of Communication, 13*(2), 21–49. doi:10.1080/01292980309364837

Hurwitz, E., & Hurwitz, S. (1994). *Working together against homelessness*. New York, NY: Rosen.

Huspek, M. (1991). Taking aim on Habermas's critical theory: On the road toward a critical hermeneutics. *Communication Monographs, 58*, 225–233. doi: 10.1080/03637759109376226

Icaza, R. (2010). *Networked activisms and regionalism: Power and resistance across borders*. New York, NY: Routledge.

Iraq Body Count. (2011, May 10). *Documented civilian deaths from violence*. Retrieved from http://www.iraqbodycount.org/database

Iraq Coalition Casualty Count. (2011a, May 10). *Afghanistan: Coalition military fatalities by year*. Retrieved from http://icasualties.org/OEF/index.aspx

Iraq Coalition Casualty Count. (2011b, May 10). *Iraq: Coalition military fatalities by year*. Retrieved from http://icasualties.org/Iraq

Iraq Coalition Casualty Count. (2011c, May 10). *Iraq coalition casualties: U.S. wounded totals*. Retrieved from http://icasualties.org/Iraq/USCasualtiesByState.aspx

Jagger, A. M. (Ed.). (2008). *Just methods: An interdisciplinary feminist reader*. Boulder, CO: Paradigm.

James, C., Bernard, W. T., Este, D., Benjamin, A., Lloyd, B., & Turner, T. (2009). *Race & well-being: The lives, hopes and activism of African Canadians*. Black Point, Canada: Fernwood.

Jansen, S. C. (2008). Rethinking social justice scholarship in media and communication [Review of the books *Communication activism* (2 Vols.), by Lawrence R. Frey & K. M. Carragee, Eds.]. *Communication, Culture & Critique, 1*, 329–334. doi:10.1111/j.1753-9137.2008.00026.x

Jason, L. A., Keys, C. B., Suarez-Balcazar, Y., Taylor, R. R., & Davis, M. I. (Eds.). (2003). *Participatory community research: Theories and methods in action*. Washington, DC: American Psychological Association.

Jennings, J. (Ed.). (1997). *Race and politics: New challenges and responses for black activism*. New York, NY: Verso.

Jensen, K. B. (1990). Television futures: A social action methodology for studying interpretive communities. *Critical Studies in Mass Communication, 7*, 129–146. doi:10.1080/15295039009360169

Jeske, C. (2010). *Into the mud: Inspiration for everyday activists: True stories of Africa*. Chicago, IL: Moody.

Joachim, J., & Locher, B. (Eds.). (2008). *Transnational activism in the UN and the EU: A comparative study*. New York, NY: Routledge.

John, S., & Thompson, S. (Eds.). (2003). *New activism and the corporate response*. New York, NY: Palgrave Macmillan.

Johnson, A. P. (2008). *A short guide to action research* (3rd ed.). Boston, MA: Pearson/Allyn and Bacon.

Johnson, J. M. (2008). *Southern women at the Seven Sister colleges: Feminist values and social activism, 1875–1917*. Athens: University of Georgia Press.

Johnson, T. R. (1996). *The occupation of Alcatraz Island: Indian self-determination and the rise of Indian activism*. Urbana: University of Illinois Press.

Johnson, T., Nagel, J., & Champagne, D. (Eds.). (1997). *American Indian activism: Alcatraz to the Longest Walk*. Urbana: University of Illinois Press.

Jones, J. L. (2002). Performance ethnography: The role of embodiment in cultural authenticity. *Theatre Topics, 12*, 1–15. doi:10.1353/tt.2002.0004

Jones, O. O. J. L., Moore, L. L., & Bridgforth, S. (Eds.). (2010). *Experiments in a jazz aesthetic: Art, activism, academia, and the Austin Project*. Austin: University of Texas Press.

Jones, T. S., & Bodtker, A. (1998). A dialectical analysis of a social justice process: International collaboration in South Africa. *Journal of Applied Communication Research, 26*, 357–373. doi:10.1080/00909889809365514

Joy, M. (2008). *Strategic action for animals: A handbook on strategic movement building, organizing, and activism for animal liberation*. New York, NY: Lantern Books.

Joyce, M. (Ed.). (2010). *Digital activism decoded: The new mechanics of change*. New York, NY: International Debate Education Association.

Kahn, R., & Kellner, D. (2004). New media and internet activism: From the "battle of Seattle" to blogging. *New Media & Society, 6*, 87–95. doi:10.1177/1461444804039908

Kahn, S. (2010). *Creating community organizing: A guide for rabble-rousers, activists, and quiet lovers of justice*. San Francisco, CA: Berrett Koehler.

Kahn, S., & Lee, J. (Eds.). (2011). *Activism and rhetoric: Theory and contexts for political engagement*. New York, NY: Routledge.

Kamberg, M.-L. (2009). *Bono: Fighting world hunger and poverty*. New York, NY: Rosen.

Kapoor, D., & Jordan, S. (Eds.). (2009). *Education, participatory action research and social change: International perspectives*. New York, NY: Palgrave Macmillan.

Keck, M. E., & Sikkink, K. (1998). *Activists beyond borders: Advocacy networks in international politics*. Ithaca, NY: Cornell University Press.

Keck, T. M. (2004). *The most activist Supreme Court in history: The road to modern judicial conservatism*. Chicago, IL: University of Chicago Press.

Kecskes, K. (Ed.). (2006). *Engaging departments: Moving faculty culture from private to public, individual to collective focus for the common good*. Bolton, MA: Anker.

Kedrowski, K. M., & Sarow, M. S. (2007). *Cancer activism: Gender, media, and public policy*. Urbana: University of Illinois Press.

Kemmis, S., & McTaggart, R. (2005). Participatory action research: Communication action and the public sphere. In N. K. Denzin & Y. S. Lincoln (Eds.), *The Sage handbook of qualitative research* (3rd ed., pp. 559–603). Thousand Oaks, CA: Sage.

Kennedy, D. (1997). *Academic duty*. Cambridge, MA: Harvard University Press.

Kerns, A. (2011). *Who will shout for us?: Student activists and the Tiananmen Square protest, China, 1989*. Minneapolis, MN: Twenty-first Century Books.

Kerr, H. P. (1959). The rhetoric of political protest. *Quarterly Journal of Speech, 45*, 146–152. doi:10.1080/00335635909385733

Kershaw, T. (2003). The black studies paradigm: The making of scholar activists. In J. L. Conyers, Jr. (Ed.), *Afrocentricity and the academy: Essays on theory and practice* (pp. 27–36). Jefferson, NC: McFarland.

Kibler, R. J., & Barker, L. L. (Eds.). (1969). *Conceptual frontiers in speech communication: Report of the New Orleans Conference on Research and Instructional Development*. New York, NY: Speech Association of America.

Kilmartin, C., & Allison, J. (2007). *Men's violence against women: Theory, research, and activism*. Mahwah, NJ: Lawrence Erlbaum.

Kim, I., & Dutta, M. J. (2009). Studying crisis communication from the subaltern studies framework: Grassroots activism in the wake of Hurricane Katrina. *Journal of Public Relations Review, 21*, 142–164. doi:10.1080/10627260802557423

Kindon, S., Pain, R., & Kesby, M. (Eds.). (2007). *Participatory action research approaches and methods: Connecting people, participation, and place*. New York, NY: Routledge.

Kirby, E. L., Feldner, S., B., Leighter, J., McBride, M. C., Murphy, B. O., Tye-Williams, S., ... Turner, L. H. (2009). "Exploring the basement of social justice issue": A graduate upon graduation. In L. M. Harter, M. J. Dutta, & C. C. Cole (Eds.), *Communicating for social impact: Engaging theory, research, and pedagogy* (pp. 63–77). Cresskill, NJ: Hampton Press.

Klawiter, M. (2008). *The biopolitics of breast cancer: Changing cultures of disease and activism*. Minneapolis: University of Minnesota Press.

Klimke, M., & Scharloth, J. (Eds.). (2008). *1968 in Europe: A history of protest and activism, 1956–1977*. New York, NY: Palgrave Macmillan.

Knight, G., & Greenberg, J. (2002). Promotionalism and subpolitics: Nike and its labor critics. *Management Communication Quarterly, 15*, 541–570. doi:10.1177/0893318902154002

Knight, G. L. (2009). *Icons of African American protest: Trailblazing activists of the civil rights movement*. Westport, CT: Greenwood Press.

Knight, M. G. (2000). Ethics in qualitative research: Multicultural feminist activist research. *Theory into Practice, 39*, 170–179. doi:10.1207/s1543042tip3903_8

Kosokoff, S., & Carlmichael, C. W. (1970). The rhetoric of protest: Song, speech, and attitude change. *Southern Speech Journal, 35*, 295–302. doi:10.1080/10417947009372062

Kowal, D. M. (2000). One cause, two paths: Militant vs. adjustive strategies in British American women's suffrage movements. *Communication Quarterly, 48*, 240–255. doi:10.1080/01463370009385595

Krone, K. J., & Harter, L. M. (Eds.). (2007). Organizational communication scholars as public intellectuals [Special forum]. *Management Communication Quarterly, 21*, 75-136.

Krouse, S. A., & Howard, H. A. (Eds.). (2009). *Keeping the campfires going: Native women's activism in urban communities.* Lincoln: University of Nebraska Press.

Kuypers, J. A. (2000). Must we all be political activists? *American Communication Journal, 4*(1). Retrieved from http://acjournal.org

Ladson-Billings, G., & Donner, J. (2005). The moral activist role of critical race theory scholarship. In N. K. Denzin & Y. S. Lincoln (Eds.), *The Sage handbook of qualitative methods* (3rd ed., pp. 279-301). Thousand Oaks, CA: Sage.

Ladwig, J. G., & Gore, J. M. (1994). Extending power and specifying method within the discourse of activist research. In A. Gitlin (Ed.), *Power and method: Political activism and educational research* (pp. 227-338). New York, NY: Routledge.

Lampert, K. (2005). *Traditions of compassion: From religious duty to social activism.* New York, IL: Palgrave Macmillan.

Lassiter, L. E. (2005). *The Chicago guide to collaborative ethnography.* Chicago, IL: University of Chicago Press.

Lawston, J. M. (2009). *Sisters outside: Radical activists working for women prisoners.* Albany: State University of New York Press.

Lawston, J. M., & Lucas, A. (Eds.). (2011). *Razor wire women: Prisoners, activists, scholars, and artists.* Albany: State University of New York Press.

Lawton, W. (1968). Thoreau and the rhetoric of dissent. *Today's Speech, 16*(2), 23-25. doi:10.1080/01463376809385477

Lazar, M. M. (2007). Feminist critical discourse analysis: Articulating feminist discourse praxis. *Critical Discourse Studies, 4*, 141-164. doi:10.1080/17405900701464816

Lea, V., & Sims, E. J. (Eds.). (2008). *Undoing whiteness in the classroom: Critical educultural teaching approaches for social justice activism.* New York, NY: Peter Lang.

Lederach, J. P. (1995). *Preparing for peace: Conflict transformation across cultures.* Syracuse, NY: Syracuse University Press.

Lederach, J. P. (1997). *Building peace: Sustainable reconciliation in divided societies.* Washington, DC: United States Institute of Peace Press.

Lee, F. L. F. (2008). Local press meets transnational activism: News dynamics in an anti-WTO protest. *Chinese Journal of Communication, 1*, 55-76. doi:10.1080/17544750701861921

Lemisch, J. (2003). 2.5 cheers for bridging the gap between activism and the academy; or, stay and fight. *Radical History Review, 85*, 239-248. doi:10.1215/01636545-2003-85-239

Lemish, D. (2002). Gender at the forefront: Feminist perspectives on action theoretical approaches in communication research. *Communications: The European Journal of Communication Research, 27*, 63-78. doi:10.1515/comm.27.1.63

Lempert, R. O. (2001). Activist scholarship. *Law & Society Review, 35*, 25-32. Retrieved from http://www.jstor.org/action/showPublication?journalCode=lawsocietyreview

Lengel, L. B. (1998). Researching the "other," transforming ourselves: Methodological considerations of feminist ethnography. *Journal of Communication Inquiry, 22*, 229-250. doi:10.1177/0196859998022003001

Lewis, F. P. (1999). *The context of judicial activism: The endurance of the Warren Court legacy in a conservative age.* Lanham, MD: Rowman & Littlefield.

Leyland, W. (Ed.). (2002). *Out in the Catsro: Desire, promise, activism.* San Francisco, CA: Leyland.

Li, X. (2007). *Voices rising: Asian Canadian cultural activism.* Vancouver, Canada: University of British Columbia Press.

Liamputtong, P., & Rumbold, J. (Eds.). (2008). *Knowing differently: Arts-based and collaborative research methods.* New York, NY: Nova Science.

Lievrouw, L. A. (2011). *Alternative and activist new media.* Malden, MA: Polity Press.

Lindquist, S. A., & Cross, F. B. (2009). *Measuring judicial activism.* New York, NY: Oxford University Press.

Liu, M., Geron, K., & Lai, T. A. M. (2008). *The snake dance of Asian American activism: Community, vision, and power in the struggle for social justice, 1945–2000.* Lanham, MD: Lexington Books.

Lomas, C. W. (1960). The agitator in American politics. *Western Speech, 24,* 76–83.

Lomas, C. W. (1963). Agitator in a cassock. *Western Speech, 27,* 14–26.

Love, J. (1985). *The U.S. anti-apartheid movement: Local activism in global politics.* New York, NY: Praeger.

Lovitz, D. (2010). *Muzzling a movement: The effects of anti-terrorism law, money, and politics on animal activism.* New York, NY: Lantern Books.

Lukes, S. (2005). *Power: A radical view* (2nd ed.). New York, NY: Palgrave MacMillan.

Lykke, N. (2010). *Feminist studies: A guide to intersectional theory, methodology and writing.* New York, NY: Routledge.

MacDonald, K. (2008). *Understanding Jewish influence: A study in ethnic activism.* Augusta, GA: Washington Summit.

Maddison, S., & Scalmer, S. (2006). *Activist wisdom: Practical knowledge and creative tension in social movements.* Sydney, Australia: University of New South Wales Press.

Madison, D. S. (2005a). *Critical ethnography: Method, ethics, and performance.* Thousand Oaks, CA: Sage.

Madison, D. S. (2005b). Critical ethnography as street performance: Reflections of home, race, murder, and justice. In N. K. Denzin & Y. S. Lincoln (Eds.), *The Sage handbook of qualitative research* (3rd ed., pp. 537–546). Thousand Oaks, CA: Sage.

Madison, D. S. (2006). The dialogic performative in critical ethnography. *Text & Performance Quarterly, 26,* 320–324. doi:10.1080/10462930600828675

Madison, D. S. (2010). *Acts of activism: Human rights as radical performance.* New York, NY: Cambridge University Press.

Mahrouse, G. (2009). The compelling story of the white/Western activist in the war zone: Examining race, neutrality, and exceptionalism in citizen journalism. *Canadian Journal of Communication, 34,* 659–673. Retrieved from http://www.cjc-online.ca

Maier, E., & Lebon, N. (Eds.). (2010). *Women's activism in Latin America and the Caribbean: Engendering social justice, democratizing citizenship.* New Brunswick, NJ: Rutgers University Press.

Maigushca, B., & Thornton, M. (Eds.). (2006). Activism, academia and education [Special section]. *Millennium: Journal of International Studies, 35,* 101–165.

Makau, J. M. (1996). Notes on communication education and social justice. *Communication Studies, 47*, 135–141. doi:10.1080/10510979609368469

Maloney, W. A., & van Deth, J. W. (Eds.). (2010). *Civil society and activism in Europe: Contextualising engagement and political orientation.* New York, NY: Routledge.

Markowitz, L. (2000). *Worker activism after successful union organizing.* Armonk, NY: M. E. Sharpe.

Marlow, L. (2009). *Mothers in prison: Women's autobiography and activism.* Saarbrücken, Germany: VDM Verlag.

Marshall, C., & Anderson, A. L. (Eds.). (2009). *Activist educators: Breaking past limits.* New York, NY: Routledge.

Martin, H. H. (1966). The rhetoric of academic protest. *Central States Speech Journal, 17*, 244–250. doi:10.1080/10510976609362843

Martin, R. (2009). Academic activism. *PLMA, 24*, 838–849. doi:10.1632/pmla.2009.124.3.838

Martinez-Saenz, M. (2009). Creating change: Arts, activism, and the academy. *Diversity & Democracy, 12*(2), 16–17. Retrieved from http://www.diversityweb.org/DiversityDemocracy

Mauch, C., Stolzfus, N., & Weiner, D. R. (Eds.). (2006). *Shades of green: Environmental activism around the globe.* Lanham, MD: Rowman & Littlefield.

Maxey, I. (1999). Beyond boundaries? Activism, academia, reflexivity and research. *Area, 31*, 199–208. doi:10.1111/j.1475-4762.1999.tb00084.x

Maynard, J. (2007). *Fight for liberty and freedom: The original of Australian Aboriginal activism.* Canberra, Australia: Aboriginal Studies Press.

Mayock, E. C., & Radulescu, D. (Eds.). (2010). *Feminist activism in academia: New essays on personal, political and professional change.* Jefferson, NC: McFarland.

Mbazira, C. (2009). *Public interest litigation and judicial activism in Uganda: Improving the enforcement of economic, social and cultural rights.* Kampala, Uganda: Human Rights & Peace Centre, Faculty of Law, Makerere University.

McCall, M. M. (2000). Performance ethnography: A brief history and some advice. In N. K. Denzin & Y. S. Lincoln (Eds.), *Handbook of qualitative research* (2nd ed., pp. 421–433). Thousand Oaks, CA: Sage.

McCaughey, M., & Ayers, M. D. (Eds.). (2003). *Cyberactivism: Online activism in theory and practice.* New York, NY: Routledge.

McChesney, R. W. (2004). Media policy goes to main street: The uprising of 2003. *Communication Review, 7*, 223–258. doi:10.1080/10714420490492139

McEdwards, M. G. (1968). Agitative rhetoric: Its nature and effect. *Western Speech, 32*, 36–43. doi:10.1080/10570316809389547

McEvoy, K., & McGregor, L. (Eds.). (2008). *Transitional justice from below: Grassroots activism and the struggle for change.* Portland, OR: Hart.

McGee, J. J. (2003). A pilgrim's progress: Metaphor in the rhetoric of Mary Fisher, AIDS activist. *Women's Studies in Communication, 26*, 191–213. doi:10.1080/07491409.2003.10162459

McGregory, J. (2010). *Downhome gospel African American spiritual activism in Wireglass Country.* Jackson: University Press of Mississippi.

McGuire, M., & Slembeck, E. (1987). An emerging critical rhetoric: Hellmut Geissner's sprechwissenschaft. *Quarterly Journal of Speech, 73*, 349–358. doi:10.1080/00335638709383813

McHale, J. P. (2004). *Communicating for change: Strategies of social and political advocates*. Lanham, MD: Rowman & Littlefield.

McHale, J. P. (Producer/Director), Wiley, R. (Producer/Editor), & Huck, D. (Producer/Assistant Editor). (2002). *Unreasonable doubt: The Joe Amrine case* [Videotape]. Available from John P. McHale, School of Communication, Illinois States University, 453 Fell Hall, Normal, IL 61761-4480

McHale, J. P. (Producer/Director), Wylie, R. (Producer/Editor), & Huck, D. (Producer/Assistant Editor). (2005). *Picture this: A fight to save Joe Amrine* [DVD]. Available from https://www.createspace.com

McKinnon, S., Chávez, K. R., & Way, D. (2007). Toward a healthy dialogue: A further consideration of ethics for feminist ethnography. *Kaleidoscope: A Graduate Journal of Qualitative Communication Research, 6*, 1–20.

McIntyre, A. (2006). Activist research and student agency in universities and urban communities. *Urban Education, 41*, 628–647. doi:10.1177/0042085906292510

McIntyre, A. (2008). *Participatory action research*. Thousand Oaks, CA: Sage.

McKerrow, R. E. (1989). Critical rhetoric: Theory and praxis. *Communication Monographs, 56*, 91–111. doi:10.1080/03637758909390253

McKerrow, R. E. (1991). Critical rhetoric in a postmodern world. *Quarterly Journal of Speech, 77*, 75–78. doi:10.1080/00335639109383945

McKerrow, R. E. (1993). Critical rhetoric and the possibility of the subject. In I. Angus & L. Langsdorf (Eds.), *The critical turn: Rhetoric and philosophy in postmodern discourse* (pp. 51–67). Carbondale: Southern Illinois University Press.

McKerrow, R. E., & St. John, J. (2006). The public intellectual and the role(s) of criticism. *Quarterly Journal of Speech, 92*, 310–319. doi:10.1080/00335630600938799

McNiff, J., & Whitehead, J. (2002). *Action research: Principles and practice* (2nd ed.). New York, NY: RoutledgeFalmer.

McNiff, J., & Whitehead, J. (2006). *Action research: Living theory*. Thousand Oaks, CA: Sage.

McNiff, J., & Whitehead, J. (2009). *Doing and writing action research*. Thousand Oaks, CA: Sage.

McNiff, J., & Whitehead, J. (2010). *You and your action research project*. New York, NY: Routledge.

Meikle, G. (2002). *Future active: Media activism and the internet*. New York, NY: Routledge.

Merriam-Webster Online. (2011, May 3). *Activism*. Retrieved from http://www.merriam-webster.com/dictionary/activism

Messer-Davidow, E. (2002). *Disciplining feminism: From social activism to academic discourse*. Durham, NC: Duke University Press.

Mienczakowski, J. (1995). The theatre of ethnography: The reconstruction of ethnography into theatre with emancipatory potential. *Qualitative Inquiry, 1*, 360–375. doi:10.1177/107780049500100306

Mikula, M. (Ed.). (2008). *Women, activism and social change: Stretching boundaries*. New York, NY: Routledge.

Miller, B. A. (2000). *Geography and social movements: Comparing antinuclear activism in the Boston area*. Minneapolis: University of Minnesota Press.

Miller, S. (2008). *Edible action: Food activism and alternative economics*. Halifax, Nova Scotia, Canada: Fernwood.

Minkler, M., & Wallerstein, N. (Eds.). (2008). *Community-based participatory research for health: From process to outcomes* (2nd ed.). San Francisco, CA: Jossey-Bass.
Mische, A. (2008). *Partisan politics: Communication and contention across Brazilian youth activist networks.* Princeton, NJ: Princeton University Press.
Mitchell, T. D. (2007). Critical service-learning as social justice education: A case study of the Citizen Scholars Program. *Equity & Excellence in Education, 40,* 101–112. doi:10.1080/10665680701228797
Mohapatra, P. K. (Ed.). (1999). *Social justice: Philosophical perspectives.* New Delhi, India: D. K. Printworld.
Monbiot, G. (2010, June 7). The oil firms' profits ignore the real costs. *The Guardian.* Retrieved from http://www.guardian.co.uk
Monks, R. A. G. (1999). *The emperor's nightingale: Restoring the integrity of the corporation in the age of shareholder activism.* Reading, MA: Perseus Books.
Moore, L. N. (2010). *Black rage in New Orleans: Police brutality and African American activism from World War II to Hurricane Katrina.* Baton Rouge: Louisiana State University Press.
Moreno, J. (2007). *Dancing in dissent: Poetry for activism.* San Diego, CA: Dolphin Calling Press.
Mukherjee, A. (2009). *Frontiers in PRA and PLA: PRA & PLA in applied research.* New Delhi, India: Academic Foundation.
Muller, S. (1969). The limits of scholarly activism. *PS: Political Science & Politics, 2,* 582–590. Retrieved from http://www.jstor.org/action/showPublication?journalCode=ps
Mumby, D. K. (1993). Critical organizational communication studies: The next 10 years. *Communication Monographs, 60,* 18–25. doi:10.1080/03637759309376290
Munger, F. (2001). Inquiry and activism in law and society. *Law & Society Review, 35,* 7–20. Retrieved from http://www.jstor.org/action/showPublication?journalCode=lawsocietyreview
Munson, Z. W. (2008). *The making of pro-life activists: How social movement mobilization works.* Chicago, IL: University of Chicago Press.
Murphy, J. M. (1995). Critical rhetoric as political discourse. *Argumentation & Advocacy, 32,* 1–15.
Murray, C., Parry, K., Robinson, P., & Goddard, P. (2008). Reporting dissent in wartime: British press, the anti-war movement and the 2003 Iraq War. *European Journal of Communication, 23,* 7–27. doi:10.1177/0267323107085836
Nabhan-Warren, K. (2005). *The Virgin of el barrio: Marian apparitions, Catholic evangelizing, and Mexican American activism.* New York: New York University Press.
Nagengast, C., & Vélez-Ibáñez, C. G. (Eds.). (2004). *Human rights: The scholar as activist.* Oklahoma City, OK: Society for Applied Anthropology.
Nah, S., Veenstra, A. S., & Shah, D. V. (2006). The internet and anti-war activism: A case study of information, expression, and action. *Journal of Computer-Mediated Communication, 12*(1), Article 12. doi:10.1111/j.1083-6101.2006.00323.x
Naples, N. A. (2003). *Feminism and method: Ethnography, discourse analysis, and activist research.* New York, NY: Routledge.

Naples, N. A., & Steck, L. W. (2004, August). *Activist scholarship and academic activism: Towards an action plan for SWSD activism* [Report]. Kingston, RI: Sociologists for Women in Society.

Napoli, P. M. (2009). Public interest media advocacy and activism as a social movement. In C. S. Beck (Ed.), *Communication yearbook* (Vol. 33, pp. 384–429). New York, NY: Routledge.

Napoli, P. M., & Aslama, M. (Eds.). *Communications research in action: Scholar-activist collaborations for a democratic public sphere.* New York, NY Fordham University Press.

Nawab, M., & Ali, F. (Eds.). (2009). *Igniting thought, unleashing youth: Perspectives on Muslim youth and activism in Singapore.* Singapore: Select.

Nelson, C. (2009). Afterword: Activism and community in the academy. In M. Rothberg & P. K. Garrett (Eds.), *Cary Nelson and the struggle for the university: Poetry, politics, and the profession* (pp. 221–230). Albany: State University of New York Press.

Nelson, C., & Watt, C. (2004). *Office hours: Activism and change in the academy.* New York, NY: Routledge.

Newman, K. S., & Jacobs, E. S. (2010). *Who cares?: Public ambivalence and government activism from the New Deal to the second gilded age.* Princeton, NJ: Princeton University Press.

Newman, L. R., & Kurs, D. J. (2009). *I fill this small space: The writings of a deaf activist.* Washington, DC: Gallaudet University Press.

Nichter, M. (2006). Anthropology and global health: Reflections of a scholar-activist. *India Review, 3–4,* 343–371. doi:10.1080/14736480600939124

Nickitas, D. M., Middaugh, D. J., & Aries, N. (Eds.). (2011). *Policy and politics for nurses and other health professions: Advocacy and action.* Sudbury, MA: Jones & Bartlett.

Nielsen, J. M. (Ed.). (1990). *Feminist research methods: Exemplary readings in the social sciences.* Boulder, CO: Westview Press.

Noffke, S., & Somekh, B. (Eds.). (2009). *The Sage handbook of educational action research.* Thousand Oaks, CA: Sage.

Norman, J. M. (2009). Creative activism: Youth media in Palestine. *Middle East Journal of Culture & Communication, 2,* 251–274. doi:10.1163/187398509X12476683126464

Novek, E. (2005). "The devil's bargain": Censorship, identity and the promise of empowerment in a prison newspaper. *Journalism: Theory, Practice & Criticism, 6,* 5–23. doi:10.1177/1464884905048950

Nygreen, K. (2006). Reproducing or challenging power in the questions we ask and the methods we use: A framework for activist research in urban education. *Urban Review, 38,* 1–26. doi:10.1007/s11256-006-0026-6

Ochoa, E. C., & Ochoa, G. L. (Eds.). (2005). *Latino Los Angeles: Transformation, communities, and activism.* Tucson: University of Arizona Press.

Offord, B. (2003). *Homosexual rights as human rights: Activism in Indonesia, Singapore, and Australia.* New York, NY: Peter Lang.

Okafor, O. C. (2007). *The African human rights system, activist forces, and international institutions.* Cambridge, United Kingdom: Cambridge University Press.

Olesen, T. (Ed.). (2011). *Power and transnational activism.* New York, NY: Routledge.

Oleson, V. (2005). Early millennial feminist qualitative research: Challenges and contours. In N. K. Denzin & Y. S. Lincoln (Eds.), *The Sage handbook of qualitative methods* (3rd ed., pp. 235–278). Thousand Oaks, CA: Sage.

Oliver, B. (2007). *Jean Beadle: A life of labor activism*. Crawley: University of Western Australia Press.

Ollman, B. (1993). A model of activist research: How to study class consciousness ... and why we should. In B. Ollman (Ed.), *Dialectical investigations* (pp. 147–179). New York, NY: Routledge.

Olomo, O. O. O. (2006). Performance and ethnography, performing ethnography, performance ethnography. In D. S. Madison & J. Hamera (Eds.), *The Sage handbook of performance studies* (pp. 339–345). Thousand Oaks, CA: Sage.

Olson, K. M., & Olson, C. D. (2003). Problems of exclusionary research criteria: The case against the "usable knowledge" litmus test for social justice communication research. *Communication Studies, 54*, 438–450. doi:10.1080/10510970309363302

Online Etymology Dictionary. (2011, May 10). *Theory*. Retrieved from http://www.etymonline.com/index.php?term=theory

Ono, K. A., & Sloop, J. M. (1992). Commitment to "telos"—A sustained critical rhetoric. *Communication Monographs, 59*, 48–60. doi:10.1080/03637759209376248

Opel, A. (2004). *Micro radio and the FCC: Media activism and the struggle over broadcast policy*. Westport, CT: Praeger.

Orta, A. (2008). Remembering the Ayllu, remaking the nation: Indigenous scholarship and activism in the Bolivian Andes. *Journal of Latin American Anthropology, 6*, 198–201. doi:10.1525/jlca.2001.6.1.198

Palacios, J. M. (2007). *The Catholic social imagination: Activism and the just society in Mexico and the United States*. Chicago, IL: University of Chicago Press.

Palczewski, H. (2001). Cyber-movements, new social movements, and counterpublics. In R. Asen & D. C. Brouwer (Eds.), *Counterpublics and the state* (pp. 161–186). Albany: State University of New York Press.

Palmeri, T. (2006). Media activism in a "conservative" city: Modeling citizenship. In O. Swartz (Ed.), *Social justice and communication scholarship* (pp. 149–173). Mahwah, NJ: Lawrence Erlbaum.

Panitch, M. (2007). *Disability, mothers, and organization: Accidental activists*. New York, NY: Routledge.

Patterson, D. S. (2008). *The search for negotiated peace: Women's activism and citizen diplomacy in World War I*. New York, NY: Routledge.

Pearce, W. B. (1998). On putting social justice in the discipline of communication and putting enriched concepts of communication in social justice research and practice. *Journal of Applied Communication Research, 26*, 272–278. doi:10.1080/00909889809365505

Peeples, J. A. (2003). Trashing South-Central: Place and identity in a community-level environmental justice dispute. *Southern Communication Journal, 69*, 82–95. doi:10.1080/10417940309373280

Pestello, F. G., Saxton, S. L., Miller, D. E., & Donnelly, P. G. (1996). Community and the practice of sociology. *Teaching Sociology, 24*, 148–156. Retrieved from http://www.jstor.org/action/showPublication?journalCode=teacsoci

Peterman, F. P. (2008). *Partnering to prepare urban teachers: A call to activism*. New York, NY: Peter Lang.

Pezzullo, P. C. (2001). Performing critical interruptions: Stories, rhetorical invention, and the environmental justice movement. *Western Journal of Communication, 65*, 1–25. doi:10.1080/10570310109374689

Pezzullo, P. C. (2003). Resisting "National Breast Cancer Awareness Month": The rhetoric of counterpublics and their cultural performances. *Quarterly Journal of Speech, 89*, 345–365. doi:10.1080/0033563032000160981

Pezzulo, P. (2009). [Review of the books *Communication activism* (2 Vols.), by L. R. Frey & K. M. Carragee, Eds.]. *Journal of Communication, 59*, E1–E6. doi:10.1111/j.1460-2466.2009.01426.x

Phillips, P., & Project Censored. (Eds.). (2003). *Project Censored guide to independent media and activism*. New York, NY: Seven Stories Press.

Phillips, S. D. (2008). *Women's social activism in the new Ukraine: Development and the politics of differentiation*. Bloomington: Indiana University Press.

Pickerill, J. (2003). *Cyberprotest: Environmental activism online*. New York, NY: Manchester University Press.

Pierson, P., & Skocpol, T. (Eds.). (2007). *The transformation of American politics: Activist government and the rise of conservatism*. Princeton, NJ: Princeton University Press.

Pilotta, J. J., McCaughan, J. A., Jasko, S., Murphy, J., Jones, T., Wilson, L., ... Endress, K. (2001). *Communication and social action research*. Cresskill, NJ: Hampton Press.

Pini, B., Brown, K., & Previte, J. (2004). Politics and identity in cyberspace: A case study of Australian women in agriculture online. *Information, Communication & Society, 7*, 167–184. doi:10.1080/1369118042000232639

Pinsky, D. (2010). *Jewish feminists: Complex identities and activist lives*. Urbana: University of Illinois Press.

Piper, N., & Uhlin, A. (Eds.). (2004). *Transnational activism in Asia: Problems of power and democracy*. New York, NY: Routledge.

Platt, S. N. (2011). *Art and politics now: Cultural activism in a time of crisis*. New York, NY: Midmarch Arts Press.

Pollock, D., & Cox, J. R. (1991). Historicizing "reason": Critical theory, practice, and postmodernity. *Communication Monographs, 58*, 170-178. doi:10.1080/03637759109376221

Pollock, M. A., Artz, L., Frey, L. R., Pearce, W. B., & Murphy, B. A. O. (1996). Navigating between Scylla and Charybdis: Continuing the dialogue on communication and social justice. *Communication Studies, 47*, 142–151. doi:10.1080/10510979609368470

Pulido, L. (2006). *Black, brown, yellow, and left: Radical activism in Los Angeles*. Berkeley: University of California Press.

Quigley, D., Sanchez, V., Handy, D., Goble, R., & George, P. (2000). Participatory research strategies in nuclear risk management for native communities. *Journal of Health Communication, 5*, 305–331. doi:10.1080/10810730050199123

Quinn, T., & Meiners, E. R. (2009). *Flaunting it!: Queers organizing for public education and justice*. New York, NY: Peter Lang.

Rael, P. (Ed.). (2008). *Africa-American activism before the Civil War: The freedom struggle in the antebellum North*. New York, NY: Routledge.

Rakow, L. F. (2005). Why did the scholar cross the road? Community action research and the citizen-scholar. In S. H. Priest (Ed.), *Communication impact: Designing research that matters* (pp. 5–17). Lanham, MD: Rowman & Littlefield.

Ralston, M., & Keeble, E. (2009). *Reluctant bedfellows: Feminism, activism, and prostitution in the Philippines*. Sterling, VA: Kumarian Press.

Rambo, K. S. (2009). *Trivial complaints: The role of privacy in domestic violence law and activism in the U.S.* New York, NY: Columbia University Press.

Rao, H. (2009). *Market rebels: How activists make or break radical innovations*. Princeton, NJ: Princeton University Press.

Raunig, G. (2007). *Art and revolution: Transversal activism in the long twentieth century* (A. Derieg, Trans.). Los Angeles, CA: Seiotext(e).

Real, M. (1984). Debate on critical theory and the study of communications: A commentary on ferment in the field. *Journal of Communication, 34*(4), 72–80. doi:10.1111/j.1460-2466.1984.tb02189.x

Reason, P., & Bradbury, H. (Eds.). (2008). *The Sage handbook of action research: Participative inquiry and practice* (2nd ed.). Thousand Oaks, CA: Sage.

Reber, B. H., & Berger, B. K. (2005). Framing analysis of activist rhetoric: How the Sierra Club succeeds or fails at creating salient messages. *Public Relations Review, 31*, 185–195. doi:10.1016/j.pubrev.2005.02.020

Reed, R. (2009). At the intersection of scholarship and activism. *Anthropological Quarterly, 82*, 1065–1068. doi:10.1353/anq.0.0096

Reed, T. V. (2005). *The art of protest: Culture and activism from the civil rights movement to the streets of Seattle*. Minneapolis: University of Minnesota Press.

Reidner, R., & O'Conner, N. (Eds.). (1999). Activism and the academy [Special section]. *Minnesota Review, 50/51*, 55–160.

Reimann, K. D. (2009). *The rise of Japanese NGOs: Activism from above*. New York, NY: Routledge.

Reinharz, S. (with Davidman, L.). (1992). *Feminist methods in social research*. New York, NY: Oxford University Press.

Reitan, R. (2007). *Global activism*. New York, NY: Routledge.

Reydams, L. (Ed.). (2011). *Global activism reader*. New York, NY: Continuum.

Rho, H.-K. (2007). *Shareholder activism: Corporate governance reforms in Korea*. New York, NY: Palgrave Macmillan.

Rhoads, R. A. (1998). *Freedom's web: Student activism in an age of cultural diversity*. Baltimore, MD: John Hopkins University Press.

Rimmerman, C. A. (2010). *The new citizenship: Unconventional politics, activism, and service* (4th ed.). Boulder, CO: Westview Press.

Riser, R. V. (2010). *Defying disfranchisement: Black voting rights activism in the Jim Crow South, 1890–1908*. Baton Rouge: Louisiana State University Press.

Ristock, J. L., & Pennell, J. (1996). *Community research as empowerment: Feminist links, postmodern interruptions*. New York, NY: Oxford University Press.

Roces, M., & Edwards, L. (Eds.). (2010). *Women's movements in Asia: Feminisms and transnational activism*. New York, NY: Routledge.

Rodger, E., & Field, J. B. (2010). *Social justice activist*. New York, NY: Crabtree.

Rodriguez, C. (1996). African American anthropology and the pedagogy of activist community research. *Anthropology & Education Quarterly, 27*, 414–431. doi: 10.1525/aeq.1996.27.3.04x0356r

Rogers, E. M. (1994). *A history of communication study: A biographical approach.* New York, NY: Free Press.

Rosaen, C. L., Foster-Fishman, P. G., & Fear, F. A. (2001). The citizen scholar: Joining voices and values in the engagement interface. *Metropolitan Universities: An International Forum, 12*(4), 10–29.

Rosenfield, L. W. (1983). Ideological miasma. *Central States Speech Journal, 34,* 119–121. doi:10.1080/10510978309368128

Rudacille, D. (2006). *The riddle of gender: Science, activism, and transgender rights.* New York, NY: Anchor Books.

Rude, L. G. (1969). The rhetoric of farmer–labor agitators. *Central States Speech Journal, 20,* 280–285. doi:10.1080/10510976909362979

Rushing, J. H., & Frentz, T. S. (1991). Integrating ideology and archetype in rhetorical criticism. *Quarterly Journal of Speech, 77,* 385–406. doi:10.1080/00335639109383970

Ryan, C. (1991). *Prime time activism: Media strategies for grassroots organizing.* Boston, MA: South End Press.

Ryan, C., Carragee, K. M., & Meinhofer, W. (2001). Theory into practice: Framing, the news media, and collective action. *Journal of Broadcasting & Electronic Media, 45,* 175–182. doi:10.1207/s15506878jobem4501_11

Ryan, C., Carragee, K. M., & Schwerner, C. (1998). Media, movements, and the quest for social justice. *Journal of Applied Communication Research, 26,* 165–181. doi:10.1080/00909889809365500

Sagor, R. (2010). *Collaborative action research for professional learning communities.* Bloomington, IN: Solution Tree Press.

Sanchez, J., & Stuckey, M. E. (2000). The rhetoric of American Indian activism in the 1960s and 1970s. *Communication Quarterly, 48,* 120–136. doi: 10.1080/01463370009385586

Sanchez, M. C. (2009). *Reforming the world: Social activism and the problem of fiction in nineteenth-century America.* Iowa City: University of Iowa Press.

Sandell, R., Dodd, J., & Garland-Thompson, R. (Eds.). (2010). *Re-presenting disability: Activism and agency in the museum.* New York, NY: Routledge.

Sandler, R., & Pezzullo, P. C. (Eds.). (2007). *Environmental justice and environmentalism: The social justice challenge to the environmental movement.* Cambridge, MA: MIT Press.

Sandmann, L. R., & Gillespie, A. (1991). Land grant universities on trial. *Adult Learning, 3*(2), 23-25.

Sanford, V. (2009). Gendered observations: Activism, advocacy, and the academy. In M. K. Huggins & M.-L. Glebbeek (Eds.), *Women fielding danger: Negotiating ethnographic identities in field research* (pp. 123–146). Lanham, MD: Rowman & Littlefield.

Sanford, V., & Angel-Ajani, A. (Eds.). (2006). *Engaged observer: Anthropology, advocacy, and activism.* New Brunswick, NJ: Rutgers University Press.

Santiago, C. D. (1972). *A century of activism.* Manila, The Philippines: Rex.

Saunders, P. C. (2006). *China's global activism: Strategy, drivers, and tools.* Washington, DC: National Defense University Press.

Saxton, S. (1993). Sociologist as citizen-scholar: A symbolic interactionist alternative to normal sociology. In T. R. Vaughan, G. Sjoberg, & L. T. Reynolds (Eds.), *A*

critique of contemporary American sociology (pp. 232–251). Dix Hills, NY: General Hall.
Schell, E. E., & Rawson, K. J. (Eds.). (2010). *Rhetorica in motion: Feminist rhetorical methods and methodologies*. Pittsburgh, PA: University of Pittsburgh Press.
Schneider, E. M. (2003). Afterword: The perils and pleasures of activist scholarship. *American University Journal of Gender, Social Policy & Law, 11*, 965–967. Retrieved from http://www.wcl.american.edu/journal/genderlaw
Schoening, G. T., & Anderson, J. A. (1995). Social action media studies: Foundational arguments and common premises. *Communication Theory, 5*, 93–116. doi:10.1111/j.1468-2885.1995.tb00100.x
Schramm, W. (1997). *The beginnings of communication study in America: A personal memoir* (S. H. Chaffee & E. M. Rogers, Eds.). Thousand Oaks, CA: Sage.
Schurman, R., & Munro, W. A. (2010). *Fighting for the future of food: Activists versus agribusiness in the struggle over biotechnology*. Minneapolis: University of Minnesota Press.
Scott, R. L., & Smith, D. K. (1969). The rhetoric of confrontation. *Quarterly Journal of Speech, 55*, 1–8. doi:10.1080/00335636909382922
Schwichtenberg, C., & Davis, D. K. (1989). Feminist cultural studies. *Critical Studies in Mass Communication, 6*, 202–208. doi:10.1080/15295038909366745
Seaton, C. E. (1996). *Altruism and activism: Character disposition and ideology as factors in a blockade of an abortion clinic: An exploratory study* (2nd ed.). Lanham, MD: University Press of America.
Seibold, D. R. (2000). Applied communication scholarship: Less a matter of boundaries than of emphases. *Journal of Applied Communication Research, 28*, 183–187. doi:10.1080/00909880009365566
Seibold, D. R. (2008). Applied communication research. In W. Donsbach (Ed.), *The international encyclopedia of communication* (Vol. 1., pp. 189–194). Malden, MA: Wiley-Blackwell.
Seidman, G. W. (2007). *Beyond the boycott: Labor rights, human rights, and transnational activism*. New York, NY: Russell Sage Foundation.
Self, L. (Ed.). (1988). What distinguishes/ought to distinguish feminist scholarship in communication studies?: Progress toward engendering a feminist academic practice [Special issue]. *Women's Studies in Communication, 11*(1).
Seliktar, O. (2005). "Tenured radicals" in Israel: From new Zionism to political activism. *Israel Affairs, 11*, 717–736. doi:10.1080/13537120500233979
Sender, K. (2001). Gay readers, consumers, and a dominant gay habitus: 25 years of the *Advocate* magazine. *Journal of Communication, 51*, 73–99. doi:10.1111/j.1460-2466.2001.tb02873.x
Senker, C. (2011). *Strength in numbers: Industrialization and political activism, 1861–1899*. New York, NY: Chelsea House.
Senn, C. Y. (2005). You can change the world: Action, participatory, and activist research. In F. W. Schneider, J. A. Gruman, & L. M. Coutts (Eds.), *Applied social psychology: Understanding and addressing social and practical problems* (pp. 355–373). Thousand Oaks, CA: Sage.
Seo, H., Kim, J. Y., & Yang, S.-U. (2009). Global activism and the new media: A study of transnational NGOs' online public relations. *Public Relations Review, 35*, 123–126. doi:10.1016/j.pubrev.2009.02.002

Shah, P. (Ed.; with Aziz, N., & Chamberlain, P.). *Defending justice: An activist resource kit*. Somerville, MA: Political Research Associates.
Shaw, T. C. (2009). *Now is the time!: Detroit black politics and grassroots activism*. Durham, NC: Duke University Press.
Sheffield, A. D. (1926). *Creative discussion: A statement of method for leaders and members of discussion groups and conferences* (3rd ed.). New York, NY: American Press.
Shepard, B. (2010). *Queer political performance and protest: Play, pleasure and social movement*. New York, NY: Routledge.
Sheridan-Rabideau, M. (2008). *Girls, feminism, and grassroots literacies: Activism in the GirlZone*. Albany: State University of New York Press.
Sherrod, R. (2006). *Youth activism: An international encyclopedia*. Westport, CT: Greenwood Press.
Shi, Y. (2005). Identity construction of the Chinese diaspora, ethnic media use, community formation, and the possibility of social activism. *Continuum: Journal of Media & Cultural Studies, 19*, 55–72. doi:10.1080/1030431052000336298
Shragge, E. (2003). *Activism and social change: Lessons for community and local organizing*. Orchard Park, NY: Broadview Press.
Shreve, B. G. (2011). *Red power rising: The National Indian Youth Council and the origins of Native activism*. Norman: University of Oklahoma Press.
Silliman, J., & Bhattacharjee, A. (1999). Relocating women's studies and activism: A dialogue. *Women's Studies Quarterly, 27*, 122–136. doi:10.2307/40004483
Silversides, A. (2003). *AIDS activist: Michael Lynch and the politics of community*. Toronto, Canada: Between the Lines.
Simpson, J. L., & Shockley-Zalaback, P. (Eds.). (2005). *Engaging communication, transforming organizations: Scholarship of engagement in action*. Cresskill, NJ: Hampton Press.
Singh, P. (Ed.). (2009). *Indigenous identity and activism*. Delhi, India: Shipra.
Sirianni, C., & Friedland, L. (1997, January/February). Civic innovation & American democracy. *Change*, pp. 14–23.
Slaughter, L. D. (2008). TreeHuggerTV: Re-visualizing environmental activism in the post-network era. *Environmental Communication, 2*, 212–228. doi:10.1080/17524030802141760
Smale, R. L. (in press). *I sweat the flavor of tin: Labor activism in early twentieth-century Bolivia*. Pittsburgh, PA: University of Pittsburgh Press.
Smart, P. G. (2011). *Sacred modern: Faith, activist, and aesthetics in the Menil collection*. Austin: University of Texas Press.
Smith, A. (2007). Social-justice activism in the academic industrial complex. *Journal of Feminist Studies in Religion, 23*, 140–145. doi:10.1353/jfs.2007.0043
Smith, D. H. (1967). Social protest ... and the oratory of human rights. *Today's Speech, 15*(3), 2–8. doi:10.1080/01463376709368830
Smith, R. A., & Siplon, P. D. (2006). *Drugs into bodies: Global AIDS treatment activism*. Westport, CT: Praeger.
Solomon, R. C. (1980). The emotions of justice. *Social Justice Research, 3*, 345–374. doi:10.1007/BF01048082
Sowards, S. K., & Renegar, V. R. (2004). The rhetorical functions of consciousness-raising in third wave feminism. *Communication Studies, 55*, 535–552. doi:10.1080/10510970409388637

Sowards, S. K., & Renegar, V. R. (2006). Reconceptualizing rhetorical activism in contemporary feminist contexts. *Howard Journal of Communications, 17*, 57–74. doi:10.1080/10646170500487996

Spalter-Roth, R., & Hartmann, H. (1996). Small happinesses: The feminist struggle to integrate social research with social activism. In H. Gottfried (Ed.), *Feminism and social change* (pp. 206–224). Urbana: University of Illinois Press.

Speed, S. (2008). At the crossroads of human rights and anthropology: Toward a critically engaged activist research. *American Anthropologist, 108*, 66–76. doi:10.1525/aa.2006.108.1.66

Speer, S. A. (2002). What can conversation analysis contribute to feminist methodology? Putting reflexivity into practice. *Discourse & Society, 13*, 783–803. doi:10.1177/0957926502013006757

Sprague, J. (2005). *Feminist methodologies for critical researchers: Bridging differences*. Walnut Creek, CA: AltaMira Press.

Spry, T. (2011). Performative autoethnography: Critical embodiments and possibilities. In N. K. Denzin & Y. S. Lincoln (Eds.), *The Sage handbook of qualitative research* (4th ed., pp. 497-511). Thousand Oaks, CA: Sage.

Staggenborg, S. (1991). *The pro-choice movement: Organization and activism in the abortion conflict*. New York, NY: Oxford University Press.

Stammers, N. (2009). *Human rights and social movements*. New York, NY: Pluto Press.

Staudt, K. (2008). *Violence and activism at the border: Gender, fear, and everyday life in Ciudad Juárez*. Austin: University of Texas Press.

Stearman, K. (2010). *Taking action against homelessness*. New York, NY: Rosen Central.

Stengrim, L. (2005). Negotiating postmodern democracy, political activism, and knowledge production: Indymedia's grassroots and e-savvy answer to media oligopoly. *Communication & Critical/Cultural Studies, 2*, 281–304. doi:10.1080/14791420500332527

Stevens, S. M. (2006). Activist rhetoric and the struggle for meaning: The case of "sustainability" in the reticulate public sphere. *Rhetoric Review, 25*, 297–315. doi:10.1207/s15327981rr2503_4

Stevens, S. M., & Malesh, P. (Eds.). (2009). *Active voices: Composing a rhetoric for social movements*. Albany: State University of New York Press.

Stevenson, M. R., & Cogan, J. C. (Eds.). (2003). *Everyday activism: A handbook for lesbian, gay, and bisexual people and their allies*. New York, NY: Routledge.

Still, B. (2008). *Online intersex communities: Virtual neighborhoods of support and activism*. Amherst, NY: Cambria Press.

Stockdill, B. C. (2003). *Activism against AIDS: At the intersection of sexuality, race, gender, and class*. Boulder, CO: Lynne Rienner.

Stokes, A. Q., & Rubin, D. (2010). Activism and the limits of symmetry: The public relations battle between Colorado GASP and Philip Morris. *Journal of Public Relations Research, 22*, 26–48. doi:10.1080/10627260903150268

Stole, I. L. (2006). *Advertising on trial: Consumer activism and corporate public relations in the 1930s*. Urbana: University of Illinois Press.

Storey, D. (2005). Academic boycotts, activism, and the academy. *Political Geography, 24*, 992–997. doi:10.1016/j,polgeo.2005.06.007

Strain, C. B. (2005). *Pure fire: Self-defense as activism in the civil rights era*. Athens: University of Georgia Press.
Strine, M. S. (1991). Critical theory and "organic" intellectuals: Reframing the work of cultural critique. *Communication Monographs, 58*, 195–201. doi:10.1080/03637759109376223
Stringer, E. T. (1999). *Action research* (2nd ed.). Thousand Oaks, CA: Sage.
Strossen, N. (2005–2006). Wearing two hats: Life as a scholar and activist. *Tulsa Law Review, 41*, 611–624. Retrieved from http://heinonline.org/HOL/Index?collection=journals&index=journals/tlj
Sudbury, J., & Okazawa-Rey, M. (Eds.). (2009). *Activist scholarship: Antiracism, feminism, and social change*. Boulder, CO: Paradigm.
Sutherland, C. M. (2002). Feminist historiography: Research methods in rhetoric. *Rhetoric Society Quarterly, 32*(1), 109–122. doi:1080/02773940209391224
Swan, S. (2002). Rhetoric, service, and social justice. *Written Communication, 19*, 76–108. doi:10.1177/074108830201900104
Swartz, O. (1997). *Conducting socially responsible research: Critical theory, neopragmatism, and rhetorical inquiry*. Thousand Oaks, CA: Sage.
Swartz, O. (2004). Partisan, empathic and invitational criticism: The challenge of materiality. *Ethical Space: The International Journal of Communication Ethics, 1*, 28–33.
Swartz, O. (2005). *In defense of partisan criticism*. New York, NY: Peter Lang.
Swartz, O. (Ed.). (2006). *Social justice and communication scholarship*. Mahwah, NJ: Lawrence Erlbaum.
Switzer, J. V. (2003). *Environmental activism: A reference handbook*. Santa Barbara, CA: ABC-CLIO.
Taft, J. K. (2011). *Rebel girls: Youth activism and social change across the Americas*. New York: New York University Press.
Tasker, E., & Holt-Underwood, F. B. (2008). Feminist research methodologies in historic rhetoric and composition: An overview of scholarship from the 1970s to the present. *Rhetoric Review, 27*, 54–71. doi:10.1080/07350190701738833
Tate, W. (2007). *Counting the dead: The culture and politics of human rights activism in Columbia*. Berkeley: University of California Press.
Tenopir, C. (2004a). Online databases-online scholarly journals: How many? *Library Journal, 2*. Retrieved from http://www.libraryjournal.com
Tenopir, C. (2004b). *User behavior across international and disciplinary boundaries*. Paper presented at the Fiesole Collection Development Retreat, Fiesole, Italy. Retrieved from http://www,ini.it/retreat/2004_docs/Tenopir.pdf
Thayer, M. (2010). *Making transnational feminism: Rural women, NGO activists, and northern donors in Brazil*. New York, NY: Routledge.
Theodore, A. (2002). "A right to speak on the subject": The U.S. women's antiremoval petition campaign, 1829–1831. *Rhetoric & Public Affairs, 5*, 601–624. doi:10.1353/rap/2003.0018
Thomas, J. (1993). *Doing critical ethnography*. Newbury Park, CA: Sage.
Thompson, H. A. (Ed.). (2010). *Speaking out: Activism and protest in the 1960s and 1970s*. Upper Saddle River, NJ: Pearson Prentice Hall.
Thorson, K., Ekdale, B., Borah, P., Namkoong, K., & Shah, C. (2010). YouTube and Proposition 8: A case study in video activism. *Information, Communication & Society, 13*, 325-349. doi: 10.1080/13691180903497060

Timmerman, C., Hutsebaut, D., Mels, S., Nonneman, W., & Van Herck, W. (Eds.). (2007). *Faith-based radicalism: Christianity, Islam and Judaism between constructive activism and destructive fanaticism*. Brussels, Belgium: Peter Lang.

Toch, H. H., Deutsch, S. E., & Wilkins, D. M. (1960). The wrath of the bigot: An analysis of protest mail. *Journalism Quarterly, 27*, 173–185.

Tompkins, P. K. (2009). *Who is my neighbor?: Communicating and organizing to end homelessness*. Boulder, CO: Paradigm.

Tonello, M. (2008). *Hedge fund activism: Findings and recommendations for corporations and investors*. New York, NY: Conference Board. Retrieved from http://www.infoedge.com/toc_new/CB-1434toc.pdf

Townes, E. M. (2009). Walking on the rim of nothingness: Scholarship and activism. *Journal of the American Academy of Religion, 77*, 1–15. doi:10.1093/jaarel/lfp006

Tracy, J. F. (2007). A historical case study of alternative news media and labor activism: *The Dubuque Leader* 1935–1939. *Journalism and Communication Monographs, 8*, 269–343.

Trent, J. S. (2000). Prospects for the future: The communication scholar as citizen. *Communication Studies, 51*, 189–194. doi:10.1080/10510970009388518

Tretheway, A. (1999). Critical organizational communication theory, feminist research methods, and service-learning: Praxis as pedagogy. In D. Droge & B. O. Murphy (Eds.), *Voices of a strong democracy: Concepts and models for service-learning in communication studies* (pp. 177–189). Washington, DC: National Communication Association.

Trigg, M. K. (Ed.). *Leading the way: Young women's activism for social change*. New Brunswick, NJ: Rutgers University Press.

Turbin, C. (1996). Reflections on feminist activism and scholarship: Sarah Eisenstein's *Give us bread but give us roses*. *Gender & History, 8*, 252–257. doi:10.1111/j.1468-0424.1996.tb00046.x

Turner, V., & Turner, E. (1982). Performing ethnography. *TDR: The Drama Review, 26*, 33–50. Retrieved from http://www.jstor.org/action/showPublication?journalCode=dramareviewtdr

Turner, V., & Turner, E. (1988). Performance ethnography. In V. Turner, *The anthropology of performance* (pp. 139–155). New York, NY: Performing Arts Journal.

U.S. Department of State. (2010, June). *Trafficking in persons report* (10th ed.). Retrieved from http://www.state.gov/documents/organization/142979.pdf

Urrieta, L., Jr. (2009). *Working from within: Chicana and Chicano activist educators in whitestream schools*. Tucson: University of Arizona Press.

Urrieta, L., Jr., & Méndez Benavídez, L. R. (2007). Community commitment and activist scholarship: Chicana/o professors and the practice of consciousness. *Journal of Hispanic Higher Education, 6*, 222–236. doi:10.1177/1538192707302535

Valentine, A. (1936). The scholar as citizen. *Vital Speeches of the Day, 2*, 583–561.

Valocchi, S. (2009). *Social movements and activism in the USA*. New York, NY: Routledge.

Van Alest, P., & Walgrave, S. (2002). New media, new movements? The role of the internet in shaping the "anti-globalization" movement. *Information, Communication & Society, 5*, 465–483. doi:10.1080/13691180208538801

Van de Donk, W., Loader, B. D., Nixon, P. G., & Rucht, D. (Eds.). (2004). *Cyberprotest: New media, citizens, and social movements.* New York, NY: Routledge.

Van de Ven, A. H. (2007). *Engaged scholarship: A guide for organizational and social research.* New York, NY: Oxford University Press.

Van de Ven, A. H., & Zlotkowski, E. (2005). Toward a scholarship of engagement: A dialogue between Andy Van Ven and Edward Zlotkowski (A. Kenworthy-U'Ren, Ed.). *Academy of Management Learning & Education, 4,* 355–362.

VanderPlaat, M. (1999). Locating the feminist scholar: Relational empowerment and social activism. *Qualitative Health Research, 9,* 773–785. doi:10.1177/104973299129122270

Varallo, S. M., Ray, E. B., & Ellis, B. H. (1998). Speaking of incest: The research interview as social justice. *Journal of Applied Communication Research, 26,* 254–271. doi:10.1080/00909889809365504

Vargas, R. (2008). *Family activism: Empowering your community, beginning with family and friends.* San Francisco, CA: Berrett-Koehler.

Varsanyi, M. (Ed.). (2010). *Taking local control: Immigration policy activism in U.S. cities and states.* Stanford, CA: Stanford University Press.

Vassallo, F. (2010). *France, social capital, and political activism.* New York, NY: Palgrave McMillan.

Vijayalakshmi, V. (2005). *Feminist politics in India: Women and civil society activism.* Bangalore, India: Institute for Economic and Social Change.

Wagstaff, A. E. (2009). A review of Lawrence R. Frey and Kevin M. Carragee's (2007) two-volume text *Communication Activism. Rocky Mountain Communication Review, 6*(2), 38–41. Retrieved from http://www.rmcr.utah.edu

Walsh, K. C. (2009). Scholars as citizens: Studying public opinion through ethnography. In E. Schatz (Ed.), *Political ethnography: What immersion contributes to the study of power* (pp. 165–183). Chicago, IL: University of Chicago Press.

Wander, P. (1983). The ideological turn in modern criticism. *Central States Speech Journal, 34,* 1–18. doi:10.1080/10510978309368110

Wander, P. (1984). The third persona: An ideological turn in rhetorical theory. *Central States Speech Journal, 35,* 197–216. doi:10.1080/10510978409368190

Wander, P., & Jenkins, S. (1972). Rhetoric, society, and the critical response. *Quarterly Journal of Speech, 58,* 441–450. doi:10.1080/00335637209383142

Ward, J. (2008). *Respectably queer: Diversity culture in LGBT activist organizations.* Nashville, TN: Vanderbilt University Press.

Ward, S. (2001). "Scholarship in the context of struggle": Activist individuals, the Institute of the Black World, and the contours of black power radicalism. *Black Scholar, 31*(3/4), 42–51.

Warren, J. T. (Ed.). (2006). Performance ethnography [Symposium]. *Text and Performance Studies, 26,* 317–346.

Warren, M. R. (2010). *Fire in the heart: How white activists embrace racial justice.* New York, NY: Oxford University Press.

Warwick, A., & Auchmuty, R. (1995). Women's studies as feminist activism. In G. Griffin (Ed.), *Feminist activism in the 1990s* (pp. 182–191). Bristol, PA: Taylor & Francis.

Weaver, C. K. (2010). Carnivalesque activism as a public relations genre: A case study of the New Zealand group Mothers against Genetic Engineering. *Public Relations Review, 36,* 35–41. doi:10.1016/j.pubrev.2009.09.001

Weber, C. (2006). An activist and a scholar: Reflections of a feminist sociologist negotiating academia. *Humanity & Society, 30,* 153–166.
Weiss, A. (2002). *Principles of spiritual activism.* Hoboken, NJ: KTAV.
Weiss, A. (2008). *Spiritual activism: A Jewish guide to leadership and repairing the world.* Woodstock, VT: Jewish Lights.
Weissberg, R. (2005). *The limits of civic activism: Cautionary tales on the use of politics.* New Brunswick, NJ: Transaction.
West, M., & Gastil, J. (2004). Deliberation at the margins: Participant accounts of face-to-face public deliberation at the 1999–2000 world trade protests in Seattle and Prague. *Qualitative Research Reports in Communication, 5,* 1–7.
Whisenhunt, D. W. (2011). *Veterans of Future Wars: A study in student activism.* Lanham, MD: Lexington Books.
White, L. E., & Perelman, J. (Eds.). (2011). *Stones of hope: How African activists reclaim human rights to challenge global poverty.* Stanford, CA: Stanford University Press.
Whitt, J. (2010). *Burning crosses and activist journalism: Hazel Brannon Smith and the Mississippi civil rights movement.* Lanham, MD: University Press of America.
Wigginton, E. (Ed.). (1991). *Refuse to stand silently by: An oral history of grass roots social activism in America, 1921–64.* New York, NY: Doubleday.
Wolfe, C. (1997). *Judicial activism: Bulwark of freedom or precarious society?* (Rev. ed.). Lanham, MD: Rowman & Littlefield.
Wood, J. T. (1996). Social justice research: Alive and well in the field of communication. *Communication Studies, 47,* 128–134. doi:10.1080/10510979609368468
Woodhouse, E. Hess, D., Breyman, S., & Martin, B. (2002). Science studies and activism: Possibilities and problems for reconstructivist agendas. *Social Studies of Science, 32,* 297–319. doi:10.1177/0306312702032002004
Wright, R. E., Barber, E., Crafton, M., & Jain, A. (Eds.). (2004). *History of corporate governance: The importance of stakeholder activism.* London, England: Pickering & Chatto.
Wright, W., & Middendorf, G. (Eds.). (2008). *The fight over food: Producers, consumers, and activists challenge the global food system.* University Park: Pennsylvania State University Press.
Wuthnow, R., & Evans, J. H. (Eds.). (2002). *The quiet hand of God: Faith-based activism and the public role of mainline Protestantism.* Berkeley: University of California Press.
Xie, L. (2009). *Environmental activism in China.* New York, NY: Routledge.
Yackle, L. (2007). *Regulatory rights: Supreme Court activism, the public interest, and the making of constitutional law.* Chicago, IL: University of Chicago Press.
Yang, G. (2009). *The power of the internet in China: Citizen activism online.* New York, NY: Columbia University Press.
Yep, G. A. (2008). The dialectics of intervention: Toward a reconceptualization of the theory/activism divide in communication scholarship and beyond. In O. Swartz (Ed.), *Transformative communication studies: Culture, hierarchy and the human condition* (pp. 191–207). Leicester, United Kingdom: Troubador.
Yoder, J. (1969). The protest of the American clergy in opposition to the war in Vietnam. *Today's Speech, 17*(3), 51–59. doi:10.1080/01463376909368896

Young, M., Boyd, S. B., Brodsky, G., & Day,. S. (2008). *Poverty: Rights, social citizenship, and legal activism*. Vancouver, Canada: University of British Columbia Press.

Zake, I. (Ed.). (2009). *Anti-communist minorities in the U.S.: Political activism of ethnic refugees*. New York, NY: Palgrave Macmillan.

Zamarrón, S.E. (2009). Trabajar haciendo: Activist research and interculturalism. *Intercultural Education, 20*, 39–50. doi:10.1080/14675980802700680

Zerai, A. (2002). Models for unity between scholarship and grassroots activism. *Critical Sociology, 28*, 201–216.doi:10.1177/08969205020280011201

Zine, J. (2004). Creating a critical faith-centered space for antiracist feminism: Reflections of a Muslim scholar-activist. *Journal of Feminist Studies in Religion, 20*, 167–187.

Zoch, L. M., Collins, E. L., Sisco, H. F., & Supa, D. H. (2008). Empowering the activist: Using framing devices on activist organizations' web sites. *Public Relations Review, 34*, 351–35 358. doi:10.1016/j.pubrev.2008.07.005

Zompetti, J. P. (1997). Toward a Gramscian critical rhetoric. *Western Journal of Communication, 61*, 66–86. doi:10.1080/10570319709374562

1

OPENING COMMUNICATION PATHWAYS IN PROTRACTED CONFLICT

From Tragedy to Dialogue in Cyprus

Benjamin J. Broome
Arizona State University

Harry Anastasiou
Portland State University

Maria Hajipavlou
University of Cyprus

Bülent Kanol
Management Centre of the Mediterranean, Cyprus

The eastern Mediterranean island of Cyprus, famous since antiquity as the birthplace of Aphrodite (the goddess of love, beauty, and fertility), is divided by a buffer zone that runs east–west across the entire length of the island, including through the middle of the capital city, Nicosia (see Figure 1.1). The buffer zone was established as a cease-fire line in the 1974 war, in which a Greek-led coup against the elected government of the Cyprus Republic was followed by Turkish military intervention, leading to the creation of two ethnic zones on the island. "Temporarily" separating the two sides until negotiations could establish an agreement to end the conflict, the buffer zone remains in place today and continues to divide the Greek-Cypriot and Turkish-Cypriot populations. United Nations (UN) peacekeeping forces, which have been on the island since intercommunal fighting in 1964 led to a division of Nicosia, patrol the buffer zone and maintain observation posts along its 180-kilometer (112-mile) length.

With its coiled barbed wire, sand bags, machine gun emplacements, tire stacks, rusting oil drums, and buried landmines, the buffer zone, often called the "Green Line," is an ugly scar across the island. For the Turkish Cypriots in the north, whose self-declared state is not recognized by the international community (other than Turkey), the buffer zone provides a sense of security, but at the same time, it isolates them from the rest of the world. For the Greek Cypriots in the south, whose history on the island goes back much further than that of the Turkish Cypriots, the zone is like a dagger that cuts through the heart of their history and identity. Perhaps most important, the buffer zone has resulted in an almost complete cutoff of communication between the two sides for more than 3 decades (see the next section for a more detailed overview of the Cyprus conflict).

Since its establishment in 1974, there have been only a few violent incidents along the buffer zone, mostly involving single civilians or soldiers stationed there. In August 1996, however, violent clashes between opposing sets of demonstrators took place in the buffer zone, leading to the tragic death of two Greek-Cypriot civilians. In the aftermath of those clashes and the resulting deaths, the rhetoric in the news media and from politicians on both sides became more extreme and uncompromising. There was very little, if any, public examination about what led to those events, and neither side shouldered any responsibility for what happened. However, a few Greek-Cypriot and Turkish-Cypriot peace activists, who had been communicating with one another and working together prior to the buffer-zone incidents, held separate meetings on each side of the dividing line to analyze the events and find ways to restart intercommunal contacts.[1] This group attempted to understand why the events had spiralled out of control, how the incidents might be perceived by the other community, how the one-sided rhetoric was hurting the cause of each side and the image of Cyprus to the outside world, and what might be done to prevent such events in the future. The members of this group provided a moderating voice in the midst of an otherwise extreme and narrow discussion of blame and accusations.

More important, the members of this group organized bicommunal gatherings during the 3 months following the incidents, reopening channels of communication between members of the two communities and setting the stage for a surge in bicommunal activities that would take place during the following year. Their voices did not receive news media attention but they helped to prevent a negative spiral toward further separation and, possibly, additional violence between the two sides.

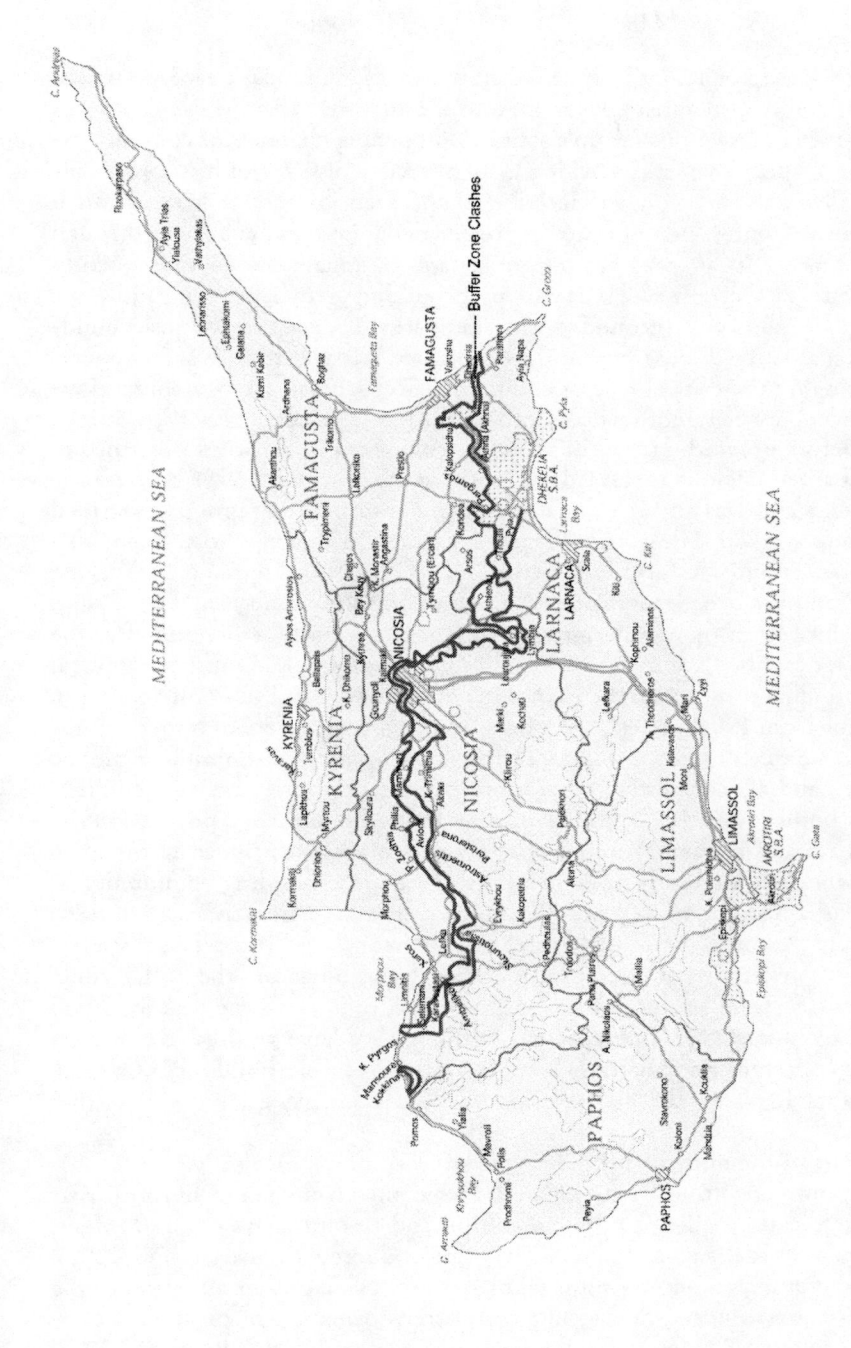

Fig.1.1. Map of Cyprus showing buffer zone, Nicosia, and Dherinia (based on a UN map; source: UN Cartographic Section)

This chapter tells the story of how this bicommunal peace group, of which we were members, responded to the 1996 buffer-zone events, examining the effects of this group's actions on opening channels of communication in Cyprus. We first provide a brief overview of Cypriot history to contextualize the situation we describe in the sections that follow. We then explain the buffer-zone events in greater detail and analyze them through the frameworks of protracted conflict and nationalism. We subsequently explicate the activist work of our peacebuilding group, showing how the group's actions were grounded in frameworks of dialogue and peacebuilding. Finally, we discuss important lessons we learned from this experience, focusing on the critical role of communication scholar-activists in developing links between unofficial and official efforts in resolving conflict.

Before proceeding, we situate our involvement in the work described in this chapter. Each of us resided in Cyprus at the time of the 1996 buffer-zone incidents and was an active member of the peacebuilding groups described (although Hadjipavlou was abroad temporarily during those incidents). Anastasiou and Hadjipavlou, both Greek Cypriots, and Kanol, a Turkish Cypriot, have been leaders in the peacebuilding community since the 1980s, and, along with their colleagues, have organized, both before and after the events described, numerous bicommunal meetings and initiated several bicommunal projects on the island. Broome was a U.S. Fulbright Scholar in Cyprus from 1994 to 1996, working closely with members of both communities in peacebuilding activities, primarily facilitating bicommunal dialogue groups and agenda-setting workshops (for descriptions of these activities, see Broome, 1997, 2004, 2006). Since resuming his academic position in the United States at the beginning of 1997, Broome has continued to organize workshops and consult with members of the peacebuilding community in Cyprus, returning more than 20 times to the island to assist with various projects. All of us have made substantial personal and professional investments to promote communication and cooperation across the buffer zone; at the same time, each of us has stepped back to analyze the peacebuilding work from a scholarly perspective. Although we have worked together on many communication activism projects related to peacebuilding in Cyprus, this is the first time that we have coauthored a scholarly examination of that work.

Part of the impetus for telling the story of how peace activists can positively influence the course of a conflict comes from our conviction that communication is key to the prevention and resolution of ethnic conflict, particularly in the case of civil-society peacebuilding (see Anastasiou, 2002), and, therefore, communication scholars should give greater attention to the successful resolution, management, and transformation of protracted conflicts (Albert, 2009; Broome, Carey, De La Garza, Martin, & Morris, 2005; Ellis, 2006).[2] Unfortunately, communication scholarship about protracted conflicts is quite limited. A number of studies have appeared in recent years—most notably, about the Middle East and about Northern Ireland (e.g., Carcasson, 2000; Ellis, 2005; Ellis & Maoz, 2002, 2007; Frosh & Wolfsfeld, 2007; Klang-Maoz, 1997; Maoz, 1999, 2000a, 2000b, 2000c, 2001, 2002, 2004; Maoz & Ellis, 2001, 2008; Maoz, Steinberg, Bar-On, & Fakhereldeen, 2002; Rogers & Ben-David, 2008; Spencer, 2003, 2004; Wolfsfeld, 1997; Wolfsfeld, Khouri, & Peri, 2002; Zupnik, 2000), including some communication activism peacebuilding research (e.g., Albeck, Adwan, & Bar-On, 2006; Bar-On & Kassem, 2004; Maoz & Ellis, 2006)—but communication scholars have not led the way in developing and facilitating peacebuilding practices. This chapter hopefully adds to the body of communication research on intrastate and international ethnic conflict by bringing more attention to both the need for such research and its potential contributions to dealing effectively with protracted conflicts.

OVERVIEW OF THE CYPRUS CONFLICT[3]

Situated approximately 40 miles south of the Turkish coast and 60 miles west of Syria, Cyprus is home to two primary ethnic communities, Greek Cypriots and Turkish Cypriots, that are distinguished by differences in language, cultural heritage, and religion, as well as divided by seemingly incompatible views of the past, politics of the present, and visions of the future. Greek Cypriots, who primarily are Christian Orthodox, with cultural and linguistic ties to Greece, comprise approximately 80% of the population, whereas Turkish Cypriots, who predominately are Muslim, with cultural and linguistic ties to Turkey, make up approximately 20% of the population. Greek Cypriots trace their presence on the island back to the eighth century BCE, and they have identified with the Hellenic world since Greek colonists settled on the island around 1500 BCE. Turkish Cypriots first established a presence in Cyprus after the Ottoman conquest of the island in 1571. Although Greek and Turkish Cypriots have close relations with their respective "motherlands," Greece and Turkey, they maintain a distinct common Cypriot component to their identity, although that aspect of their identity has been suppressed by the ethnocentric nationalism that has dominated the political public culture of each community.

The UN-patrolled buffer zone that divides the island was created following intercommunal hostilities that began in 1963, but it was limited at that time to the capital city, Nicosia. In 1974, the buffer zone was extended to the entire island following a brutal war that started after an overthrow of the elected government of Cyprus, carried out by forces acting under the direction of the ruling military junta in Greece, which provoked Turkey to send military forces to the island. During the ensuing conflict, most of the

Greek Cypriots living in the north of Cyprus were driven from their homes and businesses. Overnight, one third of the Greek-Cypriot population became refugees in the south of the island. The northern 40% of the island fell under Turkish control, and nearly all Turkish Cypriots living in the south of Cyprus fled to the Turkish-controlled area. The southern 60% of the island remained under the administration of Greek Cypriots, who continue to hold the government of the internationally recognized Republic of Cyprus. As a result of the 1974 war, two ethnically homogeneous zones were created, and after nearly 400 years of living together in mixed and adjacent towns and villages scattered throughout the island, Greek Cypriots and Turkish Cypriots forcibly were divided into two geographic zones. Today, Turkish troops still maintain a strong presence in the north (for a more detailed description, see UN Peacekeeping Force in Cyprus, 2009).

Since the cease-fire that was arranged immediately after the war in 1974, UN-led negotiations have failed to reach agreement on the island's future, and over the more than 3 decades of separation, the two communities have grown further apart. Greek Cypriots view themselves as victims of Turkish aggression who are denied access to their homes, lands, and businesses in the island's north by an illegal occupying army. They envision the future of Cyprus as a unified state consisting of two primary communities (Greek Cypriot and Turkish Cypriot) under a single national identity. Turkish Cypriots, who operate under a self-declared government, feel isolated and trapped by international embargoes and dependence on Turkey that prevent them from developing their economic potential and building fully functioning democratic institutions. They envision the future of Cyprus as a confederation functioning loosely under a weak bicommunal national governmental structure. Because of past actions by each side toward the other that brought disruption, displacement, loss of life, and other forms of suffering, both sides see themselves as victims of aggression and neither side trusts the other. These perceptions and feelings, coupled with the strong desire of the Turkish Cypriots to maintain a separate ethnic zone and the equally strong desire of the Greek Cypriots to regain their lands and their former dominance within a unitary state, set the stage for the violent clashes along the buffer zone in 1996 that are described next.

THE BUFFER-ZONE INCIDENTS

On August 11, 1996, a group of Greek-Cypriot motorcyclists staged an "anti-occupation" rally along the buffer zone in Cyprus. Organized under the Cyprus Motorcyclists Federation, they were protesting the continued division of the island, the presence of Turkish troops in the north, and their inability to return to the homes, towns, and lands they fled during the war

22 years earlier. The demonstrators rode under the banner "Ride to Kyrenia," which referred to the beautiful harbor town on the north coast that, for Greek Cypriots, serves as a symbol of their life before the division of the island. Their plan was to gather at a crossing point by the village of Dherinia, located on the eastern edge of the buffer zone (see Figure 1.1).

With the exception of a few moderate voices that declared the pending event unwise and dangerous, many Greek-Cypriot political leaders openly endorsed the motorcyclists' preparatory efforts, and banks and cooperatives (co-ops) in the south opened accounts for citizens to contribute money to support the motorcyclists' forthcoming event. Meanwhile, the UN warned that the possible entry of nonauthorized persons into the buffer zone would constitute a violation of the cease-fire agreement and could lead to dangerous consequences. None of these warnings, however, were heeded.

The UN secretary general at that time, Boutros Boutros-Ghali, made a last-minute intervention, issuing a statement the day before the main event that expressed his hope that event organizers would avoid provocative actions and that called on the Cyprus government to take effective measures to prevent the motorcyclists from making any unauthorized entry into the UN buffer zone. After an appeal from the government's president, the leader of the Cyprus Motorcyclists Federation agreed to cancel the event and hold a rally in a stadium in Nicosia. However, because momentum for the protest had been building for weeks through nationalist rhetoric, agitation, and invocation, it became practically impossible to deter or stop the originally planned event at a last-minute notice; consequently, hundreds of motorcyclists, joined by others arriving in vehicles, gathered at the Dherynia checkpoint.

In preparation for a likely confrontational encounter at the buffer zone, extremist forces gathered on the Turkish-Cypriot side, including members of the Gray Wolves, a far right-wing nationalist organization in Turkey. The voices of some moderate Turkish-Cypriot party leaders, who were calling on Turkish Cypriots not to participate in the escalation of events, were drowned out by the media-backed, top-level Turkish-Cypriot and Turkish nationalist leadership, who declared themselves determined to "teach the Greek Cypriots a lesson."

Thus, on both sides, preparations throughout the run-up to the bufferzone encounter drew together into a critical mass the most nationalistically oriented citizens on each side of the ethnic divide, setting the stage for a dangerous confrontation between the most uncompromising and belligerently inclined members of each community. The collective mobilization and subsequent inflation of adversarial nationalist sentiments among the Greek-Cypriot and Turkish-Cypriot populations was fueled by two groups on each side of the ethnic divide: (a) civil and political older generation leaders, who, in advance and in the background of the events, furnished the nationalist rationales, support structures, and incentives; and (b) excitable youths, who, after being cheered and mobilized into belligerent nationalism, became the main actors at the forefront of the motorcyclists' events. On both sides of the ethnic divide, the long-standing socialization of youths into the polarizing ethnocentric narratives of their respective communities rendered them extremely vulnerable to confrontational and highly dangerous interactions with youths from the other side. The mass gathering of agitated young Greek-Cypriot motorcyclists and their supporters on the southern side of the Dherynia crossing, and the simultaneous mass gathering of opposing and equally agitated Turkish-Cypriot youths and their supporters on the northern side, formed the powder keg that waited igniting.

As tensions heightened during the mass gatherings, many of the Greek-Cypriot demonstrators rushed into the buffer zone, overwhelming their police forces and UN peacekeepers, and hurling rocks at soldiers and police on the other side. The Turkish-Cypriot police and demonstrators gathered on the north side moved toward the Greek-Cypriots and clashes broke out. In the resulting melee, a Greek Cypriot who had become entangled in the barbed wire was beaten and killed. The episode was captured on videotape, showing Turkish-Cypriot police participating in the killing of the young man. The videotape immediately was broadcast all over Cyprus, enraging Greek Cypriots and bringing a great deal of worry to Turkish Cypriots, foreign residents of the island, and the international diplomatic community (for a documentary of the buffer-zone clashes, see ABC Australia, 1998; see also the report of the incidents by the UN, 1996).

Three days later, after the funeral of the victim, more demonstrations occurred, again at the Dherynia crossing, and when a Greek Cypriot ran into the buffer zone and climbed the flagpole that was flying the Turkish flag, with what appeared to be an intention of bringing down the flag, he was shot and killed by the Turkish military. Captured, again, on videotape, this incident further exacerbated the situation, leading to nearly constant replays of the two killings on Greek-Cypriot television stations. These images were accompanied by uncompromising nationalist rhetoric, domination of the airwaves by hard-line views, and increasingly vocal anti-Turkish sentiment. For Greek Cypriots, the incidents were evidence of the "barbaric" nature of Turks. In the Turkish-Cypriot community, the nationalist voices used the incidents to buttress their arguments against a unitary state, arguing that the provocative actions of the Greek Cypriots and their harsh rhetoric afterward were proof that the presence of the Turkish army in Cyprus was essential to protect Turkish Cypriots and that they never would be able to live peacefully together with Greek Cypriots.

Clearly, any goodwill that had existed between the two sides quickly disappeared, and even those in the Greek-Cypriot community who normally took a more moderate stance on the conflict were silenced. The buffer-zone incidents made their way into mainstream news media around the world, creating a dark impression regarding future prospects for the island. Many in the international community believed that the incidents and the strong responses to them in the Greek-Cypriot and Turkish-Cypriot communities would likely set back negotiations for years, if not ending altogether the hope of reuniting the island under a single governmental structure.

The buffer-zone incidents, seen in the broader context of the Cyprus conflict, can be interpreted as an example of protracted interethnic conflicts that exhibited many features of ethnocentric nationalism. Such conflicts, as discussed in the next section, are subject to a set of negative dynamics that are self-perpetuating and extremely difficult to resolve.

PATTERNS OF PROTRACTED CONFLICT AND THE ROLE OF NATIONALISM

Although some conflicts are "resolvable" through negotiations and well-timed interventions, leading to successfully implemented agreements over disputed issues, other conflicts belong to a special class known as "protracted" or "intractable" conflicts. Such conflicts are exceptionally complex; usually involve issues of identity, meaning, justice, and power; and often resist even the most determined attempts at resolution (Coleman, 2000, 2003). Intractable conflicts frequently are characterized by ethnic victimization, unaddressed historical grievances and traumas, economic asymmetries, unequal distribution of resources, and structural inequalities (see, e.g., Azar, 1983, 1986, 1990; Bar-Tal, 1988; Burgess & Burgess, 1996; Burton, 1990; Kriesberg, 1993; Kriesberg, Northrup, & Thorson, 1989; Rouhana & Bar-Tal, 1998).

Protracted conflicts often are embedded in a context of long-standing differences and inequalities stemming from colonialism, ethnocentrism, and human rights abuses. The hatred, fear, and atrocities committed by parties against each other create a tendency for opponents in ethnonational conflicts to "demonize" each other and to attribute the causes of their suffering and experiences of injustice exclusively to the other side. This essentialist view puts all of the blame on the "enemy" and excludes situational factors. "Our side" is righteous and justified in its actions; the "other side" inherently is aggressive and acts the way it does because "it has always acted like that."

In deeply divided societies, where barbed-wire barriers and police checkpoints prohibit freedom of movement of both ideas and goods, an environment is created in which a culture of conflict, mistrust, and suspicion, as well as a flourishing of "enemy images," is reinforced. According to "enemy system theory" (Mack, 1990; Montville, 1990; Volkan, 1990), humans have a deep-rooted psychological tendency, at both individual and group levels, to dichotomize by creating "enemies" and "allies." According to this view, primitive and unconscious impulses are mobilized that often result in former neighbors harming and killing each other simply because they belong to different national/ethnic groups.

One of the primary factors that creates and sustains protracted/intractable conflict is *ethnocentric nationalism*, in which a nation is viewed as "absolute and sacred in value, mono-ethnic in nature, collectivist and narcissistic in mentality, conflictual in predisposition, and militant in its concept of defense and in its means of freedom" (Anastasiou, 2008a, p. 153). As such, ethnocentric nationalism "conceptualizes society in terms of a single homogeneous ethnic identity, thus rendering the existence of other ethnic groups a national anomaly—and in times of conflict a national blemish that needs cleansing" (Anastasiou, 2008a, p. 153).

Individuals in protracted conflicts who have been shaped and directed by a nationalist mindset tend to integrate the accompanying loss and suffering back into the nationalist framework, thus converting tragedy to fuel for further conflict and alienation. By doing so, nationalists become driven toward a partisan, skewed, and unilateral declaration of grievances, and toward a fierce preoccupation with an abstract assertion of rights that renders them blind to the need for attending to and mending interethnic relations. Sadly, the abstract assertion of grievances and rights deepens the estrangement of the communities in conflict, at the expense of concretely engaging each other in solution-seeking endeavors—the fundamental prerequisite for any meaningful resolution of the conflict.

In Cyprus, these patterns of abstract partisan assertions and alienating interactions between Greek Cypriots and Turkish Cypriots can be understood fully only when they are contextualized within the respective nationalist narratives and related events and phenomena that historically have led to, shaped, and structured over time the Cyprus conflict. Both Greek nationalism and Turkish nationalism among Greek Cypriots and Turkish Cypriots, respectively, developed and crystallized during the British colonial era in Cyprus (1878–1960), particularly after World War II. However, whereas the nationalism of Greek Cypriots was configured around the idea of *enosis*, the union of all of Cyprus with Greece, the nationalism of Turkish Cypriots was configured around the idea of *taksim*, the ethnic partition of Cyprus. Although these two nationalist agendas, in principle, were irreconcilable, they both were premised on the same nationalist concept of nationhood and statehood, which views the nation and state (i.e., the nation-state) as primarily and exclusively ethnocentric and mono-ethnic in nature. Once nationalism is adopted, the nation and state are seen as an extension and projection of a singular concept of ethnicity. In the nationalist mind, not only is the nation-state viewed as having an ethnic identity but it also has only one ethnic identity.

Hence, Greek-Cypriot nationalism revolved around the idea that because the majority of the inhabitants of Cyprus were Greek, the island, essentially and primarily, was a Hellenic state. According to this nationalist assumption, the Greek majority had the right to rule and, therefore, to unite Cyprus with its motherland, Greece. This approach was in line with *ethnic irredentism* (a territory historically or ethnically related to one political unit but under the political control of another), an integral part of the nationalist phenomenon ever since its historical advent in the 19th century (see, e.g., Alter, 1994; Anastasiou, 2008a). By the same logic, Turkish-Cypriot nationalism pursued ethnic partition, because by geographically segregating the ethnic communities, Turkish Cypriots would become the ethnic majority in the territory they controlled and, as such, would create a mono-ethnic state, as the projection of their ethnic identity. Just like the nationalism of Greek Cypriots, the nationalism of Turkish Cypriots was premised on the idea that the basis for self-determination and the nation-state, and its governance, in principle, is the ethnic majority within the state's territory. In their similarly premised ethnonationalism, these communities developed conceptions of nationhood, statehood, identity, society, and territory that were mutually exclusive, and, hence, irreconcilable.

Forged by Greece, Turkey, and Britain, the founding of the Republic of Cyprus in 1960 as a biethnic independent state marked a meager attempt to supersede the irreconcilable agendas of Greek-Cypriot and Turkish-Cypriot nationalism. However, because nationalism was not addressed adequately in the structures and constitution of the Republic, it resulted in the constitutional crisis and interethnic violence of the 1960s, culminating in the 1974 Athens-led coup d'état and Turkish military intervention in Cyprus. Through massive displacement, prisoner exchange, and relocation of Greek Cypriots and Turkish Cypriots, the island became de facto divided into a Turkish north and a Greek south.

After 1974, the respective nationalisms metastasized into new patterns, incorporating the events and residual effects of both the Greek coup and the Turkish military control of northern Cyprus. Greek-Cypriot nationalism subsequently focused on reuniting the divided island by restoring the sovereignty and territorial integrity of the Republic of Cyprus and, thus, restoring the human rights of all Greek-Cypriot refugees by allowing their unimpeded return to their ancestral homes. In contrast, Turkish-Cypriot nationalism, backed by the might of the more powerful Turkish army, focused on entrenching the ethnic partition of the island by pursuing international recognition of the breakaway state, conceived as a purely Turkish state as the basis of Turkish-Cypriot self-determination, identity preservation, and security. Hence, both sides remained fixed on their respective mono-ethnic and exclusivist notions of statehood—the very condition that created the conflict in the first place.

The juxtaposition of these two nationalisms was the context within which the motorcyclists' protest on Cyprus took place. Although motivated by a sense of injustice that resulted from the 1974 massive displacement of Greek Cypriots from their homes in the north of the island, the Greek Cypriots at the center of the escalating motorcyclists' events reawakened and reasserted the idea of Cyprus as a Hellenic state, which rung more "true" with the Turkish army preventing Greek-Cypriot refugees from accessing their properties in the north. The motorcyclists, thus, saw their actions as asserting their patriotism, loyalty to their ethnic community, and right to restore the integrity of their presumed Hellenic island state, with the Turks appearing to confirm the terrible enemy image that such nationalism espoused. The motorcycle protesters, however, seemed unaware that the pursuit of nationalist ethnocentric agendas, with their mono-ethnic notions of statehood, had led to the demise of Cypriot society in the first place.

Similarly, the Turkish-Cypriots and Turkish army at the center of the confrontation with the Greek-Cypriot motorcyclists operated under an ethnocentric nationalist perspective. Their mono-ethnic, secessionist approach to statehood drove them to the forceful assertion of the purely Turkish nature of their breakaway state. The actions of Turkish-Cypriot and Turkish nationalists engaged in the motorcyclists' events was based on the presumed "right" of opposing any non-Turk from entering their space, even to the point of killing any Greek Cypriot who crossed the buffer zone. This presumed right was configured by integrating the 1960s suffering of the Turkish Cypriots into their Turko-centric nationalist concept of identity and statehood, with its projected and generalized enemy image of Greeks as "sly haters and killers of Turks." The Turkish-Cypriot and Turkish nationalists, thus, shared the same blind spot as did the Greek-Cypriot nationalists: They would not acknowledge that the human suffering that befell the island over the years was the direct outcome of competing and exclusivist ethnocentric nationalistic perspectives.

Throughout its struggle for interethnic communication and peacebuilding, the fledgling civil-society peace movement of Cyprus strove to transcend the impasse of ethnocentric nationalism. One key aim of the bicommunal movement in confronting this phenomenon was to dissociate the human aspects of the conflict—the loss of life and suffering on both sides of the ethnic divide—from the adversarial frameworks of the respective nationalism of the rival ethnic communities—the very frameworks that produced the conflict in the first place. Unfortunately, the buffer-zone events, and the adversarial frameworks they reinforced, threatened both the past accomplishments of the bicommunal movement and its members' hopes for the future. Although the movement had been gaining strength during the 2 years prior to the buffer-zone incidents (see Broome, 2005; Hadjipavlou, 2004), there seemed to be little possibility of holding bicommunal meetings in the foreseeable future. It was in this context that we met with our colleagues to discuss what we could do to reopen communication across the buffer zone.

CONFRONTING NATIONALISM AND REOPENING COMMUNICATION

The grim events associated with the buffer-zone incidents were particularly distressing for those of us who had worked so hard to promote communication across the Green Line. As we witnessed the escalating belligerency, fear, and confusion of the events leading up to the clashes, the delirium that overcame the crowds of Greek Cypriots and Turkish Cypriots violently entangled in the buffer zone, and the intensifying anger, frustration, and animosity in public opinion on both sides that followed in the days after the clashes, an array of unanswered, oppressive questions streamed through our minds: Is this the definitive end of all the peace work that we had done over the years? Will all the bicommunal peace work be lost forever? Are the buffer-zone incidents the beginning of another flare-up of the Cyprus conflict? Some nationalist voices among the Greek Cypriots were calling for citizens to step back and allow the army to take over, but if that happened, would we see another deadly clash between the Greek-Cypriot National Guard and the Turkish army that could even escalate to a full-scale war? If that happened, would Greece and Turkey subsequently become embroiled in the conflict in Cyprus that possibly could extend to an all-out war between Greece and Turkey along their border? Would the Turkish navy and air force then blockade Cyprus? Will we all end up entrapped and under siege within a war zone? Should we take our families and leave Cyprus as soon as possible?

Having spent years struggling to build intercommunal contacts, we were discouraged and unsure what actions we could take to further the aims of the peace movement. However, we found solace in talking with peace-oriented friends and colleagues, meeting informally in homes or at cafes and restaurants, escaping for a short while from the nationalist rhetoric that surrounded us nearly every minute of our waking hours. As we discussed the situation, we began to consider another stream of questions that prodded us in a different direction: Is it not now that bicommunal work and engagement is needed the most? Are there ways to prevent the animosity triggered by the buffer-zone incidents from closing in on us and pervading the entire political culture of the island? What about the Turkish-Cypriots living in the south—is there anything we can do to protect them from the vengefulness of hard-liners? Should we bring together leaders of the bicommunal peace movement to brainstorm strategies and actions that can deescalate the tension? Should we contact friends in Greece and Turkey who can infuse into policy leaders' discussions our suggestions for nonbelligerent responses to the crisis? Is there anything we can do jointly with leaders of the other community that can be enacted immediately to curb the alienation that has befallen the two communities? Can authoritative third parties, such as the UN and foreign embassies, be resources in our struggle to strategize and devise actions to reframe and reorient the trends toward greater separation?

As we pondered these two sets of conflicting questions, it became clear that if the projections of the first set of question prevailed, disaster would be imminent and certain; if, however, the projections of the second set of question prevailed, there would at least be a chance of averting the worst, although there was no certainty, just a possibility of doing so. After a great deal of soul-searching and intense discussion among ourselves and with other colleagues, we opted for the latter—the uncertainty of a hopeful possibility over the certainty of disaster.

The members of the Greek-Cypriot and Turkish-Cypriot peacebuilding groups could not meet together, but Broome, in his role as an external third party, was able to cross the buffer zone to meet with each group separately.[4] Although Broome had acted over the past several years primarily in the role of facilitator with the mono-communal and bicommunal groups (see Broome, 2006, 2009), in this case, he served primarily as a communication link between the two sides, shuttling across the buffer zone to carry information back and forth, and as a mediator, helping each group to negotiate differences about how to move forward. Anastasiou and Kanol were part of the discussions in their respective communities, serving as key players who raised questions, offered insights, and made suggestions for action. The deliberations within each group used an open discussion process, with no designated moderator, facilitator, or group leader. Hadjipavlou was in a unique position, temporarily abroad in the United States while on sabbatical. During the buffer-zone incidents, she was part of a bicommunal workshop with Greek-Cypriot and Turkish-Cypriot educators meeting in Boston, simultaneously experiencing the events from afar and observing the anger, fear, and confusion within the bicommunal workshop setting. She used that workshop setting to help those educators search for ways to deal with the tension they were feeling in relation to the buffer-zone incidents and to examine what contribution they could make in their role as peacebuilders.

At first, there was a sense of helplessness pervading both the Greek-Cypriot and Turkish-Cypriot peacebuilding groups. Everyone involved felt constrained in terms of how to respond, recognizing that anything the group said or did could cause a backlash. Some members suggested that the bicommunal groups should be brought together to engage in discussions about the buffer-zone events; others advocated speaking out in the news media and other public forums against the nationalist rhetoric; and several members thought that it would be better to simply "lay low" until more time had passed and the atmosphere was more conducive to taking action.

As each group discussed the three options, a general agreement was reached, after some "shuttle diplomacy" across the Green Line, that taking a passive stance would only reinforce the divide. It was likely that the messages emanating from politicians and the news media, reflected in local conversations occurring in coffee shops and workplaces, and around the dinner table, would continue for a long period of time and push the communities even further apart. Under that scenario, we might have to wait years before starting bicommunal meetings again. The urge was strong, particularly in the Greek-Cypriot group, to take some action, as many believed that it was very important to offer the public an alternative to the rhetoric that permeated that society, replacing the seemingly mindless nationalist oratory that filled the airwaves and newspapers with messages of balanced, reasoned analysis. We feared, however, that if we took a strong public stance against the prevailing language, not only would we be accused by the larger society as failing to uphold the cause of justice (as seen by each side) but, potentially, we could harm the long-term cause of peace itself. By challenging the views that nearly the entire population seemed to hold about the cause of the bufferzone events and the nature of the other side, we could create negative perceptions of the peacebuilding movement, reinforcing the image of peace activists as naïve, collaborators with the enemy, and traitors to the national cause on each side. Group members in each community believed that, eventually, we had to offer more persuasive messages of peace to the general public, but that the time was not right for such a move.

Opinion within both groups slowly shifted toward finding ways to restart the bicommunal meetings, providing people with opportunities to exchange ideas and views with members of the other community. We knew, however, that it would not be possible on our own to obtain the necessary permissions to bring together people living on different sides of the Green Line, as the usual avenues for gaining permissions through the Fulbright office or working directly with the UN no longer offered viable possibilities for convincing authorities to allow Greek Cypriots and Turkish Cypriots to meet together. We needed a set of allies that, collectively, would be strong enough to break through the barrier of the buffer zone to allow bicommunal groups to start meeting again.

After much discussion within each group and shuttling of messages back and forth across the Green Line, both groups agreed on a course of action: to organize a single bicommunal event and invite those Greek Cypriots and Turkish Cypriots who had participated in past bicommunal events, as well as the diplomatic core of all foreign embassies serving in Cyprus. We decided to use the occasion of the International Day of Peace

(Peace Day), a yearly global holiday in which individuals, communities, and nations highlight efforts to end conflict and to promote peace.[5] Our strategy of involving the international diplomatic community as sponsors for this event not only created pressure on authorities to grant permissions for the bicommunal event but also legitimized the strategy in a way that would not be possible if it primarily had been associated with peace activists.

After an array of inquiries, consultations, and exchange of ideas, we gained the support of nearly all of the diplomatic entities on the island, including the four largest and most influential offices: the UN, U.S. Embassy, Office of the European Commission, and British Embassy. With their support, we organized and successfully held the first bicommunal gathering after the buffer-zone incidents, a little more than 6 weeks after they occurred. Approximately 150 people, including ambassadors from most of the embassies, came together for an evening of speeches and discussions focused on the possibilities that still existed for rapprochement, even in the face of the tragedies and setbacks. The recent buffer-zone incidents inevitably were at the center of both the formal presentations and the informal discussions that occurred throughout the bicommunal event. Working in dyads or groups, Greek Cypriots, Turkish Cypriots, diplomats, and UN personnel reflected, analyzed, and deciphered the recent escalation of conflict, and jointly explored where things could evolve and whether there were ways to defuse the negative effects of the incidents and redirect developments in constructive directions.

The success of that event had a significant influence on the evolution of sociopolitical phenomena in the aftermath of the buffer-zone incidents. Third-party diplomats and UN personnel who attended the bicommunal gathering were amazed that despite the recent tragic incidents and the interethnic alienation that ensued, Greek Cypriots and Turkish Cypriots still were willing to meet with their ethnic counterpart from the other community. They were surprised to see that the disastrous incidents had failed to blunt the relationships that these Greek Cypriots and Turkish Cypriots had developed through their involvement over the years in bicommunal peace-enhancing initiatives, and they were impressed by the commitment and determination of these Cypriots to move forward and supersede the anger and negativity that had engulfed the island. Seeing the energy and engagement of these Turkish Cypriots and Greek Cypriots, the diplomats and UN personnel realized that perhaps not all had been lost, as had been suggested by the spectacle of the buffer-zone killings and their hyped media coverage.

Following the Peace Day gathering, we and other peace activists engaged in informal talks with the UN and other third parties, arguing that despite all that had happened, the "reality" in Cyprus was not limited to the *adversarial Cyprus* of ethnonationalist polarization but also included the *peacebuilding Cyprus* of the bicommunal movement, which was strong and poised to become a more influential force. Although the number of people subscribing to the alternative reality was much smaller than the more visible nationalists, it was possible that many more Cypriots in both communities were at least sympathetic to peacebuilding and potentially open to reconciliation. We further argued that the best antidote to the buffer-zone incidents was not to simply accept the entrenched reality of hyper-nationalism but, rather, to further promote and expand bicommunal contacts and communication between the two communities. The critical question we posed to the third parties was where members of the diplomatic community should invest energy and resources—in the Cyprus of interethnic estrangement or that of bicommunal peacebuilding. We also asked whether they would support the definitive finality of the negative impact of the buffer-zone incidents by resigning to their immediate impact or invest their energy in opening up new paths of interethnic communication that, in time, could reenergize bicommunal rapprochement.

In the days that followed the Peace Day event, it became clear that the international diplomatic community had regained a degree of faith in the potential contribution of bicommunal contacts. Under the leadership of the UN envoy to Cyprus, the third-party diplomats from the various embassies who attended the Peace Day event met to forge a joint position and strategy for moving forward in the aftermath of the buffer-zone incidents. The outcome was a joint communiqué—the first of its kind—that called on leaders of the Greek-Cypriot and Turkish-Cypriot communities to permit and encourage the immediate commencement of bicommunal gatherings as a way to curb the negative impact of the buffer-zone incidents. Behind the scenes, at the highest levels, third parties also exerted pressure on leaders of the two communities to support bicommunal gatherings and rapprochement projects.

Although we knew that it might take some time to regain momentum in the bicommunal movement, we decided to build on the success of the Peace Day event and direct our efforts toward organizing another gathering on UN Day (October 24), when UN forces in Cyprus usually schedule a bicommunal reception and sponsor activities for children.[6] After the buffer-zone clashes, this event already had been cancelled for the current year, partly because of security concerns but also because, at the time, there was no evidence that members of the two communities would attend such a bicommunal get-together. However, with Peace Day demonstrating that an alternative reality still was alive in Cyprus, the UN was willing to go forward with the celebrations, convinced, in part, by our group's promise to bring people to the event. Our hope was to bring together not only people who previously had experienced bicommunal activities but also those we knew to be open to contacts across the Green Line. We knew that UN Day offered an opportunity not only to make another strong statement about the possibilities for peace on the island but that it also was a good opportunity to expose a large number of people in a relatively safe environment to the possibility of contact across the Green Line. If we could bring people to this social event, perhaps we could convince them to join us later in more sustained dialogue activities.

The UN Day event exceeded everyone's expectations, with more than 1,000 Greek Cypriots and Turkish Cypriots gathering at the Ledra Palace Hotel, a former luxury hotel in central Nicosia that had become the home for UN peacekeeping troops and the only place where bicommunal meetings could be held. The atmosphere was full of excitement, as old friends met for the first time in years, as those new to bicommunal activities found themselves in conversations with people from the other community, and as "veterans" of the bicommunal movement enjoyed the gratification of seeing their vision and hard work pay off. In addition to bringing people to the event, the peace activists organized the program of speeches and activities, which emphasized the youth of Cyprus, using a theme of building a shared future and leaving younger generations an island where they could live in peace. This decision to focus on youth became particularly important in the steps we took after UN Day to reopen communication across the buffer zone.

Even though both Peace Day and UN Day kept alive the hope of intercommunal reconciliation and produced much-needed bright spots after the August clashes, we knew that much more work was needed to turn the tide of negativity and slow the drifting of the two communities away from a shared future. We also needed to go beyond large one-time events, which have significant symbolic and motivational value but do not allow in-depth discussion of difficult issues or the building of relationships that is required for long-term results. We believed that the best way to proceed was to start more dialogue groups, which would allow participants opportunities to explore the tough issues and share deeply held feelings in a safe environment, offering potential for developing closer ties across community lines. To accomplish that goal, however, we needed help, again, from the diplomatic community, particularly in gaining the necessary permissions for meeting at the Ledra Palace Hotel.

We were hopeful about obtaining assistance from third parties, but we were not sure which group should become the focus of our efforts. In the year prior to the buffer-zone incidents, we had worked with groups of young business and political leaders, teachers, and artists, as well as with a group whose members came from across professional sectors. One group that we had not brought together previously, however, was university students, primarily because we perceived them to be relatively closed to the idea of bicommunal contacts. Given that most of the students at that time were born after the 1974 division of the island, they had no experience of that war, had most likely never met anyone from the other community, and were products of an educational system that promoted a highly negative view of the other community. As a result, student groups tended to express highly nationalistic sentiments and often engaged in provocative acts toward the other side, such as painting anti-Turkish and anti-Greek graffiti on walls near the buffer zone and sometimes gathering for protests against the other side. Hence, we were hesitant to start a student group despite the fact that this group clearly was important for the future viability of the peace movement. We decided, however, to make students the focus of our next effort, swayed by two factors: First, the dangers of ignoring this group was driven home to us by the fact that the buffer-zone incidents themselves had involved mainly the youth; second, bringing together students now would be an effective follow-up to the youth emphasis of UN Day. Fortunately, we obtained support from one of the diplomatic offices for bringing together a university student group. Initially, we encountered some difficulty finding enough students with sufficient interest to meet in a bicommunal setting, but we were able to organize a meeting in early December 1996, less than 4 months after the buffer-zone clashes.

The bicommunal meetings with university students were facilitated by Broome (and later by Fulbright Scholar Philip Snyder, who continued working with bicommunal groups after Broome returned to the United States in 1997). The initial session was devoted primarily to icebreaker (get-acquainted) exercises, reducing some of the tension associated with the bicommunal setting and giving students a chance to become comfortable with one another. Establishing a positive climate was particularly important, especially because none of these students had ever met anyone from the other community. Their images of the other community came from heavily biased school textbooks, one-sided media portrayals, and self-serving political messages. They, thus, went into the meeting expecting to find people who were very different from them, with little anticipation that they would find the students from the other side either likable or open.

This initial meeting of the students went surprisingly well. They quickly discovered that they had many things in common, particularly in relation to popular culture, university experiences, and global awareness. They came away from that meeting questioning the messages they had heard all their lives about the other community, and they were eager to continue their discussions in future meetings. For those of us who had hesitated to start a students' group, it left us wondering why it had taken us so long to focus on them.

Subsequent meetings were held with the students, using a structured dialogue process that helped them to explore special topics related to university student concerns, develop a deeper understanding of the perspectives of the other community, recognize the diversity of views that existed within each community, improve their ability to listen and communicate in productive ways, and form relationships that could be sustained outside the meetings.[7] After meeting five times, we arranged a visit for the students (as a bicommunal group) with both the Greek-Cypriot leader, Glafcos Clerides, and the Turkish-Cypriot leader, Raulf Denktash. We subsequently received funds from the Council of Europe to take the group on a 4-day trip outside Cyprus, which cemented the bonds of friendship between the students and allowed them to develop several ideas for projects that they eventually implemented in Cyprus (for more complete descriptions of the student group, see Broome, 1998, 1999).

These three bicommunal events, coming so soon after the buffer-zone incidents, set in motion a sequence of further bicommunal gatherings that continued throughout the following year. From fall 1996 to the end of 1997, the peace movement grew from the 150 individuals who had been involved before the buffer-zone calamity to more than 2,000 Greek Cypriots and Turkish Cypriots participating in dozens of dialogue and project groups focused on a diverse array of issues pertinent to Cyprus. They became biethnically engaged in numerous activities, ranging from conflict resolution workshops to think tanks and joint projects having a bearing on various sociopolitical aspects of the Cyprus problem.

As often is the case when significant change occurs, the vastly increased number of Greek-Cypriot and Turkish-Cypriot participants in bicommunal meetings during this period of time was due to many factors. Although we cannot know with certainty how our original decision to proceed with bicommunal gatherings a few weeks after the buffer-zone clashes affected the general population, we believe that these meetings provided for many people an alternative response to the heightened animosity and polarization that had been generated around the buffer-zone incidents. In view of the dangerous escalation of tension, many Turkish Cypriots and Greek Cypriots, who had misgivings about the confrontational approaches of nationalists on each side of the ethnic divide, were looking for something to counterbalance the negative dynamics that had developed. Perhaps because they wanted to be part of something more constructive, these individuals saw the opportunity to participate in bicommunal gatherings as a viable path of conflict de-escalation and rapprochement. Throughout the year, Greek Cypriots and Turkish Cypriots who never before had been active stepped forward and became involved in bicommunal contacts and projects, and many of them indicated that becoming involved in such activities lifted a heavy psychological burden from their shoulders. Doing so gave them hope for the future and confidence that the two ethnic groups could learn to live together peacefully.

In our view, this renewed effort at reactivating the rapprochement process contributed to defusing some of the explosive climate created by the buffer-zone incidents, and it served as an impetus for the general growth of interethnic contacts. It is possible, however, that none of this activity would have transpired had it not been for the decision by the peacebuilding community to prod the UN to hold the two bicommunal events in fall 1996, and the subsequent organization of dozens of other bicommunal events over the following year. As an antidote to the buffer-zone incidents, the bicommunal phenomenon gave rise to the first sign of a new demarcation around the Cyprus conflict, contrasting the numerous pro-peace groups of Greek Cypriots and Turkish Cypriots to the polarizing nationalist images that prevailed at the time.

As members of the peace activist community deeply involved in the activities described above, the four of us shared a strong sense of satisfaction in seeing our work play a role in turning around a dangerous situation, but in addition to the practical results, we also were gratified to gain confirmation for some of the theoretical principles that guided our choices. In the next section, we examine how our work was grounded in theories of conflict transformation.

PROACTIVE PEACE THEORIES INFORMING OUR WORK

The bicommunal events that the peacebuilders pursued in the immediate aftermath of the buffer-zone crisis, highlighted by the gathering of Greek Cypriots and Turkish Cypriots on Peace Day, directly challenged ethnocentric nationalism and asserted that multiethnic rapprochement, cooperation, inclusivity, and interethnic relationship building is the necessary path for transcending past tragedies of nationalist belligerency. The peacebuilders' concrete actions in response to the buffer-zone incidents marked a strategy and an orientation that not only broke free from the clutches of nationalism but, by working together across ethnic lines, also exemplified a postnationalist stance that confronted the negative impact of the incidents. These actions demonstrated in tangible ways that, both as an intellectual theory and a general mindset, ethnonationalism was not the way of the future (Anastasiou, 2008b; Broome, 1997, 2004; Hadjipavlou, 2007). Rather, against the backdrop of the alienating buffer-zone incidents, a joint peace-insistent presence—also in the buffer zone—embodied the hope of a new postnationalist paradigm that pointed to the replacement of nationalist zealotry with conciliatory courage, the defiance of nationalist animosity through interethnic friendship, and the expansion of people's sense of community by including more than members of their immediate ethnic identity group.

Transcending ethnonationalism after the buffer-zone clashes was enabled by implementing an approach to dialogue based in the works of

Bohm (1996), Buber (1958), Pearce and Littlejohn (1997), Stewart (1978, 1983), and others. These theorists consider *dialogue* to be a collective process of communicative engagement that has the propensity of building relational empathy by creating a third culture shared by participants (see Broome, 2009), one that expands people's horizons, synthesizes hitherto disparate facts, and creates new, more inclusive and polycentric perspectives that can facilitate conflict analysis, conflict resolution, and, ultimately, peace (Anastasiou, 2007). Through persistent and innumerable engagement in these bicommunal dialogic encounters, Greek Cypriots and Turkish Cypriots who participated developed an alternative, nonadversarial experience of each other, a more sophisticated and nuanced understanding of the Cyprus conflict, and a shared conflict-transcending perspective grounded in creative peace-enhancing strategies.

More important, the game-changing gathering on Peace Day, and the array of bicommunal groups subsequently formed in the year following the buffer-zone incidents, presented for the broader Greek-Cypriot and Turkish-Cypriot communities an alternative constructive image of Greek-Cypriot–Turkish-Cypriot relations. To employ Bohm's (1996) terminology, the polarizing news media *representations* of the horrible buffer-zone incidents in terms of generalized nationalist enemy stereotypes were countered by images of interethnic communality in concrete *presentations* of joint Greek-Cypriot–Turkish-Cypriot peace-seeking engagements. The abstract and highly negative images of the "Other," in which the buffer-zone events were nationalistically integrated, were contested and offset by the positive and tangible bicommunal confidence-building engagements, thereby *dis*-integrating those terrible incidents. In this way, the bicommunal actions of peacebuilders took exception to the generalizations of nationalist enemy stereotypes and deconstructed and disempowered those images.

The overall strategy of bringing people together across the divide through bicommunal events was rooted in Lederach's (1995, 1997) theory of transformative peacebuilding. Lederach described a systemic approach to peacebuilding, using a "pyramid" with three major categories of actors. At the top of the pyramid (Level 1) are high-level leaders, including military, political, and national religious leaders with high visibility. The focus of peacebuilding at Level 1 is on official negotiations, often led by a recognized external mediator. At the bottom of the pyramid (Level 3) is grassroots leadership, consisting of local actors, including indigenous nongovernmental organizations, community developers, and leaders of relief projects, who usually focus on survival in the aftermath of destruction brought about by the violence of war. In the middle of the pyramid (Level 2) is middle-range leadership, consisting of respected leaders in various societal sectors (e.g., business and education), local ethnic and religious leaders, academics and other intellectuals, and humanitarian leaders. Middle-level leaders are positioned such that they are known by or have connections with top-level leaders and have good links with grassroots leaders. Often, middle-level leaders have preexisting professional or personal relationships with their counterparts on the other side of the conflict; consequently, they are ideally positioned to participate in peacebuilding and reconciliation activities.

Lederach (1995, 1997) placed strong emphasis on the peacebuilding potential of the middle level of this pyramid, for such individuals are in a unique position to influence both policy leaders and common grassroots citizens. Hence, the core of bicommunal peacebuilders in Cyprus came primarily from the middle level of that society and acted from that middle-level vantage point. As Lederach (1995, 1997) noted, peacebuilders at the middle level are free from the constraints of a constituency and the protocols of high office typical of top political leaders, and, therefore, they usually have greater flexibility and creativity in seeking and developing peace-enhancing perspectives and actions than those at the other levels of the pyramid. The bicommunal peacebuilders of Cyprus both discovered and acted on this unique capacity of their standing in their respective communities.

Lederach (2003) used the concept of *conflict transformation* to describe the goal of peacebuilding: engaging in constructive change initiatives that help both to resolve particular problems and to build a strong basis for productive relationships afterward. Conflict transformation views peace as centered and rooted in the quality of relationships at both the microlevel and macrolevel, including quality face-to-face interactions and the ways in which social, political, economic, and cultural relationships are structured. Viewing peacebuilding as a process of transformation, bicommunal activists in Cyprus pursued the mending of interethnic relations as a step-by-step engagement, erecting peace-enhancing building blocks that could prove catalytic to a final settlement of the Cyprus problem and that, one day, could reach a critical mass, replacing polarizing nationalist culture with an all-inclusive peace culture.

Finally, it is important to note that peacebuilding is a process that plays out over a long period of time, not something that can be accomplished overnight. The Turkish-Cypriot and Greek-Cypriot peacebuilders' years of bicommunal work, including their response to the 1996 buffer-zone incidents, was marked by perseverance, patience, and an ongoing insistence on employing peace-promoting strategies and actions that moved beyond the frustrating searches for quick fixes (Anastasiou, 2008a). By adopting a process-focused perspective, these peacebuilders took a long-term view and "absorbed" many of the difficulties, disappointments, and setbacks that occurred along the way. This stance allowed their peacebuilding efforts to continue, even in the face of seemingly "game-ending" events, such as the buffer-zone clashes.

LESSONS LEARNED ABOUT COMMUNICATION ACTIVISM SCHOLARSHIP

Reflecting on the peacebuilding process described in previous sections, we draw several important lessons about communication activism scholarship. First, we saw how important it is for unofficial civil society peacebuilding groups to develop effective communication links with official diplomatic entities. Often referred to as "Track I" (official) and "Track II" (unofficial) diplomacy (see Chigas, 2003; Nan, 2003), conflict resolution theorists, such as Fisher (1997) and Kelman (2002), have long made a strong case for their complementarity, and other scholars have expanded such thinking to discuss "multitrack diplomacy" (e.g., Diamond & McDonald, 1996). Although no one argues that citizen peace initiatives should substitute for official negotiations, the theory of parallel tracks generally is premised on the idea that inasmuch as protracted conflict impacts and conditions both the official high-level politics of government and the lives and culture of a society's citizens, the process of moving from conflict to resolution and, eventually, to a peace culture requires orientations, actions, and strategies at the levels of both formal politics *and* civil society.

The idea of multitrack approaches to conflict transformation generally has been conceptualized in terms of peace-enhancing initiatives that move *in parallel* to each other, with political elites and citizens both doing their part and contributing to conflict transformation in different ways. However, what is unique about the way that the Cyprus peacebuilders responded to the buffer-zone clashes and the challenges those clashes posed to peace, and particularly the manner in which the peacebuilders opened channels of communication through an increasingly closed wall of separation, adds a new dimension to conflict transformation that moves the process beyond the idea of parallel tracks. In effect, the peacebuilders' responses illustrate the complementary idea of *crisscrossing tracks* as yet another vital modality of conflict transformation, in which the peacebuilders crossed over to the domain of official politics, offering political officials well-reasoned interpretations of the developments and constructive input on possible ways forward that would both contain and supersede the negative impact of the tragic events (for further discussion of the possible interface of official and unofficial diplomacy in the interest of peace, see Strimling, 2006). At the most critical moment in the escalation of events, the peacebuilders, after consulting with each other on both sides of the ethnic divide, turned their communication focus to UN officials and embassy personnel. Although their interactions with these persons were unofficial, their input ended up shaping official policy and related actions taken by the UN and other third-party diplomats in Cyprus. Under the circumstances, had communication by the peacebuilders remained confined to the track of civil society, working in parallel to whatever was happening at official levels, the chances of curbing the negative effects of the buffer-zone incidents would have been minimal, if not altogether negligible. However, by crossing over from the civil society track to the official politics track, the peacebuilders momentarily but strategically influenced the course of events in the immediate aftermath of the tragic incidents of summer 1996.

The work of the Cyprus bicommunal peacebuilders, thus, opens up new vistas for peace scholarship and, in particular, for communication activism scholarship in the service of conflict transformation, as it expands and complements the concept of parallel tracks in conflict transformation with the addition of crisscrossing tracks. Theory and practice, consequently, need to be broadened to focus on analyses and designs that differentiate the appropriateness and underscore the complementarity of parallel and crisscrossing tracks as pathways to peace.

A second lesson from our peacebuilding efforts relates to how culture affects communication and peacebuilding processes. It commonly is accepted that cultural differences affect conflict communication in both obvious and subtle ways. As LeBaron (2003) pointed out, conflicts are not just about territorial, boundary, and sovereignty issues; they also are about *acknowledgment, representation,* and *legitimization of different identities,* as well as ways of *living, being,* and *making meaning.* The peacebuilding group in Cyprus paid special attention to cultural issues, particularly those related to the concerns identified by LeBaron. Both the Greek-Cypriot and Turkish-Cypriot groups, during their meetings after the buffer-zone incidents, were careful to acknowledge the views and feelings of the other ethnic group, recognizing that the impact of the incidents might be different in each community. In organizing the bicommunal gatherings, there was general agreement to seek equality of representation, even though one community (Greek Cypriots) constituted the numerical majority in Cyprus. Moreover, despite the call by some to emphasize a pan-Cypriot identity as a way of developing solidarity, the groups agreed to recognize community identities (Greek Cypriot and Turkish Cypriot). This move was particularly important in keeping Turkish Cypriots onboard with the process, because for them, the notion of a pan-Cypriot identity would lead to the assimilation or absorption of the Turkish-Cypriot identity into the larger Greek-Cypriot identity.

A third lesson from our work concerns the need to find an appropriate mix of local and "imported" conflict-resolution approaches and methodologies, many of which have been developed in the United States or in other Western countries. Third-party interventions based on Western political experiences sometimes are criticized for exporting communication values that promote a more individualized form of democratic input into decision making at the expense of the more collective approach that often is found outside Western democracies. At the same time, although most societies have developed mediation and problem-solving methods to manage disputes at the local level (see Augsburger, 1992), many conflicts exist because there has been a breakdown of these approaches. Hence, the introduction of external approaches sometimes can provide an important and even necessary stimulus for moving groups in conflict toward more positive outcomes. The key question, thus, revolves around how to introduce external methodologies in ways that are culturally compatible with local settings.

In Cyprus, the situation was even more complex, because there were two communities involved and the local styles of communication and decision-making methods differed between them. For example, the general Greek-Cypriot communication style is more expressive and emotional than is the Turkish-Cypriot style, and Greek Cypriots tend to be more action oriented in response to problems, whereas Turkish Cypriots are more likely to take a low-profile approach to dealing with issues, at least in the initial stages. For these reasons, the Western emphasis on self-expression and problem solving is a closer fit for Greek Cypriots, although some aspects of U.S. approaches to dialogue, such as an emphasis on thorough analysis of the problem before proposing solutions, is a better fit for Turkish-Cypriot culture. We believe that the peacebuilding groups in Cyprus achieved a healthy balance of local (from both communities) and imported (U.S.-based) approaches, leading participants from the two communities to compromise in areas in which they differed among themselves. By applying these approaches constructively, the groups enriched both the processes and outcomes of the peacebuilding efforts.

Finally, we learned that communication scholarship, particularly theory and research on dialogue, could make significant contributions to building peace in protracted conflict situations. Communication served as the focus of this activist effort in three major ways. First, the peacebuilding communities on each side of the Green Line came together for a series of discussions in which *open and reflective communication* within their respective groups, as well as between the groups through an intermediary, helped them to process the events and to strategize about how to respond to them. Second, their deliberations led to a series of *bold communication initiatives* that brought together hundreds of people from the two communities in a bicommunal setting, defying the general consensus, shared by both local communities and by the international community, that the division of Cyprus had been cemented. Third, they implemented a *dialogic communication process* that pulled the two communities away from ethnonationalist rhetoric and toward a more meaningful exchange of viewpoints and greater cooperation in accomplishing common goals. This combination of practices represents a potent form of communication activism, in which communication is both the goal of peacebuilding activists' efforts and the means by which that goal is accomplished.

The bicommunal groups that met regularly prior to the buffer-zone incidents, guided by communication principles and practices, developed into a core group of peacebuilders who were motivated and prepared to respond quickly and insightfully to the ethnonationalist rhetoric by reopening channels of communication across the buffer zone. Because of their previous experience working across community lines, these peacebuilders were sensitized to the concerns of the other community, allowing them to address the cultural issues (acknowledgment, representation, and identity confirmation) discussed previously. They also understood the importance of opening lines of communication, even in the face of a seemingly unscalable wall that divided the two communities after the clashes. Although there were many personal and contextual factors that influenced their choices, the peace movement leaders all had received communication training—in listening, perspective taking, intercultural sensitivity, and expressing ideas in an open, nonjudgmental, and respectful manner, among other practices—which they put to good use during the crisis.

As noted earlier, it is unfortunate that so few communication scholars focus on protracted conflicts, given how crucial communication is to resolving, managing, and transforming such situations, especially in the arena of intergroup dialogue and peacebuilding. Hopefully, this chapter stimulates more interest in, and exploration of, this important area of study.

CONCLUSION

The primary aim of the activist efforts described in this chapter was to open pathways of communication across community lines in Cyprus, following a traumatic set of events that effectively had blocked all contact for the foreseeable future. Although these efforts had a significant, even game-altering effect in the year that followed the buffer-zone events, the new environment for peacebuilding did not last. Bicommunal meetings were dealt a severe blow at the end of 1997 when the Turkish-Cypriot authorities implemented a policy that denied permission for Turkish Cypriots to attend meetings in the buffer zone. This new policy was partly a response to a negative decision taken by the European Union toward starting membership talks with Turkey, and partly a reaction to the explosive growth of the bicommunal movement, which was not viewed positively by the Turkish-Cypriot leadership. The ruling party in the north at that time believed that bicommunal contacts undermined its goal of creating a separate state, and it was upset that Greek-Cypriot officials sometimes pointed to the bicommunal meetings as evidence that Turkish Cypriots had nothing to fear from life as a minority under a Greek-Cypriot government. Additionally, there were some who feared that the bicommunal movement could turn into a political movement in opposition to the ruling party in the north.[8]

Fortunately, the severe restrictions of Turkish Cypriots crossing the checkpoint in Nicosia did not fully stop the bicommunal work, for by the time of the closure, there were dozens of projects up and running, and the international community, particularly the U.S. Agency for International Development, had committed substantial funds to support bicommunal projects. Thus, a number of groups received funding for meetings held outside Cyprus, mainly in Europe and the United States, and groups started meeting in the mixed village of Pyla, located in the buffer zone but within British sovereignty, about an hour's drive from Nicosia.[9] Additionally, the first internet service providers were established in Cyprus in 1997, allowing groups to communicate via electronic means. Perhaps ironically, the continuation of the bicommunal contacts was led primarily by youths, the very group that we had been hesitant to work with before the buffer-zone incidents, but which, fortunately, was the focus of our efforts afterward.

In recent years, several important developments have affected the bicommunal peace movement, including a relaxing of restrictions on intercommunal contact in 2003, a failed 2004 referendum on a carefully negotiated UN peace plan (rejected by Greek Cypriots and accepted by Turkish Cypriots), the entry of Cyprus into the European Union in 2004 (applied only in the Greek-Cypriot south), and intensified negotiations under the auspices of the UN that started in 2008, continuing through this writing. Although the failed referendum in 2004 led to great disappointment within the peacebuilding community, and the UN-led negotiations have not produced a settlement of the conflict, the ability to hold bicommunal meetings without the need to obtain permissions has opened new possibilities for dialogue and cooperation across the Green Line. Although there is still much to be done, the peace process in Cyprus has come a long way since the 1996 buffer-zone incidents.

Although there are clear indications that bicommunal contacts and intergroup dialogue have made significant contributions to the overall peace process in Cyprus (see Broome & Jakobsson-Hatay, 2006), it is more difficult to link peace activists' activities with specific political events. As with any conflict, progress in reaching a viable and sustainable political settlement depends on many factors, including regional and international developments that are beyond the control of those involved in activities at the level of civil society. We believe, however, that the communication activism of peacebuilders described in this chapter, which opened communication pathways between the two communities after the 1996 buffer-zone clashes effectively had closed down the possibility of regular contact, played an important role in turning Cyprus away from a course of permanent separation. Today, Cyprus has an opportunity to transform a tragic past into a shared future, although both communities need to take bold steps to make that happen. If political leaders reach an agreement to reunite the island, and if the two communities accept this agreement, it will be only the next step in a long process of conflict transformation.

NOTES

1. As discussed later in more detail, in the period prior to the buffer-zone incidents, a number of bicommunal groups had been meeting regularly in the buffer zone; the peace activists who came together in each community after the clashes had been leaders in these bicommunal dialogue groups.
2. Distinctions are made in conflict studies between conflict "resolution," "management," and "transformation." *Conflict resolution*, the term used most widely, refers to the search for a stable solution that identifies and deals with the underlying sources of the conflict. *Conflict management* was introduced into the discourse by those who argued that resolution is not always possible and, therefore, it often is more important to find ways to manage the situation such that it is more constructive and less destructive, by intervening in ways that make the ongoing conflict more beneficial and less damaging to all sides. *Conflict transformation* is a more recent term that emphasizes modification of the relationships and social structures that drive conflict, by seeking improved understanding despite differing or even irreconcilable interests, values, and needs of the parties in conflict (for further discussion of these distinctions, see Lederach, 1995). In Cyprus, all three terms are used by the peacebuilding community, but because the dominant referent is conflict resolution, we mostly employ it in this chapter.
3. The material in this section is based on Broome (2006); for additional treatments of the Cyprus conflict, see Anastasiou (2008a, 2008b), Attalides (1979), Calotychos (1998), Gazio lu (1990), Hitchens (1989), Joseph (1997), Koumoulides (1986), Markides (1977), Mirbagheri (1998), Papadakis (2006), Richmond (1998), Stearns (1992), Theophanous (1996), Uludag (2006), and Volkan (1979); for recent research on the Cyprus conflict, see publications by the International Peace Research Institute of Oslo (PRIO; http://www.prio.no/Cyprus), which maintains an office in Cyprus.
4. The Greek Cypriots and Turkish Cypriots who participated in these discussions represented a wide cross-section of Cypriot society, both in terms of occupation (educators, business persons, shop owners, civil servants, and even elected officials) and political affiliation (although almost by definition, none of the members represented hard-line extreme nationalist views). For all of the peace activists, there was a great deal of personal sacrifice associated with their participation in bicommunal activities, for not only was it a considerable commitment of personal time and expense but they also often were criticized in the news media, as well as by coworkers, neighbors, friends, and, even sometimes, family members. They were accused of betraying the national cause, collaborating with the enemy, and interfering in areas best left to politicians and diplomats. In some cases, they even received threatening phone calls and other forms of harassment. They were well aware of the dangers, but fully committed to the cause of promoting dialogue across community lines.

5. Originally established by a UN resolution in 1981, the General Assembly, in resolution 55/282, of September 7, 2001, decided that, beginning in 2002, the International Day of Peace should be observed each year on September 21. The Assembly declared that it be observed as a day of global cease-fire and nonviolence—an invitation to all nations and people to honor a cessation of hostilities during that day. All member states, organizations of the UN system, regional and nongovernmental organizations, and individuals were invited to commemorate the day in an appropriate manner, including education and public awareness events, and to cooperate with the UN in establishing a global cease fire (see UN, 2008a).
6. UN Day commemorates the anniversary of the entry into force of the UN Charter on October 24, 1945, and has been celebrated since 1948. The day traditionally has been marked throughout the world by meetings, discussions, and exhibits on the achievements and goals of the organization. In 1971, the UN General Assembly recommended that member states observe it as a public holiday (see UN, 2008b).
7. The structured dialogue process employed with the students was similar to that used with the core group of peacebuilders and other groups in the 2-year period before the buffer-zone clashes (for detailed descriptions, see Broome, 1997, 2004, 2005).
8. The fear that the bicommunal movement could have a political impact had some basis in reality, as demonstrated in 2003, when the main opposition party, which had long supported the bicommunal peace movement, came to power on a pro-unification platform that departed in significant ways from nearly 30 years of policies that sought a political division of the island.
9. When Cyprus achieved independence from Great Britain in 1960, nearly 259 square kilometers (100 square miles) of the island remained under British sovereignty. Known as Sovereign Base Areas, they are located in Akrotiri (near the city of Limasol) and Dhekelia (near the eastern edge of the buffer zone). These areas are considered part of the United Kingdom, with British law applying within their borders.

REFERENCES

ABC Australia (Producer). (1998). *Divided we stand—Cyprus* [Motion picture]. (1998). United Kingdom: Journeyman Pictures. Retrieved from http://www.youtube.com/watch?v=H7CbIYGhWSA

Albeck, J. H., Adwan, S., & Bar-On, D. (2006). Working through intergenerational conflicts by sharing personal stories in dialogue groups. In L. R. Frey (Ed.), *Facilitating group communication in context: Innovations and applications with natural, groups: Vol. 1. Facilitating group creating, conflict, and conversation* (pp. 155–181). Cresskill, NJ: Hampton Press.

Albert, R. D. (2009). Communication for social impact: What communication scholars and practitioners can contribute to the prevention and resolution of ethnic conflicts worldwide. In L. M. Harter, M. J. Dutta, & C. C. Cole (Eds.),

Communicating for social impact: Engaging theory, research, and pedagogy (pp. 127–143). Cresskill, NJ: Hampton Press.
Alter, P. (1994). *Nationalism* (2nd ed.). New York, NY: Edward Arnold.
Anastasiou, H. (2002). Communication across conflict lines: The case of ethnically divided Cyprus. *Journal of Peace Research, 39,* 581–596. doi:10.1177/0022343302039005005
Anastasiou, H. (2007). The communication imperative in an era of globalization: Beyond conflict-conditioned communication. *Global Media Journal: Mediterranean Edition, 2*(1), 63–75. Retrieved from http://globalmedia.emu.edu.tr
Anastasiou, H. (2008a). *The broken olive branch: Nationalism, ethnic conflict, and the quest for peace in Cyprus: Vol. 1. The impasse of ethnocentrism.* Syracuse, NY: Syracuse University Press.
Anastasiou, H. (2008b). *The broken olive branch: Nationalism, ethnic conflict, and the quest for peace in Cyprus: Vol. 2. Nationalism versus Europeanization.* Syracuse, NY: Syracuse University Press.
Attalides, M. A. (1979). *Cyprus: Nationalism and international politics.* New York, NY: St. Martin's Press.
Augsburger, D. W. (1992). *Conflict mediation across cultures: Pathways and patterns.* Louisville, KY: Westminster/John Knox Press.
Azar, E. E. (1983). The theory of protracted social conflict and the challenge of transforming conflict situations. In D. A. Zinnes (Ed.), *Conflict processes and the breakdown of international systems: Merriam seminar series on research frontiers* (pp. 81–99). Denver, CO: Graduate School of International Studies, University of Denver.
Azar, E. E. (1986). Protracted international conflicts: Ten propositions. In E. E. Azar & J. W. Burton (Eds.), *International conflict resolution: Theory and practice* (pp. 28–39). Boulder, CO: Lynne Rienner.
Azar, E. E. (1990). *The management of protracted social conflict: Theory and cases.* Brookfield, VT: Gower.
Bar-On, D., & Kassem, F. (2004). Storytelling as a way to work through intractable conflicts: The German–Jewish experience and its relevance to the Palestinian–Israeli situation. *Journal of Social Issues, 60,* 289–306. doi:10.1111/j.0022-4537.2004.00112.x
Bar-Tal, D. (1998). Societal beliefs in times of intractable conflict: The Israeli case. *Journal of Conflict Management, 9,* 22–50. doi:10.1108/eb022803
Bohm, D. (1996). *On dialogue* (L. Nichol, Ed.). New York, NY: Routledge.
Broome, B. J. (1997). Designing a collective approach to peace: Interactive design and problem-solving workshops with Greek-Cypriot and Turkish-Cypriot communities in Cyprus. *International Negotiation, 2,* 381–407. doi:10.1163/15718069720848022
Broome, B. J. (1998). Views from the other side: Perspectives on the Cyprus conflict. In J. N. Martin, T. K. Nakayama, & L. A. Flores (Eds.), *Readings in cultural contexts* (pp. 422–433). Mountain View, CA: Mayfield.
Broome, B. J. (1999, September). Greek and Turkish Cypriot university students have more in common than expected. *Washington Report on Middle East Affairs,* pp. 82–84. Retrieved from http://www.wrmea.com

Broome, B. J. (2004). Reaching across the dividing line: Building a collective vision for peace in Cyprus. *Journal of Peace Research, 41*, 191–209. doi: 10.1177/0022343304041060

Broome, B. J. (2005). *Building bridges across the Green Line: A guide to intercultural communication in Cyprus.* Nicosia, Cyprus: United Nations Development Programme. Retrieved from http://www.undp-act.org/main/data/articles/building_bridges_english.pdf

Broome, B. J. (2006). Facilitating group communication in protracted conflict situations: Promoting citizen peace-building efforts in Cyprus. In L. R. Frey (Ed.), *Facilitating group communication in context: Innovations and applications with natural groups: Vol. 1. Facilitating group creation, conflict, and conversation* (pp. 125–154). Cresskill, NJ: Hampton Press.

Broome, B. J. (2009). Building relational empathy through an interactive design process. In D. J. D. Sandole, S. Byrne, I. Sandole-Staroste, & J. Senehi (Eds.), *Handbook of conflict analysis and resolution* (pp. 184–200). New York, NY: Routledge.

Broome, B. J., Carey, C., De La Garza, S. A., Martin, J., & Morris, R. (2005). In the thick of things: A dialogue about the activist turn in intercultural communication. In W. J. Starosta & G. M. Chen (Eds.), *Taking stock in intercultural communication: Where to now?* (pp. 145–175). Washington, DC: National Communication Association.

Broome, B. J., & Jakobsson-Hatay, A. S. (2006). Building peace in divided societies: The role of intergroup dialogue. In J. Oetzel & S. Ting-Toomey (Eds.), *Handbook of conflict communication* (pp. 627–662). Thousand Oaks, CA: Sage.

Buber, M. (1958). *I and thou* (2nd ed., R. G. Smith, Trans.). New York, NY: Scribner.

Burgess, H., & Burgess, G. (1996). Constructive confrontation: A transformative approach to intractable conflict. *Mediation Quarterly, 13*, 305–322. doi: 10.1002/crq.3900130407

Burton, J. W. (1990). *Conflict: Resolution and prevention.* London, England: Macmillan.

Calotychos, V. (Ed.). (1998). *Cyprus and its people: Nation, identity, and experience in an unimaginable community, 1955–1997.* Boulder, CO: Westview Press.

Carcasson, M. (2000). Unveiling the Oslo narrative: The rhetorical transformation of Israeli–Palestinian diplomacy. *Rhetoric & Public Affairs, 3*, 211–245. doi: 10.1353/rap.2010.0145

Chigas, D. (2003, August). *Track II (citizen) diplomacy.* Retrieved from http://www.beyondintractability.org/essay/track2_diplomacy/

Coleman, P. T. (2000). Intractable conflict. In M. Deutsch, P. T. Coleman, & E. C. Marcus (Eds.), *The handbook of conflict resolution: Theory and practice* (pp. 553–559). San Francisco, CA: Jossey-Bass.

Coleman, P. T. (2003). Characteristics of protracted, intractable conflict: Toward the development of a metaframework—I. *Peace and Conflict: Journal of Peace Psychology, 9*, 1–37. doi:10.1207/S15327949PAC091_01

Diamond, L., & McDonald, J. (1996). *Multi-track diplomacy: A systems approach to peace* (3rd ed.). West Hartford, CT: Kumarian Press.

Ellis, D. G. (2005). Intercultural communication in intractable conflicts. In G.-M. Chen & W. J. Starosta (Eds.), *Taking stock in intercultural communication: Where to now?* (pp. 45–69). Washington, DC: National Communication Association.

Ellis, D. G. (2006). *Transforming conflict: Communication and ethnopolitical conflict.* Lanham, MD: Rowman & Littlefield.

Ellis, D. G., & Maoz, I. (2002). Cross-cultural argument interactions between Israeli-Jews and Palestinians. *Journal of Applied Communication Research, 30,* 181–194. doi:10.1080/00909880216583

Ellis, D. G., & Maoz, I. (2007). Online argument between Israeli Jews and Palestinians. *Human Communication Research, 33,* 291–309. doi:10.1111/j.1468-2958.2007.00300.x

Fisher, R. J. (1997). *Interactive conflict resolution.* Syracuse, NY: Syracuse University Press.

Frosh, P., & Wolfsfeld, G. (2007). ImagiNation: News discourse, nationhood and civil society. *Media, Culture & Society, 29,* 105–129. doi:10.1177/0163443706072001

Gazioglu, A. C. (1990). *The Turks in Cyprus: A province of the Ottoman Empire (1571–1878).* London, England: K. Rüstem & Brother.

Hadjipavlou, M. (2004). The contribution of bicommunal contacts in building a civil society in Cyprus. In A. H. Eagly, R. M. Baron, & V. L. Hamilton (Eds.), *The social psychology of group identity and social conflict: Theory, application, and practice* (pp. 193–213). Washington DC: American Psychological Association.

Hadjipavlou, M. (2007). The Cyprus conflict: Root causes and implications for peacebuilding. *Journal of Peace Research, 44,* 349–365. doi:10.1177/0022343307076640

Hitchens, C. (1989). *Hostage to history: Cyprus from the Ottomans to Kissinger.* New York, NY: Noonday Press.

Joseph, J. S. (1997). *Cyprus: Ethnic conflict and international politics: From independence to the threshold of the European Union.* New York, NY: St. Martin's Press.

Kelman, H. C. (2002). Interactive problem-solving: Informal mediation by the scholar-practitioner. In J. Bercovitch (Ed.), *Studies in international mediation: Essays in honour of Jeffrey Z. Rubin* (pp. 167–193). New York, NY: Palgrave Macmillan.

Klang-Maoz, I. (1997). A decade of structured educational encounters between Jews and Arabs in Israel. In D. S. Halpérin (Ed.), *To live together: Shaping new attitudes to peace through education* (pp. 47–56). Paris, France: United Nations Educational, Scientific and Cultural Organization. Retrieved from http://unesdoc.unesco.org/images/0010/001085/108501eo.pdf

Koumoulides, J. T. A. (Ed.). (1986). *Cyprus in transition: 1960–1985.* London, England: Trigraph.

Kriesberg, L. (1993). Intractable conflict. *Peace Review: A Journal of Social Justice, 5,* 417–421. doi:10.1080/10402659308425753

Kriesberg, L., Northrup, T. A., & Thorson, S. J. (Eds.). (1989). *Intractable conflicts and their transformation.* Syracuse, NY: Syracuse University Press.

LeBaron, M. D. (2003). *Bridging cultural conflicts: A new approach for a changing world.* San Francisco, CA: Jossey-Bass.

Lederach, J. P. (1995). *Preparing for peace: Conflict transformation across cultures.* Syracuse, NY: Syracuse University Press.

Lederach, J. P. (1997). *Building peace: Sustainable reconciliation in divided societies.* Washington, DC: United States Institute of Peace Press.

Lederach, J. P. (2003). *The little book of conflict transformation*: Intercourse, PA: Good Books.

Mack, J. (1990). The enemy system. In V. D. Volkan, D. A. Julius, & J. V. Montville (Eds.), *The psychodynamics of international relationships: Vol. 1. Concepts and theories* (pp. 83–95). Lexington, MA: Lexington Books.

Maoz, I. (1999). The impact of third-party communications on the Israeli–Palestinian negotiations. *Harvard International Journal of Press Politics, 4*(3), 11–25. doi:10.1177/1081180X99004003003

Maoz, I. (2000a). An experiment in peace: Reconciliation-aimed workshops of Jewish-Israeli and Palestinian youth. *Journal of Peace Research, 37,* 721–736. doi:10.1177/0022343300037006004

Maoz, I. (2000b). Multiple conflicts and competing agendas: A framework for conceptualizing structured encounters between groups in conflict—The case of a coexistence project between Jews and Palestinians in Israel. *Peace and Conflict: Journal of Peace Psychology, 6,* 153–156. doi:10.1207/S15327949PAC0602_3

Maoz, I. (2000c). Power relations in intergroup encounters: A case study of Jewish–Arab encounters in Israel. *International Journal of Intercultural Relations, 24,* 259–277. doi:10.1016/s0147-1767(99)00035-8

Maoz, I. (2001). Participation, control, and dominance in communication between groups in conflict: Analysis of dialogues between Jews and Palestinians in Israel. *Social Justice Research, 14,* 189–208. doi:10.1023/A:1012893003614

Maoz, I. (2002). Conceptual mapping and evaluation of peace education programs: The case of education for coexistence through intergroup encounters between Jews and Arabs in Israel. In F. Salamon & B. Nevo (Eds.), *Peace education: The concept, principles, and practices around the world* (pp. 259–271). Mahwah, NJ: Lawrence Erlbaum.

Maoz, I. (2004). Coexistence is in the eye of the beholder: Evaluating intergroup encounter interventions between Jews and Arabs in Israel. *Journal of Social Issues, 60,* 437–452. doi:10.1111/j.0022-4537.2004.00119.x

Maoz, I., & Ellis, D. G. (2001). Going to ground: Argument between Israeli-Jews and Palestinians. *Research on Language and Social Interaction, 4,* 399–419. doi:10.1207/S15327973RLSI3404_01

Maoz, I., & Ellis, D. G. (2006). Facilitating groups in severe conflict: The case of transformational dialogue between Israeli-Jews and Palestinians. In L. R. Frey (Ed.), *Facilitating group communication in context: Innovations and applications with natural groups: Vol. 1. Facilitating group creating, conflict, and conversation* (pp. 183–203). Cresskill, NJ: Hampton Press.

Maoz, I., & Ellis, D. G. (2008). Intergroup communication as a predictor of Jewish-Israeli agreement with integrative solutions to the Israeli–Palestinian conflict: The mediating effects of out-group trust and guilt. *Journal of Communication, 58,* 490–508. doi:10.1111/j.1460-2466.2008.00396.x

Maoz, I., Steinberg, S., Bar-On, D., & Fakhereldeen, M. (2002). The dialogue between the "self" and "other": A process analysis of Palestinian–Jewish encounters in Israel. *Human Relations, 55,* 931–962. doi:10.1177/0018726702055008178

Markides, K. C. (1977). *The rise and fall of the Cyprus Republic.* New Haven, CT: Yale University Press.

Mirbagheri, F. (1998). *Cyprus and international peacemaking*. New York, NY: Routledge.
Montville, J. (1990). The psychological roots of ethnic and sectarian terrorism. In V. D. Volkan, D. A. Julius, & J. V. Montville (Eds.), *The psychodynamics of international relationships: Vol. I. Concepts and theories* (pp. 121–134). Lexington, MA: Lexington Books.
Nan, S. A. (2003, June). *Track I diplomacy*. Retrieved from http://www.beyondintractability.org/essay/track1_diplomacy/?nid=1327
Papadakis, Y. (2006). *Echoes from the dead zone: Across the Cyprus divide*. New York, NY: I. B. Tauris.
Pearce, W. B., & Littlejohn, S. W. (1997). *Moral conflict: When social worlds collide*. Thousand Oaks, CA: Sage.
Richmond, O. P. (1998). *Mediating in Cyprus: The Cypriot communities and the United Nations*. Portland, OR: Frank Cass.
Rogers, R., & Ben-David, A. (2008). The Palestinian–Israeli peace process and transnational issue networks: The complicated place of the Israeli NGO. *New Media & Society, 10*, 497–528. doi:10.1177/1461444807085321
Rouhana, N. N., & Bar-Tal, D. (1998). Psychological dynamics of intractable ethnonational conflicts—The Israeli–Palestinian case. *American Psychologist, 53*, 761–770. doi:10.1037/0003-066x.53.7.761
Spencer, G. (2003). Pushing for peace: The Irish government, television news and the Northern Ireland peace process. *European Journal of Communication, 18*, 55–80. doi:10.1177/0267323103018001226
Spencer, G. (2004). The impact of television news on the Northern Ireland peace negotiations. *Media, Culture & Society, 26*, 603–623. doi:10.1177/0163443704044218
Stearns, M. (1992). *Entangled allies: U.S. policy toward Greece, Turkey, and Cyprus*. New York, NY: Council on Foreign Relations Press.
Stewart, J. (1978). Foundations of dialogic communication. *Quarterly Journal of Speech, 64*, 183–201. doi:10.1080/00335637809383424
Stewart, J. (1983). Interpretive listening: An alternative to empathy. *Communication Education, 32*, 379–391. doi:10.1080/03634528309378559
Strimling, A. (2006). Stepping out of the tracks: Cooperation between official diplomats and private facilitators. *International Negotiation, 11*, 91–127. doi:10.1163/157180606777835766
Theophanous, A. (1996). *The political economy of a federal Cyprus*. Nicosia, Cyprus: Research and Development Center, Intercollege Press.
Uludag, S. (2006). *Oysters with the missing pearls: Untold stories about missing persons, mass graves and memories from the past of Cyprus*. Nicosia, Cyprus: IKME Socio-political Studies Institute; BILBAN Sociopolitical Studies Institute.
United Nations. (1996). *The demonstrations of 11 August 1996*. Retrieved from http://www.hri.org/MFA/foreign/cyprus/UN2.htm
United Nations. (2008a). *International Day of Peace 21 September 2008*. Retrieved from http://www.un.org/events/peaceday/2008
United Nations. (2008b). *United Nations Day 24 October 2008*. Retrieved from http://www.un.org/events/unday/2008

United Nations Peacekeeping Force in Cyprus. (2009). *The buffer zone*. Retrieved from http://www.unficyp.org/nqcontent.cfm?a_id=1592

Volkan, V. D. (1979). *Cyprus—War and adaptation: A psychoanalytic history of two ethnic groups in conflict*. Charlottesville: University Press of Virginia.

Volkan, V. D. (1990). An overview of psychological concepts pertinent to interethnic and/or international relationships. In V. D. Volkan, D. A. Julius, & J. V. Montville (Eds.), *The psychodynamics of international relationships: Vol. 1. Concepts and theories* (pp. 31–46). Lexington, MA: Lexington Books.

Wolfsfeld, G. (1997). Fair weather friends: The varying role of the news media in the Arab–Israeli peace process. *Political Communication, 14*, 29–48. doi: 10.1080/105846097199524

Wolfsfeld, G., Khouri, R., & Peri, Y. (2002). News about the other in Jordan and Israel: Does peace make a difference? *Political Communication, 19*, 189–210. doi:10.1080/10584600252907443

Zupnik, Y.-J. (2000). Conversational interruptions in Israeli–Palestinian "dialogue" events. *Discourse Studies, 2*, 85–110. doi:10.1177/1461445600002001004

2

NEGOTIATING DIALECTICAL TENSIONS IN COMMUNICATION ACTIVISM

A Decade of Working in the Countertrafficking Field

Christopher Carey
Portland State University

On the edge of Kolkata, India—a city of 13 million people situated between two enduring holy sites—sits Khalighat, one of the most desperate places in India. It is a place of many truths: crushing poverty, river-soaked sewage flooding the streets every full moon, and many women and children who make a living by selling themselves for a few rupees. Khalighat, however, also is a place of corner temples and deeply religious worship, and where Kalam: Margins Write, a human rights-based creative writing program for marginalized youth in red-light districts and railway stations, creates poetry with the city's youth.

In India, stories never seem to end, and although it is difficult to pinpoint a beginning for a journey that would take me to the paper temples of Khalighat, steaming heat of Dhaka, and pungent smells of Kathmandu, it would be that first day traveling with my students in summer 2000. As we began our ascent up the long, steep trail to Dubachowr—the village that would be our home for the next several days—my friend, Shreesta, told me to look at the roofs in Dubachowr and the other villages we passed. "Those roofs tell stories," she said. "You know the home of a woman who has returned from India: Her family can afford a tin roof." As we weaved our way up the trail through terraced farms and past teahouses and women working in the fields, we looked out over the Sindupalchuk Valley and caught the occasional glint of a tin roof. We didn't just look; we met, talked to, worked alongside, and ate and drank with many of the people who lived in Dubachowr. The experience changed the students' lives, as well as mine.

Returning to Kathmandu and meeting with Nepalese lawyers, judges, and activists, we learned about the tragic stories of trafficked women from Nepal. The international community estimates that 1 out of 10 Nepalese girls ends up a slave in a brothel in another country, with the number of Nepalese girls currently languishing in brothels in large cities in India alone ranging from 100,000 to 300,000. That realization, coupled with my experiences in South Asia, paved the way for the formation of The Daywalka Foundation, a nonprofit organization dedicated to alleviating human trafficking.

For the past 10 years, I have combined activism and research in the countertrafficking field. For 4 of those years, starting in 2003, I served as executive director of The Daywalka Foundation (TDF), providing oversight of its organization, direction, and operations, as well working with U.S. funders and South Asian partners. My communication activism research includes developing stakeholder engagement and dialogue strategies for TDF's programs, and conducting evidence-based research to develop new programs for that organization. This chapter explains that work by first providing an overview of the problem of human trafficking, then detailing TDF's specific interventions during the time I served as its executive director, and concluding with a discussion of three dialectical tensions experienced in my communication activism in the countertrafficking field and lessons learned about managing those tensions.

HUMAN TRAFFICKING

Human trafficking, commonly known as "trafficking in persons" (TIP), encompasses human smuggling, forced labor, child labor, bonded labor, and sexual slavery, and is the third top income-generating illicit crime in the world today (U.S. Department of State, 2004), after arms and drug trafficking. The United Nations (UN, 2000) Protocol to prevent, suppress, and punish TIP, one of two Protocols known as the "Palermo Protocol," defined *trafficking in persons* as:

> the recruitment, transportation, transfer, harbouring or receipt of persons, by means of the threat or use of force or other forms of coercion, of abduction, of fraud, of deception, of the abuse of power or of a position of vulnerability or of the giving or receiving of payments or benefits to achieve the consent of a person having control over another person, for the purpose of exploitation. Exploitation shall include, at a minimum, the exploitation of the prostitution of others or other forms of sexual exploitation, forced labour or services, slavery or practices similar to slavery, servitude or the removal of organs. (p. 2)

TIP crimes involve several parties: traffickers; trafficking survivors or victims; and usually if an intervention has occurred, various government and nongovernmental organization (NGO) workers charged with the capture and prosecution of traffickers, and with the prevention and protection of trafficked persons. *Traffickers* are those persons who are responsible for, or knowingly participate in, the trafficking of human beings, including agents, employers, madams, pimps, pimp–boyfriends, recruiters, and owners of venues that exploit trafficked persons (Bertone, 1999). Police and other law enforcement, government, and authority figures that are complicit in the act of trafficking also are considered to be traffickers. *Trafficked persons* refer to men, women, and children (under the age of 18) who have experienced or currently are experiencing a state of being trafficked.

The U.S. Department of State (2010) estimated that the TIP trade enslaves an estimated 12.1 million individuals around the globe, with some estimates as high as 27 million people (Leuchtag, 2003), although reliable numbers are difficult to obtain because of the underground nature of the crime and the problem of assessing the size of hidden populations. The roots of one significant aspect of trafficking, commercial sexual exploitation, have been tied to organized crime, gender discrimination, poverty, government corruption, and childhood abuse. The proliferation of such trafficking reflects many of today's social and economic ills—a second wave of slavery stemming from the commodification of human beings.

Of the various groups involved in TIP, international organized crime has capitalized on the increased movement of people, poverty, and gender discrimination to maintain trafficking for sexual exploitation as part of its global market economy. Many case studies have noted that traffickers generally comprise a small network (two to three individuals), which, according to U.S. federal law, constitutes an organized crime group. Along with low penalties and high profits associated with TIP worldwide (estimates range from 600,000 to 800,000 individuals trafficked yearly across international borders; U.S. Department of State, 2007), a large number of those persons are forced into labor or other exploitative circumstances (Banerjee, 2002; Leuchtag, 2003; O'Beirne, 2002).

Increasing attention is being paid to human trafficking within countries, which the U.S. Department of State (2007) estimated to be much higher worldwide than is cross-border trafficking. For example, in India, 90% of human trafficking is believed to be internal, with people transported from one place to another in India (U.S. Department of State, 2010). The U.S. Department of State (2010) estimated that although between 14,500 and 17,500 persons are trafficked into the United States each year, there also are a significant number of trafficked Americans (generally, underage children who have run away from exploitative or abusive family situations only to be forced or pressured into prostitution from "friends" they meet on the street).

Commercial trafficking of children, in particular, steadily is increasing and occurs on large regional and global levels (Clark, 2003). The United Nations Children's Fund (http://www.unicef.org) estimated that children constitute at least 30% of the total individuals trafficked for the commercial sex industry (Leuchtag, 2003). A decade ago, conservative estimates put the number of child sex workers in Asia at 1 million, with Kuo (2000) indicating upward trends of as much as 20% per year. In the 1990s, the mean age of trafficked children was 14 years, but in the 21st century, that number is showing signs of falling even lower (Clark, 2003).

Even though trafficking in children appears to be decreasing in some places, other evidence suggests a mere shift in where children are trafficked. For instance, although Cambodia, which has a long history of child commercial sex work, has seen a decrease in its numbers due to heavy international pressure, other Southeast Asian countries are taking up the slack to provide child sex workers (Beyrer & Stachowiak, 2003). Child sex workers also demonstrate high rates of HIV infection, with, for example, in 1995, about half of the known trafficked Nepali children in Mumbai, India infected (Marble, 1995). Leaders of local NGOs note that children are more prone to HIV infection, because they do not have the power to say no to sex without a condom.

TIP is not an isolated social problem but, instead, is intimately linked to the rapid urbanization of many developing countries, uneven economic opportunities, and vast movement of people migrating for economic, political, and social reasons. Public health and, particularly, the spread of HIV and AIDS are interwoven with TIP. In India alone, 5.7 to 7 million people are infected with the HIV virus (Parsons, 2006), with 75% to 85% of infections transmitted through heterosexual contact (National AIDS Control Organization, 1997). Sarkar et al. (2006) indicated that trafficked women engaged in sex work in India are two to four times more likely to be infected with the HIV virus than are nontrafficked sex workers. In one astonishing statistic, Nepalese women who worked in brothels for less than 5 years had a 48% HIV infection rate (Parsons, 2006).

Because the problem of TIP is complex and requires the collaboration of a variety of stakeholders with diverse worldviews, effective communication holds the key to alleviating this problem. The communication discipline, thus, has much to offer the countertrafficking field, but, unfortunately, has produced very little about TIP. What work does exist, although informative, tends to focus on discursive and rhetorical aspects of human trafficking policies (Heiss, 2007; Isgro, 2005; Soderlund, 2005). A notable exception is Steinfatt's (2002) observation over a 12-year period of more than 4,000 sex workers and interviews conducted with 2,445 of them to examine the exchange of sex for money from both economic and (health) communication perspectives. Although Steinfatt's explicit focus was on the implications of sex work for the spread of sexually transmitted diseases (AIDS, in particular), his study offered insights into the communication patterns and practices that encompass the world of sex work.

THE DAYWALKA FOUNDATION

In 1995, I had just graduated from law school and was entering a world about which many young law graduates dream: a high-paying job at a ritzy firm in Chicago with a million-dollar view (and billable hours to match). Those first years of practice flew by in a blur, but I soon began to experience restlessness and some pretty pronounced jitters in my stomach. My closest friend was on the road traveling the world with nothing but a backpack, and we agreed to meet in Nepal. At the time, I thought that getting off "the grid" was a necessary step to being prepared to continue in the world of corporate law, and that all I needed was a good dose of no cell phones, e-mails, or business suits for a couple of weeks. I wanted an adventure in a place that I had never been to before, staring at and hiking the Himalayas, drinking butter tea, and hanging out with sherpas. I had no idea that this first trip to the Sindupalchuk region of Nepal would catapult me on a journey that would consume much of the next 12 years of my life.

The town of Dubachowr, Nepal was exactly what we were looking for; it was marginally on a trekking trail, had limited facilities but a warm guesthouse, and, best of all, one had to walk 2 miles to get there from the nearest drivable road. I thought we were making good time, when I realized that there was a line of Nepalis behind me patiently waiting for me to step aside to let them pass. They each carried at least 50 pounds of rice sacks and water, and most were at least twice my age. Staring at the line of Nepalis waiting patiently for the out-of-shape Western tourist to let them pass, I was reminded that my sense of place was not as secure as I perceived. My sense of place and perception would be challenged and displaced over the next decade as a result of my work in the countertrafficking field.

After arriving in Dubachowr and settling in for a few days, we began to develop friendships by playing, working, and eating with our gracious hosts. It did not take long to realize that something was missing in the village: young women. At first, I thought perhaps there was a cultural convention where young women simply did not appear in public and interact with strangers. Later, however, over evening tea, we were talking to a friend and she explained that most of the young women from poor families had left the village to go work in the carpet factories of India. It was not until later that I learned that the term "carpet factories" was a pseudonym for forced labor and, in many cases, for work in brothels.

I returned to the United States and continued my work as a lawyer. At night, however, I thought about Dubachowr, remembering the smell of dhal bhat (essentially, rice and lentil soup) cooking over an open fire, the pungent taste of Nepalese tea, and the missing young women. Still, it was easy to be distracted by the billable hours, high pay, and million-dollar views, distractions that lasted 3 years, until my eagerness to return to courtroom practice and my desire to do something more meaningful led me to accept a position as a deputy district attorney in Portland, Oregon. Practicing daily in the criminal justice system exposed me to the cruelty that human beings can inflict on one another, but I also felt empowered that I could do something about that cruelty. I also began to seek other avenues of change.

In 2000, I was invited to teach a service-learning course on human rights for Seattle University, taking 13 undergraduate students to Nepal. It was the combination of teaching, the law, and those students that inspired a group of us to put our ideas into practice, and, in 2002, TDF officially was incorporated. TDF began with an operating budget of $5,000, four board members, a few paid staff, and an abundance of energy and desire to create an organization that promoted collaboration among stakeholders within the countertrafficking community.

For the first 2 years, TDF concentrated on scholarship programs to provide schooling for Dubachowr's young women and children in a very informal and inexpensive manner. We were attuned to the top-down nature of international development that included paying high salaries to expatriate employees, meeting the formalistic and overly rational performance objectives of the U.S. Department of State, and, most important, what we called the "white Land Rover syndrome," which meant that whenever an international NGO received a large grant, its first purchase usually was a white Land Rover. From our perspective, this display of opulence and excessiveness represented everything that was wrong with international development, with the Land Rover serving as a significant symbol that further divided the powerful from those who were powerless. In contrast, we wanted to develop an organization that would stay close to the ground, work without the bureaucratic hassles and costs of most international organizations, and stay focused on the people it was designed to assist.

Within 3 years, we had obtained sufficient funding for TDF from the U.S. Department of State and several private sources. In 2003, we opened our first full-time center in Nepal, and within the next 2 years, we opened centers in India, Bangladesh, and Mexico. As TDF's executive director, I participated in all aspects of the organization's antitrafficking work, from interacting with policymakers in Washington, DC to training police officers in South Asia. TDF's other programs, many of which are described later, included providing vocational training to trafficking survivors, judicial awareness and training, police investigation training, alternative educational programs, public health training, scholarship programs, trafficking awareness training for religious leaders, and the development of several law libraries. To accomplish these programs, as described next, TDF adopted an approach that differed in important ways from traditional approaches to international development.

APPROACHES TO INTERNATIONAL DEVELOPMENT

The United States has been involved in foreign trade and relations since before the signing of the Declaration of Independence. With such a history, the United States should have become an expert at understanding, communicating, and reaching agreement with other cultures, but, unfortunately, that is not the case. Indeed, it was not until the middle part of the 20th century that the U.S. Department of State understood that there might be something more to communicating with other countries than just translating their languages. Practical issues arising from the massive post-World War II global rebuilding and reconstruction in the years immediately following the war, and the concerns of diplomats and international business personnel as they expanded their efforts to develop global commerce led to the establishment of the U.S. Foreign Service Institute in 1947, through which anthropologist Edward T. Hall and other scholars developed methods for training U.S. workers to live overseas (see Leeds-Hurwitz, 1990; Rogers & Hart, 2002). Such efforts also led communication scholars to create the subfield of intercultural communication (Martin & Nakayama, 1999).

Although the primary emphasis in the early years of intercultural communication development was practical training of relatively privileged white U.S. professionals working overseas, the civil rights movement during the 1960s led scholars to call for more attention to issues of power and social justice (see, e.g., Smith, 2007), paving the way for advances in development theory and practice. However, over the past 50 years, although paying some attention to power and social justice, the United States primarily has become skillful at solving engineering problems of the developing world, such as building dams, drilling wells, mining natural resources, and discovering future resources, although many of those engineering marvels have come at the cost of local populations and cultures (Kidder, 2003). Hence, what the United States is not particularly skilled at, and what continues to plague its relationships with other countries, is working with human beings—work that requires social and humanistic solutions. Consequently, problems such as alleviating poverty, promoting civil rights, protecting children, and stopping TIP are more difficult for the Unites States to understand and confront. Similar to new models of holistic health care that treat people's physical, emotional, and spiritual needs, scholars and practitioners now are beginning to understand that international development programs must address the intangible qualities of humans as well (see, e.g., Kincaid & Figueroa, 2009).

Hence, there has been a significant theoretical shift in development communication from a focus on modernization to that of empowerment (White, 2004). Historically, communication scholarship privileged models of development that viewed modernization (meaning Westernization) as central to increasing the quality of life in the developing world, which was especially true in Mexico and Latin America (see, e.g., Huesca, 2000; Huesca & Dervin, 1994). In contrast, the recent theoretical shift to empowerment focuses on cultural, religious, and other local practices within countries, as well as, significantly, on power relationships inherent in the development process (Melkote & Steeves, 2001). As White (2004) noted:

> The current research on communication for development tends to stress, rightly I would say, that empowerment is the affirming of the dignity and value of one's own identity and re-evaluation of the local culture. It also means resignifying the cultural institutions so that one's own cultural capital is given greater recognition and is seen as more valuable. The resignification is also important so that the price of changing power relations is not to give up one's own identity. With the premise that all cultural identities that contribute to justice and community are valued, the world needs a rich variety of cultural identities. (p. 21)

Unfortunately, this theoretical shift has not been accompanied by changes in applied international development practices. The work described in this chapter is a step toward filling that gap between contemporary theory and practice in international development.

The concept of *capacity building* (assistance provided to governments, organizations, groups, and people of developing countries to acquire certain skills or competencies, or to create appropriate institutions and policies, to function more effectively) has been introduced as a way to work with both the human and organizational realities of the developing world. Because capacity building is a long-term process, it must be done in a manner that ensures its longevity and sustainability. Hence, the challenge of international development is to create infrastructures, policies, and programs that outlive the limited duration funding cycles of international aid.

Although much has been written about TIP, especially its victims and, survivors, surprisingly, limited work has explored the people, groups, and organizations involved in the antitrafficking community. In particular, few mainstream writers and even fewer academics have paid attention to the fissures that separate those working in the antitrafficking community. Moreover, although TIP has been reported on widely (for recent work, see, e.g., Aronowitz, 2009; Bickerstaff, 2010; Cullen-DuPont, 2009; Ebbe & Das, 2008; Hart, 2009; Jonsson, 2009; Kara, 2009; Limoncelli, 2010; McCabe, 2008; Winckelmann, 2009) and several mainstream films and documentaries have been produced about it (e.g., the Academy award-winning *Born into Brothels*; Kauffman & Briski, 2005), many of those texts follow the same narrative familiar to Western audiences and, particularly, the narrative of 20th-century America: The story of the American hero who comes to the rescue of a poor segment of the developing world. Indeed, this narrative is as familiar to U.S. audiences as the tale of the American cowboy conquering the old West (West & Carey, 2006).

This narrative continues in the antitrafficking movement today, where perhaps nowhere else in law enforcement do victims have fewer rights and say about what happens to them in the legal process. Rarely are TIP survivors consulted about their desires or wishes prior to the start of legal proceedings. In most instances, a rescued victim has limited legal rights and may be in a country illegally, which means that she must actively participate in prosecution of traffickers.[1] In India, for example, this process can take years, with 80% of TIP trials resulting in acquittals (Parsons, 2006).

TIP, thus, is a complex transnational problem that requires dialogue with and decision making by a number of stakeholders, including public health officials, law enforcement agents, judicial officers, social service providers, immigrant rights advocates, academics, and international policy experts. Furthermore, stakeholders generally have different ways of framing TIP and are hard-pressed to agree on how to alleviate the problem. Figure 2.1 represents the stakeholder engagement process at the macrolevel developed by TDF, providing a visual representation of the diverse stakeholders involved in constructing antitrafficking policy.

The fact that TIP involves human movement (although not always across borders) makes this an intercultural and transnational problem. Even in India, where a majority of the trafficking is internal, there are 12 official

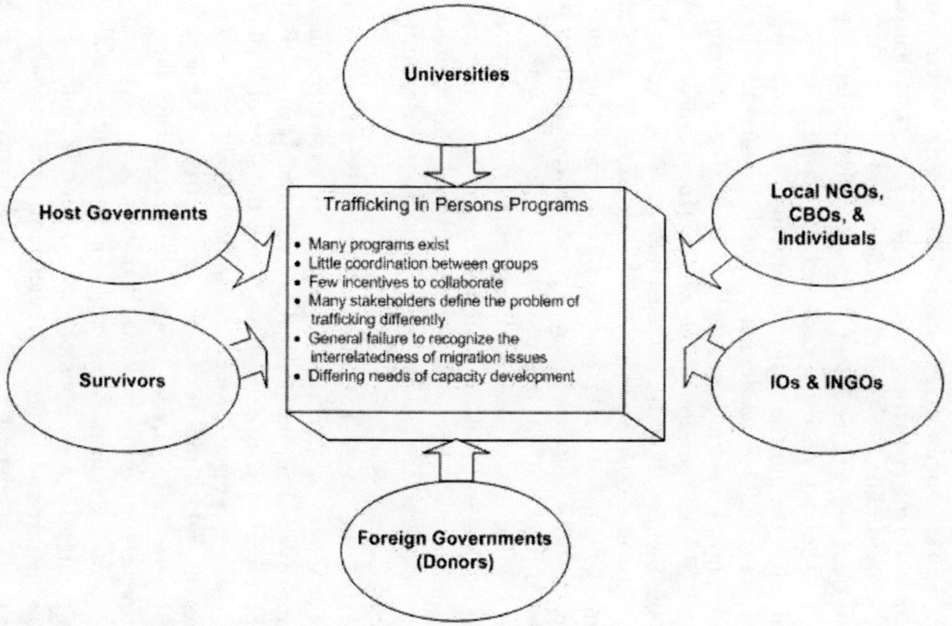

Trafficking in Persons Programs
- Many programs exist
- Little coordination between groups
- Few incentives to collaborate
- Many stakeholders define the problem of trafficking differently
- General failure to recognize the interrelatedness of migration issues
- Differing needs of capacity development

Stakeholders: Local NGOs, CBOs, & Individuals; IOs & INGOs; Universities; Foreign Governments (Donors); Host Governments; Survivors

Note: NGOs are nongovernmental organizations, CBOs are community-based organizations, IOs are international organizations, and INGOs are international nongovernmental organizations

Fig. 2.1. Trafficking in persons macrolevel stakeholder model.

languages, hundreds of regional dialects, and literally thousands of distinct cultural groups and patterns. Any particular trafficking case involves coordination of distinct cultural, social, and political groups; consequently, solving this problem means examining how TIP is discussed in local and international circles, and bringing engaged stakeholders into meaningful dialogue about this important issue.

Carey (2008), based on observation of and interviews conducted with several of the stakeholders listed in Fig. 2.1, identified four approaches in the international development field to human trafficking: expert/didactic, moral, justice/equality, and postcolonial/resistance. The *expert/didactic approach*, the dominant approach to international development in the antitrafficking community (Soderlund, 2005), views TIP as a specialized problem that requires expertise to understand and alleviate. Expertise is gained by people achieving advanced degrees, working in the field, and participating in conferences on the topic. Most of these experts are consultants who offer lectures and specific training programs about the problem. These powerful experts sit on advisory panels and determine the type and subject manner of the grants that fund much of the antitrafficking community. In this approach, expert knowledge replaces and, in many cases, trumps local, indigenous forms of knowledge. Policy implications include a top-down model of development, where conditions are set by the funding authority, as illustrated, for instance, by the U.S. government's policy on affirmative declarations against prostitution for organizations receiving financial support.

The *moral approach* is driven by the belief that values and worth are not defined by individual cultures but, instead, are derived from an external, overriding grand narrative. Many advocates of this approach view the fight against TIP as part of a larger, morally driven crusade against evil. This fight takes on the characteristics of a holy war and does not end with the conviction of traffickers but with the redemption, healing, and restoration of victims' souls. Although not all of the religious-based antitrafficking programs are steeped in this approach, generally there is a strong religious or faith-based element to such programs.

The *justice/equality approach* draws on elements of both the expert/didactic and moral perspectives to view knowledge about rights and values as most valuable when understood in light of local culture. From such a perspective, understanding TIP in India, for example, requires understanding how childhood is viewed and defined in India, as opposed to how the UN or other countries define it. This approach seeks to educate local communities in rights granted to them within the international community, collaborating with local communities to create opportunities to empower themselves to obtain agency and legitimacy within the international community.

The final approach, the postcolonial/resistance approach, to international development views communication and identity as sites of resistance where bodies, spaces, and ideas collide in an ever-changing landscape of, in this instance, postcolonial South Asia. This approach is founded on the agency of individuals and, consequently, focuses not on the end result but on a journey of self-discovery. The conceptualization of identity as fluid, constantly in flux, and changing is the key difference from the other three approaches. With regard to antitrafficking work, the postcolonial approach focuses on TIP victim survivors from their perspective. For example, many TIP women and children survivors have no desire to engage in a criminal legal action and simply want to return home; consequently, many programs that require active participation by victims with law enforcement are not available to them. The postcolonial approach, thus, strikes at the heart of traditional international development and, specifically, the history of colonial rule, because it does not rely on an external legal framework that, in this instance, defines "success" in stopping TIP.

The following dialogue that I had with Sahar, a TDF fieldworker involved in the Kalam: Margins Write poetry program (described later), illustrates the postcolonial/resistance approach:

Chris: Sahar, we need to talk about the program goals, objectives, and program measures for the Kalam program.

Sahar: Well, Chris, you know that Kalam is a poetry program that works with marginalized youth in Kolkata. It's focused on helping children who are at high risk of being trafficked. It is about the students recrafting their identities and developing agency to do so. The postcolonial psychological oppressions run deep, so I don't really see that measuring the program in a rationalistic manner fits with what we are trying to do. This is about the students' experience.

Chris: Well, okay, that is fine, but this program is funded by the U.S. government, which needs something to measure success by.

Sahar: Chris, dude, listen, this is not about performance measures or reaching some artificial goal to meet the government's requirements, the same government that has contributed to most of the colonialist empire in the last 2 centuries. Kalam is a journey of self-discovery.

Silence for about a minute and then I finally speak.

Chris: Well, I am not sure I can get a journey of self-discovery funded.

That exchange perhaps is when I first understood that it is not just the practical aspects of working in the international development field—specifically, working with programs that address TIP—that divides those in the countertrafficking community but the worldviews that guide their behavior.

Although TIP has captured the world's attention as one of the major humanitarian issues of the 21st century, as the very nature of enslaving millions around the globe to perform some of the worst forms of labor is an aberration to the modern human rights movement, these different worldviews have prevented effective collaboration on the problem. Thus, TDF's main focus was working through these differences to understand and intervene appropriately with various stakeholders in the countertrafficking community.

The lack of dialogue among stakeholders involved in this issue is particularly acute. Interviews conducted with stakeholders of international organizations devoted to solving this problem revealed a lack of trust, competition for funding, and few appropriate forums or training programs for meaningful dialogue to occur (Carey, 2008). Moreover, stakeholders, at both the organizational and individual level, often hold different deep-seated moral beliefs about sexual behavior. Although these beliefs ultimately may be irrelevant to focusing on the intersection of HIV and sex trafficking, they have prevented meaningful dialogue among stakeholders. For example, stakeholders that frame TIP as a public health issue identify HIV prevention as the most important objective and, consequently, work with brothel owners, mobilize sex worker communities, and are tolerant of prostitution, whereas stakeholders that identify TIP as a law enforcement issue, and particularly view sex trafficking within a Judeo–Christian moral frame, refrain from working directly with brothel owners or even sex workers because they believe that prostitution inherently is immoral. These differences in worldviews prevent meaningful collaboration among stakeholders that cannot get past their divergent philosophies.

One of the significant issues facing the antitrafficking community, thus, is the divergence in worldviews about human trafficking. These worldviews are not merely tangible disagreements about who should receive funding and for which programs but, rather, represent differences in core assumptions about the world—about the nature of good and evil, and agency and self-determination—and, consequently, about the right courses of action in antitrafficking programs.

THE DAYWALKA FOUNDATION'S APPROACH AND PROGRAMS

The following discussions describe some of TDF's interventions over the past several years to prevent human trafficking. With the understanding that the key to effective antitrafficking programs is communication (and, more specifically, dialogue), TDF first developed a stakeholder engagement model that focused on identifying the programmatic stakeholders working on countertrafficking strategies (see Figure 2.2).

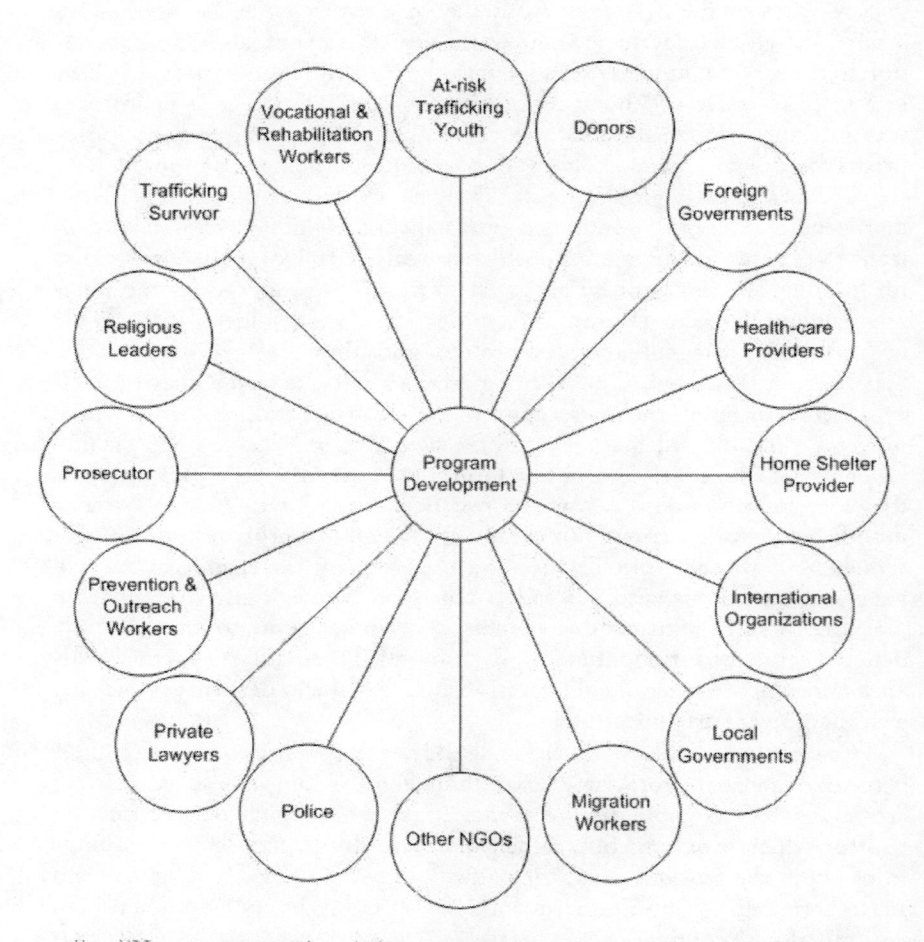

Fig. 2.2. Trafficking in persons programmatic stakeholder model.

The challenge for TDF and its stakeholders was that most antitrafficking programs rarely are singularly focused and that developing capacity-building programs necessitates the incorporation of several perspectives. Here, I first discuss TDF's theoretical influences and methodological approach, and then highlight five of its programs and briefly discuss their results/outcomes: (a) a scholarship program for at-risk youth, (b) Women's and Children's Security Resource Centers, (c) criminal justice and prosecution capacity building, (d) National Consultation on Better Legal Response to Human Trafficking, and (e) the "Kalam: Margins Write" poetry program for at-risk youth.

Theoretical Influences

From TDF's inception, the board of directors discussed the importance of using theory and practical knowledge to develop countertrafficking programs. Specifically, we understood culture, in general, and intercultural communication, more concretely, within a *dialectical perspective* (see, e.g., Martin & Nakayama, 1999) that acknowledged the inevitability of some uncertainty or tension in TDF's communication with stakeholders. This perspective required flexibility in TDF's programs that allowed for change depending on the particular cultural forces affecting specific programs. For example, TDF's first program—the scholarship program for at-risk youth in the Sindupalchuk region of Nepal (described later)—began with the understanding that we would fund only young girls from Dalit families that met certain financial and need-based criteria.[2] Our fieldworkers met separately with each family and determined whether the criteria had been met, but we immediately ran into problems with the village development council (VDC), the governing board of the village, in terms of village hierarchy and gender issues. The VDC explained that the established forums it had in place should decide who should be funded. Additionally, by excluding boys, we immediately challenged 4,000-year-old cultural norms surrounding gender and, specifically, the social bias in favor of males.

Along with the dialectical perspective, sociopsychological theories that had been applied to intercultural communication, such as the *contact hypothesis*, which asserts that interpersonal contact is one of the most effective ways of reducing prejudice (see Allport, 1954), weighed heavily in TDF's models of stakeholder engagement and collaboration. For example, there is a deep-seated distrust of the police and courts in many places in South Asia, but many stakeholders had limited contact with those institutions, meaning that if TDF could provide a neutral and comfortable place for all parties to gather, talk, and share chai (tea), some of the stereotypes and mistrust might diminish.

Third, one of the most important influences was *dialogue theory*, which was key to working through group, organizational, and cultural challenges. We understood *dialogue* to be consistent with Cissna and Anderson's (2002) definition and perspective:

> A special kind of communicative act that differentiates from other forms of communication in its focus on the interaction between process and content. It [dialogue] implies more than a simple back-and-forth message exchange in interaction. ... It points to a particular process and quality of communication in which the participants "meet," which allows for changing and being changed. In dialogue, we do not know exactly what we are going to say, and we can surprise not only the other but ourselves. (p. 10)

Specifically, TDF sought to create spaces and programs for dialogic conversations in which people can:

- recognize that their perspective is one of many and tell their story in a way that acknowledges others;
- know that there are good reasons for people's perspectives within their social worlds;
- allow space for others to express what is most important to them;
- honor the life experiences that lead to this moment in the conversation;
- believe that it is possible to be open to the life experiences of others without negating or undermining the significance of their experiences, beliefs, and values; and
- together, create ways to move forward constructively in managing and coordinating diverse opinions, ideas, and goals (see, e.g., Littlejohn & Domenici, 2001; Pearce & Littlejohn, 1997; Spano, 2001).

Pearce and Littlejohn (1997) referred to the type of discourse that TDF promoted as "transcendent" or "transformative," and Pearce and Pearce (2000) termed it dialogic virtuosity. Regardless of the label, such discourse leads participants to work through issues in new ways, transcending conflict and promoting productive discussions in which healthy cocreation of meanings occur. Such discussion is educative in that participants learn significant new things, generative because it leads to newly shared insights, and reflective because it encourages participants to explore the power and limits of their ideas and those of others.

Practically, the extensive applied work done with transformative dialogue in deep-rooted conflict situations involving religious, ethnic, national, or tribal disputes, such as with Palestinians and Israeli-Jews (for overviews, see, e.g., Albeck, Adwan, & Bar-On, 2006; Maoz & Ellis, 2006), and with Greek Cypriots and Turkish Cypriots on Cyprus (see Broome, Anastasiou, Hajpavlov, & Kanol, this volume), influenced the design of TDF's programs. That dialogic approach embraces analytical and noncoercive approaches to solving problems, abandons power-oriented techniques, and works through open-sourcing of discussion. Specifically, such dialogue asks members of each "side" to talk about their personal experiences and feelings that formed their worldviews, resulting in equal power sharing of the facilitated space. Such dialogue also focuses on reconciliation—not merely an exchange of ideas but an understanding and acceptance of others' points of view, within the context of developing long-term relationships.

Another example of employing dialogue that served as a cautionary tale for TDF was the World Health Organization's (WHO) 1977 Healthy

Cities/Healthy Communities project in response to urban decay, in which WHO envisioned community members engaging in dialogue to define the meaning of a "healthy city" and how to achieve it (see, e.g., Hancock, 1993; Norris & Pittman, 2000; Zoller, 2000). Turning that project into a movement, however, demonstrated mixed results, especially with respect to the implementation process. Zoller's (2000) 6-month field study of a group of trained citizens initiating the Healthy Communities process in their city revealed important tensions between trainers and participants with respect to the balance between collaboration and imposing one's will on others, whether communication is an essential element or an impediment to social change, and the desire to maintain diversity versus the desire to reach consensus. Zoller concluded that engaging in dialogue is vital, but that the results of the study point "to the importance of encouraging interactants to cultivate responsive relationships more than emphasizing techniques and steps in the process" (p. 205), a suggestion adopted by TDF.

Methodological Approach

TDF employs qualitative and quantitative methods in both formative and summative evaluation research about whether program goals are met. In particular, in-depth interviews are conducted with selected knowledgeable community leaders and other members to explore the following evaluation themes:

- Identify and understand the beneficiary population's overall priorities for action and its ranking of different program activities.
- Identify and understand the beneficiary population's specific priorities within a specific sector of the antitrafficking community.
- Identify and understand underlying reasons for problems before developing solutions.
- Identify and understand the beneficiary population's language, concepts, and beliefs surrounding specific behaviors/situations targeted for change.
- Assess stakeholders' reactions to programs to adapt implementation and evaluate (subjectively) the immediate effects of those programs.

TDF also continuously surveyed local NGO partners to develop the most effective and powerful responses to human trafficking. Moreover, because dialogue is key to understanding stakeholders' worldviews, TDF's programs encouraged dialogue at every methodological stage of the development process; consequently, this methodological rubric guided decisions regarding program development and evaluation. These methodological considerations informed the development of the following programs.

Scholarship Programs for At-Risk Youth

One of TDF's first interventions was the offering of scholarships to at-risk youth in Dubachowr, Nepal. This program began with 25 girls and boys from Dalit castes who were most susceptible of being trafficked to India. TDF provided scholarships for those children to attend school and a small stipend for their families to offset the loss of income from the children not working in the fields. The results of this program were immediately realized, as 80% of those scholarship recipients attended school on a regular basis and returned the following school year.

TDF also provided English-language education to both those students and their teachers, and I participated in the teacher training. As the program developed, four female teachers (the first in the village) from Dalit classes were hired to serve as role models for the students and, thereby, deconstruct the stereotypes that still plague many Dalits from South Asia. Several of those teachers went on to secure permanent positions within the Nepalese education system.

Women's and Children's Security Resource Centers

The Women's and Children's Security Resource Centers (WCSRC) perhaps was the core of TDF's programs, with theories of dialogue, conflict management, intercultural communication, and organizational communication imbedded into its programs. The first Women's Security Resource Center was developed in Nepal to bring together prosecutors, investigators, judges, trafficking survivors, shelter home workers, and other stakeholders to coordinate their efforts in the fight against TIP networks. The center then expanded, with, at one point, a total of four centers operating with varying degrees of programmatic capability in Kathmandu, Nepal; Dhaka, Bangladesh; Kolkata, India; and Mexico City, Mexico.

The centers provided a shared space where stakeholders could interact and obtain information regarding TIP. Computer databases and research support also were provided to countertrafficking organizations that identified TIP networks and prosecuted their members. Survivor-based training in the form of dance therapy, cooking instruction, and HIV and AIDS awareness programs also were offered through the WCSRC.

The Kathmandu WCSRC generated unique, critical returns in the fight against TIP by coordinating the efforts of local and international NGOs, law enforcement, and other government ministries. Over 4 years, that

WCSRC increased the number of prosecutions and convictions of traffickers, and it reduced duplication and the zero-sum, competitive climate that existed among aid recipients in Nepal.

The centers also served as information hubs in a regional network to increase cooperation of law enforcement officials across South Asia. Based on the track record of the Katmandu WCSRC in fiscal year 2003–2004, TDF partners strongly supported broadening the South Asian regional countertrafficking network to Kolkata and Dhaka, with those centers including computer and legal training for local NGOs. Those centers also commenced survivor training and reintegration programs in carpet factories, schools, and local shelters. Small business cooking and bakery training facilities, in combination with microfinance, allowed one survivor to successfully open a small tea shop and restaurant in Kathmandu, which made her economically self-sufficient. TDF subsequently expanded this training and microfinance pilot project to help more TIP survivors open businesses with WCSRC support.

Criminal Justice and Prosecution Capacity Building

These interventions focused on capacity building at the local, regional, and national law enforcement levels. The interventions included technological support for law enforcement professionals and strengthening the criminal enforcement network by providing funds for prosecutors, criminal investigators, and witness documentation techniques in high-TIP areas. Criminal investigators of countertrafficking are in great demand in India and Nepal, and hiring and training them in investigation, deception, and compliance-gaining techniques are the most immediate ways to boost enforcement of TIP laws and subsequent convictions of traffickers. Additionally, TDF provided a subgrant to the Rescue Foundation, a shelter organization in Mumbai, India that houses more than 40 TIP survivors, to support the shelter's retention of local private counsel to assist public prosecutors in ongoing criminal cases against human traffickers.

Programs designed to identify TIP victims in government care also are in great need. TDF's research indicated that more than 80% of rescued TIP survivors responded that they had not been trafficked, despite the fact that their circumstances fell under the Palermo Protocol's definition of trafficking. Consequently, a training was initiated to educate shelter workers and researchers to create communication techniques (e.g., avoiding defensive communication, and understanding language, identity, and notions of time in South Asia culture) that were consistent with the local culture to collect accurate data and, more important, to identify trafficked persons in government care. Critical to that endeavor was an understanding the concept of "face" in South Asia. Although *face* is defined in different ways in the communication literature, a common element is how a public image is negotiated, understood, and respected (Okun, Fried, & Okun, 1999). Face, thus, includes aspects of identity, status, power, courtesy, interpersonal relations, and respect. Significantly, it was important to have participants craft their stories and identities, and understand how they viewed their roles in specific programs, which entailed sometimes long meetings, active listening, and inclusion of most participants in program design and implementation. However, these procedures paid off, as TDF, with its local partners, identified scores of minors with potential trafficking cases, many of whom had been in both private and government-sponsored care for years, with little or no action on their cases pending before the criminal justice system. Some of those minors never had a First Information Report (the first police complaint) filed. TDF also developed a law enforcement training that reached approximately 900 new and experienced police officers and law enforcement representatives.

National Consultation on Better Legal Response to Human Trafficking

In April 2006, TDF and the West Bengal National University of Judicial Science sponsored a 2-day consultation on human trafficking, the design and implementation of which was carried out by local stakeholders in India in response to the lack of face-to-face dialogue among stakeholders in the countertrafficking community. Specifically, we recognized that typical conferences, where experts lecture audience members, who then may have the opportunity to ask questions after a presentation, are of little value to most conference attendees. Hence, we designed a consultation where individuals involved in antitrafficking work came together and dialogued about issues that were important to them.

The consultation began with an explicit recognition by the opening speakers that TIP, especially in South Asia, involves a mix of cultures, nationalities, and languages, as well as, perhaps more important, the variety of worldviews explained earlier that reflect deep-seated beliefs within the countertrafficking community that influence with whom stakeholders work. The consultation also pointed out that there were very few formal mechanisms to promote collaboration either within or between countries (e.g., for a prosecutor in West Bengal, India to discuss a case with a police officer in Nepal or Bangladesh), which was ineffective because many TIP cases involve cross-border movement and, therefore, different law enforcement agencies need to work together to build a successful case.

One hundred seventy-seven people attended the consultation, representing in excess of 50 groups drawn from prosecutors, police, investigators, immigration and asylum attorneys, judges, legislators, activists, social service providers, victim rights groups, and academicians; and representing the countries of Bangladesh, India, Nepal, Thailand, and the United States. Pilot interviews revealed that because trust is such a significant concept in many South Asian communities, a familiar or recognizable person would better facilitate the consultation dialogues than an outside person who first would need to establish rapport and trust. Facilitators, chosen on the basis of their familiarity with the South Asian countertrafficking community, were trained to use a very basic participatory procedure for the dialogue sessions. Specifically, everyone seated at a table introduced themselves and talked briefly about their background and interests. A topic then was raised by the facilitator and everyone was encouraged to participate, with the facilitator pointing out that there were no right or wrong points of view, and that a plurality of ideas was desired. Drawing on the respect of and principles of transformative dialogue, collaborative learning practices as employed in conflict situations (see, e.g., Daniels & Walker, 1996, 2001; Daniels, Walker, Carroll, & Blatner, 1996; Walker, Daniels, & Cheng, 2006), and the core principle of interactive management (see, e.g., Warfield, 1976, 1994; Warfield & Cárdenas, 1994) that participants take responsibility for the processes and products of their group work (see, e.g., Broome, 1995, 2006; Broome, DeTurk, Kristjansdottir, Kanata, & Ganesan, 2002), participants were encouraged to respond to the ideas discussed and to direct their comments to the facilitator instead of the other individuals. Finally, some sessions focused on a task to be accomplished, such as the development of a training manual for police or prosecutors.

The conference was divided into 12 concurrent dialogue sessions (all conducted in English[3]), each facilitated by a person in the antitrafficking community. Group discussion sessions on day 1 were guided by questions posed from the facilitators; for day 2, topics generated locally, prior to the conference, were discussed, and included evidence, international law, police investigation, due process of law, trial strategies, victim-centered lawyering, judicial response, comparative law, training manuals, methods of TIP investigation/research, and coordination among government agencies. Results from the consultation included an increase in local prosecutions in Bengal, several new cross-border collaborations, and a model trafficking manual for prosecutors in West Bengal, India.

Kalam: Margins Write—A Poetry Program for At-Risk Youth

I am
I am the closed door to the south
Faded, rain—wet, always the same;
I don't make much noise:
Just creak as I shut.
I hate being blocked behind this rotten wood.
Looking for a long-lost dream.
—Saraswati Mondal (who lives in a shelter and is in high school; originally written in Bangla)

One of the most successful programs that TDF sponsored over the past few years was a poetry program for second- and third-generation TIP victims in Kolkata, India. Kalam: Margins Write[4] is a rights-based writing program that builds critical and creative voices among marginalized youth living in Kolkata's slum areas, red-light districts, railway platforms, and shelters. The program provided opportunities for youth living at the margins to discover themselves as creative writers and cultural thinkers by promoting their critical consciousness and engaged imaginations, leading these young people to claim their right over their lives by rewriting their identities, communities, and worlds, from their perspectives.

The Kalam program has been an overwhelming success, with more than 100 students participating. The young poets produced three poetry books (Kalam: Margins Write, 2005a, 2005b, 2005c) and have been featured in *The New York Times* (Kristof, 2006), with many continuing their education and schooling (see also the annual magazine that the program publishes; http://marginswrite.wordpress.com). Interviews conducted with these young poets indicated that many have developed a strong sense of self-esteem and confidence that they had not experienced before. Even the simple act of walking into a bookstore in India was something many of them would not have imagined doing prior to participating in the program; now, many of them not only visit bookstores but give poetry readings there.

COMMUNICATION ACTIVISM REVISITED: LIVING WITHIN THE TENSIONS

For me, South Asia is a place of constant transition, from developing world to developed, economic instability to stability, and from air-conditioned minivan to the suffocating heat of Dhaka's streets and constant movement of people on unimaginable scales. The air-conditioned minivan is supposed to make me comfortable but, instead, it marks my difference and power imbalance. The sweat on my white skin also marks me, making me aware of my privileges and that despite the air conditioning, I am ill-equipped to survive here. This is the ultimate irony that many Westerners take for granted: That our luxuries inevitably make us weaker and unable to adapt outside our immediate (and controlled) environment. Indeed, I cannot even enjoy the energy it takes to enjoy those luxuries—more energy than most South Asians use in a year—for the transitions from the air-conditioned minivan to the sweltering heat are much harder to endure when the shock is so dramatic.

As we enter the building for a meeting with a local partner, we are met by two attorneys and a social worker of the Bangladesh Legal Defense Coalition. In the usual South Asian style, we are ushered into a room and served tea and biscuits. I am thankful for this nourishment, as it quells the rumble in my stomach that armoring up has left in my body. It is the intricacies of my immediate surroundings that I always notice when I am in these meetings. The aging buildings tell of a colonial period when the country was subjugated but the buildings shone, but today, of course, it is the opposite. Bangladesh, formerly known as East Pakistan, was a geographical creation of the British, with the country's boundaries making absolutely no sense physically or culturally. Even today, in the heightened awareness of global terrorism, there are Indian villages on the Bangladeshi side and Bangladeshi villages on the Indian side. People cross the unmarked border at their leisure, leaving security experts to ponder how to alter thousands of years of migration in the name of "national security." Bangladesh and India both are struggling with messy democracies and working out the rule of law for over a billion people in the two countries.

Cleaning its buildings is not at the top of the government's priorities. Our conference room is one long wood table in a room illuminated by fluorescent light, with wires hanging everywhere. I am both horrified and intrigued by the bundles of wires that are wrapped like snakes around each other, a situation that would not even come close to passing an electrical code back home in the United States. I think that the wires are a metaphor for my cultural understanding of this place: messy but workable. For despite appearances, everything functions; we have web access and PowerPoint, as well as the thankful hum of an ancient window air conditioner that has been turned to its maximum output, no doubt on my behalf, for every Bangladeshi in the room is wearing a sweater.

As I reflect on my time spent working with TDF[5] and the narratives I wrote about my experiences, I am reminded of the statement by McKenna (1996) that the *"felt presence of immediate experience* [emphasis added] is the surest dimension, the surest guide that you can possibly have" (para. 3). Consequently, this section discusses lessons that I have learned from this work in the form of three dialectical tensions—local–external knowledge, protocol–purpose, and representation–objectification—and how TDF managed them. I begin by briefly explaining a dialectical perspective, followed by a discussion of the three tensions.

A dialectical perspective emphasizes four main concepts: contradictions, totality, processes, and praxis. First, *contradictions* are the dynamic interplay between unified oppositions. Second, *totality* suggests that contradictions are part of a unified whole and cannot be understood in isolation; in other words, dialectics cannot be separated, for they intrinsically are related to each other. Third, relational dialectics must be understood in terms of social processes, with movement, activity, and change being functional properties. Fourth, *praxis* is a philosophical term for the concept of "practical behavior" or, sometimes, "the experience of practicing." In praxis, dialectic tensions are created and recreated through people's active participation and interaction (Baxter, 1988). The following tensions illustrate these dialectical concepts within the context of the antitrafficking community.

Tension 1: The Local–External Knowledge Dialectic

The first dialectical tension is the contrast between local and external knowledge within the antitrafficking community. As explained previously, international development generally employs an expert-based didactic approach that leaves little room for local actors and indigenous knowledge. Grant funding is awarded based on U.S. national priorities and, many times, the local cultural frame is a secondary consideration. Assessment of the success of antitrafficking programs works in a similar fashion, with achievements measured in terms of externally produced performance objectives and further broken down into unit costs for granting agencies. However, as highlighted previously in the interaction that I had with Sahar (TDF's fieldworker involved in the Kalam: Margins Write program), some of the most effective antitrafficking programs simply cannot fit into these measures. These external controls further isolate and marginalize local actors, who are unable to operate within this external knowledge base.

The need for international development policies to include local knowledge frames was apparent in conversations I had with South Asian countertrafficking activists. As Sahar explained:

> The ideas need to come from within, because there is Indian feminism and there is human rights from an Indian perspective. All these things are indigenous. You could go to a village in some place where you feel like there are no ideas as feminism or whatever, but it's there, it's present in its own form and it just needs to be rediscovered, but it's not an external idea, it's not an imported idea. If NGOs can support that, the change will just be much more exponential compared to coming in with their ideas and implementing them. (personal communication, October 17, 2005)

As executive director of TDF, I understood this dialectic to be the greatest challenge. My task was to first learn local knowledge and then translate it into a framework that granting agencies could understand and that was consistent with their funding guidelines. For example, the Kalam: Margins Write program did not fit readily into the predefined grant categories of supply-and-demand programs, and it took some thought to make connections that the granting agency wanted and to frame the program in such a way as to correspond to those categories. In this instance, TDF argued that Kalam qualified as a demand-side program because it helped young poets to recast their identities within the larger Indian society.

Tension 2: The Protocol–Purpose Dialectic

The second dialectical tension highlights the complexities of translating local programs not only into the language of funding agencies but into the funding culture as well. This tension occurs because there are many formal rules for conducting development work in the international arena, including local government laws, visa restrictions, and customs, as well as an array of U.S. laws and regulations regarding spending federal funds, and many of the practices associated with the central purpose of the antitrafficking community—to alleviate immediate suffering—are at odds with many of those external rules or protocols. For example, much of South Asia does business on a cash-only basis; receipts sometimes are available, but much of this work includes hidden charges that crop up at the most crucial times when executing a program. Hence, many times, the choice is whether to distribute funds and continue a program, or stop and confirm the expense with the granting agency, which can take from a few days to several weeks. The immediate needs of programs, thus, must be balanced with the need for financial transparency. It may be impossible to fully resolve differences between financial requirements and immediate programmatic needs, but it is possible to manage them through dialogue; specifically, by involving both grantors and grantees in the financial accounting from the beginning and, together, developing a workable framework within the context of local environments.

Another important example of the tension between protocol and purpose is the U.S. policy, as mentioned previously, that any entity that receives, directly or indirectly, U.S. government funds is prohibited from promoting or advocating the legalization or practice of prostitution or sex trafficking. Additionally, any foreign recipient of such funds must have a policy explicitly opposing, in its activities outside the United States, prostitution and sex trafficking (U.S. Department of State, 2006). Although this policy supports a well-documented principle that prostitution is related to an increase in TIP, it complicates matters on the ground. Additionally, given the documented connections between HIV, AIDS, prostitution, and TIP, with a large portion of the transmission of HIV occurring in brothels, antitraffickers must work with brothel owners to gain access to those sites, but rarely is such access granted without compensation for the time and preparation of the site visit or intervention. Consequently, restrictions on the use of U.S. funds prohibit such collaboration because it violates the U.S. government's policy on prostitution. Hence, U.S. policies about international aid (which, by far, is the largest source of funding for countertrafficking work) polarize stakeholders and force them to adopt a fixed identity on certain issues to qualify for U.S. government funds.

Informal rules of protocol also complicate the antitrafficking work on the ground. As explained previously, interviews conducted with stakeholders of international organizations revealed a lack of trust, competition for funding, and limited forums or training for meaningful dialogue to occur. Furthermore, notions of identity, moral behavior, and immigration hamper discussions of the interlocking oppressions of TIP. For instance, as discussed earlier, although there is a strong link between HIV and sex-trafficking victims, stakeholders working on these issues, rarely, if ever, engage in dialogue about their programs because of their deep-seated differences in moral beliefs about sexual behavior.

Tension 3: The Representation–Objectification Dialectic

In the last decade, there has been an increased acceptance of ethnographic writing that centers on (co-)participants' voices and performances (see, e.g., Conquergood, 2002). However, an important dialectical tension apparent in any performative or ethnographic-based scholarship stems from a fear that researchers are not up to the task of representing the experiences and suffering of those the research is intended to benefit. Although many scholars have called for more collaboration between researchers and social actors, others have explored problems associated with such collaboration, including issues of representation, speaking on behalf of others (especially those who are disenfranchised), and objectification of people as "research subjects" (see, e.g., Alcoff, 1991–1992). Scholars' attempts to connect with and "give voice" to the less powerful through community-based activist research often result in the appropriation of that experience—paternalistic, at best, and self-aggrandizing, at worst (Shugart, 2003).

This dialectical tension of representation–objectification becomes more apparent when examined in light of power relationships and historical forces that dominate international development, in general, and the antitrafficking community, in particular. Shome (2002) argued that power dynamics, especially in relationship to the history of postcolonialism in South Asia, permeate all areas of development and can manifest themselves in issues such as representation, objectification, and looking to outside conditions for assistance. Tensions, thus, arise, specifically, in the application of any fixed moral framework to any culture.

The representation–objectification dialectical tension probably was the most difficult tension to manage. TDF entered the South Asian development field within the larger historical perspective of colonial rule, but instead of guns enforcing development rules, TDF had money. That funding meant that priorities were determined outside of the host country, were subject to outside political forces, and involved putting in place outside conditions for assistance. Additionally, given the variety of cultures and identities involved in TDF's work, this dialectic of difference was critical to the inclusion of all stakeholders in TDF's programs. Managing this tension required TDF to engage in multiple discussions, hold meetings to hear all participants voice their concerns, and be as transparent as possible in making decisions. The ultimate lesson from this dialectic is that time and dialogue can manage most of these tensions; however, in my experience, nothing can aggravate this tension more than imposing timelines and deadlines that are not in accordance with specific cultural norms in South Asia.

CONCLUSION

As I reflect on my time working in the antitrafficking community, a journal entry that I wrote seems particularly appropriate:

I am tired, I smell, and I have had stomach problems since I arrived in India 2 weeks ago. I am waiting in the international airport terminal in New Delhi, after many delays on what should have been a short flight from Kolkata. The delay bumped me from my earlier flight, and airport rules dictate that I cannot leave the sparse waiting area for my next flight. I have been in this room for 6 hours and, thankfully, the arrival of my plane back home has just been announced. My saving grace is that I have finally saved enough miles to fly business class for the 16-hour flight, and I am looking forward to some luxury. The time spent in the airport, however, has allowed me to reflect on these past 2 weeks in India, where I participated in the National Consultation on Better Legal Response to Human Trafficking, along with 176 other participants.

I was impressed with the participants and the content of the consultation, but, ultimately, I feel as if it was a failure. What I wanted was a safe place for participants to engage in a meaningful exchange of ideas; a place where dialogue could overcome, or at least manage, the challenges of culture, gender, and power. What I witnessed was mostly people talking at one another as opposed to talking with one another. Gender, language, competition, and cultural conventions all prevented a dialogic frame for achieving shared meaning between participants.

I also know, however, that the consultation in the funders' and many of the participants' views was a success. The fact that it was held at all, was attended by 177 people, and was keynoted by the attorney general of West Bengal all mark significant gains and recognition for the antitrafficking com-

munity. It also was a success because a conference report was produced and distributed to participants. The conference highlights a successful collaboration between an NGO, the United States, and the Indian government. The ambassador and the counsel general held press conferences and released press statements, and they seem pleased with the results.

I am left with mixed feelings: Part of me is happy that the consultation was well received, but part of me is left with the question of what actually was accomplished by this consultation and whether the cause of the antitrafficking was advanced. I keep returning to the thought that although knowledge was conveyed, it was not created.

It is those tensions that I remember most about my communication activism work with The Daywalka Foundation to prevent trafficking in persons. Those tensions are not obstacles to that work but, rather, reminders that competing worldviews must always be understood when attempting to confront large, complex problems. Moreover, as the work of The Daywalka Foundation shows, communication is key to managing those tensions and preventing the tragedy of human trafficking.

NOTES

1. Of the estimated 800,000 trafficking victims each year, at least 80% are women (U.S. Department of State, 2008).
2. *Dalit* is a term used in parts of South Asia to refer to a member of a social class regarded as below the four divisions within the traditional Hindu caste system because the person is viewed as not possessing any *varnas*, which refers to the Hindu belief that most humans, supposedly, were created from different parts of the body of the divinity.
3. Pilot interviews revealed that English was the language of compromise and practicality because all participants spoke it. Speaking Hindi would have been unacceptable to many of the participants from West Bengal and Bangladesh, just as Bengali would have been for individuals residing outside of those areas, and most participants outside of Nepal did not speak Nepali; hence, conference organizers decided that English should be the language used in the sessions.
4. *Kalam* (ka-lum), a noun (Hindi, Urdu, Bangla, Nepali, Farsi, Arabic), means (a) an instrument to write with and (b) a pen or pencil.
5. Four years of trying to run this nonprofit organization, complete a dissertation, and meet the demands of a tenure-track faculty position took its toll, and in May 2007, after a lengthy search for a new executive director, I resigned. In early 2010, TDF closed its doors and transferred its programs to local partners. The reason given for the closure was that TDF was unable to obtain additional grants from public or private sources for its programs and operations. I suspect that it fell victim to what plagues many small businesses and nonprofits: poor succession planning, lack of dedication to the foundation's mission, and the

inability to obtain the necessary funding to maintain the organization's administrative operations.

REFERENCES

Albeck, J. H., Adwan, S., & Bar-On, D. (2006). Working through intergenerational conflicts by sharing personal stories in dialogue groups. In L. R. Frey (Ed.), *Facilitating group communication in context: Innovations and applications with natural groups: Vol. 1. Facilitating group creating, conflict, and conversation* (pp. 155–181). Cresskill, NJ: Hampton Press.

Alcoff, L. (1991–1992). The problem of speaking for others. *Cultural Critique, 20*, 5–32. Retrieved from http://www.jstor.org/action/showPublication?journalCode=culturalcritique

Allport, G. W. (1954). *The nature of prejudice.* Cambridge, MA: Addison-Wesley.

Aronowitz, A. A. (2009). *Human trafficking, human misery: The global trade in human beings.* Westport, CT: Praeger.

Banerjee, U. (2002, June). *Globalization, crisis in livelihoods, migration, and trafficking of women and girls: The crisis in India, Nepal, and Bangladesh.* Paper presented at the Third Conference on Women, Work, and Health, Stockholm, Sweden.

Baxter, L. A. (1988). A dialectical perspective of communication strategies in relationship development. In S. Duck (Ed.), *Handbook of personal relationships: Theory, research, and interventions* (pp. 257–273). New York, NY: Wiley.

Bertone, A. M. (1999). Sexual trafficking in women: International political economy and the politics of sex. *Gender Issues, 18*(1), 4–22. doi:10.1007/s12147-999-0020-x

Beyrer, C., & Stachowiak, J. (2003). Health consequences of trafficking of women and girls in Southeast Asia. *Brown Journal of World Affairs, 10*, 105–117. Retrieved from http://www.bjwa.org

Bickerstaff, L. (2010). *Modern-day slavery.* New York, NY: Rosen.

Broome, B. J. (1995). The role of facilitated group process in community-based planning and design: Promoting greater participation in Comanche tribal governance. In L. R. Frey (Ed.), *Innovations in group facilitation: Applications in natural settings* (pp. 27–52). Cresskill, NJ: Hampton Press.

Broome, B. J. (2006). Facilitating group communication in protracted conflict situations: Promoting citizen peace-building efforts in Cyprus. In L. R. Frey (Ed.), *Facilitating group communication in context: Innovations and applications with natural groups: Vol. 1: Facilitating group creation, conflict, and conversation* (pp. 125–154). Cresskill, NJ: Hampton Press.

Broome, B. J., DeTurk, S., Kristjansdottir, E. S., Kanata, T., & Ganesan, P. (2002). Giving voice to diversity: An interactive approach to conflict management and decision-making in culturally diverse work environments. *Journal of Business and Management, 8*, 239–264.

Carey, C. (2008). *Collaboration and conflict: Exploring the worldviews within the anti- trafficking community* (Unpublished doctoral dissertation). Arizona State University, Tempe.

Cissna, K. N., & Anderson, R. (2002). *Moments of meeting: Buber, Rogers, and the potential for public dialogue*. Albany: State University of New York Press.

Clark, M. A. (2003). Trafficking in persons: An issue of human security. *Journal of Human Development, 4*, 247–263. doi:10.1080/1464988032000087578

Conquergood, D. (2002). Performance studies: Interventions and radical research. *TDR: The Drama Review, 46*(2), 145–156. doi:10.1162/105420402320980550

Cullen-DuPont, K. (2009). *Human trafficking*. New York, NY: Facts on File.

Daniels, S. E., & Walker, G. B. (1996). Collaborative learning: Improving public deliberation in ecosystem-based management. *Environmental Impact Assessment Review, 16*, 71–102. doi:10.1016/0195-9255(96)00003-0

Daniels, S. E., & Walker, G. B. (2001). *Working through environmental conflict: The collaborative learning approach*. Westport, CT: Praeger.

Daniels, S. E., Walker, G. B., Carroll, M. S., & Blatner, K. A. (1996). Using collaborative planning learning in fire recovery. *Journal of Forestry, 94*(8), 4–9.

Ebbe, N. I., & Das, D. K. (Eds.). (2008). *Global trafficking in women and children*. Boca Raton, FL: CRC Press.

Hancock, T. (1993). The evolution, impact and significance of the Healthy Cities/Healthy Communities movement. *Journal of Public Health, 14*, 5–17. Retrieved from http://www.jstor.org/action/showPublication?journalCode=jpublhealpoli

Hart, J. (2009). *Human trafficking*. New York, NY: Rosen.

Heiss, B. (2007, May). *New challenges for transnational social movement networks: Studying framing in the U.S.-led response to sex trafficking*. Paper presented at the meeting of the International Communication Association, San Francisco, CA. Retrieved from http://www.allacademic.com/meta/p_mla_apa_research_citation/1/7/1/9/4/p171949_index.html

Huesca, R. (2000). Communication for social change among Mexican factory workers of the Mexico–United States border. In K. Wilkins (Ed.), *Redeveloping communication for social change* (pp. 73–88). Lanham, MD: Rowman & Littlefield.

Huesca, R., & Dervin, B. (1994). Theory and practice in Latin American alternative communication research. *Journal of Communication, 44*(4), 53–73. doi:10.1111/j.1460-2466.1994.tb00699.x

Isgro, K. (2005, May). *Human price tags and the politics of representation: An analysis of UN sex trafficking discourses*. Paper presented at the meeting of the International Communication Association, New York, NY. Retrieved from http://www.allacademic.com/meta/p_mla_apa_research_citation/0/1/4/0/3/p14032_index.html

Jonsson, A. (Ed.). (2009). *Human trafficking and human security*. New York, NY: Routledge.

Kalam: Margins Write. (2005a). *Poetic spaces*. Calcutta, India: Seagull Books.

Kalam: Margins Write. (2005b). *Poetry junction*. Calcutta, India: Daywalka Foundation.

Kalam: Margins Write. (2005c). *The world and I*. Calcutta, India: Daywalka Foundation.

Kara, S. (2009). *Sex trafficking: Inside the business of modern slavery*. New York, NY: Columbia University Press.

Kauffman, R. (Producer & Director), & Briski, Z. (Director). (2005). *Born into brothels* [Motion picture]. United States: Thinkfilm.
Kidder, T. (2003). *Mountains beyond mountains*. New York, NY: Random House.
Kincaid, D. L., & Figueroa, M. E. (2009). Communication for participatory development: Dialogue, action, and change. In L. R. Frey & K. N. Cissna (Eds.), *Routledge handbook of applied communication research* (pp. 506–531). New York, NY: Routledge.
Kristof, N. D. (2006, January 23). Anti-trafficking groups. *The New York Times*. Retrieved from http://www.nytimes.com
Kuo, M. (2000). Asia's dirty secret. *Harvard International Review, 22*(2), 42–45.
Leeds-Hurwitz, W. (1990). Notes in the history of intercultural communication: The Foreign Service Institute and the mandate for intercultural training. *Quarterly Journal of Speech, 76*, 262–281. doi:10.1080/00335639009383919
Leuchtag, A. (2003). Human rights sex trafficking and prostitution. *Humanist, 63*(1), 10–16.
Limoncelli, S. A. (2010). *The politics of trafficking: The first international movement to combat the sexual exploitation of women*. Stanford, CA: Stanford University Press.
Littlejohn, S., & Domenici, K. (2001). *Engaging communication in conflict: Systemic practice*. Thousand Oaks, CA: Sage.
Maoz, I., & Ellis, D. (2006). Facilitating groups in severe conflict: The case of transformational dialogue between Israeli-Jews and Palestinians. In L. R. Frey (Ed.), *Facilitating group communication in context: Innovations and applications with natural groups: Vol. 1: Facilitating group creation, conflict, and conversation* (pp. 183–203). Cresskill, NJ: Hampton Press.
Marble, M. (1995, September 4). Group exposes trans-border sex slavery between Nepal and India. *Women's Health Weekly*, pp. 9–10.
Martin, J. N., & Nakayama, T. K. (1999). Thinking dialectically about culture and communication. *Communication Theory, 9*, 1–25. doi:10.1111/j.1468-2885.1999.tb00160.x
McCabe, K. A. (2008). *The trafficking of persons: National and international responses*. New York, NY Peter Lang.
McKenna, T. (1996, April 25). *Culture is not your friend*. Speech presented at St. John the Divine's Cathedral, Synod Hall, New York. Retrieved from http://www.salvia-divinorum-scotland.co.uk/quotes/mckenna/cultureisnotyourfriend.htm
Melkote, S. R., & Steeves, H. L. (2001). *Communication for development in the Third World: Theory and practice for empowerment* (2nd ed.). Thousand Oaks, CA: Sage.
National AIDS Control Organization. (1999). *Surveillance for HIV infection/AIDS cases in India*. New Delhi: Government of India.
Norris, T., & Pittman, M. (2000). The healthy communities movement and the coalition for healthier cities and communities. *Journal of Public Health, 115*, 118–124. Retrieved from http://www.jstor.org/action/showPublication?journalCode=jpublhealpoli
O'Beirne, K. (2002, March 11). Of human bondage. *National Review*, pp. 20–22. Retrieved from http://www.nationalreview.com

Okun, B. F., Fried, J., & Okun, M. L. (1999). *Understanding diversity: A learning-a-practice primer*. Pacific Grove, CA: Brooks/Cole.
Parsons, S. (2006, November). *Trafficked minor immigrants and refugees and HIV rate increases in India*. Paper presented at the meeting of the American Public Health Association, Boston, MA.
Pearce, W. B., & Littlejohn, S. W. (1997). *Moral conflict: When social worlds collide*. Thousand Oaks, CA: Sage.
Pearce, W. B., & Pearce, K. A. (2000). Combining passions and abilities: Toward dialogic virtuosity. *Southern Communication Journal, 65*, 161–175. doi: 10.1080/10417940009373165
Rogers, E. M., & Hart, H. B. (2002). The histories of intercultural, international, and development communication. In W. B. Gudykunst & B. Mody (Eds.), *Handbook of international and intercultural communication* (2nd ed., pp. 1–18). Thousand Oaks, CA: Sage.
Sarkar, K., Bal, B., Mukherjee, R., Saha, M., Chakraborty, S., Niyogi, S., & Bhattacharya, S. (2002). Young age is a risk factor for HIV among female sex workers: An experience from India. *Journal of Infection, 53*, 255–259. doi: 10.1016/j.jinf.2005.11.009
Shome, R. (2002). Interdisciplinary research and globalization. *Communication Review, 9*, 1–36. doi:10.1080/10714420500500828
Shugart, H. A. (2003). An appropriating aesthetic: Reproducing power in the discourse of critical scholarship. *Communication Theory, 13*, 275–303. doi: 10.1111/j.1468-2885.2003.tb00293.x
Smith, L. (2007). *From Congress to the brothel: A journey of hope, healing, and restoration*. Vancouver, WA: Shared Hope International.
Soderlund, G. (2005). Running from the rescuers: New U.S. crusades against sex trafficking and the rhetoric of abolition. *NWSA Journal, 17*(3), 64–87. Retrieved from http://muse.jhu.edu/journals/nwsa
Spano, S. (2001). *Public dialogue and participatory democracy: The Cupertino community project*. Cresskill, NJ: Hampton Press.
Steinfatt, T. (2002). *Working at the bar: Sex work and health communication in Thailand*. Westport, CT: Ablex.
United Nations. (2000). *Protocol to prevent, suppress and punish trafficking in persons, especially women and children, supplementing the United Nations convention against transnational organized crime*. Retrieved from http://untreaty.un.org/English/TreatyEvent2003/Texts/treaty2E.pdf
U.S. Department of State. (2004, June). *Trafficking in persons report* (U.S. Department of State Publication No. 11150 Rev.). Retrieved from http://www.state.gov/documents/organization/34158.pdf
U.S. Department of State. (2006, June). *Trafficking in persons report* (U.S. Department of State Publication No. 11335 Rev.). Retrieved from http://www.state.gov/documents/organization/66086.pdf
U.S. Department of State. (2007, June). *Trafficking in persons report* (U.S. Department of State Publication No. 11407 Rev.). Retrieved from http://www.state.gov/documents/organization/82902.pdf
U.S. Department of State. (2008, June). *Trafficking in persons report* (U.S. Department of State Publication No. 11407 Rev.). Retrieved from http://www.state.gov/documents/organization/105501.pdf

U.S. Department of State. (2010, June). *Trafficking in persons report* (10th ed.). Retrieved from http://www.state.gov/documents/organization/142979.pdf
Walker, G. B., Daniels, S. E., & Cheng, A. S. (2006). Facilitating dialogue and deliberation in environmental conflict: The use of groups in collaborative learning. In L. R. Frey (Ed.), *Facilitating group communication in context: Innovations and applications with natural groups: Vol. 1: Facilitating group creation, conflict, and conversation* (pp. 205–238). Cresskill, NJ: Hampton Press.
Warfield, J. N. (1976). *Societal systems: Planning, policy, and complexity.* New York, NY: Wiley.
Warfield, J. N. (1994). *A science of generic design: Managing complexity through systems design* (2nd ed.). Ames: Iowa State University Press.
Warfield, J. N., & Cárdenas, A. R. (1994). *A handbook of interactive management* (2nd ed.). Ames: Iowa State University Press.
West, M., & Carey, C. (2006). (Re)enacting frontier justice: The Bush administration's tactical narration after September 11th. *Quarterly Journal of Speech, 92*, 379–412. doi:10.1080/00335630601076326
White, R. A. (2004). Is "empowerment" the answer?: Current theory and research on development communication. *Gazette, 66,* 7–24. doi: 10.1177/0016549204039939
Winckelmann, T. (2009). *Human trafficking*. Yankton, SD: Erickson Press.
Zoller, H. (2000). A place you haven't visited before: Creating the conditions for community dialogue. *Southern Communication Journal, 65,* 191–207. doi: 10.1080/10417940009373167

3

STAGING SUDANESE REFUGEE NARRATIVES AND THE LEGACY OF GENOCIDE

A Performance-Based Intervention Strategy

Linda Welker

Grand Valley State University

> Social theatre may be generally described as theatre practiced in times/places of crisis.
> —Thompson and Schechner (2004, p. 14)

I began to experience the fuzzy sensation of increasing enlightenment. I could not quite catch everything that my student "Mary"[1] was saying. A student in my oral rhetoric class, Mary had requested permission to "say something at the end of class" that was not related to the course curriculum or pedagogy, or so I thought at the time. As I listened to what turned out to be an impassioned appeal, my consciousness was drawn inexorably out of the classroom "present" and into the virtual present of the characters inhabiting her short, vivid tale. I began not to hear words but to see pictures in my mind's eye of a horrible (and as Mary explained it), all-too-real scene taking place in the real present of the now, in a place on the other side of the world. In this unfamiliar world and fuzzy state of mind, all I knew for sure was that I was seeing something to which I had been ignorantly blind until that very moment. Her plaintive expressions swirled across my perception field: "Thousands killed ... millions displaced ... orphans ... hunger ... Africa ... rape ... GENOCIDE. ... So will you please sign this petition in support of the suffering people of South Sudan?" I snapped back to the actual present, and, although I did not know it at the time, my community-based production of *A Prayer for Sudan* began that very moment.

* * *

[Close-up shot of Sudanese woman in agony, projected on upstage screen. Performers enter in darkness from the back of the theatre, moving to the beat of Dinka music. Stage lights up. Performers take their positions on stage facing audience. Music fades out under the next line. Slide changes to photograph of a Sudanese person holding a soccer ball and standing next to a freshly dug grave.]

    Person 1: More than 2 million people in South and Central Sudan have died in the past 21 years as a result of Sudan's civil war,[2] and more than 4 million have become internally displaced.[3]
    Person 2: Twelve Sudanese die every hour from war-related causes.
    Person 3: Sudan's civil war is the longest African civil war on record.
    Person 4: The massive loss of life in Sudan has surpassed the civilian death toll in any war since World War II.
[Slide changes to a photograph of young Sudanese men, rifles on their shoulders, wading waist-deep across a river.]
    Person 5: At least one out of every five Southern Sudanese has died because of this protracted war.
    Person 2: Women are openly raped. Women and young boys are forced into slavery.
[Simultaneous with the line below, the slide changes to large white numerals on a black screen: 200,000.]
    Person 3: Human rights and local tribal groups estimate the number enslaved could be as high as 200,000 people.
    Person 5: [breaks through, running in and out of the "rumbling facts," and shouts] More than [simultaneous with the speaker's enumeration, corresponding numbers appear on the screen] 2 million people in South and Central Sudan have died in the past 21 years.

Thus, did the community-based performance (CBP), titled *A Prayer for Sudan*, begin as it played in late spring 2005 in two primary settings: a U.S. university auditorium filled with more than 200 college students, faculty, and Sudanese friends; and a large Episcopal church nave filled with Southern Sudanese refugees living in the midwest United States, many of whom contributed their individual stories to this production. Reprised in 2006, the production also was performed for other audiences: members of six regional churches, participants and audience members of a regional performance and social justice conference, student and faculty audience members of a campuswide evening performance at a university in Indiana, and performance and other scholars at the Central States Communication Association conference held in Indianapolis, Indiana.

The primary goals of the performances were to elevate people's consciousnesses about the genocide in South Sudan and to stimulate them to participate in social justice activities, including signing already prepared petitions and letters to then-President George W. Bush, Secretary of State Condoleezza Rice, Michigan Senators Deborah Stabenow and Carl Levin, and Michigan Congressperson Pete Hoekstra and Vern Ehlers; and to donate to organizations that are working for peace and social justice in South Sudan, such as the Office of the United Nations High Commissioner for Refugees (UNHCR), Human Rights Watch, and Amnesty International. In summary, our activist theatrical goal was to lay bare the manifold injustices perpetrated by the powerful against the vulnerable, and to induce all who were stirred by these revelations to become activists working to stop the violence in South Sudan. This is the story of how that brief student announcement (above) led to the creation and performance of the advocacy project, *A Prayer for Sudan*, and its effects on audiences.

This chapter begins with an overview of CBP, examining various purposes and goals of this alternative type of theatrical offering, and paying particular attention to activist interventionist CBP. I then explain the CBP class and detail specific challenges involved in teaching it. That discussion includes an explication of the performance composition process that students and I employed to research and create *A Prayer for Sudan*. Portions of the script with commentary also are provided.

An interpretive ethnography of the production also is included, as is an analysis of the "TalkBack" session held after each performance, a question-and-answer period wherein audience members, cast and crew, and the director process and respond to a production. I then reflect on and evaluate the impact of this project on the primary CBP participants and stakeholders, including the student researchers–performers, myself as adapter–director, the Sudanese individuals interviewed, non-Sudanese audiences, and audiences of Sudanese refugees. I then offer a critical analysis of the production, informed by P. H. Collins's (2000) perspective of the "matrix of domination," to ask, "How has *A Prayer for Sudan* served (if at all) to loosen the grip of hegemonic powers at work in this particular matrix of domination, and can I claim to have been involved in a successful activist endeavor?"

Finally, I share lessons learned about the power of CBP as a form of communication activism in the service of social justice. In line with the focus of this volume, I explain how differences in culture, race, ethnicity, class, and religion (between thoroughly U.S. American, mostly white, Christian students and that of black, Anglican Africans) both enrich and challenge the acts of engagement, interpretation, perspective taking, identification, and representation requisite for effective performance activism.

COMMUNITY-BASED PERFORMANCE

CBP has evolved into its present form(s) via its historical linkages with political theatre. Specifically, CBP's "immediate roots are in the turbulent 1960s and early 1970s, when nationwide questioning of the status quo led to significant expansion of art" (Cohen-Cruz, 2005, p. 1). Cohen-Cruz (2005), a leading CBP theorist and practitioner, asserted that a

> community-based production is usually a response to a collectively significant issue or circumstance. It is a collaboration between an artist or ensemble and a "community" in that the latter is a primary source of the text, possibly of performers as well, and definitely a goodly portion of the audience. (p. 2)

Weinberg (2000) fleshed out this "response" by identifying the activist goal of such collaborative work, asserting that CBP "seeks social change rather than stasis, transformation rather than consolidation of power" (p. 22).

This practice also is known as "community-based theatre" (Brady, 2000; Haedicke, 1998; Haedicke & Nellhaus, 2008; Kuftinec, 1997, 2003; Lev-Aladgem, 2004; Plastow, 1997; Seda, 2008; Weinberg, 2000), "devised theatre" (Brian, 2005; Plastow, 1997), "documentary theatre" or "theatre of testimony" (e.g., Ben-Zvi, 2006), "theatre for development" (Seda, 2008), "grassroots theatre" (McConachie, 1998), "community-based drama" (Kemp, 2006; Mbugguss, 1999; "U of M Stages Drama," 2005), and even "group performance of oral history" (Armstrong, 2000; Raphael, 2006).[4]

Despite the different terms, a similar type of performance practice is signified: one that brings community members together so that their heretofore muted/unspoken/unheard voices might be helped collectively by intoning heart-piercing stories in ways that only embodied evocation can accomplish. Thus, CBP can offer unique viewpoints on a range of social justice topics, from everyday social concerns to cataclysmic crises, because community members themselves are observers of or participants in the events that constitute their narratives.

Taylor (2003) created the master term of *applied theatre* to describe this particular performance genre that enables "individuals to connect with and support one another [even as it provides opportunities for] groups to voice who they are and what they aspire to become" (p. xviii). Thompson and Schechner (2004) employed a different master term, *social theatre*,

> defined as theatre with specific social agendas; theatre where aesthetics is not the ruling objective. ... [Such] theatre takes place in diverse locations—from prisons, refugee camps, and hospitals; to schools, orphanages, and homes for the elderly. ... [It is theatre in which] participants ... [are] often from vulnerable, disadvantaged, and marginalized communities. (p. 12)

Unlike *aesthetic theatre* (in which the text usually is written by a solo playwright to provide commercial entertainment), CBP is created or composed collectively among artists, activists, and community members; and it employs performance techniques (including dance, acting, simplified spectacle, and mediated images/sounds) to address the needs/desires/problems of a particular community. Although CPB has other laudable purposes (e.g., celebration and historical reflection), it primarily is directed toward community activist intervention.

Although they cluster along an activist performance continuum, these practices do not exactly duplicate one another. Overlaps do exist, however, and may be explained by analyzing the name of each practice. Theorists and practitioners adopt language that best suits their vision of the generic category, production modality, aesthetic qualities, rhetorical or dramatic goals, and evolutionary history of their chosen practice. For instance, the term "drama" traditionally refers to a literary form and, consequently, might be more apropos for those who place more significance on the created text. In contrast, "community-based *theatre*" or "devised *theatre*" is semantically differentiated from *drama* in that it primarily emphasizes live enactment on a stage as opposed to the written dramatic text. Community-based *performance*, on the other hand, is used by theoreticians and practitioners who wish to broaden the scope of the enterprise to include not only traditional theatre praxis but also such performance practices as dance, media, movement, and art installations. The term *documentary* theatre, moreover, indicates its practitioners' view of the enterprise in terms of its creative modality, generic classification, and rhetorical purpose.

The term *devised* in devised theatre foregrounds its compositional strategy, meaning that performers create a theatrical piece via a quasi-improvisational process that then is worked and set into a repeatable performance. Although devised theatre does not always explore social justice issues, it often does. "Grassroots theatre" and "community-based theatre" have been used interchangeably by practitioners whose creative impulses are informed by and privilege the creation of ideological interaction between audience and performers, which, of course, is part of most human interactions, aesthetic or otherwise. In summary, all of these endeavors may be conceptualized as a "matrix of performative resistance" that (although comprised of various theatrical practices) shares the common goal of destroying all "matrixes of domination."

A SEED TAKES ROOT: CULTIVATING CROSS-CULTURAL RELATIONSHIPS IN AND THROUGH COMMUNITY-BASED PERFORMANCE

In the months that followed Mary's plea on behalf of people in Sudan, I experienced a quite common phenomenon: I became increasingly sensitive to references about the ongoing rape, murder, hunger, and genocide there. In particular, *The Lost Boys of Sudan* (Mylan & Shenk, 2003), an Emmy-nominated, feature-length documentary that followed two Sudanese refugees on their journey from Africa to the United States, was playing at the local contemporary art museum, and although I did not see it at the time, just talking about it with colleagues led me to discover that some "Lost Boys" actually were living nearby. I contacted the director of the social justice division of a local denominational headquarters who had met a Sudanese man, Madit, just a few days before in his office.

Within 2 weeks, I had met with Madit and two other Sudanese men (Abraham and Thon) who were members of this midwest Sudanese diaspora. It was only because of the assistance and kindness of a second man, Abraham, that I became connected to the Sudanese Anglican Christian community that worshiped at this same place, every Sunday at 11 a.m. I worshiped with members of that community over a period of 5 months (September through January), during which time, I grew quite close to many of the 50 or so people in the congregation, such that by the time my class started in February, I was able to be a liaison between the Sudanese congregants and students in my COMM 303 CBP course.

Ten students (three men and seven women) registered for the CPB course that winter semester. They represented a wealth of demographic differences. One woman was black, another woman was from the United Arab Emirates, and a third woman was a second-generation immigrant from India. One man was a blond white son of U.S. missionaries serving in the

Caribbean; his cultural identification and sometimes linguistic leanings were more Caribbean than U.S. American. The other six students were whites who had been born in the United States. Although I made it clear from the beginning that they would be doing cross-gender and cross-ethnic performances, some students balked at what they saw as an unethical practice, asking, "How can we, who have nothing in common with these African people, dare to adequately understand and represent their experiences?"

Such a position is common among beginning and even intermediate performance students, especially among those with a highly developed respect of the different Other. Some of the students in the class, however, understood either intuitively or through their performance education that taking on the actions of the different Other—becoming hermeneutic instruments that both come to know and then evoke the Other—facilitates a rich sense of that person's perspective and experiences. Eventually, everyone apprehended the value of performing difference as we discussed Conquergood's (1985) assertion that the refusal to perform someone because of difference "is the most morally reprehensible [stance] ... because it forecloses dialogue" (p. 8). Because we sought dialogue with the living "texts" who were victims of violent oppression and witnesses to genocidal acts, we came not just to accept but to embrace the performance of difference.

The purpose of this three-credit-hour, general education, "cross-cultural engagement" core course was fourfold:

1. to come to know others who were different from ourselves,
2. to create a dramatic evocation of their stories,
3. to demonstrate solidarity with these South Sudanese refugees, and
4. to advocate on their behalf and on behalf of their innocent friends and relatives, who, at that very moment, were being raped, enslaved, killed, or otherwise terrorized by the oppressive Arab and renegade Muslim forces led by Omar Hassan Ahmad al-Bashir, President of Sudan.

To prepare the students to achieve these objectives, I required much of them. I also required much of myself, as I was challenged in many ways, but especially in my ability to deftly teach a performance class comprised of five advanced theatre majors with abundant experiences on the stage and the rest who never had performed in their lives. Although self-identified theatrical neophytes, these "others" were highly accomplished in their respective fields (art history, graphic art, international studies, and pre-med) and they provided a mixture of skills, interests, and expertise that greatly enhanced the whole gestalt.

The course curriculum consisted of readings about the following:

1. adapting and staging nonliterary and ethnographic texts for group performance (Yordon, 1997),
2. writing the new ethnography (Goodall, 2000),
3. CPB (e.g., Brady, 2000; Haedicke, 1998; Kuftinec, 1997; Lev-Aladgem, 2004; Little, 2004; Weinberg, 2000),
4. oral history and its performance (Pollock, 1990; Stucky, 1995),
5. showing hospitality to strangers (Smith & Carvill, 2000),
6. living a compassionate life in service to others (McNeill, Morrison, & Nouwen, 1982), and
7. interpretive ethnography (Geertz, 1973).[5]

Two videos also informed our work: *Blue Train: Making History Dance* (Bowers & Spence, 1998) provided a CBP study of the historic influence of trains on various segments of the inhabitants of Lincoln, Nebraska; and stories documented in *Lost Boys of Sudan* (Mylan & Shank, 2003) framed our inquiry into the parallel journeys of the Southern Sudanese we were coming to know.

The following is a brief explanation of the course structure, assignments, and pedagogical activities of the 15-week semester. Upon entering the course, most students knew little to nothing about the Sudan civil war; therefore (as planned), we spent the first 2 weeks learning about the war-torn circumstances there and the resulting refugee situation in the United States. To provide that background, I gave a brief introductory lecture (with handouts) accompanied by projected images of the war and its concomitant state of affairs. At the same time, students were working on individualized research assignments that asked them to (a) probe the situation in Sudan in more detail, (b) write a two- to three-page report about it, (c) distribute handout summaries of it to class members, and (d) present a brief oral report on it in class. Deep discussions about the disturbing circumstances resulted. By the end of week 3, students had sufficient background knowledge and personal commitment to the project to move ahead to the next unit of the course.

We spent the next 2 weeks learning about CBP from my lectures and from research projects that required students to (a) read an assigned CBP article, (b) write a one-page summary of it, (c) distribute copies of the summary to all students, and (d) give a brief class report about CBP (e.g., a particular case, theoretical stance, or creative process). My educational goals for both assignments were informed by my belief that students learn best by "doing"; consequently, I employed a pragmatic pedagogy shaped by the founder of pragmatism, John Dewey (1925/1958). Simultaneously, in the classroom, we doubled up on curricular emphases: studying ethnography and oral history methods alternately with group performance principles and techniques.

By week 5, students were conducting practice ethnographies and mock interviews, and were engaged in scripting and performance exercises. They learned about creating and using interview protocols and techniques, principles and techniques of effective observation and participation, and how to record findings by taking good fieldnotes and using reliable recording devices. Students also learned how to transcribe their recordings and to interpret their fieldnotes. As part of this research-oriented instruction, we also discussed the nature and importance of using informed consent forms in human research projects. Students then received an informed consent form that I had crafted, which was to be filled out by their cultural partners and attached to students' final projects.

We covered particularly appropriate performance principles, including performing ethnographies, personal narratives, and how to use chamber theatre techniques to adapt an individual's story to a group performance. We also learned how to select, structure, and stage disparate texts into an organic whole according to themes. In the end, we structured the production according to an "augmented" (Yordon, 1997, p. 66) musical structure. Beginning with text (the scholar's lament about genocide in Sudan), we enlarged the genocide theme by adding other texts (e.g., refugees' testimonies and news reports), and returned periodically to the scholar's lament as the central controlling idea (Yordon, 1997).

Over time, students learned that this was no ordinary "theatre" course, as there was no ready-made script; they would not be performing fictive characters that they could research in the text; and the kind of "acting" they would be doing was not pure "acting," as they had been taught, but was more a performance interpretation practice used in performance studies. They acknowledged the unique *presentational modality* that the production would take, which involves using a primarily offstage focus, wherein performers acknowledge their awareness of and often address the audience. Moreover, they began to accept this modality as much as they had heretofore embraced representational theatre—the practice of adopting actor-to-actor onstage focus wherein actors/characters face each other and do not acknowledge the presence of an audience.

After 5 weeks of classroom instruction, we traveled on a bitterly cold Sunday to the Episcopal church to attend the 11 a.m. Sudanese service. We filled the second row and played the role of "foreigners" who moved to the rolling drums and strained to comprehend the strange-to-us language. The students' first entry into this site prompted a range of responses, including fear, excitement, and alienation. One woman student, who left early, later explained that "they were so different, strange, and frightening. I felt like running from the sanctuary and them as fast as I could." This xenophobic response to being immersed in a new culture demonstrates that no matter how smooth I *thought* I had made the path, some student-initiates traveled it with difficulty—finding real or perceived stumbling blocks along the way. Crossing such borders requires determination, hardiness, and bravery that a few students had in short supply.

Pastor Deng asked me to explain why we were there, so I made a brief announcement to the group (who, by then, knew me fairly well) about our desire to meet with individuals over the course of the semester, to become friends and to share experiences. I further explained that our ultimate goal was to create a dramatic production of their stories from Sudan, which elicited a somewhat encouraging response from members of the assembly.

Following the service, students (some timidly and others boldly) approached Sudanese individuals to strike up a conversation. The Sudanese men easily became interlocutors (as they spoke English), but nearly all of the women were inaccessible, as most of them spoke only Dinka or (in some cases) Arabic.[6] We pressed hard, although sensitively, to find individuals who would be cultural informants/teachers. Moving around from student to student, I facilitated their interactions with the cultural Others. Abraham served in the same manner to steer some Sudanese people into conversations with the different cultural U.S. Others. Like Basenji (African herding dogs), we herded these two groups, leading them to prospective ethnographic mates. In the end, we found only two Sudanese women who spoke English. Another elderly, Dinka-speaking woman expressed through her son, who spoke English, that she would like to be interviewed, but when the actual interview occurred weeks later, the son and his friend ignored his mother and talked directly with the student cultural learner. That experience revealed potential multiple lessons about Sudanese males' attitudes toward women, although it also could have been merely an example of two persons hogging the stage.

Eventually, all of the students were coupled in some way with a member of the Sudanese community and met at least six times in places of their mutual choosing. Equipped with informed consent forms, field notebooks, cameras, and micro-recorders, students were charged to first develop friendships through pleasant conversations with their partners. Notebooks were to be used only after each interaction, and cameras could be used only after trust had been established. It was only after they had met for awhile that students were to ask their partners to talk about their experiences in Sudan, their displacement experience, and their experiences coming and adjusting to life in the United States.

Some dyads connected easily and developed a special closeness. For example, an older Sudanese woman, Martha, invited the female student to her home several times and showed her how to cook Sudanese meals. A mixed-gender dyad also was successful, with the female student meeting 10 times with Ackech, mostly in the college coffee shop. For a variety of reasons (e.g., fear, complicated schedules, and miscommunication were most voiced), some students' experiences were less involving. Because of "obstacles" unique to them, two students never did connect with a Sudanese person; they did not fare well in the course and had only peripheral responsibilities vis-à-vis the production (discussed in more detail later). Despite this glitch, by the end of their 8-week ethnography, practically everyone had deeply moving encounters with their cultural teachers—becoming close to and learning much from them. Such familiarity and understanding served the students well as they began to create empathic evocations for the stage.

By the end of their 8-week ethnography, we had good ideas about what should be in the performance; however, before students could move to the production of the group script, they had to accomplish an intermediate performance step. They were assigned to craft and present a solo performance built from a select part(s) of their partner's story. They transcribed their audiotaped interviews and conducted a phenomenological analysis on the transcripts and their fieldnotes, looking for emergent themes. In addition to the resources mentioned earlier, students drew on photographs and audiorecordings to craft their performative enactments.

Adapting their interview transcripts into a solo performance script was the next step in their process, and after rehearsing at least six times, they each performed before the entire class. To help them both match and evoke their partners, we worked together as a class on their dialects. We created phonetic transcriptions of select interview tapes, which we followed as we listened to the audiotapes and repeated the discourse numerous times; eventually, each performer achieved an acceptable version of the inflection patterns and English pronunciations of this sub-Saharan African linguistic community. Embodying and envoicing particular living individuals without moving to caricature is a performative challenge of the first order.

As we proceeded to craft the group performance script, our process involved taking secondary research material about the situation in Sudan and compiling it into a foundational narrative that we augmented (see Yordon, 1997) with individual narratives that had been thematized according to the structure of our interview protocol, which consisted of three open-ended primary questions about their experiences of (a) the war in South Sudan and how it affected them, their families, and their communities; (b) trying to escape/deal with the violence, including both their time on the run and their experiences in refugee camps; and (c) coming to the United States and living here as refugees—separated from their homes and families.

Accordingly, the overarching structure of *A Prayer for Sudan* was comprised of three seamless acts that evoked the experiences of these Sudanese: in Sudan, as displaced people, and coming and adjusting to life in the United States. The performance script was written for an ensemble that moved in and out of choric and character roles evoking and commenting on horrific experiences.

The ensemble consisted of six student performers, with the other four students in charge of technical aspects of the production, including creating and running the projector, music, and sound effects; creating and disseminating advertising; and serving in the role of a dramaturg, whose major responsibilities included oversight of the historical accuracy of the work and the creation of a large preperformance dramaturgical display. Set up weeks before the first performance, that display was located in the college theatre lobby—a major thoroughfare for students, faculty, and staff. With its artistic renderings of design elements, enlarged articles about and photographs of the genocide in Sudan, photographs of our production process, and a horizontal exhibit of fieldnotes and other research materials/tools, the display was a striking invitation to the performance and a persuasive advocacy initiative in its own right.

A Prayer for Sudan involved the interlacing of individual stories and choric narrative commentary. After providing narrative commentary, troupe members transitioned back into Sudanese characters by singing a song in Dinka as they moved to the next episode (a loose Anglicized transliteration is offered below the Dinka lyrics):

Gai wen de David ace ben panhial,
Eben Ke Malaika ne puyennom,
Ku Chok wo chok edek
Ne peu kai peu atheer Ne puyennom

Loose translation:
Wonderful Son of David has come from heaven,
He came with angels to this Earth,
To give us eternal water [not] of this Earth

We also used this Dinka song as a turn-taking technique, as if one person were asking another to relinquish the storytelling place.

THE "WORLD PREMIERE" OF A *PRAYER FOR SUDAN*

A medium-sized midwest U.S. college was the setting for the premiere performance of *A Prayer for Sudan*. Students, faculty, administrators, and a small number (10–12) of Sudanese friends filled the mainstage theatre house three-fourths full, with more than 200 or more attendees that night. Prior to that performance day, we had worked with the college social justice student organization to promote both the cause and the production. Their members set out a table in the lobby covered with stacks of leaflets, flyers, pamphlets, and other informative materials testifying to the situation in South Sudan. As mentioned previously, we made available contact information and already prepared petitions and letters to important politicians, as well as information about donating to organizations working for peace and social justice in South Sudan. The social justice student organization staffed this table both before and after the production—serving as a close advocacy partner for this cause.

Under the direction of the dramaturg, the CBP class displayed a PowerPoint presentation on a large television located in the lobby. The projected images of the destruction in South Sudan were augmented by recorded sound effects and indigenous music. Serving as welcoming ushers, one nonperforming class member and two of her friends staffed a table next to the social justice table. As ushers, they also were responsible for disseminating the production programs, which included the following: (a) an overview of the situation in South Sudan, (b) director's notes about the nature and purpose of CBP, (c) names of performers and their role portrayals, and (d) an invitation to stay following the production for a TalkBack session. An insert also was included that informed about and solicited funds for the "Sudan School for Orphans" being built in South Sudan.

All persons stationed at these tables were enthusiastic advocates who reached out to passers-by in a style that might loosely be compared to that of carnival barkers on a midway. Their vernacular, although less crass, was no less passionate, as their appeals invited support of others rather than personal gain. Thus, in addition to the performance, we provided both a pre- and postperformance advocacy event for attendees, enveloping them in all-encompassing sound, vivid images, and tactile connections with the activists and their messages.

* * *

The house lights dim. With a boost of the base and overall volume, the preshow cadence overpowers recorded ethnic vocals, creating a metrically ordered acoustic world into which six individuals (in maroon tops and black pants—shades that hinted at colors in South Sudan's flag) move down the aisles toward a dimly lit theatrical frame, which outlines a dramatic playing space. The playing space was encoded by simple sign vehicles (six short stools arranged in a semicircle, African pottery, and large projected images behind the stools); this dreamlike location becomes a liminal space in which past can become present; make-believe, reality; horror, hope; and is, ought. The procession arrives at its on-stage destination, lured (it would seem) by a beguiling theatrical corona, a luminous synechdotal marker of a theatrical world of total possibility.

When functioning together, the six performers formed a chorus; when members performed individually, they stood in for persons from South

Sudan whose story gripped the heart and incited the spirit. Choric exclamations of death, destruction, rape, and enslavement spill out rapid-fire at anyone in the performers' acoustic field. A lone scholarly voice steps out of the chorus and begins to theorize about the terrible facts encircling her. "The point is," she begins, "if there is credible evidence that the broad definition of genocide is met in a particular case, then we have a moral obligation to prevent it." The vocal horde continues its proclamations: "At least one out of every five Southern Sudanese has died because of the 21-year war!" "Women are openly raped and young boys are forced into slavery!" The theorist continues, "But as with any case of domestic criminal law violations, what we need is *evidence* of law violations, you know, their forensic evidence or witness testimony." With that, the horde turns sharply toward the theorist and, in unison, shrieks its frustration and incredulity: "Witness testimony?! Witness Testimony?! Witness Testimony?!" Finally, one individual who can take it no longer screams directly into the theorist's face, "People are dying!" All action freezes as she repeats more softly and mournfully, "People are dying!" She turns to the audience and announces to those who share this moment, "Tonight we *bear witness* through the *testimony* of our Sudanese friends."

[Slide changes to black with select (italicized) words from the dialogue below emerging on screen as they are spoken. Performers break from chorus configuration. The theorist continues to listen and watch with increasing interest. All others counter cross to designated downstage spots on their lines below.]

> Person 1: This is the story of one *journey*.
> Person 2: Individual stories serve as *milestones* while *joy* and *fear*
> Person 3: *desperation* and *determination*
> Person 4: *anger* and *love*, and
> All: *HOPE!* ... show the way.
> Person 1: This is a story of *Sudan and her people*.
> [Theorist (person 6) joins the chorus and crosses to her downstage center spot.]
> Person 6: It is *one* of many.
> Person 5: It has been a *source of pain and pride*.
> Person 4: It is a *history*.
> Person 3: It is a *song*.
> Person 6: It is a *gift*.
> All: It is a *prayer*!
> [Person 4 picks up his drums and begins to play the rhythmic transition into the first testimony.]

Horrific details of pain, persecution, slavery, and death materialize in a series of testimonies punctuated by choric commentary. Individuals stand in for others whose experiences simultaneously are told and dramatically evoked in the playing space—the liminal world where cruelty now plays within the margins.

Tales of raids on villages, bombardments of homes from camouflaged planes, desperate running to escape killers, and separation from loved ones fill each testimony. Poignant escape accounts of "no-good-outcome" choices gush without restraint as person after person recounts the shared experience of deciding to cross the raging Nile River (where human-eating crocodiles swam in wait) to get to safety in Ethiopia or to face the reckoning wrath of their oppressors—bloodthirsty tormenters on horseback. Motivated by the promised 72 virgins awaiting them in heaven, these Jihadists hounded their targets into the hazardous torrent. Struggling to make it to the other side of the river, this swimming prey watch helplessly as companions to their right and left are pulled under by the predatory crocodiles or by the raging torrent itself.

Unfathomable persecution and loss regularly repeat. Poetry, songs, and stylized movement poeticize the exposition, making the evocations all the more captivating. As recounted later in the TalkBack session, audience members began to realize that, at the time these sickening acts transpired, they likely were engaged in any number of carefree activities, knowing nothing about nor doing anything for our Southern Sudanese kin. It took two brave documentarians (Mylan & Shank, 2003) to awaken the Western world to the "invisible" atrocities.

In due course, different dramatic evocations emerge in the playing space. Cruelty is dislodged and, in its place, hope, ever so tentatively, begins to dance. Here, the refugee lexis is endowed with an extensive vernacular of sanctuary and respite. Such vocabulary developed first in refugee camps, such as Kakuma, about which the Sudanese said: "At least I had a chance to live in Kakuma. I didn't have that in Sudan" or "When we were in the camps, we had food to eat and a safe place to sleep, and we didn't have to run anymore." "It was in 2000 when people from the UN said, 'We will send you to America.'"

Each person speaks of culture shock, estrangement, and apprehension endemic to radical relocation, and yet, without exception, all expressed the excitement they felt, along with the fear. "Here in the United States, my children have a future," says Achol. "They will be able to learn, go to college, and get good jobs."

Some discovered, however, that living in the United States was no panacea. As Ackech laments:

> Being in this foreign land has made me lonely, and I don't like it. One thing I fear about this place is being alone. If my friends are not here then I am depressed and I have nowhere to go. It is really very hard for me. When I am by myself, I think, "Why am I here?"

A few more stories about work, school, homesickness, and other things follow Ackech's lament. Not everyone expresses Ackech's sadness but nearly to a person, all appear torn between enjoying the freedoms and opportunities in their new homeland and fretting about their friends and relatives who remain in Sudan. Accounts of loss after loss reach each refugee. Souls shrink, scars mend slowly, and hope plays hide and seek. Although they still walk through the valley of shadow and death, they press on, and, in so doing, inspire those of us whose lives they touched.

The performance draws to a close as members of the chorus drop their Sudanese characters and, in a choreographed manner, bid two Southern Sudanese sitting in the front row to join them in the playing space.

> [As the Sudanese men come to center stage, the ensemble surrounds them in a semicircle]
> Person 5: Today, we take a small step to support you on your journey.
> All: You sojourners have traveled far.
> Person 2: It is our true prayer that you, our Sudanese friends, will realize your own true peace, one that you so richly deserve. Let us pray the prayer our Lord (The Prince of Peace) has taught us.
> [Two Sudanese men join the ensemble on stage and recite the Lord's Prayer in Dinka.]
> Fin

The TalkBack Session

TalkBack sessions are standard postperformance discussions employed in two primary theatrical genres: social theatre (including CBP) and new aesthetic theatrical performances. TalkBack sessions, according to Fox (2006), extend the activist agenda by "providing a space for audience members to articulate their responses to" (p. 50) performances. Perhaps the most important part of activist performances, TalkBack sessions enable audience members to share and compare their reactions to performances, to challenge propositions articulated by the enactments, and to ask for further explication of select points made in performances.

According to Goodwin (2004), this communication event, whether it is called "community conversation," "talkback," or "postshow," is a relatively recent cultural phenomenon that is beginning to excite interest not only within but beyond the theater and dance community. Audience is where the action is, and in a productive postshow one can observe and contribute to the public formulation of positions and relationships, and their transformation. In a productive postshow, audiences talk back, talk to each other, and (with good facilitation) also listen to one another, making sense together of common experience in the advantageously liminoid atmosphere that lingers following a powerful performance. (p. 317)

As announced in the preshow welcoming comments, the TalkBack session began after a brief pause to let those who wanted to leave do so, although few did. The performers returned to the stage and I moved to an onstage right position where I invited audience members to ask questions or make comments on any aspect of the production. At first, they sat silently, but after a few moments, they hesitantly began to respond. As one audience member eventually expressed it, "I was just too stunned to talk and needed a few more minutes to process what we'd witnessed." Soon, however, the auditorium was abuzz with comments and questions for the two Sudanese men who had participated in the performance and for a handful of Sudanese who had attended and sat in the back of the theatre, but now made their way down to the stage.

Often, the cast and director participate in TalkBack discussions, but these audience members wanted to talk primarily with the Sudanese men to learn more about their experiences and opinions. Audience members' responses ranged from incredulity about to certainty that genocide was being perpetrated in South Sudan, just as we had portrayed it. Questions flew across the auditorium: "How can we help"? "What, specifically, can I do"? "What's President Bush doing about this"? "Why isn't the UN able to stop this slaughter"? "Are any of you going back to Sudan?" "What can we do from here?"

Patiently and with seriousness of purpose, the Sudanese men answered the questions. One of them gave an impassioned speech about the geopolitical consequences of not stopping al-Bashir and his army. "This is happening now in South Sudan, yes," he said, "but soon, it will move out to contiguous countries. They will do the same in other places as they have been doing in our part of the country." Sadly, his prediction soon came true, for within weeks, al-Bashir turned his killing machine on African Muslims in the western region of Sudan called Darfur.

Some audience members did not let us off the hook when it came to key issues that were absent from our text. One person strongly asserted (in the form of a rhetorical question) that he believed the government of North Sudan had the right to govern all parts of Sudan because of its sovereignty over the entire country. Before we could react, he challenged us, again, by asking us from where the guns used in South Sudan had come. The answer to his question came quickly roaring from the back of the auditorium, voiced by an apparently irritated professor of African national heritage. "I can tell you," the professor bellowed, "they come from the United States!"

The not-so-subtle subtext of both comments was a strong reminder of our complicity as U.S. Americans in the genocide, and they rightly called attention to the absence of this national self-critique in the midst of our performative finger-pointing. The comments made us realize that to advocate against the Sudanese genocide, we also must intervene within our country to prevent the proliferation of guns in that nation.

Through the TalkBack session, we extended our activist agenda and worked hard to elicit audience members' responses that created (in a certain fashion) an old-time, town-hall community meeting, where citizens engage in cooperative and competitive interactions—a space where pertinent questions can be posed, such as "What are we supposed to do with this now that we have seen it?" "Can we accept what we have witnessed as the truth, the whole truth, and nothing but the truth?" We attempted to do what Ellis (2000) identified as the purpose of TalkBack sessions: to challenge

> the passivity of audiences by providing structured opportunities for immediate feedback. Using performance not as an object of art to be studied and appreciated but rather as a catalyst for dialogue about issues of particular interest to an audience, community-based performers are engaging audiences in startling conversations precipitated by performances. These conversations allow audiences to give feedback that does more than provide evaluation of the work: When carefully organized and facilitated, these dialogues can contribute to the process of forming community self-awareness. (p. 92)

RETURNING STORIES TO THE PEOPLE: PERFORMING *A PRAYER FOR SUDAN* FOR THE MIDWEST SUDANESE COMMUNITY

The second performance of *A Prayer for Sudan* occurred that next weekend and was nearly identical to what took place at the college. This performance, however, was enacted not on a stage in an auditorium but, rather, on the altar of the Episcopal church's sanctuary, with more than 50 Sudanese occupying the pews that we had sat in during our weeks of observation and participation. Unlike the previous audience, this was an informed one, as members had lived the stories being enacted before them.

After a preperformance run-through in which we adjusted our blocking to this sacred space, we began the performance with a procession from the back of the nave. An hour later, when the TalkBack session began, we realized that this audience's response was qualitatively different than that of the college audience, as no one asked questions aloud before the group; instead, silence and stares greeted us. I later discovered many reasons for their seeming lack of response. First, they were not used to clapping in church; in fact, doing so is commonly frowned on, even in U.S. church culture. Second, they are a publicly quiet people, especially in the presence of outgoing U.S. Americans. Most important, they recently had lived these stories (and were still living them each day in various ways, especially as communiqués carrying news of tragic loss regularly reached them). It is no wonder, then, that they did not (perhaps could not) respond publicly in the TalkBack session.

On the day of the performance, we were mindful that the college audience had taken some time to warm up; consequently, we were not alarmed by the slow reaction of the Sudanese. After a few minutes, I recognized that they probably preferred not to respond and closed down the discussion time—inviting individuals to talk with us one-on-one. For a time, no one stirred, but people then moved gradually toward us (cast, crew, and director). Their hands reached out to shake ours, hug us, and pat us on the back. The physical contact was accompanied by phrases of gratitude and appreciation, which flowed freely from their lips as they got about an arm's length from us: "Thank you for this!" "I can't believe you care enough about us to do this." "This is exactly what happened to us." "This was so wonderful, thank you." "You must really perform this again for many other audiences so that people will know and will help us."

Clearly, *A Prayer for Sudan* voiced these people's real-life sagas. The dramatic mirror projected their already experienced world and, along with it, the comforting awareness that others knew about and felt their plight. Empathy moved back and forth through this performative evocation, with give and take reverberating throughout the performance and beyond; we recognized (with delight) that the genuine dialogue we had sought had been achieved. However, this "theatre of war [was] not used by the practitioners [as mere] "raw material" (Thompson & Schechner, 2004, p.16) for artistic purposes; rather, it was living memory sewn in our hearts and handled with needed care. It was the kind of history making and sharing unachievable in the flattened world of printed test. As Lippard (1997) put it so well, "Memory replaces official history, especially when a group of people is displaced geographically or culturally" (p.102).

IMPACT ON THE COMMUNITY-BASED PERFORMANCE PARTICIPANTS

A Prayer for Sudan worked on those who participated in multiple and profound ways. Although not all of the students were "on board" from the beginning of the course, by the time of *the performance*, all expressed genuine appreciation for the opportunity to have been involved in it. This section thematizes the impact of this communication activism on the students, the director, and the Sudanese who were interviewed and who attended the production.

Students expressed their reactions in end-of-the-semester response papers and casual conversation. A prevailing and uniformly expressed experience regarded how personally moved students were by their partners' stories and how those storied led to expanded interactions with those persons. For example, as Steve admitted:

> The stories of Jacob's life were unimaginable, to say the least. I became so interested in his stories and life. I looked forward to helping him out with certain tasks or papers that he needed looked over or advice on.

Sarah expressed a similar reaction:

> I actually met up with Ackech simply to hear his stories for my benefit and just to spend time with him as a friend. We went out for meals, built our first snowman, and called each other up at least once a week. I was glad that I was able to get to know him as a friend and not just meet up with him because I had to act out his life at the end of the semester.

Most students expressed similar reactions, which make for engaged activists, for as Seda (2008) asserted, "participation allows the use of people's forms of cultural expression and creates rapport as well as a sense of sharing" (p. 184). Performance calls on persons to transport themselves (via empathic engagement) from a state of self-concern to an other-orientation, resulting in a fruitful merger of self and other, which phenomenologists and performance scholars call "embodied knowing." As Weinberg (2000) contended, "Embodied participation in the process of theatre-making—performance itself—is the most subversive element in participatory community-based theatre … [because it] mobilizes all resources—experiential and embodied, as well as intellectual" (p. 28).

Such empathic engagement and merger insist on the mobilization of researchers' entire set of epistemic resources, as Samantha's disclosure illustrates: "I didn't begin to understand the depth of their [the Sudanese] pain until I had to take on Niahlic's emotions and imagine the horror of being raised around hate and being constantly dehumanized." Sarah's pithy comment also captured the value of embodied knowing: "The day we went on the stage, I felt like I was in Ackech's shoes." Some student-performers even were moved to tears by their performance experience; for example, Julie (who typically presents a somewhat stoic and disengaged persona, and, therefore, played the part of the theorist) confessed:

> I'm not sure if anyone noticed but I had to hold back tears. I had said the line a million times, "Forcing women and children into slavery, and performing ethnic cleansing through calculated famine," but something was different on Sunday [in the performance for the Sudanese]. As I looked out into the audience of people who had actually lived through that kind of hell, it was like I listened to myself for the first time. The sterile harshness of the words struck me and my voice caught for a second, and then I realized a removed theorist wouldn't tear up like that, so I pulled myself together and finished.

A few students expressed a residue of their initial concern regarding performing roles that required cross-gender, cross-ethnic, and cross-linguistic enactments. Although we repeatedly discussed the value of performing difference as a way of knowing diverse Others, some students remained a bit reluctant to do so because they thought that we might cause offense. Bob's comment best illustrated this concern:

> The applause and smiles from the Sudanese were encouraging—dispelling big concerns of mine concerning cultural sensitivity and relevancy in performance. I was concerned that the mimicry of the dialect and the overlapping of gender in the performance might result in unintended offense to the Sudanese. In retrospect, I see that it wasn't a central issue.

The next emergent theme of the performance changing participants as people reverberated throughout students' writings and in their public discourse. For example, several students indicated a profound change vis-à-vis their general fear of people they do not know and, in a few cases, their specific fear of "black people." According to Julie, who took weeks to get up the nerve to go to her partner's apartment:

> Before this class, I would never even think of going into that part of town, let alone knocking on a door in a predominantly black apartment building. I have been sheltered all my life and living in my exclusively

white world. I've always been afraid of blacks no matter where I was, and until now, I didn't even recognize how wrong that was. But now, I'm not afraid like I was before."

Although not a complete conversion, her change represented personal growth nonetheless.

Another student changed her aesthetic preference for "great art" in the form of theatrical stage productions, explaining "I'm no longer the theatre snob I have been all my life. I now value theatrical practice that can do what we did in *A Prayer for Sudan*—serve and advocate." Others reported that their worldviews had expanded and with that change had come recognition of how selfish they had been to be concerned only about people in their small spheres of interest. As Steve admitted:

> I never watched the news or read a newspaper and have been so caught up in my little world that I had no clue about other situations in the world. I recognize how limiting this is. ... It's like I've awakened into a different world—one that I now want to participate in more fully.

One final theme emerged from students' responses: The vast majority expressed appreciation for, and interest in, continuing to participate in activist interventionist endeavors. As Samantha wrote, "I love how this form of theatre can be used to call people out of their indifference and awaken their social consciences. I especially noticed this after our performance at the Episcopal church." Amy planned to devote her career to such endeavors and immediately jumped into an advocacy role, by becoming a member of a local chapter of Darfur Matters, a national advocacy nongovernmental organization (NGO). According to Amy, "I realize that's what our class had equipped us to do. Now this time, instead of Sudan, it will be Darfur." Students' appreciation was evident in the plans made by several to keep doing what we had done in *A Prayer for Sudan*. For instance, Bob expressed a serious desire to continue to be a change agent:

> In the future, I intend to go to grad school for ethnomusicology on a PhD track. I need to learn a third language, and I'm very seriously considering Arabic. With a new sensitivity to our Sudanese brothers and sisters, I am hoping that I can use the abilities of language and of music to provoke greater change—a desire that this project has sparked within me.

A female student in the original production was headed to medical school and told me in a private conversation that she intended to return to India, her parents' homeland, to work among subjugated and otherwise marginalized women of the countryside. She was determined to combine her work as a physician with being a CBP facilitator. Her desire to advocate in this way demonstrated a clear, holistic, communal approach to health and well-being. Another person, also headed to medical school, expressed a similar desire to include performance activism, in conjunction with his medical practice. As the reprised performance tour ended, another performer already was raising funds to go to South Sudan to interview orphaned children there. Stories such as these speak to the potential multiplication of advocacy efforts birthed by the meaningful participation of performers in such aesthetic communication activism.

I also have been radicalized by serving as an advocate for my Sudanese friends over the past 5 years. As a part-time volunteer coordinator at a local Lutheran church, I have worked with a refugee resettlement organization to coordinate volunteers to prepare homes for new arrivals—collecting household furnishings, food, and clothing. Welcoming refugees on their arrival at the local airport, volunteers also transport them to the fully furnished homes and warm meals waiting for them. My intervention efforts also have included organizing and staffing English-as-a-second-language classes, as well as being a liaison to schools, physicians, and government agencies. Currently, I volunteer with a new NGO, "Hope for Women and Children of South Sudan" to coordinate a national conference of Sudanese women.

Members of the Sudanese community were variously impacted by *A Prayer for Sudan*. Interviewees expressed their appreciation for the opportunity to get to know their partners and interacting so personally with U.S. Americans. As new residents of the United States, the Sudanese enjoyed having their new world enlarged by people who not only listened to their stories but also talked about their experience as U.S. Americans. Although they did not identify this experience as cross-cultural engagement, it is reasonable to assume that they valued engaging in more than phatic communication with people outside their Sudanese community.

The Sudanese interviewees and those who attended the performance of *A Prayer for Sudan* were deeply touched by seeing "their" stories enacted before them. Because Sudanese refugees' experiences were so similar, everyone could identify personally with the narratives enacted before them. They appreciated the fact that U.S. Americans cared enough about what had happened to them to produce such a public communication of the story, which acknowledged and validated both their suffering and triumph. Many Sudanese said that they were comforted by looking back on their amazing journey in this way, although they also expressed deep-seated sorrow over their losses and worry over loved ones they had left in the path of the Jihadists.

The impact of the performance went beyond the theatrical frame of *A Prayer for Sudan*. Our "participatory theatre mobilize[d] all resources—

experiential and embodied, as well as intellectual" (Weinberg, 2000, p. 28). In addition to the preperformance and performance activist outcomes, there were radical postperformance modifications of individuals' life callings.

PERFORMATIVELY CHALLENGING POWERS OF DOMINATION

One clear goal of *A Prayer for Sudan* was to enflesh ideologies of identity by means of the embodied practice of performance. Because the identities being embodying were/are oppressed, altered, hurt, or otherwise defiled, this CBP became "an activist form of [theatre], which aim[ed] to influence and alter the actual world, not just reflect it" (Haekicke, 1998, p. 132). The performance provided a pathway to individual and group empowerment for those who were/are oppressed, their performer counterparts, and their dialogical partners. The performance intervention "add[ed] to, contradict[ed], and /or renegotiate[d] how Southern Sudanese are spoken of both in Sudan and in [part of] the US" (Román, 1998, p. 7) culture, with the intent of calling dominant ideologies into question.

Drawing on P. H. Collins's (2000) conceptualization of the "matrix of domination," which is "organized via four interrelated domains of power, namely, the structural, disciplinary, hegemonic, and interpersonal domains" (p. 276), I incorporate and integrate race, gender, religion, and ethnicity into my analysis of performance as a method of opposing power and oppression. *A Prayer for Sudan*, like many CBPs, was part of that "wider struggle for human dignity and social justice" (p. 276) to which that matrix may be applied.

Central to the struggle to unseat domination is the epistemological tenet regarding the value of dialogue in the exploration of empowerment (see Papa, Papa, & Buerkel, this volume), with performance being an exceedingly dialogical tool available to those who seek to understand and challenge social injustice. Stucky (1995) argued that empowerment

> arises from enactment, through body-knowledge, [that] takes place in dialogic encounters between the performers and the person whose histories are represented, as well as between the performers and the audience. Dialogic engagement allows the participants to understand something of the "cultural and personal identity" of the person performed. (p. 2)

Our dialogical enactments "situated the ethnographer [and performers] as a part of rather than apart from the [cultural] performance[s] [it evoked]"

(Raphael, 2006, p. 14). The performance became a "voice" that called out for social justice; it was the "enunciation and the acknowledgement [sic] of the obligations and anxieties of [all who live] in the [human] community" (Watts, 2001, p. 179).

In this section, I briefly explicate the interrelated domains of power associated with the matrix of domination and explore specific ways that performance, in general, and our performance, in particular, may have worked within and against the powers of oppression and domination. In so doing, I underscore the "power of performance to challenge the master narratives and discourses of history" (Ben-Zvi, 2006, p. 45).

A Prayer for Sudan is well suited to P. H. Collins's (2000) analytic framework, offering assorted exemplars of ways in which performance can work to decenter instruments of power. For instance, the testimonial narratives and the choric commentary exposed unambiguous powers of domination that oppress and discriminate against individuals and groups. By their oppressive actions, these powers of domination situate innocent inhabitants outside the world of human significance. My analysis explores ways that the performed text, at once, revealed and resisted the matrix of domination, as well as how the process of producing the CBP transformed the adapter–director, performers, and production staff into nonviolent activist interventionists.

First, the performance exposed key structural domains of power: "large-scale, interlocking social institutions" (P. H. Collins, 2000, p. 277) that both created and reproduced the subordination of Southern Sudanese. A particularly serious local Sudanese leader we interviewed pointed to a specific institutional power nexus in his story:

> So, what happened is that, uh, the Sudan government is fighting for land in the South, so they [sic] train people and they call them "the Jihad," and then they send them to the South ... and they have this principle that if you kill 70 people in the South, here's the key, you go to heaven.

A Prayer for Sudan singled out Sudan's president al-Bashir as the supreme puppet master who (along with a cadre of radical Arabic Muslims) convincingly deluded many of its male citizens to accept as true this "Jihad" guarantee. Inspired by this assurance and fortified with lethal weaponry, Jihadists carried out their genocidal orders—making it much easier for al-Bashir to claim South Sudan's resource-rich land for the North's uses (see note 2). The production called into question a counternarrative advanced by some who claim that the conflict, at best, merely is a civil war in which both sides are equally complicit or, at worst, the result of the South's rebellious attacks against the North after a long period of peace (see note 2). For instance, Abdullah (2001) accused the Southern Sudanese of being responsible for the conflict:

> The war is usually described as a conflict between the Arabic-speaking Muslim North and the black African Christian or animist South. This description fits the two sides well enough, but their religious and ethnic differences are not the main causes of the war. Basically, the war is a case of Sudan's South against Khartoum. Nearly half a century ago, in 1955, the Southerners took to arms. Apart from a peaceful break between 1972 and 1983, they have continued to fight ever since (para. 17–18).

In contradistinction, *A Prayer for Sudan* shed light on the North's conflation of religious and governmental power structures to extend its Islamic ways of being and the implementation of Sharia law into and throughout South Sudan. The performance asserted that the purpose of taking up weapons by those in the South was to defend themselves from the North's hegemonic actions. Multiple signifiers (linguistic signifiers included Jihad, Sharia, Mosque, and Muslim) peppered the performed testimonies and choric reportage—pointing to the commingling of the North's governmental entities and its extreme version of Islam.

A member of the chorus addressed North Sudan's institutional complicity as she filled in historic facts about Islamic groups that worked hand-in-glove with governmental powers of domination: "After staging a military coup in 1989, the National Islamic Force based in Northern Sudan began a civil war dividing the Islamic North from the Christian and tribal South." Mayom testified to his desire to fight from within the forces of domination when he asserted, "Since I was young, I thought that I was going to grow up and join the army and fight. Our people are fighting for their freedom!" Both religious and geographic signifiers, Muslim North and Christian South—like their respective human signifieds—exist in semantic opposition.

Some might argue that Arabic Muslim domination is no different than that of Christian missionaries who came to Sudan in the 19th century and whose efforts went hand-in-glove with British imperialism powers of domination. I assert, however, that the missionaries' methods of persuasion likely did not include death threats, as done by the Jihadists, and, therefore, the missionaries' rhetorical endeavors differed both in manner and scope from that of the Jihadists.

Second, *A Prayer for Sudan* revealed hidden disciplinary domains of power operating within Northern Sudanese institutional bureaucracies. As a way of ruling over those they oppress, social institutions rely on "bureaucratic hierarchies and techniques of surveillance" (P. H. Collins, 2000, p. 280). The Southern Sudanese were disciplined by means of surveillance, threats of violence, refusal of jobs, and exclusion from higher education, to name a few techniques. The production revealed examples of these disciplining phenomena occurring, especially (but not exclusively) in schools and workplaces. For example, Martha related an account of being pushed to the floor and then fired by her Muslim boss who scrutinized her every move:

In Sudan, I worked in a small company. It was a good job, but all my coworkers were Muslim. Again and again, they invited me to come to the mosque with them for prayers, but I refused each time. The next day, my boss called me into his office. He told me that it was very important that all those working for him go to mosque together. He asked me, again, if I would go with them. When I told him I was a Christian, he pushed me on the ground and scraped my knees. Then he told me never to come back.

The boss's actions were meant to discipline Martha because she stood her ground. Although she did lose her job, nevertheless, in that small act of defiance, she bravely carried out what P. H. Collins (2000) has labeled as "resistance from inside the bureaucracy" (p. 281).

Niahlic's story exposed another case of an oppressive disciplining strategy—this one taking place in an educational institution. "It's kind of hard to get into college over there," she lamented. "They just make you fail in your classes. They don't treat you like they treat the other kids. They make you pay money." Although she did not label it as such, clearly, Niahlic was the victim of discrimination, extortion, and exclusion—concrete disciplining strategies meted out to her because she was neither Arabic nor Muslim.

Of course, the most pervasive and harshest disciplining strategies were the threats or executions of rape, murder, and enslavement of Southern Sudanese—acts that were "witnessed" to in both the testimonies and evocations on the production's public stages. Mayen's testimony was a salient case in point: "So they train them [the members of Jihad]; they give them weapons, horses, and they give them cars, and they go to the South. When they go there, wherever they go there, people will be killed." In response to such violence, the Sudan People's Liberation Army/Movement (SPLA/M) was formed and became the chief organized form of resistance to the slaughter.

Third, *A Prayer for Sudan* unmasked the veiled tactics used by the Northern Sudanese hegemonic domain of power. According to P. H. Collins (2000), the hegemonic domain of power "aims to justify dominating practices, by manipulating ideology and culture" (p. 284). By creating and maintaining "a popular system of 'commonsense' ideas that support [the dominant group's] right to rule" (P. H. Collins, p. 284), hegemons justify their oppression of others.

Bureaucratic agents of the Arabic Muslim North Sudan perpetuated a "commonsense" notion that the cattle-herding Dinka tribes of the South were inferior in every respect. The Dinka's Christian religion was viewed as antithetical to Islam, their simple rural existence was unsophisticated, and their technological knowledge was nil, meaning that they could never recover/use the rich resources beneath their soil. Their women and children had no worth and, therefore, could be treated as slaves. Above all, their dark-skinned African physiognomy was seen as inferior by those of Northern Sudanese Arabic ethnicity.

Because of these views, the Northern hegemons sought to destroy key positive self-perceptions held by Southern Sudanese regarding their (a) ethnic worth as members of royal tribal blood lines, (b) meaningful way of life in the ownership and trading of cattle, and (c) religious practice. The hegemons, thus, attempted to replace the Southern Sudanese biographies with "a commonsense" ideology that negated their deep-seated affirmative self-knowledge. Our production pulled back the curtain on this hegemonic ideological practice, as Niahlic's simple statement about her experience of ethnic and religious prejudice instantiates: "Sometimes, they don't, you know, like the Southern people. ... They just always say, 'Christians, they have bad manners; they're wrong, Islam came first,' and all that stuff." In contrast, *A Prayer for Sudan* rendered a potent, positive alternative interpretation of the Southern Sudanese that invalidated the Northern Sudanese's commonsense hegemonic rhetoric. Standing in for those who themselves represented other oppressed Southern Sudanese, cast members (and those who worked behind the scenes) produced a powerful nullification of the hegemonic ideology behind the oppressors' powers of domination.

Finally, *A Prayer for Sudan* offered all witnesses (cast and crew, and U.S. and Sudanese audiences) a vision of how they might work against what P. H. Collins (2000) called "interpersonal domains of power" (p. 287). In particular, the production did not portray the Southern Sudanese only as submissive, ill-fated heirs of mistreatment; instead, our enactments drew attention to strong people who, by their acts of individual resistance, impacted the power dynamics, at least in some small measure, as seen in Martha's testimony. The production also featured people who planned to take action against the oppression when they returned to Sudan. According to Mayom, for instance, "The Muslim government set all kinds of laws that we cannot follow. We have to fight. It is a good thing to fight for our freedom. We cannot follow the Sharia. ... I will go back—I will go back to help my country." Abden related a similar intent:

> My thought right now that I am in America is that my country is very, very, very behind right now. In development, even in knowledge, in technologies, in everything, it's behind. Best thing we should do is that we go to school 'til we can get everyone educated, get technology into [our] head, and take this technology home and spread it everywhere, give it to everyone. ... After I am done with my education, I'm going back. I have to go back.

These two individuals were not alone in their intent to return to resist the matrix of domination, which, by 2005 (the year of the Comprehensive Peace

Agreement between the SPLA/M and the government of Sudan; see note 2), had cost "3.5 million Southern lives and the displacement of 5.5 million more (Nasong'o & Rapando, 2005, p. 67).

LESSONS LEARNED ABOUT COMMUNICATION ACTIVISM AND COMMUNITY-BASED PERFORMANCE

As a communication scholar whose focus is the nexus of culture, organizations, and community, and whose methods include ethnography and performance, my understanding and practice of communication activism is grounded in distinctly embodied and aesthetic ways of knowing and being. Frey and Carragee's (2007; this volume) challenge to communication scholars "to engage in direct vigorous action in support of needed social change" (p. 3) has been met through the research and production of *A Prayer for Sudan*. Through its energetic ethnographic explorations, enthusiastic performative evocations, and hearty dialogical TalkBack sessions, *A Prayer for Sudan* embodies the vigorous action-based research in support of social change called for by Frey and Carragee.

Expressed from a first-person perspective, this chapter has sought to bring readers as close as possible to the embodied experiences of the researchers and their cultural partners, as well as to those who attended the production. Through the CBP (a first-stage product of the research), we sought to move audiences to action on behalf of the Sudanese through an aesthetic form of communication. Hence, given that our communication activist texts primarily included interview narratives, ethnographic conversations, and dramatic presentations, my analysis of the lessons learned about communication activism necessarily should be viewed primarily through ethnographic and performance lenses.

Because *A Prayer for Sudan*, first and foremost, was the product of a 15-week semester college course, many (although not all) of the lessons learned emanate from its particular educational context, curricular goals, and pedagogical strategies, and their concomitant timeboundedness. Here, I discuss lessons learned about the educational particulars of this communication activism, as well as lessons that pertain to CBP practice, in general.

The first lesson is to have sufficient time to achieve one's activist agenda. An activist performance could have been constructed merely from secondary research about the conflict in Sudan; alternatively, I could have conducted primary research and created a ready-made script for students to have at the beginning of the semester. Because it was one of several cross-cultural engagement core curriculum offerings, the CBP course was required to help students learn about a culture different from theirs, but because the manner or mode of that guideline was not specified, I required students to learn about the Sudanese through one-on-one interactions with them and then to advocate on their behalf. My choice was not the easiest route to performance activism but I believed that it would lead to effective experiential learning and advocacy.

Except for the limited knowledge of the situation in Sudan that I brought to the course, students constructed the activist production almost ex nihilo; consequently, the production clock started ticking early, loudly, and increasingly faster throughout the semester, causing our already jittery nervous systems and racing heartbeats to meld into one giant, synchronized, stressed-out organism. We had much to do in the 15 weeks if we were to become knowledgeable and effective activists.

It was not until week 12 that the script was finalized and we mounted the production; that is, blocked the onstage movements; integrated East African live drumming throughout; and coordinated the mediated images, sound effects, and prerecorded music. Most play productions normally take 4 to 6 weeks, with the benefit of months of preproduction dramaturgical research, script analysis, and coordination of design elements. Our comparatively short 20-day production schedule required acute single-mindedness, concentrated twice-a-day and weekend rehearsals, and extreme individual focus. Throughout this truncated rehearsal period, fear and dread were my constant companions, but they remained contained and unexpressed, for I had long ago learned to perform "as if" success was a foregone conclusion and to "confidently" push through to accomplish that which even I perceived as being terribly difficult.

In the end, we successfully achieved our performance activist goals and felt exceedingly privileged to have engaged with these Sudanese. Students were activated because of their close relationships with the people for whom they advocated. The stories sank deep into their souls and then poured out of them in their everyday discussions and subsequent social justice endeavors.

When the production was reprised the next academic year (2006), many of the original performers returned to continue the cause, and their persuasive activist rhetoric enticed others to join the performance troupe, with audience responses mirroring those of the original production. Having had a year to "massage the script," I refined and updated the text. That process opened my eyes to the potential value of having extra time, and it led me to consider making the course a two-semester offering, which would bring its own set of challenges, particularly recruiting students, given their difficulty incorporating that into their 4-year graduation plan. In the end, I decided not to change the format because of the recruitment issue but made other adjustments that simplified the work and made my next CBP process more manageable.[7]

A second lesson about CBP activism emanated from the experience of producing *A Prayer for Sudan*: Activism involving crossing boundaries constituted by numerous and deep-seated differences requires open attitudes and, especially, skillful communication. Most students were well intentioned in their desire to become activists on behalf of the Sudanese refugees, many had experienced other cultures either through travel or social exposure, and several were committed social justice advocates, but other students had neither crossed cultures nor taken any interest in activism. None of the students, however, had ever engaged with native Africans whose lives involved subsistence-level nomadic cattle herding, tribal loyalty and royalty, bride-price marriage contracts, fleeing for one's life, and watching family members being killed and/or raped. Nor had any of the students encountered people who, for more than 10 years, had lived in the quasi-safe world of a refugee camp.

Given these differences between the students and the Sudanese, to be effective advocates, I had to prepare students (no matter their level of awareness, experiences, expertise, or interests) not to be afraid but to push past hesitancy to find common ground within difference. Two students, unfortunately, never did find that common ground because of their immutable stance vis-à-vis these different Others, and their inaction perfectly demonstrated the cultural paralysis caused by an unwarranted sense of superiority, overt racism, and/or ill-founded phobia.

Students who successfully found common ground with the Sudanese did so by emptying themselves of (or at least putting in check) nationalist, racist, and classist ideologies that can emanate from one's ethnocentric positionality. To accomplish this objective, students learned to employ three communication skills that involve letting go of the primacy of ego and its selfish orientation: mindfulness and mindful listening, mutual disclosure, and empathic engagement.

According to Brown and Ryan (2003), *mindfulness* involves "attention to and awareness of present events and experience" (p. 3). Consequently, students developed heightened states of wakefulness in their ethnographic interactions with the Sudanese. Mindful listening became an essential part of this activist endeavor, regardless of the stage of the ethnographic or performance work. As Wood (2010) contended, when ethnographic Others "sense [that] we are really listening, they tend to elaborate on their ideas and express themselves in more depth" (p. 147). Greene (2000) similarly theorized the importance of being in the state of "*wide*-awakeness [that] Albert Camus had described ... if people [are] to become aware of deficiencies in the world and take action to repair them" (p. 313). Students' preparation for activist engagement included working hard to achieve both wide-awakeness and mindful listening, efforts that paid off, as evidenced by the rich dialogical interactions recorded in students' transcripts and the number of "thick descriptions" (Geertz, 1973, p. 2) recorded in their field notebooks.

Finding common ground also involves appropriate self-disclosure that fosters trust, which, in turn, cultivates a robust dialogue. Such endeavors take time and risk, but students who sought that dialogue found that the benefits of sharing themselves offset those risks. Relational equilibrium between self and other in performance-based communication activist contexts can yield mutual understanding and close relationships between the knower and the known. Indeed, the knower–known distinction is called into question in this state, as the perpetually shifting standpoints of relational equilibrium do not verify such traditional, static epistemological role definitions; instead, both interactants, at once, are the knower and the known.

Students' ability to find common ground with the Sudanese also was facilitated by their successful empathic engagement with them at every stage and level of association. From their ethnographic connections to their performative evocations, students who engaged the qualitative process and came to understand and share the Sudanese's feelings achieved empathy that moved them from self-absorption and primacy of ego to the other-orientation essential for advocacy.

Those who were most successful on stage sincerely incorporated Pelias's (1992) three-step empathic performance work: recognition, convergence, and adoption. For instance, Sarah's rehearsal/performance work not only involved numerous hours engaging in a variety of activities with Ackech but when it came time to create an evocation of him, she "worked to understand as fully as possible what [he had] experience[ed] emotionally ... [and] why [he felt] that way" (p. 90). Sarah soon became part of Ackech's "affective world" (Pelias, p. 93) and began to "merge with" (Pelias, p. 95) him. According to Pelias, such convergence involves performers "tap[ping] and pull[ing] into play their own feelings ... based upon the [Other's] utterances" (p. 93). Sarah's resultant "adjustive identification" with Ackech enabled her to "perceive [his] situation through [his] eyes" (Pelias, p. 94).

Sarah "adopted [Ackech's] stance" (Pelias, 1992, p. 94) by evoking a version of Ackech that so closely resembled him, that if her non-African pigmentation were not obvious to the audience, she easily could have been taken as a Sudanese man playing himself. Her empathic rendering helped audience members to feel the thorns scratching Ackech's feet as he fled for his life, the grief he felt after his mother's murder, and the loneliness he now feels living in the United States far away from his family and friends.

No playwright had created Ackech and no "character notes" (dialogues spoken by other characters about Ackech) or portrayals of him were available. Instead, this activist ethnoperformer took as her source the lived experience shared by Ackech himself; he was her guide in his creation and evocation. Although her rendering, like all ethnoperformances, could only imaginatively point to Ackech's ontic status, to the degree that Sarah found common ground with Ackech, developed relational equilibrium with him through mutual disclosure, and achieved empathic engagement with him, her portrayal of a person different from her by gender, nationality, ethnicity, culture, and life experience was a superb example of performance advocacy that affected not only others but her as well, making her a stronger, more committed advocate—a personal transformation experienced by most of the student performers. As demonstrated in comments offered during the TalkBack session, performances like Sarah's inspired some audience members to advocate on behalf of persons they witnessed before them.

Another related lesson learned about CBP activism concerns the often-preferred practice of having community members play themselves in such performances. Our experience suggests that having performers play community members should not necessarily be eschewed by CBP practitioners, or even always be a second choice. In this case, students portrayed members of the Sudanese community because the enterprise, first and foremost, was a college course project. This decision also was impacted, however, by two pragmatic obstacles that precluded the Sudanese from portraying themselves: (a) few could speak English well enough to be understood by U.S. theatrical audiences and (b) they had overly full schedules, as most of them both worked and went to school full time. To compensate for their absence from the production, two Sudanese men (and they had to be men because, at that time, few women spoke English) always joined the cast to say the ending prayer in Dinka. Having them speak with the audience during the TalkBack sessions also greatly enhanced this communication activism and emblematized the joint nature of the entire venture.

One final lesson was a heartbreaker: The formation of strong friendship bonds in successful activism can result in the experience of great loss for community members when those student friends graduate and move on. Ackech, for instance, found it very difficult to no longer have a regular tete-â-tete with Sarah. Although for a time, Sarah touched base with him, their contact eventually ended. Each time I saw him at the church in the months following our performances, he would ask me if I had heard from Sarah, and I was greatly saddened to have to tell him that she had moved to a different continent.

This lesson learned is apropos for all communication activists who invest time and energy into forming a bond between themselves and those for and with whom they advocate: Because we should do no harm in our efforts to help, we should be vigilant at every step of the advocacy process to assure those with whom we are privileged to be involved of our post-advocacy relational intentions. This vigilance is especially true with people who have been marginalized and oppressed. Will we honestly continue to communicate with one another or is it likely that after a time, we will not? Thus, I offer a cautionary note: Potentially intimate relationships demand forthright communication by ethnoperformers (and those with more privilege) regarding the dyad's possible future, even if it means the loss of "good performance material" or rich research capta. I realized too late that I should have encouraged the students to seek understanding about future contact with their partners. Ackech's felt loss of Sarah became one more painful and unnecessary loss in a far-too-long string of them.

CONCLUSION

A Prayer for Sudan turned out to be a workable form of communication activism because it operated in "the realm of cultural politicization and community action" (Haedicke, 1998, p. 130). It also served as a "vehicle of teaching through testimony" (Raphael, 2006, p. 1), bringing public attention, not only through the performance but also via follow-up news stories about the performance,[8] to the genocide and its impact on Sudan and the lives of these Sudanese people. Our audiences were "encouraged … to ask questions, detail observations, and draw inferences" (Kuftinec, 1997, p 172) about how their lack of awareness and inaction could be considered as complicity with the heinous acts shown throughout the performance.

Through our performative enactments, TalkBack sessions, use of literature, select news coverage, and the one-to-one conversations between U.S. Americans and Sudanese, *A Prayer for Sudan* as a communication activism endeavor called attention to and urged resistance to oppression. Based on observations of many audience members taking advocacy literature with them after the performances of *A Prayer for Sudan*, the production may have helped "to create a sense of community in which [hundreds of] people [could] participate as agents of change" (Weinberg, 2000, p. 27).

The situation in South Sudan remains bleak, for as Dennis C. Blair (2010), director of U.S. National Intelligence, explained, mass killings are to be expected in the coming years:

> Looking ahead over the next five years, a number of countries in Africa and Asia are at significant risk for a new outbreak of mass killing. All of the countries at significant risk have or are at high risk for experiencing internal conflicts or regime crises and exhibit one or more of the additional risk factors for mass killing. Among these countries, a new mass killing or genocide is most likely to occur in Southern Sudan. (p. 37)

Given such expectations, another reprise of *A Prayer for Sudan* seems in order. Indeed, the perilous prospects in South Sudan cry out for all manner of intervention, including (and perhaps especially) by communication scholar-activists. Hopefully, this chapter functions as a form of communication advocacy, mobilizing others across the world community to intervene on behalf of those in imminent peril who face every day the prospects of another genocide in South Sudan.[9]

NOTES

1. All names referencing students or our Sudanese friends are pseudonyms. Some Sudanese people refer to themselves in public by their Christian, baptismal names (e.g., Mary, Jacob, Matthew, and William); others use their indigenous names (e.g., Ackech, Madit, Thon, Atem, and Niahlic). I refer to individuals by whichever name version they used in conversations with us, but I change their name to equivalent alternative names (Christian or indigenous).
2. The recent civil war in South Sudan is just the latest in a series of conflicts fought over the East African nation since the mid-19th century. European traders who worked their way up the Nile were the first wave of invaders who sought to conquer that nation. With their superior technology, the traders forced their way into the predominantly tribal populations and "caused a serious clash of cultures out of which rose a violent new world" (R. O. Collins, 2006, p 13). *A Prayer for Sudan* was produced during a contemporary period of conflict "when the extremist National Islamic Front (NIF), based in the North usurped power through a military coup" (Robinson, 2003, p. 17). Since 1989, the extremist Muslim government in the North "has been waging a declared *jihad* against ethnic and religious communities that resist Arabization and Islamization" (Sliwa, 2004, p. 343). NIF has been fighting the rebel soldiers from the Sudan People's Liberation Army/Movement (SPLA/M). General Omar al-Bashir led the NIF, consolidated its power, and then "seized [government control] through a military coup that in 1989 overthrew the elected government" (Human Rights Watch [HRW], 1994, Human Rights Development section, para. 2). As Jesper Strelsholm, the Africa correspondent for *Politken*, asserted, "The battle is over land, oil, power and religion, by a government that is made up of some of Africa's most aggressive Islamists" (as cited in Silwa, 2004, p. 343).

   In 1994, HRW identified NIF and al-Bashir's "radical agenda [of imposing] its version of Shari'a (Islamic) law and convert[ing] [of] Sudan into a totalitarian Islamic state" (Human Rights Developments section, para. 2). HRW also asserted that "Sudan's thirty million citizens would be ranked according to religion, sect, political affiliation and sex and granted or deprived of rights accordingly" (Human Rights Developments section, para. 2).

   The war has become increasingly complex the longer it has been fought. Numerous regional injustices have created abundant reasons "for armed confrontation and shifting alliances within the wider conflict [and] have produced a pattern of interlocking civil wars now being fought on different levels" (Johnson, 2003, p. 127). Although all parties in the conflict have committed human rights abuses, according to Sapienza (2003), "the Sudanese government [in North Sudan] is responsible for the bulk of the violence ... [including] aerial raids over southern villages often targeting churches, hospitals, and international aid groups" (p. 889).

A Prayer for Sudan is set during the latter part of the conflict between 1998 and 2003, within the memories and experiences of the mostly young men and women we interviewed. This conflict continued until November 21, 2006, and ended with the signing of The Comprehensive Peace Agreement (CPA; aka Naivasha Agreement) between the SPLA/M and the government of Sudan. When the production was reprised in 2006, it was revised to reflect this change and the tentative peace it wrought.

3. In addition to incorporating the narratives of interviewed Sudanese individuals in our script, *A Prayer for Sudan* included facts and statistics drawn from secondary sources, including Deng (2001), McClelland (2003), Means (2004), Palmberg (2004), Robinson (2003), Sapienza (2003), and Sliwa (2004).
4. Of all these designations, I prefer the term "community-based *performance*" because, as Cohen-Cruz (2005) explained, the term includes "not only dance and music but also a much larger category of heightened behavior intended for public viewing" (p. 1).
5. In subsequent years, I used Cohen-Cruz's (2005) germinal work, as well as readings from Leonard and Kilkelly's (2006) collection, both of which were not available until after this class had been taught (for another powerful collection, see Haedicke & Nellhaus, 2008).
6. Most of the Sudanese men had taken English lessons in refugee camps, plus they arrived in the United States years before many of the women. Consequently, the men became the spokespersons for the women, as translators and, as I discovered eventually, as their mind guards who shielded them from much information.
7. I limited the unit on past CBP performances to a few short assignments, omitted other readings and collapsed their main points into one or two lectures, and taught ethnographic and oral history methods concurrent with study of the historic background of community issues. One 90-minute in-class session per week was omitted and, instead, the class met for 5 to 6 hours on each Saturday, with me driving everyone in a college van to meet with community members, which required prior notification of potential CBP students before they registered for the course. Surprisingly, this requirement did not seem to deter many students, as the class size was about on par with the Southern Sudanese semester.
8. News coverage consisted of stories and announcements in local newspapers, as well as on the college website (see, e.g., "Multimedia Show Tells Tale of the Sudanese," 2006; "A Prayer for Sudan," 2005; "Sudanese Church in Grand Rapids," 2005).
9. As this chapter goes to print, South Sudan is preparing for a July 9, 2011 celebration to mark its status as an independent country, a move approved overwhelmingly in a referendum vote held during January 2011 and accepted by al-Bashir ("South Sudan Backs Independence," 2011). Even as the young country gets ready for this joyous fete, violence continues to erupt across the region. Weeks of spotty conflicts have, according to Boswell (2011), left hundreds dead. Additionally, "rebel militias in Southern Sudan have united in a new armed movement against the young southern government, raising the prospect of civil war even before South Sudan declares independence in July" (Boswell, para. 1). Clearly, this region must remain a central concern and focus of international oversight and communication activism endeavors.

REFERENCES

Abdullah, O. B. (2001, January 13). Muddling through Sudan's critical state of affairs. *Islam Online.net*. Retrieved from http://www.islamonline.net

A prayer for Sudan. (2005, May 3). Retrieved from http://www.calvin.edu/news/2004-05/sudan.htm

Armstrong, A. E. (2000). Paradoxes in community-based pedagogy: Decentering students through oral history performance. *Theatre Topics, 10*, 113–128. Retrieved from http://www.press.jhu.edu/journals/theatre_topics

Ben-Zvi, L. (2006). Staging the other Israel: The documentary theatre of Nola Chilton. *TDR: The Drama Review, 50*(3), 42–55. Retrieved from http://www.mitpressjournals.org/loi/dram

Blair, D. C. (2010, February 2). *Annual threat assessment of the US intelligence community for the Senate Select Committee on Intelligence*. Retrieved from http://intelligence.senate.gov/ 100202/blair.pdf

Boswell, A. (2011, April 6). Latest challenge for South Sudan: Armed internal rebellion. *McClatchy*. Retrieved from hppt://www.mcclatchydc.com

Bowers, M., & Spence, J. (Directors/Producers). (1998). *Blue train: Making history dance* [DVD]. Available from http://www.lightstruckpress.com/bt.htm

Brady, S. (2000). Welded to the ladle: Steelbound and non-radicality in community-based theatre. *TDR: The Drama Review, 44*(3), 51–74. doi:10.1162/105420400565170

Brian, C. (2005). Devising community. *Theatre Topics, 15*, 1–13. doi:10.1353/tt.2005.0003

Brown, K. W., & Ryan, R. M. (2003). The benefits of being present: Mindfulness and its role in psychological well-being. *Journal of Personality and Social Psychology, 84*, 822–848. doi:10.1037/0022-3514.84.4.822

Cohen-Cruz, J. (2005). *Local acts: Community-based performance in the United States*. New Brunswick, NJ: Rutgers University Press.

Collins, P. H. (2000). *Black feminist thought: Knowledge, consciousness, and the politics of empowerment* (Rev. ed.). New York, NY: Routledge.

Collins, R. O. (2006). *The Southern Sudan in historical perspective*. New Brunswick, NJ: Transaction Books.

Conquergood, D. (1985). Performing as a moral act: Ethical dimensions of the ethnography of performance. *Literature in Performance, 5*(2), 1–13. doi:10.1080/10462938509391578

Deng, F. M. (2001). Sudan—Civil war and genocide. *Middle East Quarterly, 8*(1), 13–21. Retrieved from http://www.meforum.org/meq

Dewey, J. (1958). *Experience and nature*. New York, NY: Dover. (Original work published 1925)

Ellis, A. (2000). The art of community conversation. *Theatre Topics, 10*, 91–100. doi:10.1353/tt.2000.0010

Fox, R. (2006). Negative: Using performative interventions to explore HIV-negativity. *Theatre Topics, 16*, 47–64. doi:10.1353/tt.2006.0007

Frey, L. R., & Carragee, K. M. (2007) Introduction: Communication activism as engaged scholarship. In L. R. Frey & K. N. Carragee (Eds.), *Communication activism* (2 Vols., pp. 1–64). Cresskill, NJ: Hampton Press.

Geertz, C. (1973). *The interpretation of cultures: Selected essays*. New York, NY: Basic Books.

Goodall, H. L., Jr. (2000). *Writing the new ethnography*. Walnut Creek, CA: AltaMira Press.

Goodwin, J. L. (2004). The productive postshow: Facilitating, understanding and optimizing personal narratives in audience talk following a personal narrative performance. *Theatre Topics, 14*, 317–338. doi:10.1353.tt.2004.004

Greene, M. (2000). The sixties: The calm against the storm, or, levels of concern. *Educational Theory, 50*, 307–320. doi:10.1111/j.1741-5446.2000.00307.x

Haedicke, S. C. (1998). Dramaturgy in community-based theatre. *Journal of Dramatic Theory and Criticism, 13*(1), 125–132. Retrieved from http://journals.ku.edu/index.php.jdtc

Haedicke, S. C., & Nellhaus, T. (Eds.). (2008). *Performing democracy: International perspectives on urban community-based performance*. Ann Arbor: University of Michigan Press.

Human Rights Watch. (1994). *Sudan*. Retrieved from http://www.hrw.org/legacy/reports/1994/WR94/Africa-09.htm

Johnson, D. H. (2003). *The root causes of Sudan's civil wars*. Bloomington: Indiana University Press.

Kemp, M. (2006). Promoting the health and wellbeing of young black men using community-based drama. *Health Education, 106*, 186–200. doi:10.1108/09654280610658532

Kuftinec, S. (1997). Odakle ste? (Where are you from?): Active learning and community-based theatre in former Yugoslavia and the US. *Theatre Topics, 7*, 171–186. Retrieved from http://www.press.jhu.edu/journals/theatre_topics

Kuftinec, S. (2003). *Staging America: Cornerstone and community-based theatre*. Carbondale: Southern Illinois University Press.

Leonard, R. H., & Kilkelly A. (2006). *Performing communities: Grassroots ensemble theaters deeply rooted in eight U.S. communities* (L. F. Burnham, Ed.). Oakland, CA: New Village Press.

Lev-Aladegm, S. (2004). Whose play is it?: The issue of authorship/ownership in Israeli community-based theatre. *TDR: Drama Review, 48*(3), 117–134. doi:10.1162/1054204041667721

Lippard, L. R. (1997). *The lure of the local: Senses of place in a multicentered society*. New York, NY: New Press.

Little, E. (2004). Towards a poetics of popular theatre. *Canadian Theatre Review, 117*, 29–32.

Mbugguss, M. (1999, November 19). Community-based drama with a noble message. *East African Standard*. Retrieved from http://www.indexkenya.org/citation.asp?control=E00167

McClelland, S. (2003, November 10). "I'd rather die than be a slave": Francis Bok tells of his life in slavery. *Macleans.ca*. Retrieved from http://www.macleans.ca

McConachie, B. A. (1998). Approaching the "structure of feeling" in grassroots theatre. *Theatre Topics, 8*, 33–53. Retrieved from http://www.press.jhu.edu/journals/theatre_topics

McNeill, D. P., Morrison, D. A., & Nouwen, H. J. M. (1982). *Compassion, a reflection on the Christian life*. Garden City, NY: Doubleday.

Means, A. K. (2004, September–October). "Genocide" in Sudan. *Tikkun Magazine*, *19*(5), 55–58.
Multimedia show tells tale of the Sudanese. (2006, April 1). *Grand Rapids Press*, p. E8.
Mylan, M., & Shank, J. (Directors/Producers). (2003). *Lost boys of Sudan* [DVD]. Available from http://www.lostboysfilm.com
Nasong'o, S. W., & Rapando, G. (2005). Lack of consensus on constitutive fundamentals: Roots of the Sudanese civil war and prospects for resettlement. *African and Asian Studies*, *4*, 51–82. doi:10.1163/1569209054547328
Palmberg, E. (2004, September). A passion for peace: Even as atrocities in Western Sudan have drawn the world's focus in recent months, there are signs of hope elsewhere in the nation, which has been ravaged by civil war for three or four decades. *Sojourners Magazine*. Retrieved from http://www.sojo.net
Pelias, R. J. (1992). *Performance studies: The interpretation of aesthetic texts*. New York, NY: St. Martin's Press.
Plastow, J. (1997). The Eritrea community-based theatre project. *New Theatre Quarterly*, *13*, 386–395. doi:10.1017/S0266464X00011544
Pollock, D. (1990). Telling the told: Performing *Like a Family*. *Oral History Review*, *18*(2), 1–36. doi:10.1093/ohr/18.2.1
A prayer for Sudan. (2005, May 3). Retrieved from http://www.calvin.edu/news/2004-05/sudan.htm
Raphael, T. (2006). Something to declare: Performing oral history. *Transformations: The Journal of Inclusive Scholarship and Pedagogy*, *17*(1), 13–31.
Robinson, J. (2003, March–April). Hope for Sudan: A grassroots movement stars down an oil company. *Sojourners Magazine*. Retrieved from http://www.sojo.net
Román, D. (1998). *Acts of intervention: Performance, gay culture, and AIDS*. Bloomington: Indiana University Press.
Sapienza, L. (2003). Classifying the killings in Sudan as genocide. *New York Law School Journal of Human Rights*, *19*, 889–894.
Seda, O. (2008). Border crossings—A transatlantic project in community-based theatre: Performing the *Bus Stop Journals*. *Theatre Topics*, *18*, 183–190. doi:10.1353/tt.0.0039
Sliwa, M. (2004, June). The rape of slave boys in Sudan. *Contemporary Review*, pp. 343-345. Retrieved from http://findarticles.com/p/articles/mi_m2242/is_1661_284/ai_n6140462
Smith, D. I., & Carvill, B. (2000). *The gift of the stranger: Faith, hospitality, and foreign language learning*. Grand Rapids, MI: Wm. B. Eerdmans.
South Sudan backs independence—Results. (2011, February 7). *BBC News*. Retrieved from http://www.bbc.co.uk/news
Stucky, N. (1995). Performing oral history: Storytelling and pedagogy. *Communication Education*, *44*, 1–14. doi:10.1080/03634529509378993
Sudanese church in Grand Rapids offers outreach, service. (2005, May 11). *East Grand Rapids Cadence*, p. 8.
Taylor, P. (2003). *Applied theatre: Creating transformative encounters in the community*. Portsmouth, NH: Heinemann Press.
Thompson, J., & Schechner, R. (2004). Why "social theatre"? *TDR: The Drama Review*, *48*(3), 11–16. doi:10.1162/1054204041667767

U of M stages drama to raise awareness about HIV/AIDS. (2005, May 2). Retrieved from http://www1.umn.edu/news/news-releases/2005/UR_RELEASE_MIG_2244.html

Watts, E. K. (2001). "Voice" and voicelessness" in rhetorical studies. *Quarterly Journal of Speech, 87,* 179–196. doi:10.1080/00335630109384328

Weinberg, M. S. (2000). Community-based theatre: A participatory model for social transformation. In J. W. Frick (Ed.), *Theatre at the margins: The political, the popular, the personal, the profane* (pp. 22–33). Tuscaloosa: University of Alabama Press.

Wood, J. T. (2010). *Interpersonal communication: Everyday encounters* (7th ed.). Boston, MA: Cengage Wadsworth.

Yordon, J. E. (1997). *Experimental theatre: Creating and staging texts*. Prospect Heights, IL: Waveland Press.

4

CHALLENGING DOMESTIC VIOLENCE

Trickle-Up Theorizing About Participation and Power in Communication Activism

Charlotte Ryan
Media Research Action Project
Karen Jeffreys
Rhode Island Coalition for the Homeless

On New Year's Eve 2000, Central Falls police arrested Rhode Island state legislator, Michael Farrell, for battering his girlfriend. Supported by the statewide Rhode Island Coalition against Domestic Violence (RICADV), domestic violence (DV) activists in Central Falls and neighboring Pawtucket, RI pressed for Farrell's resignation in a campaign that integrated grassroots organizing, lobbying of legislators, and direct outreach to the news media. At first, Farrell refused to resign, but after several weeks of sustained pressure from activists, the news media, and fellow legislators, he stepped down.

RICADV's victory went far beyond toppling a state legislator who had battered a partner. Coalition calls to politicians got swifter attention, and

RICADV's standing as a news source grew, signaling a shift in a journalistic convention that had long troubled anti-DV activists: Although media outlets routinely welcomed public service announcements from organizations opposing DV, reporters typically reverted to the sensationalized crime-beat formula when covering DV crimes. The resulting stories privileged official sources and bystanders (including victims' families and neighbors) over experts, advocates, and activists (Bullock, 2008; Ryan, Anastario, & DaCunha, 2006).

Building on the success of the Farrell case, RICADV worked systematically with professional communicators and communication scholars to shift news media sourcing practices to better promote their movement's framing of DV. For RICADV and movement allies, far from being a private family tragedy or an inexplicable mystery, DV is a social problem demanding societal solutions; failure to publicly address violence in the home ensures that DV will continue.

By 2002, after 7 years of systematic communication work, RICADV and allies opposing DV no longer were occasional sources; they had joined police as common lead sources in DV news (Ryan et al., 2006). Other changes in DV reporting appeared concomitantly, including a measurable cultural shift in the RI media market, with sources unrelated to RICADV—even police—framing DV as a social issue requiring community intervention (see Ryan, Anastario, & Jeffreys, 2005).

In the context of longstanding frustrations with DV news coverage, this shift in sourcing patterns and in news discourse about DV took on national importance. When RICADV reported its success at a national meeting of state DV coalitions, attendees broke into applause. Given that RICADV's communication successes facilitated major legislative gains, DV coalitions in other states asked RICADV for coaching. Spurred by these requests, RICADV pursued a U.S. Department of Health and Human Services grant to organize a training institute, called "Media Matters," attended by 37 state coalitions, where RICADV and the DV survivors group Sisters Overcoming Abusive Relationships (SOAR), joined by partnering communication scholars and professionals, shared communication strategies for influencing news coverage of DV.

Among the scholars who accompanied RICADV in this growth were members of the Media Research Action Project (MRAP; http://www.mrap.info), whose mission is to strengthen local and national social movements promoting social justice and inclusive, participatory democracy. In this chapter, we link our grounded theorizing about confronting DV to communication activism for social justice scholarship, a field that now represents both a general perspective (see Frey, Pearce, Pollock, Artz, & Murphy, 1996) and a growing body of empirical research and pedagogical practice (see Frey & Carragee, 2007; Frey & Palmer, in press). The Farrell case serves as an exemplar of a sustained activist–scholar partnership that originated in communication activism, but evolved into a series of communication activism scholarly projects. When the Farrell case arose, scholarship was not our primary objective; instead, RICADV (supported by MRAP) sought to challenge an immediate injustice. Addressing this injustice, however, also had the potential to strengthen RICADV's "rapid-response capacity"—its ability to function as a routine source for breaking news. To help RICADV achieve standing as a routine source, Jeffreys, as RICADV's communication director, tapped Ryan, a MRAP codirector, and other communication scholars and professionals.

A more theoretical project lurked in the background, however. We were familiar with Freirian-influenced participatory communication and organizing theories common in the Global South,[1] and we gravitated toward justice-centered organizing models that embedded community empowerment in popular education (see, e.g., www.thepraxisproject.org; www.Highlandercenter.org). Consequently, we wanted to develop a participatory communication model for social movements functioning in the heavily media-dominated Global North; in our case, in Rhode Island, a midsized U.S. media market.

Rhode Island represents a valuable testing ground for social theorizing, generally, and communication activism scholarship, in particular. First, the state approximates the demographic profile of the United States. Second, given the state's small size—less than 50 miles north to south or east to west—a social movement organization with modest resources can launch a viable statewide campaign. Third, Rhode Island's media market, 43rd largest in the nation, is sufficiently large to reflect trends, yet sufficiently small to permit organizers to launch market-wide campaigns. Finally, Rhode Island's political borders coincide with the boundaries of its media market and service catchment areas, making it possible for resource-strained movement organizations to launch multiarena organizing strategies, such that grassroots mobilization and legislative and media outreach synergistically reinforce each other.

The Farrell case marked a turning point vis-à-vis both our practical and theoretical goals. On the practical front, RICADV helped a member organization, Blackstone Valley Advocacy Center (Called Blackstone Shelter at that time; http://www.bvadvocacyce.org), which "provides services to women and their children who are in crisis as a result of domestic violence and/or homelessness" (Judiciary of Rhode Island, n.d., para. 1), to conduct a sustained news media campaign that conveyed its framing of DV and achieved its desired objective of forcing Farrell's resignation. Drawing on this and subsequent campaigns, we—Jeffreys at RICADV and Ryan at MRAP—fused Global North social marketing with Global South participatory communication theories to distill a movement-centered communication model that could support anti-DV movement efforts to gain broader access to mainstream media. As our partnership deepened and our communication activism research grew, we engaged in additional rounds of grounded theorizing, with problems that surfaced in practice spurring us to address basic conceptual gaps in Global South and North communication theory.

This chapter describes that continuum of practical theorizing and theorizing practice, departing from the organizing opportunity represented by the Farrell case and continuing with our efforts to address the undertheorizing of participation, power, and empowerment in communication activism scholarship. We explain that activists, among themselves and in dialogue with scholars, constantly theorize but they do not necessarily present their ideas in formal scholarly venues. Theorizing, thus, is not the exclusive domain of academics, and scholarship that ignores organizers' theorizing risks losing valuable insights. To prevent this fate, we call for "trickle-up theorizing": theories that percolate up from and are tested in sustained collaboration with collective actors representing those directly affected by an inequality. Trickle-up theorizing certainly has its disadvantages; most obviously, it is slow and its quality is not assured. Collaboration with an engaged collective actor, however, permits emerging theories to be tested, debated, and refined in practice, an advantage worth noting.

We first sketch the media context, conditions, and contradictions that produce challenges faced by U.S.-based social movements, in general, and the movement against DV, in particular. We then review communication activism scholarship that addresses the interplay between social movements and the news media. Turning to Global South participatory communication models, we summarize their strengths, particularly their systematic attention to grassroots involvement, and we identify their conceptual gaps, such as insufficient definitions of power and participation. Once the conceptual landscape is identified, we describe the growing cross-organizational partnership between RICADV and MRAP, and explain how we used learning community approaches to transcend differences in experience and conceptualization between activists and scholars. Turning to the Farrell case, we explain the practices we developed to implement our emerging communication model. We then discuss the concepts of "power" and "participation" in more depth, concluding with lessons learned about communication activism scholarship.

THE MEDIA CONTEXT, SOCIAL MOVEMENTS, AND THE MOVEMENT AGAINST DOMESTIC VIOLENCE

Media, according to Castells (2004), represent "the space of politics in the information age" (p. 371). Put differently, media form a convening system whose logic (Altheide & Snow, 1979) permeates social and political contests. News media systems channel information, shaping whether and what audiences hear, believe, and question about conflicts and disparities, locally, nationally, and globally (Herman & McChesney, 1997; Kellner, 2005; McChesney, 1999; Schiller, 1996). News media institutions become *the* "master forum, the major site of contest politically, in part because all of the would-be or actual sponsors of meaning—be they authorities, members or challengers—*assume* pervasive influence" (Gamson 1998, p. 59). Accepting this influence, politicians turn to media outlets to affect public opinion, as well as to promote elite "agenda-setting, policy enactment and implementation and the acquisition of political power" (Andrews, 2002, p. 106). Not only politicians but other established social actors, including corporations, churches, and cultural institutions, seek news media coverage to influence public perceptions, strengthen their bases of support, amass resources, call for action, and support or challenge existing elites, policies, or social practices (see, e.g., Alimi, 2007a; Castells, 2007; Curren, 2002; Edelman, 1988; the essays in Graber, 2011). Journalists, operating from news norms and routines, serve as gatekeepers who choose which social actors gain standing as reliable sources (Gans, 1979; Soley, 1992) and choose which happenings gain traction (Bennett, 1990). Conversely, accounts ignored by the news media lose legitimacy (Gamson, 1992). Hence, far from neutral hosts of public discourse, the news media heavily influence social priorities and inequalities in access-hampered democratic debate (Aufderheide, 1999; Gans, 2003).

Also aware of the influence of the news media, social movement organizations, operating from the challenged end of the power spectrum, often join with established social actors to seek coverage to set and shape agendas, policies, and public perceptions (Alimi, 2007b; Gitlin, 1980; Morris & Staggenborg, 2004; Rohlinger, 2002). Systemic obstacles, however, stymie organizers' efforts to tap mainstream news media (Bennett, 2009; Croteau & Hoynes, 1994, 2001; Herman & Chomsky, 1988; Herman & McChesney, 1997). As connective tissue integrating information flow among political, social, and economic arenas, the news media are bound tightly to the transnational economy and governance (Croteau & Hoynes, 1994, 2001; Herman & McChesney, 1997; McChesney, 1999). Most news media stories, consequently, are sponsored by government sources, corporations, or public relations firms working for corporate clients (Nimmo & Combs, 1990; see also Drake, this volume), with these insiders holding crucial advantages, including plentiful resources, communication infrastructure, messages that reinforce rather than question accepted values, and organizational cultures well suited to mainstream news conventions (Ryan, 1991). Hence, as Herman (1985) explained, the news media marginalize constituencies not by conspiracy but though the cumulative effects of industry structure, common sources, ideology, patriotism, and the power of government and top media sources to define newsworthiness and frameworks of discourse. Self-censorship, market forces, and norms of news practices may produce and maintain a particular viewpoint as effectively as formal state censorship. (p. 137)

As a result, even when social movement organizers promote newsworthy stories, they often meet resistance from reporters. To facilitate quick and efficient production, journalists prefer sources that they, reporters, already have anointed as reliable, and they hesitate to cultivate sources among more controversial and more easily challenged marginalized constituencies (Huesca, 1996; Ryan, 1996; van Dijk, 1991). Cumulative obstacles to becoming routine sources, thus, face those marginalized by inequalities such as age, class, gender, sexuality, and race, as well as those whose views or situations fall outside established social norms.

DV represents a case in point, as it was not widely recognized as a social problem until raised by the women's movement in the 1970s (Tierney, 1982). Despite gains in public awareness, however, news coverage continues to frame DV as a private tragedy, not as a social problem; consequently, atomized victims struggle for protection as the social dimensions of DV remain obscured (Meyers, 1997; Soothill & Walby, 1991). News media's coverage often implies complicity by DV victims: that they were masochistic, provoked batterers, deserving of the crime, or failed to leave the situation (Consalvo, 1998; Pagelow, 1981). These patterns also are heavily gendered, for "when women are the perpetrators and men the victims, active voice becomes more common … resulting in descriptions that highlight women's responsibility and deemphasize men's responsibility for acts of interpersonal violence" (Frazer & Mitchell, 2009, p. 68).

In tone, news coverage of DV incidents has ranged from the sensational (highlighting garish crime details) to the poetic (profiling abusers as tragic figures), but only infrequently has linked DV to broader social analyses, focusing, more typically, on specific incidents (Maxwell, Huxford, Borum, & Hornik, 2009). Lacking context (Iyengar, 1994), crime-driven stories divert attention from efforts to change public policy and consciousness (Loseke, 1989). DV activists have critiqued these patterns (see, e.g., Bart & Moran, 1993; Caputi, 1993; Johnson, 1994; Soothill & Walby, 1991) and how they intensify when victims are poor or working-class women and/or women of color (Benedict, 1992; hooks, 1992; Meyers, 1997; van Dijk, 1991), with the perpetrator's race adding yet more complexity (Enck-Wanzer, 2009). Both scholars and activists have recommended reforms in news institutions and journalistic education to support more contextualized coverage, including (a) changes in news practices (Benedict, 1992; Byerly, 1994; Jones, 2000; Meyers, 1997; RICADV, 2000), (b) journalist professional training and in-service education (Berkeley Media Studies Group, 2003; Byerly, 1994; Jones, 2000; Park & Bye, 2005), and (c) institutional guidelines for DV coverage (Benedict, 1992; Johnson, 1994; Meyers, 1997).

Although practical and compelling, the recommendations offered have not addressed formidable barriers to changing news practices. Market-driven news operations, like most institutions, resist change. Media critics generally concur that U.S. media systems, especially in the second half of the 20th century, have served democracy poorly (see, e.g., Gans, 2003; Herman & Chomsky, 1988; McChesney, 1999). Media reform efforts tend to stall unless grounded in broader movement building, in which individual activists and organizations work in concert to challenge systemic inequalities (Croteau & Hoynes, 2001; Morris, 1984; Ryan, 2004).

Marginalized populations' lack of access to the news media is not easily remedied. Using news media to engage in public debates requires skill and infrastructure—resources rarely at the command of individuals. Unorganized workers receiving pink slips do not issue media advisories condemning their layoffs, for instance; similarly, DV victims do not call press conferences. Hence, to gain access to mainstream news media, marginalized voices need support from organized sponsors with a communication infrastructure. In the absence of such support, they need to form collective actors that, in addition to promoting a defined political agenda, can build and sustain the communication infrastructure, analyze barriers to news media access, and develop strategies for challenging them. Here, the need for collaboration between communication activists and scholars becomes apparent.

INTEGRATING MOVEMENTS AND NEWS MEDIA: ACTION AND REFLECTION

To overcome barriers to accessing the news media and to promote the anti-DV movement's messages, Ryan and Jeffreys, representing the two organizations of MRAP and RICADV, respectively, worked to build a shared reflexive practice. Practically speaking, we wanted to engage in communication activism to lessen interpersonal violence, a real and present danger that affects one in every four women over their lifetimes (Tjaden & Thoennes, 2000), not including child witnesses who often reproduce violent patterns in later relationships. On another level, we wanted to challenge communication scholarship that underplayed or overplayed individual or organizational potential (power) to exercise effective agency vis-à-vis media institutions. Existing models of media–movement interaction left unanswered many questions regarding how skillful social actors, understanding media contexts, develop effective media strategies (Ryan, 1991). We shared Morris and Staggenborg's (2004) view that media systems may constrain movement options but do not determine them, such that "social structures cannot deliberate, imagine, strategize or engage in decision-making; human actors, navigating a matrix of social structures, initiate these activities. Strategic decisions figure prominently in determining movement outcomes" (p. 188). In other words, informed leaders engaged in collective decision making maximize their movements' efficacy (Morris & Staggenborg, 2004; see also Ganz, 2000; Jasper, 2004).

How do movement organizers know, however, which strategies are best? Rooted in the Greek word for generalship (*strategia*), strategy assumes a unit of analysis greater than the individual. Although individuals can position themselves to maximize their power *within* existing structures, individuals rarely amass sufficient resources to launch structural challenges. Efforts to challenge power relations in political, economic, or media institutions, therefore, generally presuppose one or more collective actors working in concert — sharing grievances, worldviews, analyses, identities, and resources. Collaboration is even more critical when the challenging group is comprised of constituencies facing multiple structural inequalities, such as age, class, colonialisms past and present, ethnicity and race, gender, language, and sexuality.

Movement strategists' goal is to channel limited resources to best advance the goals of marginalized constituencies that those movements represent. Access to mainstream news media, communication equipment, cultural resonances (e.g., a history of struggle and a shared understanding of equality and civil rights), labor, movement-controlled media, social networks, and space are among the resources that social movement actors tap in building sustained protest against identified structural inequalities (Gamson, 1990; Morris, 1984).

To act strategically, social movement actors evaluate existing historical conditions and then position their forces (e.g., allies, base, and networks) and resources (e.g., cultural, financial, political, and social) to best advantage. Speaking from the Chilean experience, Harnecker (2001) conceptualized this strategic positioning as the conjuncture of social forces (*la coyuntura de fuerzas*). Her focus on *conjuncture* embeds actors in historical relationships located in specific spaces and times; her emphasis on *forces* highlights *collective* actors as dynamic, intentional subjects who mobilize — for or against — other social forces, arrangements, and practices. This approach avoids the determinist bent of studies that focus on how existing social arrangements reproduce inequality and marginalization, yet it allows social movement organizers to develop strategies as they weigh their best "options under pressure" (Williams, 1976, p. 87).

Successful challengers — in this case, DV survivors and allies — form a collective force that breaks through structural barriers by leveraging resources and relationships at their command. Often, successes reap modest results—*reforms*, in political science parlance. Should the social movement strategy produce cumulative victories, structural inequalities become more vulnerable to attack and the social movement gains ground.

Strategists' approaches vary to match not only the general historical period but the conditions within specific institutional arenas (Rucht, 1988), as a winning strategy in one political or economic area may not work in another arena. Cutting and Themba-Nixon (2006) also stressed that strategies vary with each constituency's culture and history of struggle. Moreover, state actions and reactions vary in intensity (Alimi, 2007b). Thus, strategists must concretely assess shifting forces, positioned actors, and related conditions in each arena before deciding the best overall strategy (and related incremental tactics) for moving their players.

Although overall strategy guides a movement's news media strategy, that strategy requires additional research on the news media arena at that moment in time. In planning media strategy, collective actors (within their capacity) assess the news media arena as a whole, but they also consider variations in power dynamics in relevant local news markets. They map the discursive opportunities presented by news media institutions of interest, estimating the relative standing of their movement (Ferree, Gamson, Gerhard, & Rucht, 2002), and they weigh news media and public familiarity with their issues and frames. They also may consider conjunctures and tensions between governmental communication policies and business initiatives.

On the level of a single institution, as contrasted to the news media arena, collective strategists consider how reporters' news-gathering practices and news norms shape the conjuncture within which the social movement must negotiate. For instance, social movement actors must accommodate reportorial deadlines and pitch their story ideas within the conventions of mainstream news criteria that stress "balanced "accounts, even in situations of profound imbalance. Institutional news norms and news-gathering routines, therefore, shape not only access but also how news is framed.

Movement organizations also enter framing contests under conditions not of their making, generally struggling uphill against cultural norms. Social movements seek to highlight inequalities so chronic that they become taken for granted, accepted as norms (normal) for all. Additionally, movement organizers must challenge mainstream news conventions that typically interpret power in individual terms and, thereby, obscure systemic disparities. They must maneuver around the news media's penchant for proximate events, such as the weather, traffic, and flu season. They take advantage of the news media's interest in the unexpected in daily life, be it humorous or tragic. In initiating strategic challenges to existing media arrangements, collective actors must incorporate small openings in news norms to build toward larger ones. In all of the above, from structural analyses on a meta-industry level to news routines within institutions to framing strategies and news tactics, communication scholars may be of use.

New media—such as cable, satellite, internet, and cell phones—offer new possibilities for leveling the media playing field.[2] In many cases, a blogger, alternative news website, or independent journalist with a handheld camera not only breaks a story but reaches vast audiences. Despite increased opportunities to disseminate movement messages via new media, however, the digital divide remains significant and communication via new media remains labor intensive. To attract traffic, websites need constant refreshing with new content. If movement organizations lack the infrastructure and labor power to sustain traditional media campaigns, they may encounter comparable problems with new media. Websites may be launched but irregularly updated, as an overburdened staff person assumes the additional role of webmaster. Opposition and alternative journalists themselves are underresourced, with few receiving regular salary or benefits.

Moreover, movement messages are not posted in a vacuum. Corporate marketers with hefty budgets incorporate new media in their integrated marketing campaigns to woo the critical youth audience. With websites such as YouTube, powerful sponsors, as well as individual bloggers, flood the web with content, with anti-immigrant blogging offering a case in point (see Ryan, 2007). Social movement organizations must not only attract kindred spirits but position their voices strategically in a noisy, competitive environment. Although the media have changed, the challenges of inequality and marginalization continue. New media provide possibilities but no escape from the challenges of planning, implementing, and sustaining a movement-building media strategy from a position of disadvantage. Tasks shift but still demand labor time, technical skill, group consensus, message clarity, sustainability, and a collective assessment of discursive opportunities (Ferree et al., 2002). There also is a danger of overestimation: Attracted by the promised ease of virtual communities, movement communicators may underestimate the difficulty of building trust and sociability online (Barab, 2008; Lazar & Preece, 2002).

Given these ongoing challenges, studies of media–movement interactions (e.g., Barker-Plummer, 2002; Gamson, 2000; Gamson & Goodson, 2000; Gitlin, 1980; Hoynes, 2005) remain valuable. More recently, researchers have collaborated with activists to advance understanding of strategic choices (Jasper, 2004) entailed in movement communication work (see, e.g., Carragee, 2005; Dichter, 2005; Kidd, Barker-Plummer, & Rodríguez, 2005; see also the essays in Frey & Carragee, 2007). Although scholars and activists alike recognize the constraints imposed by mainstream news conventions and routines, we hesitate to boycott mainstream news media, given their convening authority in U.S. society (Gamson, 1998). Movement activists seek news media access in "hope ... at least of breaking the appearance of unanimity which is the greater part of the symbolic force of the dominant discourse" (Bourdieu, 1999, p. viii).[3]

Communication activism scholarship provides a framework for creating and integrating knowledge that addresses the issues just described. Relevant literature is threaded throughout many disciplines—political science, sociology (particularly, social movement studies), organizational studies, planning, marketing, political economy, cultural studies, and, especially, communication (e.g., Barker-Plummer, 1996; Carragee & Roefs, 2004; Dagron, 2001; Frey & Carragee, 2007; Huesca, 1996; Kidd, 2003; Riaño, 1994; Servaes, 2008; Waisbord, n.d.; White, 1994). Still, much remains unknown about interactions between movements and media. Few studies track media–movement interaction for any sustained period of time (Klandermans, 1992); consequently, movement successes or failures in negotiating within media logics and arenas remain poorly understood and undertheorized. Moreover, as new media rework conventional media–movement interactions, attending to these dynamics becomes an even more acute concern for democracies (Castells, 2007; Dichter, 2005; Gans, 2003).

GLOBAL SOUTH PARTICIPATORY MODELS

We focus here on participatory communication, a Global South approach to countering lost public communication space. In recent years, social movements in the Global North have experimented with participatory communication models (de Jong, Shaw, & Stammers, 2005; Kidd, 2003), drawing from similar developments in the Global South (Dagron, 2001; Melkote & Steeves, 2001; Okigbo & Festus, 2004; Riaño, 1994), to stress communicative democracy as a core component of attempts to challenge structural inequalities of power.

Participatory approaches diverge from top-down communication models typical of neoliberal development strategies in several ways (see Bah, 2008). Influenced by Brazilian philosopher and educator, Paolo Freire and other proponents of liberation theology (Steeves, 2001), grassroots women's movements (Riaño, 1994), and peasant (Harter, Sharma, Pant, Singhal, & Sharma, 2007) and youth movements (Dichter, 2005), participatory communication models employ community dialogue to link individual transformation with broader social changes. Such dialogue encourages community-generated content and dissemination, strengthening local leadership in the process (Servaes, 2008; White, 1994).

Participatory communication models privilege human development, not necessarily on an individual level but as a collective process of empowerment (e.g., increasing the ability of disempowered groups to affect desired change). A first step involves mapping underrepresentation and misrepresentation of marginalized communities, such as people of color, people who are working class or poor, and gays and lesbians. A second step involves mapping inequalities in communication systems. Working in tandem with marginalized communities, participatory communicators then develop strategic responses that strengthen the abilities of marginalized constituencies to communicate on their behalf. Communicative democracy, participatory communicators argue, is fundamental to democratic change, for without it, marginalized groups lose "the right and power to intervene in the social order and change it through political praxis" (Freire, 1994, p. xiii).

Participatory models encourage learning through the planning and assessment of communication activist projects, and through reflection on those activist experiences (Chakravartty, 2006; Dichter, 2005; Harter et al., 2007; Kincaid & Figueroa, 2009). This emphasis facilitates collaborations between scholars and activist groups, which are eager to work with scholars to articulate systematically their communication models. The expansion of participatory action research methods and projects reflects this trend.

Communication theorists, however, have flagged conceptual gaps in participatory models that often are obscured by enthusiastic rhetoric. White (1994), for instance, noted the dramatic language linking participation and grassroots empowerment, arguing that

> the euphoric word "participation" has become a part of development jargon. Now, no respectable development project can be proposed without using this "in" word. More than this, a project proposed nowadays can rarely be funded without some provision of the "participation" of the people. ... Provision for "participation of the people" is likely to become as integral to any project as "evaluation." (p. 16)

What passes as participation, however, varies from project to project, making comparison and evaluation difficult. Although interpersonal and group communication experiments can define and measure participation relatively easily (Waisbord, n.d.), measuring participation in mediated communication projects is more problematic. Community radio provides a case in point, with some community radio experiments operationalizing participation as the creation of media content by marginalized individuals or by organized groups comprised of marginalized constituencies; at other times, participation refers to creating media in indigenous languages, with participation measured by audience size (Dagron, 2001).

At present, there is little uniformity in definitions or measures of participation; scholars have yet to clarify how much and what type of participation suffices for a communication initiative to be called "participatory,"[4] and which constituencies need be involved for a communication initiative to be considered as participatory. As Waters (2000) concluded, "Surprisingly few communication researchers have attempted to develop methodological tools to inform this practice" (p. 98).

In the last decade, a host of scholars have clarified core concepts in participatory communication models, such as participation, power, empowerment, community, and control. Concomitantly, social movement scholars (e.g., Staggenborg, 2002) and communication theorists (e.g., Kincaid & Figueroa, 2009; Melkote & Steeves, 2001; Rozario, 1997; Wilkins, 2000) have noted the need to clarify relationships between concepts, such as between participation and empowerment. These concepts and interrelations, critics stress, need to be tested and refined in recurring cycles of concrete engagement.

These issues remain when U.S. activists apply Freirian participatory models to mediated Global North conditions. In the current U.S. climate, social movements are weak and fragmented, isolated from communication scholars and existing media. Movement-controlled media have not operationalized consistent measures of participation, and although U.S. political parties claim that new media allow for broader participation in fund-raising and mobilization, control tends to remain centralized.

Perhaps the most consistent experiments in participatory methods have emerged in marketing, where researchers have perfected nonempowering participatory techniques that solicit audiences' opinions and discard self-actualizing aspects of Freirian pedagogy. Focus groups represent one such technique that taps citizens' opinions without forming ongoing learning communities (*comunidades de base*) that act and reflect together on a shared goal. Without the collective, empowerment-focused dialogue of Freirian-inspired learning communities, marginalized constituencies lose opportunities to map existing power relations; consequently, power inequalities remain both unnamed and unaddressed.

How participatory communication models address conflicts within social movements and between movements and allies also warrants further attention. Communication can be undermined by power disparities within movements, as well as by power dynamics among academics, community-based organizations, funders, government officials, movement groups, nongovernmental organizations, and nonprofit organizations. Such power asymmetries undercut claims regarding empowerment via participation. For instance, Kincaid and Figueroa (2009) noted that "scholars and practitioners agree that community members should determine the goals of development themselves, but the problem-specific nature of funding often means that external change agents impose development goals on communities" (pp. 507–508). Moreover, funding controls, program controls, and related problems compound, leading to "conceptualizations of power as possibly the thorniest problematic issue facing researchers" (Huesca, 2001, p. 430).

Without attending to power inequalities, communication researchers cannot assess empowerment claims of participatory communication initiatives. Although activist and advocacy groups may espouse participatory communication, in practice, it often falls to group leaders to negotiate entry to multiple power arenas—legislatures, media, private foundations, and state and local regulatory agencies. Moreover, these groups do not operate in a vacuum; other advocates and activists compete for influence in culture, politics, and other arenas. In fluid, shifting environments, some organizations may lack skills, resources, and infrastructure to gain or sustain influence; other groups may compromise, drifting toward projects that minimally challenge existing inequalities of power (Bah, 2008; Rozario, 1997).

In summary, to maximize and sustain structural gains (in contrast to short-term gains or gains that advance a leader or group at the expense of a broader movement), social movement organizations must understand how power relations are structured concretely and how these structures are best challenged under actual conditions. U.S. social movement theorists call these power dynamics the "structuring of political opportunity" (see, e.g., Gamson & Meyer, 1996, p. 276; Meyer, 2004, p. 127), and Latin-American theorists speak of a precise assessment of the "political conjuncture" (Harnecker, 2001, p. 127). In either case, mapping power and negotiating contested terrain necessitate intentional collective activity that is both skillful and sustainable.

Social movement organizations that adopt a poorly conceived strategy, cannot implement a strategy effectively and consistently, or cannot adapt as conditions shift may worsen their situations. For example, rising news media visibility can exacerbate intergroup competition, inadvertently undermining trust between movement partners. Given their single-issue, single-constituency structure, most U.S. social movements attempting participatory communication models need to address infrastructure, resource, skill, and size disparities that hamper establishing participatory communication processes. Diverging interests also arise *between* researchers and movement actors (see, e.g., Cagle, 2007; Waters, 2000). Insufficiently addressed, these differences undermine the democratic impact of participatory processes (Waters, 2000); in fact, "liberating processes (participation in the collective construction of identity) can generate oppressive consequences" (Huesca, 2001, p. 430).

These examples suggest the challenges we have faced as members of a scholar–activist team working together for almost 2 decades. Our collaboration grew from shared values, theories, methods, and experiences in U.S. social movements; we both embraced Freirian-influenced models of community organizing and participatory action research, although in distinct settings. Ryan had encountered Freirian organizing methods in Chile during Allende's Popular Unity government, as well as in U.S. adult education projects that used liberation educational approaches. Jeffreys had been trained in popular education as advanced by the Highlander Center, which served as a halfway house in the civil rights movement (see, e.g., Durham, 2005; Gaventa, 1991; Morris, 1984; Murphy, 2003; Wyatt, 2002). Additionally, we each had worked in a variety of learning communities (Senge, 2006). We shared criticisms of the Saul Alinsky-inspired, pragmatic models of organizing (see, e.g., Alinsky, 1971) that had dominated U.S. activism and wanted to develop an alternate organizing model resonant with black organizers, such as Septima Clark and Ella Baker, who fostered

> emancipatory dialog that leads to expanded individual and communal consciousness and power, with no hierarchical distinction among participants in dialog. ... The central focus should be face-to-face egalitarian dialog to initiate and sustain a collective process of reflection and action. (Steeves, 2001, p. 400)

We, thus, saw participatory communication as central to building a new model of organizing for the Global North. Whereas other nations might have multigenerational social movements, U.S. movements tended to rise and fall within one generation. Our first step, therefore, was to form a sustainable collective actor that could undertake systematic dialogue. To accomplish this goal, we had to build a shared culture and identity. In that effort, "dialogic praxis offer[ed] a promising mode of entrée" (Huesca, 2001, p. 429).

FORMING COLLECTIVE ACTORS: THE MEDIA RESEARCH ACTION PROJECT

Catalyzed by the social movements of the mid-20th century, U.S. social movement scholarship blossomed in the mid-1980s. As part of that trend, pioneering social movement scholar William A. Gamson formed, with colleagues (Ryan among them), the MRAP. MRAP members have met weekly for 20 years, producing several generations of scholars, research action projects, simulation games, and related publications (see Carragee, 2005; Croteau & Hoynes, 1994, 2001; Croteau, Hoynes, & Carragee, 1993, 1996; Croteau; Hoynes, & Ryan, 2005; Gamson, 1992; Gamson & Goodson, 2000; Goodson, 2005; Hoynes, 1994; Hoynes & Croteau, 1990; Ryan, 1991; Ryan et al., 2006; Ryan, Carragee, & Schwerner, 1998; Ryan & Gamson, 2006; Schwerner, 2005).

Although many MRAP members had activist roots, academic–activist collaboration proved harder to sustain than envisioned. Although scholars in relatively new fields of study (e.g., Africana, Chicano, and other ethnic studies; environmental studies; gender studies; labor studies; and queer studies) had maintained ties to the movements from which those fields emerged, researchers in the more generic field of social movements lacked common projects and languages. Moreover, by the mid-1980s, when social movement studies gained legitimacy as an academic field, many social movements were experiencing a downturn, marked by burnout, conflicts, and resource reduction (Springer, 2005). As a result of social movement scholars focusing heavily on academic publishing, scholarly works with obvious value for activists (e.g., Gamson, 1990; Gitlin, 1980; Morris, 1984) remained largely unknown in social movement circles (Bevington & Dixon, 2005).

Additionally, although MRAP members had roots in various social movements, as a collective actor, MRAP had yet to earn standing in community, labor, and movement circles. Although members thought that their work was of direct utility, many movement groups had negative experiences with researchers and, consequently, were hesitant to collaborate again.

To address negative experiences and to test the utility of its work, MRAP needed to establish routine dialogues; members wanted activists and scholars to reflect on movement experiences and to link their experiences to relevant cases, concepts, and methods from other movements and scholars. MRAP members would serve both as receptive audiences for activists' experiences and as conduits carrying activists' unanswered questions back to the academy.

Keeping in mind the issues that had arisen in prior MRAP workshops with activist groups, Ryan began to distill concepts and tools from works by U.S. and British social movement and communication theorists (e.g., Gamson & Lasch, 1983; Gitlin, 1980; Golding, Murdoch, & Scheslinger, 1986; Tuchman, 1978). Building on that work and in dialogue with movement activists, MRAP sought to identify communication opportunities for movements challenging power inequalities. Group members respected incisive critiques that highlighted structural inequalities permeating mainstream media systems (see, e.g., Herman & Chomsky, 1988), but they wanted to explore how organized movements could challenge structural inequalities and press for broader communication opportunities. Beginning in 1987, MRAP members worked with anti-intervention (opposing U.S. interference in the internal affairs of other sovereign nations), community, and labor groups to create workshops addressing patterns of misrepresentation and underrepresentation in news content and barriers to access. After each workshop, MRAP trainers reviewed participating groups' successes, failures, and best practices, distilling these for workshops and publications (see Ryan, 1991).

The workshops diverged from standard public relations training in recognizing that mainstream news media offer an uneven playing field that favors organizations with ample resources and relatively mainstream messages (see Drake, this volume). Individuals, and even groups, attempting to raise grievances, thus, face serious obstacles glossed over by pragmatic movement organizers intent on creating coalitions around programmatic demands. MRAP found that groups were preoccupied with two recurring obstacles: (a) inequalities in communication infrastructure (e.g., framing tools, media databases, news archives, and sustained relations with news media institutions), labor power, and skills; and (b) disadvantages faced by movements attempting to develop and promote frames that challenged mainstream views.

In terms of resources and skills, coalitions were not homogenous but, instead, included a wide range of "media-haves," larger movement groups and well-resourced nonprofits with considerable communication capacity, mixed with "media-have-nots," small nonprofits and movement groups with limited labor power and little sustainable communication capacity. Media-haves could move quickly to implement media plans, and, with the best intentions, take charge, leaving media-have-nots in their wake. The resulting divisions and resentments undermined movement building, which grows by strengthening not dominating allies.

Moreover, coalitions often faced tensions over how their messages would be framed, especially with regard to whether frames should challenge underlying assumptions about marginalized constituencies. Grassroots and more radical groups often thought that they should and, consequently, used a political moment to promote frames challenging mainstream assumptions. Others in the coalition, intent on winning short-term battles, preferred to link programmatic demands (e.g., no cuts in human services) to existing, widely accepted news frames. Despite being in the same coalitions and movement groups, the media-have-nots often found themselves outvoted or their messages minimized.

MRAP argued that this condition would not change without sustained attention to *communication capacity building*, establishing resources and routines for communication strategizing, coordination, training, message development, and postcampaign evaluation. Explaining that the most successful movement groups had developed their communication capacity over several years, Ryan suggested that groups "start small, build big." Influenced by resource mobilization scholars (e.g., Gamson, 1990) and organizational theorists (e.g., Senge, 2006), MRAP attempted to consolidate and share what it had learned.

Jeffreys, a community organizer planning media strategies for a movement challenging defunding of subsidized housing and welfare programs, attended a 1990 MRAP workshop, and we began to work together regularly after that, even when Jeffreys shifted jobs. By the mid-1990s, we joined with other local communication activists to create Media Fellows, a media capacity-building program for community organizations. Building on past MRAP workshops, the Media Fellows curriculum stressed that communication strategy grew from organizing strategy. We urged activists to involve those directly affected by issues when framing their messages. We reaffirmed the importance of activists "talking politics" (Gamson, 1992), understood broadly as talking about power, with each other and with potential allies, and we stressed the need for a communication infrastructure and long-term consistency. "It takes a whole movement to raise an issue" became our general slogan.

ESTABLISHING COLLABORATION: THE RHODE ISLAND COALITION AGAINST DOMESTIC VIOLENCE

Just as the Media Fellows program began in 1996, Jeffreys assumed a new position as communication coordinator for RICADV. For the next 10 years, this organization provided a valuable laboratory for our shared communication activism and research. Our activism built the communication capacity of the movement against DV in Rhode Island; our research distilled lessons about communication activism, linking those lessons to the theories and practices of other social movements.

Before we summarize the specific work that is the focus of this chapter, a brief description of methods used to construct that summary is warranted. Jeffreys kept notes on every meeting, phone conversation, and group session that involved framing messages (called a "message caucus"). After each major campaign or landmark, we met with participating RICADV members and staff to reconstruct events and to reflect on outcomes. Our approach creates a shared history (Portelli, 1997) in the tradition of critical oral histories (Blight & Lang, 1995) and history from below (Burke, 2001). This description of our collaboration used both RICADV archives and transcripts of the shared history interviews.[5]

A women's movement offshoot, RICADV, at that time, was a small statewide organization working to improve state policies and services about DV. Organized as a coalition, its six service and advocacy organizations covered each of Rhode Island's six counties. Additionally, RICADV included SOAR, the DV survivors group. In 1995, RICADV received a U.S. Department of Health and Human Services discretionary grant that enabled it to hire for a year its first communication staff person. As Deb Debare, the executive director, recalled:

> It was a big risk for us because I don't like to hire people with a 1-year commitment, not knowing where follow-up funding will come from. What we did as an organization was "start small, build big." We added resources one step at a time—one staff person at a time, one computer at a time, one database at a time. Through these little steps, we built sys-

tems, weaving them into a communications department. But it started with one small step—hiring communication staff in February 1996. (personal communication, March 25, 2004)

Prior to Jeffrey's hiring, RICADV communication initiatives mostly were internal. Its newsletter, for example, was circulated only to members, and public education occurred via a yearly conference. Staff spent time on community outreach, but not on communication. To illustrate the low level of press work, Linda Impagliazzo, executive director of Blackstone Valley Advocacy Center, one of RICADV's six member agencies, offered the following story:

> In 1988, a Pawtucket, RI woman, Maria Correira, was beaten to death in a particularly brutal murder by her husband, who was convicted. We decided not to do outreach to the press, although we responded when they [reporters] called us. But we did not reach out to the media, and this was pretty much the norm before Karen [Jeffreys] came. We knew some people in the media, some of us more than others, but none of us maintained a routinely updated press list. We didn't proactively call reporters; we expected them to call us. (personal communication, May 21, 2004)

RICADV's members already were heavily burdened and were not particularly interested in adding more work. As, Diane D'Errico, a staff member at the DV shelter, Elizabeth Buffam Chase House, remembered:

> At this point, no one had communication staff. We were about client services and constantly pulled into funding work on top of service work. The last thing we were thinking about was communication, much less developing a strategic plan for it. (personal communication, May 21, 2004)

Nor did member organizations expect much support from RICADV. "At the time, I mostly considered coalition meetings a nuisance. I had to go to stay in touch, but I didn't think that our organization was getting much from the coalition per se," said Impagliazzo (personal communication, May 21, 2004). Member organizations, therefore, greeted Jeffreys's hiring with benign indifference.

SYSTEMATIZING THE COMMUNICATION OF THE RHODE ISLAND COALITION AGAINST DOMESTIC VIOLENCE

Jeffreys and Ryan adapted the Media Fellows curriculum for RICADV's purposes and brainstormed regularly by telephone about specific RICADV projects. Jeffreys started to develop communication systems, including a media caucus that helped groups to frame political messages; available RICADV members and organizers would "caucus" to develop and refine messages in teams to allow the broadest participation possible in the creation of messages (Ryan, Jeffreys, & Blozie, in press). Increasingly, communication was integrated into the organization's overall strategic planning. As we reflected on what did and did not work, our model's core tenets began to emerge (see the Appendix) and they continue to evolve with every project.

Taking to heart MRAP's slogan of "Start Small, Build Big," Jeffreys began her work at RICADV by assessing the existing situation. She first interviewed the executive directors of RICADV's six county-level organizations, asking how they envisioned making progress on DV issues in Rhode Island and what role communication could play. She also asked about their existing communication infrastructure and systems—such as clipping files, databases, fax systems, and newsletters—and what communication training and technical assistance they wanted to receive.

The executive directors initially were dubious. As Impagliazzo, the first director interviewed, explained:

> I appreciated the effort at outreach, but was only cautiously optimistic. We brainstormed for a long time. I was surprised; I had good ideas, lovely ideas that hadn't occurred to me until we made the time to sit down and talk. But I didn't necessarily think anything would happen. (personal communication, May 21, 2004)

Despite the executive directors' hesitation, Jeffreys slowly strengthened her working relationships with member groups by building communication tools and infrastructure, and making them readily available.

After nearly 5 years (1996–2000), increasingly, member groups turned to Jeffreys for substantive communication support. Together, Jeffreys and member groups chose audience-appropriate communication venues, including face-to-face communication, such as door-knocking and lobbying; developed news media databases and protocols; and, using a participatory caucus format, framed messages. This combined strengthening of internal communication systems and communication with members, base supporters, and news media outlets was evidence of a solid communication infrastructure.

By Jeffreys's fifth year (2000), RICADV could provide reliable news media outreach for both policy initiatives and direct actions (e.g., demonstrations and rallies). The Farrell case then arose, providing, as explained below, an opportunity for RICADV to demonstrate its growing ability to integrate organizing on three fronts: the legislative arena, the news media, and grassroots participation of movement members and supporters.

The Farrell Case

Located in Pawtucket, the Blackstone Valley Advocacy Center (hereafter Blackstone) serves the densely populated Blackstone Valley, including the towns of Central Falls, Cumberland, Lincoln, and Pawtucket. On New Year's Day, January 1, 2000, Central Falls police arrested Michael Farrell, the town's state representative, on domestic assault charges for punching his girlfriend in the face. Impagliazzo explained how she learned of the incident 3 days later when her local daily newspaper reported it in a front-page story:

> On Tuesday, January 4, 2000, I went to Memorial, our local hospital, to receive a contribution for Blackstone's work. As I waited for the hospital's community relations officer, I opened our local daily newspaper, the *Pawtucket Times*. There, plastered across the front page in bold type, was the headline "Rep. Farrell Charged in Assault on Girlfriend." (O'Connor, 2000, p. A1)
>
> I stood there, my mouth open in disbelief. I couldn't wait to call Karen [Jeffreys, RICADV's director of communication]. As soon as I left the hospital, I called RICADV. I said, "Karen, we have to do something. I don't know *what* we can do but we have to respond to this." We took off from there, working together.
>
> Karen asked me, "What do you want to do? Ask him to resign?" I told her that I had to check with my board of directors before taking things that far, but short of calling for his resignation, I did want to make a strong statement. He needs to be held accountable! (personal communication, May 21, 2004)

Blackstone and RICADV agreed that an effective reaction needed to be immediate. "We seized the moment," said Jeffreys." If we had waited a day, it would have been old news. I bagged everything planned for that day to work with Linda" (personal communication, May 21, 2004).

Impagliazzo had called Jeffreys at 11 a.m. and by lunchtime, they had conducted a media caucus to clarify Blackstone's message. They cowrote a press release expressing Blackstone's disappointment and outrage over Farrell's DV arrest. Blackstone's (2000d) press release stated that Farrell's alleged behavior calls to question his fitness for elected office. We question his ability to lead our community given these actions. If proven guilty, his behavior as a perpetrator of domestic violence sends the wrong message, especially to our young people who need to learn that there is no excuse for abuse.

The press statement also commended Central Falls police for insisting that "all perpetrators of domestic violence will be held accountable," and it praised community residents who contacted police, stressing that "domestic violence is everyone's business." The press release concluded by stating that "it is only through the continued involvement of all of us in the community—police, courts, media, friends, co-workers, neighbors, and family—that we will end domestic violence."

The next day, Wednesday, January 5, 2000, a second front-page article in the *Pawtucket Times* reported "Farrell's 'Fitness for Office' Questioned: Director of Women's Shelter 'Outraged' by State Lawmaker's Alleged Assault on Girlfriend" (Baron, 2000a, p. A1). The article drew heavily from Impagliazzo's press statement; indeed, the article's continuation inside the newspaper was subtitled, "Women's Shelter Speaks Out" (Baron, 2000b, p. A6). Farrell declined to comment on the article, citing advice of counsel.

In close consultation with Blackstone's board of directors, Impaglizzo and staff decided to keep pressure on Farrell. "We were going to try to get this representative to resign," Impaglizzo explained. "This was unacceptable in our district—anywhere for that matter. We were going to work to get him to resign, regardless of the consequences" (personal communication, May 21, 2004).

The "consequences" were not spelled out, but a state representative has power and can retaliate in both direct and indirect ways. In this case, Farrell could informally label Blackstone's staff as troublemakers, suggest that state human service agencies reconsider contracts with the shelter, or simply ask the state treasurer to review Blackstone's financial records.

When Farrell pleaded no contest to assault 16 days later on January 20, 2000, Blackstone called for his resignation, garnering prominent articles in the *Pawtucket Times* (Baron, 2000b) and in the statewide newspaper of record, the *Providence Journal* (Hill, 2000; Laplante, 2000). Both articles in the *Providence Journal* quoted Blackstone's (2000b) press statement flagging Farrell's history of DV (his prior DV assault charge had been expunged at his request).

Building on this coverage, Impaglizzo at Blackstone and Jeffreys at RICADV mapped a three-prong communication campaign involving outreach to legislators, the news media, and Farrell's constituents with the goal of forcing Farrell's resignation. With the coalition's support, Blackstone selected three tactics (actions):

1. Blackstone (2000a) would prepare a bilingual (Spanish and English) mailing to 10,000 voters in Farrell's district, urging them to call Farrell's office and demand his resignation.
2. Blackstone would lobby key political figures, including Central Falls' mayor and other legislators, urging them to press for Farrell's resignation as well.
3. Blackstone and RICADV scheduled a rally demanding Farrell's resignation for January 27 at the State House rotunda.

For their part, RICADV statewide staff members would lobby their news media and statehouse contacts, asking them to press for Farrell's resignation.

News media interest in this story continued. In addition to print coverage, a local radio talk show host, WPRO-AM's Dan Yorke, took up and kept the case alive by interviewing the victim and polling listeners. With a rally scheduled and flyers about be mailed to his entire district, Farrell resigned on Tuesday, January 25, offering a "personal apology for my actions on New Year's Day" and stating that "I am seeking professional counseling for domestic abuse, alcohol abuse and anger management" (Baron, 2000c, p. A10). Using RICADV's communication infrastructure, Blackstone (2000c) immediately praised Farrell's decision.

The *Providence Journal* reported Farrell's resignation on the front page (Saltzman, 2000) and, in an editorial titled "These Batterers Should Go" (2000), cited "public opinion" as the force compelling Farrell's "belated" (p. A18) resignation. A January 27 front-page *Pawtucket Times* story by Madden (2000) opined that all three of RICADV's tactics had contributed to Farrell's resignation—calls from the legislature for his ouster, a sustained "media firestorm" (p. A1), and mobilization by groups opposed to DV.

The case was not over, however, as Farrell began to claim that the physical abuse had been "mutual," and he suggested that gender bias was at play, stating that "abuse is a two-way street. Unfortunately, abuse against men is never reported" (Madden, 2000, pp. A6, A1). Continuing in this vein, 3 days later, Farrell announced in the *Providence Journal* that he would run in the special election being held for the legislative seat he just had vacated, and that he would "tell his side of the story" (Schaefer, 2000, p. A1) by going door to door and holding community meetings.

Impagliazzo and Jeffreys brainstormed about how to respond. Instead of challenging Farrell's right to run, they decided that Impagliazzo (2000) should write an op-ed in the *Pawtucket Times*. The op-ed mentioned Farrell briefly but then segued to a general explanation of batterers' urge to control their victims, stressing that DV is not a private matter; its elimination depends on public will. Facing growing resistance, Farrell decided not to run. Meantime, we had educated thousands of people about DV (Bakst, 2000). We moved on but met later to distill lessons from the case, as such reflection serves both movement and theory building.

Aftermath and Reflection

Our success in forcing Farrell to resign provided an external measure of RICADV's growing communication strength. MRAP had estimated that an underresourced movement organization typically works for 5 to 7 years to create the communication systems required to function as a routine news source. RICADV's success in the Farrell case documented that RICADV's standing had risen in the 5 years since Jeffreys's hiring. This success had been achieved incrementally in steps that involved RICADV strengthening organizational communication internally, establishing communication systems, and building ongoing working relations with reporters. By 2000, RICADV could support a 30-day communication campaign. RICADV's communication capacity, carefully constructed and tested in practice, underpinned Blackstone's effective campaign to area news media. RICADV had made strides in becoming recognized as a serious news source, which buttressed its confrontation with a public official who battered his partner. When RICADV and Blackstone won this case, their power grew yet again.

DISCUSSION

By 2000, U.S. women's movements and allies had been working for 3 decades to end DV and could claim significant progress, including the establishment of support services, preventive education, research, and the training of public safety, social service, and health-care providers (Bart & Moran, 1993; Tierney, 1982). Many advocacy groups had pursued proactive communication strategies to raise public awareness and to stimulate public dialogue about DV as a social problem. To this end, they had worked to become routine news sources, familiarizing themselves with news norms (e.g., deadlines, mainstream news criteria, and story formats) and establishing ongoing working relationships with journalists, and they had recommended shifts in news practices as well.

Despite these efforts, organized voices for the movement against DV, such as RICADV, seldom achieved standing as news sources, which MRAP and RICADV recognized as a measurable marker of power inequality. Global South models were appealing for their emphasis on participation but they did not address clearly how this power inequality could be challenged, and Global North power definitions (described later) did not clarify how to operate from a position of relative disempowerment. Hence, to catalyze change on a practical level, we, Ryan at MRAP and Jeffreys at RICADV, recognized a mutual need to develop a more robust concept of "power." Moreover, participatory communicators would benefit if we could clarify how participation influences empowerment. However, without clear definitions of participation, power, and empowerment, it was unclear how to assess whether participation increases power or represents little more than busy work. For instance, some critics have argued that neoliberal participatory practices in the Global South employ democratic rhetoric and forms but ignore, and, thereby, reinforce existing power inequalities (Bah, 2008; Rozario, 1997). Clarifying whether and how participation encourages empowerment was especially important in the Global North, where calls for participation coexist with widening power inequalities. Building on the Farrell case, we turn to our expansion of a definition of power in participatory communication.

Defining Power

As a starting point, we adopt Lukes's (2005) three-dimensional understanding of power, a conceptualization that is popular with both activists and scholars (Gaventa, 1982; Healey & Hinson, 2005). Lukes's model explains how established political, social, and cultural practices tend to reproduce existing power inequalities. Building on other scholar-activists' application of Lukes's model to U.S. social movement contexts (see, e.g., the Grassroots Policy Project; http://www.grassrootspolicy.org/power), we explore the model's utility for clarifying power dynamics in participatory communication organizing cases, such as the Farrell case.

Increasingly, social movements recognize communication inequality as a critical social disparity. Participatory communicators ask, "How can communication work support marginalized groups as they challenge inequalities of power that underlie communication disparities?" Addressing these disparities requires an understanding of how power and inequalities of power operate, and how they can be altered.

Power represents sustained capacity to operate within institutions, across institutions, throughout multi-institutional arenas, and, ultimately, in complex, multiarena fields comprised of all of the above. Through this elaborate mesh, societies set social agendas, allocate resources, make rules and contracts, enforce compliance, and develop shared beliefs, knowledge, and interpretations of social reality. When acting alone, individuals rarely can surmount inequalities of power embedded in cultural, economic, political, and social institutions. To become empowered change agents, individuals need to form collective actors that focus strategically on reshaping societal meaning making, priorities, rules, and resource allocation. However, left underdeveloped in existing participatory communication models is the process by which participation translates into collective empowerment, not for the single individual who gains standing but for the entire constituency grappling with systemic marginalization. To address this issue, we turn to Lukes's (2005) conception of "multidimensional power."

Lukes (2005) identified the first face of power as *decision making*, the ability/power to move a policy agenda in established institutional arenas; most notably, in government. The second face of power is less formal *agenda setting* via other social networks, and the third face represents the internalization of power inequalities as normal and uncontestable. Increasingly, social movement support organizations, such as Grassroots Policy Project and the globally focused Development Research Center (http://www.drc-citizenship.org), recognize the need for participatory movements to address the many layers of disempowerment that reinforce and often precede policy making. In other words, prior to arriving on the policy agenda, an issue needs to be recognized as worthy of society's attention; power, thus, rests in naming the issue as worthy of attention (see Drake, this volume). Conversely, power also rests in rejecting an issue, such as DV, as worthy of society's attention. Moving an issue from personal trouble to social problem meriting policy reform involves the second and third faces of power. Social institutions that control agenda setting and broader cultural norms may ignore a social problem and, thereby, keep it out of public discourse. Without public attention, social movements cannot mobilize for desired changes.

The anti-DV movement had long attended to Lukes's (2005) third face of power—ideology. Mainstream news media routinely treated DV incidents as private family tragedies that were no one else's business. To put the issue on the public's agenda, DV opponents needed to tackle many taken-for-granted assumptions about families, privacy, women's roles, and more. DV victims and their supporters found themselves, as do most social movements, confronting layers of structural inequalities. As Gaventa (1982) explained:

> Continual defeat gives rise not only to the conscious deferral of action but also to a sense of defeat, or a sense of powerlessness, that may affect the consciousness of potential challengers about grievances, strategies or possibilities for change. Participation denied over time may lead to acceptance of the role of non-participation, as well as to a failure to develop the political resources—skills, organization, consciousness—of political action. Power relationships may develop routines of non-challenge which require no particular action on the part of power holders to be maintained. (p. 255)

Delineating the routine practices of power holders begins to clarify how power works, why participation matters, and why members of marginalized communities so often remain unengaged. As Gaventa (1982) concluded:

> The total impact of a power relationship is more than the sum of its parts. Power serves to create power. Powerlessness serves to reinforce powerlessness. ... Historical investigation must occur to discover whether routines of non-conflict have been shaped, and, if so, how they are maintained. (p. 256)

Lukes's (2005) model cogently explains the longevity of established *power holders*, those social players with institutionalized capacity to influence agenda setting, cultural arenas, and decision making. As such, the model provides a *power lens* that dissects existing relations between the powerful and powerless. The model, however, does not provide a sufficient framework for establishing an *empowerment lens*. In focusing on power holders, the model assumes the existence of two additional dimensions of power—*the ability (or inability) to exercise physical force* and *the ability (or inability) to establish collective actors*—that are taken for granted by powerful forces. However, each dimension must be addressed as a precondition for communication empowerment for marginalized constituencies.

Operating within the movement against DV, it becomes abundantly clear that freedom from force/abuse is a dimension of communication empowerment. We, thus, pose as a fourth face of power *the ability to exert force over others;* in many cases, the ability to use violence with impunity. Speaking conversely from an empowerment lens, this fourth face represents the ability to not be subjected to abuse, as well as the ability to defend oneself when abuse occurs. Self-defense alone is not empowerment; empowerment would mean the right to walk the Earth without fear. For anyone who has experienced violence on a personal, community, or state level, physical force is a central element of power. Although the first face of power, formal decision making, at times, can control the use of force, such as the regulation of a state's police or a country's decision to go to war, we argue that, as with the informal agenda setting of the second face of power, systematic social patterns perpetrate, and they perpetuate physical control over marginalized constituencies. Although many in democratic societies probably take their physical safety—freedom from violence—for granted, it is not a given for DV survivors or members of other disempowered communities (e.g., gay, lesbian, and transgendered people; and people of color in the Global North and South). Nor have workers challenging inequitable distributions of capital been assured of freedom from violence. Unless this power dimension is explicitly named, violence as a core component of nonparticipation and forced participation remains obscured. The fear of violence works synergistically with the other faces of power to increase the risk associated with challenging the status quo and, thus, hampers the growth of social movements. An empowerment lens identifies and addresses this and other barriers to the formation of collective actors.

It is important to stress that collections of individuals with common grievances are not automatically collective actors; a collective actor assumes an organizational capacity to forge shared and sustainable change strategies, and to amass the skills, resources, and knowledge needed to refine and execute those strategies in multiple arenas, including the media and politics. Achieving this goal depends on intentional relationship building that entails talking politics, experimentation, and shared reflection. As Gamson's (1990) survey of 2 centuries of social protest concluded, "There is nothing natural about the ability to organize successfully" (p. 142). Organizing assumes the ability to construct cultures, infrastructures, networks, policy platforms, social identities, and strategies that can sustain ongoing efforts to counter the status quo.

In short, although individuals can resist existing power arrangements or can position themselves to maximize their power *within* existing power arrangements, efforts to change power structures generally presuppose the establishment of one or more collective actors working in concert. Those collective actors share grievances, develop a shared vision and worldview, analyze how power is maintained in their historical setting, and decide how they can best leverage their pooled resources to challenge and reconstruct those arrangements.

Scholars and activists applying Lukes's (2005) model implicitly flag this fifth power dimension. Stressing collective responses, scholar-activist Gaventa (1982) suggested that "the powerless must undergo a process of mobilization ... develop their own resources for challenge—organization, information, sustaining values—to counter the prevailing mobilization of bias" (p. 257). Similarly, Healey and Hinson (2005) urged that Lukes's model must address the need of marginalized constituencies to construct sustainable political and social infrastructure.

Not by chance does this insight emerge from scholars who have embedded themselves with movement actors. The need to expand the definition of power becomes clear when the shift is made from asking, "How does power work?" to asking the movement-building question, "How does empowerment work?" An empowerment lens recognizes that collective actors must attend to the physical safety of individuals challenging their marginalization. Without collective actors, members of marginalized communities cannot protect themselves, much less establish and sustain infrastructure needed to build movement strength in agenda setting, counterculture/knowledge production, decision making, and resource accumulation.

In summary, Lukes's (2005) three-dimensional power lens aptly analyzes existing power dynamics; specifically, how vested actors with standing maneuver in political power games. Attention to the two additional dimensions of power identified here, however, is a precondition for shifting from a power lens to an empowerment lens that informs challenges to power arrangements in any given historical conjuncture.

As noted earlier, social movements may encourage participation without encouraging empowerment. To clarify this distinction, a participatory approach to communication operating from an empowerment lens would include these questions when mapping strategic choices:

- In the face of violence, does the communication model address the risk for violence should members speak out against power inequality? Does the model help members to anticipate risks and prepare to protect themselves?
- In the face of established resource inequalities, does the communication model support the development of collective and sustainable communication infrastructures (e.g., archives, hardware, networks, skills, and systems) to advance the ability of marginalized constituencies to navigate other power dimensions?
- In the face of cultural domination, does the communication model recognize the importance of nurturing oppositional identities, frames, and narratives that challenge dominant stereotypes, reframe social issues, and shift policy agendas?
- In the face of the ability of established forces to set agendas informally, does the communication model identify the need for disempowered constituencies to launch multiarena campaigns that democratize agenda setting (e.g., including opposition perspectives in the media and demanding more transparency in governance and budgeting)?
- Finally, in the face of formal decision-making bodies, does the communication model include as an important component increasing the ability of disempowered constituencies to influence formal decision making in the political arena or, for that matter, in other institutional arenas?

Applying the Model to the Farrell Case

In applying the communication model to the Farrell case, to address the first added power dimension, the threat of violence, RICADV supported SOAR, a collective actor organized by and for DV survivors. Each survivor had a support network to facilitate recovery. Additionally, she received speaker training and was supported by a "buddy" when she spoke publicly. More important, RICADV never expected any DV victim, witness, or survivor to play a role publicly that could put the speaker in harm's way. By participating in media caucuses, victims, witnesses, and survivors could contribute to the creation of messages without being personally vulnerable. When reporters covering an active DV case, such as the Farrell case, sought victims' perspectives, RICADV would provide survivors further along in the healing process and less vulnerable than victims still in crisis, as the vulnerability of survivors, even after batterers have been convicted, is a serious issue.

RICADV spent perhaps the most time addressing the second added dimension of power: the formation of a collective actor with sustainable infrastructure. Jeffreys's decision on joining the coalition to establish a collaborative working relationship with each participating organization bore fruit when the Farrell crisis hit, as a member group, Blackstone, already knew and trusted Jeffreys. Over the previous 4 years, RICADV's members had built a shared understanding of communication routines that encouraged the collaborative planning of communication strategies. RICADV also had established media databases and other tools that allowed it to effectively approach news media outlets.

With regard to creating shared culture, ideology, and worldview, RICADV had discussed for 4 years, internally and externally, that far from being a private tragedy, DV was a social responsibility requiring community-level intervention. Speaking for Blackstone, Impagliazzo argued forcefully that leaving an accused batterer in office sent a chilling message to every DV victim still living in fear, for if a leading public figure could engage in such violence with impunity, how could an unknown victim expect protection? Talking politics (in this case, discussing DV in terms of power inequalities and needed policy shifts) had been an integral part of RICADV's communication work, especially by making the message caucus a routine practice involving available members and staff.

In terms of agenda setting, RICADV reached out to reporters, police, court officers, teachers, teens, emergency room staff, and others to argue that DV is "everyone's business." For each social arena and its constituencies, RICADV prepared talking points and strategic communication priorities.

Finally, in the most visible power dimension, formal decision making, RICADV was poised to press legislative leaders to recognize that state lawmakers would lose credibility if they allowed a fellow legislator to serve after he had broken the state's DV law. Moreover, in the aftermath of Farrell's departure, RICADV pressed for broader policy initiatives to hold batterers accountable and to keep victims and witnesses safe, turning a crisis into a proverbial opportunity.

The five dimensions of power act synergistically, with each dimension forming a unique arena but actively influencing the other dimensions. Decision-making processes recur in every arena, but in the legislative arena, decision making is the first face of power. Understanding power as multifaceted helps to map more precisely how power and disempowerment work, and, ultimately, how social movement practices can support empowerment.

LESSONS LEARNED ABOUT COMMUNICATION ACTIVISM AND SCHOLARSHIP

In addition to reconceptualizing power and empowerment, our collaboration produced five insights about a learning community approach to communication activism and scholarship about it. We begin with three lessons that illustrate the added value to activists of tapping into the growing reservoir of communication activism scholarship, and then close with two lessons about the added value of sustained partnerships with activists from scholars' perspectives.

First, we learned to treat communication as an independent arena of social contest; that is, as a complex system demanding close analysis, infrastructure, resource allocation, and skill building, in its own right. This insight drove us to attend to RICADV's internal communication systems and to analyze regional news media outlets, with our skill growing as we documented and reflected systematically on what did or did not work.

Second, and conversely, we learned to treat communication as an integral component of all social movement arenas. U.S. social movement culture tends to engage in communication work at the last minute (e.g., writing press releases and calling press conferences). In contrast, we viewed communication as a nervous system spreading ideas, resources, and skills, as well as absorbing learning across arenas. Beginning with the Farrell case, RICADV worked with MRAP to integrate communication into every component of movement building. RICADV's plan identified communication opportunities in every exchange between RICADV staff and members and other individuals and groups involved in DV work, be they emergency room workers, high school guidance counselors, postal clerks, or probation officers. RICADV's media plan similarly considered all forms of media. Our collective sophistication grew as we built and refined RICADV's communication infrastructure to serve as connective tissue integrating input from each campaign into each institutional arena. Everyone became a communicator in each interaction; as Gretchen Nelson, a DV survivor, concluded, "I went from being talked about to being part of the talk" (personal communication, February 15, 2003).

Third, an empowerment focus means that social movement members must reflect on how power works in their groups and organizations. We analyzed power inequalities permeating our work, and acknowledged the need to create a sustainable collective team that could build a communication infrastructure. Power establishment institutions and media consultants accustomed to working with those institutions could take this step for granted, but we could not. Forming a collective actor was the first step to challenging not only marginalization from communication systems but the multidimensional experience of disempowerment. Consolidating our relationship as thought partners was one element of team building.

Related to our thought partnership are two final reflections on sustaining partnerships that advance communication activism and communication activism scholarship. First, building viable partnerships between communication activists and scholars demands acknowledging border tensions, because activism and scholarship are arenas with unique rules of entry and engagement (see Cagle, 2007). Interests and questions often diverge, although this tension can be useful.

Second, communication activism scholars face the same challenges as those in other justice-laden fields that emerged from social movements, including Africana studies, gender and queer studies, Latino/a and other ethnic studies, and labor studies. Ultimately, these fields struggle over their relation to activism (Croteau, 2005; Hu-Dehart, 2001; Reed, 2001). To engage activists in critical reflection on movement–media interaction, communication activism scholars must be both connected to and sufficiently distant from activist partners. From this dialectic, scholars help activists to structure cycles of dialogue, action, and reflection, offering insights, language, and methods from other social movements, as well as establishing evidence-based evaluation and encouraging activists to name and disseminate their experiences. Activists, in turn, take responsibility for providing both connection and sufficient distance from scholar partners, with the intention of helping scholars to recognize the academy itself as a positioned location with interests not always aligned with movements. In deepening and sustaining working relations, both activists and scholars maximize learning and theorizing from practice.

To facilitate these goals, scholar-activists must be firmly grounded in both academic and activist realms. The burden of bridging those two worlds—of achieving dual cultural competence and establishing infrastructure to sustain that bridgework—falls primarily on scholar-activists, doubling their work in many cases. Maintaining the right tension between distance and engagement is an ongoing challenge: Too distant a relationship leaves activism scholarship without a raison d'etre; too close a relationship may weaken opportunities to reflect critically and to add fresh perspectives from other fields.

CONCLUSION

After 2 decades of collaboration as thought partners engaged in common practice, we recognize hard-won gains: RICADV's communication tools have been shared with domestic violence coalitions in every state, and multiple movements have adapted RICADV's messaging and communication strategy tools. We continue to engage in collaborative theorizing even as we recognize its drawbacks. Because the process is slower than academic theorizing, we describe it as "trickle-up theorizing." Theoretical constructs not only illuminate social dynamics but they also inform strategies for social transformation. Additionally, prior to theorizing collaboratively, activists and scholars must develop shared language, concepts, and approaches, testing and refining them over the course of projects (and years). This work easily could be considered a sixth face of power, with the academy representing the traditional institutional arena for knowledge production. Collaborative theorizing, thus, represents an empowerment approach to this sixth dimension, to which communication activism scholarship speaks directly. By distilling and disseminating the learning that results from communication activism, scholars and activists can promote more effectively the social justice causes for which they fight.

APPENDIX
ELEMENTS OF PARTICIPATORY COMMUNICATION FOR SOCIAL CHANGE

1. Challenge power inequalities by organizing: Organizers challenge power inequalities by building social networks and collective infrastructure that can launch and sustain collective resistance.
2. Build a sustainable collective actor: Assume group not individual action. Individuals can oppose and resist, but not change systems/relations. To sustain resistance, groups need infrastructure.
3. Support independent collective actors for those directly affected by inequality: Without an independent collective actor, those directly affected cannot gain systematic access to decision making.
4. Link values and worldviews to daily organizational routines: Shared values (e.g., respect, diversity, and equality), underlie participatory processes that support transparency, reflexivity, and accountability.
5. Strategize—detailed power and empowerment analyses inform work plans: Strategy requires that group resources be weighed against analysis of historical conditions.
6. Take a long view and build infrastructure: Because movement building is a long-term project, groups build infrastructure (e.g., systems and practices) that sustain group initiatives over time.

7. Form a reflexive learning community: Reflect on collective experience as learning communities. With reflection part of routine, the collective actor measures results and makes strategic adjustments.
8. Reflect on practice: When reflection links daily work to core values, the collective actor becomes a safer space.
9. Treat framing as dialogic and dynamic: A collective actor involves members and supporters in every widening discussions of strategy. Framing involves dialogues over strategy.
10. Apply core values in all aspects of work: Core values of respect, equality, and diversity apply in coalitions not only within a collective actor.

NOTES

1. Riaño (1996) used the term *Global South* to refer to nations, often in the Southern hemisphere, that are economically dependent on and, from a model of industrial capitalism, are seen as "less developed" than those countries in the North. These words are used to avoid negative connotations that terms such as *developing countries* or *Third-World* countries may have. Riaño noted a resonance between Global South communicative practices and those of social movements and marginalized groups in North America.
2. We touch on this development only briefly, as the Farrell case preceded the explosion of new media.
3. Bourdieu (1999) proactively extended Brecht's (1964) remark that "Anybody who advises us not to make use of such new apparatus just confirms the right of the apparatus to do bad work; he forgets himself out of sheer open-mindedness, for he is thus proclaiming his willingness to have nothing but dirt produced for him" (p. 4).
4. The Communication for Social Change Consortium (www.communicationforsocialchange.org), an international nonprofit organization that builds the local capacity of people living in poor and marginalized communities to use communication to improve their lives, is working to address this need.
5. Excerpts from the shared histories are cited as "personal communication." Each interview was conducted in the presence of at least two actors who had engaged in the original events, and many interviews involved six or more participants. Hence, we constructed the history of RICADV's organizing campaigns by creating a setting in which key participants could spark and challenge each other's recollections.

ACKNOWLEDGMENTS

This chapter would be unthinkable without our colleagues at the Media Research and Action Project and the Rhode Island Coalition against Domestic Violence. We dedicate this to RICADV's staff member, Alice Trimieu.

REFERENCES

Alimi, E. (2007a). Discursive contention: Palestinian media discourse and the inception of the "first" Intifada. *Harvard Journal of Press/Politics, 12*(4), 71–91. doi:10.1177/1081180X07307412

Alimi, E. Y. (2007b). *Israeli politics and the first Palestinian Intifada: Political opportunities, framing processes and contentious politics.* New York, NY: Routledge.

Alinsky, S. (1971). *Rules for radicals: A practical primer for realistic radicals.* New York, NY: Random House.

Altheide, D. L., & Snow, R. P. (1979). *Media logic.* Beverly Hills, CA: Sage.

Andrews, K. T. (2002). Creating social change: Lessons from the civil rights movement. In D. S. Meyer, N. Whittier, & B. Robnett (Eds.), *Social movements: Identity, culture, and the state* (pp. 105–120). New York, NY: Oxford University Press.

Aufderheide, P. (1999). *Communications policy and the public interest: The telecommunications act of 1996.* New York, NY: Guilford Press.

Bah, U. (2008). Daniel Lerner, Cold War propaganda and US development communication research: An historical critique. *Journal of Third World Studies, 25,* 183–198. Retrieved from http://www.bnet.com

Bakst, C. (2000, January 27). Farrell case fallout: Good can emerge from this ugliness. *Providence Journal,* p. A19.

Barab, S. (2008). *Theoretical inspirations—Communities of practice.* Retrieved from http://inkido.indiana.edu/research/community.htm

Barker-Plummer, B. (1996). The dialogic of media and social movements. *Peace Review: A Journal of Social Justice, 8,* 27–34. doi:10.1080/10402659608425926

Barker-Plummer, B. (2002). Producing public voice: Resource mobilization and media access in the National Organization for Women. *Journalism & Mass Communication Quarterly, 79,* 188–205.

Baron, J. (2000a, January 5). Farrell's "fitness for office" questioned: Director of women's shelter "outraged" by state lawmaker's alleged assault on girlfriend. *Pawtucket Times,* pp. A1, A5.

Baron, J. (2000b, January 21). Farrell pleads no contest to assault on woman. *Pawtucket Times,* pp. A1, A6.

Baron, J. (2000c, January 26). Farrell resigns. *Pawtucket Times,* pp. A1, A10.

Bart, P. B., & Moran, E. G. (Eds.). (1993). *Violence against women: The bloody footprints.* Newbury Park, CA: Sage.

Benedict, H. (1992). *Virgin or vamp: How the press covers sex crimes.* New York, NY: Oxford University Press.

Bennett, W. L. (1990). Toward a theory of press–state relations in the United States. *Journal of Communication, 40*(2), 103–127. doi:10.1111/j.1460-2466.1990.tb02265.x

Bennett, W. L. (2009). *News: The politics of illusion* (8th ed.). New York, NY: Pearson Longman.

Berkeley Media Studies Group. (2003). *Distracted by drama: How California newspapers portray intimate partner violence*. Retrieved from http://www.bmsg.org/pdfs/Issue13.pdf

Bevington, D., & Dixon, C. (2005). Movement-relevant theory: Rethinking social movement scholarship and activism. *Social Movement Studies, 4*, 185–208. doi:10.1080/14742830500329838

Blackstone Valley Advocacy Center. (2000a, January 21–26). *Atencion residentes de Central Falls: Usted quiere que este hombre los represente?* [Attention Central Falls residents: Do you want this man representing you?; Flyer]. Pawtucket, RI: Author.

Blackstone Valley Advocacy Center. (2000b, January 20). *Blackstone shelter calls for Farrell's resignation* [Press release]. Pawtucket, RI: Author.

Blackstone Valley Advocacy Center. (2000c, January 26). *Domestic violence advocates hail Farrell's resignation as victory for victims* [Press release]. Pawtucket, RI: Author.

Blackstone Valley Advocacy Center. (2000d, January 4). *Press statement by Linda Impagliazzo, Executive Director*. Pawtucket, RI: Author.

Blight, J. G., & Lang, J. M. (1995). Burden of nuclear responsibility: Reflections on the critical oral history of the Cuban missile crisis. *Peace and Conflict: Journal of Peace Psychology, 1*, 225–264. doi:10.1207/s15327949pac0103_1

Bourdieu, P. (1999). *Acts of resistance: Against the tyranny of the market* (R. Nice, Trans). New York, NY: New Press.

Brecht, B. (1964). *Brecht on theater: The development of an aesthetic* (J. Willet, Ed. & Trans.). New York, NY: Hill & Wang.

Bullock, C. F. (2008). Official sources dominate domestic violence reporting. *Newspaper Research Journal, 29*(2), 6–22. Retrieved from http://www.bnet.com

Burke, P. (2001). *New perspectives on historical writing* (2nd ed.). University Park: Pennsylvania State University Press.

Byerly, C. M. (1994). An agenda for teaching news coverage of rape. *Journalism Educator, 49*(1), 59–69.

Cagle, V. M. (2007). Academia meets LGBT activism: The challenges incurred in utilizing multimethodological research. In L. R. Frey & K. M. Carragee (Eds.), *Communication activism: Vol. 2. Media and performance activism* (pp. 155–194). Cresskill, NJ: Hampton Press.

Caputi, J. (1993). The sexual politics of murder. In P. B. Bart & E. G. Moran (Eds.), *Violence against women: The bloody footprints* (pp. 5–25). Newbury Park, CA: Sage.

Carragee, K. M. (2005). Housing crisis: Gaining standing in a community coalition. In D. Croteau, W. Hoynes, & C. Ryan (Eds.), *Rhyming hope and history: Activists, academics, and social movement scholarship* (pp. 79–96). Minneapolis: University of Minnesota Press.

Carragee, K. M., & Roefs, W. (2004). The neglect of power in recent framing research. *Journal of Communication, 54*, 214–233. doi:10.1111/j.1460-2466.2004.tb02625.x

Castells, M. (2004). *The information age: Economy, society and culture. Vol. 2: The power of identity* (2nd ed.). Malden, MA: Blackwell.

Castells, M. (2007). Communication, power and counter-power in the network society. *International Journal of Communication, 1*, 238–266. Retrieved from http://ijoc.org/ojs/index.php/ijoc

Chakravartty, P. (2006, January 21). Who speaks for the governed? World summit on the information society, civil society, and the limits of "multistakeholderism." *Economic & Political Weekly*, pp. 250–257.

Consalvo, M. (1998). "3 shot dead in courthouse": Examining news coverage of domestic violence and mail-order brides. *Women's Studies in Communication, 21*, 188–211.

Croteau, D. (2005). Which side are you on? The tension between movement scholarship and activism. In D. Croteau, W. Hoynes, & C. Ryan (Eds.), *Rhyming hope and history: Activists, academics, and social movement scholarship* (pp. 20–40). Minneapolis: University of Minnesota Press.

Croteau, D., & Hoynes, W. (1994). *By invitation only: How the media limit political debate*. Monroe, ME: Common Courage Press.

Croteau, D., & Hoynes, W. (2001). *The business of media: Corporate media and the public interest*. Thousand Oaks, CA: Pine Forge Press.

Croteau, D., Hoynes, W., & Carragee, K. M. (1993). *Public television "prime time": Public affairs programming, political diversity, and the conservative critique of public television*. Unpublished manuscript.

Croteau, D., Hoynes, W., & Carragee, K. M. (1996). The political diversity of public television: Polysemy, the public sphere, and the conservative critique of PBS. *Journalism & Mass Communication Monographs, 157*, 1–55.

Croteau, D., Hoynes, W., & Ryan, C. (Eds.). (2005). *Rhyming hope and history: Activists, academics, and social movement scholarship*. Minneapolis: University of Minnesota Press.

Curren, J. (2002). *Media and power*. New York, NY: Routledge.

Cutting, H., & Themba-Nixon, M. (Eds.). (2006). *Talking the walk: A communications guide for racial justice*. Oakland, CA: AK Press.

Dagron, A. G. (2001, January 1). *Making waves: Stories of participatory communication for social change*. New York, NY: Rockefeller Foundation. Retrieved from http://www.comminit.com/en/ node/3713

Dichter, A. (2005, June 8). *Together, we know more: Networks and coalitions to advance media democracy, communication rights and the public sphere 1990–2005*. Retrieved from Media Action Grassroots Network website: http://www.mag-net.org/media-justice-resource-library

Durham, F. (2005). Media tactics and taste: Organising the Southern labour movement at Highlander Folk School, 1938–1946. *Javnost—The Public, 12*(1), 33–47. Retrieved from http://www.javnost-thepublic.org

Edelman, M. (1988). *Constructing the political spectacle*. Chicago, IL: University of Chicago Press.

Enck-Wanzer, S. M. (2009). All's fair in love and sport: Black masculinity and domestic violence in the news. *Communication & Critical/Cultural Studies, 6*, 1–18. doi:1080/14791420802632087

Ferree, M. M., Gamson, W. A., Gerhard, J., & Rucht, D. (2002). *Shaping abortion discourse: Democracy and the public sphere in Germany and the United States.* New York, NY: Cambridge University Press.

Frazer, A. K., & Miller, M. D. (2009). Double standards in sentence structure: Passive voice in narratives describing domestic violence. *Journal of Language and Social Psychology, 28*, 62–71. doi:10.1177/0261927X08325883

Freire, P. (1994). Foreword. In S. A. White (Ed., with K. S. Nair & J. Ascroft), *Participatory communication: Working for change and development* (pp. 12–14). Thousand Oaks, CA: Sage.

Frey, L. R., & Carragee, K. M. (Eds.). (2007). *Communication activism* (2 Vols.). Cresskill, NJ: Hampton Press.

Frey, L. R., & Palmer, D. L. (Eds.). (in press). *Communication activism pedagogy.* Cresskill, NJ: Hampton Press.

Frey, L. R., Pearce, W. B., Pollock, M. A., Artz, L., & Murphy, B. A. O. (1996). Looking for justice in all the wrong places: On a communication approach to social justice. *Communication Studies, 47*, 110–127. doi:10.1080/ 10510979609368467

Gamson, W. A. (1990). *Strategy of social protest* (2nd ed.). Belmont, CA: Wadsworth.

Gamson, W. A. (1992). *Talking politics.* New York, NY: Cambridge University Press.

Gamson, W. A. (1998). Social movements and cultural change. In M. G. Giugni, D. McAdam, & C. Tilly (Eds.), *From contention to democracy* (pp. 57–77). Lanham, MD: Rowman & Littlefield.

Gamson, W. A. (2000). Framing social policy. *Nonprofit Quarterly, 6*(2), 40–42. Retrieved from http://www.nonprofitquarterly.org

Gamson, W. A., & Goodson, A. (2000, Fall). Social movements and children's policy. *Insight*, pp. 5–8.

Gamson, W. A., & Lasch, K. (1983). The political culture of social welfare policy. In S. E. Spiro & E. Yuchtman-Yaar (Eds.), *Evaluating the welfare state: Social and political perspectives* (pp. 397–415). New York, NY: Academic Press.

Gamson, W. A., & Meyer, D. (1996). Framing political opportunity. In D. McAdam, J. D. McCarthy, & M. N. Zald (Eds.), *Comparative perspectives on social movements: Political opportunities, mobilizing structures, and cultural framings* (pp. 275–290). New York, NY: Cambridge University Press.

Gans, H. J. (1979). *Deciding what's news: A study of CBS Evening News, NBC Nightly News, Newsweek, and Time.* New York, NY: Pantheon Books.

Gans, H. J. (2003). *Democracy and the news.* New York, NY: Oxford University Press.

Ganz, M. (2000). Resources and resourcefulness: Strategic capacity in the unionization of California agriculture, 1959–1966. *American Journal of Sociology, 105*, 1003–1062. doi:10.1086/210398

Gaventa, J. (1982). *Power and powerlessness: Quiescence and rebellion in an Appalachian valley.* Urbana: University of Illinois Press.

Gaventa, J. (1991). Toward a knowledge democracy: Viewpoints on participatory research in North America. In O. Fals-Borda & M. A. Rahman (Eds.), *Action and knowledge: Breaking the monopoly with participatory action research* (pp. 121–131). New York, NY: Apex Press.

Gitlin, T. (1980). *The whole world is watching: Mass media in the making and unmaking of the New Left*. Berkeley: University of California Press.

Golding, P., Murdock, G., & Schlesinger, P. (1986). *Communicating politics: Mass communications and the political process*. New York, NY: Holmes & Meier.

Goodson, A. D. (2005). Building bridges, building leaders: Theory, action, and lived experience. In D. Croteau, W. Hoynes, & C. Ryan (Eds.), *Rhyming hope and history: Activists, academics, and social movement scholarship* (pp. 206–221). Minneapolis: University of Minnesota Press.

Graber, D. A. (Ed.). (2011). *Media power in politics* (6th ed.). Washington DC: CQ Press.

Harnecker, M. (2001). *Los conceptos elementales de materialismo historico* [Basic concepts of historical materialism]. Mexico City, Mexico: Siglo XXI. Retrieved from http://www.salvador-allende.cl/Biblioteca/Marta-Harnecker%20-%20 Los%20conceptos%20elemetales%20del%20materiali.pdf

Harter, L., Sharma, D., Pant, S., Singhal, A., & Sharma, Y. (2007). Catalyzing social reform through participatory folk performances in rural India. In L. R. Frey & K. M. Carragee (Eds.), *Communication activism: Vol. 2. Media and performance activism* (pp. 285–314). Cresskill, NJ: Hampton Press.

Healey, R., & Hinson, S. (2005). Movement strategy for organizers. In D. Croteau, W. Hoynes, & C. Ryan (Eds.), *Rhyming hope and history: Activists, academics, and social movement scholarship* (pp. 57–77). Minneapolis: University of Minnesota Press.

Herman, E. S. (1985). Diversity of news: "Marginalizing" the opposition. *Journal of Communication, 35*(3), 135–147. doi:10.1111/j.1460-2466.1985.tb02454.x

Herman E. S., & Chomsky, N. (1988). *Manufacturing consent: The political economy of mass media*. New York, NY: Pantheon Books.

Herman, E. S., & McChesney, R. W. (1997). *The global media: The new missionaries of corporate capitalism*. Washington, DC: Cassell.

Hill, J. (2000, January 22). Police: Expunged record eased penalty in R.I. legislator's case. *Providence Journal*, pp. A3, A4.

hooks, b. (1992). *Black looks: Race and representation*. Boston, MA: South End Press.

Hoynes, W. (1994). *Public television for sale: Media, the market, and the public sphere*. Boulder, CO: Westview Press.

Hoynes, W. (2005). Media research and media activism. In D. Croteau, W. Hoynes, & C. Ryan (Eds.), *Rhyming hope and history: Activists, academics, and social movement scholarship* (pp. 97–114). Minneapolis: University of Minnesota Press.

Hoynes W., & Croteau, D. (1990, April). *All the usual suspects*: MacNeil/Lehrer *and* Nightline. New York, NY: FAIR.

Hu-Dehart, E. (2001). Ethnic studies in U.S. higher education: The state of the discipline. In J. E. Butler (Ed.), *Color-line to borderlands: The matrix of American ethnic studies* (pp. 103–112). Seattle: University of Washington Press.

Huesca, R. (1996). Diversity in communication for social change. *Peace Review: A Journal of Social Justice, 8*, 69–74. doi:10.1080/10402659608425932

Huesca, R. (2001). Conceptual contributions of new social movements to development communication research. *Communication Theory, 11*, 415–433. doi: 10.1111/j.1468-2885.2001.tb00251.x

Impagliazzo, L. (2000, February 1). Farrell case sheds needed light on problems of domestic abuse [Op-Ed]. *Pawtucket Times*, p. A11.

Iyengar, S. (1994). *Is anyone responsible? How television frames political issues.* Chicago, IL: University of Chicago Press.

Jasper, J. M. (2004). A strategic approach to collective action: Looking for agency in social-movement choices. *Mobilization, 9,* 1–16. Retrieved from http://www.mobilization.sdsu.edu

Johnson, D. (1994). *A dangerous pattern: Media coverage of violence against women in California.* Unpublished manuscript.

Jones, A. (2000). *Next time she'll be dead: Battering & how to stop it* (Rev. ed.). Boston, MA: Beacon Press.

Jong, W. de, Shaw, M., & Stammers, N. (Eds.). (2005). *Global activism: Global media.* Ann Arbor, MI: Pluto Press.

Judiciary of Rhode Island. (n.d.). *Blackstone Shelter: About.* Retrieved from http://www.courts.ri.gov/domesticnew/resources/blackstone_about.htm

Kellner, D. (2005). *Media spectacle and the crisis of democracy: Terrorism, war, and election battles.* Boulder, CO: Paradigm Press.

Kidd, D. (2003). Indymedia.org: A new communications commons. In M. McCaughey & M. D. Ayers (Eds.), *Cyberactivism: Online activism in theory and practice* (pp. 47–69). New York, NY: Routledge.

Kidd, D., Barker-Plummer, B., & Rodríguez, C. (2005). *Media democracy from the ground up: Mapping communication practices in the counter public sphere.* Retrieved from http://mediaresearchhub.ssrc.org/media-democracy-from-the-ground-up-mapping-communication-practices-in-the-counter-public-sphere/resource_view

Kincaid, D. L., & Figueroa, M. E. (2009). Communication for participatory development: Dialogue, action, and change. In L. R. Frey & K. M. Cissna (Eds.), *Routledge handbook of applied communication research* (pp. 506–531). New York, NY: Routledge.

Klandermans, B. (1992). The case for longitudinal research on movement participation. In M. Diani & R. Eyerman (Eds.), *Studying collective action* (pp. 55–75). Newbury Park, CA: Sage.

Laplante, J. (2000, January 21). Legislator pleads no contest to assaulting woman. *Providence Journal,* pp. A1, A14.

Lazar, J., & Preece, J. (2002). Social considerations in online communities: Usability, sociability, and success factors. In H. van Oostendorp (Ed.), *Cognition in the digital world* (pp. 112–132). Mahwah, NJ: Lawrence Erlbaum.

Loseke, D. R. (1989). Violence is "violence" ... or is it? The social construction of "wife abuse" and public policy. In J. Best (Ed.), *Images of issues: Typifying contemporary social problems* (pp. 191–206). New York, NY: Aldine de Gruyter.

Lukes, S. (2005). *Power: A radical view* (2nd ed.). New York, NY: Palgrave MacMillan.

Madden, D. (2000, January 27). Farrell: Physical abuse "mutual" in relationship with mother of his son. *Pawtucket Times,* pp. A1, A6.

Maxwell, K. A., Huxford, J., Borum, C., & Hornik, R. (2000). Covering domestic violence: How the O.J. Simpson case shaped reporting of domestic violence in the news media. *Journalism & Mass Communication Quarterly, 77,* 258–272.

McChesney, R. W. (1999). *Rich media, poor democracy: Communication politics in dubious times*. Urbana: University of Illinois Press.

Melkote, S. R., & Steeves, H. L. (2001). *Communication for development in the Third World: Theory and practice for empowerment* (2nd ed.). Thousand Oaks, CA: Sage.

Meyer, D. S. (2004). Protest and political opportunities. *Annual Review of Sociology, 30*, 125–145. doi:10.1146/annurev.soc.30.012703.110545

Meyers, M. (1997). *News coverage of violence against women: Engendering blame*. Thousand Oaks, CA: Sage.

Morris, A. D. (1984). *The origins of the civil rights movement: Black communities organizing for change*. New York, NY: Free Press.

Morris, A. D., & Staggenborg, S.. (2004). Leadership in social movements. In D. A. Snow, S. A. Soule, & H. Kriesi (Eds.), *The Blackwell companion to social movements* (pp. 171–196). Malden, MA: Blackwell.

Murphy, T. A. (2003). Civil society, the Highlander Folk School, and the cultivation of rhetorical invention. *Communication Review, 6*(1), 1–23. doi:10.1080/10714420390184132

Nimmo, D., & Combs, J. E. (1990). *Mediated political realities* (2nd ed.). New York, NY: Longman.

O'Connor, K. (2000, January 4). Rep. Farrell charged in assault on girlfriend. *Pawtucket Times*, pp. A1, A6.

Okigbo, C. C., & Festus, E. (Eds.). (2004). *Development and communication in Africa*. Lanham, MD: Rowman & Littlefield.

Pagelow, M. D. (1981). *Woman battering: Victims and their experiences*. Beverly Hills, CA: Sage.

Park, G., & Bye, G. (2005). Domestic violence presentation raises awareness in student reporters' stories. *Newspaper Research Journal, 26*(2/3), 113–118.

Portelli, A. (1997). *The battle of Valle Guilia: Oral history and the art of dialogue*. Madison: University of Wisconsin Press.

Reed, T. V. (2001). Heavy traffic at the intersections: Ethnic, American, women's, queer, and cultural studies. In J. E. Butler (Ed.), *Color-line to borderlands: The matrix of American ethnic studies* (pp. 273–292). Seattle: University of Washington Press.

Rhode Island Coalition Against Domestic Violence. (2000). *Domestic violence: A handbook for journalists*. Warwick, RI: Author.

Riaño, P. (1994). *Women in grassroots communication: Furthering social change*. Thousand Oaks, CA: Sage.

Rohlinger, D. A. (2002). Framing the abortion debate: Organizational resources, media strategies, and movement–countermovement dynamics. *Sociological Quarterly, 43*, 479–507. doi:10.1111/j.1533-8525.2002.tb00063.x

Rozario, S. (1997). Development and rural women in South Asia: The limits of empowerment and conscientization. *Bulletin of Concerned Asian Scholars, 29*(4), 45–53. Retrieved from http://criticalasianstudies.org

Rucht, D. (1988). Themes, logics and arenas of social movements: A structural approach. In B. Klandermans, H. Kriesi, & S. Tarrow (Eds.), *International social movement research: Vol. 1. From structure to action: Comparing social movement research across cultures* (pp. 305–328). Greenwich, CT: JAI Press.

Ryan, C. (1991). *Prime time activism: Media strategies for grassroots organizing.* Boston, MA: South End Press.
Ryan, C. (1996). The media war over welfare. *Peace Review: A Journal of Social Justice, 8,* 13–19. doi:10.1080/10402659608425924
Ryan, C. (2004). It takes a movement to raise an issue: News coverage of the 1997 U.P.S. strike. *Critical Sociology, 30,* 483–511. doi:10.1163/156916304323072189
Ryan, C. (2007, December). Who are these people?: Implied and under-recognized internet audiences. *Revista Iberoamericana de Comunicación,* pp. 11–26.
Ryan, C., Anastario, M., & DaCunha, A. (2006). Changing coverage of domestic violence murders: A longitudinal experiment in participatory communication. *Journal of Interpersonal Violence, 21,* 209–228. doi:10.1177/0886260505282285
Ryan, C., Anastario, M., & Jeffreys, K. (2005). Start small, build big: Negotiating opportunities in media markets. *Mobilization, 10,* 111–128. Retrieved from http://mobilization.sdsu.edu
Ryan, C., Carragee, K. M., & Schwerner, C. (1998). Media, movements, and the quest for social justice. *Journal of Applied Communications Research, 26,* 165–181. doi:10.1080/00909889809365500
Ryan, C., & Gamson, W. A. (2006). The art of reframing politics debates. *Contexts, 5*(1), 13–18. doi:10.1525/ctx.2006.5.1.13
Ryan, C., Jeffreys, K., & Blozie, L. (in press). It's like a bread slicer: Strategic uses of publicity in movement building. In G. M. Maney & R. V. Kutz-Flamenbaum (Eds.), *Strategy in action: Movements and social change.* Minneapolis: University of Minnesota Press.
Saltzman, J. (2000, January 26). Legislator resigns over abuse incident. *Providence Journal,* pp. A1, A6.
Schaefer, E. (2000, January 29). Farrell may run for House seat he just vacated. *Providence Journal,* pp. A1, A5.
Schiller, H. I. (1996). *Information inequality: The deepening social crisis in America.* New York, NY: Routledge.
Schwerner, C. (2005). Building the movement for education equity. In D. Croteau, W. Hoynes, & C. Ryan (Eds.), *Rhyming hope and history: Activists, academics, and social movement scholarship* (pp. 157–175). Minneapolis: University of Minnesota Press.
Senge, P. M. (2006). *The fifth discipline: The art and practice of the learning organization* (Rev. and updated ed.). New York, NY: Doubleday/Currency.
Servaes, J. (Ed.). (2008). *Communication for development and social change.* Thousand Oaks, CA: Sage.
Soley, L. C. (1992). *The news shapers: The sources who explain the news.* New York, NY: Praeger.
Soothill, K., & Walby, S. (1991). *Sex crime in the news.* New York, NY: Routledge.
Springer, K. (2005). *Living for the revolution: Black feminist organizations, 1968–1980.* Durham, NC: Duke University Press.
Staggenborg, S. (2002). The "meso" in social movement research. In D. S. Meyer, N. Whittier, & B. Robnett (Eds.), *Social movements: Identity, culture, and the state* (pp. 124–139). New York, NY: Oxford University Press.
Steeves, H. L. (2001). Liberation, feminism, and development communication. *Communication Theory, 11,* 397–414. doi:10.1111/j.1468-2885.2001.tb00250.x

Tjaden, P., & Thoennes, N. (2000, July). *Extent, nature and consequences of intimate partner violence: Findings from the National Violence against Women Survey.* Washington, DC: U.S. Department of Justice, National Institute of Justice. Retrieved from http://www.ojp.usdoj.gov/nij/pubs-sum/181867.htm

These batterers should go [Editorial]. (2000, January 26). *Providence Journal*, p. A18.

Tierney, K. J. (1982). The battered women movement and the creation of the wife-beating problem. *Social Problems, 29*, 207–219. doi:10.1525/ sp.1982.29.3.03a00010

Tuchman, G. (1978). *Making news: A study in the construction of reality.* New York, NY: Free Press.

van Dijk, T. A. (1991). *Racism and the press.* New York, NY: Routledge.

Waisbord, S. (n.d.). *Family tree of theories, methodologies and strategies in development communication.* New York, NY: Rockefeller Foundation. Retrieved from Communication for Social Change Consortium website: http://www.communicationforsocialchange.org/pdf/familytree.pdf

Waters, J. (2000). Power and praxis in development communication discourse and method. In K. G. Wilkins (Ed.), *Redeveloping communication for social change: Theory, practice, and power* (pp. 89–101). Lanham, MD: Rowman & Littlefield.

White, S. A. (1994). The concept of participation: Transforming rhetoric to reality. In S. A. White (Ed., with K. S. Nair & J. Ascroft), *Participatory communication: Working for change and development* (pp. 15–32). Thousand Oaks, CA: Sage.

Wilkins, K. G. (2000). Accounting for power in development communication. In K. G. Wilkins (Ed.), *Redeveloping communication for social change: Theory, practice, and power* (pp. 197–210). Lanham, MD: Rowman and Littlefield.

Williams, R. (1976). Notes on Marxism in Britain since 1945. *New Left Review, 100*, 81–94. Retrieved from http://newleftreview.org

Wyatt, N. (2002). Foregrounding feminist theory in group communication research. In L. R. Frey (Ed.), *New directions in group communication* (pp. 43–56). Thousand Oaks, CA: Sage.

5

FOOD FIGHTS

Reclaiming Public Relations and Reframing a Runaway Food System through a Grassroots Movement

Jeanette L. Drake
The University of Findlay

Even before opening the sliding glass door, I heard the buzzing coming from my parents' sunroom, but neither that nor my mother's forewarnings prepared me for what I was about to witness. The floor, walls, and windows were black—covered with flies in every stage of life. As journalists would describe it, it was a fly population of "Biblical proportions."

  A nearby concentrated animal feeding operation, with its acres of manure piled up on a concrete floor, had precipitated the plague that hit hundreds of homes in this small rural community in central Ohio. This feeding operation wreaked so much havoc that people across the country would come to know it by name: Buckeye Egg Farm. This now infamous icon of industrialized agriculture has influenced my scholarship in profound ways, leading me to engage in communication activism to promote sustainable living as a form of social justice.

"Words matter," Barack Obama (2007) said as a presidential candidate, and communication scholars know the truth of that statement. The power of communication, even in the reverberation of a single voice, never should be underestimated. Proof of that power hit home one winter day in 1998, even though I would not fully grasp the significance of the event until years later, when Lowell Lufkin, Director of the Marion County, Ohio Health Department, after receiving several complaints about the fly infestation, decided to examine the problem himself.

I was looking after my ill father while my mother went grocery shopping, so I was the one who answered the door. Upon learning who Lufkin was and why he was there, I showed him the sunroom, where the flies were the worst, and implored him to do something about the problem.

Later that evening, I recounted his visit to my parents. At one end of the dinner table, I sat with my dad, who was suffering from nonalcoholic cirrhosis of the liver and, as a result, was losing mobility and barely able to eat on his own. At the other end of the table, my mother sat perched with a fork in one hand and a flyswatter in the other.

My 65-year-old parents had a lot on their plates. Their lives revolved around my father's emergency trips to the hospital and his daily bodily functions, which, in his condition, meant life or death. All their lives they had trusted the government to ensure safeguards regarding basic needs, such as clean air and water, as well as safe food. In fact, as former farmers for some 25 years, they experienced firsthand the production of food. More recently, however, my parents, along with many of their neighbors, had discovered a hole in the system that led them to become citizen-activists.

Their plight was painful to watch, but it inspired me to join what I now call the "food fight." I believe that everyone deserves clean air and water, and that citizens have the right to know where their food comes from, what is in it, and how it is produced. I also believe that every living being deserves to be treated humanely, although farm animals neither can defend that basic right nor are protected under the law. Although every state in the country has animal anti-cruelty statutes, most explicitly exempt farm animals, as does the federal Animal Welfare Act.

As it turns out, these beliefs are widespread, which is why a large number of citizens and advocacy groups oppose animal confinement and other unsustainable practices of industrialized agriculture. Although there is no consensus on the term, according to the United Nations General Assembly (1987), *sustainable development* "meets the needs of the present without compromising the ability of future generations to meet their own needs" (para. 2). Doing so involves reconciling environmental, social, and economic demands, which concentrated animal feeding operations (CAFOs) are unable to do. Taxpayer subsidies support these resource-intensive plants, using large amounts of electricity, tremendous quantities of fuel, and millions of gallons of clean fresh groundwater every day.

In Ohio alone, Sharp (2008) reported that 30% to 40% of citizens are "very concerned" about large-scale poultry and livestock development, 57% believe that their food is not as safe as it was 10 years ago, and 45% are "very concerned" about food that travels more than 100 miles to reach them. Moreover, 63% are "very concerned" about the loss of family farms and farmland, and 56% believe that increased regulation of animal treatment in farming is needed. U.S. Americans, in general, agree with the latter view by an overwhelming majority, with a 2003 Zogby International poll finding that 80% of those surveyed believe that there "should be effective laws to prevent farm animal cruelty" (The Humane Society of the United States, n.d., para. 5).

Nevertheless, in the face of wide-ranging protest by citizens, in 1996, the state of Ohio granted to Buckeye Eggs (BE; then called AgriGeneral and now called Ohio Fresh Eggs) a permit to build the first of several new confinement facilities, an egg-laying plant. Reporters quoted industry sources that discredited concerned citizens by saying their knowledge of the egg business was "scrambled." However, it was the agricultural industry that would wear egg on its face and local citizens who would suffer for the duration of BE's turbulent history.

To some Ohioans, the granting of this permit was déjà vu all over again, as AgriGeneral had opened and operated since the 1980s a similar plant in Newark County, Ohio. Anton Pohlmann, the company's owner, already had earned a reputation as a bad environmental neighbor. Nonetheless, despite the company's history of environmental wrongdoing, increasing protests surrounding factory farms, and what would turn out to be repeated infestations of flies and beetles, and other violations, the state continued over the next few years to grant permits for the company to expand and build additional facilities.

This study examines the ideological conflict between the company and agricultural industry, on one side, and activists, on the other, over the legitimacy of factory-farmed animals. Among the dimensions of the controversy, framing (how something is presented) was central, as words do matter in creating meaning, shaping public opinion, and forging public policy. Unlike the mythical tale of David and Goliath, framing battles typically are determined by the side that has more resources, and this fight was no exception. Although citizens realized short-term victories, the agricultural industry (led by the Ohio Department of Agriculture [ODA] and the Farm Bureau [FB]) prevailed and used lessons learned from the BE fiasco to streamline the permit process. As a result, the number of animal-feeding operations in Ohio more than tripled in the 1990s, with nearly 140 by 2002 (Environmental Integrity Project, 2006).

In this chapter, I reflect on the journey that took me from corporate public relations practitioner to citizen-advocate and communication activist-scholar. I began applying public relations as a communication activist when I counseled Concerned Citizens of Central Ohio (CCCO), a nonprofit grassroots organization that formed to protest BE. This chapter explores conflicts I encountered and growth I experienced as a communication scholar engaged in promoting social justice for rural residents and for farmed animals, along with advocating for sustainable practices in the production of food.

According to Frey, Pearce, Pollock, Artz, and Murphy (1996), *social justice* involves "engagement with and advocacy for those in our society who are economically, socially, politically, and/or culturally underresourced" (p. 100), with communication scholars called on to lay bare the "grammars that oppress or underwrite relationships of domination" (p. 112), and then to reconstruct those grammars in more just ways. To accomplish that goal, I first provide background about CAFOs and then examine theoretical perspectives, including media framing, which informed this social justice communication intervention. I then describe the site of this community's particular struggle, followed by details about the context, including my activities and journey from naïve practitioner-participant to engaged communication activist-scholar. I conclude the chapter by sharing the results of this effort, including lessons learned about communication activism scholarship, and by making the case for social justice advocates to reclaim public relations.

A SOCIAL JUSTICE ISSUE: CONCENTRATED ANIMAL FEEDING OPERATIONS

CAFOs have radically transformed the U.S. rural landscape in the past 2 decades, supplanting less resource-intensive forms of agriculture, such as family farming and ranching practices. This relatively new phenomenon, also known as "megafarms" or "factory farms," entails giant feedlots that amass thousands of animals in warehouses, often in unspeakable conditions, where they produce more fecal matter than does a large city. Although CAFOs have been banned in some European countries and significantly restricted in others, they have mushroomed in the United States, in part, because emigrating European producers are drawn to the abundant, relatively cheap land across rural America, where factory farms are allowed and government regulations are lenient.

Unlike traditional family farms, which are owned and run by a family that lives on the land, factory farms usually are owned, managed, and operated by different entities—often large corporations. Using vertical integration, these farms create monopolistic conditions, with the same corporation often controlling all aspects of production. For instance, just four companies market 57% of the hogs produced in the United States (Environmental Integrity Project, 2006). In fact, CAFOs dominate the beef, dairy, pork, poultry, and egg-laying industries, with just 3% of U.S. farms producing more than 60% of America's agricultural goods ("Emerging Farm Powers," 2004).

Meat production is big business, with, according to the Environmental Integrity Project (2006), the poultry industry generating more than $21 billion in on-farm revenue in 1997 and the swine industry generating approximately $10 billion per year at the production level and revenue from consumer sales often exceeding $20 billion. Large agribusinesses realize the lion's share of the profits, with Tyson Foods, the world's largest meat producer, reporting $26.4 billion in sales and $1.9 billion in gross profits in 2004, and Smithfield Foods, the nation's largest hog producer, recording $9.3 billion in sales and $227 million in net income that same year (Environmental Integrity Project).

Industrialized meat production practices yield unprecedented high volume and profit, with companies having little regard for unintended consequences, such as the astounding environmental impact of factory farms. In the United States, these facilities produce 2.7 trillion pounds of animal waste each year that often leaks into rivers, killing fish and contaminating drinking water (Fauth, 2002). In Ohio, CAFOs generate more than 10 million tons of manure each year, with, as an example, one factory farm of 4,500 dairy cattle in Hardin County producing the waste of 95,000 people, exceeding the population of the state's seventh largest city of Youngstown (Environmental Integrity Project, 2006). What to do with the untreated waste is one of the largest problems resulting from intensive agriculture. Additionally, the gases from CAFO waste are ventilated from barns and lagoons, and foul the air with ammonia, hydrogen sulfide, and other contaminants. CAFOs, thus, pollute the air and water, spreading disease via the unprecedented high concentration of animals.

The intensive practices of factory-farmed animals raise myriad other public health concerns involving the overuse of antibiotics and the increased risk for mad cow disease, Escherichia coli (E. coli), and pandemic diseases (such as swine flu). Moreover, studies have shown that CAFOs have negative effects on neighbors (Okun, 1999; Southwest Utah Board of Health, 2001; Thu et al., 1997), property values (Hopey, 2003), and quality of life (Wing & Wolf, 2000), along with detrimental effects on communities (Goldschmidt, 1978; Lobao & Saenz, 2002), the environment (O'Brien, 2001; S. Williams, 2004), and, of course, on abused farmed animals (Coats, 1989).

Because of the implications of factory farms on public health, effective regulatory oversight is critical, but regulators have not kept up with changes in the industry. Factory farms also enjoy exemptions realized by no other industry; for example, President George W. Bush's administration reduced federal regulations on CAFOs, exempting them from air pollution standards. The factory farm industry, and its political allies, "leverage vast wealth and influence to undermine efforts at the federal, state, and local level to regulate factory farms effectively" (Environmental Integrity Project, 2006, Introduction section, para. 1). A lack of federal regulation has resulted in competition among states to attract agribusiness and, as a result, that industry has targeted environmentally lax states, such as Ohio, that have allowed factory farms to develop unhindered.

Although factory farms have "an unprecedented [negative] impact on the environment, health, and society of neighboring rural communities and downstream cities" (Environmental Integrity Project, 2006, Introduction section, para. 1), structural barriers make a mockery of democratic principles and social justice. Right-to-farm legislation restricts local governments from controlling the location and impacts of factory farms; trade secret laws are misused to allow factory farms to conceal where manure will be applied in communities; and food ("veggie") libel laws (passed in 13 states), a common scare tactic used by the livestock industry, have a chilling effect on free speech by threatening citizens who might talk "disparagingly" about food, those who produce it, or how it is produced, by making it easier for food producers to sue their critics (see, e.g., Collins, 2000).

The FB and livestock industry defend CAFOs, and, in fact, partnerships between industry and government have left little room for small, sustainable farms (Nestle, 2002). CAFO defenders claim that such intensive practices are the only way to keep food prices down and to feed the world's growing population, but defenders do not factor in nor pay for the true costs of these operations, which include significant, long-term environmental damage. Favoring sustainable agriculture, opponents criticize factory farms for consuming inordinately more resources than other food production methods and actually being less able to end world hunger. Citizen-activists decry inhumane animal treatment, environmental degradation, public health threats, and inappropriate powerful government–industry alliances.

The environmental stakes associated with factory farms are high, but political hurdles to stopping them are even higher. The diffusion of CAFOs across the United States has "created a disturbing dynamic of increasingly grave environmental risk combined with increasingly well-funded opposition to environmental regulation and enforcement" (Environmental Integrity Project, 2006, Introduction section, para. 1). During the last half of the 20th century, when the food-agricultural industry grew to be the second-most profitable industry in the country, behind pharmaceuticals

(Magdoff, Foster, & Buttel, 2000), farming became almost entirely removed from the daily lives of most citizens. Hence, at the exact time that personal experience dwindled and, thereby, created dependence on the news media, industrialized agriculture intensified, but news media reporting of agricultural issues significantly declined in quantity and quality (Pawlick, 2001), which means decreased citizen participation in, and increased politicization of, food.

Throughout my work with CCCO, I came to better comprehend the growth of animal feeding operations and how the controversy evolved in the news media. As explained here, that understanding is informed by theories about how news and meaning are produced, and about how innovations diffuse throughout a society. Of utmost concern is the role that power plays and the influence of political and social inequalities on public dialogue, public policy and, in this case, on public health.

THEORETICAL UNDERPINNINGS: THE SOCIAL CONSTRUCTION OF RURALITY

A common thread woven throughout this case study is the theoretical perspective that meaning is socially constructed (P. L. Berger & Luckmann, 1966) and, therefore, is a product of social interaction. All reality is produced through an ongoing symbolic contest; however, the playing field is grossly skewed by asymmetrical power relationships among political and social actors. This perpetual rhetorical battle over "what is" and "what will be" may be better understood through framing (Goffman, 1974) and social movement theories, which inform both my communication activism, in general, and the analysis of this particular case.

As a public relations strategist, I was influenced by a working knowledge of media effects. Over the course of my work with CCCO, I evolved from a public relations practitioner to communication activist-scholar. Thus, linkages, albeit fragmented, unfolded between the following theories and my work with this grassroots organization.

The cliché, "perception is reality," sums up both the mantra for public relations professionals and the theoretical essence of the social construction of reality. The social production of meaning is evident in this case study, as everything regarding intensified, industrialized food production, including public policy, has been predicated on whether it is viewed as "farm" or "factory." Proponents apply the former symbol, whereas many citizens argue the latter, with the "truth" being whichever frame and frame sponsor dominate at the time.

Entman (1993) defined *framing* as the process of emphasizing and deemphasizing aspects of a text to identify problems, pinpoint causes, level moral judgments, and recommend solutions. Framing has been referred to as a type of *conceptual scaffolding* that helps people to make sense of the world (Snow & Benford, 1988). Frames are ubiquitous; framing occurs within senders, receivers, texts, and cultures.

As stated previously, the power to influence symbolic imagery through frames is significant in shaping prevailing reality. Paramount to this discussion of power is that frames are associated with interests that are not equal (Reese, 2003). Gamson (1989) identified the sources of imbalance as access to and control of resources, strategic alliances, and a cache of knowledge not only of the issue at hand but also about the skills of frame sponsorship.

For example, public relations strategists (employed mostly by corporations and the government) affect public discourse by influencing news frames, developing relationships with media practitioners (e.g., key journalists) to whom they provide prepackaged information reflecting their organization's perspective on various issues. These "information subsidies" reduce the cost of information and, thereby, boost the likelihood that the media will use it (Gandy, 1982). Also called a "web of subsidies," with *subsidies* being a collection of human, material, and knowledge resources that "political actors weave ... to privilege the dissemination and packaging of information to their advantage" (Pan & Kosicki, 2003, p. 44), this concept references the influence and imbalance of power behind frame sponsorship. Griffin and Dunwoody (1995), for instance, showed that these information subsidies augmented local press coverage of environmental issues. However, in some cases, strategists have crossed the ethical line to weave a *web of impediments*, which are "activities to obstruct or disadvantage other actors who are not conforming to the desired framing" (Drake, 2004, p. 164).

Pan and Kosicki (1993) identified the news frame as the most exigent element of a news story because of its dual function of shaping ways that reporters write a story and guiding how readers decode it. Iyengar (1991) demonstrated how news coverage about political issues more often follows an episodic (i.e., examination of specific cases) rather than a thematic (i.e., ongoing contextualized discussion) frame, with the former resulting in superficial reporting.

The role of the news media in the progression of social movements is paramount (DeLuca, 1999; Gamson, 1989; see also Ryan & Jeffreys, this volume) because, like socially constructed reality, social problems are not naturally occurring. Although organization and resources are needed to elevate a condition to problem status via a social movement (McCarthy & Zald, 1977), social problems are not objective and identifiable conditions but, rather, outcomes of *collective action frames*, the cohesive articulation and definition of particular situations (Spector & Kitsuse, 1977). Put simply, situations are not social problems until they are labeled as problems. Gamson (1992) explained that collective action frames are derived through public discourse that affirms the possibility of altering conditions through collective action. This type of frame is not always present but involves three components: (a) injustice (a sense of being wronged), (b) agency (a sense of power to do something about a situation), and (c) identity (an adversarial sense of "us" against "them"). Gamson (1992) found that the news media often avoid collective action frames in their reporting of issues. Despite a large body of knowledge about framing, however, social justice advocates do not appear to employ it to their benefit, with Zoch, Collins, Sisco, and Supa (2008) finding that activist organizations' websites failed to make use of most framing devices, rendering those organizations less effective than they could be.

Although the impact of framing has long been understood, much of the public relations scholarship has looked uncritically at framing, addressing media effects of framing or positing framing models for media relations (e.g., Hallahan, 1999; Zoch & Molleda, 2006), but largely ignoring the more heuristic sociological and communication perspectives. Carragee and Roefs (2004) argued that framing research must go beyond media effects to examine broader issues of political power and structural imbalance involved in media hegemony. In other words, in studying framing, it is imperative to consider *ideological domination*, the set of ideas within a group that has the greatest power and the adherence of the greatest number of people at any given time (Hall, 1997). Framing studies that examine news coverage of political issues are especially fruitful because interests of the existing power structure are reflected in the media (Herman & Chomsky, 1988).

The literature is replete with research on the framing of farming, with scholars content analyzing news to illustrate ideological battles over animal rights (Packwood Freeman, 2009), bioengineered foods (Durham, 2005; Henderson, 2005; Nucci & Kubey, 2007), environmental justice (Burch & Harry, 2004), and, as in the present case, factory farms (C. B. Glenn, 2004; Kunkel, 1995; McMillan, 2000). Using a social justice perspective, this study scrutinizes factory farm frames and frame sponsorship, resources available to sponsors, and the political and social environments within which framing contests occur.

Reese (2003) argued that the most effective power prevents issues from surfacing and frames from materializing in the first place, which was the state of agriculture during the last quarter of the 20th century, when both people's direct experience with food production and news coverage of farming simultaneously plummeted (Pawlick, 2001), and was a time when meat production was changing radically. Given that the media shape people's perceptions of that which they do not directly experience (see, e.g., Lippmann, 1922), when news coverage of farming all but disappeared, the industry essentially operated out of public sight and, thereby, avoided public scrutiny. As a result, the sudden appearance and surge in mammoth CAFOs at the turn of the millennium caught many people off-guard. However, the rapid diffusion of CAFOs eventually triggered a growing social movement against them.

THE GRASSROOTS CAMPAIGN AGAINST CONFINED ANIMAL FEEDING OPERATIONS IN CENTRAL OHIO

Lufkin's visit that afternoon in March 1998 changed everything in the small Ohio community's struggle against BE. Via the local newspaper, this county official declared the situation "a clear threat to public health" (cited in Moore, 1998, p. A1) and publicly opposed additional permits for the facility. This single communication event turned the tide, with journalists and other elites subsequently becoming critical of the factory farm. Lufkin's criticism represented *indexing*, or conflict among elites that moderates the degree to which the news media support the status quo (Bennett, 1990). That one rhetorical act from an official, expert source gave concerned citizens instant credibility and turned the issue into a "problem."

The nonpartisan Environmental Integrity Project (2006) summed up this problem:

> After flouting environmental regulations for nearly two decades beginning in the early 1980s, Buckeye Egg Farm and owner Anton Pohlmann earned one of the most notorious reputations among the nation's CAFOs. These exploits included numerous pollution incidents, such as a large manure spill into Otter Creek in 1983 that killed 150,000 fish. According to former OPEA [Ohio Environmental Protection Agency] Director Chris Jones, Buckeye Egg's "failure to properly manage the large volume of manure generated by its 15.5 million chickens has resulted in severe fly infestation on several separate occasions," citing court documents that described Buckeye Egg's fly problem as reaching "Biblical proportions." Former Attorney General Betty Montgomery called the company "the most recalcitrant corporate polluter" her office had ever seen. (Case Studies section, para. 1)

In all, BE accrued more than $1 million in fines for egregious violations, including fly and beetle infestations, fish kills, and selling backdated eggs. Lufkin provided neither the first nor the only public condemnation of the company; the Natural Resources Defense Council (1998) cited Ohio as having the worst environmental record with factory farms, a designation brought about by this single operation, which, at its peak, produced 2.6 billion eggs, or 4% of the nation's eggs.

Intense citizen protest, news media coverage, and the company's continual wrongdoing led to changes in state regulations and a state order to close the factory farm. However, although citizens were effectual in bringing attention to and an order to close down the egg-laying plant, the facilities never closed; they merely changed ownership in 2003 and continued operating as Ohio Fresh Eggs. In doing so, the ODA "had turned over the reins of one of the nation's most disreputable CAFOs to one of the nation's most disreputable CAFO owners" (Environmental Integrity Project, 2006, Case Studies section, para. 3).

Ohio has been at the forefront of the rising predominance of factory farms, with the number of CAFOs more than tripling in the 1990s. Although the number of hog farms in Ohio fell from 20,062 to 4,976 from 1974 to 2002 (a 75.2% drop), the number of hogs sold rose from 3,165,535 to 4,609,153, which was a 45.6% spike (Environmental Integrity Project, 2006). Paralleling the shift to CAFOs, the livestock industry has lobbied aggressively to consolidate regulatory oversight within the ODA.

This case focuses on the time period of the most intense public scrutiny, from 1995, when BE announced its intent to build facilities in Marion County, to 2003, when those facilities were ordered to be closed and then sold. Communication activism in this case included consulting, grassroots organizing, leading protest events, developing communication tools, engaging in media relations, and employing frame analysis. That activism was done with a newly formed grassroots organization in Marion, Ohio, CCCO. Other organizations joined the protest against BE, including the Sierra Club, Ohio Environmental Council, Humane Society of the United States, and People for the Ethical Treatment of Animals.

The Journey of a Public Relations Scholar: From Apathy to Activism

After reflecting on this grassroots campaign, I realized that I never intended to be an activist; in fact, even now, it is not a label I use to describe myself. However, somewhere along the way, my path as a scholar took a decidedly critical cultural turn. In this section, I retrace that journey and discuss my work with CCCO—my debut in social justice work.

Before returning to the academy, I managed strategic communication for corporate and nonprofit organizations in Columbus, Ohio. My work included generating positive publicity for organizations and attempting to influence what was said about them—that is, public relations. The term "framing," in its technical sense, had entered neither my vocabulary nor public consciousness, even though scholars in many disciplines had been studying frame analysis for the previous quarter century. My knowledge of framing theory would not occur until a few years later, when I became a doctoral student at Bowling Green State University (BGSU).

Those professional experiences privileged me with insider knowledge of the news media. I knew that *how* something is communicated is as significant as *what* is communicated. Still, I remember when my interest in news did not go deeper than hunting for newspaper clips about clients and judging whether those clients were presented in a positive, negative, or neutral light.

In 1995, I first heard about the controversy that had arisen in Marion County, Ohio, which is 50 miles northwest of Columbus: an egg-laying operation being proposed in Marion, Wyandot, and Hardin counties. The operation of 14 million chickens would fall within a 7-mile radius, but in a "divide-and-conquer" strategy, the facilities were separated into those three counties, confounding citizens' organizing efforts, diluting news media attention, and dividing attempts at regulation. I learned about the factory farm from relatives who lived in Marion County and, subsequently, from newspaper clippings that my mother began saving, as the planned facilities would be within miles of my family's farm, where my mother still lives today.

My father had traded in farming for small business ownership 2 decades earlier; consequently, I long ago had lost track of the state of agriculture, and I suspect others in my family had as well, except for my sister's family, who continued running the family farm. When relatives started telling me about the factory farm that was going to be built in their community, I had no idea what they were talking about. I also had no idea that my life's work would be shaped by this new phenomenon of CAFOs, or that I would go on for more than a decade to study how the news media frame food and farming, and the impact of those frames on public policy.

I was unaware of the issues involved, for I had never heard of farms housing millions of chickens, and I was not sure what community residents were so upset about. My initial thoughts were that times change and technological advances maximize efficiency. I had uncritically bought into a "progress" frame and was ignorant of its full ramifications—economic or otherwise. Hence, it did not seem surprising that agriculture was beginning to do what other fields had done long ago—get bigger. Working and making my home in Columbus all those years, however, had distanced me from everyday life in the community where I had grown up.

As the controversy continued, I found myself becoming interested, increasingly informed, and actively involved in it. At my brother's urging, CCCO approached me for public relations advice, and I agreed to help as time allowed. I met regularly with that group and moved from a bystander to a part-time participant who provided strategic counsel to the group. The group was loosely organized, with barely a half-dozen members regularly attending meetings, although on several occasions, the group motivated upward of 400 citizens to attend public forums about the factory farm.

The contrast of how the debate about the factory farm was playing out in the local newspaper versus how community members were talking about it resulted in two vastly different realities. The local press was giving the issue substantial coverage, which seemed, on the surface, to promote a vigorous public debate. However, even though the controversy was making the front page and the reporting appeared fair, the coverage was superficial in that it focused on the fight rather than on the issues. I read the newspaper articles from start to finish, poring over word choices, sources, and quotations. At the time, I did not know the theoretical constructs involved in framing but I was keenly aware that the way the issue was presented in the newspaper eventually would affect policy decisions about the factory farm. Also remarkable was the reliance by the news media on official sources and CCCO's reliance on news coverage.

Not long after the formation of CCCO, a career change took me to The University of Findlay in northwest Ohio to teach public relations. Soon thereafter, I began work on a doctorate in communication at BGSU, where I learned about theories that, in turn, induced new perspectives about the controversy transpiring in Marion County. Thus, I focused on the phenomenon of CAFOs and how the ensuing social protest over this factory farm played out in the news media. Along with what I came to understand were framing issues, I was particularly interested in power differences in this rural community and policymaking about public health.

The goal of the loosely organized grassroots group had evolved over time. At first, the goal was to prevent the CAFO from locating in the community, but once the facility permits were approved, the goal shifted to ensuring proper regulation of it and, finally, to shutting it down. By allowing its gaze to be limited to this single company, CCCO unknowingly would be less effectual accomplishing the goals of a larger justice movement, which, for example, would question the very existence of factory farms. Although most CCCO members questioned the legitimacy of factory farms from the beginning and some continue to work as part of the larger movement crusading against those farms more than 15 years later, in the end, the ODA was successful, in large part, at containing this controversy to a local issue.

My intermittent involvement with CCCO included both paid consultancy and pro bono work, but the members of CCCO did the heavy lifting day-to-day, 365 days a year. I helped to develop communication strategies, including advising the group about organizing, generating publicity for it, identifying and training spokespersons, creating key messages, and seeking needed resources. Activities in which I engaged included penning letters to newspaper editors, joining marches at the statehouse, establishing contacts with media representatives, and producing a quarterly newsletter. However, my involvement throughout was limited by time and distance, given that I lived and worked an hour away.

Communication Activities of Concerned Citizens of Central Ohio

The successes of this grassroots effort may be attributed to the work of CCCO members, whose dogged determination for the better part of a decade was significant in bringing the factory farm issue to light. In particular, CCCO was effective in influencing the local news media agenda (McCombs & Shaw, 1972) and obtaining significant publicity focused on the controversial egg facility. Over the course of 8 years (1995–2003), the debate generated 487 articles by the local newspaper, with most articles being allocated at least 20 to 40 column inches and 71% receiving front-page placement (Drake, 2004).

Early on, protesters intuited the *barter principle* (Gamson, 1989), the implicit agreement that activists provide visually exciting action that makes good pictures in exchange for news media coverage. For instance, a march on the statehouse with one person dressed as a chicken hit the front pages of local and regional newspapers and topped the nightly television news. As one reporter wrote, "People who wear life-size chicken outfits will always get attention" (Baker, 1995c, p. A1); consequently, the chicken often appeared in public and continued to get publicity.

News coverage demonstrated the *protest paradigm* (Chan & Lee, 1984), which questions protesters' legitimacy and employs a battle metaphor that focuses on conflict between players at the expense of the content of an issue. In the beginning, episodic framing often trumped thematic framing, which resulted in superficial coverage that assigned responsibility to individuals rather than holding societal or institutional factions accountable (Iyengar, 1991). For instance, the bulk of news media coverage from 1995 to 2002 focused on events surrounding this particular CAFO rather than examining factory farms, in general; as a result, all eyes were focused on BE and not on the larger issue of such farms.

Despite the impressive quantity of news coverage, the challenges for CCCO seemed insurmountable. The core group struggled mightily in each of the three essential aspects of movement development described previously: resources, organization, and collective action frames. Many members did not have computers or internet access, further confounding attempts at organization; in fact, about the only presence the group had was a post office box. Nor did the group understand the nuances and need to develop and repeat key messages as a means of influencing news coverage, public understanding, and public opinion. Messages were haphazard and reactive, and resources were paltry. By way of comparing the asymmetrical resources, BE employed 480 workers and brought in an estimated $125 million in revenues (Byron, 1999). In 2003, the ODA had a budget of $52.5 million, with $335,000 earmarked for communications just for that year (Drake, 2006), and its communications budget nearly tripled during the 8-year controversy, whereas the entire 8-year budget of CCCO was less than $25,000.

CCCO applied for and received a $10,000 grant from Farm Aid, an organization that provides financial resources and celebrity backing by way of country singer Willie Nelson's support. CCCO used the grant to hire an attorney who pursued litigation and lobbying strategies. (The attorney's fees, although reduced, were the single biggest expense and one that the group continues whittling away at today via garage sales.) In 1998, at the same time that the health director declared BE a public health threat, other organizations with divergent missions joined with CCCO to focus on factory farms. CCCO attracted a coalition of 10,000 people that included members from the Ohio Farmers Union, Ohio Sierra Club, Humane Society of the United States, and the Ohio Catholic Conference, to sign a letter to state officials calling for a moratorium on factory farms, but the state's Republican-led Senate Agriculture Committee swiftly blocked it.

Opponents of the factory farm were most successful when they used an "injustice" frame in relation to the farm. In one incident, members of the animal rights group, Mercy for Animals (http://www.mercyforanimals.org), made a videotape about BE that revealed the injustice done to its farmed animals, creating a significant buzz among the general public about the deplorable conditions depicted. In another case that resonated with the public, a CCCO leader was quoted in the local newspaper asserting that everyone deserved clean air and water. As described throughout this case, the most attention and change came when groups and organizations aligned their voices in collective action frames; their effectiveness broke down when their individual interests took priority over common goals.

A portion of the Farm Aid grant to CCCO funded advertisements, as well as the creation of a quarterly printed newsletter, for which I was responsible. I first designed a logo for the group and a name for the quarterly publication, *Beneath the Shell*. The newsletter was a four-page, black-and-white hardcopy publication with a distribution that exceeded 100 people, including journalists and elected officials.

The newsletter accomplished the multiple objectives of framing explained earlier by articulating the problems and the cause of the problems; making moral judgments about the factory farm and the resultant situation, particularly regarding environmental justice issues; and recommending solutions. Additionally, the newsletter satisfied other framing needs by (a) creating identity, or the sense that those affected by this issue were like the newsletter readers and that this could happen to them; (b) generating agency, or the sense that people can do something about this problem; and (c) articulating the environmental injustice of factory farms.

Producing this newsletter gave CCCO a way to create a narrative about BE rather than rely only on news media narratives. To create this narrative,

I interviewed CCCO members and asked them to tell their stories by contributing the major articles, which added credibility to the newsletter among its recipients. The newsletter also highlighted specific actions that recipients could take to confront the problem, such as attending public forums, writing letters to newspaper editors and elected officials, and supporting CCCO via donations and volunteering.

Another way that I lent support to CCCO was through proactive media relations activities. During a march at the statehouse, I discussed the situation with the agricultural beat reporter from *The Columbus Dispatch*, after which he regularly reported on BE. I also contacted an Associated Press reporter in Cleveland, who began following the issue, and I frequently wrote letters to editors of various newspapers in affected communities, as well as op-ed columns that were published in Ohio's major newspapers.

CCCO activities induced constant local and regional publicity, and, at times, national attention. Group members maintained a clip file of news coverage, and I monitored that file regularly to informally content analyze the stories and tone of the coverage. Eventually, I conducted a longitudinal frame analysis of the issue as it played out in local news media to discover what master frames evolved over time and how proponents and opponents were framed (Drake, 2006). That study was the culmination of my experience as a naïve participant, my activist work with this group, my professional work in the communications industry, and my initiation into communication scholarship on framing and environmental reporting. Although truncated, the next section summarizes key findings of that work, highlights the influence of frame sponsors, and illuminates the substantial difference in power and resources among them.

THEORIZING SUBTERFUGE

What was remarkable about this public debate was that, at face value, CCCO had great influence in shaping the issue and power in moving it forward to problem status. *The Marion Star*, with a circulation of 14,000, published nearly 500 articles about the issue over an 8-year period from mid-1995 (when it first reported that the facility planned to open) through 2003 (when BE was ordered to close). Indeed, CCCO was effective at shaping the news media agenda, with publicity peaking in 1998 and 1999 at 116 and 80 articles, respectively, in that local newspaper, and other years averaging 47 articles. However, closer inspection of the master frames that evolved reveals that although CCCO had minor victories, by and large, the group was less effective at frame dominance. The state–industry partnership dwarfed CCCO in terms of financial, political, strategic, and human resources, and, as a result, it regained frame dominance over the issue.

With their "spiral of opportunity," Miller and Reichert (2003) illustrated four key stages through which an issue advances: emergence, definition/conflict, resonance, and equilibrium/resolution—each providing diminishing opportunities to reframe the issue. The development of the factory farm issue mirrored this evolution. The framing of opponents, proponents, and other agents ebbed and flowed throughout the debate, during which four nondiscrete master frames evolved: (a) progress is good, (b) clear threat to health, (c) Buckeye is a bad egg and more regulations are necessary, and (d) ODA will fix everything (see Table 5.1 for headlines of articles published in *The Marion Star* that illustrate these four master frames).

During the emergence phase, the frame of "progress is good" dominated. Government and industry sources praised the economic benefits of the factory farm, which was effective because U.S. cultural frames default to the script that privileges economic progress. Additionally, by not addressing the issue or engaging with CCCO, top government officials delegitimized CCCO, denied the existence of a problem, and, thus, prevented the issue from gaining even more traction in the news. CCCO, however, kept the issue in the local newspaper by providing a steady flow of news events, such as by demonstrating, lobbying, writing letters to newspaper editors, marching on the statehouse, attending public forums, filing appeals to the Ohio Environmental Protection Agency (OEPA), exploring multiple regulatory avenues, filing formal complaints against BE, and organizing letter-writing campaigns.

During the definition/conflict phase, CCCO gained legitimacy through frame realignment, which resulted in the dominant frame that BE was a "clear threat to health." Five major variables caused a sea change during this time:

1. effective organization by CCCO that represented its most successful attempt at collective action,
2. increasing corporate malfeasance by BE,
3. criticism against BE from government sources,
4. news coverage that described the human impact from BE and portrayed citizens as victims, and
5. an election during which Ohio's Governor George V. Voinovich ran for and was elected to the U.S. Senate.

CCCO was more effectual at this time than any other, with its efforts shaping the dominant frame. Communication activism included securing grant resources and celebrity backing; creating the monthly newsletter; lobbying for local government support; collaborating with religious, environmental, and animal rights organizations and activists; and earning national news coverage, including reporting in *The Wall Street Journal* and on the National

TABLE 5.1. *The Marion Star* Headlines Illustrating Phases and Master Frames

Phases, Master Frames, and Illustrative Headlines	Date
Phase I: Progress is Good (1995–1996; economics, growth, expert support)	
Politicians Support Claim of Economic Benefits	Sept. 4, 1995
Team to Free Expanding Farmers from Red Tape	Dec. 24, 1995
Policy Experts: Public has it Wrong	March 9, 1996
Phase II: Clear Threat to Health (1997–1998; unhealthy, unsafe, expert opposition)	
A "Clear Threat to Health": Health Official Opposes Permits for Egg Farm	March 11, 1998
"Dateline" Scrutinizes Local Egg Farm [for back-dated eggs]	April 7, 1998
Boyle Blasts Buckeye Egg Farm's Growth	Nov. 23, 1998
Ohio Gets Pummeled for Factory Farms; Egg Operations are Targeted	Dec. 4, 1998
Phase III: Buckeye is a Bad Egg and More Regulations are Necessary (1999–2001; scapegoating)	
Buckeye Egg Farm Gets Violation Notice from OEPA	Jan. 4, 1999
[Senator] Mumper Introduces New Factory Farm Bill	May 15, 1999
[Governor] Taft Stands Tall on Need for Factory Farm Rules	Aug. 2, 1999
Farm Bureau: Buckeye Egg not Typical Farm; Farmers Call for Clear Rules	Dec. 3, 1999
State Tells Buckeye Egg to Stop Being a Nuisance	Dec. 3, 1999
State's Suit against Buckeye Egg One of the Largest this Decade	Dec. 19, 1999
[Attorney General] Montgomery: Buckeye Egg's a "Flagrant Violator"	May 3, 2000
Phase IV: Ohio Department of Agriculture (ODA) Will Fix Everything (2002–2003; resolution)	
State to Court: Close Buckeye Egg Barns	Nov. 20. 2001
ODA Scrambles to Crack Down on BE; Dailey Wants to Revoke Farm's Permits	Aug. 20, 2002
Egg Farm Foes Wait, Watch New Enforcer [ODA]	Aug. 26, 2002
ODA Answers Dairy Farm Questions	Jan. 9, 2003
"Honest Egg" Eyeing Egg Facilities	Jan. 29, 2003
Buckeye Egg Told to Close; Locals Welcome News, but Expect Appeals	July 9, 2003
If Egg Farm Cleans Up Act, Finds Buyer, Everyone Wins	July 24, 2003

Broadcasting Corporation's television program *Dateline*. News coverage peaked in 1998, with 116 articles appearing, a 100% surge in coverage over the previous year. Approximately 50 articles from 1997 to 1998 legitimized the problem and CCCO by advancing the "clear threat to health" frame. Surprisingly, in this context, the OEPA granted two more permits to build or expand BE's facilities.

At this time when CCCO achieved frame dominance, the proverbial gloves came off. The factory farm threatened to sue the health director. The local FB launched public relations efforts that manifested in defensive headlines, such as "[Farmers are] doing the best we can," and in signs that simultaneously minimized the problem and denounced concerned citizens through the message that bad odors are just the way it is in rural areas. The governor and other state officials, who had for the previous 3 years remained silent on the sidelines, now engaged in the dialogue to quell public opinion. With an election looming, the state–industry partnership was able to table the issue by putting BE's pending permits on hold for a year. The governor literally put the issue on hold from July to November 1998 and, thereby, preempted coverage prior to the election; the closer to election day, the fewer articles there were, with 25 and 19 in March and April, respectively, in contrast to just 7, 6, and 0 articles in September, October, and November, respectively. Preemption is a common tactic in public relations to keep something out of the news or to minimize news coverage. This cooling-off period would be followed by a proactive "shock-and-awe" strategy from state officials to regain control of the issue by dominating the conversation, vindicating citizens, punishing the villain, and resolving the problem through new regulations.

During the resonance phase, the frame of "Buckeye is a bad egg and more regulations are necessary" dominated. This phase, more than any other, was replete with political spectacle. The state–industry-sponsored frame dominated, with BE cast as the villain, citizens cast as victims, and state agents playing heroes. Citizens had gained legitimacy, but ironically, as citizens' voices became more important, they became less potent. News coverage revealed a marked increase in top leaders engaging the issue. Casting BE as the villain was a necessary strategy shift for both the state and industry to regain control of what had become a big problem. By scapegoating, the state–industry partnership diverted attention from the livestock industry at large. Citizens' voices largely were overshadowed by government sources effectively co-opting the issue with a steady stream of government-sponsored events that fed the news media and filled the news hole. Citizens found it hard to disagree with the master frame that "Buckeye is a bad egg and more regulations are necessary"; consequently, this frame found the most resonance. CCCO essentially sat back and watched the spectacle play out, in part, because the grant money and other resources had been depleted. On one level, defining BE as a "bad egg" was a victory for CCCO; on another level, the industry–state effectively limited the problem to one company and, thereby, neglected the broader and systemic problems associated with factory farms.

During the equilibrium/resolution phase, an "ODA will fix everything" frame dominated. ODA cast itself as the vindicator and, at the same time, took over from the OEPA control of the permitting and regulating processes for factory farms. Cable and Benson (1993) predicted that organizations would become skilled at managing environmental conflicts and framing relevant issues, asserting that organizations "will not simply acquiesce to attempts to limit their profitability ... [but] will fight back" (p. 474). In this case, the state–industry partnership fought back and regained control of the issue. Part of the fight included tactics based on subterfuge, a strategy to circumvent democratic participation.

Diffusion and Subterfusion of Innovations

Given that animal feeding operations are controversial, it would be natural to wonder how the livestock industry so efficiently supplanted traditional farming and ranching practices over the course of a couple of decades without widespread public controversy or debate. Typically, a new phenomenon, such as factory farms, would follow the *diffusion of innovations* model (Rogers, 1995), which explains how sources use communication to raise people's awareness of an innovation and to get them to consider, try, and, ultimately, adopt it. In this case, however, the livestock industry resorted to *subterfusion of innovations*, a process by which an innovation, as it is being rapidly diffused within an industry, is effectively hidden from public view to avoid scrutiny (Drake & McCoy, 2009). Consequently, the new phenomenon of CAFOs was explicitly adopted by producers, but unknowingly adopted by consumers. By using this model, the livestock industry averted public scrutiny long enough for a critical mass of diffusion and adoption to occur.

Krackhardt (1997) argued that a small minority of innovators can take over a system if *viscosity* is present, the lack of free movement of people and exchange of ideas throughout a system. In this case, viscosity represented the lack of communication among the public at large regarding a radically changing livestock industry. Such structural variables explain the diffusion of controversial innovations, but they ignore the rationality of actors and strategic behavior that dominate 21st-century communication and diminish authentic public dialogue.

Subterfusion, thus, seeks to leapfrog legitimacy questions by masking a controversial innovation. As explained below, this case study revealed five methods of subterfuge: (a) rural redlining to target areas with fewer resources and less political muscle, (b) preemptive framing to keep an innovation out of the news, (c) manipulating definitions of key concepts to maintain frame dominance and issues management, (d) employing misleading names and frames to mask an innovation and to circumvent democratic participation, and (e) creating a "web of impediments" or roadblocks to prevent opposing voices from influencing an issue (Drake, 2004).

Rural Redlining. Residents in more sparsely populated, remote areas are especially vulnerable to a new form of discrimination that I call *rural redlining*, a practice to demarcate areas for unwanted land-use facilities that unfairly discriminates against rural residents, often those of lower socioeconomic status. This intention was obvious, as stated in two newspaper articles: The first article argued that "the spread of factory farms ... has been shaped by the industry's search for regions of the country where local control is weak" ("In Defense of Local Control," 2004, p. A13); the second article maintained that "factory farms often create problems of environmental injustice when they are located (as they often are) in poor communities with no political power" (S. Williams, 2004, para. 8). Socioeconomic data from the U.S. Census Bureau (2009) for Hardin County, Ohio, where the bulk of BE facilities were concentrated, fall well below the state average, with the median household income in 2007 being $41,546 (more than 10% below the state average), the median value of owner-occupied housing in 2000 being $73,800 (30% below the state average), and 15% of Hardin County residents falling below the poverty line in 2007 (nearly 3% below the state average).

Preemptive Framing. *Preemptive framing*, keeping issues out of the news, is the most powerful framing of all. In this case, preemptive framing by state–industry agents started early on. Deciding where to locate CAFOs begins years in advance, with the general public being the last to be informed and only after decisions have been made. Molotch and Lester (1975) explained how a dominant coalition of several actors who hold power in the community (e.g., realtors, landowners, and politicians) often are privy to information well in advance and are involved in behind-the-scenes planning, which was the case in this community, where, as it turned out, BE had been quietly trying to build for the better part of a decade (Baker, 1995a), although in a different part of the county. This preemptive "decide, announce, defend" decision-making strategy is common to unwanted land-use facilities because it circumvents democratic participation (Inhaber, 1992). Testimony to the success of the livestock industry in keeping the "new" industrialized processes out of the news is the fact that although CAFOs had been around for several decades, the general public just began to learn about them at the turn of the millennium.

Manipulating Definitions for Frame Dominance. This case illustrated classic strategies of persuasion and intentionality in framing. The president of the Ohio Senate warned against regulating confined livestock facilities by saying that "telling an owner how to use his property is risky," and he explained the lack of regulations by asserting that "he's not aware of a definition in Ohio of what constitutes an 'industry-sized' farm for the purposes of regulation" (cited in D. Glenn & Williams, 1998, pp. A1, A2). Only after permits were granted and the facilities built did state agents define and propose regulations for CAFOs.

Defining CAFOs has been equally problematic and has been part of the subterfuge; without a name or definition, an issue cannot be a problem. However, once established, CAFOs needed the permanent legitimacy that comes with regulation. The OEPA subsequently reclassified such farms as large, medium, and small, with large farms having more than 1,000 beef cattle, 2,500 hogs, or 82,000 laying hens ("House Passes Bill," 2003). The battle lines were drawn, with opponents urging legislators to "treat factory farms as what they truly are: factories, requiring regulations, zoning, and taxing different from small-scale farms" (Holmes, 2003, p. A8). Proponents continue to call confinement facilities "farms," and some owners develop a facility to fall a few animals short of the official definition and, thereby, avoid regulations.

Misleading Frames to Circumvent Democratic Participation. Clearly, some of the chief functions of framing are the power to name, label, and define the players and problems. Agrarian symbols, such as "farming" or "agriculture," often are employed to serve ideological ends because they are associated with broader U.S. ideals, such as God, family, moral integrity, independence, and hard work (Dalecki & Coughenour, 1992). These symbols, however, have not kept up with the industry and, consequently, people "continue to use agriculture as an overall term that obscures most of its industrial character" (Friedland, 2002, pp. 352–353). By retaining these symbols, the industry not only maintains valuable widespread positive perceptions but it avoids very real burdens of legislation, regulation, and taxation imposed on every other industry.

Although proponents of CAFOs have rejected symbols of industry (e.g., factories and plants) and clung to antiquated terminology (e.g., farms and barns), in practice, they have promoted industrialization. Journalists are caught in the middle. Using terminology that no longer fits results in general-interest newspapers' farm writing that is superficial, stereotyped, and crisis oriented (Reisner & Walter, 1994). To another extreme, farm magazine writing tends to be uncritical of agriculture and unconcerned with social and environmental issues. Overall, print media coverage tends to polarize the industry and the public, which bodes poorly for the public's understanding of and participation in agricultural policymaking (Reisner & Walter, 1994).

Additionally, Walter (1996) found that U.S. farm magazines from 1934 to 1991 consistently constructed the meaning of a successful farmer in a coherent, one-sided model that privileged commercial-industrial methods. As Walter noted, "Successful farmers populating the narrative typically have been aggressive pursuers of higher production, greater efficiency, and, often, more farmland or livestock" (p. 604). Few publications offered alternatives to this paradigm, even though less explicitly commercial criteria for success existed; for example, successful farmers rarely were linked with soil conservation, land stewardship, or involvement in alternative agriculture movements. Walter concluded that the findings revealed "an underlying editorial bias toward agricultural industrialization and the interests of major advertisers" (p. 604).

News media coverage of BE throughout this study revealed a strong tendency to default to traditional agricultural terminology. Headlines disguised the industrial nature of the innovation, with 464 out of 487 referencing "egg farms" or "farms." Once CAFOs entered public dialogue, industry agents developed a street-friendly name, "megafarms," which retains the misleading term of "farm" to combat opponents' descriptors of "factory farms." A recent trend is to drop "concentrated" or "confined" and call them simply "animal feeding operations."

The first newspaper article announcing the new CAFO illustrated the naming problem, with Baker (1995d), at various points, calling AgriGeneral's operation an "egg plant," a "farm," and an "egg-laying and washing operation." During the first year of coverage, virtually all of the subsequent articles coalesced into naming BE an "egg farm," aligning with the agrarian mythology. In fact, it was not until the seventh month of the controversy that the alternative term, "factory farm," surfaced in a headline (Baker, 1995b). In response, proponents actively denounced the term "factory." As B. Williams (1995) explained:

> Some say the sprawling egg farms are egg "factories," a view that AgriGeneral and the Ohio Poultry Association call nonsense, because eggs cannot be manufactured. Others say the complex may not be a factory, but it is more like an industrial operation than a traditional farm. Factory farming, corporate farming, industrial farming, intensive farming—whatever it's called—is big and it's raising a stink in some parts of rural Ohio. (p. G1)

During the height of its crisis, AgriGeneral exercised the ultimate power by changing its name to Buckeye Egg Farm as part of an image makeover. The new name made it virtually impossible for journalists to avoid calling the industrial operation a farm.

Creating a Web of Impediments. This communication activism scholarship also revealed a new construct, the *web of impediments*, which references those subsidies that serve as a series of roadblocks to prevent opposing voices from influencing an issue (Drake, 2004). Proponents of CAFOs in this case included BE, the livestock industry (e.g., FB and the Poultry Association), and the state government (i.e., ODA)—groups and organizations that dominate lobbying and public relations activities via a larger web of subsidies or resources and access (Gandy, 1982; Pan & Kosicki, 2003). However, evidence in this case pointed to an aggressive proponent strategy of getting out desired messages and, simultaneously, muting opponents. A web of bureaucratic impediments, consequently, blocked outsiders from industry knowledge.

Further impediments were used to first minimize public awareness of the innovation and then to demonize and discredit critics via the news media. Multiple state–industry agents tried to marginalize citizens and to put more power in the hands of the livestock industry. The state–industry muscle can be seen in Table 5.2, which includes selected examples, out of dozens, of article headlines published in *The Marion Star* where agents delegitimized, regulated, litigated, threatened, bribed, or otherwise coerced opponents. For example, one headline revealed the company's offer to pay township trustees if they voted in its favor: "Egg Farm Company Offers Cash Incentive; AgriGeneral Wants Township Not to Use Certain Fire Codes" (1997).

Although legislation would be developed to "free expanding farmers from red tape" (McKee, 1995), endless bureaucratic and regulatory roadblocks were set up to stymie citizens. Major decisions and public forums consistently were scheduled during the Christmas and year-end holiday season to minimize public engagement. Public meetings and hearings were held in rooms too small to accommodate citizens who attended, and they literally were left standing out in the hall on more than one important occasion. New legislation that "limits local government's role" ("New Law," 2003) was enacted. A three-strike proposal to make a felony out of three false accusations was so ludicrous that it failed even in Ohio's industry-friendly political setting: "Residents Claim Bill Would Stifle Them; Egg Farm Neighbors Claim Intent is to Silence Them" (Warsmith, 1998). Additionally, as demonstrated in Table 5.2, state–industry agents followed the public relations playbook to alternately deny, defend, denounce, distract, and, finally, to defuse the problem, regardless of physical realities.

The web of impediments created by state–industry agents includes stifling debate and circumventing dialogue in the news media. Dozier and Lauzen (2000) warned that this type of public relations "may have profound harmful effects on society's political and mass media systems" (p. 18). In this case, to gain final frame dominance, experts bullied, punished, and otherwise

TABLE 5.2. Impediments Created by State–Industry Agents

The Marian Star Headlines Illustrating Web of Impediments	Date
Politicians Support Claim of Economic Benefits	Sept. 4, 1995
Team to Free Expanding Farmers from Red Tape	Dec. 24, 1995
Poultry Experts: Public has it Wrong	March 9, 1996
EPA Inspector No Longer at Egg Farm Site	Dec. 27, 1996
AgriGeneral: Group Lying about Its Eggs	May 2, 1997
Egg Farm Offers Cash Incentive; AgriGeneral Wants Township Not to Use Fire Codes	Aug. 12, 1997
AgriGeneral Denies 29 Violations Filed by OSHA	Sept. 10, 1997
AgriGeneral has New Boss, Name	Oct. 7, 1997
Buckeye Egg Farm Threatens Action against Citizens' Group	Oct. 23, 1997
Residents Claim Bill Would Stifle Them	Jan. 9, 1998
Senate Leaders Pull Moratorium Bill	March 11, 1998
Egg Farm Threatens Legal Action; Lufkin [health director] Named in Letter	March 17, 1998
[Buckeye Egg COO] Hansen: They're Not Our Flies	March 20, 1998
Poultry Industry Tries to Solve Manure Problem	Aug. 25, 1998
Judge Sides with Buckeye Egg: Megafarm can Re-open, Sell Barns near Marion	Feb. 25, 2003
New Law Reclassifies Megafarms, Limits Local Govt.'s Role	Aug. 7, 2003

exerted undue influence on newspapers throughout the state to end the controversy.

First, in 2002, the state's capital newspaper quietly dropped the agricultural beat altogether, even though "the need for agricultural reporting was greater than ever" (B. Williams, agriculture beat reporter at *The Columbus Dispatch*, personal communication, June 2, 2003). In another incident, after a reporter at the *Cleveland Plain Dealer* produced in-depth coverage of the factory farm problem, the ODA "made further information seeking [for her] more difficult" (F. Henry, *Cleveland Plain Dealer* reporter, personal communication, July 14, 2003). The FB, in the words of Cornely, one if its public relations executives, then "picked a fight" (as cited in Drake, 2004, p. 163) with the *Dayton Daily News*, with Cornely visiting the newspaper that had earned awards for its coverage of factory farms and confronting journalists about their critical coverage of the livestock industry. Finally, after 8 years of reporting on the factory farm problem, the local newspaper dropped its coverage of the issue almost entirely in the midst of the precedent-setting decision regarding whether BE would remain open. When asked about the lack of coverage, the editor revealed that he had been contacted by the livestock industry for being too critical, saying:

> If we're not doing our job in this matter, then why were we the only Ohio newspaper the Agriculture Department called following the announcement of the closings of Buckeye Egg? They [sic] felt our article took too critical a viewpoint on how long this "due process" was taking. (B. Guth, personal communication, August 12, 2003)

The local newspaper's sudden noncritical coverage was a sign that, by 2003, the ODA was successfully regaining framing control of the issue.

It was in this local newspaper that Lufkin first declared BE a threat to public health, and, in 1999, the newspaper issued the first of many calls to shut down this factory farm. However, the livestock industry's influence was seen in an editorial published in 2003 in *The Marion Star*, which showed a complete reversal of its position through its headline, "If Egg Farm Cleans Up Act, Finds Buyer, Everyone Wins." The editorial may well have been taken straight from an ODA press release in the way that it ignored environmental justice issues, along with issues of animal care ethics, quality of life, and other negative effects on the community.

In 2003, the state of Ohio reversed its decision to close down the facility and, instead, allowed the owner of BE to sell the facilities without any interruption in the operation. The agricultural industry practiced successful frame realignment and regained final control of the issue by using BE's owner as a scapegoat and diverting attention away from the larger question of the legitimacy of factory farms, in general. Government officials appeased opponents with the threat to close down BE, but through the sale of BE, the state created the perception that it got rid of the problem, despite the physical reality that the factory farm remained.

Since 2003, CCCO has become mostly inactive as an organization. It is one of many groups linked to social movements that "spring up, flourish, and fade as those movements evolve" (Dozier & Lauzen, 2000, p. 13). Such social movements, however, can bring about slow, but profound, societal changes by way of the cumulative efforts of these diverse ad hoc groups. In addition to contributing to the larger sustainable agriculture movement, CCCO was influential throughout the debate, as detailed throughout this case study. Similarly, in addition to influencing decisions, particularly regarding the BE facilities, communication activism by CCCO members was instrumental in moving journalists and the news media on the issue of animal feeding operations along the continuum from predominantly episodic framing to regular and sustained thematic framing. By earning significant news media coverage, communication activism by citizens intensified public awareness and shaped public opinion concerning CAFOs, as seen in biennial public attitude surveys (Sharp, 2008). That communication activism was in line with Krackhardt's (1997) explanation that the success of a controversial innovation does not depend on the quality of the innovation itself but on the ability to build a critical mass of support for the innovation by way of rhetorical strategy, which suggests a significant role and responsibility for public relations practitioners in promoting social justice issues.

LESSONS LEARNED ABOUT COMMUNICATION ACTIVISM SCHOLARSHIP

During the course of this project, I learned a great deal about communication activism scholarship. As explained here, by the time the campaign reached its apogee, I had to grapple with two major issues: (a) the application of public relations practices for social justice purposes and (b) the dialectical tensions inherent in communication activism that involves speaking for others.

Reclaiming Public Relations to Promote Social Justice

Perhaps the strongest dialectical tension I experienced throughout this journey is the paradox of public relations. The academy teaches students that public relations is about doing the right thing and communicating it, but that oversimplified vision fails to account for power relationships between entities, a long history of corporate bias, and inherently asymmetrical structural variables. Using a critical lens, I explore and echo the call for justice advocates to reclaim public relations and for public relations scholars to expand their intellectual domain.

Public relations has been defined as "the management function that builds and maintains mutually beneficial relationships between an organization and the publics upon whom its success or failure depends" (Cutlip, Center, & Broom, 2006, p. 5). Bernays, who, early on, candidly called public relations "propaganda" (1928) and, later, "engineering consent" (1955), described how the profession evolved from a "public be damned" mentality at the turn of the 20th century through stages of "public information," "mutual understanding," and, finally, to the era of "adaptation and adjustment" marked by organizations' growing need from 1960 to 1990 to accommodate activist and societal demands.

Practitioners were warned to "protect" their companies from activists by "aggressively applying public relations" (Rose, 1991, p. 32). Effective social movements of the past have resulted in redoubled efforts in the academy and in the field to master crisis communication—a branch of public relations that makes a science out of battling activists and defusing crises, such as corporate malfeasance (see, e.g., Coombs, 2007; Coombs &

Holladay, 2010; Heath & O'Hair, 2008; Seeger, Sellnow, & Ulmer, 2003; Ulmer, Sellnow, & Seeger, 2007; Zaremba, 2009). L. A. Grunig (1992) elaborated on how activism limits the effectiveness of corporations, and how the world's largest firms have become über experts at dodging activists' bullets. The efforts of socially beneficial campaigns, such as the Mothers Against Drunk Driving, notwithstanding, countless exposés of less than ethical public relations have led critics to suggest that the practice has devolved to a "public be scammed" (Drake, 2007, p. 31) era.

Spotlighting the final quarter of the 20th century, Stauber and Rampton (1995) chronicled case after case of front groups, fake news, disinformation, obfuscation, and other impediments that public relations firms use to sway public opinion and systematically mute concerned citizens' voices. Among the most atrocious instances, the authors detailed how, in 1990, the Kuwaiti government paid $10.8 million to Hill & Knowlton (H&K), then the world's largest public relations firm, to mastermind what became a deceitful and unethical campaign to "sell the war" in the Persian Gulf. Stauber and Rampton detailed how 119 H&K executives from 12 offices across the United States ran the campaign that included staging a Congressional hearing with fabricated testimony from a 15-year-old Kuwaiti girl (who turned out to be a member of the Kuwaiti royal family who was coached on what to say) who said that she saw Iraqi soldiers take hundreds of babies from hospital incubators and leave them on the cold floor to die. The story spread like wildfire, and the U.S. Senate voted to support a declaration of war against Iraq (Stauber & Rampton, 1995). Stauber and Rampton also examined numerous deceptive practices used by the tobacco and chemical industries. Underhanded public relations tactics, thus, transpire daily.

Alas, the ideals portrayed by the two-way symmetrical view of public relations (J. E. Grunig & Hunt, 1984) and the Excellence Study (Dozier, 1995)—designed to answer the how, why, and to what extent communication affects the achievement of organizational objectives—lull even well-intentioned practitioners into a blind spot where they do not see the enormous resource disparity between corporations and activist publics (Karlberg, 1996) or between corporations and powerless publics (Dozier & Lauzen, 2000) whose lives are affected by the behavior of organizations but do not have the resources necessary to command mutually beneficial relationships with those organizations. Nor do those ideals account for the possibility of irreconcilable differences between a company and any one of its key publics. All of this suggests the need to study public relations and activism through a critical lens.

Working with CCCO took me outside of the corporate box to consider public relations from a broader perspective, and to reject hegemonic views that believe "the behavior of activist groups is a growing problem for [corporate] organizations" (Werder, 2006, p. 342). Derville (2005) argued that by using a corporate paradigm, public relations scholars misinterpret activism and overlook the valuable role that even radical activists play in raising public awareness about social issues. Dozier and Lauzen (2000) urged public relations scholars to apply a critical perspective to consider unintended consequences of public relations at both macro- and microlevels. They added that a critical approach is beneficial in revealing moral and ethical contradictions inherent in the practice of public relations. Dozier and Lauzen argued that the myopic empirical–administrative focus privileging the corporate agenda and informing much scholarship about public relations does not accommodate social movements and activism.

I would go further to claim that not only do public relations scholars need to apply a critical lens in shaping their intellectual domain but that scholars and practitioners should consider their role and responsibility in reclaiming public relations for civic purposes—that is, as a tool for activism (see also Holtzhausen, 2010). Recent headlines about some of the failures of the biggest industries (e.g., oil, pharmaceuticals, tobacco, and banking) reveal the need to reclaim public relations in this way. Communication professionals owe a debt to society, with Mannes (1955/1964) saying it best: "For it is not enough to show people how to *live* better: There is a mandate for any group with enormous powers of communication to show people how to be better" (p. 34). Hence, public relations tactics should be used to benefit social movements and, most pressing, for efforts such as my work with CCCO in media advocacy and public education to secure social justice.

Even if public relations practitioners want to "do the right thing," they may be limited by complex power relationships (B. K. Berger, 2005) of the dominant coalition (Dozier, 1995) and other structural constraints. Holtzhausen and Voto (2002) found that some practitioners counter this limitation by assuming activist roles within their companies, serving as a conscience. In some cases, a desire for change or a concern for employee representation motivate professionals to practice dissensus, dissymmetry, and other powerful forms of resistance that can give rise to new ideas and solutions. Hence, postmodern public relations practitioners can be a positive force for change by resisting authority, even when they are part of the dominant coalition.

For a better balance, a social justice perspective should be included in public relations education. Critical theories of public relations, along with social justice literature, belong on the bookshelf side-by-side with traditional public relations texts that privilege corporate over civic interests (Duffy, 2000). By incorporating activism into an introductory public relations course, Opt (2005) demonstrated how educators can "empower students by giving them a voice in social issues while they simultaneously learn public relations skills" (p. 47).

Third, the post-9/11 world begs for more academic departments of public relations to specialize in social justice issues. If public relations education fails to seize this opportunity, other disciplines will continue to claim this focus and the benefits of communication scholarship will not be obtained. Not only will a social justice focus recast public relations but it also will make public relations education increasingly more relevant within society.

Speaking for Others

In addition to recognizing the need for activists to reclaim public relations, my growth as a communication scholar-activist was evident in another realm: experiencing and coming to appreciate the dialectical tensions inherent in engaging in communication activism with people or groups that have backgrounds and experiences different from mine. Other-directed social movements include those that "are created, led, and populated primarily by those who do not perceive themselves to be dispossessed, and are struggling for the freedom, equality, justice, and rights of others rather than selves" (Stewart, 1999, p. 92). In the case discussed in this chapter, "other" refers both to farmed animals and rural residents.

With the latter group, instant rapport and credibility with CCCO members suggest that I enjoyed insider status because it was the community where I had grown up. Insider status resulted in authentic narratives by me and others in the newsletters and editorials. Occasionally, however, I sensed "otherness," but at the time, I was not always cognizant of its presence or cause in this hodgepodge group that did not fit into a single stereotype. Cloke and Little (1997) underscored the diversity found in rural locales, pointing out that there is no essential rural condition but, instead, multiple realities that are becoming increasingly complex. Aside from ethnic homogeneity (Caucasian), CCCO comprised a disparate group—teachers, business owners, farmers, and office professionals of various incomes, as well as working- and middle-class women and men ages 25 to 65—connected simply by the map and their mission. Thus, the outsider status I felt may be attributed to a divide as great as class and race: the urban–rural dialectic.

Although geographic and social terrains between rural and urban may appear less distinct than they were 50 years ago, the personal terrain and politics of identity are widening (Ching & Creed, 1997). It was on this murky ground between city and country that I detected differences had developed. For instance, CCCO members confounded me when they voted against their self-interests and remained loyal to politicians who consistently undermined CCCO's efforts. Area residents voted largely Republican, despite the fact that other politicians were sympathetic to their cause. At state and federal levels, CAFOs thrived under Republican leadership beholden to corporate interests and blind to the unintended consequences of CAFOs in nonmetropolitan areas. Rural communities are suffering direct and immediate repercussions of CAFOs, and Spurlock (2009), noting the urban–rural divide, observed that "predictably, 'the rural' has once again become a figure of ecological and cultural loss" (p. 8).

This dialectic is compounded by a contemporary challenge of defining the term "rural." Depending on which definition is used, 23% to 25% (i.e., of the population) and 84% to 98% (i.e., of land area) of the United States is considered *rural* (John, 2008). As John (2008) explained, "Metro/urban areas can be defined using several criteria. Once this is done, nonmetro/rural is then defined by exclusion—any area that is not metro/urban is nonmetro/rural" (Introduction section, para. 3). Given that definition, it is easy to understand how the rural perspective has been relegated to the bottom of the cultural hierarchy, with urban beliefs privileged; indeed, the "urban has come to be the assumed reference" (Ching & Creed, 1997, p. 3).

Consequently, the urban–rural dialectic is predicated both on social and physical handicaps. In point of fact, populations in small towns are less able than those in cities to mobilize formal bureaucratic resources to react effectively to ecological crises (Couch & Knoll-Smith, 1994). These structural inequities faced by residents of nonmetropolitan areas hampered the CCCO via double jeopardy: first by way of the hardship itself of not being able to effectively mobilize formal bureaucratic resources, and then, again, by resultant disenfranchisement.

Traditionally, a seeming contradictory gap also has existed regarding the environment, such that rural residents typically are slightly less concerned with environmental issues than are urban residents (Tremblay & Dunlap, 1978). Whereas individuals who live in agricultural areas tend to embrace *stewardship*—a conservationist view that focuses on preserving natural resources for human use—Shiva (2000) and others have criticized this perspective for its environmental shortfalls, including a disregard for or need to dominate the nonhuman world.

Along with most CCCO members, my philosophical outlook shifted throughout our work from that of stewardship to one of *deep ecology* that looks holistically at the connectedness and ethical implications of plant, animal, and human life—a shift that instantiates Patterson's (2003) assertions of an earthkeeping tendency toward agricultural stewardship that "recognizes that the Earth is not solely for people's use and that ecological diversity and stability are important values which agriculture must not prejudice" (p. 57). From that perspective, everyone is involved in agricultural stewardship—consumers, manufacturers, and policymakers alike.

Just as rural is relegated to the last rung, this case revealed a hierarchy among nonhuman beings. Farmed animals have not resounded the same "irresistible call of conscience" (Black, 2003, p. 316) as do, for example, dogs, which is even truer in agricultural areas. Although an overwhelming majority of U.S. Americans agree with the right of farmed animals to "live decently," animal rights activists go further to argue that all animals have "the right not to be killed" (Black, 2003, p. 316). A focus on the animals hidden, and their inhumane treatment, in factory farms has sparked more concern for animals raised for food (see Mercy for Animals' website).

Clearly, the fight against factory farms has attracted unusual bedfellows, which can be advantageous if participants can successfully negotiate the disparate terrain. In this case, those opposing BE included, on one end of the spectrum, animal rights activists from the political left and primarily from urban areas, and, on the other end, conservative Christians primarily from rural settings. Black (2003) explained how these seemingly politically disjointed groups actually find common ground on the "sanctity of life," demonstrating that "opposite agitative units can mesh into a joint rhetoric calling for the rights of the marginalized, the sensate other" (p. 313).

Many individuals and groups, representing different ideological movements (e.g., animal rights, sustainability, and social justice), are speaking out against factory farms. Communication activists can be instrumental in mining joint rhetoric among these disparate groups, in speaking up for those beings that literally have no voice, and in helping muted voices to be heard.

CONCLUSION

Helping to amplify rural voices and magnify animal care ethics has been rewarding, but being an activist sometimes is too much to bear, as I found out in 2003, when the BE saga played out to its end. That year, I was consumed with the convalescence and, ultimately, the death of my father. Consequently, my family was absent during the Ohio Department of Agriculture's final public hearings that, after 8 long years, would determine the fate of this factory farm and community; in that moment, the outrage of factory farms paled next to personal grief. The struggle was over.

My story is not unique, as *struggle*—"to make strenuous or violent efforts in the face of difficulties or opposition" (Merriam-Webster Online, 2011)—is a part of, and aptly describes, the essence of communication activism, in general, and the decade-long ordeal of Buckeye Egg Farm, in particular. For that reason, it is especially vital to reflect on successes.

This chapter focused on the fight of a grassroots organization against factory farms in the sustainable agriculture movement, but that organization made a difference in many ways. Through communication activism, that organization had a hand in bringing about stepped-up regulations and oversight, cash awards and settlements to citizens who had suffered damages, fines against BE for environmental violations, and an order from the state to shut down the facilities, although it resulted, instead, in the sale of the confined animal feeding operation that still operates today.

Although communication activism in this one community did not ameliorate the devastating effects of confined animal feeding operations, this effort did advance the movement. Communication activism eventually affected more thematic coverage of factory farms, spawned nearly 500 articles in the local newspaper of the Ohio community affected by Buckeye Egg Farm, and obtained equally impressive coverage in regional and national news media. Media advocacy increased concern about factory farms in Ohio (Sharp, 2008) and it fueled debate on the topic throughout the state and at the national level.

The Environmental Integrity Project (2006) called Buckeye Egg Farm one of the "dirty half dozen" that represent "a range of regulatory challenges and failures in Ohio" (Case studies section, para. 1). Pressured by protesters, the livestock industry said it will phase in some improvements in animal conditions, but this particular operation, now doing business as Ohio Fresh Eggs, remains, even today, a powerful symbol of the injustice of factory farms. In fact, a recent fire at one of the plants drew 100 firefighters from 35 departments, drained more than 500,000 gallons of water (some from a nearby wildlife preserve), and led to 250,000 chicken deaths when electricity was shut off to prevent the fire from spreading (Zachariah, 2010).

Hence, the struggle continues. Concerned Citizens of Central Ohio and countless other grassroots groups worldwide have engaged in communication activism to promote sustainable food production, a movement that is stronger now than at any time in recent history. Communication scholar-activists have much to add to this movement, for by opening our mouths about food issues, we open minds and paths to social justice.

REFERENCES

Baker, D. (1995a, November 13). AgriGeneral still trying after all these years; egg company approached Marion area in late 1980s. *The Marion Star*, p. A1.
Baker, D. (1995b, September, 20). Coalition asks OEPA to study factory farm operations more. *The Marion Star*, p. A1.
Baker, D. (1995c, April 15). Ruffling feathers: Giant chicken demonstrators against Marseilles egg farm. *The Marion Star*, p. A1.
Baker, D. (1995d, March 1). Wyandot egg plant planned. *The Marion Star*, p. A1.
Bennett, W. L. (1990). Toward a theory of press–state relations in the United States. *Journal of Communication*, 40(2), 103–127. doi:10.1111/j.1460-2466.1990.tb02265.x
Berger, B. K. (2005). Power over, power with, and power to relations: Critical reflections on public relations, the dominant coalition, and activism. *Journal of Public Relations Research*, 17, 5–28. doi:10.1207/s1532754xprr1701_3
Berger, P. L., & Luckmann, T. (1966). *The social construction of reality: A treatise in the sociology of knowledge*. Garden City, NY: Doubleday.
Bernays, E. L. (1928). *Propaganda*. New York, NY: Horace Liveright.

Bernays, E. L. (1955). The engineering of consent. *ANNALS of the American Academy of Political and Social Science, 250,* 113–120. doi:10.1177/00027 1624725000116

Black, J. E. (2003). Extending the rights of personhood, voice, and life to sensate others: A homology of right to life and animal rights rhetoric. *Communication Quarterly, 51,* 312–331. doi:10.1080/01463370309370159

Burch, E. A., & Harry, J. C. (2004). Counter-hegemony and environmental justice in California newspapers: Source use patterns in stories about pesticides and farm workers. *Journalism & Mass Communication Quarterly, 81,* 559–577.

Byron, N. (1999, January). How we did last year. *Smart Business Columbus.* Retrieved from http://www.sbnonline.com

Cable, S., & Benson, M. (1993). Acting locally: Environmental injustice and the emergence of grass-roots environmental organizations. *Social Problems, 40,* 464–477. doi:10.1525/sp.1993.40.4.03x0092n

Carragee, K. M., & Roefs, W. (2004). The neglect of power in recent framing research. *Journal of Communication, 54,* 214–233. doi:10.1111/j.1460-2466.2004.tb02625.x

Chan, J. A., & Lee, C. C. (1984). The journalistic paradigm on civil protests: A case study of Hong Kong. In A. Arno & W. Dissanayake (Eds.), *The news media in national and international conflict* (pp. 183–202). Boulder, CO: Westview Press.

Ching, B., & Creed, G. W. (Eds.). (1997). *Knowing your place: Rural identity and cultural hierarchy.* New York, NY: Routledge.

Cloke, P., & Little, J. (Eds.). (1997). *Contested countryside cultures: Otherness, marginalisation and rurality.* New York, NY: Routledge.

Coats, C. D. (1989). *Old MacDonald's factory farm: The myth of the traditional farm and the shocking truth about animal suffering in today's agribusiness.* New York, NY: Continuum.

Collins, R. K. L. (2000). Free speech, food libel, and the First Amendment ... in Ohio. *Ohio Northern University Law Review, 26,* 1–40. Retrieved from http://heinonline.org/HOL/LuceneSearch?collection=journals&searchtype=fi eld&journal=onulr

Coombs, W. T. (2007). *Ongoing crisis communication: Planning, managing, and responding* (2nd ed.). Thousand Oaks, CA: Sage.

Coombs, W. T., & Holladay, S. J. (Eds.). (2010). *The handbook of crisis communication.* Malden, MA: Wiley-Blackwell.

Couch, S. R., & Kroll-Smith, S. (1994). Environmental controversies, interactional resources, and rural communities: Sitting versus exposure disputes. *Rural Sociology, 59,* 25–44. doi:10.1111/j.1549-0831.1994.tb00520.x

Cutlip, S. M., Center, A. H., & Broom, G. M. (2006). *Effective public relations* (9th ed.). Upper Saddle River, NJ: Pearson Prentice-Hall.

Dalecki, M. G., & Coughenour, C. M. (1992). Agrarianism in American society. *Rural Sociology, 57,* 48–64. doi:10.1111/j.1549-0831.1992.tb00456.x

DeLuca, K. M. (1999). *Image politics: The new rhetoric of environmental activism.* New York, NY: Guilford Press.

Derville, T. (2005). Radical activist tactics: Overturning public relations conceptualizations. *Public Relations Review, 31,* 527–533. doi:10.1016/j.pubrev.2005.08.012

Dozier, D. M. (with Grunig, L. A., & Grunig, J. E.). (1995). *Manager's guide to excellence in public relations and communication management.* Mahwah, NJ: Lawrence Erlbaum.

Dozier, D. M., & Lauzen, M. M. (2000). Liberating the intellectual domain from the practice: Public relations, activism, and the role of the scholar. *Journal of Public Relations Research, 12,* 3–22. doi:10.1027/s1532754xjprr1201_2

Drake, J. (2004). *Would a farm by any other frame smell as sweet? News frames, factory farms, and social protest* (Doctoral dissertation). Available from ProQuest Dissertations and Theses database. (UMI No. 3159603)

Drake, J. (2006). Is agriculture spinning out of control? A case study of Buckeye Egg Farm: Environmental communication, news frames, and social protest. In S. May (Ed.), *Case studies in organizations: Ethical perspectives and practices* (pp. 185–198). Thousand Oaks, CA: Sage.

Drake, J. (2007, Fall). PRSA at 60: Golden or gilded age for public relations? *Public Relations Strategist,* pp. 30–32.

Drake, J. W., & McCoy, J. R. (2009). Subterfusion of innovations: PR methods used to diffuse and defuse controversial new processes in food production. *Ohio Communication Journal, 47,* 1–25.

Duffy, M. E. (2000). There's no two-way symmetric about it: A postmodern examination of public relations textbooks. *Critical Studies in Media Communication, 17,* 294–315. doi:10/1080/15295030009388397

Durham, F. (2005). Public relations as structuration: A prescriptive critique of the StarLink global food contamination case. *Journal of Public Relations Research, 17,* 29–47. doi:10.1207/s1532754xjprr1701_4

Egg farm company offers cash incentive; AgriGeneral wants township not to use certain fire codes. (1997, August 12). *The Marion Star,* p. A1.

Emerging farm powers sow seeds of agriculture problems for U.S. (2004, July 1). *Toledo Blade,* pp. B6, B9.

Entman, R. M. (1993). Framing: Toward clarification of a fractured paradigm. *Journal of Communication, 43*(4), 51–58. doi:10.1111/j.1460-2466. 1993.tb01304.x

Environmental Integrity Project. (2006, October). *Giving away the farm: Why U.S. EPA should reject the Ohio Department of Agriculture's bid to administer the Clean Water Act.* Washington, DC: Author. Retrieved from http://waterkeeper.org/ht/a/GetDocumentAction/i/14071

Fauth, L. (2002, March). Victory: No more manure, say Michiganders. *Planet, 9*(2), Article 2. Retrieved from http://www.sierraclub.org/planet

Frey, L. R., Pearce, W. B., Pollock, M. A., Artz, L., & Murphy, B. A. O. (1996). Looking for justice in all the wrong places: On a communication approach to social justice. *Communication Studies, 47,* 110–127. doi:10.1080/10510979609368467

Friedland, W. H. (2002). Agriculture and rurality: Beginning the "final separations"? *Rural Sociology, 67,* 350–371. doi:10.1111/j.1549-0831.2002.tb00108.x

Gamson, W. A. (1989). Reflections on "The strategy of social protest" [Review of the book *The strategy of social protest* by W. A. Gamson]. *Sociological Forum, 4,* 455–467. doi:10.1007/BF01115022

Gamson, W. A. (1992). *Talking politics.* Cambridge, MA: University Press.

Gandy, O. H., Jr. (1982). *Beyond agenda-setting: Information subsidies and public policy.* Norwood, NJ: Ablex.

Glenn, C. B. (2004). Constructing consumables and consent: A critical analysis of factory farm industry discourse. *Journal of Communication Inquiry, 28,* 63–81. doi:10.1177/0196859903258573

Glenn, D., & Williams, B. (1998, March 10). Neighbors ask state to block farm growth. *The Columbus Dispatch*, pp. A1–A2.
Goffman, E. (1974). *Frame analysis: An essay on the organization of experience*. Cambridge, MA: Harvard University Press.
Goldschmidt, W. (1978). *As you sow: Three studies in the social consequences of agribusiness*. Montclair, NJ: Alanheld, Osmun.
Griffin, R. J., & Dunwoody, S. (1995). Impacts of information subsidies and community structure on local press coverage of environmental contamination. *Journalism & Mass Communication Quarterly, 72*, 271–284.
Grunig, J. E., & Hunt, T. (1984). *Managing public relations*. New York, NY: Holt, Rinehart & Winston.
Grunig, L. A. (1992). Activism: How it limits the effectiveness of organizations and how excellent public relations departments respond. In J. E. Grunig (Ed.; with D. M. Dozier, W. P. Ehling, L. A. Grunig, F. C. Repper, & J. White), *Excellence in public relations and communication management* (pp. 503–530). Hillsdale, NJ: Lawrence Erlbaum.
Hall, S. (1997). The spectacle of the "other." In S. Hall (Ed.), *Representation: Cultural representations and signifying practices* (pp. 223–279). Thousand Oaks, CA: Sage.
Hallahan, K. (1999). Seven models of framing: Implications for public relations. *Journal of Public Relations Research, 11*, 205–242. doi:10.1207/s1532754xjprr1103_02
Heath, R. L., & O'Hair, D. (Eds.). (2008). *Handbook of risk and crisis communication*. New York, NY: Routledge.
Henderson, A. (2005). Activism in "paradise": Identity management in a public relations campaign against genetic engineering. *Journal of Public Relations Research, 17*, 117–137. doi:10.1207/s1532754xjprr1702_4
Herman, E. S., & Chomsky, N. (1988). *Manufacturing consent: The political economy of the mass media*. New York, NY: Pantheon Books.
Holmes, M. (2003, June 8). Cracking open Ohio's egg mega-farms for a close look [Letter to the editor]. *Toledo Blade*, p. A8.
Holtzhausen, D. R. (2010). *Public relations as activism*. New York, NY: Routledge.
Holtzhausen, D. R., & Voto, R. (2002). Resistance from the margins: The postmodern public relations practitioner as organizational activist. *Journal of Public Relations Research, 14*, 57–84. doi:10.1207/s15327544xjprr1401_3
Hopey, D. (2003, June 7). Hog heaven? Study finds large hog farms lower property values. *Pittsburgh Post-Gazette*, p. D3. Retrieved from http://www.post-gazette.com
House passes bill to align megafarm rules with federal guidelines. (2003, May 21). *Daily Chief Union*, p. 6.
The Humane Society of the United States. (n.d.). *Fact sheet*. Retrieved from http://www.hsus.org/web-files/PDF/109_stewardship_factsheet.pdf
If egg farm cleans up act, finds buyer, everyone wins. (2003, July 24). *The Marion Star*, p. A8.
In defense of local control [Op-ed]. (2004, January 7). *The New York Times*, p. A13. Retrieved from http://www.nytimes.com
Inhaber, H. (1992). Of LULUs, NIMBYs, and NIMTOOs. *National Affairs, 107*, 52–64. Retrieved from http://www.nationalaffairs.com

Iyengar, S. (1991). *Is anyone responsible?: How television frames political issues.* Chicago, IL: University of Chicago Press.

John, P. L. C. (2008, September). *What is rural?* [Rev. by Reynells, L., & John, P. L. C.; Report for the Rural Information Center]. Beltsville, MD: U.S. Department of Agriculture, National Agricultural Library, Rural Information Center. Retrieved from http://www.nal.usda.gov/ric/ricpubs/what_is_rural.shtml

Karlberg, M. (1996). Remembering the public in public relations research: From theoretical to operational symmetry. *Journal of Public Relations Research, 8*, 263–278. doi:10.1207/s1532754xjprr0804_03

Krackhardt, D. (1997). Organizational viscosity and the diffusion of controversial innovations. *Journal of Mathematical Sociology, 22*, 177–199. doi: 10/1080/0022250X.1997.9990200

Kunkel, K. R. (1995). Down on the farm: Rationale expansion in the construction of factory farming as a social problem. In J. Best (Ed.), *Images of issues: Typifying contemporary social problems* (2nd ed., pp. 239–256). Hawthorne, NY: Aldine De Gruyter.

Lippmann, W. (1922). *Public opinion.* New York, NY: Harcourt, Brace.

Lobao, L., & Saenz, R. (2002). Spatial inequality and diversity as an emerging research area. *Rural Sociology, 67*, 497–511. doi:10.1111/j.1549-0831. 2002.tb00116.x

Magdoff, F., Foster, J. B., & Buttel, F. H. (2000). An overview. In F. Magdoff, J. B. Foster, & F. H. Buttel (Eds.), *Hungry for profit: The agribusiness threat to farmers, food, and the environment* (pp. 7–21). New York, NY: Monthly Review Press.

Mannes, M. (1964). *But will it sell?* New York, NY: J. B. Lippincott. (Original work published 1955)

McCarthy, J. D., & Zald, M. N. (1977). Resource mobilization and social movements: A partial theory. *American Journal of Sociology, 82*, 1212–1241. doi: 10.1086/226464

McCombs, M. E., & Shaw, D. L. (1972). The agenda-setting function of mass media. *Public Opinion Quarterly, 36*, 176–187. doi:10.1086/267990

McKee, T. (1995, December 24). Team to free expanding farmers from red tape. *The Marion Star*, p. A1.

McMillan, M. (2000). *"Your freedom ends where my nose begins": Conflicting views of large-scale hog farms in eastern North Carolina* (Doctoral dissertation). Available from ProQuest Dissertations and theses database. (UMI No. 9988890)

Merriam-Webster Online. (2011, May 4). *Struggle.* Retrieved from http://www.merriam-webster.com/dictionary/struggle

Miller, M. M., & Reichert, B. P. (2003). The spiral of opportunity and frame resonance: Mapping the issue cycle in news and public discourse. In S. D. Reese, O. H. Gandy, Jr., & A. E. Grant (Eds.), *Framing public life: Perspectives on media and our understanding of the social world* (pp. 107–120). Mahwah, NJ: Lawrence Erlbaum.

Molotch, H. L., & Lester, M. (1975). Accidental news: The great oil spill as local occurrence and national event. *American Journal of Sociology, 81*, 235–260. doi:10.1086/226073

Moore, K. A. (1998, March 11). A "clear threat to health"; health official opposes permits for egg farm. *The Marion Star*, p. A1.

Natural Resources Defense Council. (1998, December). *America's animal factories: How states fail to prevent pollution from livestock waste*. New York, NY: Author. Retrieved from http://devstaging.win.nrdcdev.org/water/pollution/factor/aatinx.asp

Nestle, M. (2002). *Food politics: How the food industry influences nutrition and health*. Berkeley: University of California Press.

New law reclassifies megafarms, limits local government's role. (2003, August 7). *The Marion Star*, p. A1.

Nucci, M. L., & Kubey, R. (2007). "We begin tonight with fruits and vegetables": Genetically modified food on the evening news 1980–2003. *Science Communication, 29*, 147–176. doi:10.1177/1075547007308173

Obama, B. (2007, February 17). *Words matter* [Speech]. Retrieved from http://www.youtube.com/watch?v=SgMcht-EW6I

O'Brien, T. (2001, June 1). Factory farming and human health. *Ecologist*, pp. 12–23.

Okun, M. (1999, January). *Human health issues associated with the hog industry*. Raleigh, NC: Carolina Association of Local Health Directors. Retrieved from http://agrienvarchive.ca/bioenergy/download/okun_human_health_hogs.pdf

Opt, S. K. (2005). Learning activism in the basic public relations course. *Texas Speech Communication Journal, 30*, 47–56.

Packwood Freeman, C. (2009). This little piggy went to press: The American news media's construction of animals in agriculture. *Communication Review, 12*, 78–103. doi:10.1080/10714420902717764

Pan, Z., & Kosicki, G. M. (1993). Framing analysis: An approach to news discourse. *Political Communication, 10*, 55–75. doi: 10.1080/10584609.9962963

Pan, Z., & Kosicki, G. M. (2003). Framing as a strategic action in public deliberation. In S. D. Reese, O. H. Gandy, Jr., & A. E. Grant (Eds.), *Framing public life: Perspectives on media and our understanding of the social world* (pp. 35–65). Mahwah, NJ: Lawrence Erlbaum.

Patterson, J. L. (2003). Conceptualizing stewardship in agriculture within the Christian tradition. *Environmental Ethics, 25*, 43–58.

Pawlick, T. F. (2001). *The invisible farm: The worldwide decline of farm news and agricultural journalism training*. Chicago, IL: Burnham.

Reese, S. D. (2003). Prologue—Framing public life: A bridging model for media research. In S. D. Reese, O. H. Gandy, Jr., & A. E. Grant (Eds.), *Framing public life: Perspectives on media and our understanding of the social world* (pp. 7–31). Mahwah, NJ: Lawrence Erlbaum.

Reisner, A., & Walter, G. (1994). Agricultural journalists' assessments of print coverage of agricultural news. *Rural Sociology, 59*, 525–537. doi:10.1111/j.1549-0831.1994.tb00546.x

Rogers, E. M. (1995). *Diffusion of innovations* (4th ed.). New York, NY: Free Press.

Rose, M. (1991). Activism in the 90s: Changing roles for public relations. *Public Relations Quarterly, 36*(3), 28–32.

Seeger, M. W., Sellnow, T. L., & Ulmer, R. R. (2003). *Communication and organizational crisis*. Westport, CT: Praeger.

Sharp, J. S. (2008, October). *Summary report: 2008 Ohio survey of food, agriculture, and environmental issues* (Report No. SRI-08-01). Columbus: The Ohio State University. Retrieved from http://ohiosurvey.osu.edu/pdf/2008OHSurveyConcernIssueSummaryRpt.pdf

Shiva, V. (2000). *Stolen harvest: The hijacking of the global food supply*. Cambridge, MA: South End Press.
Snow, D. A., & Benford, R. D. (1988). Ideology, frame resonance, and participant mobilization. In B. Klandermans, H. Kriesi, & S. Tarrow (Eds.), *International social movement research: Vol. 1. From structure to action: Comparing social movement research across cultures* (pp. 197–217). Greenwich, CT: JAI Press.
Southwest Utah Board of Health. (2001, February). *An evaluation of health concerns in Milford, Utah and the possible relationship of Circle Four Farms to those concerns*. St. George: Southwest Utah Public Health Department. Retrieved from http://www.waterquality.utah.gov/documents/Milfdrpt_ 2-2001.pdf
Spector, M., & Kitsuse, J. I. (1977). *Constructing social problems*. Menlo Park, CA: Cummings.
Spurlock, C. M. (2009). Performing and sustaining (agri)culture and place: The cultivation of environmental subjectivity on the Piedmont Farm Tour. *Text & Performance Quarterly, 29*, 5–21. doi:10.1080/10462930802514305
Stauber, J., & Rampton, S. (1995). *Toxic sludge is good for you: Lies, damn lies and the public relations industry*. Monroe, MA: Common Courage Press.
Stewart, C. J. (1999). Championing the rights of others and challenging evil: The ego function in the rhetoric of other-directed social movements. *Southern Communication Journal, 64*, 91–105. doi:10.1080/10417949909373125
Thu, K., Donham, K., Ziegenhorn, R., Reynolds, S., Thorne, P. S., Subramanian, P., . . . Stookesbery, J. (1997). A control study of the physical and mental health of residents living near a large-scale swine operation. *Journal of Agricultural Safety and Health, 3*, 13–26.
Tremblay, K. R., Jr., & Dunlap, R. E. (1978). Rural–urban residence and concern with environmental quality: A replication and extension. *Rural Sociology, 43*, 474–491.
Ulmer, R. R., Sellnow, T. L., & Seeger, M. W. (2007). *Effective crisis communication: Moving from crisis to opportunity*. Thousand Oaks, CA: Sage.
U.S. Census Bureau. (2009, July 10). *State & county quickfacts*. Retrieved from http://quickfacts.census.gov/qfd/states/39/39065.html
United Nations General Assembly. (1987, December 11). *Report of the World Commission on Environment and Development*. Retrieved from http://www.un.org/documents/ga/res/42/ares42-187.htm
Walter, G. (1996). The ideology of success in major American farm magazines, 1934–1991. *Journalism & Mass Communication Quarterly, 73*, 594–608.
Warsmith, S. (1998, January 9). Residents claim bill would stifle them; egg farm neighbors claim intent is to silence them. *The Marion Star*, p. A1.
Werder, K. P. (2006). Responding to activism: An experimental analysis of public relations strategy influence on attributes of publics. *Journal of Public Relations Research, 18*, 335–356. doi:10.1027/s1532754xjprr1804_3
Williams, B. (1995, December 3). A new pecking order: Big egg farms not going over easy. *The Columbus Dispatch*, p. G1.
Williams, S. (2004, February 6). Factory farms deemed unhealthy. *Johns Hopkins News-letter*. Retrieved from http://media.www.jhunewsletter.com/media/storage/paper932/news/2004/02/06/Science/Factory.Farms.Deemed.Unhealthy-2245631.shtml

Wing, S., & Wolf, S. (2000). Intensive livestock operations, health, and quality of life among eastern North Carolina residents. *Environmental Health Perspectives, 108,* 233–238. doi:10.2307/3454439

Zaremba, A. J. (2009). *Crisis communication: Theory and practice.* Armonk, NY: M. E. Sharpe.

Zachariah, H. (2010, March 24). Fire destroys egg farm warehouse, leads to quarter-million chicken deaths. *The Columbus Dispatch.* Retrieved from http://www.dispatch.com

Zoch, L. M., Collins, E. L., Sisco, H. F., & Supa, D. H. (2008). Empowering the activist: Using framing devices on activist organizations' websites. *Public Relations Review, 34,* 351–358. doi:10.1016/j.pubrev.2008.07.005

Zoch, L. M., & Molleda, J. C. (2006). Building a theoretical model of media relations using framing, information subsidies, and agenda-building. In C. H. Botan & V. Hazleton (Eds.), *Public relations theory II* (pp. 279–310). Mahwah, NJ: Lawrence Erlbaum.

6

SAVING KENNETH FOSTER

Speaking with Others in the Belly of the Beast of Capital Punishment

Jennifer Asenas
California State University, Long Beach

Bryan J. McCann
Wayne State University

Kathleen Feyh
Dana Cloud
The University of Texas at Austin

The end of August is a familiar time of transition for most academics, with new students and cooler weather awaiting. However, for communication scholars involved in the campaign to save Austin, Texas death row inmate Kenneth Foster, Jr., August 30, 2007 was a day haunted by the specter of uncertainty. At 6 p.m. CST that day, Foster was scheduled to enter the Huntsville execution chamber and receive a lethal injection. Our summer of struggle—filled with rallies, press conferences, news releases, organizing meetings, and acts of civil disobedience—came down to this day.

By that point, almost every major newspaper in Texas had published an editorial in Kenneth's favor.[1] High-profile public figures, including

Archbishop Desmond Tutu, President Jimmy Carter, actress Susan Sarandon, and Catholic nun and death penalty abolitionist Sister Helen Prejean, had sent letters to the members of the Texas Board of Pardons and Paroles, and to Texas Governor Rick Perry, asking them to spare Kenneth's life. In fact, the Texas Board of Pardons and Paroles had received 11,815 communications and 5,470 petition signatures opposing the execution, with only 12 communications in favor of it (Gloria, 2007). The Coliseum in Rome was even lit up in Kenneth's honor (Goodman & Gonzalez, 2007b). The campaign to save Kenneth Foster, thus, had given Governor Perry every reason to spare Kenneth, but we could not be sure that it was enough, given that he had presided over more executions than any U.S. governor in modern history in the state that, since 1976, has executed more than half as many people (487) as all of the other states *combined* (827 people; Death Penalty Information Center, 2011).

Kenneth's pro bono appeals attorney, Keith Hampton, had been cautious about embracing the activist campaign to save his client, but that afternoon, he called communication activist and scholar Bryan McCann, who had become a liaison between Keith and the campaign, to share the news that Perry had commuted Kenneth's death sentence to life imprisonment. We had won. The sense of joy and relief we felt at that moment is difficult to describe.

Across from the Texas governor's mansion, activists who had protested the executions of Gary Graham (aka Shaka Sankofa), Frances Newton, and Karla Faye Tucker, among countless others, found themselves in an unusual position—celebrating (see Bruni, 2000; Staunton, 2005; Verhovek, 1998). This incredible victory for Kenneth and his family, and for abolition of the death penalty, had been difficult to imagine just 90 days prior when the campaign began.

On May 30, 2007, approximately 50 people gathered at the Carver Library in Austin to discuss the prospect of saving Kenneth Foster's life. Although those in attendance shared a desire to halt Kenneth's execution, their ideas about how to do so differed dramatically. Such differences were not surprising, for as Gamson and Meyer (1996) observed, social movements contain "a field of actors, not a unified entity" (p. 283). Some people present (including the authors who attended[2]) supported a vibrant and community-based grassroots campaign, but others feared that such an effort would alienate the powers that be and seal Kenneth's fate. Complicating this debate over strategy was a more fundamental question of representation: Who had the right to represent Kenneth—his new wife from Denmark, the grandfather who raised him, the lawyer who represented him, or the experienced activists who befriended him? This question provoked passionate pleas, divisive remarks, and even threats of litigation that would color the dynamics of the ensuing 90-day campaign.

This chapter documents the difficult questions of ethics and strategies that informed our participation in the Save Kenneth Foster Campaign (SKFC). Through an analysis of that campaign, we demonstrate how solidarity among Kenneth's supporters was forged through an ethical and strategic position of speaking *with* rather than speaking *for* others; taking this stance offers the possibility of communicating across differences of identity, strategy, and political orientation. By illuminating debates that occurred during this campaign and strategies that emerged from them, we highlight not only the ethical balancing act emanating from the cacophony of voices within the struggle to save Kenneth's life but also the very strategies of communication activism that gained this victory.

This work, thus, fits with the growing "diverse array of activist–scholars and scholarly activists dedicated to using communication theories and research for the greater social good" (Artz, 2007, p. 34). A number of communication scholars, for instance, have studied the intersection between activism and teaching in the prison system, and, more specifically, the use of writing to enable people who are incarcerated to be authors of their experiences (Corcoran, 1985; Hartnett, 2003; Novek, 2005a, 2005b; Novek & Sanford, 2007; Valentine, 1998, 2006). Communication scholars also have written about the need for activism to address the prison–industrial complex and the systemic inequalities that the system replicates and perpetuates (e.g., Hartnett & Larson, 2006; McHale, 2007; PCARE, 2007), and nowhere are these inequalities more apparent than in capital punishment cases (see, e.g., Sunwolf, 2006, 2007). Most communication scholarship on capital punishment, however, analyzes public discourse surrounding that topic (e.g., Dardis, Baumgarten, Boydstun, De Boef, & Shen, 2008; Hartnett, 2010; Hartnett & Larson, 2006; Moore, 2006; Wood, 2005), with only a few scholars intervening to change that discourse; a notable example is McHale's (2007) use of video documentary as an activist tool to prevent the execution of Joe Amrine, "a Missouri man living on death row for 17 years ... despite there being neither witnesses nor evidence against him" (p. 196).

To clarify the ethical and strategic contours of the SKFC campaign, we first briefly sketch social injustices associated with the death penalty. Second, we describe Kenneth Foster's case and explain the difference in opinion over the campaign's strategy that emerged at the inception of our organizing efforts. Third, we outline our theoretical orientation regarding the "problem of speaking for others" that we encountered in this campaign. Fourth, we follow these foundational descriptions with an analysis of the campaign that explores problems of credibility, organizing, and representation. Fifth, we conclude the chapter with lessons learned through the campaign and how those lessons might be applied to a broader terrain of struggle.

REALITIES OF THE DEATH PENALTY

Even as it acts on the body in obvious and profound ways, the death penalty also is a fundamentally communicative phenomenon. Several scholars have engaged public debates about capital punishment, noting how rhetors struggle over particular tropes, such as the question of who may and may not lay claim to the status of "victim" (e.g., Hartnett & Larson, 2005, 2006; McCann, 2007). Conquergood (2002) described executions themselves as "awesome rituals of human sacrifice through which the state dramatizes its absolute power and monopoly on violence" (p. 342). Communication about the death penalty, thus, is connected to the exercise of power through broader institutional structures.

Many U.S. Americans believe that the death penalty is reserved for the most heinous crimes, but in reality, people sentenced to death are treated as though they are politically, socially, and economically expendable. Although the spectacle of the death penalty portrays a mode of punishment considered rightfully applied to society's villains, the reality of the death penalty is that people of color and people who are poor are most likely to be sentenced to death.

Race and the Death Penalty

The criminal justice system has been and continues to be a structural form of racism where the legacy of slavery still survives (Rizer, 2003). Although whites constitute 75.1% of the U.S. population and blacks represent only 12.3% (U.S. Census Bureau, 2001), blacks are overrepresented on death row and executions. A report prepared for the National Association for the Advancement of Colored People Legal Defense and Educational Fund found that in 2009, 1,457 whites (44.4%) and 1,364 blacks (41.67%) were on death row (Fins, 2009). Between 1930 and 2010, of the 1,193 prisoners executed, whites accounted for 668 (57%) and blacks accounted for 415 (34%) of the executions (Death Penalty Information Center, 2010a). Finally, 52 people were executed in 2009, of whom 23 were white (44.2%), 22 were black (42.3%), and 7 were Latino (13.4%; Death Penalty Information Center, 2009a).

Evidence of the racist nature of the death penalty has been brought before the U.S. Supreme Court as a violation of equal protection. In *McCleskey v. Kemp* (1987), the Supreme Court considered the Baldus Study, which found that "a black perpetrator is eleven times more likely to get the death penalty than a white criminal charged with the same crime. Moreover, a black defendant is twenty-two times more likely to get the death penalty if the victim is white" (Rizer, 2003, p. 852). However, the Supreme Court refused to halt executions, in part, because of its opinion that "disparities in sentencing are an inevitable part of our criminal justice system" (*McCleskey v. Kemp*, p. 312).

Racism also is an important component of public support for the death penalty. Numerous studies have found that whites draw on negative racial stereotypes of blacks when they consider crime and punishment (e.g., Gilliam & Iyengar, 2000; Peffley & Hurwitz, 2002). A more recent study by Peffley and Hurwitz (2007) confirmed the findings of previous studies: The majority of whites who support the death penalty believe that black criminality is the result of dispositional characteristics rather than a racist justice system, and refuse to abandon their support for the death penalty, even when faced with evidence that the practice is flawed (see also Bobo & Johnson, 2004). Peffley and Hurwitz (2007) also found that whites who were told that the death penalty is racist actually become more supportive of it. Given these findings, it will take public education and multiracial organizing to break this association. However, to address the systemic discrimination of the death penalty system, we also must consider how the death penalty system targets the poor.

Poverty and the Death Penalty

In a nation that valorizes the accumulation of wealth, those who are poor become morally suspect and legally vulnerable. The U.S. criminal justice system reinforces the "familiar American association between wealth and virtue, poverty and moral bankruptcy ... [and] sends the message that it is the poor, not the rich, who commit crimes and whom the middle class should fear" (Rizer, 2003, p. 858). Those general perceptions are reflected in Marquart, Ekland-Olson, and Sorenson's (1994) interviews with death row inmates, which showed that they shared a few common characteristics: They were poor, poorly educated, from the social fringes, and had family problems.

The meagerness of resources available to defend people who are poor in capital cases compared with the resources of the state and the high cost of trial almost guarantees an inadequate defense. For instance, between 1995 and 2004, the state of New York spent $23 million per death sentence (Mello, 2008). Defendants who cannot afford the cost of retaining attorneys are assigned poorly compensated, inadequately prepared, and sometimes incompetent lawyers who are under extraordinary stress because their errors might result in the death of their client (see, e.g., Sunwolf, 2006, 2007). A survey of defense attorneys revealed that "the average hourly rate for retained criminal work in Texas is $135.98 per hour. ... However, when defense counsel are [sic] assigned to represent indigent clients, they report that they receive, on average, $39.81 per hour" (Butcher & Moore, 2000, p. 15). During George W. Bush's tenure as governor of Texas, the *Chicago Tribune* found that in 40 death penalty cases, defense attorneys presented at most one witness or no mitigating evidence during the sentencing phase (Solar, 2004). In 43 of 131 cases, capital defense trial lawyers already had been or were later disbarred, suspended, or otherwise sanctioned for misconduct; three of them actually were convicted of felonies (Solar, 2004). The cost of defending oneself against the state, which has considerable resources and little motivation to equip the defense, makes people who are poor more likely to be sentenced to death (Death Penalty Information Center, 2009b).

THE CAMPAIGN TO SAVE KENNETH FOSTER, INMATE AND ACTIVIST

On the night of August 14, 1996, Kenneth Foster, Mauriceo Brown, Julius Steen, and Dewayne Dillard planned and committed two separate robberies. Brown, Steen, and Dillard accosted the victims; Kenneth was the getaway driver. After the two robberies, Kenneth asked Dillard to persuade Brown and Steen to stop. On their way home, they saw a woman in front of her residence who appeared to be waving them down. Brown wanted to talk to the woman, so Kenneth stopped the car and Brown exited and started talking to the woman. The woman's boyfriend, Michael LaHood, approached the two from the driveway, exchanged words with Brown, and was then shot and killed by Brown. According to Dillard, Kenneth looked shocked and started to drive away, but stopped at Dillard's request.

Unlike Julius Steen and Dewayne Dillard, Kenneth Foster was tried with the shooter, Mauriceo Brown. During the trial, Brown testified that he had no plans to rob the woman or Michael LaHood, and that he had acted on his own. Brown was executed in 2005 for his crime.

Kenneth also was sentenced to die based on a deeply flawed and inappropriately used law in this case. Commonly known as the "Law of Parties," the Criminal Responsibility for Conduct of Another Act of the Texas Penal Code (1973) states that a person is criminally responsible for another person's actions if

> acting with intent to promote or assist the commission of the offense, he [or she] solicits, encourages, directs, aids, or attempts to aid the other person to commit the offense; or ... if, in the attempt to carry out a conspiracy to commit one felony, another felony is committed by one of the conspirators, all conspirators are guilty of the felony actually committed, though having no intent to commit it, if the offense was committed in furtherance of the unlawful purpose and was one that should have been anticipated as a result of the carrying out of the conspiracy. (Sec. 7.02)

The imposition of the death penalty under the Law of Parties violates the U.S. Supreme Court's ruling in *Enmund v. Florida* (1982) that a death sentence is a disproportionate punishment when the defendant was not present at the killing, did not kill, and did not intend that the victim(s) be killed or did not anticipate that lethal force might be used in the course of a robbery or to effect a safe escape. Nonetheless, the judge in Kenneth's case told the members of the jury that they could "find the defendant Kenneth Foster guilty of the offense of capital murder, though he may have had no intent to commit the offense" (Jacobs, 2007, para. 16). Under those instructions, a jury can impose the death penalty for a defendant's mental status no greater than negligence and jury members are asked to evaluate whether a defendant should have foreseen that a crime would take place—a difficult task given that the jury already knows that a crime did take place. Consequently, Kenneth was sentenced to death for being in the wrong place at the wrong time.

Kenneth's relationship to the Texas anti-death penalty movement was not always a matter of the Law of Parties or saving his life; rather, members of the Campaign to End the Death Penalty (CEDP; http://nodeathpenalty.org/content/index.php) came to know Kenneth as part of a broader movement against the death penalty. Kenneth is one of five founding members of the Death Row Inner-Communalist Vanguard Engagement (DRIVE; http://drivemovement.org), whose purpose is to protest the conditions on death row at the Polunsky Unit (previously named the Terrell Unit) in Livingston, Texas. There, death row inmates are kept in 23-hour administrative segregation inside 60-square-foot cells with sealed steel doors, deprived of sensory stimulation and physical contact. Their nutritional and health-care needs are substantially substandard (for a narrative of life in Polunsky, see Nealy, n.d.). Their connection to loved ones is limited to one 5-minute telephone call every 6 months and their mail often is censored. To address these issues, DRIVE members engaged in coordinated acts of civil disobedience.

Kenneth's political involvement in DRIVE encouraged him to forge relationships with anti-death penalty and leftist activists outside the prison. Kenneth first contacted a CEDP member by mail in 2000 and has remained in contact with one or more members since. Kenneth's political activism in prison made sustained grassroots action for SKFC members far more realistic than if he had remained silent for his 10 years on death row. A prolific writer with a sharp political critique, he shared essays, poems, and instructions with us by mail. The lines from one of Foster's (2006) poems described his writing as a way of understanding his situation and expressing his agency in resisting it:

I can't get the gun shots out my head!
Can't get the pen out of my hand!
The penitentiary is out of hand.

His critique of the criminal justice system gave us reason to believe that the tone of a campaign to save his life would be forceful and political.

The Problem of Speaking for Others: A Common Goal, Differing Means

Kenneth Foster was given an execution date of August 30, 2007. McCann, a member of CDEP and one of Kenneth's pen pals, alerted CEDP of the impending execution date. CEDP decided to call a community meeting on May 30 at Carver Library in Austin to bring together Kenneth's family, friends, and community members to fight for his life.

CEDP spent 2 weeks advertising and encouraging attendance at the community meeting. We invited Kenneth's lawyer, Keith Hampton, to speak to the group, and CEDP's Lily Hughes presided over the meeting. We knew that there were relational strains between some of Kenneth's family members and his fiancée Tasha Foster, and his close friend and civil attorney, Mary Felps. We were surprised to find that Tasha questioned the right of CEDP to be involved. Before the meeting began, Felps pulled McCann aside and threatened to sue him if he or CEDP engaged in any political action that "resulted" in Kenneth's death. After convincing her—at least for the moment— that we all had a common goal, the meeting began.

After Keith delivered his opening remarks, Tasha and Mary stood up and read a letter from Kenneth explaining that they should have complete control over any campaign to save Kenneth. Tasha and Mary wanted the campaign to focus solely on Kenneth, not on the death penalty or its racial and class politics. Citing the much-publicized failed campaign to stop the execution of Stanley "Tookie" Williams in California, Tasha and Mary feared any political activism that might offend or alienate Governor Perry, Texas lawmakers, or Texans, in general, would cost Kenneth his life. Tasha claimed that California executed Tookie to prove that it could and would execute its citizens, and she feared that Kenneth would be treated the same in Texas. Instead of a public campaign, they favored a letter-writing campaign to Perry and the Texas Board of Pardons and Parole, as well as hiring Sheila Murphy of Chicago's John Marshal Law School (to gain an audience with the governor to plead Kenneth's case).

CEDP members and other anti-death penalty activists, along with some of Kenneth's other family members, such as Kenneth's grandfather, Lawrence, however, envisioned a public campaign that would be built around petitions, rallies, and marches. Based on Kenneth's activism in DRIVE and previous successful campaigns, CEDP believed that efforts would be best spent creating a climate that would make it, in the words of MOVE's[3] Mario Africa, "politically untenable" for Texas to execute Kenneth. After a range of impassioned arguments, it was unclear whether those in attendance could work together; much less decide on a strategy.

Regardless of CEDP members' desire to save Kenneth, the organization was faced with some significant ethical dilemmas. Because of Kenneth's limited ability to represent himself publicly, the problem of representation in such a campaign loomed large. First, what right did CEDP, as a group of primarily white, educated, and privileged people, have to "speak for" Kenneth, a black man of modest means and little formal education? Second, what role could CEDP members play to encourage solidarity despite our differences to create a campaign that would effectively "speak with" Kenneth? Third, what was our responsibility as scholar-activists to involve ourselves in such a campaign?

Advocating for those who are oppressed and exploited in any given society sometimes may conflict with the imperative for those very individuals to articulate their experiences in their voices; this dilemma is what Alcoff (1991–1992) named the "problem of speaking for others" (p. 6). Regardless of how well meaning, persons of privilege (including academics) must consider the political ramifications of representing the concerns of those who are oppressed and exploited. Who gets to speak for whom is "politically constituted by power relations of domination, exploitation, and subordination. Who is speaking, who is spoken of, and who listens is a result, as well as an act, of political struggle" (Alcoff, p. 15). For scholar-activists, "the question is how to keep the ethnocentric Subject from establishing itself by selectively defining an Other. This is not a program for the Subject as such; rather it is a program for the benevolent Western intellectual" (Spivak, 1988, p. 293). People of privilege have assumed in the past (and some continue to assume) that they can "give voice" or "empower" marginalized groups to speak. This practice reifies the structures that create marginalized people by assuming that they cannot organize but, instead, need those who are privileged to speak on their behalf.

However, even though the attempt to speak for another person is necessarily problematic, that does not mean that those who are privileged should stand idly by as others are oppressed and exploited (see Welker, this volume) As Alcoff (1991–1992) noted:

> It is not always the case that when others unlike me speak for me I have ended up worse off, or that when we speak for others they end up worse off. Sometimes ... we do need a "messenger" to advocate for our needs. ... The point is not that for some speakers the danger of speaking for

others does not arise, but that in some cases certain political effects can be garnered in no other way. (pp. 29, 18)

In addition to the propositional content of speech/representation, Alcoff argued that when people speak, they must consider the "probable or actual effects of the words on the discursive and material context," as well as "where the speech goes and what it does there" (p. 26).

Speaking To and With Kenneth Foster and the Community

As a group of pen pals with and activists for Kenneth, CEDP members knew that Kenneth did not need us to speak for him. Rather, as the following analysis demonstrates, we employed a politics of speaking *with* Kenneth, doing so in three main ways. First, we spoke to Kenneth, as well as to his biological and extended family, to create credibility as activists who desired to conduct a public campaign. Second, we helped to build a grassroots movement about Kenneth in communities sensitive to issues of race and class. Third, we actively sought ways for Kenneth to express himself through his poetry, family, and political allies.

Creating credibility: Speaking to Kenneth Foster. Spivak (1988) argued that those who are in positions of privilege should not be silenced by their privilege but, instead, should unlearn it. That is, privileged activists must question the limitations on knowledge and understanding that their privilege creates and acknowledge the knowledges of those who are oppressed before assuming the role of spokespersons (see also Landry & MacLean, 1996). To undertake the necessary unlearning, people who are privileged must

> work hard at gaining some knowledge of the others who occupy those spaces most closed to our privileged view. Attempting to *speak to* [emphasis added] those others in such a way as they might take us seriously and, most important of all, be able to answer us back. (Landry & MacLean, 1996, pp. 4–5)

In other words, because the authors, as well as many members of CEDP, are people who have a degree of privilege in society, we had to find ways to learn about Kenneth's situation in conversation with him and with his family.

One important aspect of unlearning one's privilege is to engage in dialogue with others as equals. CEDP members had been in contact with Kenneth and DRIVE for some time, but at the beginning of the campaign to save Kenneth, that relationship was strained. After the contentious first community meeting, McCann received a letter from Kenneth that chastised CEDP for desiring to control the campaign and disrespecting Tasha and Mary. The letter was quite a blow, as CEDP had devoted considerable energy and resources to his case. After speaking with some of Kenneth's family members, we learned that Kenneth had been misinformed about what had happened at the first meeting. Nonetheless, we realized that if Kenneth did not want us to represent him, we would respect his wishes.

CEDP members felt confident in their relationship with Kenneth to communicate with him directly about our involvement in his campaign. McCann wrote back to Kenneth, explaining our intentions for and perspective on that first meeting, and expressing our frustration and hurt about the accusation that we had attempted to usurp power from Tasha and Mary. Our open and honest communication with Kenneth proved successful, as, in subsequent letters, he approved of CEDP's involvement and encouraged CEDP members to write to him, which many did. This correspondence strengthened the solidarity between CEDP members and Kenneth, and among campaign members. Letter writing also increased the frequency and amount of information that Kenneth received about the campaign and provided him with greater opportunity to offer input into how it was to be run.

Gathering support, engaging in bold action: The grassroots movement. CEDP also had to gain credibility with Kenneth's family members, as they, too, had a personal stake in how he would be represented. It was important for CEDP members to demonstrate a genuine desire to help Kenneth and not just use his case for political purposes. We laid the groundwork for this type of relationship with his family at the second community meeting. We also had to mediate some differences between the vision that Tasha and Mary had for the campaign and that of other members of Kenneth's family, some of whom were a bit skeptical of the plan to raise money to hire Murphy to gain an audience with Governor Perry to plead Kenneth's case. We asked Mary to cochair the meeting along with CEDP member Jennifer Asenas, and we invited any of Kenneth's family still interested in a coalition to meet us at the Austin History Center. To allay Tasha and Mary's fears of opportunistic activism, we agreed to engage only in public displays approved by SKFC members. We also paired Tasha and Mary's idea for a letter-writing campaign with a public event to increase our visibility in the community by planning to have an information booth at the Austin Juneteenth celebration on June 19.[4] At that celebration, campaign members could gather petitions and letters of support for Kenneth, speak to people about Kenneth's case, and invite people to our weekly meetings. Finally, we asked Beverly Fisher, Kenneth's cousin and a friend to CEDP, to chair the next meeting.

Through dialogue, compromise, shared responsibilities, and good-faith effort to promote Kenneth's cause, CEDP began to gain credibility with Kenneth and his other supporters. However, CEDP members knew that credibility among people who supported Kenneth would not be enough to spare his life. We still had to prove to some SKFC members who favored working with professional politicians and lawyers that a grassroots campaign was not only tenable but also necessary to save Kenneth's life. A grassroots strategy also would maintain an ethical relationship between campaign members and Kenneth, allowing us to speak *with* him rather than *for* him.

The growing support and positive response to the campaign's framing of Kenneth's plight with the slogans, "Wrong Place at the Wrong Time" and "Death for Driving a Car?" enabled SKFC to take more risks. For example, our protest in front of the church that Governor Perry attends could be viewed as questionable, but we felt confident that the ad hoc picket would draw public support and news attention, and we were not disappointed.[5]

The campaign also made the difficult decision to perform an act of civil disobedience. Modeled after a similar tactic employed during the 2000 campaign to halt the execution of Texas death row inmate Shaka Sankofa,[6] six activists (including McCann and Kathleen Feyh) sat down in front of the gated entrance to the driveway of the governor's mansion following a rally that had begun at the nearby Capitol (see Gold, 2000). Those participating in this civil disobedience action refused to surrender their locations unless Perry or one of his representatives agreed to collect letters of appeal written by Lawrence, Tasha, and Nydesha Foster (Kenneth's daughter). After 2 hours, it became clear that no letters would be collected or arrests made. Shifting strategies, the six sitting activists abandoned their original positions, joined 200 others blocking traffic, and declared via bullhorn that the governor would rather see activists break the law by blocking his driveway and city traffic than look Kenneth Foster's family in the face.[7]

Some scholars have argued that changes to society have rendered traditional models of social change irrelevant. For instance, DeLuca's (1999) work on image politics, focused on media products of new social movements, argued for the efficacy of "mind bombs" (p. 1)—spectacular, newsworthy image events that explode the public's consciousness on a particular issue. This type of social change strategy jettisons community-based politics in favor of gaining a media audience to change people's minds and actions. Greene (2006) argued for an "orator communist" who assembles a "multitude" for a "refusal or defection from the commands of money/speech" (p. 86) and against an instrumental politics of direct struggle for both the hegemony of ideas and achievement of concrete political goals. This perspective emphasizes communication technologies as resources for escape from, rather than for a direct challenge to, the system (of capital, capital punishment, and actual existing conditions).

The use of media and communication technologies and grassroots organizing are not necessarily mutually exclusive. Indeed, grassroots organizations, like the Student Nonviolent Coordinating Committee and the Congress of Racial Equality, certainly harnessed the power of technology to dramatize and address racism by creating newsworthy events, such as the lunch counter sit-ins and the Freedom Rides. The question is one of focus. In contrast to professionalized, media-driven, or individualist forms of social change, SKFC focused its efforts on local organizing to craft its message and to build support for Kenneth's cause. In their classic work on social movements, Bowers, Ochs, and Jensen (1973) highlighted the importance of day-to-day organizing in the potential success of social campaigns and movements. Bowers et al. argued that an absolutely central component of successful movement organizing is *solidification*, the "rhetorical process by which an agitating group produces or reinforces the cohesiveness of its members, thereby increasing responsiveness to group wishes" (p. 24). Mobilizing at the community level to build support for Kenneth through face-to-face meetings of campaign members *and* use of appeals to news outlets by campaign members gave SKFC the ability to speak *with* Kenneth to lawmakers and the public.

Struggling from the ground up: "Speaking with" Kenneth Foster. Our regular contact with Kenneth and his family, particularly his daughter Nydesha, were weekly reminders of what was at stake in our campaign. Through our meetings, e-mails, phone calls, and information tables, SKFC members cultivated our political messages, organized campaign tasks, and encouraged each other to persevere against the odds that Kenneth would not be spared.

Significantly, Kenneth's correspondence with SKFC activists influenced our work and kept it connected to him and his case. That correspondence allowed Kenneth to speak to us and with us on his terms. For instance, on July 8, 2007, Kenneth wrote to Dana Cloud:

> Though I've been fussy about the late starts,[8] I'm still grateful to what's taking place. I see very great and powerful things being done. Things started off rocky (as can be expected), but it does seem like things have smoothed out.
>
> I've just been sitting back smiling at what's going on, because for 10 years now, I've become accustomed to telling everyone what to do, but I see everyone is doing it. ... I'm so very thankful. I know there is a long road ahead. ... Keep the strength. I close in solidarity!

Kenneth, thus, acknowledged the early struggles over the right to speak for him and heralded the solidarity that emerged in the collective process of the campaign. Corresponding with Kenneth solidified activists around his case and provided us with the resources to construct his story in ways that were faithful to his experience and to his critique of racism and the justice system.

Constructing an Alternative Counter-Narrative to Dominant Narratives of Race and Capital Punishment

A significant challenge to the campaign was how to speak *with* Kenneth to articulate and disseminate an alternative version to the dominant narrative of the Kenneth Foster story, which suggested that Kenneth was guilty of a crime deserving death. This dominant narrative is steeped in racialized discourses of criminality and Texas's will to execute death row prisoners. Historically, U.S. master narratives portray black men as criminal threats to the social order (Jones, 2005). Blacks continue to be "singled out" for "wholesale criminalization" (Stabile, 2006, p. 8), as suggested by the 2008 Pew Center study that found that one in nine black men between the ages of 20 and 34 is in prison, which is significant because it is "easier to gain a capital conviction against someone with a prior record" (Solar, 2004, p. 32).

SKFC also had to work against Texas's macabre ritual of capital punishment. Before the advent of lethal injection, Texans affectionately referred to the electric chair as "Old Sparky," which was used to execute 361 prisoners and now is showcased at the Texas Prison Museum in Huntsville. Texas cares little about the opinions of other states and nations on the issue of capital punishment. Amidst protests on two occasions—the eve of Texas's 400th execution and the 2008 execution of Mexican national José Medellin—Governor Perry asserted the state's right to put criminals to death, saying, "Texans are doing just fine governing Texas" (Office of the Governor Rick Perry, 2007, para. 1).

The convergence of these two rhetorical obstacles meant that SKFC needed to talk about Kenneth's case as a specific example of the justice system's incommensurate punishment for his crime and its connection to racism and the political enjoyment of the death penalty. In our efforts, as explained below, we constructed a counter-narrative in three ways: promulgation of movement aims to gather popular support for Kenneth's cause, forefronting Kenneth's family, and capturing news attention to these efforts to frame the movement in human terms.

Organizing to tell Kenneth's story: Gathering support. The initial effort to interrupt the dominant narratives of racist criminalization and Texas's "states' rights" discourse was at the annual Juneteenth festivities in Austin on June 19, 2007. In Austin, Juneteenth is a lively block party held on the city's predominantly black east side. SKFC believed that the celebration represented an excellent opportunity to spread the message of Kenneth's case to a population disproportionately affected by the criminal justice system and, therefore, more likely to recognize the gross injustices at the core of Kenneth's case. Throughout the day, a rotating group of campaign members sat under an elevated tarp in the Texas summer heat, talking to passersby about the misapplication of the Law of Parties, seeking signatories to the petition demanding a halt to Kenneth's impending execution, and inviting them to our weekly campaign meetings.[9]

The petition, both in paper and digital form, was a growing testament to Kenneth's wide base of support, with more than 5,000 signatures collected. We printed the petitions, several clemency letters, and editorials calling for the commutation of Kenneth's death sentence from every state newspaper, and delivered these documents to judges on the Texas Court of Criminal Appeals and to the Texas Board of Pardons and Parole members. We also attached them to placards and banners, which we used as visual support at protests in front of the governor's mansion and in front of the Methodist church that the governor attends during Sunday services. The visual display of these messages of support was a reminder that political momentum was on our side.

SKFC also used the petitions as a tool to organize the local community by providing space on them for signatories to share their contact information if they wanted to know about future campaign events. The result was a growing database of people willing to dedicate even modest amounts of time and energy to saving Kenneth's life. Additionally, SKFC members visited local churches to collect signatures, spoke to citizens about Kenneth's case, and established relationships with sympathetic community members, some of whom were influential in local and state politics and/or society. Circulation of the petition increased attendance at our weekly meetings and brought together such forces as local congregations, the Nation of Islam, hip-hop artists, and local branches of the National Association for the Advancement of Colored People, Amnesty International, CEDP, and the International Socialist Organization.

Family as the face of the Save Kenneth Foster Campaign. The challenge in representing Kenneth Foster and the death penalty was twofold for SKFC: (a) we needed people to speak who were able to communicate credibly the counter-narrative about Kenneth and (b) we needed to make sure that the counter-narrative was heard. Thus, SKFC decided that Kenneth's family members should tell an alternative to the dominant narrative about black men and crime. To clarify what the alternative to the dominant discourses of Texas crime and punishment looked like in this campaign, we turn to the strategies we employed to provide Kenneth and his family with opportunities to express themselves publicly about their experiences.

The counter-narrative we offered came out in public speeches, public readings of Kenneth's letters and essays, and interpersonal interactions at SKFC events. The story was compelling and believable, in part, because of the significant involvement of Kenneth's family. Family members of death row inmates face considerable financial and emotional challenges in speaking out, as they typically receive little assistance or sympathy from their social support networks and suffer publicly because the news media often present "one-sided" and completely "inaccurate" (King, 2005, p. 10) coverage of the crime. Despite the difficulties of families being involved in an anti-death penalty campaign, Kenneth's family articulated both the emotional harm and political injustice of Kenneth's sentence, and of the death penalty, in general.

In July 2007, SKFC planned as the major initial public push of the campaign a rally to be held a month before the scheduled execution. With few exceptions, campaign participants enthusiastically were in favor of a large rally that connected the death penalty to issues of race and class, and that connected this campaign with the broader abolitionist movement. Beverly Fisher, Kenneth's cousin, was the moderator of the rally, and speakers included exonerated death row inmates Shujaa Graham and Darby Tillis, professor and activist Cloud, Felps, and, at Kenneth's request, New York hip-hop group The Welfare Poets and Philadelphia MOVE activist Mario Africa. We played a recorded message from Kenneth, and his 11-year-old daughter, Nydesha, spoke and dedicated a dance performance to her father. Kenneth and his family already had taken the lead in organizing the campaign, but with this rally, they became its public face, its spokespeople.

The July 21, 2007 rally contributed significantly to promoting the counter-narrative about Kenneth, which positioned Kenneth and his family as potential victims of the death penalty. This counter-narrative did not negate the importance and terrible grief of Michael LaHood's family or our sympathy for them[10] but it did increase public sympathy for Kenneth and his family. The discourse of agency began to shift as well, with Kenneth, his family, the families of other condemned inmates, and exonerated death row inmates coming out of the obscurity in which these *other* victims of capital punishment traditionally have been wrapped and speaking for themselves. Nydesha's speech at that rally contains both the cry of a daughter who may lose her father to the death penalty (after already losing him as a physical presence in her life to incarceration) and a confident and angry clarion call for justice:

> What is justice? It seems that justice is just us, meaning me and my dad, eye to eye, loving each other behind the glass that they thought would separate us. ... I'm 11 and wondering if this is what Texas has in the wings for me. I could be Frances Newton.[11] She could be me. ... So what is justice? Shame on you, Texas! This time you are really wrong!

> This is my poem, my prayer, my song, that you be known for something other than killing and ignoring the truth. We all make mistakes, even you. ... You tell my dad to take responsibility? Well, he has for 10 years! We're tired of tears. July 21st today we make a stand to end this injustice. Just us was my dad and DRIVE saying it's enough. Today, I stand as his testament, saying we can't accept no less than liberation. ... Today we make this statement, a statement to Texas. Give us justice![12]

Kenneth's family members also spoke at a public forum on August 14, 2007, where they were joined by families of other inmates on death row; at an August 15 press conference; and at marches and rallies in San Antonio and Austin on August 18, 22, and 25. During our weekly campaign meetings, Kenneth's grandfather, father, cousins, other relatives, and friends were central to proposing, planning, and carrying out these actions. They spoke to their pastors, local government officials, and to the press. Nydesha continued to speak at rallies and to participate as permitted by her family, who also had to consider her emotional well-being and the consequences of such public exposure. In summary, their voices combined with those of SKFC supporters and activists in chanting, shouting, and speaking out.

Through their speeches, Kenneth's family grew their base of support for the campaign in the community. One of the most moving voices of support for Kenneth came from Sean-Paul Kelley (2007), a close friend of Michael LaHood, who later wrote, "He did not pull the trigger, or encourage Mr. Brown to pull it in any way, nor was he even aware that the murder was being contemplated or had been committed until after the fact. His punishment should not be execution" (para. 3). Through the efforts of Kenneth's loved ones, the campaign mobilized an ever-growing activist base, from anarchists to Nation of Islam members to church ministers to socialists. Through CEDP's network, the campaign reached all over the United States, and through mobilization of other networks, including Amnesty International, the campaign reached into Europe.

Capturing news media attention. Although we were not primarily focused on gaining news attention, it was important to our campaign. The news media play an important role in the process of social change because they are "a site on which various social groups, institutions, and ideologies struggle over the definition and construction of social reality" (Gurevitch & Levy, 1985, p. 19; see Drake, this volume). However, the relationship between campaigns for social change and the news media is complex. Activists need the news media to communicate their dissent, win public support, mobilize supporters, and broaden the scope of the conflict (Gamson & Wolfsfeld, 1993). Movements also can measure their success by "how well their preferred meanings and interpretation are doing in various media arenas" (Gamson & Stuart, 1992, p. 56; see Ryan & Jeffreys, this volume).

Successful movements must draw on a diverse range of media to effectively publicize a message. As McHale (2004) demonstrated in his study of various activist campaigns, media are best understood broadly as constituting a vast tapestry of communication strategies (e.g., interpersonal, group, print, and electronic) that coalesce to transform social reality around a specific issue. Drawing from his experiences as an anti-death penalty organizer and documentary filmmaker, McHale (2007) noted that diverse strategies are mutually beneficial. For example, news coverage can draw attention to a movement, which increases participation in public demonstrations, which attracts further news coverage, and so on. However, campaigns today have become "reflexively conditioned by their pursuit of media attention" (Cottle, 2008, p. 853). Rather than viewing news coverage as but one element of a complex social movement strategy, contemporary organizers far too often privilege media strategies at the expense of others. This tension was present for SKFC inasmuch as we needed news outlets to portray Kenneth in a different light than they had previously and therefore, we had to escalate our efforts to keep their attention.

We were encouraged by the increasing number of media outlets showing interest in Kenneth's case throughout the summer. Interviews with family and campaign members and articles written about the case began to appear in various progressive and mainstream media in the United States and Europe (particularly in Italy and France). In August, coverage of Kenneth's case appeared in *The New York Times*, *The Guardian* (United Kingdom), *The Independent* (United Kingdom), *MSNBC.com*, *Commondreams.org*, *The Nation*, *Le Monde*, *ABC News Online*, *The Huffington Post*, and on National Public Radio and the television/radio show *Democracy Now!*. Coverage also appeared in every major Texas newspaper and on television and in print news outlets in the Austin area. Part of the reason for the broad exposure was the thorough and strategic local media work of SKFC. This local work was complemented by the work of CEDP nationally, with both local chapters and the national organization using their press networks to maximize coverage of Kenneth's case and to gain new supporters. Most of the coverage that the campaign received was favorable or neutral toward Kenneth and either questioned his death sentence or opposed it outright (see, e.g., "Another Stain on Justice," 2007; "Backward Texas Law," 2007; Blumenthal, 2007; Chapa, 2007; Chasnoff, 2007; Glaister, 2007; Goodman & Gonzalez, 2007a).

Two final rallies in Austin escalated the SKFC's confrontation with the state of Texas and sustained positive news attention. As previously mentioned, on August 22, hundreds of activists marched around the Capitol building in Austin and to the governor's mansion, where six people engaged in civil disobedience. Three days later, on August 25, activists linked the hundreds of petition pages we had collected with ribbon and, once again, marched on the governor's mansion and surrounded it with the chain of documents. Each of these actions fed into other organizing efforts, garnering press coverage, increasing the involvement and confidence of Kenneth's loved ones, and bringing ever-greater numbers of activists into the fight to save Kenneth's life. At every turn, SKFC resisted the temptation to fetishize the potential visibility of news media coverage, choosing instead to recognize that a successful movement must integrate a wide range of mutually interactive and beneficial communication strategies (see McHale, 2004, 2007).

ANATOMY OF A VICTORY: LESSONS LEARNED ABOUT COMMUNICATION ACTIVISM SCHOLARSHIP

On August 30, 2007, in an unprecedented move, Governor Perry commuted Kenneth's sentence from the death penalty to life in prison. It was an outcome that Kenneth's lawyer attributes to the hard work of SKFC members who conducted a campaign that found the right combination of political calculation, media savvy, and personal passion among its members. In a victory toast given soon after Kenneth's execution was stopped, Feyh called SKFC a campaign "where family became activists and activists became family."

There were many lessons learned from this campaign. Here, we offer five lessons that we, as activist-scholars, learned from this campaign that can be generalized to others who engage in communication activism scholarship.

First, communication scholar-activists should not be discouraged from becoming involved in a movement or campaign because of their privilege or the accusation that their involvement is narcissistic. In their highly influential book on social movements, Stewart, Smith, and Denton (2007) distinguished between self-directed and other-directed movements, with their descriptions of these movements suggesting that difference is a barrier to solidarity. They argued that although a chief goal of self-directed movements is to improve the impoverished self-image of those who are oppressed and downtrodden, other-directed movements must reaffirm the messianic posture of those self-fashioned saviors who leverage their social privilege to improve the lot of people who are marginalized.

Solidarity among people of different races and privilege is not only possible but also critical to the success of organizing around issues such as the criminal justice system, where people of color are disproportionately affected. Following the experiences and lessons of the SKFC, we wholeheartedly reject the brittle dichotomy that Stewart et al. (2007) described between those who are marginalized and those who are privileged. Although we readily acknowledge that our structural relationship to Kenneth's incarceration and impending execution was significantly different from his, his family, or the 3,242 men and women who were are on death row in the United States as of October 1, 2010 (Fins, 2010), nonetheless, we understand our participation in SKFC as something other than an act of charity. We agree with Sarat (2001), a legal scholar, who eloquently described the death penalty as "a strategy of governance that makes us fearful and dependent on the illusion of state protection, that divides rather than unites, that promises simple solutions to complex problems" (p. 247). Because we view the death penalty, in particular, and the prison–industrial complex, in general, as colossal failures of public policy that are at odds with the aims of a democratic society, helping to save the life of Kenneth Foster represented a strategic step forward in a broader effort to cultivate a more just society for everyone. Thus, our experience with the SKFC highlights how scholar-activists might find solidarity across lines of difference by imagining diverse relationships among members with respect to the specific policy issue at hand. One need not occupy a death row cell or be a member of a demographic group more likely to do so to recognize a significant and compelling interest in abolishing executions. Campaigns and movements, therefore, would do well to appeal to citizens' *interest* rather than identities that divide us when pursuing a specific change in public policy.

Second, prisoners and their families, when they have the opportunity to engage in communication activism, can be more effective in persuading others and shifting narratives of victimhood, humanity, worth, and justice than can scholar-activists or activists, in general, speaking in their stead. Prisoners and their families can counter standard narratives of victimhood and justice, and represent their experiences with an ethos that is difficult to obtain from outside. That said, their voices must be part of a strategy of organizing that also includes instrumental communicative actions, such as working with the news media, lobbying officials, demonstrating, and engaging in civil disobedience. Furthermore, the confidence that they gain through their active participation in organizing has the potential to transform them from victims of capital punishment into activists in their own right. For example, Kenneth's father and grandfather have continued to speak out in campaigns about other prisoners and in other political venues. Sandra Reed, the mother of another Texas prisoner, and Jeannine Scott, a prisoner's wife, both serve on CEDP's Board of Directors. They and many other family members and former prisoners have been part of regional and national speaking events, and have become instrumental in CEDP's fight for abolition of the death penalty.

Third, both interracial organizing and the development of prisoners and their family members as activists require organizers to actively integrate their ideas and experiences into the campaign. Indeed, prisoners and their families must be encouraged to speak for themselves as part of a movement's strategy and must be supported by activists in doing so. They are not movement mouthpieces but must be active participants whose ideas are heard and respected. Communication scholar-activists and activists, in general, must not, however, refrain from arguing with them about strategies and tactics. Communication scholar-activists and seasoned activists bring expertise based on their experiences and research on coordinating and conducting rallies and marches, creating media packets, press releases, and memory of previous struggles. However, family members and communication scholar-activists must engage in decision making as equals, drawing on each other's strengths and expertise in a climate of mutual trust in each other's good faith, judgment, and desire to prevail.

Fourth, it is important for scholar-activists engaged in anti-death penalty or prison work to interact with prisoners who also are aligned with similar kinds of political work. To find ways to create solidarity despite our differences, scholar-activists should learn about the experiences of prisoners from prisoners themselves such that they can struggle *with* rather than *for* them. That relationship needs to be mutually beneficial as activist-prisoners, like Kenneth and members of DRIVE, and scholar-activists learn and are energized by one another. CEDP and SKFC members' correspondence with Kenneth and other death row inmates who are actively involved in the political struggle against the death penalty created the possibility of a unified front against the injustices of the death penalty and the prison–industrial complex described in this chapter. Knowing Kenneth personally allowed SKFC to present his case to the public with a richness and complexity that would not have been possible if we knew him only in name and as a cause.

Fifth, scholar-activists should seek to reproduce in their academic writing the values they embraced during a particular campaign or movement. Although we did not write this chapter with Kenneth or any of his family members, we did attempt to write it with the same honesty and sincerity that we maintained during SKFC. We also included portions of Kenneth's letters and poetry, as well as Nydesha's words, to have Kenneth and his family represent themselves. This chapter would have been incomplete and our campaign, quite possibly, unsuccessful had their voices not been included.

CONCLUSION

Currently, Kenneth Foster is off death row and serving a life sentence in a prison in Beeville, Texas. He continues to correspond and work with the Campaign to End the Death Penalty, and, as indicated earlier, we maintain contact with his family. As of 2011, the national tide is turning against capital punishment. Although a majority of U.S. Americans still support the death penalty, their numbers have declined significantly since the 1990s

(Newport, 2007). Sixteen states plus the District of Columbia have abolished capital punishment altogether and other states are considering doing so. It is, of course, impossible to credit one victory in Texas with a broader trend against executions, but we believe that the success and visibility of the Save Kenneth Foster Campaign, at least in part, is both a cause and a consequence of that wider political trend.

During Texas's 2008–2009 legislative session, Rep. Terri Hodge, a Dallas Democrat, drafted a bill, entitled "The Kenneth Foster, Jr. Act," which, if passed, would have automatically severed codefendants' trials in capital cases and removed the death penalty as a sentencing option in Law of Parties cases. Although the bill passed the Texas House, it died in the Senate after a veto threat from Governor Perry altered and subsequently stalled the bill, preventing senators from debating it before the session ended (Ward, 2009). This outcome was disappointing, but this effort to change Texas law inspired a number of new family members of prisoners affected by the Law of Parties to become politically active.[13] This is what we hope the legacy of the SKFC will be. Although the road between Kenneth's commutation and the outright abolition of the death penalty is a long one, we remain invested in struggles that place the experiences of those most directly impacted by capital punishment at the center. It is their judgment and experience, combined with activism by communication scholars and others, that shall determine the legitimacy, strength, and outcomes of this life-and-death struggle.

At the beginning of summer 2007, the members of SKFC were certain of only one thing: If we did nothing, the state of Texas would execute Kenneth. Without the determination of Kenneth, his family and friends, and other community members to work together to overcome our differences, the campaign could have easily fallen apart before it began. Fighting for Kenneth's life, however, was the right thing to do and those who decided to stay and fight became a powerful force in Texas as we supported, struggled, and succeeded together in the belly of the beast.

NOTES

1. See the archive of media coverage and editorials at the Save Kenneth Foster! blog at http://savekenneth.blogspot.com.
2. Not all of us were in Austin during the entire campaign but our involvement both in and out of Austin spanned the length of the campaign. By referring to "we" or the Campaign to End the Death Penalty (CEDP), we are expressing our political position in the campaign. To be clear, Dana Cloud and Bryan J. McCann were in Austin working on the campaign from beginning to end; Katie Feyh flew back from visiting Russia early to be at the July 21, 2007 rally and to join the campaign; and Jennifer Asenas worked on the campaign from the beginning before leaving Austin August 8, 2007 to begin teaching at California State

University, Chico (where she taught before going to California State University, Long Beach).
3. MOVE (not an acronym and spelled in all uppercase), an organization of people who follow the teachings of John Africa, with members all having adopted the last name "Africa," works to stop humans from polluting the Earth and enslaving life (see http://www.onamove.com).
4. Juneteenth is the oldest known celebration commemorating the ending of slavery in the United States, dating back to June 19, 1865, when Union soldiers, led by Major General Gordon Granger, landed at Galveston, Texas with news that the war had ended and that the enslaved now were free (for more information, see http://www.juneteenth.com/history.htm).
5. See video footage of this picket at http://www.veoh.com/videos/v1044912W3xASwp8?jsonParams=%257B%2522query%2522%253A%2522%252Bmedia.collectionIds%253Adeathpenalty%2B-metadata%253A%2528%255C%2522fullLength%253D1%255C%2522%2529%2Border%253Armdf%253DepisodeNumber%2522%252C%2522veohOnly%2522%253Atrue%252C%2522collection%2522%253A%2522deathpenalty%2522%257D&c=deathpenalty&context=CHANNEL&viewType=channel.
6. To protest the scheduled execution of Sankofa, anti-death penalty activists around the United States scheduled a day of action on June 19, 2000. In Austin, 200 demonstrators marched from the state capitol to the governor's mansion, where 15 activists sat down in the driveway and were arrested. Ultimately, Sankofa was executed, but the civil disobedience action brought a lot of attention to the case.
7. See video footage of this protest at http://www.youtube.com/watch?v=ff6yXkybadw
8. The year prior to his scheduled execution date, Kenneth had expressed frustration that activist groups had not been working on his case in a sustained way. He had written CEDP members Randi Jones and McCann to this effect. Although the CEDP had been in touch and working with Lawrence Foster, Kenneth's grandfather, for some time, when a person is in prison, it is difficult for him or her to have a sense of the real constraints and possibilities for action at any given moment. We did not believe we could have launched the campaign earlier.
9. Several individuals who added their signatures reflected on their encounters with law enforcement, knowing all too well the types of corrupt logic that drove a piece of legislation such as the Law of Parties.
10. The LaHood family was not in favor of Kenneth's clemency (for an example of the type of narratives that argued Kenneth should be executed for his role in LaHood's murder, see http://blogs.dailymail.com/donsurber/2007/08/27/screw-foster-who-is-michael-lahood-jr).
11. Newton was executed in Texas on September 14, 2005, despite grave doubts about her guilt (see Smith, 2005).
12. See video footage of this speech at http://www.youtube.com/watch?v=y5wjK0PXuCg.
13. Terri and Stephen Been, as well as their children (relatives of Jeff Wood); Crystal Wilson (wife of Randy Halprin); and the families of Humberto Garza and

Robert Garza have become politically active to challenge the Law of Parties on behalf of their loved ones.

REFERENCES

Alcoff, L. (1991–1992). The problem of speaking for others. *Cultural Critique, 20*, 5–32. doi:10.2307/1354221

Another stain on justice, Texas style [Editorial]. (2007, August 28). *Austin American-Statesman*, p. A10.

Artz, L. (2007). Re-defining activism, re-constructing change [Review of the book *Communication activism*, 2 volumes, by L. R. Frey & K. M. Carragee]. *Communication Research Trends, 26*, 33–36.

Backward Texas law may make man pay with life for deed he didn't do [Editorial]. (2007, July 28). *Austin American-Statesman*, p. A18.

Blumenthal, R. (2007, August 30). Not the killer, but still facing a date with the executioner. *The New York Times*. Retrieved from http://www.nytimes.com

Bobo, L. D., & Johnson D. (2004). A taste for punishment: Black and white Americans' views on the death penalty and the war on drugs. *Du Bois Review: Social Science Research on Race, 1*, 151–180. doi:10.1017/S1742058X04040081

Bowers, J. W., Ochs, D. J., & Jensen, R. J. (1993). *The rhetoric of agitation and control* (2nd ed.). Prospect Heights, IL: Waveland Press.

Bruni, F. (with Yardley, J.). (2000, June 23). With Bush assent, inmate is executed. *The New York Times*, p. A1. Retrieved from http://www.nytimes.com

Butcher, A. K., & Moore, M. K. (2000, September 22). *Muting Gideon's trumpet: The crisis in indigent criminal defense in Texas*. Retrieved from Department of Political Science, University of Texas at Arlington website: http://www.uta.edu/pols/moore/indigent/last.pdf

Chapa, R. (2007, August 29). Lone Star State's broken system metes out irreversible "justice." *San Antonio Express-News*. Retrieved from http://www.mysanantonio.com

Chasnoff, B. (2007, August 25). Death debate centers on intent. *San Antonio Express-News*. Retrieved from http://www.mysanantonio.com

Conquergood, D. (2002). Lethal theatre: Performance, punishment, and the death penalty. *Theatre Journal, 54*, 339–367. doi:10.1353/tj.2002.007

Corcoran, F. (1985). Pedagogy in prison: Teaching in maximum security institutions. *Communication Education, 34*, 49–58. doi:10.1080/03634528509378582

Cottle, S. (2008). Reporting demonstrations: The changing media of the politics of dissent. *Media, Culture & Society, 30*, 853–872. doi:10.1177/0163443708096097

Criminal Responsibility for Conduct of Another Act, Texas Penal Code § 7.02. (1973 & Amended 1993).

Dardis, F. E., Baumgarten, F. R., Boydstun, A. E., De Boef, S., & Shen, F. (2008). Media framing of capital punishment and its impact on individuals' cognitive responses. *Mass Communication & Society, 11*, 115–140. doi:10.1080/15205430701580524

Death Penalty Information Center. (2009a, December). *Executions in the United States in 2009*. Washington, DC: Author. Retrieved from http://deathpenaltyinfo.org/executions-united-states-2009

Death Penalty Information Center. (2009b, October). *Smart on crime: Reconsidering the death penalty in a time of economic crisis*. Washington, DC: Author. Retrieved from http://www.deathpenaltyinfo.org/documents/CostsRptFinal.pdf

Death Penalty Information Center. (2010, January). *National statistics on the death penalty and race*. Washington, DC: Author. Retrieved from http://www.deathpenaltyinfo.org/race-death-row-inmates-executed-1976

Death Penalty Information Center. (2011, May 18). *Facts about the death penalty*. Washington, DC: Author. Retrieved from http://www.deathpenaltyinfo.org/documents/FactSheet.pdf

DeLuca, K. M. (1999). *Image politics: The new rhetoric of environmental activism*. New York, NY: Guilford Press.

Enmund v. Florida, 458 U.S. 782 (1982).

Fins, D. (2009, Winter). *Death row U.S.A*. Retrieved from NAACP Legal Defense and Educational Fund website: http://www.naacpldf.org/content/pdf/pubs/drusa/DRUSA_Winter_2009.pdf

Fins, D. (2010, Fall). *Death row U.S.A*. Retrived from NAACP Legal Defense and Educational Fund website: http://naacpldf.org/files/publications/DRUSA_Fall_2010.pdf

Foster, K. (2006, May 1). *La vista*. Retrieved from http://drivemovement.org/#/la-vista/4519632549

Gamson, W., & Meyer, D. (1996). Framing political opportunity. In D. McAdam, J. D. McCarthy, & M. N. Zald (Eds.), *Comparative perspectives on social movements: Political opportunities, mobilizing structures, and cultural framings* (2nd ed., pp. 275–290). New York, NY: Cambridge University Press.

Gamson, W., & Stuart D. (1992). Media discourse as symbolic contest: The bomb in political cartoons. *Sociological Forum*, 7, 55–86. doi:10.1007/BF01124756

Gamson, W., & Wolfsfeld, G. (1993). Movements and media as interacting systems. *Annals of the American Academy of Political and Social Science*, 528, 114–125. doi:10.1177/0002716293528001009

Gilliam, F. D., Jr., & Iyengar, S. (2000). Prime suspects: The influence of local television news on the viewing public. *American Journal of Political Science*, 44, 560–573. doi:10.2307/2669264

Glaister, D. (2007, August 20). Texas defies federal court with plan to execute man who did not kill. *Guardian*. Retrieved from http://www.guardian.co.uk

Gloria. (2007, September 26). *Kenneth Foster—Public information act request* [Web log post]. Retrieved from http://www.breakallchains.blogspot.com/2007/09/kenneth-foster-public-information-act.html

Gold, R. (2000, June 20). Protesters of Graham execution arrested at governor's mansion. *San Antonio Express-News*, p. A5.

Goodman, A., & Gonzalez, J. (Producers). (2007a, July 23). Supporters of death row prisoner Kenneth Foster rally in Texas [Television/radio/video and audio podcast]. *Democracy Now!* Retrieved from http://www.democracynow.org

Goodman, A., & Gonzalez, J. (Producers). (2007b, August 29). Jimmy Carter, Desmond Tutu urge Texas to stay execution of Kenneth Foster

[Television/radio/video and audio podcast]. *Democracy Now!* Retrieved from http://www.democracynow.org

Greene, R. W. (2006). Orator communist. *Philosophy & Rhetoric, 39,* 85–95. doi:10.1353/par.2006.0008

Gurevitch, M., & Levy, M. (1985). Introduction. In M. Gurevitch & M. Levy (Eds.), *Mass communication review yearbook* (Vol. 5, pp. 11–22). Beverly Hills, CA: Sage.

Hartnett, S. J. (2003). *Incarceration nation: Investigative poems of hope and terror.* Walnut Creek, CA: AltaMira Press.

Hartnett, S. J. (2010). *Executing democracy: Capital punishment & the making of America, 1683–1807.* East Lansing: Michigan State University Press.

Hartnett, S. J., & Larson, D. M. (2005). Moving beyond the rhetorics of dignity and depravity; or, arguing about capital punishment [Book review essay]. *Rhetoric & Public Affairs, 8,* 477–498. doi: 10.1353/rap.2005.0060

Hartnett, S. J., & Larson, D. M. (2006). "Tonight another man will die": Crime, violence, and the master tropes of contemporary arguments about the death penalty. *Communication and Critical/Cultural Studies, 3,* 263–287. doi:10.1080/14791420600984102

Jacobs, R. (2007, July 4). The disturbing case of Kenneth Foster: Texas wants to kill another man, the law be damned. *CounterPunch.* Retrieved from http://www.counterpunch.org

Jones, D. M. (2005). *Race, sex, and suspicion: The myth of the black male.* Westport, CT: Praeger.

Kelley, S.-P. (2007, July 31). Kenneth Foster, Jr.: An innocent man will soon execute. *The Huffington Post.* Retrieved from http://www.huffingtonpost.com

King, R. (2005). *Capital consequences: Families of the condemned tell their stories.* New Brunswick, NJ: Rutgers University Press.

Landry, D., & MacLean, G. (1996). Introduction: Reading Spivak. In D. Landry & G. MacLean, *The Spivak reader: Selected works of Gayatri Chakravorty Spivak* (pp. 1–14). New York, NY: Routledge.

Marquart, J. W., Ekland-Olson, S., & Sorenson, J. R. (1994). *The rope, the chair, and the needle: Capital punishment in Texas, 1923–1990.* Austin: University of Texas Press.

McCann, B. J. (2007). Therapeutic and material <victim>hood: Ideology and the struggle for meaning in the Illinois death penalty controversy. *Communication and Critical/Cultural Studies, 4,* 382–401. doi:10.1080/14791420701632931

McCleskey v. Kemp, 481 U.S. 279 (1987).

McHale, J. P. (2004). *Communicating for change: Strategies of social and political advocates.* Lanham, MD: Rowman & Littlefield.

McHale, J. P. (2007). Unreasonable doubt: Using video documentary to promote justice. In L. R. Frey & K. M. Carragee (Eds.), *Communication activism: Vol. 2. Media and performance activism* (pp. 195–222). Cresskill, NJ: Hampton Press.

Mello, M. (2008). Certain blood for uncertain reasons: A love letter to the Vermont Legislature on not reinstating capital punishment. *Vermont Law Review, 32,* 765–876. Retrieved from http://lawreview.vermontlaw.edu

Moore, M. P. (2006). To execute capital punishment: The mortification and scapegoating of Illinois Governor George Ryan. *Western Journal of Communication, 70,* 311–330. doi:10.1080/10570310600992129

Nealy, C. (n.d.). *From the Ellis unit to the Terrell unit.* Retrieved from http://www.deathrow.at/welcometohell/from.html

Newport, F. (2007, October 12). Sixty-nine percent of Americans support death penalty: Majority say death penalty is applied fairly. *Gallup.* Retrieved from http://www.gallup.com

Novek, E. M. (2005a). "The devil's bargain": Censorship, identity and the promise of empowerment in a prison newspaper. *Journalism, 6,* 5–23. doi:10.1177/1464884905048950

Novek, E. M. (2005b). "Heaven, hell, and here": Understanding the impact of incarceration through a prison newspaper. *Critical Studies in Media Communication, 22,* 281–301. doi:10.1080/07393180500288410

Novek, E., & Sanford R. (2007). At the checkpoint: Journalistic practices, research reflexivity, and dialectical tensions in a women's prison. In L. R. Frey & K. M. Carragee (Eds.), *Communication activism: Vol. 2. Media and performance activism* (pp. 67–95). Cresskill, NJ: Hampton Press.

Office of the Governor Rick Perry. (2007, August 21). *Statement by Robert Black, spokesman for Texas Governor Rick Perry, concerning the European Union's appeal that Texas enact a moratorium on the death penalty* [Press release]. Retrieved from http://www.governor.state.tx.us/news/press-release/129

PCARE. (2007). Fighting the prison-industrial complex: A call to communication and cultural studies scholars to change the world. *Communication and Critical/Cultural Studies, 4,* 402–420. doi:10.1080/14791420701632956

Peffley, M., & Hurwitz, J. (2002). The racial component of "race-neutral" crime policy attitudes. *Political Psychology, 23,* 59–75. doi:10.1111/0162-895X.00270

Peffley, M., & Hurwitz, J. (2007). Persuasion and resistance: Race and the death penalty in America. *American Journal of Political Science, 51,* 996–1012. doi:10.1111/j.1540-5907.2007.00293.x

Rizer, A. L., III. (2003). The race effect on wrongful convictions. *William Mitchell Law Review, 29,* 845–867. Retrieved from http://www.wmitchell.edu/lawreview

Sarat, A. (2001). *When the state kills: Capital punishment and the American condition.* Princeton, NJ: Princeton University Press.

Smith, S. W. (2005, September 14). Frances Newton executed in Texas: Is 3rd woman, and 1st black woman, put to death in state since '82. *CBS News.* Retrieved from http://www.cbsnews.com

Solar, S. L. C. (2004). *No justice, no victory—The death penalty in Texas* (S. Bright, Ed.). Austin, TX: Plain View Press.

Spivak, G. C. (1988). Can the subaltern speak? In C. Nelson & L. Grossberg (Eds.), *Marxism and the interpretation of culture* (pp. 271–313). Urbana: University of Illinois Press.

Stabile, C. A. (2006). *White victims, black villains: Gender, race, and crime news in US culture.* New York, NY: Routledge.

Staunton, D. (2005, September 9). Texas executes woman for murder. *Irish Times.* Retrieved from http://www.irishtimes.com

Stewart, C. J., Smith, C. A., & Denton, R. E., Jr. (2007). *Persuasion and social movements* (5th ed.). Long Grove, IL: Waveland Press.

Sunwolf. (2006). Empathic attunement facilitation: Stimulating immediate task engagement in zero-history training groups of helping professionals. In L. R. Frey (Ed.), *Facilitating group communication in context: Innovations and applications with natural groups: Vol. 1. Facilitating group creation, conflict, and conversation* (pp. 63–92). Cresskill, NJ: Hampton Press.

Sunwolf. (2007). Facilitating death talk: Creating collaborative courtroom conversations about the death penalty between attorneys and jurors. In L. R. Frey & K. M. Carragee (Eds.), *Communication activism: Vol. 1. Communication for social change* (pp. 287–323). Cresskill, NJ: Hampton Press.

U.S. Census Bureau. (2001, May). *Profiles of general demographic characteristics: 2000 Census of population and housing: United States.* Washington, DC: U.S. Department of Commerce. Retrieved from http://www.census.gov/prod/cen2000/dp1/2kh00.pdf

Valentine, K. B. (1998). "If the guards only knew": Communication education for women in prison. *Women's Studies in Communication, 21,* 238–243. doi:10.1080.07491409.1998.10162558

Valentine, K. B. (2006). Unlocking the doors for incarcerated women through performance and creative writing. In D. S. Madison & J. Hamera (Eds.), *The Sage handbook of performance studies* (pp. 309–324). Thousand Oaks, CA: Sage.

Verhovek, S. H. (1998, February 4). Execution in Texas: The overview; divisive case of a killer of two ends as Texas executes Tucker. *The New York Times.* Retrieved from http://www.nytimes.com

Ward, M. (2009, May 21). Veto threat alters death-penalty bill. *Austin American-Statesman.* Retrieved from http://www.statesman.com

Wood, J. K. (2005). Balancing innocence with guilt: A metaphorical analysis of the US Supreme Court's rulings on victim impact statements. *Western Journal of Communication, 69,* 129–146. doi: 10.1080/10570310500076817

7

DISRUPTING WHITENESS AT A FIREHOUSE

Promoting Organizational Change through Relational Praxis

Chris Groscurth
Trinity Health

There have been certain historical events in the United States that have shaped public perceptions of fire and emergency response organizations, and the individuals who work in them. On the one hand, events such as September 11, 2001 cultivate images of emergency workers selflessly risking their lives for the public good. Thus, for some people, the uniforms of public service workers stand as symbols of bravery, heroism, and protection (see Scott & Myers, 2005; Tracy & Scott, 2006). On the other hand, the race riots of the 1960s and more contemporary events, such as Hurricane Katrina, plague U.S. social consciousness (see, e.g., Dyson, 2005), with the sirens, lights, and uniforms of emergency responders standing to many members of marginalized groups (e.g., blacks) as symbols of danger, exploitation, and violence. Hence, for many marginalized people in the United States, because of fear of exploitation and a history of unjust exercises of power, there is an understandable mistrust of emergency response workers.

Part of the reason for people's perceptions may be due to emergency response workers' communication with marginalized populations. Unfortunately, we know little about the communication processes that constitute emergency response organizations and the individuals who work in those organizations. The research that does exist primarily has focused on the gendered aspects of firefighting (Desmond, 2006; Tracy & Scott, 2006) and on assimilation into (Myers, 2005) and leadership processes within firefighting organizations (Cragan, 2008; Ziegler & DeGrosky, 2008). The activist research reported in this chapter extends that literature by examining how racial identities, power, privilege, and organizational discourse function in constituting a fire department (hereafter referred to as "Fire Services"). The project grew from my desire to understand the individual–institutional dynamics of how Fire Services, a racially homogeneous (i.e., white) organization, operates in the racially and ethnically diverse community in the southeastern United States in which it is located.

My interest in observing and intervening in the multileveled discourses of Fire Services, wherein social justice was implicitly—if not explicitly—at issue, stems from my doctoral dissertation. Ultimately, the changes that I sought in that organization were increased reflection among key stakeholders about diversity-related matters, such as inclusion of marginalized people, culturally competent patient care, and diversity training for the staff. To accomplish these goals, I assisted in efforts to form a diversity relations committee, design diversity training, and facilitate managerial dialogue about the implications of diversity on this organization's services.

Although structural transformation was the ultimate goal of the project, I also was interested in learning more about how discourse shapes the cultural identities of individuals and organizations (see Tracy, Myers, & Scott, 2006; Tracy & Scott, 2006). Understanding how discourse constitutes individual and organizational identity requires a theoretical sensibility for ways in which power is produced, distributed, and resisted through the process of organizing, a term I use to signify the emergent nature of organizations. In other words, organizations, such as fire departments, are the result of individual and interactional communication processes (see also Fairhurst & Putnam, 2004). The racial dynamics between Fire Services and the culturally diverse community it serves provides a unique opportunity to observe these communication processes in action. Moreover, this context provides an opportunity for disruptive praxis aimed at promoting greater reflexivity about whiteness and white privilege at the individual and organizational levels.

This chapter is organized into four sections. The first section locates my theoretical approach to the racial subject and to power. Like many scholars (e.g., Barge, 2001; Craig & Tracy, 1995; Frey, Pearce, Pollock, Artz, & Murphy, 1996; Tracy, 2007), I assume that applied communication research (including activism research) inherently is theoretical, practical, and—to a greater or less degree—political (see also Frey, 2006). To situate my particular approach to communication activism scholarship, this section describes how the principles of dialogism and power articulated by Bakhtin and Foucault, respectively, informed my intervention. The second section provides a justification for communication activism scholarship that is critical of whiteness and white privilege. *Whiteness*, a concept that grew out of literary, legal, education, and cultural studies, refers not to white people per se but to the set of dynamic historical, cultural, and political narratives that shape (and are shaped by) race relations. Whiteness is the subject of critical inquiry, particularly in the United States, because of its ubiquity and influence, which results in unwarranted social advantages, privileges, and injustices (Cooks, 2003; Jackson, 1999; McIntosh, 1998; Nakayama & Krizek, 1995). Following the discussion of critical whiteness studies, the third section explains the stages of my activist research at Fire Services and analyzes the individual and organizational changes that resulted. The final section discusses lessons learned from the intervention for communication scholar-activists who design, implement, and assess the impact of their interventions directed at issues of race, power, and/or identity.

A DIALOGIC APPROACH TO THE RACIAL SUBJECT AND POWER

The writings of Mikhail Bakhtin and Michel Foucault shape my philosophical assumptions about the relationship between the individual and the social/institutional (cf. Hermans, Kempen, & van Loon, 1992; Holland, Lachicotte, Skinner, & Cain, 1998; Tracy & Trethewey, 2005). When juxtaposed, these authors' writings illuminate how subjectivity is forged through discursive acts exercised within a field of ongoing tensions and power relations. Moreover, Bakhtin and Foucault provide insight for theorizing (a) the relational nature of the racial subject, (b) the contingency of subjectivity, and (c) the relations of power that shape and are shaped by the subject (see also Holland et al., 1998; Johnson, 2003). I drew on these principles to design and implement my communication activism with Fire Services.

From a dialogic perspective, the subject "I" is a fleeting discursive location rather than a static self-referential essence (see, e.g., Deetz, 2001; Hermans et al., 1992; Holland et al., 1999; Johnson, 2003). Hermans et al.

(1992) conceptualized the dialogic subject as a "dynamic multiplicity of relatively autonomous 'I' positions in an imaginal landscape" (p. 28). The dialogic subject is constituted through the use of multiple voices, communicated in response to (and anticipation of) the response of another (see also Baxter, 2004). Both the subject and the social context in which the subject acts are *in process* or *becoming* someone (or something) else—hence, the communication processes used by the subject (voice) both shape and are shaped by the context in which they are uttered (i.e., a shifting or "imaginal" landscape; see also Barge & Little, 2002; Baxter, 2004). In other words, there are multiple "I" positions that are constructed through situated speech acts or utterances in what Shotter (2004) called the "moment of acting." In moments of acting, dialogic subjects agree, contradict, argue, reinforce, challenge, and accept their social positions from one context to the next. In short, the dialogic subject is in a continual state of becoming. When conceived as such, there is no essential or internally located "I"; rather, subjectivity continually is produced in response to an external other or an "I" of another time–space—that is, either a past or future (anticipated) "I."

The notion of a "dialogic subject" fleshed out by Bakhtin (1984) and Hermans et al. (1992) raises important questions about the social construction of racial identities (see also Johnson, 2003). Although identities can be conceived of as contingent discursive relations (see, e.g., Deetz, 2001; Tracy & Trethewey, 2005), there are important social and material consequences associated with racial identities (see, e.g., Cooks, 2003; Harris, Groscurth, & Trego, 2007; Warren, 2001). For example, Johnson's (2003) analysis of racial identity as performed through gospel music examined the limits of "authentic" racial identities, highlighting the cultural, material, spiritual, and historical significance of gospel music for black people, as well as the tension produced by the performance of gospel by white Australians. His analysis provided evidence that race has both discursive and physical elements. Put simply, race simultaneously is a physical phenomenon *and* a discursive production, the meanings of which are negotiated through social interaction.

The meanings surrounding race, although deeply entrenched in material relations of economic power and material bodies, are changeable. Discourse is the means by which social relations, in general, and race relations, in particular, are created, maintained, and opposed; however, the interplay between material and discursive relations are always enabled and constrained by relations of power, a subject that Bakhtin does not fully flesh out in his discussion of the subject. Foucault (1978, 2001), in contrast, argued that the construction of alternative forms of subjectivity is a primary means for resisting hegemonic exercises of power, which function to constrain the subject. Therefore, by disrupting whiteness through communication activism (i.e., interrogating its form and function), thereby influencing how people construct meanings about themselves, others, and the world around them, scholar-activists can create more socially just communities and organizations. One way of intervening in the production of racial meaning (and racial identity) is to surface assumptions about race, identity, and power that are evident in organizational discourses (e.g., printed materials, conversations, and strategic plans). Once these assumptions and discursive practices have been raised, communication activists are responsible for facilitating more just communication practices (e.g., by initiating reflective discussion about race, conducting training, documenting activist interventions for public consumption, and raising awareness about these issues in the community). Reflecting and acting (praxis) are interdependent processes for social change.

For this project, I use Foucault's work on the subject and power to augment the Bakhtinian principles that inform my approach to the racial subject. Although Bakhtin's work provided clear principles for understanding the relational and contingent nature of the subject, he was less explicit about how relations of power influence (and are influenced by) the actions of the subject. Hence, Foucault's (1977, 1978, 2001) writing about power helped to tease out Bakhtin's seemingly metaphorical discussions of "authority" and "monologue" (read: power; see Bakhtin, 1981). In the Foucaultian sense, power is not a top-down or repressive structural phenomenon, nor is it a finite thing that can be pointed to; rather, power is a generative process, exercised and produced through social relations. Power produces identities, institutions, knowledge, and truth (Foucault, 1977; see also Tracy & Trethewey, 2005). Organizationally, power is produced and distributed through innumerable discourses articulated by individuals coordinating their action in groups. As such, understanding the perceptions, motives, and communication actions of organizational stakeholders is a first step in the process of disrupting and redistributing relations of power in a more socially just manner (see Foucault, 2001).

In summary, Foucault's principle of relational power and Bakhtin's dialogic principle provide a theoretical framework for understanding relations between the racial subject, discourse, and power. Within that framework, the subject is viewed as relationally interdependent, contextually contingent, and enmeshed within power relations. Given that power can be exercised from any social position, there are innumerable points of entry for disrupting unjust exercises of power, which crystallize in domination. Privilege, such as white privilege, is one such crystallization of power. Thus, the Bakhtinian–Foucaultian lens is effective for understanding how power and discourse shape the subject and, as such, how communication scholars might begin to disrupt the reproduction of racial power and privilege through criticism, activist research, civic participation, and community intervention.

THE NEED FOR INTERVENTIONIST PRAXIS IN CRITICAL WHITENESS STUDIES

The theoretical approach brought to this intervention makes a unique contribution to the communication literature on whiteness and white privilege. Within the communication field, critical whiteness studies (CWS) engage the discourses through which racist power and privilege are created and maintained (see, e.g., Nakayama & Krizek, 1995). The work of CWS often intersects with other subfields, such as communication education (e.g., Cooks, 2003; Cooks & Simpson, 2007; Endres & Gould, 2009; Giroux, 2003; Harris et al., 2007; Orbe, Groscurth, Jeffries, & Prater, 2007), communication and rhetorical theory (e.g., Jackson, 1999; Kennedy, Middleton, & Ratcliffe, 2005; Lacy, 2008; Nakayama & Krizek, 1995; Simpson, 2008), critical media studies (e.g., Brown, 2009; Butterworth, 2007; Calhoun, 2005; Chidester, 2008; Dubrofsky, 2006; Fraley, 2009; Grealy, 2008; Hess, 2005; Lavelle, 2010; Mayer, 2005; Moon & Nakayama, 2006; Projansky & Ono, 1999; Tierney, 2006; Watts, 2005), interracial and intercultural communication (e.g., Bahk & Jandt, 2008; Martin & Davis, 2001; Miller & Harris, 2005; Nakayama & Martin, 1999; Orbe, Smith, Groscurth, & Crawley, 2010), performance studies (e.g., Warren, 2001; Warren & Kilgard, 2001), and organizational communication (e.g., Ashcraft & Allen, 2003; Grimes, 2001, 2002). For more than a decade, communication scholars in these and other areas have made significant theoretical, empirical, and pedagogical contributions to the emergence of CWS.

Although communication scholars who are critical of whiteness all seek to produce theory, research, criticism, and pedagogy related to whiteness and white privilege, these scholarly objectives are pursued in various ways. For example, Cooks (2003) and Warren (2001) used interdisciplinary theories of performance and performativity to examine articulations of privilege in the university classroom (see also the essays in Cooks & Simpson, 2007; Harris et al., 2007; Warren & Kilgard, 2001). These studies provide readings of the communication of whiteness and white privilege as they emerge through classroom interaction (see also the essays in Lea & Sims, 2008; Miller & Harris, 2005; Warren & Hytten, 2004).

In a different way, cultural and rhetorical critics draw on critical and poststructuralist theories of race and identity (e.g., Jackson, 1999; McPhail, 2002, 2004; Nakayama & Krizek, 1995) to examine how power and privilege are reproduced through media texts. For example, Hess (2005), Moon and Nakayama (2005), and Watts (2005) contributed to CWS by critically examining popular films and print media (see also Dyer, 1997; Mukherjee, 2006; Projansky & Ono, 1999; Wiegman, 1999). Examinations through these theoretical lenses expose the complexities and challenges that whiteness poses for coherent race relations and interracial harmony (McPhail, 2004; Simpson, 2008).

Although these studies have established a strong theoretical and empirical basis for CWS, there is much work yet to be done. The continued legitimacy of CWS as an antiracist form of scholarly praxis hinges on two important considerations. First, if CWS is to become a catalyst for social change, as often claimed, scholars must diversify the contexts in which whiteness is interrogated, as, to date, it has been explored in a limited number of contexts. The most heavily researched/critiqued institutional site is the university classroom followed closely by textual analyses of popular media. Although classroom interactions and popular media are important (and certainly readily accessible) contexts for interrogating whiteness, there is more to how whiteness operates than these contextual analyses have demonstrated. For example, with rare exception (e.g., Watts, 2005), critical analyses of whiteness in communication do not interrogate how whiteness intersects with other aspects of identity, such as social class, gender, sexuality, or religion. Moreover, CWS tend not to directly engage people living racial lives (e.g., at work, watching or interacting with media, at church, or in their communities). This lack of research raises important questions about whiteness: For instance, do older white women, who identify as lesbian, communicate about whiteness differently than do 18- to 22-year-old college students? How does communication about race among "blue-collar" whites compare with other populations focused on in CWS? Do the most socially disenfranchised (e.g., people who are homeless and/or imprisoned) communicate in ways that contribute to white power and privilege? If CWS are going to be a force for social justice, intervening into these culturally complex relationships is a necessary direction for communication scholar-activists.

In particular, organizations, such as workplaces, churches, educational institutions and government organizations, and public services deserve critical attention. If CWS is to live up to its "radical" or transformational claims, future work must engage the individuals, organizations, and communities where whiteness is constructed and where racial injustices are negotiated. One way for critical whiteness scholars to make a difference in these contexts is to adopt a communication activist or interventionist approach (see Frey, 2006, 2009; Frey & SunWolf, 2009). When viewed from the perspective of communication activism, scholar-activists engage in forms of critical whiteness practice that actively seek to promote racial justice and to eliminate white power and privilege.

Although such a turn toward critical whiteness practice might be unique to the study of whiteness and related identities, interventionist praxis has roots in the well-established subfield of applied communication research (Frey & SunWolf, 2009). The emerging literature on communication activism situates intervention as a particular way of mobilizing communication principles, theories, and practices to promote social justice on local and global scales (e.g., Carragee & Frey, this volume; Frey, 2006, 2009; Frey &

Carragee, 2007a, 2007b). The topics and contexts that communication scholars engage should do more than produce knowledge (theory) for the sake of knowledge; communication scholars should make society better by changing it (e.g., building communities, managing conflicts, improving literacy, advocating for those who are disadvantaged, and redistributing power relations). The emergence of communication activism research demonstrates the potential difference that communication scholars can make in the world (see Frey, 2009). The call for communication activism, thus, compels scholars from different subdisciplinary fields to examine how their work is addressing social injustices (e.g., racism, heterosexism, and classism) by changing (or at least attempting to change) unjust social conditions. Although scholarly reports (e.g., journal articles) are necessary for the continuity of the field, they will not help individuals to improve their material conditions, make workplaces more satisfying, or make communities more just.

The form of critical whiteness practice described here was an attempt to make a difference at Fire Services by changing the discourses of whiteness that were observed. Additionally, my critical whiteness practice took a particular antiracist political orientation. Critical whiteness practice, by nature, cannot be complicit, as complicity naturally reproduces the taken-for-granted privileges that constitute white power (see McPhail, 2004; Simpson, 2008). Following Laclau and Mouffe (1985), "Radical politics should concern 'life' issues and be 'generative,' allowing people and groups to make things happen; and democracy should be envisioned as a form of a 'dialogue,' controversial issues being resolved through listening to each other" (p. xv).

In summary, to make a difference, CWS must actively engage (and change) the discourses and contexts in which whiteness, power, and privilege are created and maintained. Communication activism provides critical whiteness scholars with a framework and practices to conceive and implement interventionist projects related to race and social justice. Thus, I situate this project alongside other activist research that promotes dialogue, reflection, and systemic change about pressing sociopolitical issues (e.g., Groscurth & Orbe, 2006; Jovanovic, Steger, Symonds, & Nelson, 2007; Shields & Preston, 2007).

In seeking to meet the goals of communication activism scholarship, CWS and critical whiteness practice must address the tension between observation and intervention. As Frey (2009) noted, graduate students receive extensive training in observation (method) and the production of understanding (theory) that, for the most part, privileges observation and interpretation over reflexive action (see also Carragee & Frey, this volume; Craig & Tracy, 1995; Freire, 1970; Frey & Carragee, 2007b). However, most graduate programs pay almost no attention to what communication research can do to change the social phenomena of interest and of political importance (in this case, race relations). This condition certainly was the case in my graduate program of study. Thankfully, through collaborative projects with established scholars, I learned how to mobilize observation for the purposes of community assessment and intervention (see, e.g., Groscurth & Orbe, 2006). Moreover, the emerging literature on communication activism scholarship has been invaluable in my research related to race relations, in general (including other social identities tacit in such discussions), and whiteness, power, and privilege, in particular (see also Nicotera, Clinkscales, Dorsey, & Niles, 2009).

From a communication activism perspective, observation and intervention are both necessary to alter the unjust distribution of power and privilege in society, and to promote social justice (see Bok's, 2006, discussion of the role of publicly funded scholarship). However, if "critical" observations of whiteness become habitual, and if European-American scholars continually engage in activities that are devoid of reflexive action (i.e., not intervening to enact structural and/or social change), they risk benefiting from the very structures of domination that they purportedly aim to transform (e.g., in the form of tenure and promotion). Hence, scholars must be suspicious of the growth and institutionalization of CWS. A turn toward critical whiteness practice and activist intervention is a promising means for reducing the threat of perpetuating unjust relations of power and racial privilege through CWS—even if the observational methods (e.g., textual analysis) are critical in nature. The following description documents the practices, processes, and outcomes of my communication activism research, and offers a glimpse of what critical whiteness praxis might look like in the future.

CRITICAL WHITENESS PRAXIS: ENGAGING THE INDIVIDUAL, CHANGING THE INSTITUTION

Fire Services is one of the largest tax-based fire and emergency response organizations in the southeastern United States, employing nearly 800 men and women. The community that Fire Services is located in has been one of the fastest growing counties in the nation for several decades, and is located outside a major metropolitan area. The population of this community is nearly 800,000. The economic base is comprised of retail; government, legal, professional, and technical services; and industry (particularly technology), with the major employers being public schools, county government, Wal-Mart, and another "big-box" retailer headquartered nearby. The median annual income in this community in 2007 was approximately $65,000; however, for whites, the median annual income was $72,000 compared with $66,100 for Asians, $52,300 for blacks, and $41,200 for Hispanics and

Latino/as. The annual median income for firefighters in this region ranges between $34,000 and $50,000, depending on experience, training, certification, and rank. These data illustrate the range of socioeconomic differences among members of the community in which Fire Services operates (U.S. Census Bureau, 2008).

Over the past 2 decades, the community has experienced tremendous racial and ethnic diversification. Latino/a, Korean, and blacks now account for approximately 44% of the county's total population (U.S. Census Bureau, 2008), making it nearly a "majority-minority" community. In fact, whites account for only 60% of the population, which is 14% below their representation in the United States (U.S. Census Bureau, 2008). Paradoxically, less than 5% of Fire Services' firefighters and emergency medical technicians are persons of color. As with many cases of so-called "white flight," it comes as no surprise, due to the earning potential at Fire Services, that many Fire Services employees live in wealthier suburbs or rural areas where they purchase large pieces of land. Many of the individuals interviewed for this study commute more than an hour to work every third day to work their 24-hour shift (although data pertaining to the percentage of employees who commute from outside of the service area were unavailable).

The clash of racial and socioeconomic status between the employees of Fire Services and the diverse community that the organization serves poses a number of communication challenges, including language barriers, religious and socioeconomic differences, lack of multicultural communication competence in patient care, lack of community outreach and education, recruitment, and promoting antiracist organizational policies. As a citizen-activist living in this community, these factors, in part, piqued my interest in the relationship between emergency service organizations and the cultural communities they serve. My interest also was motivated by two related news stories of alleged racial discrimination among fire and emergency service workers in surrounding communities. The first case related to alleged discrimination in employment practices at a nearby county fire department; the second controversial case was related to the alleged murder of a black citizen by white police officers. In the wake of these controversies, I became interested in how public service organizations in my community (in particular, Fire Services) were responding in policy and practice to matters of racial and ethnic difference.

In light of these events, I decided to research for my doctoral dissertation how whiteness operated through a critical analysis of individual and organizational discourses at Fire Services. My original intention for the project was to describe (observe) racialized communication processes at Fire Services, but as the research unfolded, I became interested in influencing communication phenomena through intervention. Thus, my dissertation involved both observing and intervening into the discourses of Fire Services. The experience of transitioning from observer to activist was personally and professionally transformative. In addition to expanding the range of possibilities that I saw for communication and social justice work, the research shaped my decision to direct my professional energies toward intervention into discourses. Finally, my experiences observing and intervening into the discourses of whiteness and white privilege altered my perception of CWS (see earlier discussion) and the role of critical whiteness practice in social justice struggles. Below, I describe the phases of my project, outcomes, and lessons learned about communication activism scholarship through the process.

Intervention Process

In this section, I detail the phases of the intervention, which included collection of textual artifacts, critical discourse analysis (CDA), data feedback and critical reflection with key stakeholders, and action planning (for similar examples, see Coates, 1997; Orbe, 2007; Sline, 2006). During each phase, I reflect on tensions experienced as I transitioned from observer to activist.

My process of becoming a scholar-activist began with a thorough CDA (see, e.g., Fairclough, 1995; Fairclough & Wodak, 1997; Locke, 2004; van Leeuwen, 2008; Weiss & Wodak, 2003; Wodak & Meyer, 2009) of public artifacts produced by Fire Services. Critically interrogating textual and visual organizational discourses exposes the *espoused values* and *tacit assumptions* that underlie these discursive practices (Schein, 2004) and that contribute to the perpetuation of racial privilege. This phase involved a close reading of public documents, such as information posted on Fire Services' website and videos produced by Fire Services intended for community outreach, as well as the organization's annual report for the preceding year, demographic statistics for the region, diversity community materials produced by Fire Services, and a national report addressing the importance of diverse community relations committees for fire and emergency organizations, published by the International Association of Fire Fighters, which was used to contrast "best practices" with the practices of Fire Services.

More than 200 pages of single-spaced text were reviewed, which provided one layer of evidence regarding Fire Services' espoused values and tacit assumptions about race, equality, and community responsibility. Additionally, this discourse analysis provided a rich context for understanding how issues of racial difference (see, e.g., Reisigl & Wodak, 2000, 2001) are situated within the fire and emergency service fields at local, state, and federal levels. A close reading of these texts revealed a number of important insights regarding the discursive construction of racial privilege and organizational participation. For example, a number of paradoxical themes are expressed through the public discourse of Fire Services that relate to the simultaneous *inclusion* and *exclusion* of underrepresented individuals in the emergency response discourse, with the organization touting its commitment to "equal opportunity" and "community," yet this rhetoric contradicts the actual representation of racial/ethnic minorities in the organization. Additionally, the public discourse of Fire Service perpetuates an ideology of *color-blindness* by failing to speak to the importance of a diverse staff to better serve a diverse community. Color-blindness is articulated by positioning the human experiences of loss, grief, and tragedy as universal and devoid of any culturally specific variability.

The reoccurrence of privilege, color-blindness, and constrained participation identified during this phase of inquiry were essential themes for understanding the problem of whiteness at Fire Services. Through this research, I began to understand how white privilege was tacitly communicated through organizational discourse. For example, the overwhelming absence of messages about the diverse nature of the community, educational materials in languages other than English, and outreach efforts to specific cultural communities all reinforced the pervasive presence of whiteness in the organizational rhetoric of Fire Services. The discursive exercise of power centralized Euro-American language, religious values, and cultural norms as the "standard" to which "nonwhites" in Fire Services should assimilate (see Cooks, 2003). In effect, such exclusionary practices render that which is nonwhite invisible. Such observations were useful points of reference that guided the interviews conducted in the second phase of this intervention.

This CDA was both empirically and theoretically interesting, standing alone as a useful contribution to the CWS communication literature. However, in a personal-political sense, producing such an analysis and offering the traditional "implications for future research" would not have a direct positive impact on the lives of the marginalized members of my community or on the perpetuation of privileged discourses at Fire Services. This concern led me to question how I, a white male on the verge of earning a PhD and entering the privileged space of academia, was unintentionally benefiting from the system of white privilege through a well-intentioned, yet traditional, scholarly project. Consequently, I explored how I might avoid reproducing white privilege through less traditional scholarly modes. My views of communication practice subsequently began to change, as I realized that I had to become an agent for change, and that my scholarship-activism could be a vehicle for that change. This realization led to the second phase of the intervention with Fire Services.

From Observation to Intervention

The second stage of the intervention, also a part of my dissertation work, involved personal involvement with employees of Fire Services. During the planning and implementation of this phase, the line between observer and activist became increasingly blurred and complex. Having spent several weeks analyzing the organization's public discourse, I had a good sense of the espoused values and assumptions about racial difference, which may (or may not) find their way into the language of Fire Services employees. For the most part, these values reflected the meritocratic and color-blind ideologies that consistently are observed among those who identify with whiteness (see Nakayama & Martin, 1999). As a result, the goals of the interviews and observations were twofold: (a) to collect additional information from employees about their experiences with race, their training (especially related to matters of cultural communication), and their perceptions about how racial diversity influences their work; and (b) to challenge the status quo of the organization by creating space for employees to reflect on the tacit privilege communicated through the policies and practices of the organization.

To gain access to organizational employees, I initiated contact with Fire Services over the phone and was put in contact with Lt. Cooper (a pseudonym), a senior officer of the organization. As the public information officer of the organization, Cooper was the public face of the organization. Cooper was a white man in his late 40s to early 50s, with graying hair, a moustache, a highly decorated uniform, and a calm, measured Southern drawl—he performed the "prototypical" Fire Services employee well. During our initial conversation, I told Cooper that I was a PhD candidate at the local university and that I was interested in the diversity of our community and its impact on Fire Services. I told him that I wanted to conduct on-site interviews with firefighters and paramedics to get a better sense of how diversity complicates interaction with members of the community. He told me that in addition to conducting on-site interviews, I could observe as many shifts of firefighters that I deemed appropriate, and also ride along on calls on the fire engine. Appreciating the ease with which I was gaining access, I told Cooper that, in return, I was willing to share collected information with senior staff members and to help them formulate "best practices" for employee training. He was enthusiastic about the project and moved quickly to get it approved by his superior (the county fire chief). Gaining access also required bureaucratic exchanges between Cooper and me. I needed a letter of invitation from the organization to receive institutional review board approval at my university, and Cooper had me sign a liability waiver. Cooper arranged my first meeting with the captain (the first in command in the station) of the firehouse to which I was assigned, although Cooper remained my primary point of contact for the duration of the project.

Observations and interviews took place at one of the 28 firehouses in the county, which was selected because it was in a particularly diverse part of the 437-square-mile service area and had a high volume of calls. I had no contact with other firefighters or officers at this station prior to arriving to conduct observations and interviews. In addition to conducting one-on-one interviews, I had informal group conversations with the firefighters (most of whom were white, with three being men of color) about their experiences of difference at work and in the community that they serve.

On my first day at Fire Services, I intended to introduce myself to organizational members, conduct an interview or two, get acclimated to the station, and observe from a distance. However, within an hour of my arrival, the commanding officer directed me to get on the fire engine as the firefighters scrambled to put on their gear to respond to a call about a large apartment fire near the station. I awkwardly climbed into a seat in the back of the fire engine as the siren began to blare and put on a headset to listen to the engineers communicate with each other. As we pulled out of the station onto the street, we saw a large plume of thick black smoke rising over a line of trees not far from the station. "Holy shit. We got us a fire, boys," exclaimed one of the firefighters. We arrived on the scene within minutes, and as soon as I stepped out of the truck, I was handed a large yellow hose and instructed to drag it as far and as fast as I could across the apartment parking lot. I then was told to stand back as the hose was charged with water pressure from a nearby hydrant. As the firefighters went to work, I thought, "So much for standing back and observing."

My initial orientation to Fire Services involved standing outside for more than 5 hours as the fire eventually was contained and extinguished. I, thus, did not conduct any interviews during my first 8-hour shift. Subsequent shifts were filled with emergency medical calls, car accidents, and less eventful calls, such as burn violations (e.g., burning yard clippings illegally). During the following weeks, I realized that establishing rapport and getting to know the firefighters interpersonally would be easy, given our shared experiences on ride-alongs and at the station, in general. Thus, I made the most of our time together by getting to know the firefighters, listening to their stories, answering their questions, and talking about the interracial communication between them and those whom they serve. During this phase of the research, I conducted, recorded, and transcribed seven formal interviews, and generated notes on more than 40 hours of participant observation. More important, I established relationships with more than 20 employees as we cooked, cleaned, played whiffleball, and engaged in nondirective conversations. These activities helped me to establish trust with the firefighters, which provided a relational foundation for engaging them about sensitive topics, such as race, privilege, and prejudice.

During subsequent visits to the firehouse, I conducted in-depth interviews with the firefighters to probe issues observed in my analysis of textual artifacts and preceding on-site observations. These interviews were conducted at the fire station and audio recorded for transcription at a later time. Interviews lasted 20 to 60 minutes, and were guided by a formal interview protocol. The questions/topics addressed interrogated participants' general perceptions of cultural diversity, the impact of diversity in the community, and their interpretations of whiteness and white privilege. Open-ended questions/topics included: "What are some unique qualities that members of your organization are expected to possess?" "What words come to mind when you hear the term 'diversity'?" "Tell me about a time when you interacted with someone of a different race or ethnicity on an emergency call." "How would you describe your race?" "What does it mean to be white?" I structured the interview schedule such that I had time to listen, review, and reflect on the interview transcripts; make adjustments in follow-up questions/topics; and analyze the data between each interview.

The firefighters' responses to questions about the expected qualities and characteristics of a firefighter were task-oriented, relating to such attributes as "having common sense," "being a hard worker," "being responsible," and "being dependable" In short, they identified personal attributes that would help someone to "get the job done" or to "adapt" to adversity and "overcome" a challenge in the field. None of the firefighters discussed characteristics related to being "bilingual," "culturally competent," or an "effective communicator." Additionally, firefighters' interpretations and experiences of diversity were largely apolitical, downplaying the significance of difference (e.g., arguing to "just treat everyone the same"). Firefighters who described themselves as Caucasian or white were clearly unsure and/or uncomfortable reflecting on what it means to be a white person (see Martin & Davis, 2001). Participants either avoided that issue or resisted the fact that there was any significance associated with being in the racial majority.

The color-blindness that was evident in the firefighters' responses when we discussed whiteness and white privilege explicitly, however, was paradoxically absent when they shared stories about working in the diverse community. For example, several firefighters interviewed talked about their whiteness as a "disadvantage" when entering predominantly Asian-American or African-American communities. One firefighter said that his race adds to the emotional complexity of "keeping cool" (i.e., staying composed and providing effective customer service). He shared a story of recently being called "snowman" (referring to his whiteness) as he was responding to an intentionally pulled fire alarm in an apartment complex. I probed by asking, "So, what did you say in response?" The firefighter said that he ignored the man and kept walking to avoid a potential conflict. His story was significant for several reasons. First, it pointed to the significance of race in emergency service work and the deep mistrust that exists between members of this community and white firefighters. Second, it illustrated that firefighters are well aware of the racial complexities of their interactions in the community. Finally, it demonstrated how color-blindness operates in making racial identities, paradoxically, highly visible, which, ultimately, reinforces the power of whiteness (see also Watts, 2005).

These interviews were intended to produce "actionable," or responsive, understanding (Bakhtin, 1986), which involves *talking with* (rather than *at*) others (see Asenas, McCann, Feyh, & Cloud, this volume) and is responsive to their actions (Shotter, 2004). According to Bakhtin (1986), "All real and integral understanding is actively responsive and constitutes nothing other than the initial preparatory stage of a response" (p. 69). Consequently, understanding is a continuous process of active response and management of meaning, which is rooted in moral commitment to one's interlocutor (see Barge & Little, 2002, 2008). Through this process, unanticipated aesthetic moments are created (Baxter, 2004). In the context of a dialogic interview, these moments are characterized by deep reflection, perspective sharing, and, perhaps, transformation of subsequent thought and action.

By contrast, traditional survey interviews take on a different character than dialogic speech (see, e.g., Kvale & Brinkmann, 2009). The survey interview seeks participants' monologues about a particular subject that is of interest to the researcher. The intent of survey interviews is to confirm or disconfirm the monologues (hypotheses) of the researcher, not the formation of a relationship between interviewers and interviewees. This mode of discourse, by its very nature, calls for a response that affirms rather than challenges the reproduction of the internal discourse or monologue of participants. Such an interview is focused on the outcome (i.e., the report from the research participant) rather than on the process (i.e., the struggle over meaning) between interlocutors in dialogue.

Throughout my intervention with Fire Services, I realized that the interviews I conducted were producing actionable understanding at the individual level, which, in turn, could lead to organizational transformation. The talking with or dialogic format of the interviews (Shotter, 2004) provided employees with a space to reflect on diversity matters in ways that they had not done before at the firehouse. Many of the firefighters with whom I spoke shared that they do not tend to talk about race because it is such a sensitive topic. Moreover, several reported that there "wasn't much" to talk about in terms of race, because everyone was "equal," culturally speaking, at the fire station.

Engaging firefighters about the topics of race, power, and privilege was difficult because of their reluctance (resistance?). The interviews were complicated because they involved managing the tension between nonresponsive or "passive" interviewing (i.e., listening and accepting) and active (i.e., intervention-oriented) responses that challenged firefighters to respond to new ideas related to privilege, participation, and race. The management of this tension, however, marked a turning point in the project from me being a passive observer to an agent for organizational intervention.

I view *the relationship*, formed and tested through interactions and interviews, as the principal unit for communication activism, as communication activism is performed in relation to (and with) informants, stakeholders, and community members, and in the context of macrolevel structures. From this perspective, activist intervention into social systems involves working with and changing the perceptions, attitudes, and behaviors of individuals. Social systems, including those that contribute to (in)justice are comprised of parts and wholes: The part is in the whole and the whole is in the part (see Senge, 2006). Accordingly, to create socially just groups, organizations, and communities, one must engage discourse at both the individual (micro) level and the structural (macro) level. Although individual change does not automatically affect structural change, systemic change is not possible without individuals learning how to make and manage meaning differently—particularly for promoting social justice.

I found the interview to be a useful entry point into the discourse of Fire Services. For example, I asked overt questions that challenged firefighters' color-blind ideologies when they were observed. When firefighters said things such as, "I don't really think of a person's race," I asked them to tell me about their race and how they felt about their race, in addition to posing questions that invited perspective taking by asking them, for instance, to imagine how our conversation would sound if I were an Asian woman or a member of another race. Moreover, I inquired about firefighters' meanings of the phrase "white privilege," which most had not encountered before. Such questions created a space for firefighters to reflect on and discuss the nature of both racial and economic privilege that certain groups in the community shared that others did not. For example, some firefighters believed that their services to the community were "wasted" on people who receive public assistance or "take advantage" of the system (e.g., those who "don't pay taxes," as one firefighter put it). Firefighters cited a number of instances in which citizens called 911 to take an ambulance across town, as if the ambulance were their "personal taxi service." Although interviewees saw such actions as community members' privilege, I inquired about the economic and educational disadvantages that such citizens must be facing to resort to such desperate measures in the first place. Such questions affected several firefighters' emotional responses, with clear frustration and negativity toward the socially disadvantaged. Others were not as outwardly opposed to such "abuses of the system"; in these cases, individuals said things such as, "It comes with the job." In other cases, these questions led some firefighters to empathize with those who did not enjoy the same privileges that they did.

In terms of perceptual and/or behavioral transformations among the firefighters, it often was the case that these interviews ended with more questions asked by interviewees than answers about how racial and ethnic differences could be addressed by Fire Services. Most interviews resulted in firefighters articulating intercultural curiosity and making statements such as, "I find this stuff really interesting" or "I probably could learn some more Spanish." In other interactions, however, overt resistance was apparent. For example, one older white male stated that he hated working in that county because "it just stinks from all the curry." In such cases, the discussion of cultural difference had little positive impact individually or organizationally. Where these interviews inspired reflection and curiosity, they served as a productive step for transforming the organizational climate for marginalized persons; where overt resistance was evident, the relational encounters were simply unsuccessful in promoting individual or organizational change. Such is the nature of promoting change through relational intervention.

In terms of affecting the organizational climate, this research helped to start conversations about race, privilege, and the impact of cultural difference on firefighting. These conversations were characterized by storytelling by the firefighters, and they opened space for me to share alternative perspectives, question the firefighters' intentions, and pose questions about how others' perceptions of Fire Services might have been affected by their interactions. Although I do not claim that my interactions with firefighters over the course of 8 weeks radically transformed Fire Services, it did help those individuals to reflect on the consequences that race (theirs and others) has on the relationships between Fire Services and the community it serves.

This intervention also was significant in shaping my perceptions of communication research as activism. I learned that the "line" between observation and intervention is not always clear. Frey (2006) and Frey and SunWolf (2009) described differences between observation, criticism, and recommendations, on the one hand, and activist intervention, on the other hand, as a "great divide." Although these forms of scholarly practice are divided (perhaps even to a "great" extent) in principle (e.g., objectives and assumptions about the role of "the observer"), in practice, communication activism requires that scholar-activists mobilize research skills, methods, and theories for social change. To change the communication processes of an organization that contribute to (in)justice requires observing, listening, and acting simultaneously, making intervention into discourse a reflexive process. Therefore, because the lines between observation and systemic intervention can become blurry, communication researcher-activists must be well trained in the practice of research and in modalities of social change. Given "the stakes" (e.g., social justice and equality), communication researchers must find the will, resources, and courage to step into social contexts like Fire Services and make a difference through their work (see Frey, 2006).

In summary, this communication activism research increased Fire Services employees' capacity to speak about race and privilege. Prior to beginning my activist research, such topics were not discussed openly at Fire Services and, as many of the white firefighters reported, were avoided because raising such sensitive topics can "get you in trouble" if someone is offended. Therefore, the prevailing practice was to not communicate about issues of difference. However, the opportunities to discuss matters of race and ethnicity differently (i.e., within a context that supported understanding and making race relations better) were well received by the fire and emergency service workers with whom I spoke—even when we disagreed.

The problem, on an organizational scale, was that Fire Services lacked a structured forum to engage such issues regularly and, especially, with the communities that it served. When race is silenced (invisible) in this way, whiteness has the greatest potential to contribute to injustice (see Cooks, 2003; Watts, 2005). Realizing this problem, I saw communication training for the firefighters and discussion circles about diversity among the firefighters as useful ways to increase the visibility of race within the organization. In fact, Fire Services regularly made use of both of these communication practices to address a variety of issues. For example, group discussion forums were offered to employees who experienced a difficult call resulting in the death of a firefighter or child. These sessions, facilitated by a psychologist, were perceived by employees to be very helpful for coping with the emotional challenges of their work. Additionally, employees regularly discussed various approaches to managing challenges (e.g., teamwork, safety, and specific skills) in the field during training sessions.

I subsequently probed senior staff about the intention behind such forums, and the logistics involved in coordinating them, such as who decides on the content for these sessions and whether a venue for discussing matters of cultural difference would be feasible. Although no such program existed, I explored possibilities regarding what such a program might look like with senior staff during the data feedback and action planning phase.

From Individual Reflection to Organizational Change

The final stage of this research with Fire Services involved getting feedback on the challenges and opportunities that I had identified through the previous phases of observation and relational intervention. My goal was to facilitate organizational change by helping the managing directors to design and implement a forum for addressing cultural differences and their implications for employees at Fire Services.

At that point, I had been working with Lt. Cooper for more than 2 months, frequently updating him about the progress that I had made by communicating over the phone, in person, and via e-mail. Prior to meeting with the managers and division directors, all except one of whom were white, Cooper and I had a final meeting to discuss my study and possibilities for further intervention and collaboration. Given my rapport with Cooper and the interest that the project had generated among the managers of Fire Services, this phase represented the point of intersection between the individual and institutional levels of change.

With the help of Lt. Cooper, I scheduled a 3-hour meeting with the senior operations staff of Fire Services. In addition to discussing the diversification of the communities in proximity to Fire Services, this meeting provided a space to discuss how whiteness functioned in the organization at the managerial level. Moreover, this meeting was an essential step in generating managerial buy-in for subsequent structural change in the organization (see Schein, 2004). The meeting took place at the Fire Services' headquarters building, which housed offices for business services, human resources, information management, risk management, and operations. As I prepared for the meeting with the managing directors, I knew that the presentation of findings, recommendations, and a question-and-answer period would be critical in leveraging the credibility I had gained up to that point in the intervention.

I opened the meeting with a brief summary of my goals as a researcher and as a member of the community. I offered my practical skills as an available asset for the organization to use to fulfill its mission of "protecting property and saving lives." I intentionally positioned myself in a facilitator role rather than as a communication activist because "activist" might have been misinterpreted by the white men who managed Fire Services. Activism connotes "radical transformation" and a "by-any-means-necessary" approach to social change. To achieve the social justice ends sought, I had to be more tactical in positioning my work (see the discussion of "tactics" by Moon & Nakayama, 2006). Assuming that the managers were not familiar with the notion of "communication activism research," my hunch was that they would interpret "activism" to mean "a doctrine or practice that emphasizes direct vigorous action [such as a mass demonstration] especially in support of or opposition to one side of a controversial issue" (Merriam-Webster Online, 2011).

Although activist research is direct and vigorous, mass demonstration was not my intent. Thus, positioning my work as "research findings" and my recommendations as those of a "facilitator/consultant" seemed—at the time—a better semantic choice for increasing the likelihood of making a difference in the organization. The advantage of positioning myself as a facilitator was that I would be listened to, my authority was not undermined, and I would be able to initiate a larger conversation about race with those in traditional positions of power. However, positioning myself as a facilitator also raises ethical issues concerning transparency, deception, and definition that communication activism researchers should consider. In hindsight, the "facilitator" role may have limited my ability to convey the seriousness of white privilege in perpetuating racism, thereby increasing the likelihood of perceived discrimination by employees, citizens in the community, and so forth. Consequently, there may have been a missed opportunity to broaden the meaning of who communication activists are (e.g., professionals committed to social change) and how they conduct their work (i.e., systematically, ethically, nonviolently, and in the pursuit of social justice). In light of this experience, the ethics of communication activism scholarship need to be further explored and considered in conducting and preparing others to engage in it.

During this meeting, I invited people to share their perspectives on diversity in a roundtable fashion. Each manager spoke about the challenges that his or her unit faced, ranging from matters of recruitment and retention of diverse employees to language barriers and community outreach. I then presented key themes from my discourse analysis, interviews, and participant-observational research, situating these findings with respect to existing organizational policies, training practices, and frames of meaning. For example, one insight gained from the interviews conducted was that the frequently invoked phase "adapt and overcome" was interpreted by employees to mean "make any and all adjustments and accommodations in the field to overcome challenges and to serve the public as best as the situation permits." Using this phrase as a common point of reference, I invited the managerial team to consider what existing training was in place to prepare fire and emergency responders to make the necessary cultural adaptations to effectively (and appropriately) overcome perceived intercultural barriers. I, thus, cast the challenges that whiteness created within existing frames of meaning that Fire Service managers shared.

This meeting culminated in strategies for helping emergency responders to develop their knowledge, skills, and abilities to make sound communication (cultural) judgments in the field during one-on-one interaction with diverse community stakeholders. Those strategies resonated with the operations and human resources managers, who saw effective intercultural relations as a means of reducing the risk of incompetent patient care, racial/ethnic misunderstanding, and legal grievances.

Similarly, Lt. Cooper saw the value of diversity communication training in making his job as the "public face" of Fire Services easier. As he stated, Fire Services wanted and needed to improve across cultural differences but simply did not know how or where to start. Thus, increasing discussions about diversity organization-wide, with diverse publics and through skills-based training, were effective plans for building greater competence in intercultural relations at the individual and institutional levels.

This feedback and action planning resulted in two tangible outcomes at the organizational level. First, the managerial team came to consensus that it was not doing enough to promote multicultural knowledge and communication skills training. This realization reinforced the fact that the organization could not deny its interdependence with diverse community stakeholders. Second, the meeting provided evidence that management was committed to increasing the organization's capacity to serve and become inclusive of diverse community stakeholders.

A critical turn in this meeting occurred as we moved from a definition of the problem (i.e., the lack of diversity training and communication about diversity) to action (i.e., planning a training). The group agreed that an officer-training seminar that explored the diversity of the community would be a worthwhile investment. The group committed to coordinating a half-day training seminar for officers to be held a month after our initial meeting. Following that meeting, I offered the human resources manager handouts and other materials to contribute to the seminar, but these overtures went unanswered. Perhaps because of the hierarchical nature of the organization, the managers wanted full control of the form and content of the seminar. Even after expressing my desire to attend the seminar as an observer, I was excluded from participating and received no follow-up communication from Cooper or the human resources manager who agreed to run the training seminar. At the end of the manager's meeting, the human resources manager, who was the only person of color among the managers, informed me that he was going to focus the training seminar largely on the demographics of the community (i.e., the cultural groups present in the community) and the drastic changes that the county had experienced over the years. I would have liked to design and facilitate workshops for employees that went beyond descriptive statistics about the community to engage privilege more deeply, but my repeated attempts to volunteer my services were not responded to with any enthusiasm. Although I saw my exclusion from the training process as a less than effective outcome, it also represented incremental institutional change. The officer-training session did take place as a one-time meeting, but has not resulted in noticeable differences in representation of diversity at Fire Services or efforts to further engage diverse community leaders. To my knowledge, this was the only seminar on diversity that was held.

These outcomes reveal several things about my communication activism research with Fire Services and communication activism, more broadly. First, these outcomes suggest that creating change is possible within a hierarchical organization, but that such efforts take time and sustained commitment. In all, I worked with Fire Services for 6 months, collecting data, engaging individuals about their perceptions of diversity, and helping to catalyze an officer training about diversity. This is slow progress, to say the least, but progress nonetheless. Because this project also served as a dissertation, I had competing demands on my time (e.g., teaching two classes, meeting deadlines toward completion of the degree, and applying and interviewing for jobs). These time constraints limited my ability to foster the creation of a diversity relations committee, which I envisioned as being comprised of stakeholders from various local cultural communities. Moreover, after successfully completing my degree and securing a job across the country, my commitment to Fire Services became logistically strained. Thus, communication activism scholarship requires not only time to invest in a group, organization, or community of practice; it also requires sustained effort, if not stubborn persistence to make a difference.

After completing the work with Fire Services for 6 months, I can assess the intervention along two dimensions: the intrapersonal and the institutional. On an individual level, the research engaged and challenged the perceptions of diversity among public service employees who provide essential services to many diverse citizens in the community. The changes observed were largely perceptual, in that Fire Services employees reflected about how diversity matters influence their work and, in doing so, they saw themselves and their work from a different cultural perspective. In some cases, these perceptual changes inspired curiosity and a desire to enhance personal knowledge about cultural differences in the community and/or about how to grow professionally (e.g., by learning medical terminology in a language other than English). In those instances of employee resistance or lack of change, these encounters demonstrated to me and, perhaps, to the employees that whiteness, power, and privilege are organizational realities that require persistent discursive intervention. Although these exchanges may not have culminated in radical shifts in perspective, they created space for privilege to be openly discussed through civil discourse.

At the organizational level, this research was successful in moving the conversation about diversity a small step in a productive direction. Through the relationships that I built with Lt. Cooper and other employees of Fire Services, I made a difference in their understanding of the role of race and ethnicity in Fire Services' practices. By creating space to engage diversity matters, the intervention directed attention toward the importance of diversity and the lack of training that employees of Fire Services have when it comes to managing intercultural and interracial interactions with the community members they serve. Managers gained a clearer understanding of small steps that they could take to use their privileged status to more effectively serve the diverse population. Additionally, the managing directors began to see the value of a diversity plan and diversity training. Finally, the management team began to see the value in using existing programs, such as its citizens' fire academy, to build relationships based on trust with diverse community stakeholders, increase the visibility and participation of Fire Services within these communities, and increase the recruitment and retention of diverse employees. However, as mentioned, because of legitimate constraints on my time and a cross-country move, I was unable to participate in or to document those efforts, but to my knowledge, these programs have not been undertaken.

The differences made through my communication activism research, although seemingly small in scope, would not have occurred if I had pursued a more traditional research project that only critiqued whiteness and white privilege at Fire Services. The understanding and insight produced through this activist research demonstrates that there is a need for CWS to move into institutional sites, in general, and, in particular, those organizations that serve culturally diverse communities. Moreover, this project demonstrates the potential difference that critical whiteness practice can make in shaping perceptions of race among individuals involved in diverse, politically charged community interactions. To facilitate such work, I turn to lessons that I learned about disrupting privilege through communication activism research.

LESSONS LEARNED ABOUT COMMUNICATION ACTIVISM RESEARCH

Like Frey et al. (1996), I believe that deliberate efforts should be made in the academy to link theory, research, and teaching to promote social justice (see also Frey, 2009), although exactly how such activities should be integrated is a separate issue for consideration (see, e.g., Wood, 1996). My work reflects a relational approach to social justice inquiry, as advocated by Allen (1995, 2007); Allen, Orbe, and Olivas (1999); Cornwell and Orbe (1999); Makau (1996); and Wood (1996). From this perspective, relational contexts are the spaces in which moral commitments and racial identities are forged, crystallized, and challenged. Thus, through relational praxis, scholar-activists affect the moral–aesthetic commitments that compel people to perceive and communicate in particular ways and shape how they organize (see also Barge & Little, 2002, 2008). The following lessons relate to conducting communication activism research, in general, and the role of cultural difference in communication activism, in particular.

Clearly Define the Changes Sought

Given the blurred boundaries between observation and intervention, communication activism researchers must clearly define the type of change sought at the individual and/or organizational level. Doing so is important for both researcher-activists and the organizations and individuals they engage. The lack of clearly defining such change in the early phases of my research was one limitation of my activist research. Over time observing the culture of Fire Services provided critical information about the role of training in the organization; organizational norms, rules, and values; and basic communication skills that could make a difference in intergroup relations in the field. Thus, I learned that observation and intervention are *truly* interdependent processes. Developing a local understanding of group communication practices can be achieved through systemic observation and immersion in the group, and is critical for understanding the type of social justice changes that are necessary. Based on a local understanding of the individuals, groups, organizations, and/or communities, communication activist researchers can more clearly define their social justice goals and select the most effective strategies for intervening into the discourses that define them.

Use Existing Discourses to Create Social Justice Change

Existing organizational norms, cultural practices, and stories are invaluable for catalyzing social justice change, and researcher-activists should use these discourses as vehicles for making and managing meaning around organizational practice and their implications for social justice. For example, because the managers of Fire Services value training, casting diversity, racial privilege, and communication competence within the framework of "skills training" was an important way to motivate change. Communication activists working within groups, organizations, and communities should learn their cultural norms, values, and practices quickly, and leverage them for social justice ends. Learning these organizational norms, values, and communication practices requires systematic observation; putting them into practice to promote social justice change requires sensitivity to one's identity (e.g., as facilitator, researcher, and/or activist); the patterns of discourse that constitute the groups, organizations, and communities involved; and the relations of power that define and are produced through the process of intervention.

Difference Matters

Communication activism research can make a difference in the world, but given the time commitment and energy that such work requires, prioritizing the differences that one wishes to make is important. Although injustices related to religion, gender, and socioeconomic status could have been addressed through my communication activism research, I focused on the difference that white power and privilege make on organizational and community relations. The choices that scholar-activists make have social justice implications in this way.

Difference also matters in terms of the cultural identities that scholar-activists bring to the context of their research. In my case, I approached the white firefighters as a white male with a similar social class background. My race and other visible identities provided me privileged access to inquire, interrogate, and challenge prevailing perceptions of whiteness. However, my whiteness also may have functioned as a disadvantage, particularly when it came to communicating with the managerial team. Throughout my interactions with Lt. Cooper and the management team, I wondered whether the managers would have been more willing to let me discuss issues of diversity at the officer training if I had been a person of color. That question demonstrates the need for culturally diverse activist research teams (see, e.g., Orbe, 2007). Multicultural teams (in terms of race, gender, ethnicity, and ability, etc.) of communication scholar-activists may be more effective than culturally homogenous teams at different stages of an intervention or enable the team to gather useful information from diverse segments of the organization or community. For example, had I conducted my activist research with a Latino/a or Korean collaborator(s), we would have more easily brought together members of these segments of the community to discuss issues related to their interactions with Fire Services. Although there is nothing inherently wrong with advocating for people of different cultural backgrounds and pursuing social justice through activist research, speaking on behalf of marginalized communities can be problematic (see Asenas et al., this volume). Thus, future communication activism research should bring together diverse stakeholders and mobilize the experiences, insights, and access that culturally diverse teams of communication researcher-activists afford.

Progress and Processes: Outcomes

Progress in communication activism research can be assessed in terms of both processes and outcomes. As the research described here demonstrates, there is value in facilitating conversations with organizational stakeholders to address the topic of race (see also Groscurth & Orbe, 2006; Orbe, 2007). To continue to affect organizational change, one must maintain "buy-in" among key organizational members by setting benchmarks for success (Coates, 1997; Schein, 2004). My assessment of perceptual changes among firefighters at the relational level was made through interviews (especially careful attention to their language use) and ongoing observation. Systemic progress was demonstrated through the offering of an officer training seminar, and through conversations about diversity planning (outcomes). Although changes in my personal and professional lives precluded me from sustained interactions with Fire Services (process), I learned that systemic change (and the pursuit of social justice) requires sustained commitment to the process. My work demonstrates that communication activism research promotes social justice progress by influencing communication practices (organizational outcomes) and informing processes (observation–intervention) that promote progressive change.

Ethical Reflexivity

Communication activism research raises important ethical questions. For example, my process of interviewing, observing, and facilitating dialogue was made clear to Fire Services personnel, but I could have been more forthcoming about my intentions to change Fire Services' organizational practices related to diversity. I made the decision to frame my activism as I did (as facilitation) because it was a beneficent act that would not cause harm to the individuals involved, and would promote cultural inclusion, acceptance, and intergroup coherence by avoiding backlash from the typical connotations associated with "activism." In reflecting on the ethics of my work, I wonder what difference being more explicit about my intervention intentions would have made. Is complete transparency possible when attempting to mitigate cultural injustices? What responsibility does a communication activism researcher have to gatekeepers, participants, and those who are socially disadvantaged when the lines between observation and intervention are blurred? Future work must engage the ethics of communication activism scholarship, particularly around matters of cultural difference. This work need not be purely philosophical or devoid of social context, as ethical reflexivity should be central to conducting and evaluating communication activism research (see May, this volume).

CONCLUSION

As cliché as it may be, this communication activism research was but a beginning, helping me to grow as a scholar, practitioner, activist, and professional. My understanding of what organizations, such as Fire Services, actually need in terms of knowledge, skills, sensitivity, and training, and what the literature (i.e., critical whiteness studies) provides (e.g., abstract concepts, decontextualized theoretical debates, and use of critical but nonintervention-oriented methods) are worlds apart. The employees of Fire Services and the people that they serve, most of whom will never enter a university classroom, simply do not benefit from the vast majority of critical whiteness studies conducted. Communication activism research represents a way to unite the theories, methods, and pedagogical practices that scholars have at their disposal with the significant cultural needs of individuals, groups, organizations, and communities. The needs of diverse communities, thus, can be met through sustained observation and communication intervention aimed at creating socially just intergroup relations.

REFERENCES

Allen, B. J. (1995). "Diversity" and organizational communication. *Journal of Applied Communication Research, 23*, 143–155. doi:10.1080/00909889509365420

Allen, B. J. (2007). Theorizing communication and race. *Communication Monographs, 74*, 259–264. doi:10.1080/03637750701393055

Allen, B. J., Orbe, M. P., & Olivas, M. R. (1999). The complexity of our tears: Dis/enchantment and (in)difference in the academy. *Communication Theory, 9*, 402–429. doi:10.1111/j.1468-2885.1999.tb00206.x

Ashcraft, K. L., & Allen, B. J. (2003). The racial foundation of organizational communication. *Communication Theory, 13*, 5–38. doi:10.1111/j.1468-2885.2003. tb00280.x

Bahk, C. M., & Jandt, F. E. (2008). Explicit and implicit perceptions on non-whiteness and interracial interaction reluctance in the United States. *Human Communication, 11*, 319–339. Retrieved from http://www.uab.edu/Communicationstudies/humancommunication

Bakhtin, M. M. (1981). *The dialogic imagination: Four essays* (M. Holquist, Ed.; C. Emerson & M. Holquist, Trans.). Austin: University of Texas Press.

Bakhtin, M. M. (1984). *Problems of Dostoevsky's poetics* (C. Emerson, Ed. & Trans.). Minneapolis: University of Minnesota Press.

Bakhtin, M. M. (1986). *Speech genres and other late essays* (C. Emerson & M. Holquist, Eds.; V. W. McGee, Trans.). Austin: University of Texas Press.

Barge, J. K. (2001). Practical theory as mapping, engaged reflection, and transformative practice. *Communication Theory, 11*, 5–13. doi:10.1111/j.1468-2885.2001.tb00230.x

Barge, J. K., & Little, M. (2002). Dialogical wisdom, communicative practice, and organizational life. *Communication Theory, 12*, 375–397. doi:10.1111/j.1468-2885.2002.tb00275.x

Barge, J. K., & Little, M. (2008). A discursive approach to skillful activity. *Communication Theory, 18*, 505–534. doi:10.1111/j.1468-2885.2008.00332.x

Baxter, L. A. (2004). Dialogues of relating. In R. Anderson, L. A. Baxter, & K. N. Cissna (Eds.), *Dialogue: Theorizing difference in communication studies* (pp. 107–124). Thousand Oaks, CA: Sage.

Bok, D. (2006). *Our underachieving colleges: A candid look at how much students learn and why they should be learning more*. Princeton, NJ: Princeton University Press.

Brown, C. (2009). WWW.HATE.COM: White supremacist discourse on the internet and the construction of whiteness ideology. *Howard Journal of Communications, 20*, 189–208. doi:10.1080/10646170902869544

Butterworth, M. L. (2007). Race in "the race": Mark McGwire, Sammy Sosa, and heroic constructions of whiteness. *Critical Studies in Media Communication, 24*, 228–244. doi:10.1080/07393180701520926

Calhoun, L. R. (2005). "Will the real Slim Shady please stand up?": Masking whiteness, encoding hegemonic masculinity in Eminem's *Marshall Mathers* LP. *Howard Journal of Communications, 16*, 267–294. doi:10.1080/10646170500326558

Chidester, P. (2008). May the circle stay unbroken: Friends, the presence of absence, and the rhetorical reinforcement of whiteness. *Critical Studies in Media Communication, 25*, 157–174. doi:10.1080/15295030802031772

Coates, N. (1997). A model for consulting to help effect change in organizations. *Nonprofit Management & Leadership, 8*, 157–169. doi:10.1002/nml.4130080206

Cooks, L. (2003). Pedagogy, performance, and positionality: Teaching about whiteness in interracial communication. *Communication Education, 52*, 245–257. doi:10.1080/0363452032000156226

Cooks, L. M., & Simpson, J. S. (Eds.). (2007). *Whiteness, pedagogy, performance: Dis/placing race*. Lanham, MD: Lexington Books.

Cornwell, N. C., & Orbe, M. P. (1999). Critical perspectives on hate speech: The centrality of "dialogic listening." *International Journal of Listening, 13*, 75–96.

Cragan, J. F. (2008). Designing and maintaining a communication consulting relationship: A fire officer case study. *Communication Education, 57*, 464–471. doi:10.1080/03634520701875200

Craig, R. T., & Tracy, K. (1995). Grounded practical theory: The case of intellectual discussion. *Communication Theory, 5*, 248–272. doi:10.1111/j.1468-2885.1995.tb00108.x

Deetz, S. (2001). Conceptual foundations. In F. M. Jablin & L. L. Putnam (Eds.), *The new handbook of organizational communication: Advances in theory, research, and methods* (pp. 3–46). Thousand Oaks, CA: Sage.

Desmond, M. (2006). Becoming a firefighter. *Ethnography, 7*, 387–421. doi:10.1177/1466138106073142

Dubrofsky, R. E. (2006). *The Bachelor*: Whiteness in the harem. *Critical Studies in Media Communication, 23*, 39–56. doi:10.1080/07393180600570733

Dyer, R. (1997). *White*. New York, NY: Routledge.

Dyson, M. E. (2005). *Come hell or high water: Hurricane Katrina and the color of disaster*. Cambridge, MA: Basic Civitas.

Endres, D., & Gould, M. (2009). "I am also in the position to use my whiteness to help them out": The communication of whiteness in service learning. *Western Journal of Communication, 73*, 418–436. doi:10.1080/10509200802185273

Fairclough, N. (1995). *Critical discourse analysis: The critical study of language*. New York, NY: Longman.

Fairclough, N., & Wodak, R. (1997). Critical discourse analysis. In T. A. van Dijk (Ed.), *Discourse studies: A multidisciplinary introduction* (Vol. 2, pp. 258–284). Thousand Oaks, CA: Sage.

Fairhurst, G. T., & Putnam, L. (2004). Organizations as discursive constructions. *Communication Theory, 14*, 5–26. doi:10.1111/j.1468-2885.2004.tb00301.x

Foucault, M. (1977). *Discipline & punish: The birth of the prison* (A. Sheridan, Trans.). New York, NY: Pantheon Books.

Foucault, M. (1978). *The history of sexuality* (R. Hurley, Trans.). New York, NY: Pantheon Books.

Foucault, M. (2001). The subject and power. In J. D. Faubion (Ed.), *Power: Essential works of Foucault 1954–1984* (Vol. 3, pp. 326–348; R. Hurley, Trans.). New York, NY: New Press.

Fraley, T. (2009). I got a natural skill . . . : Hip-hop, authenticity, and whiteness. *Howard Journal of Communications, 20*, 37–54. doi:10.1080/10646170802664979

Freire, P. (1970). *Pedagogy of the oppressed* (M. B. Ramos, Trans.). New York, NY: Herder & Herder.

Frey, L. R. (2006). Across the great divides: From nonpartisan criticism to partisan criticism to applied communication activism for promoting social change and social justice. In O. Swartz (Ed.), *Social justice and communication scholarship* (pp. 35–51). Mahwah, NJ: Lawrence Erlbaum.

Frey, L. R. (2009). What a difference more difference-making communication scholarship might make: Making a difference from and through communication research. *Journal of Applied Communication Research, 37*, 205–214. doi:10.1080/00909880902792321

Frey, L. R., & Carragee, K. M. (Eds.). (2007a). *Communication activism* (2 Vols.). Cresskill, NJ: Hampton Press.

Frey, L. R., & Carragee, K. M. (2007b). Introduction: Communication activism as engaged scholarship. In L. R. Frey & K. M. Carragee (Eds.), *Communication activism* (2 Vols., pp. 1–64). Cresskill, NJ: Hampton Press.

Frey, L. R., Pearce, W. B., Pollock, M. A., Artz, L., & Murphy, B. A. O. (1996). Looking for justice in all the wrong places: On a communication approach to social justice. *Communication Studies, 47*, 110–127. doi:10.1080/10510979609368467

Frey, L. R., & SunWolf. (2009). Across applied divides: Great debates of applied communication scholarship. In L. R. Frey & K. N. Cissna (Eds.), *Routledge handbook of applied communication research* (pp. 26–54). New York, NY: Routledge.

Giroux, H. A. (2003). Spectacles of race and pedagogies of denial: Anti-black racist pedagogy under the reign of neoliberalism. *Communication Education, 52*, 191–211. doi:10.1080/0363452032000156190

Grealy, L. (2008). Negotiating cultural authenticity in hip-hop: Mimicry, whiteness, and Eminem. *Journal of Media & Cultural Studies, 22*, 851–868. doi:10.1080/10304310802464821

Grimes, D. (2001). Putting our own house in order: Whiteness, change and organizational studies. *Journal of Organizational Change Management, 14*, 132–149. doi:10.1108/09534810110388054

Grimes, D. S. (2002). Challenging the status quo?: Whiteness in the diversity management literature. *Management Communication Quarterly, 15*, 381–409. doi:10.1177/0893318902153003

Groscurth, C. R., & Orbe, M. P. (2006). The oppositional nature of civil rights discourse: Co-cultural communicative practices that speak truth to power. *Atlantic Journal of Communication, 14*, 123–140. doi:10.1207/s15456889ajc1403_2

Harris, T. M., Groscurth, C. R., & Trego, A. (2007). Unmasking whiteness: Deconstructing misconceptions of race through role-play in an interracial communication classroom. In L. M. Cooks & J. S. Simpson (Eds.), *Whiteness, ped-*

agogy, performance: Dis/placing race (pp. 251–284). Lanham, MD: Lexington Books.

Hermans, H. J. M., Kempen, H. J. G., & van Loon, R. J. P. (1992). The dialogical self: Beyond individualism and rationalism. *American Psychologist, 37*, 23–33. doi:10.1037/0003-066X.47.1.23

Hess, M. (2005). Hip-hop realness and the white performer. *Critical Studies in Media Communication, 22*, 372–389. doi:10.1080/07393180500342878

Holland, D., Lachicotte, W., Jr., Skinner, D., & Cain, C. (1998). *Identity and agency in cultural worlds*. Cambridge, MA: Harvard University Press.

Jackson, R. L. (1999). White space, white privilege: Mapping discursive inquiry into the self. *Quarterly Journal of Speech, 85*, 38–54. doi:10.1080/00335639909384240

Johnson, E. P. (2003). *Appropriating blackness: Performance and the politics of authenticity*. Durham, NC: Duke University Press.

Jovanovic, S., Steger, C., Symonds, S., & Nelson, D. (2007). Promoting deliberative democracy through dialogue: Communication contributions to a grassroots movement for truth, justice, and reconciliation. In L. R. Frey & K. M. Carragee (Eds.), *Communication activism: Vol. 1. Communication for social change* (pp. 109–132). Cresskill, NJ: Hampton Press.

Kennedy, T. M., Middleton, J. I., Ratcliffe, K., Welch, K. E., Prendergast, C., Shor, I., ... Albrecht, L. (2005). Whiteness studies [Special symposium]. *Rhetoric Review, 24*, 359–402. doi:10.1207/s15327981rr2404_1

Kvale, S., & Brinkmann, S. (2009). *InterViews: Learning the craft of qualitative research interviewing* (2nd ed.). Thousand Oaks, CA: Sage.

Laclau, E., & Mouffe, C. (1985). *Hegemony and socialist strategy: Towards a radical democratic politics* (W. Moore & P. Cammack, Eds.). London, England: Verso.

Lacy, M. G. (2008). Exposing the spectrum of whiteness: Rhetorical conceptions of white absolutism. In C. S. Beck (Ed.), *Communication yearbook* (Vol. 32, pp. 277–311). New York, NY: Routledge.

Lavelle, K. L. (2010). A critical discourse analysis of black masculinity in NBA game commentary. *Howard Journal of Communications, 21*, 294–314. doi:10.1080/10646175.2010.496675

Lea, V., & Sims, E. J. (Eds.). (2008). *Undoing whiteness in the classroom: Critical educultural teaching approaches for social justice activism*. New York, NY: Peter Lang.

Locke, T. (2004). *Critical discourse analysis*. New York, NY: Continuum.

Makau, J. M. (1996). Notes on communication education and social justice. *Communication Studies, 47*, 135–141. doi:10.1080/10510979609368469

Martin, J. N., & Davis, O. I. (2001). Conceptual foundations for teaching about whiteness in intercultural communication courses. *Communication Education, 50*, 298–313. doi:10.1080/03634520109379257

Mayer, V. (2005). Research beyond the pale: Whiteness in audience studies and media ethnography. *Communication Theory, 15*, 148–167. doi:10.1111/j.1468-2885.2005.tb00330.x

McIntosh, P. (1998). White privilege: Unpacking the invisible knapsack. In P. S. Rothberg (Ed.), *Race, class, and gender in the United States: An integrated study* (pp. 165–169). New York, NY: St. Martin's Press.

McPhail, M. L. (2002). *The rhetoric of racism revisited: Reparations or separation?* Lanham, MD: Rowman & Littlefield.

Merriam-Webster Online. (2011, May 3). *Activism*. Retrieved from http://www.merriam-webster.com/dictionary/activism
McPhail, M. L. (2004). Race and the (im)possibility of dialogue. In R. Anderson, L. A. Baxter, & K. N. Cissna (Eds.), *Dialogue: Theorizing difference in communication studies* (pp. 209–224). Thousand Oaks, CA: Sage.
Miller, A. N., & Harris, T. M. (2005). Communicating to develop white racial identity in an interracial communication class. *Communication Education, 54*, 223–242. doi:10.1080/03634520500356196
Moon, D. G., & Nakayama, T. K. (2006). Strategic social identities and judgments: A murder in Appalachia. *Howard Journal of Communications, 16*, 87–107. doi:10.1080/10646170590948965
Mukherjee, R. (2006). *The racial order of things: Cultural imaginaries of the post-soul era*. Minneapolis: University of Minnesota Press.
Myers, K. K. (2005). A burning desire: Assimilation into a fire department. *Management Communication Quarterly, 18*, 344–384. doi:10.1177/0893318904270742
Nakayama, T. K., & Krizek, R. L. (1995). Whiteness: A strategic rhetoric. *Quarterly Journal of Speech, 81*, 291–309. doi:10.1080/00335639509384117
Nakayama, T. K., & Martin, J. N. (1999). Whiteness as the communication of social identity. In T. K. Nakayama & J. N. Martin (Eds.), *Whiteness: The communication of social identity* (pp. vii–xiv). Thousand Oaks, CA: Sage.
Nicotera, A. M., Clinkscales, M. J., Dorsey, L. K., & Niles, M. N. (2009). Race as political identity: Problematic issues for applied communication research. In L. R. Frey & K. N. Cissna (Eds.), *Routledge handbook of applied communication research* (pp. 203–232). New York, NY: Routledge.
Orbe, M. P. (2007). Assessing the civil rights health of communities: Engaged scholarship through dialogue. In L. R. Frey & K. M. Carragee (Eds.), *Communication activism: Vol. 1. Communication for social change* (pp. 133–156). Cresskill, NJ: Hampton Press.
Orbe, M. P., Groscurth, C. R., Jeffries, T., & Prater, A. D. (2007). "We—The militant ones": A collective autoethnographic analysis of racial standpoints, locating whiteness, and student/teacher interaction. In L. M. Cooks & J. S. Simpson (Eds.), *Whiteness, pedagogy, performance: Dis/placing race* (pp. 27–48). Lanham, MD: Lexington Books.
Orbe, M. P., Smith, D. C., Groscurth, C. R., & Crawley, R. L. (2010). Exhaling so that we can catch our breath and sing: Reflections on issues inherent in publishing race-related communication research. *Southern Communication Journal, 75*, 184–194. doi:10.1080/10417941003613305
Projansky, S., & Ono, K. (1999). Strategic whiteness as cinematic racial politics. In T. K. Nakayama & J. N. Martin (Eds.), *Whiteness: The communication of social identity* (pp. 149–176). Thousand Oaks, CA: Sage.
Reisigl, M., & Wodak, R. (Eds.). (2000). *The semiotics of racism: Approaches in critical discourse analysis*. Wien, Austria: Passagen.
Reisigl, M., & Wodak, R. (2001). *Discourse and discrimination: Rhetorics of racism and antisemitism*. New York, NY: Routledge.
Schein, E. H. (2004). *Organizational culture and leadership* (3rd ed.). San Francisco, CA: Jossey-Bass.

Scott, C., & Myers, K. K. (2005). The socialization of emotion: Learning emotion management at the fire station. *Journal of Applied Communication Research, 33*, 67–92. doi:10.1080/00909880420000318521

Senge, P. M. (2006). *The fifth discipline: The art and practice of the learning organization* (Rev. ed.). New York, NY: Doubleday/Currency.

Shields, D. C., & Preston, T. (2007). The urban debate league rhetorical vision: Empowering marginalized voices for leadership and activism. In L. R. Frey & K. M. Carragee (Eds.), *Communication activism: Vol. 1. Communication for social change* (pp. 157–194). Cresskill, NJ: Hampton Press.

Shotter, J. (2004). Expressing and legitimating "actionable knowledge" from within the "moment of acting." *Concepts and Transformation, 9*, 205–229. doi:10.1075/cat.9.2.08sho

Simpson, J. L. (2008). The color-blind double bind: Whiteness and the (im)possibility of dialogue. *Communication Theory, 18*, 139–159. doi:10.1111/j.1468-2885.2007.00317.x

Sline, R. W. (2006). Who owns the jazz festival? A case of facilitated intergroup conflict management. In L. R. Frey (Ed.), *Facilitating group communication in context: Innovations and applications with natural groups: Vol. 1. Facilitating group creation, conflict, and conversation* (pp. 239–267). Cresskill, NJ: Hampton Press.

Tierney, S., M. (2006). Themes of whiteness in *Bulletproof Monk*, *Kill Bill*, and *The Last Samurai*. *Journal of Communication, 56*, 607–624. doi:10.1111/j.1460-2466.2006.00303.x

Tracy, S. J. (2007). Taking the plunge: A contextual approach to problem-based research. *Communication Monographs, 74*, 106–111. doi:10.1080/03637750701196862

Tracy, S. J., Myers, K. K., & Scott, C. W. (2006). Cracking jokes and crafting selves: Sensemaking and identity management among human service workers. *Communication Monographs, 73*, 283–308. doi:10.1080/03637750600889500

Tracy, S. J., & Scott, C. (2006). Sexuality, masculinity, and taint management among firefighters and correctional officers: Getting down and dirty with "America's heroes" and the "scum of law enforcement." *Management Communication Quarterly, 20*, 6–38. doi:10.1177/0893318906287898

Tracy, S. J., & Trethewey, A. (2005). Fracturing the real-self <-> fake-self dichotomy: Moving toward "crystallized" organizational discourse and identities. *Communication Theory, 15*, 168–195. doi:10.1111/j.1468-2885.2005.tb00331.x

U.S. Census Bureau. (2008, January 7). *American community survey*. Retrieved from http://factfinder.census.gov/home/saff/main.html?_lang=en

van Leeuwen, T. (2008). *Discourse and practice: New tools for critical discourse analysis*. New York, NY: Oxford University Press.

Warren, J. T. (2001). Doing whiteness: On the performative dimensions of race in the classroom. *Communication Education, 50*, 91–108. doi: 10.1080/03634520109379237

Warren, J. T., & Hytten, K. (2004). The faces of whiteness: Pitfalls and the critical democrat. *Communication Education, 53*, 321–339. doi:10.1080/0363452032000305931

Warren, J. T., & Kilgard, A. K. (2001). Staging stain upon the snow: Performance as a critical enfleshment of whiteness. *Text and Performance Quarterly, 21*, 261–276. doi:10.1080/10462930128129

Watts, E. K. (2005). Border patrolling and "passing" in Eminem's *8 Mile*. *Critical Studies in Media Communication, 22*, 187–206. doi:10.1080/07393180500201686

Weiss, G., & Wodak, R. (Eds.). (2003). *Critical discourse analysis: Theory and interdisciplinarity*. New York, NY: Palgrave Macmillan.

Wiegman, R. (1999). Whiteness studies and the paradox of particularity. *Boundary 2, 26*(3), 115–150. Retrieved from http://muse.jhu.edu/journals/boundary

Wodak, R., & Meyer, M. (Eds.). (2009). *Methods of critical discourse analysis* (2nd ed.). Thousand Oaks, CA: Sage.

Wood, J. T. (1996). Social justice research: Alive and well in the field of communication. *Communication Studies, 47*, 128–134. doi:10.1080/10510979609368468

Ziegler, J. A., & DeGrosky, M. T. (2008). Managing the meaning of leadership: Leadership as "communicating intent" in wildland firefighting. *Leadership, 4*, 271–297. doi:10.1177/1742715008092362

8

ACTIVATING ETHICAL ENGAGEMENT THROUGH COMMUNICATION IN ORGANIZATIONS

Negotiating Ethical Tensions and Practices in a Business Ethics Initiative

Steve K. May
University of North Carolina at Chapel Hill

The current "economic meltdown" represents one of the most significant issues of the day, with people experiencing one of the most devastating downturns in the U.S. economy in several decades. The roots of the crisis are complex, encompassing questionable organizational strategy and culture, innovations in the design and use of nontransparent financial instruments, and promotion of new attitudes toward investment and risk, as well as the globalization of investment markets, among others. These questionable organizational practices produced a series of interdependent events, which culminated in severe investment losses for organizations and individuals, widespread mortgage failures, extensive job loss, and the rapid development and deployment of government bailout packages.

The economic meltdown of 2008–2011 is not merely an economic issue; it is, more importantly, an ethical one as well. I have argued, for example, that the current economic crisis is the result of an ongoing, systematic silencing of ethics in businesses (May, 2009). Employees of the organizations that have failed—or have been bailed out by the government—have lacked (a) requisite communication with stakeholders, (b) appropriate transparency regarding financial risk, (c) collaborative participation in key decision making, (d) courage to raise concerns about misconduct, and (e) the willingness to hold leaders accountable for behaviors that have done harm to millions of people.

If there has ever been an institution that requires renewed scrutiny and critique, it is today's U.S. business. Business organizations undoubtedly are the most powerful and influential institution in the United States, eclipsing the government, church, and family in their impact (Deetz, 1992), with, as seen recently, the ethical failures of business profoundly affecting everyone. Ironically, however, business organizations have received little attention in the communication activism literature, which to date, has focused on contexts and forms of activism related to issues of social justice, such as promoting human and civil rights (see Carey, this volume), ending the death penalty (see Asenas, McCann, Feyh, & Cloud, this volume), and providing health care to marginalized and disenfranchised populations (see Belone et al., this volume).

Questionable business practices, however, have created an important set of concerns related to social justice. As Deetz (2008) explained:

> The concern ranges through important issues such as human rights, environmental protection, equal opportunity and pay for women and various disadvantaged minorities, and fair competition. Such broad issues are instantiated in activities such as using prisoners as workers, moving operations to environmentally less restrictive communities, offering and taking bribes and payoffs, creating unsound or wasteful products, closing economically viable plants in takeover and merger games; also, including concerns about income disparity, declining social safety-nets, malingering harassment, unnecessary and unhealthy effects on employees, involuntary migration patterns, and rampant consumerism. (p. 3460)

In studies of activism related to organizations, scholars have focused on overt, public, and visible actions, such as union activism (De Witte, 2005; Markowitz, 2000), antiglobalization protests (Palmer, 2007), anticorporate campaigns (Esrock, Hart, & Leitchy, 2007), and shareholder resistance (Eisenhofer & Barry, 2006). Missing to date are studies that explore the mundane, sedimented, and often naturalized practices within organizations that, ultimately, impact a range of stakeholders. This chapter seeks to fill that void by exploring how specific business practices enable or constrain ethical behavior in a media company.

Despite the widely publicized scandals in both the for-profit (e.g., Adelphia, Arthur Andersen, Enron, Tyco, and WorldCom) and nonprofit (e.g., the Roman Catholic Church, U.S. military and government, and U.S. universities) sectors worldwide, and the subsequent interest in business ethics, in general (e.g., Parker, 1998b; Seeger, Sellnow, Ulmer, & Novak, 2009), and corporate social responsibility, in particular (see, e.g., the essays in May, Cheney, & Roper, 2007), the field of business ethics continues to hold a marginal status in the theory, research, and practice of organizational studies. This status is surprising given the variety of reasons to emphasize organizational ethics research and activism, including risk management, marketing, civic positioning, and organizational functioning. Nevertheless, within the study of organizational communication, the components, relationships, and applications of organizational ethics often remain tangential to other issues related to organizational life.

Even in the study of applied ethics, itself considered a marginal branch of moral philosophy, organizational ethics remains peripheral (Sorell, 1998). As Parker (1998c) explained, "The tension between theorizing what people should do (prescriptive ethics) and explaining what people actually do (descriptive ethics) is a fracture that threatens the [organizational ethics] project from the start" (p. 1). Philosophers and business ethics scholars have debated the relative merits of various prescriptive, theoretical frameworks for ethical behavior, reaching little consensus. Scholars have considered Aristotle's virtues, Rawls's social contract, Kant's categorical imperative, and Mill's greatest good for the greatest number, among other perspectives, with limited agreement regarding foundational prescriptions for ethical conduct in organizations. Perhaps the diversity of theoretical frameworks and the paucity of organizational applications are indicative of the range of behaviors that business ethics theories address. For example, the broad range of ethically oriented business issues include legal compliance, globalization and labor conditions, equal workplace opportunities (e.g., based on gender, race, age, and disability), corporate governance, social and environmental responsibility, employee control and discipline, fair wages and benefits, customer redress for accidents and product malfunctions, advertising and marketing (mis)representation, philanthropy and community involvement, and whistle-blowing (see, e.g., Lorsch, Berlowitz, & Zelieke, 2005; Reich, 2007). Both the scope and range of these issues create significant challenges for organizational and ethics scholars alike.

The disagreement, however, and, in some respects confusion, certainly has not stopped academics from writing about organizational ethics. For example, business scholars have explored Western philosophical ethics

(Carlin & Strong, 1995), in general, as well as more specific strands of existentialism (Argawal & Malloy, 2000), virtue (Solomon, 1992), utility (Goldman, 1980), social contract theory (Donaldson & Dunfee, 1994), cognitive philosophies (McDonald & Pak, 1996), sophism (Michaelson, 2001), relational ethics (Pelton, Chowdhury, & Vitell, 2004), and social justice (Shminke, Ambrose, & Noel, 1997). Although this work has moved ethics to a central position in the academy, organizational ethics scholars have not followed suit by developing a comprehensive, yet specific, conceptual foundation for organizations that is not necessarily beholden to many of the common philosophical perspectives of ethics.

The purpose of this chapter is to propose an activist framework that moves organizational ethics "beyond the fringe," both theoretically and practically. My goal is to build and apply a model of active, ethical engagement that entails a mode of organizational operation that, at once, is realistic and ethically critical. To construct that model, I propose five practices of ethical engagement (dialogic communication, transparency, participation, courage, and accountability) that enable and/or constrain ethical behavior in organizations (May, 2006). I then explore ways in which assessment tools, both quantitative and qualitative, were used to assess the "ethical culture" of a large media organization in the southeastern United States, revealing some common ethical dilemmas and/or dialectical tensions (e.g., truth–loyalty, short-term–long-term decision making, and individual–organizational interests) experienced by employees. I subsequently describe, in greater depth, my collaboration with the organization to develop an organization-wide values statement, an ethics code, an ethics action plan, and a process to reconsider structural constraints on ethical behavior (e.g., in new employee orientation, performance appraisal, training for dialogic communication, and training for ethical courage). The first three steps of the process—through the ethics action plan—were conducted with the entire organization in more than 20 hours of dialogue, deliberation, and decision making. In particular, diverse cross-sections (across divisions and hierarchical levels) of groups of employees were provided with opportunities to discuss—using both case studies and their personal experiences—ways in which the organization and its members enabled and/or constrained ethical behavior.

Using what emerged from these discussions as a foundation for the organization's ethical action plan, I summarize the substantive changes made (and, in some cases, lack thereof) by the organization to strengthen its ethical culture. I also describe several dialectical tensions (foundational–situational, individual–organizational, and ethics–performance) that emerged for members of the organization during the process. Finally, I conclude the chapter with lessons learned about communication activism scholarship, in general, and efforts to transform organizational cultures, more specifically.

COMMUNICATION ACTIVISM AND ETHICAL ENGAGEMENT: PRACTICES OF DIALOGIC COMMUNICATION, TRANSPARENCY, PARTICIPATION, COURAGE, AND ACCOUNTABILITY

This chapter is grounded in the belief that communication activism has a profound and largely untapped potential to create a sustainable and reciprocal relationship between research and social, political, economic, and ideological change (see Carragee & Frey, this volume; Frey & Carragee, 2007a, 2007b). To do so effectively, however, requires a heightened sense of reflexivity to better understand, at the least: (a) scholars' motivations; (b) interests of the persons, groups, organizations, and communities engaged by scholars; (c) responsible and responsive processes of engagement in any given context; (d) various uses of research—intended and unintended—by different stakeholders/constituencies; and (e) appropriate means to promote long-term change that builds capacity rather than dependence among organizational members.

Historically, organizational communication research has sought to affect change that served the interests of executives and/or owners of for-profit organizations. In recent decades, however, critical and feminist scholars have "deconstructed" this taken-for-granted managerial bias and have begun to question ways in which organizational communication researchers often have been appropriated and co-opted "against their will" to rationalize a range of decisions that have had detrimental effects on employees, their families, and their communities. Despite such recognition, however, few organizational scholars have moved beyond critique to intervene to reconstruct organizations to make them more responsive, responsible, and respectful.

In my view, then, organizational ethics research need not be unrealistic or utopian, as some of its critics have suggested (for a summary, see Donaldson & Freeman, 1994). Similarly, the practice of ethics in organizations need not be solely compliance driven, with a primary focus on abiding by the law, as commonly believed to be true by some practitioners. Rather, organizational ethics may be at an ideal nexus of research and action, given the current opportunity for more substantive discussions regarding the role and impact of organizations in people's lives, in response to organizational ethical scandals in the last decade.

Through an explication of a case study of organizational engagement in this chapter, my goal is to bridge theory and practice through the application of ethical theory to organizational change (see, e.g., Kitson & Campbell, 2001). To accomplish this goal, I suggest that ethical engagement involves the practice of ethical principles in the search for greater ethical awareness, the deliberate process of ethical decision making, and the striving for ethical behavior in organizations. As noted earlier, I identify five practices that play a significant role in the creation of ethical engagement in organizations: dialogic communication (open, honest, and reciprocal communication), transparency (visibility of governance structures, decision-making processes, policies, and procedures), participation (commitment to involving all employees in decision making), courage (doing what is right when risk is involved), and accountability (assuming responsibility for anticipating and responding to ethical challenges). Each practice has been studied, to varying degrees, in its own right (Christensen & Langer, 2009; Deetz & Irvin, 2008; Lord, 2006; Schultz, 1996; C. Stohl & Cheney, 2001; M. Stohl, Stohl, & Townsley, 2007), but only recently have scholars considered ways in which relationships between these practices can enable and/or constrain ethical behavior in organizations (May, 2006, 2008).

I argue that a low level of ethical engagement creates an organizational culture where leaders and employees fear delivering bad news, fail to explain decisions, disregard stakeholders, dismiss ethical dilemmas, and hide mistakes. By contrast, a high level of ethical engagement creates an organizational culture where leaders and employees speak up without fear of retribution, align policies and principles, account for stakeholders, integrate ethical concerns into decision making, and uphold ethical values.

Seeking organizational change of this nature is a complicated task that requires a nuanced understanding of the relationship between research and action. Moreover, given the centrality of corporations in today's culture, it is incumbent on scholars to engage and intervene in employee and organizational practices when possible. This need is particularly the case when the risk of a lack of scholarly engagement is silence on ethical issues such as unfair wages, poor working conditions, excessive workplace control and discipline, usurpation of personal values for corporate ones, and an imbalance of work and family–community life. Although scholarly engagement of organizations always is fraught with ethical dilemmas, I seek to offer insights to other scholar-activists who, hopefully, will learn from my limited successes and mistakes.

THE "ETHICS AT WORK" INITIATIVE

The organization for this project is Southeastern Broadcasting Company, Inc. (SBC), a pseudonym for a diversified communication company located in a major metropolitan area in the southeast United States. The company owns and/or operates five regional CBS TV affiliates, a digital media company, three regional radio stations, a state news network, a sports marketing firm, a satellite communication company, and a minor league baseball team.

SBC also has established real estate interests, including several urban revitalization projects that have refurbished manufacturing plants into residential, retail, and office space. Overall, the company has more than 500 employees.

Initially, the chief executive officer (CEO) of the company contacted a university ethics center to assist him to "further infuse ethics into the culture" of the company. The ethics center asked me, as one of its academic associates, to help design a theoretically informed, research-based project that would serve as the basis for a process of organizational assessment and change of ethics. Specifically, I was charged with the following:

- facilitating the process for creating a new ethics code,
- developing and implementing an online ethics questionnaire for all employees,
- conducting focus groups with a representative group of employees,
- reporting the questionnaire and focus group results, and
- facilitating the process for creating an action plan to improve the company's ethical culture.

Although the company was highly regarded within its surrounding communities and had been involved in a wide range of philanthropic activities, the CEO expressed concern about "troublesome changes" in the company's ethical culture. He saw growing evidence that the company he had "built from the ground up" was changing for the worse and that, in time, it might face scandals that would harm its reputation. For example, there had been public criticism of the company's hiring practices and the company's portrayals of minorities in its news reporting and other programming, both of which were considered to be discriminatory by community activists. The CEO also expressed frustration over the uncivil behavior of some managers toward employees, grey areas in accounting practices that were being explored in pursuit of greater profits, employees' use of company equipment for personal business, and potential kickbacks to sales and advertising employees. He also claimed that, as he neared retirement, his legacy might be tarnished by "new employees who did not share the company's values of integrity, excellence, diversity, teamwork, and community building." As a result of these concerns, he expressed an interest in rewriting the company's ethics code, which did not have full acceptance among employees, as well as the possibility of instituting a broader ethics change initiative for the company.

Based on a series of conversations I had with the CEO and the company's human resources (HR) director, the company agreed to participate in writing an ethics code that would culminate in a company action plan focused on organizational change. As a result, SBC embarked on a 4-month journey to define its core values and draft a code of ethics to provide clear guidance in putting those values into practice on the job. As the CEO noted in a memorandum sent to all employees of the company, SBC has always sought to set high ethical standards. But we realize that sustaining these standards in our modern world requires ongoing attention and conversation. A Code of Ethics stands as a strong moral compass for our everyday decisions at SBC.

In consultation with the company's executive team, the CEO agreed to a four-step process that involved:

1. reaffirming the company's mission statement,
2. using quantitative questionnaires and qualitative interviews developed and completed by employees to assess the ethical culture of the company,
3. conducting 20 hours of discussion and deliberation among all employees to develop a company values statement and ethics code, and
4. creating a company action plan for immediate implementation.

Each of these processes of the Ethics at Work initiative is discussed in the order it occurred.

As a starting point for the ethics initiative, all parties (i.e., the board of directors, CEO, leadership team, and employees) agreed that the company had a well-established and readily accepted mission statement that required reaffirmation. However, the CEO was firm in his belief that the affirmation of the mission statement should come from him in a formal manner, with little negotiation or deliberation among employees. He stated that the consensus regarding the mission statement's wording should not be disrupted. The mission statement reads as follows:

> Southeastern Broadcasting Company's legacy of hard work, creativity, and a commitment to our audiences, our clients, and our employees has made us a successful broadcasting company and industry leader in the communication field. As a business leader, SBC will continue to provide the highest level of service and expertise to our listeners and clients in order to increase our profitability and market share. As a community leader, SBC will strive to ensure that ethics and moral standards are clearly set forth in everything we do, reinforcing our belief that a company cannot meet its business responsibility without meeting its community responsibility. As a concerned employer, SBC will continue to provide our employees with quality benefits and retirement packages, training opportunities to help advance their skills and keep our workforce current and competitive, and a wholesome family environment.

The CEO used multiple communication channels (company newsletter, webcast, and monthly division/unit meetings) to reaffirm the company's mission. His intent was to generate employee interest in the ethics initiative and to produce, in his words, greater "alignment between company words and deeds" among employees. Such initial alignment, although focused on establishing a somewhat illusory sense of shared agreement within the company was deemed necessary by the CEO and me to create a safe context for difficult conversations that were likely to arise later in the process.

The second step in the process was an organization-wide assessment of the company's ethical culture—using the dimensions of dialogic communication, transparency, participation, courage, and accountability—via an online, confidential questionnaire. The questionnaire contained 118 items, including both closed- and open-ended questions. The closed-ended questions were rated using a 5-point Likert scale, with higher numbers indicating more agreement. The questions asked about business ethics, personal and organizational values, and organizational identification and sense of ownership. There also were questions regarding the practices of an ethically engaged organization, including dialogic communication, transparency, participation, courage, and accountability. Open-ended questions focused on ethical dilemmas in the company, processes for ethical decision making in the company, and overall satisfaction with the company. The response rate to the questionnaire was 78% of employees.

I also interviewed 50 employees in 10 peer-level focus groups to identify key ethics-related themes in the organization. During the focus groups, I sought to promote honest and safe discussions of ethics-related strengths and weaknesses in the company. A stratified random sample of employees (according to business unit, level, and seniority) was selected to create small, peer-level focus groups of four to five persons per group. Similar to the questionnaire, employees were guaranteed confidentiality and participants agreed not to divulge any of the focus group discussion to other employees. To participate in the focus group, employees were required to agree to a set of ground rules designed to protect them, including acknowledgment that no comments made during the focus groups would be used against other employees. After a 2-month period of data gathering, findings from the questionnaire were shared with all members of the organization in a series of meetings and became the basis for an initial, organization-wide discussion of the company's strengths and weaknesses with regard to ethics.

Ethics Assessment Findings

The survey questionnaire provided several key findings regarding how employees perceived the ethical culture of SBC, including both ethical strengths and challenges. The general ethical strengths were as follows:

- SBC valued integrity, excellence, honesty, loyalty, and pride, values that were consistent with employees' personal values;
- employees were proud to be members of SBC and wanted to contribute to its success;
- SBC had a strong commitment to ethics and to hiring people with integrity, which strengthened employees' loyalty to the company; and
- employees were aware of ethical dilemmas and tried to do the right thing.

In many respects, then, SBC might be considered an "ethics-proud" company, one with a legacy of ethical decision making on behalf of both internal and external stakeholders.

The questionnaire data also revealed some general ethical challenges facing the company:

- communication at SBC was not consistent and timely, making employees feel disconnected from one another;
- company leaders and managers were not open to discussing employees' ideas or concerns;
- decision-making processes were not visible and, as a result, employees did not know the rationales for decisions made;
- structures, policies, and procedures were vague and may have reduced employees' commitment to the company;
- inequities existed across divisions, units, and hierarchical levels in the company; and
- company leaders and managers did not engage in ethical behavior, and that raising such concerns with them would lead to retaliation.

In addition to these general findings, a number of important findings emerged from a more specific analysis of ethical engagement practices at SBC, including dialogic communication, transparency, participation, courage, and accountability. As a starting point for the analysis, mean scores were identified for each set of practices at SBC. Frequencies of key sets of employee behaviors also were noted for each ethical engagement practice. Finally, correlations were computed to better understand relationships among the ethical practices. Because the intent of the Ethics at Work initiative was to activate ethical engagement toward constructive organizational change, I focus here primarily on company challenges (as opposed to strengths) with regard to each ethical practice, noting its related risk.

Dialogic communication. The mean score for dialogic communication (open, honest, and reciprocal communication) at SBC was 3.01, which was the lowest score of all the ethical practices. For example, only 16% of employees reported that communication at SBC was accurate and timely, and, perhaps even more important, only 27% said that they could deliver bad news without fear of retribution. Additionally, only 30% of employees noted opportunities to discuss important organizational topics, and only 33% agreed that ideas were openly shared and exchanged. Finally, 44% reported that work-related expectations were expressed clearly. As one representative comment noted, "Employees share information freely, but it doesn't seem to trickle up or down very freely." Other employees said that "the delivery of information and support should be more timely and reoccurring," and that "we don't meet enough to offer ideas or raise concerns; there are no forums for discussion." Summary correlations indicated that dialogic communication at SBC was related most directly to transparency, such that when there was not open, honest, and reciprocal communication, there also was a perception that the company was not clear about its values, mission, and strategy.

Transparency. The mean score for transparency (visibility of governance structures, decision-making processes, policies, and procedures) was 3.06, the second lowest ethical practice for SBC, and, in many respects, the most contested practice among participants in the ethics initiative, as leaders and rank-and-file employees differed significantly in their perceptions of both the quality and importance of transparency at SBC. Overall, for example, only 16% of employees reported that leaders explained how and why decisions are made, whereas leaders, not surprisingly, were far more likely to believe that they explained decisions to their employees. Employees responded similarly to the lack of transparency regarding the company's performance management process, as only 23% said that it was clear how performance was evaluated. Finally, only 25% of employees agreed that they were kept well informed, and only 39% responded that stated values, mission, and goals aligned "with the way it really works around here." One representative comment from an employee sums up the common perception within the company: "I wish we had a common, shared vision." Another representative comment was that "either leaders are not setting policies and procedures, or they are not sharing them." Other employees stated directly that leaders "don't want to disclose how or why they make decisions." Interestingly, correlations showed that a lack of transparency was related to a lack of employee accountability, such that if leaders limited transparency, employees were less likely to hold themselves or others accountable for their actions.

Participation. One way to ameliorate the lack of transparency at SBC would be through greater employee participation in decision making, but the assessment findings indicated that SBC's degree of participation was average (with respect to other comparable companies that have been studied using this questionnaire), with a mean score of 3.48. Although 91% of employees reported that they were proud to be employees of SBC, a much smaller percentage felt a sense of ownership of the company. Additionally, nearly 75% of employees reported unfairness and inequalities across divisions, units, and hierarchical levels. Even more disturbing, more than 50% of the employees believed that leaders did not necessarily act according to the company's values. Importantly, there was a strong relationship between participation and courage, such that if employees had a history of participating in making decisions, they would be more likely to speak up about ethical concerns when they arose.

Courage. For SBC, the findings related to courage (doing what is right when risk is involved) offered a mixed message. On the one hand, the mean score for courage (3.53) was the highest of all of the ethical practices assessed, with 85% of employees reporting that they recognized situations that require ethical judgment. However, only 39% reported that employees took action regarding ethical dilemmas, meaning that SBC employees had a keen sense of ethical awareness, but limited willingness or capacity to act on ethical problems. Part of this difficulty may be attributed to the fact that only 26% of employees reported that they could raise questions about the behavior of their superiors. There appeared to be a fear of retaliation for discussing ethics-related issues, particularly when it involved employees' superiors. Even in cases where employees were comfortable turning to superiors, they were not confident that such problems would be addressed. As one employee explained, "I can go to my immediate supervisor with most concerns, but I am not confident it will get any further. It stops there." Another employee similarly noted that "I feel comfortable raising issues, but I don't think they are listened to." Overall, then, there was a perception, as one employee put it, that leaders "don't have the courage to do anything about problems." As might be expected, this lack of courage could negatively affect perceptions of accountability at SBC, which was evident in the positive correlation between the two practices.

Accountability. The final ethical practice assessed at SBC, accountability (company and employee responsibility for anticipating and responding to ethical challenges), had a mean score of 3.49. Although the score was lower than that of courage, there were several positive indicators on this dimension of ethics at SBC. Many employees stated that they felt a strong sense of personal accountability when they made decisions, with, for example, 85% reporting that they took responsibility for their ethical behavior. Employees also took into account a range of key stakeholders when making decisions and they sought to understand how their decisions would impact others at

SBC. Only 59% of employees, however, reported that SBC responded to ethical challenges, and only 52% said that SBC leaders addressed unethical behavior when it occurred. Open-ended employee responses noted several situations in which the company (or its leaders) had not taken actions to hold itself accountable for decisions. Not surprisingly, then, there was a strong correlation between organizational accountability and employee courage, such that when employees saw company leaders making ethical decisions, even when those decisions were against employees' best interest, they felt more comfortable speaking up about ethical issues.

Discussion of Ethics Assessment Findings With Southeastern Broadcasting Company Employees

For the company to engage in any potential organizational change, it was crucial for all employees to have a broad understanding of how they perceived the ethical culture of SBC. After extensive discussion with the CEO, I agreed to report the ethics assessment findings to the company's executive team prior to presenting them to employees, with assurances from the CEO that the findings should not be changed in any way as a result of the executive committee meeting.

For both the executive team and the company, as a whole, I had identified a range of ethics-related risks facing the company, based on the ethics assessment findings; however, I did not initially communicate them publicly so that both groups could develop an emergent understanding of those risks. According to both the executive team and the remainder of the employees, the lowest scoring ethical practice, dialogic communication, posed some of the most significant risks. They noted the following:

- a lack of timely and accurate communication causes employees to make inappropriate or poor decisions,
- a lack of clear expectations and direct feedback creates confusion regarding job responsibilities,
- a lack of involvement in decision making reduces employees' connection to SBC and limits their professional development, and
- when employees could not deliver bad news, they would hide mistakes and misconduct from their superiors.

With regard to transparency, not surprisingly, employees were more willing than company leaders to acknowledge problems. For example, leaders were more likely to question the need for greater transparency, whereas middle- and lower level employees viewed transparency as a key problem for the company. In time, the groups agreed on the following risks related to transparency:

- a lack of awareness of company values, mission, and goals caused employees to make decisions that were inconsistent with SBC's mission; they also felt a greater sense of isolation from, and dissatisfaction with, company decisions;
- when employees were not kept well informed, they did not make decisions guided by SBC's policies and procedures, and they became less connected to the company and to their specific department;
- when employees did not know how their performance was being evaluated, they perceived inequalities in personnel decisions; they also lacked clear direction regarding job-related priorities, and, as a result, their performance suffered;
- when the rationales and processes for decisions were unclear, employees perceived greater unfairness and inequity in the company, and they believed that they were less accountable for their decisions, providing opportunities for misconduct; and
- when employees perceived a disconnect between company values and actions, their perceptions of the company's ethics declined.

There also were a number of risks related to participation at SBC. After discussion of the assessment findings regarding participation, employees agreed on the following:

- a lack of ownership negatively affects employees' motivation and retention;
- a lack of awareness of ethics impairs employees' judgment during decision making;
- perceived unfairness and inequalities negatively affects cooperation across units, divisions, and hierarchical levels, producing silos; and
- leaders' actions that do not align with the company's values reduce understanding of, and commitment to, the company's mission, values, and goals.

During the discussion of risks related to courage, there was general agreement that, although the mean score was the highest of the five ethical practices assessed, there were departments in the company where the lack of ethical courage was a problem. In many respects, the discussion of courage was the most free-flowing and wide-ranging because employees seemed to recognize its potential negative impact at the company. They agreed that:

- employees who are reluctant to raise questions or concerns with others are unlikely to report misconduct or to anticipate potential problems,
- employees do not necessarily confront misconduct when they see it, and
- when employees want to address misconduct, they avoid doing so because of a lack of skills or a fear of retaliation; as a result, they expect others to address misconduct, reducing their sense of personal accountability in the company.

Finally, employees agreed on the following risks related to accountability at SBC:

- when employees perceived that leaders did not address unethical behavior, they believed that misconduct would not be punished or, worse, that it might be rewarded; and
- when employees did not hold their coworkers accountable for misconduct, inappropriate behavior was seen as more acceptable.

Developing a Values Statement and Ethics Code at Southeastern Broadcasting Company

Based on the ethics assessment findings and the related risks identified by employees, the ethics initiative proceeded with a focus on modeling key ethical practices and engaging employees in deliberation and debate regarding future directions of the company related to ethics. Because the findings related to dialogic communication indicated that employees needed an open forum for candid discussion of ethical issues at the company, the remainder of the ethics initiative was designed to be as dialogic as possible, despite the overarching limitation of meeting the communication needs of more than 500 employees.

To break the discussion into manageable units, the ethics initiative included a series of eight sessions with employees that were facilitated by trainers over a 4-month period. The trainers, all of whom had advanced degrees, were affiliated with the university ethics center and had specific content skills in law and ethics, as well as business skills in facilitation, training and development, negotiation, and conflict resolution. The sessions, which lasted 2 to 3 hours each and totaled 20 hours overall, were run by the trainers in close succession to provide employees with comparable experiences to prompt discussion within the company after each meeting concluded. Typically, 60 to 75 employees attended each session and were organized in small groups of approximately six to eight employees at round tables to facilitate discussion. Seating arrangements were rotated over the eight sessions to provide employees with alternative perspectives and to encourage discussion among the broadest possible range of coworkers.

During the eight sessions, employees were given an overview of the initiative's guidelines and processes; identified common ethical dilemmas at SBC (via employee-created scenarios and cases) and discussed means to manage them; articulated the company's core values through a process of appreciative inquiry (focusing on the company's strengths and capacities to enable constructive change; see, e.g., Cooperrider & Srivastva, 1987), which became the preamble to the company's ethics code (see the Appendix); identified the company's key stakeholders and created "do statements" (specific responsibilities/ duties) for each stakeholder; drafted the company's values and ethics code, via a "writing group" that represented all levels and units of the company; and developed an action plan for implementation and integration of the ethics code into company policies and procedures.

Guidelines and processes. The first session of the Ethics at Work initiative explained the basic guidelines and processes to employees. Given the challenges related to courage at SBC, particular attention was paid to the need for candid, yet fair, discussion of the range of ethical challenges facing the company. I also told employees that they would have opportunities to provide feedback (either confidentially or in the large plenary sessions) about the process at any stage of it. Additionally, I explained that, after the initial overview session, the initiative would continue with session 2 on employing case studies, session 3 creating a values statement, session 4 producing a stakeholder map, sessions 5 and 6 developing an ethics code, and sessions 7 and 8 creating an ethics action plan for the company.

Case studies. To further enhance dialogue regarding ethics-related issues in the company, session 2 was devoted to small group discussions of case studies and brief scenarios of common ethical dilemmas experienced by employees in the company. To acquire these case studies and scenarios, employees submitted examples of the most common ethical dilemmas that they had faced in the company (excluding any damaging, identifying information about specific employees). Additionally, a case study resource group, representing all divisions/units in the company, solicited cases from employees. That group also compiled a list of cases and evaluated their appropriateness, based on their relevance to employees' work experiences at SBC. Cases were evaluated after I screened them to make sure that no persons might be put at risk via any case discussion. Through this process, 10 case studies were developed and, during the second session, they were discussed in small groups for 90 minutes. Groups were asked to identify ethical dilemmas in the cases, how the company would expect the dilemmas to be managed, and how each employee would address the dilemmas, if his or her approach differed from that of the company. Groups then reported out in a plenary discussion for an additional 30 minutes, with the most common dilemmas tallied.

By a wide margin, the most common ethical dilemma faced by employees was truth versus loyalty. Many employees explained that, when confronted by an ethical dilemma, they often had to decide whether to tell the truth (i.e., engage in ethical courage) or remain loyal (to the company, a boss, or a coworker, in most cases). An additional common dilemma involved short- versus long-term decisions, with employees noting that, at times, they were expected to focus on short-term company goals (often focused on bottom-line, economic issues) at the expense of long-term goals (e.g., company reputation, integrity, and community involvement). Finally, in some divisions of the company, employees saw evidence of individual versus organizational dilemmas, often resulting from employees making self-interested—and sometimes, unethical—decisions at the expense of the work team or the company. Moreover, because of the competitive nature of the media industry, some employees expressed a sense of helplessness regarding coworkers' efforts to "rise on the back of others." Employees discussed ways in which such dilemmas often inhibited subordinates from speaking up when they saw their superiors engaged in misconduct to meet bottom-line business objectives.

Values statement. The findings related to transparency suggested that the company's core values and its ethics code needed to be revisited and reconsidered. Therefore, the series of employee meetings for session 3 were devoted to creating a company values statement that, ultimately, became a preamble to the ethics code. Using appreciative inquiry, employees in each session spent 3 hours identifying, discussing, and, in turn, voting on the company's core values. To prompt the widest range of values, employees had been notified in advance to prepare a list of values. The values identified in the session also were compared with the most common company values identified in the ethics assessment questionnaire. As seen in the company values statement, the most important values were (in order of greatest frequency) integrity, excellence, teamwork, work–life balance, community involvement, and diversity:

> We, the people of Southeastern Broadcasting Company, are individuals with diverse backgrounds, abilities, views, and ideas. We are SBC's most valued asset. We value the vitality of individuals and their families. We provide a work environment that is safe, compassionate, and rewarding. We commit to ensuring a healthy work–life balance that nurtures both our personal and corporate families.
>
> We commit to building teamwork in the pursuit of excellence. We believe teamwork thrives in an environment of appreciation, respect, and integrity. We practice clear, courteous, and open-minded communication, without repercussions.

> We consider it both our privilege and responsibility to serve and enrich the communities in which we work and live. We develop and support significant community projects, creating partnerships that benefit the public and SBC. As a driving force in the community, we are a catalyst for positive change.

As is fairly evident from the specific details of the values statement, employees commented not only on current practices but also on espoused, but largely absent, values. For example, the first sentence of the values statement, which focuses on "individuals with diverse backgrounds, abilities, views, and ideas," was the result of challenging discussions regarding ways in which gender, race, class, and hierarchical location in the organization affected how employees viewed ethics at the company. Moreover, the value statement's emphasis on teamwork that "thrives in an environment of appreciation, respect, and integrity" emerged out of conversations regarding perceived abuses by a leader of one of the television newsrooms. That emphasis, therefore, was a direct response to current difficulties in the company that had become more pronounced and pervasive over time. Finally, the statement that "we practice clear, courteous, and open-minded communication, without repercussions" was less about current practice and more an aspirational goal for the future. Lower level employees, whose jobs were least secure, were adamant that a statement about protecting them be included, particularly in circumstances where they raised ethical concerns about co-workers, bosses, or the company itself. Overall, the development of the values statement was an effort, albeit limited, to stimulate and manage difficult dialogue regarding ethics and to enable, as fully as possible, employees' participation in decision making regarding future company values.

Stakeholder map. Whereas session 3 focused on establishing an initial level of employee participation in organizational change, session 4 focused on external participation by identifying key company stakeholders. A stakeholder map (with a list of key stakeholders and responsibilities toward them) was designed to be the core feature of the ethics code and, as such, discussing the company's stakeholders was a critical first step in that process. Somewhat surprising, this session was one of the most hotly contested during the ethics initiative because, although employees had little difficulty identifying and agreeing on SBC's key stakeholders, there was much less agreement regarding their priority.

In a series of 3-hour sessions, most groups of employees, within approximately 30 minutes, agreed on (through a process of voting) a list of stakeholders that included employees; customers/audiences; local community members; owners/management; advertisers and sponsors; suppliers, lenders, and vendors; business affiliates; regulators and governing bodies; industry groups; and competitors. In contrast, the discussion of how to prioritize stakeholders was much more complicated and time-consuming. In many companies, owners/management often are considered a primary stakeholder and, consequently, making a profit, executing business strategies, and sustaining long-term growth are emphasized. Within minutes of discussing the priority of SBC's stakeholders, however, it was clear that employees viewed themselves as the key stakeholder and, therefore, should be listed first in the ethics code. During each session, employees expressed concern, at one time or another, that SBC treat everyone with respect and dignity, regardless of job status. Because of the importance of that view to employees, it became the first line of the ethics code. Although SBC's leaders consistently argued that the company needed to remain financially viable to be successful (and, thus, owners/management should be prioritized as the most important stakeholder), other rank-and-file employees countered that there would be no business without employees. In time, leaders conceded the point for fear of appearing too self-serving, particularly when it became clear that they would be outvoted.

Once the ranking of the stakeholders was established, the remaining 90 minutes was devoted to groups of employees creating a draft of responsibilities (do statements) for each stakeholder group. Inconsistent with earlier parts of the process, these statements were displayed to the remainder of the groups and became the basis for additional revisions. At the end of the session, employees voted on the do statements that were most important for each stakeholder group. The do statements for each set of meetings during the fourth session then were compiled by a voluntary group of "writing team" members for future discussion and revision.

Ethics code. At the beginning of session 5, the writing team offered a long list of do statements—as the basis of the ethics code—and asked for employees' feedback. Employees spent the next 2 hours in small groups, paring down the statements and refining their language. At 30-minute intervals, employee groups reported out in a plenary session to get additional feedback from coworkers. It was a tedious, arduous process, but ultimately, the depth of employees' participation led them to more readily accept and implement the ethics code; that is, the process led employees to develop a "stake" in the code, even in some circumstances when they disagreed with their coworkers. Most notably, particular attention was paid to the early portions of the ethics code, which focused on values of "respect and dignity," "honesty and moral treatment," and "clear, courteous, and open-minded communication." Similarly, given the long legacy of local community involvement by the company, extensive discussion was devoted to the local community, prioritized as the third most important stakeholder behind employees and customers. However, employees disagreed over the appropriate role of a business within a community and, as a result, fairly generic do statements were produced for the community, as a stakeholder, because of a lack of agreement.

Session 6 explored the extent to which the ethics code would work in practice. This session was deemed a "code-testing process," with employees preparing, in advance, examples of contradictions between current practices in their jobs and the ethics code. During this session, employees were comfortable addressing these contradictions in their small groups, but they were somewhat reluctant to identify those contradictions in larger plenary discussions. It quickly became evident, however, that some divisions and employee positions had more substantive ethical challenges than did others. For example, employees who worked directly with customers noted that they often faced dilemmas between economic bottom-line incentives versus "doing the right thing." Employees who had contact with suppliers and vendors struggled to understand the degree to which SBC's values and practices should be driven downward toward them, questioning whether SBC should be a catalyst for change in those organizations. Finally, employees with direct fiduciary responsibilities for the company sought to better understand the company's legal obligations—as a form of compliance—and its ethical obligations. These employees viewed legal compliance as the company's ethical obligation, whereas their coworkers viewed compliance as the bare minimum expectation for the company. The code-writing team received notes on these discussions and was asked to return by the next session with a final draft of the ethics code.

Company action plan. Within the first hour of session 7, employees at each of the meetings agreed on the ethics code and it was submitted for distribution and, ultimately, final approval at session 8, the culminating session of the initiative. The remainder of that seventh session was devoted to discussion of an action plan to implement the ethics code. Initial discussion revolved around specific means to deploy the ethics code throughout the company, including recommendations to post wall-sized plaques of the code in the company's entryways; prominently display it on the company and division websites; create a laminated, pocket-sized copy of it as an easy reference guide; introduce it to job applicants; and to include it during new employee training and ongoing employee development.

More substantive, structural recommendations focused on each of the specific ethical practices. For dialogic communication, employees recommended that a communication audit be done to identify key sources and processes for effective communication throughout SBC, with a focus on maximum integration of core ethics messages throughout the company. In the action plan, employees also proposed "candor" training that focused on engaging in open communication and providing direct feedback to coworkers; tools to be included were case studies of candor and skill-building exercises to improve employees' communication competence. To improve transparency, employees proposed that the company redeploy its mission, vision, and values during a new strategic planning process. They also suggested that the company establish a new employee orientation program that clarified SBC's mission, ethics code, policies, and procedures, as well as employees' roles and responsibilities.

To strengthen employees' participation in ethical decision making, an ethics awareness training program for employees to identify common ethical dilemmas and effective decision making about the dilemmas was recommended. To maintain active engagement of the ethics code, employees also suggested that all employees complete a daily checklist of the practices of ethically engaged organizations. For courage, employees discussed the need for a "pathways to courage" program that focused on specific issues related to employees; tools would include case studies of ethical courage and training to engage successfully in difficult dialogues regarding ethics. Finally, to improve accountability, employees recommended developing a standardized performance appraisal form and process that supported the mission and ethics code of SBC. They also suggested that employees be held accountable for the rules, regulations, and policies of the company, with particular attention devoted to employee alignment with the ethics code.

Of the recommendations offered during session 7, several were prioritized during session 8 and beyond. After the ethics code was institutionalized through a company-wide deployment process and via training for new and current employees, employees were to volunteer to participate in a pathways to courage program that integrated a focus on courage and dialogic communication. In time, this ethics training also was deployed to targeted divisions, with an emphasis on having difficult ethical conversations to give employees opportunities to voice their concerns and to have candid conversations about ethical challenges they faced at work. As a result of that communication training, each unit's weekly staff meeting now begins by presenting an ethical dilemma and, hopefully, engaging in an honest dialogue about how employees and the company can address it. The company also implemented a new ethics-oriented performance appraisal process designed to validate the importance of "integrity in action" at the company, with ethics identified as a core competency for all employees. Finally, a new employee orientation program was developed to focus on the company's mission and code of ethics, and to provide specific details regarding company rules, regulations, and policies. Later ethics efforts, not initially identified during the Ethics at Work initiative, included a leadership development program for middle managers that focuses on balancing excellence with integrity.

A DIALECTICAL ANALYSIS OF THE ORGANIZATIONAL ENGAGEMENT ACTIVISM

Any effort to engage ethical challenges in organizations to produce constructive change is fraught with difficulty. To address these difficulties, scholars have sought to identify change strategies that manage multiple stakeholders' needs (Lewis, 2007; Lewis & Seibold, 1998; for a review, see Seibold, Lemus, Ballard, & Myers, 2009). Other communication scholars have focused on how company vision (Fairhurst, 2007), organizational identity (Chreim, 2002), and participation in decision making (Seibold & Shea, 2001) affect the potential success of any organizational engagement endeavor.

For the purposes of this engaged project, however, it is most helpful to focus on dialectical tensions that emerged among SBC employees, as well as ways I used those tensions as an engaged scholar (see, e.g., Barge, Lee, Maddux, Nabring, & Townsend, 2008). Although such tensions can wreak havoc with a tightly controlled change initiative, when they emerge through a process that emphasizes dialogue, transparency, participation, courage, and accountability, they also can create conditions for productive organizational change (C. Stohl & Cheney, 2001). Because ethical practices in organizations frequently are contested based on employees' values, experiences, and positions in companies, a focus on dialectical tensions offers an opportunity to explore ways in which differing views are manifested and negotiated during a change process, such as the Ethics at Work initiative.

Different perspectives lead to quite different conclusions regarding what constitutes ethical behavior. These differences are based on fundamental assumptions about the character of reality, the nature of individuals, and the obligation of individuals to one another. Differences in these ethical perspectives also may be described as dialectical "tensions." The most relevant of these tensions for developing a model of organizational engagement are foundational–situational ethics, individual–organization, and ethics–performance.

Foundational–Situational Ethics Tension

The first dialectical tension faced by SBC employees considers whether ethics is foundational or situational; that is, whether ethical behavior is based on a set of actions that are constant or context-specific. Foundational, or universal ethics, persist, whereas situational ethics shift over time. Foundational ethics suggest that reality is given, self-evident, objective, and neutral, whereas situational ethics view reality as socially constructed, intersubjective, and interpreted.

As do organizational scholars, SBC employees struggled with whether organizational ethics should be seen as foundational or situational. Early in the process, for example, some employees resisted the assumption that an ethics code to guide all employees' behavior was necessary, or even appropriate. Their comments brought to the surface the belief, on the part of the CEO and the executive team, that organizational values should be agreed on and that all employees should conform to an accepted code of conduct. Discussions during the first two sessions of the initiative, however, made it clear that employees' differing perceptions of autonomy and control, as related to a company ethics code, were related to their location and position in the organization. Specifically, a number of lower level employees (and some middle managers) viewed the development of an ethics code, regardless of how participatory the process, as an imposition of leader directives on them. In their view, it was the most recent attempt by management to control and, in some cases, discipline them. Ironically, the CEO expressed few concerns about these employees, concentrating, instead, on an emerging and powerful group of division leaders who, in his view, were violating the company's fundamental values of integrity, excellence, diversity, teamwork, and community building. The structural conditions of organizational life, in addition to past experience in some cases, nevertheless, caused more vulnerable employees to understand that any new initiatives (such as an ethics code) would likely affect them disproportionately.

Within a process of organizational engagement, then, there should be a balance of foundational and situational approaches to ethics. From a situational perspective, it is not enough to only "follow the rules" of legal compliance; each organization has a distinct culture that applies ethical guidelines and principles differently. Organizational ethics codes, from this perspective, are conceptualized as "living documents" that change over time. From a foundational perspective, however, a code of ethics may create a degree of stability and predictability regarding ethical behavior in an organization. This perspective also does not exclude the possibility that there may be a core set of values that all organizations (and individuals) should follow to be ethical; most likely, these values would be longstanding and widely accepted (e.g., telling the truth and respecting others). Accordingly, although organizations may vary in their interpretation of a specific set of values, application of those values to their organizational culture, and the degree to which these values are stable, organizational engagement entails an awareness of such values and their operation within an organizational system, including how the use of foundational and situational perspectives may affect more profoundly some employees.

Individual–Organization Ethics Tension

A second dialectical tension confronted by SBC employees considers whether the individual (libertarian approach) or the community (communitarian approach) should be primary in organizational engagement. To date, most business ethics scholars have focused on either the individual actor/employee or on organizational features/structures. More broadly, the duality of agency and structure is central to organizational theory and research (see, e.g., Conrad & Haynes, 2001), and that duality has served as a defining characteristic of modern Western social and organizational studies (see, e.g., Clegg, 1989; Dawe, 1978; Giddens, 1979, 1984; Reed, 1985).

Three questions help to better understand this tension. First, is the advancement of the individual good for the organization or is the advancement of the organization good for the individual? Second, is the individual the source of ethics or is the collective wisdom of the organization the basis of ethical decision making? Third, is ethics better served by justice or by compassion?

With respect to organizational ethics, the individual focus is on the multiple factors that influence employees' behavior, whereas the community focus is on the processes through which employees' decision making is circumscribed by characteristics of organizational context. For example, on the individual side of the continuum, scholars interested in organizational ethics have studied moral development (Wimbush, 1999), individual decision making (Beu, Buckley, & Harvey, 2003), personal values (Fritzsche, 1995), honesty (Quinn, Reed, Browne, & Hiers, 1997), emotion (Gaudine & Thorne, 2001), and reasoning (Nell, 1975), among other factors. Guided by a focus on "social action," these studies explore subjective experience and voluntary and/or creative action (if not precursors to action). In contrast, scholars studying the organizational side of the continuum have examined organizational values (Daft, Conlon, Austin, & Buenger, 1996; Donaldson, 1996), ethics codes (Coughlan, 2005; Warren, 1993; Willmott, 1998), corporate governance (Deetz, 2007; Spira, 1999), organizational structure (James & Rassekeh, 2000; White & Lam, 2000), performance appraisals (Banner & Cooke, 1984), stakeholders (Deetz, 1992; Harrison & Freeman, 1999; Jones, Felps, & Bigley, 2007), organizational culture (Douglas, Davidson, & Schwartz, 2001; Nicotera & Cushman, 1992), dialogue (Morrell & Anderson, 2006; Nielsen, 1990), and organizational environment (Sims & Keon, 1999). Guided by a focus on "social system," these studies explore structural configurations and objective externalities of organizations.

In the Ethics at Work initiative, employees' location and position in SBC, again, made a difference in their view of how the initiative should proceed with regard to the individual–organization tension. For example, a number of employees in service/clerical positions contested the process for developing the values statement. In their opinion, ethics is a personal matter that could be managed by the company but should not be dictated. To them, any overt discussion of personal values, as they relate to the organization's values, should remain private and, as a result, should not be the basis of deliberation among coworkers. In a previous session focused on discussing common ethical dilemmas in SBC's workplace, for example, these employees balked at a request to "sort through" how they might individually approach a dilemma as opposed to how the company might approach it. For them, the very process of identifying and voting on a shared set of values (let alone discussing it in front of coworkers) was nonsensical. As one employee put it, "Why should I let anyone else change my values?"

A similar emphasis on individual values was evident among several senior SBC leaders who, although they accepted the code-writing process, viewed employee training as the preferred means for implementing an ethics initiative. In the executive committee meeting, these leaders explained that it was unnecessary for the entire organization to engage in a change initiative when, in essence, "a few bad apples are the problem." For them, ethics training that focused on altering the behavior of a few problem employees was the most strategic (and efficient and cost-effective) method.

In contrast, middle managers, as a whole, supported the chosen direction to focus on the ethical culture of the organization. This view seemed to be particularly true for managers responsible for a large numbers of employees. Perhaps because their positions required more direct supervision of employees, an ethics code was viewed by them as a means to manage the inherent ambiguity of their jobs, as well as employees who reported to them. As one middle manager explained, "We need something to work with, something that creates a common ground and a shared approach to our work."

In any type of organizational engagement, both of these perspectives need to be taken into account; consequently, individual and community emphases should be beneficially complementary. For example, although the collective wisdom of an organization may serve, in part, as the basis of ethical decision making, employees also are driven by their individual principles and judgments. Therefore, dialogue between an organization and its individual employees is needed to build the consensus that guides ethical decision making and other behavior. By recognizing the existence and persistence of these often-competing and incompatible views of agency and structure in organizations, a conceptual framework for organizational engagement must account for both human agency and institutional constraints.

Ethics–Performance Ethics Tension

A final relevant dialectical tension in organizational engagement that was experienced by SBC employees was ethics–performance. Research often has suffered from a conceptual narrowness because of a fixation on the corporate form of organization (see Werhane, 2007). Even recent arguments regarding the need for "triple-bottom-line" (i.e., a simultaneous focus on economic, social, and environmental concerns) reporting (Ganesh, 2007; Zorn & Collins, 2007) retain the taken-for-granted assumption of economic performance. That is, many business ethicists, in particular, entirely overlook the question of whether capitalism, as a form of economic organization, is ethically defensible.

For years, two primary domains have dominated ethics scholarship: moral philosophy, with its various ethical prescriptions; and the sciences of business/management, with their economic prescriptions. Scholars supporting the first perspective question the basic assumptions of business practices; scholars endorsing the latter perspective claim that business issues should not be considered in philosophical terms (see, e.g., Pearson, 1995). As Parker (1998a) explained, "Much of the debate so far has been couched in terms of intellectual abstraction versus economic pragmatism, or as it is often put more crudely, idealism versus realism" (p. 283). As a result, fundamental assumptions about the role of business in society create irreconcilable differences between the belief systems of many ethicists.

During the Ethics at Work initiative, the dialectical tension between doing the right thing (ethics) and making a profit (performance) was evident at all stages of the process. Employees' concerns about this tension emerged very early, when I was discussing with them the questionnaire and interview findings. For example, although most employees were stunned and appalled by the large discrepancy between the awareness of ethical dilemmas (85% of employees) and taking action on them (39% of employees), a number of client- and customer-facing employees readily acknowledged that they confronted ethical dilemmas regarding ethics–performance on a weekly basis. For them, this tension was a regular part of work that had to be negotiated on an ongoing basis. Not surprisingly, some employees in sales and marketing faced such tensions when making decisions regarding the content of advertising, movies, and videos. Although they recognized the dilemmas, they also believed that they had a company mandate to focus on the bottom-line performance, which was particularly true for employees, such as salespersons, with economically driven incentive systems.

The ethics–performance tension emerged, again, during the second session of the ethics initiative when employees were asked to create case studies of common ethical dilemmas they experienced working at SBC. As noted previously, the most common dilemma was truth versus loyalty. More specifically, a number of employees faced the dilemma of having to decide between telling the truth about troublesome client/customer behavior, to those employees' financial detriment, or remaining loyal to the (sometimes lucrative) relationships they had developed with those clients/customers.

Even more troubling, however, were confidential comments from several employees that stated they had been asked by their supervisors to engage in unethical behavior to maintain the company's bottom line, such as "creative" accounting practices, inappropriate "exchanges" with state legislators to limit regulations that negatively affected the company, and overcharging clients for services. In such cases, they expressed concern that they were being asked to violate their ethical standards and they feared retaliation for telling the truth.

Finally, the ethics–performance dialectical tension also was an implicit reference point for employees' discussions about the priority of stakeholders. Although some company leaders reiterated the common refrain that "the customer always comes first," a significant number of employees stated that such an emphasis on financial performance should have a limited place in the company's ethics code. Because this ethics–performance tension is likely to be common in many organizations, successful ethics engagement is more likely to occur when organizational policies, structures, and behaviors are designed and executed in line with ethically supported motives that balance the performance of the company and ethical practice.

LESSONS LEARNED ABOUT ACTIVATING ETHICAL ENGAGEMENT IN ORGANIZATIONS

Invariably, although any change process, such as the Ethics at Work initiative, includes both successes and failures, the project led to several positive outcomes. Aside from the creation of a new values statement and an ethics code, the company revised its performance appraisal process, instituted an orientation program for new employees, created a pathways to courage training program, introduced a leadership development program, and created regular, consistent opportunities to discuss ethics at SBC. Although it perhaps is the least tangible outcome, I consider the focus on more public dialogue, debate, and deliberation about ethics at SBC to be most important.

In a reassessment of the company's ethical culture that I conducted a year later, all scores on the ethical practices investigated had improved. In particular, the mean scores increased significantly for dialogic communication (from 3.01 to 4.21) and courage (from 3.53 to 4.50). Mean scores also improved for transparency (from 3.06 to 3.67), participation (from 3.48 to 3.79), and accountability (from 3.49 to 4.11), but to a lesser degree. Additionally, employees had more accurate perceptions of the company's mission, values, and future direction. According to information obtained from follow-up interviews conducted with employees, this clarity led some employees to leave the company voluntarily, and some others were fired because of unethical behavior. The renewed focus on ethics also caused the SBC to drop several of its customers and clients, at some cost to the company. Employees noted that they appreciated that decision and, as a result, faced fewer ethical dilemmas (and the stress related to them) on a regular basis. Follow-up data also indicated that employees were actively participating in making organizational decisions, with one of the indirect consequences being a greater sense of employee identification with, and ownership of, the company. Finally, employees reported some limited improvement in their fear of telling the truth about misconduct at the company.

The Ethics at Work initiative produced some lessons learned that may be relevant to other communication activism scholars. I examine four important lessons about such engaged scholarship.

Engaged Scholarship is Embedded

First, and most important, the initiative reminded me that all scholarship—whether engaged or not—is embedded within economic, political, social, and technical systems. As a result, scholars are not only "in the field" but they are "of the field"; consequently, they must recognize that they are necessarily agents of change, sometimes in intended ways and sometimes in unintended ways. When those unintended moments occur, scholars need to be reflexive about their motives and intentions, as well as flexible and responsive. In effect, scholars need to improvise, but in ways that are informed and nuanced.

For example, as engaged scholars, we must recognize and respond to how others seek to use our resources and expertise to further their interests. During the Ethics at Work initiative, employees constantly sought to use data from the questionnaire and interviews to serve their interests and, in some cases, to further their positions or to minimize those of others. Because data never are neutral, I consistently reflected on whether I was engaged or merely "complicit." As Conquergood (1995) noted, engaged scholars "take responsibility for how the knowledge that they produce is used instead of hiding behind pretenses and protestations of innocence" (p. 85). In my case, creating detailed fieldnotes at the end of each session was incredibly helpful for checking my understanding of employees' comments, events that had taken place, and my emotions. After completing those notes, I always reserved time to have a discussion with at least one of the trainers who assisted with the project to confirm or disconfirm my perceptions. Additionally, I "wrote out" any additional perspectives or points of view (both mine and those of employees) regarding the project that may be present but not articulated. For instance, one of the key ethical issues at the company—fear of retaliation for raising ethical concerns—was not evident to me until relatively late in the process. The issue had been raised briefly in the second session, but I did not initially give it the attention it deserved because it had not emerged in the questionnaire or interview data. In retrospect, I now understand that the problem was not common to all employees but was limited to a few key supervisors in the company who had threatened retaliation against their subordinates. As a result, employees of those supervisors were reluctant to raise their concerns in the public forums that were most common to the initiative. That experience taught me to balance opportunities for employees to provide sensitive information both in public and in private. In a related manner, it also reminded me that engagement always requires sensitivity to the participants and how they seek to negotiate their interests during an organizational ethics engagement.

"Difference Matters" in Engaged Scholarship

Any time that scholars work with organizations, their position is called into question because they are outsiders, persons of "difference." This inherent difference between insider and outsider provides the possibility of exploitation by various groups (e.g., by a range of organizational stakeholders). Unquestionably, communication activism scholars have paid much attention to how their projects can unintentionally further oppress marginalized groups and, therefore, any change initiatives must proceed with incredible caution and care. However, engaged scholars have paid less attention to ways in which project participants may use them as resources—as opportunities—to pursue vested interests in the process.

In many respects, my experience with SBC reflected this dilemma of competing interests in engaged projects, which is all too familiar to management consultants but little understood by academics. From the start, rumors swirled in the company about the ethics initiative, with employees believing that it was an attempt to downsize the company, and others apparently describing it as a "witch hunt" to fire disgruntled employees. Because my initial contact was with only the CEO and HR director, I had limited opportunities in the beginning to communicate directly with employees. Although the CEO and I collaboratively created messages about the initiative for dissemination throughout the organization, as often is the case with such projects, employees connected their larger workplace concerns and interests to the initiative. Some employees, for example, saw the initiative as an opportunity to air grievances and retaliate against bad bosses; others saw it as an opportunity to return the company to its previous position of ethical integrity; and still others viewed the initiative as a means to publicly laud the positive work of their units/divisions in the company. An organizational engagement initiative is like a Rorschach test for employees' concerns and, as a result, managing expectations with early, clear, and coherent messages is crucial. Doing so builds trust in both scholars and their interventions that is so crucial to long-term sustainable success.

Particularly in initiatives such as this project, with a focus on ethics, it also is important to remember that any form of engagement occurs in the midst of power dynamics in organizations. As noted in the discussion of how differing positions affected both employees' perceptions and practices of ethics at SBC, any engaged project necessarily excludes and includes people. Although great attention was given to providing the most comprehensive, full participation possible during the Ethics at Work initiative, opportunities for voice never are equitable in organizations. Perhaps even more important, regardless of the presumed safety of a discussion regarding organizational issues, scholars never fully understand the unique nuances of difference within organizations. The presumption that harm was done to any employee during an initiative does not necessarily guarantee that later harm did not occur. As a result, particular attention must be paid not only to commonly held employee differences, such as gender, race, class, ethnicity, sexual orientation, and age, but also to employees' location and position in organizations. As evidenced in employees' comments made during this initiative, credit and blame in organizations are not evenly distributed, nor are opportunities and constraints to identify concerns, speak up, and, ultimately, to affect change. As such, scholars, as change agents, must be skilled facilitators able to negotiate a range of competing—and often complicated—interests in organizations. They must serve as readily as protectors of employees as they do activists promoting change.

Engaged Scholars Must be Adept at "Holding" Dialectical Tensions

One of the means to balance the roles of protector and activist is to develop the capacity to recognize, balance, and "hold" dialectical tensions. As Seo, Putnam, and Bartunek (2004) noted, any change effort involves confronting a series of inherent dualities, including how issues are managed (negative focus–positive focus), how long the process occurs (continuous–episodic), how any interventions are timed (proactive–reactive), and how actively members participate in the change (open–closed).

In the case of SBC, an additional set of specific dialectical tensions emerged regarding foundational–situational ethics, individual–organization and ethics–performance. As these tensions became apparent, I faced some key decisions regarding how to respond to them. One option was to select a pole of the tension and focus on it, to the exclusion of the other pole. My inclination, for example, was to pay attention to ethics, at the expense of the company's bottom-line, performance-based financial needs. However, such an approach would not have been seen as realistic by many employees, managers, and the CEO, and it likely would have cost me trust and credibility in the organization. Another option was to separate the tensions and produce insights and offer recommendations that were singularly focused on each pole. For instance, I might have separated features of the company action plan that focused, in some cases, on the individual (e.g., employee training) and, in other cases, on the structural dimensions of the organization (e.g., the performance appraisal process). Yet another option was to integrate the tensions in ways that combined and creatively resolved them, such as writing the ethics code to integrate both foundational, prescriptive do statements and situational, flexible conditions for either adhering to or adapting the statements.

I learned that "holding" tensions in a sometimes difficult and contested position was most conducive to the process of organizational engagement that I sought. As best as possible, I used the struggle over the tensions as a synergistic means to, first, elucidate challenges and, second, to explore future opportunities. For each tension, similar to each ethical practice, any decision point represented, in the short term, both a loss and a gain. The company's ethics code, as written, for example, offered structure and guidance, but limited flexibility and adaptation; as a result, we spent additional time discussing how to translate the code into a "living, breathing document" with relevance to all realms of work at SBC. In so doing, the code would serve simultaneously as a centripetal and a centrifugal force within the organization, constraining action at times and enabling action at other times. Holding the dialectical tensions in place, I learned, necessarily involved a long-term view of the project—one that demanded constant care and cultivation. In particular, my aspirations for the initiative had to be tested and refined against the "the reality of life at SBC," as employees referred to it.

Engaged Scholarship Requires a Balance between a priori and Emergent Understanding

A change initiative, such as Ethics at Work, demands that scholars be conscious of their prior assumptions, based on their theoretical and practical understanding of life in organizations. For me, those assumptions are based on a critical perspective of organizational communication that pays close attention to relationships among power, knowledge, and discourse in organizations. My skepticism regarding the prospects of fundamental, structural change in organizations, even in my work, provides a necessary reality check when CEOs—or others who contact me—develop a certain, yet common, arrogance regarding their ability to transform organizational cultures.

Thankfully, this critical perspective also provides me, I hope, with an important sense of humility regarding what I may likely accomplish within an organizational system. At the same time, that perspective motivates me to use my engaged scholarship to pursue equity, fairness, respect, and, in the end, ethics in organizations.

However, one of the blind spots for critical organizational scholars is the inherent dialectical tension between stability–change. Wherever I turned at SBC, I saw opportunities for constructive organizational change. Opportunities to strengthen employees' voice, courage, and participation in making decisions immediately were apparent after the data-gathering phase of the project. At the same time, however, I recognized that change also unsettles, destabilizes, and makes organizational life uncomfortable for many employees. For some employees, stability has produced the privilege of position and status that often merits change, but for others, stability has created habits and routines that make work a matter of getting by and "making do" when life presents other, more important issues.

At SBC, I learned that resistance to change initiatives may come from the most unexpected people. For example, early advocates of the initiative on the company's executive team publicly resisted it when they realized that it might produce greater scrutiny of their actions rather than their subordinates' behaviors. Similarly, a number of lower level employees who stood to benefit the most from the company action plan expressed some of the most vocal concerns, largely, I later learned, out of fear that it would create additional work for them. This concern regarding the amount of work produced as a result of scholars' change initiative should not be underestimated, particularly in organizations. Over time, norms and routines often are well established and not changed easily, even when they may appear to be in employees' best interests. As a result, I regularly had to address explicitly the implicit question that seemed to be on everyone's mind: For whom is he working and to what end? Being able to answer that question perhaps is one of the most important lessons that I relearned via this project.

Finally, my a priori assumptions about the nature of organizational ethics, via my research on a range of ethical practices—such as dialogic communication, transparency, participation, courage, and accountability—were helpful but not necessarily taken for granted by organizational members. In fact, participants in this project taught me that my research agenda is necessarily partial, partisan, and problematic. In particular, unwillingness by SBC leaders to accept the need for, and benefits of, transparency caused me to reconsider its merits. They questioned, for example, whether there should be appropriate limits to transparency in organizations. Some employees taught me that accountability can come in various forms, some of which are not always fair or equitable. Still other employees taught me that ethical courage often can come at a cost. The process of the initiative, overall, taught me that participation is not a panacea, and that dialogic communication is complex, often contested, and always context-bound. In the end, I was reminded that engaged scholarship always is an iterative process of identifying problems; gathering data; constructing knowledge; reflecting on lessons learned; testing fundamental, taken-for-granted assumptions; and intervening in a responsive and responsible manner. Engaged scholarship, in this respect, demands that scholars simultaneously manage the dialectical tension of relying on a priori assumptions based on past research and on using emergent, local knowledge in the field.

CONCLUSION

Activating ethical engagement requires communication scholars to create a public space for themselves, whether in groups, organizations, communities, or other realms of life. Doing so also requires that communication scholars "be willing to *interrupt*, by making explicit and then disturbing habitual communicative practices to meaningfully address a range of social problems" (Krone & Harter, 2007, p. 76). However, engaging in interruption practices, as a form of communication activism, is risky. As noted in the Ethics at Work initiative at Southeastern Broadcasting Company, interrupting workplace habits with respect to ethics is likely to create discomfort, if not resistance, from a wide range of employees for disparate and sometimes unclear reasons. In particular, such engaged initiatives destabilize power dynamics and social relations that often are rooted and sedimented in a long history of organizational structures and practices. Activating the type of interruption that arises from organizational engagement also is risky because it can be time-consuming and physically and emotionally demanding. Collaborative partnerships rarely are easy and require ongoing maintenance and long-term sustainability. Engaged interruption also is risky because it typically has been devalued by the communication discipline and by the academy, more generally (Barge & Shockley-Zalabak, 2008).

Despite these difficulties, many communication scholars still take up this mode of scholarship because they have a unique obligation to help people, groups, organizations, and communities understand themselves and to become more active socially, politically, and economically by strengthening their capacities for dialogue, deliberation, and decision making (see, e.g., Cheney, 2007; Van de Ven, 2007; Weaver, 2007). The communication activism in which I engaged at Southeastern Broadcasting Company revolved around my concerns about the lack of talk—and related action—about organizational ethics. As a public, people spend limited time discussing the issue, aside from the occasional media portrayal of the most recent corporate scandal, but people spend even less time talking explicitly about ethics in their organizations, rarely problematizing common, taken-for-granted assumptions about how work gets done, by whom, and with what consequences to various stakeholders. This chapter described my, albeit limited, efforts to facilitate talk about ethics at one organization. The Ethics at Work initiative was guided by the general assumption that "talk matters" in organizations and, more specifically, that ethics talk requires a context that is based on dialogue, transparency, participation, courage, and accountability. Hopefully, such communication activism scholarship extends the boundaries of our work habits by moving us beyond good intentions to embodied practice.

APPENDIX
SOUTHEASTERN BROADCASTING COMPANY ETHICS CODE

Preamble

We, the people of Southeastern Broadcasting Company, are individuals with diverse backgrounds, abilities, views and ideas. We are SBC's most valued asset. We value the vitality of individuals and their families. We provide a work environment that is safe, compassionate, and rewarding. We commit to ensuring a healthy work–life balance that nurtures both our personal and corporate families.

We commit to building teamwork in the pursuit of excellence. We believe teamwork thrives in an environment of appreciation, respect, and integrity. We practice clear, courteous, and open-minded communication, without repercussions.

We consider it both our privilege and responsibility to serve and enrich the communities in which we work and live. We develop and support significant community projects, creating partnerships that benefit the public and SBC. As a driving force in the community, we are a catalyst for positive change.

Our responsibilities to our stakeholders are as follows:

Employees

We treat everyone with respect and dignity, regardless of job status.
We practice honesty and moral treatment.
We use clear, courteous, and open-minded communication.
We help our employees maintain a balance between their personal and professional lives.
We show appreciation for quality work and commitment to the company.
We commit to building teamwork throughout SBC. We work together and hold each other accountable at all levels to the code of ethics without repercussions.

Customers/Audience

We provide the highest quality of products and programming that we believe appeal to our customers and audiences.

We treat our audience and customers with respect and provide accurate, balanced information in a timely and professional manner.

We listen to and respect customer and audience feedback and respond to feedback in a timely and appropriate fashion.

Community

We hold ourselves to the highest community standards as individuals and as a corporation.

We commit to being a responsible, caring, corporate partner through philanthropic and active involvement in the community.

We serve as a role model of ethical and responsible business to improve the well-being of our community.

Owners and Management

We uphold our reputation and image by observing the highest standards of legal and ethical conduct in business dealings.

We practice clear, courteous, and open-minded communication between managers and employees.

We strive to make a profit ethically and legally.

We identify and execute business strategies that result in sustained growth and profitability.

Advertisers and Sponsors

We help our clients identify needs and achieve their goals with an emphasis on building long-term relationships.

We maintain fair and competitive pricing without compromising our integrity or misrepresenting our competitors or ourselves.

We work to ensure that our potential advertisers' and sponsors' content, products, and services are consistent with SBC's values.

We treat our clients with respect, maintain confidentiality, and provide exceptional customer service.

Suppliers, Lenders, and Vendors

We make every effort to seek vendor relationships that enrich the community.

We maintain positive and honest relationships while achieving competitive pricing and quality service.

We are truthful and respectful to suppliers, lenders, and vendors.

We make prompt payments when acceptable services and/or products are received.

Business Affiliates

We honor our responsibilities to our business affiliates without sacrificing our company's principles.

We are committed to building teamwork with our business affiliates in the pursuit of excellence.

We have fair and reasonable expectations of our business partners, and we communicate those expectations clearly.

Regulators and Governing Bodies

We know, understand, abide by, and, whenever necessary, challenge the rules and regulations of our governing bodies.

We strive to improve public policy.

We strive to develop and maintain open, healthy, and constructive relationships with all applicable governing bodies.

We incorporate self-regulation, self-inspection, and self-policing to address issues before they become problems, and we honestly report all violations to the governing body.

We take a proactive approach in dealing with governing bodies to ensure the growth of our industry and the relevance of our products and services.

Industry Groups

We are the epitome of positive leadership among our respective industries.

We advocate and uphold industry standards.

We stand firm against industry pressure.

We uphold SBC and community standards of decency.

We set a high standard of ethics and achievement within our respective industries.

Competitors

We compete aggressively but fairly, while maintaining professionalism, courtesy, and respect.

We create and perform at higher standards, raising the bar of quality.

We do not sacrifice our code of ethics in pursuit of winning.

We are responsible and accurate in our representation of our product, our competitors, and ourselves.

Compliance Statement

We pledge to uphold and promote this code of ethics and hold all accountable to it.

REFERENCES

Argawal, J., & Malloy, D. C. (2000). The role of existentialism in ethical business decision-making. *Business Ethics: A European Review, 9*, 143–154. doi:10.1111/1467-8608.00185

Banner, D. K., & Cooke, R. A. (1984). Ethical dilemmas in performance appraisal. *Journal of Business Ethics, 3*, 327–333. doi:10.1007/BF00381756

Barge, J. K., Lee, M., Maddux, K., Nabring, R., & Townsend, B. (2008). Managing dualities in planned change initiatives. *Journal of Applied Communication Research, 36*, 364–390. doi:10.1080/00909880802129996

Barge, J. K., & Shockley-Zalabak, P. (2008). Engaged scholarship and the creation of useful organizational knowledge. *Journal of Applied Communication Research, 36*, 251–265. doi:10.1080/00909880802172277

Beu, D., Buckley, M. R., & Harvey, M. G. (2003). Ethical decision-making: A multidimensional construct. *Business Ethics: A European Review, 12*, 88–107. doi:10.1111/1467-8608.00308

Carlin, W. B., & Strong, K. C. (1995). A critique of Western philosophical ethics: Multidisciplinary alternatives for framing ethical dilemmas. *Journal of Business Ethics, 14*, 387–396. doi:10.1007/BF00872100

Cheney, G. (2007). Organizational communication comes out. *Management Communication Quarterly, 21*, 80–91. doi:10.1177/0893318907302639

Chreim, S. (2002). Influencing organizational identification during major change: A communication-based perspective. *Human Relations, 55*, 1117–1137. doi:10.1177/0018726702055009022

Christensen, L. T., & Langer, R. (2009). Public relations and the strategic use of transparency: Consistency, hypocrisy, and corporate change. In R. L. Heath, E. L. Toth, & D. Waymer (Eds.), *Rhetorical and critical approaches to public relations II* (pp. 129–153). New York, NY: Routledge.

Clegg, S. R. (1989). *Frameworks of power*. Newbury Park, CA: Sage.

Conquergood, D. (1995). Between rigor and relevance: Rethinking applied communication. In K. N. Cissna (Ed.), *Applied communication for the 21st century* (pp. 79–96). Mahwah, NJ: Lawrence Erlbaum.

Conrad, C., & Haynes, J. (2001). Development of key constructs. In F. M. Jablin & L. L. Putnam (Eds.), *The new handbook of organizational communication: Advances in theory, research, and methods* (pp. 47–77). Thousand Oaks, CA: Sage.

Cooperrider, D. L., & Srivastva, S. (1987). Appreciative inquiry in organizational life. In R. W. Woodman & W. A. Pasmore (Eds.), *Research in organizational change and development* (Vol. 1, pp. 129–169). Greenwich, CT: JAI Press.

Coughlan, R. (2005). Codes, values, and justifications in the ethical decision-making process. *Journal of Business Ethics, 59*, 45–53. doi:10.1007/s10551-005-3409-9

Daft, R. L., Conlon, E. J., Austin, J., & Buenger, V. (1996). Competing values in organizations: Contextual influences and structural consequences. *Organization Science, 7*, 557–576. doi:10.1287/orsc.7.5.557

Dawe, A. (1978). Theories of social action. In T. Bottomore & R. Nisbet (Eds.), *A history of sociological analysis* (pp. 362–417). New York, NY: Basic Books.

Deetz, S. A. (1992). *Democracy in an age of corporate colonization: Developments in communication and the politics of everyday life*. Albany: State University of New York Press.
Deetz, S. (2007). Corporate governance, corporate social responsibility, and communication. In S. May, G. Cheney, & J. Roper (Eds.), *The debate over corporate social responsibility* (pp. 267–278). New York, NY: Oxford University Press.
Deetz, S. (2008). Organizational ethics. In W. Donsbach (Ed.), *The international encyclopedia of communication* (Vol. 8, pp. 3460–3461). Malden, MA: Wiley-Blackwell.
Deetz, S., & Irvin, L. (2008). Governance, stakeholder involvement, and new communication models. In S. Odugbemi & T. Jacobson (Eds.), *Governance reform under real-world conditions: Citizens, stakeholders, and voice* (pp. 163–180). Washington, DC: World Bank.
De Witte, H. (Ed.). (2005). *Job insecurity, union involvement, and union activism*. Burlington, VT: Ashgate.
Donaldson, T. (1996). Values in tension: Ethics away from home. *Harvard Business Review, 74*(5), 48–62. doi:10.1225/96502
Donaldson, T., & Dunfee, T. W. (1994). Toward a unified conception of business ethics: Integrative social contracts theory. *Academy of Management Review, 19*, 252–284. doi: 10.2307/258705
Donaldson, T. J., & Freeman, R. E. (1994). *Business as humanity*. New York, NY: Oxford University Press.
Douglas, P., Davidson, R., & Schwartz, B. (2001). The effect of organizational culture and ethical orientation on accountants' ethical judgments. *Journal of Business Ethics, 34*, 101–121. doi:10.1023/a:1012261900281
Eisenhofer, J. W., & Barry, M. J. (2006). *Shareholder activism handbook*. New York, NY: Aspen.
Esrock, S. L., Hart, J. L., & Leitchy, G. (2007). Smoking out the opposition: The rhetoric of reaction and the Kentucky excise tax campaign. In L. R. Frey & K. M. Carragee (Eds.), *Communication activism: Vol. 1. Communication for social change* (pp. 385–410). Cresskill, NJ: Hampton Press.
Fairhurst, G. T. (2007). *Discursive leadership: In conversation with leadership psychology*. Thousand Oaks, CA: Sage.
Frey, L. R., & Carragee, K. M. (Eds.). (2007a). *Communication activism* (2 Vols.). Cresskill, NJ: Hampton Press.
Frey, L. R., & Carragee, K. M. (2007b). Introduction: Communication activism as engaged scholarship. In L. R. Frey & K. M. Carragee (Eds.), *Communication activism* (2 Vols., pp. 1–64). Cresskill, NJ: Hampton Press.
Fritzsche, D. J. (1995). Personal values: Potential keys to ethical decision-making. *Journal of Business Ethics, 14*, 909–922. doi:10.1007/bf00882069
Ganesh, S. (2007). Sustainable development discourse and the global economy: Promoting responsibility, containing change. In S. May, G. Cheney, & J. Roper (Eds.), *The debate over corporate social responsibility* (pp. 379–390). New York, NY: Oxford University Press.
Gaudine, A., & Thorne, L. (2001). Emotion and ethical decision-making in organizations. *Journal of Business Ethics, 31*, 175–187. doi:10.1023/a:1010711413444

Giddens, A. (1979). *Central problems in social theory: Action, structure, and contradiction in social analysis.* Berkeley: University of California Press.
Giddens, A. (1984). *The constitution of society: Outline of the theory of structuration.* Berkeley: University of California Press.
Goldman, A. H. (1980). Business ethics: Profits, utilities, and moral rights. *Philosophy & Public Affairs, 9,* 260–286. Retrieved from http://www.jstor.org/action/showPublication?journalCode=philpublaffa
Harrison, J. S., & Freeman, R. E. (1999). Stakeholders, social responsibility, and performance: Empirical evidence and theoretical perspectives. *Academy of Management Journal, 42,* 479–485. doi:10.2307/256971
James, H. S., Jr., & Rassekeh, F. (2000). Smith, Friedman, and self-interest in ethical society. *Business Ethics Quarterly, 10,* 659–674. doi:10.2307/3857897
Jones, T. M., Felps, W., & Bigley, G. A. (2007). Ethical theory and stakeholder-related decisions: The role of stakeholder culture. *Academy of Management Review, 32,* 137–155. doi:10.2307/20159285
Kitson, A., & Campbell, R. (2001). Case studies in business ethics. In A. Malachowski (Ed.), *Business ethics: Critical perspectives on business and management: Vol. 4. Case studies in business ethics* (pp. 7-12). New York, NY: Routledge.
Krone, K. J., & Harter, L. M. (2007). Forum introduction: Organizational communication scholars as public intellectuals. *Management Communication Quarterly, 21,* 75–79. doi:10.1177/0893318907302637
Lewis, L. K. (2007). An organizational stakeholder model of change implementation communication. *Communication Theory, 17,* 176–204. doi:10.1111/j.1468-2885.2007.00291.x
Lewis, L. K., & Seibold, D. R. (1998). Innovation modification during intraorganizational innovation adoption. *Academy of Management Review, 18,* 322–354. doi:10.2307/258762
Lord, K. M. (2006). *The perils and promise of global transparency: Why the information revolution may not lead to security, democracy, or peace.* Albany: State University of New York Press.
Lorsch, J. W., Berlowitz, L., & Zelieke, A. (Eds.). (2005). *Restoring trust in American business.* Cambridge, MA: American Academy of Arts and Sciences.
Markowitz, L. (2000). *Worker activism after successful union organizing.* Armonk, NY: M. E. Sharpe.
May, S. K. (Ed.). (2006). *Case studies in organizational communication: Ethical perspectives and practices.* Thousand Oaks, CA: Sage.
May, S. K. (2008). Reconsidering strategic corporate social responsibility: Public relations and ethical engagement of employees in a global economy. In A. Zerfass, B. van Ruler, & K. Sriramesh (Eds.), *Public relations research: European and international perspectives and innovations* (pp. 365–383). Wiesbaden, Germany: VS Verlag fur Sozialwissenschaften.
May, S. K. (2009, May). *Silencing ethics in the U.S. financial crisis.* Paper presented at the meeting of the International Communication Association, Chicago, IL.
May, S., K., Cheney, G., & Roper, J. (Eds.). (2007). *The debate over corporate social responsibility.* New York, NY: Oxford University Press.

McDonald, G., & Pak, P. C. (1996). It's all fair in love, war, and business: Cognitive philosophies in ethical decision-making. *Journal of Business Ethics, 15*, 973–996. doi:10.1007/BF00705577

Michaelson, C. (2001). Is business ethics philosophy or sophism? *Business Ethics: A European Review, 10*, 331–339. doi:10.1111/1467-8608.00249

Morrell, K., & Anderson, M. (2006). Dialogue and scrutiny in organizational ethics. *Business Ethics: A European Review, 15*, 117–129. doi:10.1111/j.1467-8608.2006.00436.x

Nell, O. (1975). *Acting on principle: An essay on Kantian ethics*. New York, NY: Columbia University Press.

Nicotera A. M., & Cushman, D. P. (1992). Organizational ethics: A within-organization view. *Journal of Applied Communication Research, 20*, 437–462. doi:10.1080/00909889209365348

Nielsen, R. P. (1990). Dialogic leadership as ethics action (praxis) method. *Journal of Business Ethics, 9*, 765–783. doi:10.1007/bf00383275

Palmer, D. L. (2007). Facilitating consensus in an antiglobalization affinity group. In L. R. Frey & K. M. Carragee (Eds.), *Communication activism: Vol. 1. Communication for social change* (pp. 385–410). Cresskill, NJ: Hampton Press.

Parker, M. (1988a). Against ethics. In M. Parker (Ed.), *Ethics & organization* (pp. 282–296). Thousand Oaks, CA: Sage.

Parker, M. (Ed.). (1998b). *Ethics & organization*. Thousand Oaks, CA: Sage.

Parker, M. (1998c). Introduction: Ethic, the very idea? In M. Parker (Ed.), *Ethics & organization* (pp. 1–13). Thousand Oaks, CA: Sage.

Pearson, G. (1995). *Integrity in organizations: An alternative business ethic*. New York, NY: McGraw-Hill.

Pelton, L. E., Chowdhury, J., & Vitell, S. J., Jr. (2004). A framework for the examination of relational ethics: An interactionist perspective. *Journal of Business Ethics, 19*, 241–253. doi:10.1023/a:1005935011952

Quinn, J. K., Reed, J. D., Browne, M. N., & Hiers, W. J. (1997). Honesty, individualism, and pragmatic business ethics: Implications for corporate hierarchy. *Journal of Business Ethics, 16*, 1419–1430. doi:10.1023/a:1005787209221

Reed, M. I. (1985). *Redirections in organizational analysis*. New York, NY: Tavistock.

Reich, R. B. (2007). *Supercapitalism: The transformation of business, democracy, and everyday life*. New York, NY: Alfred A. Knopf.

Schultz, P. D. (1996). The morally accountable organization: A postmodern approach to organizational responsibility. *Journal of Business Communication, 33*, 165–183. doi:10.1177/002194369603300205

Seeger, M. W., Sellnow, T. L., Ulmer, R. R., & Novak, J. M. (2009). Applied communication ethics: A summary and critique of the research literature. In L. R. Frey & K. N. Cissna (Eds.), *Routledge handbook of applied communication research* (pp. 280–306). New York, NY: Routledge.

Seibold, D. R., Lemus, D. R., Ballard, D. I., & Myers, K. K. (2009). Organizational communication and applied communication research: Parallels, interactions, integration, and engagement. In L. R. Frey & K. N. Cissna (Eds.), *Routledge handbook of applied communication research* (pp. 331–354). New York, NY: Routledge.

Seibold, D. R., & Shea, B. C. (2001). Participation and decision making. In F. M. Jablin & L. L. Putnam (Eds.), *The new handbook of organizational communication: Advances in theory, research, and methods* (pp. 664–703). Thousand Oaks, CA: Sage.

Seo, M., Putnam, L. L., & Bartunek, J. M. (2003). Dualities and tensions of planned organizational change. In M. S. Poole & A. Van de Ven (Eds.), *Handbook of organizational change* (pp. 73-107). Thousand Oaks, CA: Sage.

Shminke, M., Ambrose, M. L., & Noel, T. W. (1997). The effect of ethical frameworks on perceptions of organizational justice. *Academy of Management Journal, 40*, 1190–1207. doi:10.2307/256932

Sims, R. L., & Keon, T. L. (1999). Determinants of ethical decision making: The relationship of the perceived organizational environment. *Journal of Business Ethics, 19*, 393–401. doi:10.1023/a:1005834129122

Solomon, R. C. (1992). *Ethics and excellence: Cooperation and integrity in business.* New York, NY: Oxford University Press.

Sorell, T. (1998). Beyond the fringe? The strange state of business ethics. In M. Parker (Ed.), *Ethics & organization* (pp. 15–29). Thousand Oaks, CA: Sage.

Spira, L. (1999). Independence in corporate governance: The audit committee role. *Business Ethics: A European Review, 8*, 262–273. doi:10.1111/1467-8608.00160

Stohl, C., & Cheney, G. (2001). Participatory processes/paradoxical practices. *Management Communication Quarterly, 14*, 349–407. doi:10.1177/0893318901143001

Stohl, M., Stohl, C., & Townsley, N. C. (2007). A new generation of global corporate social responsibility. In S. May, G. Cheney, & J. Roper (Eds.), *The debate over corporate social responsibility* (pp. 30–44). New York, NY: Oxford University Press.

Van de Ven, A. H. (2007). *Engaged scholarship: A guide for organizational and social research.* New York, NY: Oxford University Press.

Warren, R. C. (1993). Codes of ethics: Bricks without straw. *Business Ethics: A European Review, 2*, 185–191. doi:10.1111/j.1467-8608.1993.tb00044.x

Weaver, C. K. (2007). Reinventing the public intellectual through communication dialogue civic capacity building. *Management Communication Quarterly, 21*, 92–104. doi:10.1177/0893318907302640

Werhane, P. H. (2007). Corporate social responsibility/corporate moral responsibility: Is there a difference and the difference it makes. In S. May, G. Cheney, & J. Roper (Eds.), *The debate over corporate social responsibility* (pp. 459–474). New York, NY: Oxford University Press.

White, L. P., & Lam, L. W. (2000). A proposed infrastructural model for the establishment of organizational ethical systems. *Journal of Business Ethics, 28*, 35–42. doi:10.1023/A:1006221928960

Willmott, H. (1998). Towards a new ethics? The contributions of poststructuralism and posthumanism. In M. Parker (Ed.), *Ethics & organizations* (pp. 76–121). Thousand Oaks, CA: Sage.

Wimbush, J. C. (1999). The effect of cognitive moral development and supervisory influence on subordinates' ethical behavior. *Journal of Business Ethics, 18*, 383–395. doi:10.1023/a:1006072231066

Zorn, T. E., & Collins, E. (2007). Is sustainability sustainable? Corporate social responsibility, sustainable business, and management fashion. In S. May, G. Cheney, & J. Roper (Eds.), *The debate over corporate social responsibility* (pp. 405–416). New York, NY: Oxford University Press.

9

ORGANIZING FOR SOCIAL CHANGE

Communicative Empowerment for Small Business Development and Job Training for People Who are Poor[1]

Wendy H. Papa
Michael J. Papa
Rick A. Buerkel[2]
Central Michigan University

"Wow, there's a new buggy in town," said a passerby, a student at Ohio University (OU) in Athens, Ohio. Such was the beginning of "Good Gifts," a small business formed in fall 1999 to provide job skills training and a livable wage for people who are poor in southeastern Ohio, a part of the Appalachian region of the United States. The genesis of Good Gifts began with a series of meetings between Keith Wasserman (founder and executive director of Good Works, a nonprofit social services organization Keith founded in 1981 that offers shelter to people who are homeless, along with a variety of services and programs to create a community of support for those struggling with poverty) and Wendy and Michael Papa (then OU communication professors).

Wendy and Michael had heard about Keith and Good Works from Norman Coleman, a local Methodist minister. Reverend Coleman was familiar with Michael's work studying the microloan programs of the Grameen Bank in Bangladesh (M. H. Papa, Auwal, & Singhal, 1995, 1997), and he thought it would be a good idea for us to talk about possible collaborative work to help people who are poor in southeastern Ohio. We met for lunch at Wendy and Michael's home, and Michael started talking about the microloan programs of the Grameen Bank that helped the poorest of the poor to become self-sufficient through developing small businesses. Keith's eyes lit up and the conversation moved in the direction of what we could do in terms of economic development for local people who are poor in Athens and its surrounding rural communities.

The business that emerged started with a vending cart stationed on a street running through the OU campus. The products sold on the cart ranged from clothing and accessories to handmade toys and jewelry. The vending cart was staffed initially with community and student volunteers to build a sufficient economic base to eventually hire local people who were poor and unemployed, and to provide them with job skills training and a living wage. This business, started in fall 1999, continues to operate today; in addition to the mobile vending cart, the business now has a permanent retail facility on property owned by the Good Works organization. Importantly, in the 11 years since the founding of Good Gifts, 35 people who were poor and unemployed have learned job skills and earned a living wage from this business. Although we believe this outcome is significant, we also recognize that Good Gifts has had only a small influence on poverty as a social problem in the United States.

Our experiences in this organizing for social change initiative provided multiple opportunities for communication activism, ranging from the initial creation of Good Gifts to the recruitment of student volunteers to the actual operations of the organization and the creation of a related service-learning university course. In this chapter, we first define and describe the problem of poverty in the United States and in Athens, Ohio. We then situate the study of poverty within the extant communication literature. We subsequently describe the development of the small vending cart business, and then analyze that communication activism endeavor by linking our experiences with relevant theory and research. Finally, we provide insight into the lessons we learned about communication activism scholarship by reflecting on both our successes and failures.

POVERTY IN THE UNITED STATES AND IN ATHENS, OHIO

Webster's Dictionary defined *poverty* as a state in which "the means for mere subsistence, such as food and shelter, are lacking" (Guralink, 2008, p. 1116). As commonly defined by the U.S. Census Bureau, poverty is the state of living alone or in a family with income below the federally defined poverty line (DeNavas-Walt, Proctor, & Smith, 2009). For 2008, the poverty line was set at the following levels for households of one to four persons: (a) one person, $10,991; (b) two people, $14,051; (c) three people, $17,163; and (d) four people, $22,025 (DeNavas-Walt et al., 2009). Below the poverty threshold, people experience significant problems meeting expenses for housing, food, utilities, transportation, health care, and child care. Importantly, the effects of living in poverty go beyond just meeting expenses; Shoshani (2005) explained that poverty often leads to poor nutrition, poor health, depression, enrollment of children in low-quality schools, discrimination by wealthier community members, and higher levels of violence in the home.

Although the United States is the wealthiest nation in the world in terms of gross domestic product (World Bank Group, 2010), poverty remains a significant problem. The U.S. Census Bureau reported that in 2009, 14.3% of the U.S. population, or 46.3 million people, were living in households below the federally defined poverty line (DeNavas-Walt et al., 2010). The racial breakdown for those living in poverty was as follows: (a) non-Hispanic whites, 8.2%; (b) blacks, 24.7%; (c) Asians, 11.8%; and (d) Hispanics, 23.2% (DeNavas-Walt et al., 2009). Given the 2008 population data for each racial category, non-Hispanic whites account for 43.7% of the people living in poverty, blacks, 24.1%, Asians, 4%, and Hispanics, 28.2% (DeNavas-Walt et al., 2009).

In the setting where this activism project was conducted, Athens County, Ohio, the problem of poverty is especially significant. The Athens County Department of Job and Family Services (2006) reported that the poverty rate for individuals is 27.4% and 14% for families, the highest levels in the state of Ohio. Furthermore, in particular places within the county, levels of poverty are even higher, with Athens Township having a poverty rate of 39.9% and the city of Athens having a poverty rate of 51.1% (Athens County Department of Job and Family Services, 2006). Given that the countywide unemployment rate is only 6.1% (Athens County Department of Job and Family Services, 2006), many people in the county are working but not earning enough to rise out of poverty, producing a class of working poor. Although statistics for levels of poverty by racial group in the county are not available, the following statistics provide insight into the demographics of Athens County: (a) white, 92.9%; (b) black, 2.61%; (c) American

Indian/Alaskan Native, 0.1%; (d) Asian, 2.5%; (e) other race, alone, 0.3%; and (f) two or more races, 1.6% (Athens County Department of Job and Family Services, 2006).

Consistent with the observation made earlier concerning the relationship between poverty and health, Athens County, with its high poverty rate, has more negative health outcomes than people living in other parts of the state. In fact, the Ohio Department of Health (2003) reported that the mortality rate in Athens County is relatively high compared with state and national averages, with a significantly higher death rate for five of the six leading causes of death (heart disease, cancer, stroke, chronic lower respiratory disease, and unintentional injury) than the state and national averages. The only one of the six leading causes of death that Athens County ranks lower in is diabetes (Ohio Department of Health, 2003).

SITUATING DISCUSSIONS OF POVERTY IN THE COMMUNICATION LITERATURE

The issue of poverty and the experiences of people who are poor have been described in a variety of ways in the communication literature. First, the topic of U.S. welfare policies and programs has been discussed extensively. Among the areas covered in that literature are welfare reform (Asen, 2001; Carcasson, 2006; Shen & Edwards, 2005), welfare policy debates in the United States (Asen, 2003; de Goede, 1996; Gring-Pemble, 2003), welfare-to-work programs (Marston, 2008; Waldron & Lavitt, 2000; Waldron, Lavitt, & McConnaughy, 2001), how public perceptions of welfare are influenced by the media (Sotirovic, 2000, 2001), and how women welfare recipients communicate both acquiescence and dissent (Kingfisher, 1996).

Second, the issues of media exposure and media depictions of people who are poor have been studied. For example, Stephens (1972) studied how exposure to the media helped to modernize Appalachian people who are poor. Concerning media portrayals of poverty, scholars have examined how people who are poor are depicted in magazine photographs (Clawson & Trice, 2000), television programs (Gould, Stern, & Adams, 1981), and newspapers (Nielson, 2008). Related to this category of research is how the news media connect race and poverty. For example, Gilens (1996) found that the U.S. news media promote misperceptions of people who are poor by focusing stories on a disproportionate percentage of racial and ethnic minorities when, in fact, the majority of people who are poor in the United States are white. Similarly, Clawson and Kegler (2000) noted that there is "race-coding" in textbooks about the U.S. government, with a disproportionate emphasis of poverty among racial and ethnic minority group members.

Standing in contrast to so-called "objective" mainstream media depictions of people who are poor that are produced by writers who are not poor themselves, scholars have studied alternative news publications (Harter, Edwards, McClanahan, Hopson, & Carson-Stern, 2004; Hindman, 1998; Howley, 2003) and electronic networks (Schmitz, Rogers, Phillips, & Pascal, 1995) for their descriptions of people who are poor. For example, Harter et al. (2004) described how the newspaper *StreetWise*, founded and operated by people who are homeless, organizes and offers empowerment opportunities for people who are homeless in Chicago, providing them with an alternative to begging and panhandling. Specifically, by publishing and distributing *StreetWise*, the organization (with the same name) provides employment to men and women in Chicago who are either homeless or at risk for becoming so. The newspaper also seeks to expand public awareness of people who are homeless among those who have homes and to influence government policies and public discourse on homelessness and poverty. *StreetWise* accomplishes these goals through representing an alternative discourse community, privileging voices that often are marginalized, silenced, or rejected by mainstream media. A Labor Beat column, for instance, covered issues of unfair labor practices, rising unemployment, and the concerns of immigrant workers, janitorial workers, and the racially underprivileged (Harter et al., 2004). Furthermore, in a study that directly compared mainstream news coverage of poverty with an alternative news publication, Jeppesen (2009) found substantive differences in the approaches taken by two articles, one in *The Toronto Star*, the other in the alternative publication website the Ontario Coalition Against Poverty (OCAP). *The Toronto Star* article observed that tenants were organizing to protest substandard housing, but the conclusion was drawn that the government must act to improve housing conditions for people living in poverty because only the government has the real power to enact change. Conversely, the article on the OCAP (2007) website noted, "OCAP has been working for some weeks to mobilize tenants to challenge the appalling conditions and terrible neglect that they live with" (para. 1). Jeppesen (2009) observed that using action verbs, such as "working," "mobilize," and "challenge," is a clearly different discourse strategy than that taken by *The Toronto Star*; specifically, OCAP takes the perspective that grassroots action can produce change. Additionally, the OCAP article highlights the narratives of three tenants who were successful in forcing Toronto Community Housing to improve their apartment living conditions.

Third, organizational programs developed by, with, and for people who are poor have been described. Representative of this research is a focus on the success of microcapitalism in the Grameen Bank of Bangladesh, where people who are poor are given small loans for business development (Auwal, 1996; M. J. Papa et al., 1995, 1997; M. J. Papa, Singhal, & Papa, 2006).

Additionally, researchers have described grassroots community organizing for economic and social development, such as the efforts of rural people in India who are poor to participate in and govern their dairy cooperatives (M. J. Papa, Singhal, Ghanekar, & Papa, 2000; M. J. Papa et al., 2006), as well as community organizing to develop schools for children who are poor and to promote community health (W. H. Papa, Papa, Kandath, Worrell, & Muthuswamy, 2005). Moreover, Novak and Harter (2008) explained how people who are poor organized themselves democratically to advocate for issues related to poverty.

Fourth, educational and training programs for people who are poor have been examined. For example, Risopatron and Spain (1980) described a communication program to educate Costa Rican people who are poor about human sexuality. Additionally, M. J. Papa et al. (2000, 2006) detailed the cooperative development educational and communication programs offered to women in rural India to teach principles and practices of cooperative governance.

The final area of communication research focusing on poverty is how people who are poor experience alienation and stigma in their communities. For example, Daniel (1970) depicted how people who are poor feel alienated in the United States because that society privileges and empowers those who are affluent. Harter, Berquist, Titsworth, Novak, and Brokaw (2005) described how stigmatization was promoted through the disability-first label of "homeless people" and by how those who are wealthier respond both verbally and nonverbally in a dismissive manner to people who are homeless. Finally, W. H. Papa et al. (2005) and M. J. Papa et al. (2006) examined how people who are poor interact with one another in ways that alienate and fragment their existence by reproducing a dominant discourse that disempowers them.

Although communication research has made valuable contributions to understanding communication issues and problems related to poverty, most of this research may be characterized as "third-person-perspective research" (see Carragee & Frey, this volume; Frey & Carragee, 2007), meaning descriptive, interpretive, critical and recommendation-oriented research that is conducted about people who are poor without intervening directly to change that condition. In contrast, the present study represents "first-person-perspective research" (see Carragee & Frey, this volume; Frey & Carragee, 2007) in that we, as communication scholars, intervene to change discourses and material conditions through offering job training and employment opportunities for people who are poor in Appalachian Ohio. Importantly, these opportunities were provided as we worked alongside and in partnership with people who were poor.

CREATING GOOD GIFTS THROUGH COMMUNICATION ACTIVISM

Our individual and collective communication activism took a variety of forms. The first meeting attended by Keith, Wendy, and Michael initiated our activism. For Wendy and Michael, this meeting represented an opportunity to apply some lessons that they had learned from studying the microloan programs of the Grameen Bank in Bangladesh. In that organization, local people organized with very small startup funds to create economically viable enterprises that moved people who were poor from relations of dependency (e.g., begging for money) to economic self-sufficiency. For Keith, this meeting represented an opportunity to realize one of his dreams: creating an income-generating business that aids people struggling with poverty by providing them with training and a living wage. Our discussions during this and other meetings held during spring 1999 framed our subsequent activism.

The next step in creating such a business involved the recruitment of student volunteers during spring and summer 1999. Wendy and Michael began talking to students enrolled in their group communication and organizational communication courses at OU about the idea of Good Gifts, many of whom expressed interest in participating. Students were given the opportunity to register for an independent study course and use their volunteer hours with Good Gifts to earn academic credit by documenting and reflecting on their experiences in a research paper that integrated relevant communication theory and research.

Our efforts to establish a viable business were assisted invaluably by Heather Cluggston, an OU communication major who interned at the Good Works organization during 1999. When Heather found out about the plans for Good Gifts, she extended her internship to work on this initiative. One of the most important early developments in starting the business occurred when Heather and Michael negotiated with a local business owner to procure a vending cart that he had ceased using. Keith had only a limited amount of money that he could allocate to the business, most of which was earmarked for inventory; consequently, paying for a new vending cart was out of the question. There was, however, a local restaurant, called The Purple Chopstix, that had once operated a vending cart in uptown Athens. The vending cart was perfectly suited to our needs, as it had a roof to protect workers and products from bad weather, the side of the cart facing the public had a full drop-down panel to facilitate interacting with customers, and there were ample cabinets inside the cart to store products. A truck with a trailer hitch could pull the 8 x 10-foot single-axle vending cart.

Heather and Michael went to the owner of the restaurant, Ed Fisher, and explained the Good Gifts project being planned with Keith and the Good

Works organization. Ed's only reservation in giving us the cart was that it was not in a safe operating condition and he did not have the resources to repair it. We struck a deal with him that we would enlist Good Works' volunteers to repair the cart, and Ed allowed us to use his vending cart.

Heather, Wendy, and Michael then set up a series of meetings with the Athens Code Enforcement Office, Athens Health Department, and Mayor's Office to describe the new business. The purpose of the meeting with representatives from the Athens Code Enforcement Office was to obtain a license and a permit to operate a vending cart business, which necessitated an inspection of the cart to make sure that it was safe. We met with Athens Health Department officials to sign a statement that we would not sell food, which would require an inspection of food preparation and storage equipment. Finally, the Mayor's Office had to approve all new local businesses and was especially concerned that no laws be violated in the conduct of any business. These meetings resulted in all of the necessary approvals, clearing the way for our eventual operations.

Wendy and Michael began to search the World Wide Web to find businesses from which Good Gifts could purchase products. We came across Ten Thousand Villages, an organization located in Akron, Pennsylvania, that buys handcrafted products from around the world that are made by people who are poor and who are guaranteed a living wage. Aiding people in Third-World countries to obtain a living wage was important because we wanted to purchase products that assisted people who were poor internationally and, at the same time, operate Good Gifts to aid local people who were poor. We also purchased handcrafted products from Passion Works, an Athens-based organization that partners local artists with community members who have developmental disabilities. When we told Keith of our choices for suppliers, he immediately came up with the motto for Good Gifts: "Buy a gift, change the world!" A promotional brochure for Good Gifts, designed by Heather, Wendy, and Michael, identified the business philosophy:

> When you buy a gift, you are changing the world—really. The fact is that you are helping citizens who live in Third-World countries make a living wage for their hard work and in doing so, you are making a positive impact upon people who are living in poverty by helping them to help themselves. And, when you buy a gift from Good Gifts, you are helping citizens of our own community who are struggling with poverty issues in their lives. You are helping to provide training, education, and experiences to citizens who are moving from welfare to work.

With approval from the city of Athens to operate a vending cart business, and two suppliers, we were ready to order products. We employed two strategies to decide what products to order. First, Heather and Michael developed a market survey questionnaire that asked respondents to identify the type of products they would buy. We then secured permission from OU's Office of Information Technology to send this questionnaire via e-mail to approximately 1,000 OU students who participated in registered student organizations. Second, Michael and Wendy conducted focus groups with students from five classes that they taught at OU during spring and summer 1999, brainstorming ideas for products that would sell to OU students and to other local residents. Heather compiled a list of products to purchase from the approximately 250 questionnaires that were returned, and Michael and Wendy compiled their list from the focus group sessions. Heather, Michael, and Wendy met in July to discuss the lists and decided which products to order. Among the products that were ordered: jewelry, such as rings, bracelets, and necklaces; men's and women's shirts; women's scarves; shoes; small wooden storage boxes and jewelry boxes; candles and candlestick holders; wooden service trays; and Christmas ornaments. The initial purchase authorized by Keith Wasserman was for $1,500—another step accomplished along the road to opening day.

As fall quarter 1999 began at OU, Wendy and Michael contacted students who had expressed interest in volunteering at the Good Gifts vending cart and offered to sign independent study contracts such that they could receive academic credit for their volunteer work if they still were interested. Nine students signed independent study contracts; consequently, we had a sufficient number of volunteers, along with Michael, Wendy, Heather, and Keith. On September 20, 1999, Wendy, Michael, and Heather offered a training program to the nine student volunteers that described the programs of the Good Works organization, the philosophy and purpose of the Good Gifts business, the steps to open and close the vending cart, and the interpersonal communication skills that were important in interacting with customers, followed by role-play scenarios with "difficult" customers. Finally, we established a weekly schedule for staffing the vending cart.

September 21 marked the first day that the vending cart was parked on Union Street, a major street in uptown Athens. Michael and Jim, a Good Works employee, circled the small town streets of Athens until a parking space opened for the vending cart. On that first day of business, Michael and Heather, along with two student volunteers, Amber and Sandy, staffed the cart. Over the course of the 10-week quarter, Wendy and Michael staffed the cart once or twice each week, sometimes bringing their 7-year-old daughter, Sam, who loved helping out. Staffing the cart meant hauling it from the Good Works property to Union Street, finding a parking space for it, physically setting the cart into a secure position, displaying the inventory, interacting with customers, completing purchases, putting away display merchandise, attaching the cart to the truck, and driving it back to, and leaving the cart at, the Good Works property.

Sandy, one of the student volunteers, mentioned to Michael in October that she wanted to put some Ten Thousand Villages products on display tables to sell in OU residence halls. To do so, she needed to be a member of a registered student organization, which became the inspiration for creating the "Students for Good Gifts" (SGG) organization. Sandy became president of SGG, Amber served as vice president, Lydia served as treasurer, and Sara was the secretary, with Michael serving as faculty advisor and helping the new student group to craft bylaws. By winter quarter 2000, SGG began weekly displays of Good Gifts merchandise in the OU residence halls.

Although we had a group of 12 dedicated volunteers by October 1999, to raise sufficient money to employ local residents struggling with poverty, we needed to extend the operating hours of the business, requiring more volunteer assistance. To meet this need, Wendy and Michael proposed a new course, titled "Organizing for Social Change," to expose students to the interdisciplinary literature in the fields of communication, education, feminist studies, and psychology about processes of community organizing to produce social change, especially with regard to economic development for people who are poor. Central to participation in the course was a service-learning component; specifically, staffing the vending cart. This course was formally approved for spring semester 2000.

When fall quarter 1999 ended the Wednesday before Thanksgiving, we lost most of the student volunteers, but we added a few volunteers from the Athens community. Not wanting to lose business during the busy Christmas shopping season, Michael, Wendy, and Heather met with the owner of the Athens Mall and negotiated gaining access to floor space for Good Gifts display tables during the 3 weeks before Christmas for $300. Michael and Wendy staffed the display tables for several 2-hour shifts during that holiday shopping season. This activity was an economic success, as several thousand dollars in merchandise was sold, which allowed us to hire the first employees of Good Gifts.

The vending cart did not operate during winter quarter 2000 due to the weather (cold, snowy days) but Wendy, Michael, Keith, and Heather made plans for a busy spring. The Organizing for Social Change course filled to capacity with 35 students, and Michael and Wendy, the teachers, e-mailed those students to explain the service-learning component, and received several enthusiastic responses from them. Finally, given the economic success of Good Gifts' initial operations, Keith identified the first two hires, Elvira and Jim, neither of whom had been employed the past 6 months and both of whom had been homeless for parts of the past year.

On the first day of the Organizing for Social Change course, Keith and Heather came to talk about both Good Works and Good Gifts. We then set up a schedule to staff the vending cart Monday through Saturday, for a total of 54 hours a week over the 10-week spring quarter. In addition to the academic components of this course, we offered students job training in the tasks associated with working at the vending cart.

The final activity that Michael and Wendy performed for Good Gifts was to work alongside Elvira and Jim, helping them to develop confidence and transferable work habits and job skills to facilitate their transition to permanent employment in the future. Over the course of several shifts with Elvira and Jim, we answered questions that they had about Good Gifts and helped them to learn the tasks associated with opening and closing the cart, interacting with customers, and completing transactions. Importantly, we always were attentive to our behavior when staffing the cart to insure that we served as positive role models (e.g., interacting politely with customers). We also made sure that we worked *with* Elvira and Jim, engaging in every task that they did and having social conversations with them during downtime.

Thus, what started as a dream in spring 1999 became a reality in spring 2000; moreover, unlike so many small businesses that too often fail, Good Gifts continues to operate in 2011. We now analyze that activism from the standpoint of theoretical perspectives and research studies offered by various academic disciplines. In doing so, we make clear how our activism was informed by theory to make explicit the link between theory and practice. In other instances, we show how our activism may be interpreted from the perspective of theory and prior research.

ANALYSIS OF COMMUNICATION ACTIVISM THROUGH SMALL BUSINESS DEVELOPMENT

The analysis of this communication activism is divided into six sections. First, we explain what we learned about empowerment as a communication process. Second, we describe how our communication activism reflects a social justice rather than a charity approach. Third, we explain how our activism was influenced by feminist perspectives of organizing. Fourth, we show how our work was informed by Freire's (1970) critical pedagogy. Fifth, we connect our work to Bandura's (1977) social learning theory. Finally, we discuss the promises and pitfalls of service-learning related to this endeavor. These six perspectives were employed because each focuses on connecting people in ways where mutual learning and goal accomplishment takes place through observation and communication.

Empowerment as a Communication Process

Empowerment is a process of people communicating to achieve personal and collective goals (Alvesson & Willmott, 1992; Blau & Alba, 1982; Conger,

1989; Conger & Kanugo, 1988; Pacanowsky, 1988; M. J. Papa et al., 2006; Shehabuddin, 1992; Singhal & Rogers, 2003; Vogt & Murrell, 1990; see also Belone et al., this volume). More specifically, communication is central to coordinating the activities of multiple people, and it is part of negotiating, codetermining, and managing group-level power dynamics that pose both opportunities and barriers to empowerment.

The empowerment that we experienced through our activism was directly attributable to communication. Specifically, the numerous meetings among Wendy, Michael, Keith, and Heather moved Good Gifts from an idea to reality. These meetings truly were collaborative, in part, because we all were on unchartered ground in launching this small business venture. We respected one another's ideas and worked together diligently to move those ideas forward. Good Gifts could not have become a viable enterprise as quickly as it did were it not for our collaborative efforts.

Similarly, the formation of the SGG also provided empowerment opportunities for its members through communication. Michael collaborated with student members over several meetings to write a constitution that would be considered acceptable by OU's Office of Student Life. Over the course of several late night meetings, we worked through the wording of a constitution that was approved upon its initial submission. As Sandy, SGG president, remarked, "I can't believe how quickly this all came together, that we're now a registered student organization and can go to the residence halls to sell for Good Gifts." Of course, the reason that this student organization came together so quickly is because the four founding members were determined to reach their goal of selling Good Gifts merchandise on campus.

Communicative empowerment also was one of the most important experiences for Good Gifts' first two hires, Elvira and Jim. As Keith Wasserman noted on a number of occasions, one of the biggest communication barriers for many people who are poor in Athens is just being able to communicate with people from the university community. He explained further that the idea of attending a university as a student, let alone being a university professor or administrator, was so far removed from what people who are poor considered possible in their lives, that they felt intimidated in the presence of anyone from the university community. Wendy and Michael noticed immediately Elvira and Jim's discomfort in interacting with members of the OU community when first working with them. They felt comfortable with us because we were introduced as volunteers who worked with Keith at Good Works, not as OU professors. Whenever a customer from the OU community (whether a student wearing an OU shirt or a professor or administrator wearing professional clothing) would approach the cart, however, they would either avert their eyes or look to one of us to manage the interaction.

Wendy and Michael talked with Heather about Elvira and Jim feeling uncomfortable interacting with members of the OU community, and we devised a plan. Elvira and Jim were invited to come to the Good Works property, called Hannah House, where we had set up a display table with some Good Gifts merchandise. We then ran through several role-plays with Elvira and Jim as Good Gifts' workers, and Wendy, Michael, and SGG members as customers. Elvira and Jim were a little nervous at first, but, eventually, they performed very aptly as sales representatives. When they were told that Wendy and Michael were OU professors and that Sandy and Lydia were OU students, they both smiled. We then talked about how much people in the Athens community, including students and professors, wanted Good Gifts to succeed, which was especially salient given a recent positive article appearing in the student-run newspaper, *The Post*, titled "Good Gifts by Students" (Niederkohr, 1999). That talk encouraged Elvira and Jim to try to handle a couple of transactions the next day.

Elvira and Jim arrived together that next day at the start of Wendy and Michael's shift at the vending cart. Jim talked to an OU student who purchased a shirt made in India. After the sale, Jim looked at us with a huge smile, recognizing what he had accomplished. Elvira then interacted with an OU student and she was equally as happy with her interaction. Hence, a barrier was taken down for both of them that day, in that they now could interact with confidence with people (OU students) from whom they previously were disconnected. This empowerment arose, specifically, from the communication in which Elvira and Jim engaged with those OU students.

To understand empowerment as a communication process, it is necessary to focus on power and resistance. For example, Mumby (1997) viewed power as a productive, disciplinary, and strategic phenomenon with no specific center (e.g., the king or capitalism), meaning that power is distributed widely and unevenly; it is neither simply prohibitive nor productive but simultaneously enables and constrains human thought and action. Additionally, a number of scholars see resistance to power as a dynamic element of organizing processes that may lead to empowerment for organizational members (e.g., Bell & Forbes, 1994; de Certeau, 1984; Jenkins, 1988; Jermier, Knights, & Nord, 1994; Knights & Vurdubakis, 1984; Mumby, 1997; M. J. Papa et al., 1995, 1997, 2000; Trethewey, 1997); consequently, scholars encourage examining the discursive practices of organizational members as they resist and subvert the dominant social order. Hence, the enactment of resistance is particularly interesting to examine in its own right as a form of communicative empowerment.

Both Heather and Sandy displayed resistance in the face of a confrontation one day when they were staffing the vending cart. Two men from the Athens Code Enforcement Office approached the cart and asked Heather who was in charge, and she responded, "I am." One of the men then said that they had received a report of an illegal business operating uptown and they demanded to see the license for Good Gifts. Heather, normally a very poised person, became flustered and started to look for the license. After a minute or so, one of the officers said, "If you can't produce your license immediately, we're going to shut you down and issue a fine. I recommend you shut down now." Heather explained that she "was one of two people who went to your office to get the license. Don't you have a record of that?" The officer then took out a ticket book, leading Heather to say, "I can ask Michael Papa, a professor at OU, who got the license with me, to tell me where it is." She called Michael's office on her cell phone and, in a very harried manner, told Michael what was going on. Michael told her exactly where the license was located; she needed only to lift the money tray out of its container and the license was on the bottom. Heather did so and, with her hands shaking, showed the license to the two officers. One of them said, "Make sure you have this displayed at all times." They then left.

Michael could tell from Heather's voice that she was upset, so he left his office and walked quickly to the cart. When Heather saw him, she started to cry and told Michael the whole story. Michael comforted her and Sandy, who also was visibly shaken, telling them how proud he was of them for standing up to two code enforcement officers and not shutting down the cart. The resistance that they displayed, against two intimidating men, was remarkable. Michael was so angry that they had to experience such a power-laden interaction that he sent a letter of complaint to the Athens Code Enforcement Office. He received a brief response a month later saying, "It was unfortunate that the two officers neglected to check the licensing records before they went to the Union Street location of the Good Gifts vending cart."

The final form of communication that we link to empowerment is dialogue, which may promote individual and group empowerment through self-reflection, self-knowledge, and liberation from oppressive beliefs (see, e.g., Forester, 1989). Going back to its Greek roots, *dialogue* brings together *dia*, or meaning through, with *logos*, which translates to word or meaning; hence, dialogue involves people creating meaning together through communication. Dialogue can lead to mutual learning, appreciation of diversity, interpersonal trust, and understanding (Gronemeyer, 1993; Habermas, 1984). Furthermore, when dialogue is cultivated in democratic organizations, people feel validated speaking from personal experience because their listeners value them (Eisenberg, 1994, see also May, this volume). Dialogue is by no means, however, a simple process; it may require people to hear the voices of those whose language, meaning systems, and social locations are different from theirs, and the uniqueness of people's social locations may limit understanding of those others (Zoller, 2000). This difficulty does not mean that people should abandon the attempt to engage in dialogue but they need to recognize the challenges and complexities associated with creating and sustaining genuine dialogue.

The importance of dialogue for people who are poor became particularly clear as our relationship developed with Elvira. During our time together at the vending cart, we noticed that Elvira never talked about any of her friends. One day, she disclosed that neither she nor her husband, Fred, lived geographically close to their families, and that her neighbors were not very friendly people. Elvira and Fred, consequently, kept to themselves, with no social life. Heather and Michael encouraged her and her husband to accompany us to the Friday night supper sponsored by Good Works at the Fellowship Hall of the Central Avenue Methodist Church. Elvira was a little hesitant to commit, but we told her how much fun she would have, and she said that they would be there that coming Friday.

The Friday night suppers at Good Works have been ongoing since 1992. The idea for this weekly event emerged when Keith Wasserman and others realized that they sometimes lost track of people who had participated in Good Works' programs (e.g., as workers, volunteers, or recipients). These suppers, consequently, have become a reunion of sorts, allowing some people to reconnect and sustain friendships, and others to meet for the first time. Starting from a basic idea with a simple beginning, the community suppers have become a central part of the Good Works organization that often attract as many as 150 people.

Heather, Wendy, and Michael waited outside the Central Avenue United Methodist Church Fellowship Hall to greet Elvira and Fred. They both looked somewhat apprehensive upon seeing how many people already were in the fellowship hall. We encouraged them to sit with us at a table where there were six or seven other local members of the Athens community. We all introduced ourselves and started to talk about our families, local issues, the weather, funny things that we had experienced, television shows, and other things. Elvira and Fred were slow to join in, but within 10 or 15 minutes, they were part of the conversations. Eventually, Elvira disclosed how isolated she felt and Fred agreed, saying, "Athens can be a pretty lonely place." A young married couple, recently residents of the Good Works homeless shelter, then started talking about how many friends they had made since coming to their first Friday night supper several months ago. They encouraged Elvira and Fred to come every week, and Elvira said she believed they would start making the supper a regular event.

The night ended a couple of hours later after Elvira and Fred stayed with Heather, Michael, and Wendy to put away the last of the tables and chairs. Fred went to get their car and we waited with Elvira until he pulled up to the curb. She hugged each of us and said she had not had that much fun in a long time. She also said, "I never saw Fred talk so much. Thank you for telling us about this." Unquestionably, the evening was a success.

As this incident shows, dialogue does not always need to be about deeply personal or complex issues or problems; sometimes, dialogue just connects people, especially those who are disconnected. Elvira and Fred felt isolated before coming to that Friday night supper, but they left realizing that they had made new friends. Our conversations that evening were genuine in that we all shared personal stories, listened to one another, and laughed often. By connecting with the people seated at our table through conversation, Elvira and Fred empowered themselves, and, in so doing, their oppressed lives of isolation faded as they established connections with others in the broader Athens community, which explains why they returned to these suppers many times over the next several months.

Communication and Social Justice

Although there are numerous ways to characterize *social justice*, Cohen (1991) may have described it most succinctly when he wrote that "justice is done when those who should have, do have; when each gets his or her due; when what people do have is appropriate to what they should have" (p. 240). Unquestionably, endless arguments may surround *which people should have what*; not open to question, however, is the fact that there are people who are denied social justice, particularly those who are poor and homeless.

To promote social justice, particular types of communication need to occur between those who are oppressed and those offering assistance. Specifically, members of each group need to reflect together on the symbiotic relationship that exists between "institutionally organized social inequality and institutionally organized social services mitigating inequality" (Artz, 2001, p. 241). Others argue that people must move beyond reflection to critique and action by "challenging the norms, practices, relations, and structures that underwrite inequality and injustice" (Frey, Pearce, Pollack, Artz, & Murphy, 1996, p. 110). More specifically, to work for social justice requires "engagement with and advocacy for those in our society who are economically, socially, politically, and/or culturally under-resourced" (Frey et al., 1996, p. 110). Indeed, this view of social justice is the ultimate goal of communication activism scholarship (see Carragee & Frey, this volume).

The creation of Good Gifts, with its philosophy of aiding people to aid themselves, meshes well with a social justice communication perspective. The traditional, institutionally organized social service programs, in which so many people who are poor are embedded, traps them into dependency relationships that deny them meaningful opportunities to empower themselves. Soup kitchens, food pantries, homeless shelters, donations of money and clothing from local community groups and churches, and state aid programs, for instance, are helpful in emergency situations or for solving problems in the short term, but because such programs typically are based on charity rather than justice (see, e.g., Artz, 2001; Britt, in press; Frey et al., 1996), those receiving assistance are not connected to others in ways that enable them to learn how to manage their problems. In contrast, Good Gifts provided people in the same situation as Elvira and Jim with opportunities to develop work habits and skills that aided them in becoming self-sufficient. Elvira, Jim, and others worked diligently and, consequently, received wages that they fully earned. Empowerment is experienced genuinely when people learn how to manage their problems through their efforts, albeit often with aid from others who share resources in the pursuit of social justice.

Central to the promotion of social justice, then, is linking together two groups of people: those who have access to resources with those who are oppressed and suffering. Social justice is not promoted, however, when people are linked in a relationship in which those who have resources extend charity to those who do not because charity will not lead to sustained social critique and action to change unjust systemic structures; in fact, charity often denies the possibility for such change by "implying that the poor or oppressed are less competent and less able than those who have more social, cultural, and economic capital" (Artz, 2001, p. 240). Rather than engage in charity, social justice is grounded in people working in solidarity with those who are disadvantaged by institutionalized practices and conditions to change those practices and conditions (Britt, in press; Fernandez & Tandon, 1981). When people with such different life experiences connect with one another on on equal ground (e.g., laboring together on work tasks), it gives all involved a unique vantage point from which to see others' perspectives and experiences (Crabtree, 1998). Finally, as Frey (1998) explained, social justice communication projects should have long-term sustainability, create opportunities for community members to empower themselves, and offer possibilities for learning broadly applicable communication skills.

There are multiple connections to be made between this view of social justice and our activism in the Good Gifts business. First, our activism connected people with resources (e.g., OU students and faculty, and middle- and upper class community members) with those who are oppressed (e.g., by poverty, unemployment, and homelessness). These connections were not without problems, as there were barriers to be overcome between people who had little previous contact with those who were different in social and economic status. When these barriers were overcome (and they almost always were) through people talking and working together, a productive and empowering learning environment was created for everyone. For example, when a trailer hitch became stuck, two OU college student volunteers and a college professor could not figure out how to disconnect it, but Jim, the newest Good Gifts employee, who lacked a high school diploma, easily disconnected the hitch and proudly showed how the same could be done when he was not there.

We also worked in solidarity with people who were disadvantaged by those systemic conditions. As described earlier, when Elvira and Jim started working for Good Gifts, we did everything together, from transporting the vending cart to and from the Good Works' property to performing economic transactions to closing up the cart. We were equals working together toward a common goal: keeping the business going so that people who were poor, unemployed, and homeless could acquire the work habits and job skills to sustain themselves in the future without charity or dependence on others.

Our commitment to social justice also was shown in our dedication, along with the many Good Works staff members and volunteers, to creating a long-term sustainable enterprise. Moreover, this commitment to equality resulted in the creation of a long-term enterprise.

Importantly, the opportunities that opened up for these formally unemployed Good Gifts workers largely were a product of newly learned and broadly applicable communication skills. We explained previously that we offered a brief training program that involved role-play activities to help Elvira and Jim feel comfortable talking with customers who approached the vending cart. Later, they participated in group brainstorming sessions to decide collaboratively about which new products to order. Wendy also worked with Elvira and Jim to build their confidence to give brief presentations at local churches to describe the purpose of Good Gifts and the business's product line. The communication skills learned by Elvira, Jim, and the many other Good Gifts workers may be applied to many types of jobs in the future. Of course, we also learned much from Elvira and Jim as well, especially verifying the importance of reaching out and sustaining connections with those who are oppressed, despite the challenges of doing so. As stated eloquently by Frey et al. (1996), social justice is "done when we realize that none of us is truly free while some of us are oppressed" (p. 112).

Feminist Perspectives on Organizing

Three primary themes characterize feminist organizing processes: cooperative enactment, integrative thinking, and connectedness (Buzzanell, 1994). *Cooperative enactment* emphasizes the importance of people working together to reach individual and collective goals rather than competing against one another. *Integrative thinking* centers on the importance of considering the broader context in evaluating organizational choices and actions. Although a given action (e.g., small business development) can bring about a specific intended effect (e.g., increased income for workers or owners), feminists think in an integrated way by considering how specific actions produce both direct and indirect effects. For instance, a woman may consider how a new form of behavior displayed in the workplace (e.g., assertiveness) will affect her relationship with her husband, in-laws, children, neighbors, and community members if she exhibits that same assertiveness with them. *Connectedness* refers to people uniting their rational minds, bodies, and emotions to make sense of the world. Specifically, connectedness explains how humans are holistic beings who are not limited to displays of rationality but have an emotional side as well. Feminists argue that people thrive in environments where they have opportunities to connect with and nurture others on the path to collective success. Connectedness is consistent with the feminist ethic of care; as Gilligan (1982) explained, women display caring behavior through sensitivity to others, self-sacrifice, and peacemaking, behaviors that reflect interpersonal involvement by showing how caring comes from connection, and vice versa (Young, 1994).

Cooperative enactment was at the core of the entire Good Gifts venture, with the business designed cooperatively from the ground up. Cooperation between and among the volunteers (students and community members), workers eventually hired, and Good Works staff and administrators was critical in creating and sustaining a supportive group learning environment, executing the day-to-day operations of the business, and in growing Good Gifts.

An interesting challenge to our philosophy of cooperative enactment surfaced one day in Wendy and Michael's Organizing for Social Change course. Jim, a rather rambunctious student, suggested that the different shifts of volunteers compete against one another to see who sells the most, and, somewhat reluctantly, we agreed to try that approach. The next day, we went to the vending cart and saw Jim walking quickly back and forth in front of the cart trying to hawk people down, speaking loudly to them and making quite the commotion. The two other student volunteers inside the cart looked somewhat embarrassed by Jim's actions. Although we noted that more than the usual number of people stopped by the cart that day, our sense of the need for cooperative enactment crystallized when we reflected on Jim's behavior, as we realized that when groups or individuals compete against one another, there are winners and losers, and those who are more successful may not share with those who are less successful reasons for their success, hurting the long-term goal of sustaining the enterprise. The next day in class, Wendy and Michael talked about the competition between student groups staffing the cart (without drawing attention to Jim's behaviors), and how cooperation among participants in the Good Gifts business would most support its success in the long term. A class discussion then ensued about the strengths and weaknesses of cooperation and competition in promoting group success, ending with a collective decision to discontinue the sales competition between student groups.

The experience of integrative thinking surfaced one day when Elvira shared that although she and her husband were happy with the direct impact of her full-time employment, as they had more money to buy food and pay bills, she worried that Fred was beginning to feel uncomfortable with his contribution to the family income because he worked only 20 hours a week at a local grocery store. Elvira's worries showed her recognition of the possible indirect effects of her new employment on her husband and, perhaps, their relationship, as he was beginning to feel inadequate as a provider. Heather used this disclosure as an opportunity to talk with Keith about the possibility of part-time employment for Fred. Although there were no opportunities available at that time at Good Gifts, Keith did need some additional help at the Hannah House property. Consequently, Elvira's integrative thinking helped to build her husband's confidence and strengthened their relationship as well. The day after Fred had worked his first day at Hannah House, Elvira excitedly explained to us that Fred "talked about everything he did and about how much responsibility he was given. He's so happy to be making extra money as well."

Connectedness was a central part of our experiences working for Good Gifts. The work required our minds to develop ideas to move the business forward, our bodies to perform the labor associated with specific tasks, and our emotions to be expressed when we connected with others who were suffering or when we reflected on what we had accomplished. Heather expressed connectedness well when she stated:

> It made me feel so good to be working for Good Gifts, to be part of getting it off the ground. I was so sad to leave. I just broke down at our last meeting. It was so hard for me to leave. I didn't think the place was going to fall apart without me but it was such a huge part of my life. I focused so intensely on making sure that everything went right every day, I felt a sense of loss to leave, but I'm really glad I was able to do this before I left. It made me feel good. (personal communication, February 7, 2000)

For Michael and Wendy, this connectedness was heightened when we opened a present that Heather gave for the 1999 Christmas holiday. We had had a particularly hectic quarter with teaching duties, writing projects, and committee memberships, in addition to all the hours volunteering at the vending cart, training volunteers, and meeting with SGG members. We were standing next to our Christmas tree when we opened the present: a small red plastic heart with the inscription, "Good Gifts 1999." Tears came to our eyes, we hugged, and placed the ornament on the tree. We, too, gave of our minds, bodies, and hearts. Every year since, when we place that ornament on the Christmas tree, the same warm feelings return.

Critical Pedagogy

Freire's (1970) book, *Pedagogy of the Oppressed*, guided the content of the training session required of all volunteers. Except where noted, Friere's ideas from the first chapter of his book were loosely paraphrased in the following handout given to all volunteers:

> True solidarity consists in fighting to destroy the causes that nourish false charity. "False charity constrains the fearful and subdues them to extend their trembling hands. True generosity lies in striving with people who are poor so their hands need to be extended less and less in supplication" [Freire, p. 43]. Helping people who are poor to develop fully human hands that can work has the potential to change the world. True solidarity with people who are poor means fighting at their side to transform the objective reality which has made them "the other" (somehow apart from us). We create a relationship of solidarity with people who are poor when we stop regarding them as an abstract category and see them as individual people who have very often been unfairly dealt with and deprived of their voice. We must risk an act of love.
>
> Too often people who are poor have been told that they are good for nothing, know nothing, and are incapable of learning anything. They are told that they are sick, and lazy, and unproductive. In the end, they become convinced of their own worthlessness. We must recognize that there is something that people who are poor have to give to us. They can teach us as much as we can teach them. The least among us has the capacity to give, learn, and educate.
>
> Political action on the side of people who are poor or oppressed must be pedagogical action in the authentic sense of the word, and therefore, action with the oppressed. To help people who are poor, we must look at them as partners with us in learning and teaching, recognizing that learning and teaching are mutual interacting processes.
>
> This experience is an important part of your education. You will learn from serving other people and, in doing so, become a more complete person. As volunteers you should take a genuine interest in your work partners. Inquire about their lives. Disclose about your own life as well. Gain wisdom through listening, recognizing that it's especially important to listen to those who have too often been voiceless and powerless.

After talking through the ideas on that handout, Wendy and Michael led a discussion with the volunteers about how these ideas were central to the founding principles of the Good Gifts project. By the end of that discussion, volunteers recognized fully that this business was not a charity in which they would lend a helping hand to others in need as they remained disconnected from those persons but, instead, would be working *with* partners who were poor. Volunteers also realized the importance of forming personal relationships with their partners, with students learning from their partners as much as (if not more than) they would teach them.

Social Learning Theory

Bandura's (1973, 1977, 1986) social learning theory also guided the volunteer training program. When we reached this segment of the training program, we explained to volunteers that Bandura argued that a person can learn new behavior from observing another person perform it. We then linked Bandura's insights to the behaviors of the volunteers when working with their partners. Specifically, we emphasized that because the work partners would be observing and trying to learn from them, they needed to engage in positive work behaviors. For example, we discussed the importance of modeling professional behavior, such as using appropriate language, staying on task, dressing properly, being polite, and engaging in friendly interaction with each other and with customers.

One of the most important aspects of behavior modeling was linked to how to talk to customers. As we observed earlier, many of the people in Athens who are poor felt uncomfortable talking to people from OU. We knew that this would be an issue before we hired the first partner and it almost always was the case. Consequently, volunteers modeling positive behaviors when interacting with customers was particularly important. Elvira, one of the first partners, gave us insight into her experiences observing volunteers interacting with customers, saying:

> The first day I knew I was going to talk to a customer, I watched Wendy real careful. She was really friendly and happy, and seemed so relaxed, not nervous. She talked about the shirt the women picked out and how that color would look pretty on her. I thought, "I can do that. It's just like talking to a friend when you're shopping." And then I did it and I felt so happy. (personal communication, April 3, 2000)

Elvira's observation shows how work partners can and did learn to communicate effectively with customers by observing volunteers. Of course, observations of behaviors and interactions that are not so positive also provide learning opportunities; consequently, we ended the discussion of social learning in the training program by focusing on negative behaviors, soliciting ideas from trainees about which behaviors they should not perform (e.g., using inappropriate language, communicating angrily, and being disrespectful).

Service-Learning

Service-learning has become an important feature of experiential learning and a significant part of this endeavor. The promises of service-learning for students, discussed below, are reflected in its abilities to promote integrated learning, high-quality service, collaboration, student voice, civic responsibility, and reflection. The pitfalls of service-learning in this project involved the amount of out-of-class time required of students, students not being able to see immediate impacts of the service, university calendar constraints on continuing service during periods when students are not enrolled in courses, and the potential risks involved in service-learning.

The promises of service learning. The analysis of the service-learning component of the Good Gifts business venture is based on Wilczenski and Coomey's (2007) framework that identified several essential components for high-quality service-learning experiences that are consistent with standards identified by the Alliance for Service-Learning in Education Reform (1995). These components include integrated learning, high-quality service, collaboration, student voice, civic responsibility, and reflection.

Integrated learning refers to the link between classroom learning goals and objectives and social, emotional, and academic goals of the service-learning experience (Wilczenski & Coomey, 2007). The focus on academic goals and objectives is what differentiates service-learning projects from volunteerism (Banks, Schneider, & Susman. 2005). In a well-designed service-learning experience, students relate desired educational outcomes to social issues and concerns (Eyler, Giles, Stenson, & Gray, 2001). Furthermore, such service-learning experiences include an understanding of the institutionalized practices that lead to social injustice and encourage students to search for solutions that promote justice and the liberation of people who are poor, marginalized, and disenfranchised (Artz, 2001). For example, students in the Organizing for Social Change course discussed how welfare programs provide economic relief from poverty without assisting participants to learn to become self-sufficient, and how soup kitchens often involve people who are poor being served meals by wealthier community members who do not interact with them in any other, more substantive, way.

The experience of infusing the Good Gifts program into the framework of the Organizing for Social Change course presents a clear example of integrated learning. The course provided students with opportunities to amalgamate the knowledge that they acquired through the traditional learning techniques of reading, lecture, and class discussion with the experiential learning they gained by working to promote social justice with and for members of their community who are poor. Throughout the semester, students were exposed to information pertaining to social change that cut across the academic disciplines of communication, community psychology, and sociology. For example, students read chapters in Rogers's (1995) book *Diffusion of Innovations*, to gain an interdisciplinary perspective on how change may be introduced through change agents. They also read work by M. J. Papa et al. (1995, 1997, 2000) to gain insight into how social change often activates a dialectical struggle between forces of stability that perpetuate the status quo and forces that promote social change. As students gained an understanding of important concepts and information through traditional teaching methods, they also were asked to consider how that knowledge related to their experiences of volunteering a minimum of 20 hours with the Good Gifts project. Students synthesized the course material and their volunteer experiences in a journal that described how the academic information related to their participation in the Good Gifts project. Integrating the service-learning component into this course, thus, moved students beyond an abstract knowledge of social change and development. By working with the Good Gifts project, and applying the academic material to their experiences, students identified cultural factors that contributed to oppression in their community. For example, students recognized that they establish friendships and join groups that are comprised exclusively of members of the same socioeconomic status. They also experienced the triumphs and frustrations that arise when efforts are made to promote social justice, as shown here.

High-quality service is evidenced when service-learning projects respond to recognized community needs and provide students with social and course-related benefits from the experience (Wilczenski & Coomey, 2007). According to Strand, Cutforth, Stoecker, Marullo, and Donohue (2003), ideal service-learning projects focus on community-identified needs and issues, and are culturally sensitive. Clearly, the Good Gifts experience provided students with opportunities to meet a need in Athens, Ohio, and to use their communication skills to develop and express a sense of civic responsibility. By staffing the vending cart, students applied communication concepts to daily interactions with customers, participated in solving problems, and better understood the plight of the those who are poor in their community. Furthermore, with their help, the vending cart became successful and created opportunities for the meaningful employment of many people who were poor.

Collaboration involves the solicitation of input from all partners involved in service-learning projects: students, teachers, academic administrators, organizational members, and service recipients (Wilczenski & Coomey, 2007). Gronski and Pigg (2000) defined collaboration as "an interactive process among individuals and organizations with diverse expertise and resources, joining together to devise and execute plans for common goals as well as to generate solutions for complex problems" (p. 783). Collaboration among students, faculty, Good Works administrators, city government officials, community members, and those who were poor clearly was evident. Michael and Wendy created the Good Gifts business in collaboration with Keith Wasserman, the founder and director of Good Works. Through negotiations with city officials, Michael, Wendy, and Heather secured the necessary licenses to operate the business. Heather and several other students collaborated by organizing shifts to staff the vending cart and by participating in the decisions made to improve the enterprise. Community members were involved as well; for instance, Ed Fisher provided the cart and, thereby, made the enterprise possible. Other community members responded to the survey questionnaire that identified which products should be ordered for the cart. Elvira, Jim, and others who later staffed the cart, worked closely with Michael, Wendy, Heather, and other students to sell the products to the community.

Voice requires students to participate actively in planning service-learning projects, implementing reflection sessions, and evaluating the programs (Wilczenski & Coomey, 2007). Students' voices are important because they claim ownership of projects when they assist in making difficult decisions. The more strongly students own a project, the more beneficial the outcomes for them (Morgan & Streb, 2003). Although the vending cart already was in operation by the time that most OU students got involved, many students exercised their voices and made valuable contributions. Heather, for instance, was involved in all aspects of the planning and implementing of the Good Gifts cart. Other students, through the creation of SGG, lobbied university administrators to allow Good Gifts products to be sold on the OU campus, staffed the cart, and offered suggestions that improved the overall experience. Finally, students enrolled in the Organizing for Social Change course staffed the cart, interacted with the public, and, during class discussions, offered suggestions for improvement of the business.

Civic responsibility occurs through service-learning as students develop more respectful attitudes toward members of diverse groups (Hoover & Webster, 2004; Yates & Youniss, 1996); understand, respect, and care for service recipients and their community (Terry & Bohnenberger, 2003); and learn that they can impact their community through their involvement (Wilczenski & Coomey, 2007). Civic responsibility involves students moving beyond a charity orientation by building authentic relationships with people lacking resources (Skilton-Sylvester & Erwin, 2000), engaging in dialogue with those who are oppressed (Artz, 2001), and adopting a concern for social justice (Artz, 2001; Eyler & Giles, 1999). By participating in the Good Gifts project, students worked alongside individuals who were poor, giving those students many opportunities to talk with those who were poor and marginalized, to better understood their plight and to see firsthand the impact that their efforts can have on a community.

Reflection differentiates an authentic service-learning experience from a course with a community-service component (McEachern, 2006). Through effective reflection, students link service-learning projects to the academic curricula (Heffernan, 2001; Wilczenski & Coomey, 2007), explore their thoughts and feelings about the activity (Heffernan, 2001), and develop a better understanding of how those who are disenfranchised are victimized by institutional systems that promote the status quo (Artz, 2001). In this service-learning endeavor, students were given ample time to reflect on their experience. Through classroom discussions, learning activities, and written assignments, students investigated their thoughts and feelings about working with those who are poor, the value of the roles they played in the project, and the importance of the desired outcomes; through reflection, students saw that they can make an important difference in people's lives and in their community.

The pitfalls of service-learning. Service-learning projects also have a set of potential problems. For instance, the amount of time that such projects require may be difficult to manage if students carry a full course load, hold down a job, and/or participate in extracurricular activities. This problem was noted to some degree in the Good Gifts project, as most of the students in the Organizing for Social Change course were seniors and were somewhat reluctant to participate in the service-learning project due to the difficulty of simultaneously managing their course load and a service-learning project, working at jobs that required too much time for involvement in the project, and spending their time preparing for interviews for jobs after graduation. These reasons/excuses were remarkable because by registering for the course, students acknowledged that they would be willing to become involved with Good Gifts.

Another problem involved students' desire to see an immediate impact resulting from the Good Gifts business. Community change, particularly when poor and marginalized populations are concerned, tends to take time to demonstrate significant results (Kubisch et al., 1997). Unfortunately, when their efforts failed to bring about immediate and positive social change, some students became bored and frustrated, and lost their motivation to participate. For example, when students were scheduled for shifts that were not linked to training and working with Elvira and Jim, they could not see the benefits of their service in working with people who were poor.

Additionally, service-learning projects tend to operate on university, rather than community, time frames (Scheibel, Bowley, & Jones, 2005; Wallace, 2000). Although it may not be difficult to find students to participate in service-learning projects when school is in session, they are difficult to find when courses end, during holiday breaks, or during summer. When the fall quarter at OU ended, the Good Gifts cart lost most of its student volunteers. To keep the business running during the busy Christmas shopping season, Michael, Wendy, and the few remaining volunteers worked hard to staff the cart, and when the weather became too cold, the operation was moved into the Athens Mall. Those efforts resulted in several thousand dollars in merchandise being sold, ensuring the success of the venture.

Finally, the possible risks of participating in service-learning projects must be examined. The goal of risk management is to identify possible threats to students and the recipients of their service (Wilczenski & Coomey, 2007). To avoid liability, risk management must be considered before beginning any service-learning project (Seidman & Tremper, 1994; Wright, 2003). Although running a vending cart in Athens, Ohio was not considered to be a particularly risky venture, there was an instance where a student worker became engaged in a shouting match with a pedestrian who thought that the student was paying too much attention to his appearance (wearing makeup and a dress) as he passed by the cart. Although the problem was resolved without police intervention, such unexpected events may occur when dealing with the public.

LESSONS LEARNED ABOUT COMMUNICATION ACTIVISM IN SMALL BUSINESS DEVELOPMENT FOR PEOPLE WHO ARE POOR

The first lesson learned in this communication activism effort is the significant commitment of time and energy required to work on a project of this magnitude. Michael and Wendy each logged hundreds of hours in moving the Good Gifts idea in winter 1999 to a business capable of paying those who were poor and unemployed in spring 2000. The efforts expended were unquestionably worthwhile, as something of significance was accomplished in aligning ourselves with, and aiding, members of this oppressed group to learn to help themselves. Essentially, we learned that Freire's (1970) ideas work in action on the ground when people act side by side with those who are oppressed rather than offer charity.

The second lesson we learned is the remarkable power of connecting people who had not interacted previously. When we connected people who were poor, such as Elvira and her husband Fred, to others who were poor and to wealthier members of the Athens community, their social isolation ended. When we connected students and wealthier community members to people who were poor who were participating in the Good Works and Good Gifts programs, their lives were enriched in ways they may never have thought possible. These connections were central to the promotion of social justice, in that wealthier community members learned to work in solidarity with those who were disadvantaged, and people who were poor learned that they had things in common with wealthier neighbors. Importantly, all groups learned from one another because they worked equally hard toward a common goal.

The third lesson we learned is that the process of organizing for social change demands connections between people who are radically different from one another. People who are poor and those with resources often differ in access to and quality of education; those living in poverty often wonder where their next meal will come from, with survival being a day-to-day reality, whereas people with resources are able to plan for the future; health outcomes are more negative for people living in poverty; and people with resources often are embedded in many communication networks, whereas people living in poverty often experience a life of isolation. These differences are real and can pose significant barriers to people connecting with one another, but as this organizing for social change initiative shows, these barriers can be overcome, and when they are, people who are poor learn and accumulate experiences that can lead to their economic and social development.

The final lesson we learned is that there always is resistance to any communication activism effort. Small town politics expressed in the determination of the Athens Code Enforcement Officers to intimidate OU students working the vending cart almost shut it down that day. Heather's resistance to the officers' intimidation attempts shows what a supposedly weaker person can do to counteract ostensibly more powerful persons. We also experienced the challenges of working with students who did not share our commitment to make the Good Gifts business successful. We discovered that there is no such thing as a reluctant activist; a person either gives his or her body, heart, and mind to a project that is greater than that person, or else he or she steps aside to allow someone with such commitment to take his or her place.

CONCLUSION

This chapter described a communication activism endeavor in which a small business was created to provide a living wage and job training for people who are poor in Athens, Ohio, a community in Appalachia. To become viable, this business required the joint efforts of Ohio University students and faculty members, and workers and administrators of Good Works, a local social services organization that assists rural people suffering from poverty and homelessness. Starting as a simple vending cart business in 1999, the Good Gifts business has provided job-training experiences to 35 people over the past 12 years. This is just one small business, however, and millions remain poor in the United States. Given that poverty continues to be a significant problem in this country, and, of course, many others, there is a compelling need for many endeavors of this type, as well as governmental programs to provide people who are poor with the skills and experiences necessary to secure gainful employment. Perhaps the most important lesson learned from this communication activism endeavor is that people with and without resources can work together to spark economic and social development, and, in the process, learn from and about one another.

NOTES

1. The term "people who are poor" is used purposefully rather than the "disability-first" term "poor people."
2. Buerkel wrote the service-learning section of the chapter.

REFERENCES

Alliance for Service-Learning in Education Reform. (1995, March). *Standards of quality for school-based and community-based service-learning*. Alexandria, VA: Author. Retrieved from http://www.servicelearning.org/filemanager/download/12/asler95.pdf

Alvesson, M., & Willmott, H. (1992). On the idea of emancipation in management and organization studies. *Academy of Management Review, 17*, 432–464. doi:10.2307/258718

Artz, L. (2001). Critical ethnography for communication studies: Dialogue and social justice in service-learning. *Southern Communication Journal, 66*, 239–250. doi:10.1080/104517940109373202

Asen, R. (2001). Nixon's welfare reform: Enacting historical contradictions of poverty discourses. *Rhetoric & Public Affairs, 4*, 261–279. doi: 10.1353/rap.2001.0019

Asen, R. (2003). Women, work, welfare: A rhetorical history of images of poor women in welfare policy debates. *Rhetoric & Public Affairs, 6*, 285–312. doi: 10.1353/rap.2003.0041

Athens County Department of Job and Family Services. (2006, November). *An in-depth look at the issues of poverty*. Athens, OH: Author. Retrieved from http://jfs.athenscountygovernment.com/gfx/media/PovertyReport.2006.pdf

Auwal, M. A. (1996). Promoting microcapitalism in the service of the poor: The Grameen model and its cross-cultural adaptation. *Journal of Business Communication, 33*, 27–49. doi:10.1177/002194369603300105

Bandura, A. (1973). *Aggression: A social learning analysis*. Englewood Cliffs, NJ: Prentice-Hall.

Bandura, A. (1977). *Social learning theory*. Englewood Cliffs, NJ: Prentice-Hall.

Bandura, A. (1986). *Social foundation of thought and action: A social cognitive theory*. Englewood Cliffs, NJ: Prentice-Hall.

Banks, N., Schneider, G., & Susman, P. (2005). Paying the bills is not just theory: Service learning about a living wage. *Review of Radical Political Economics, 37,* 346–356. doi:10.1177/0486613405279034

Bell, E., & Forbes, L. C. (1994). Office folklore in the academic paperwork empire: The interstitial space of gendered (con)texts. *Text and Performance Quarterly, 14,* 181–196. doi:10.1080/10462939409366082

Blau, J. R., & Alba, R. D. (1982). Empowering nets of participation. *Administrative Science Quarterly, 27,* 363–379. doi:10.2307/239317

Britt, L. L. (in press). Service-learning in the service of social justice: Situating communication activism pedagogy within a typology of service-learning approaches. In L. R. Frey & D. L. Palmer (Eds.), *Communication activism pedagogy.* Cresskill, NJ: Hampton Press.

Buzzanell, P. M. (1994). Gaining a voice: Feminist organizational communication theorizing. *Management Communication Quarterly, 7,* 339–383. doi:10.1177/0893318994007004001

Carcasson, M. (2006). Ending welfare as we know it: President Clinton and the rhetorical transformation of the anti-welfare culture. *Rhetoric & Public Affairs, 9,* 655–692. Retrieved from http://muse.jhu.edu/journals/rhetoric_and_public_affairs

Clawson, R. A., & Kegler, E. R. (2000). The "race coding" of poverty in American government college textbooks. *Howard Journal of Communications, 11,* 179–188. doi:10.1080/10646170050086312

Clawson, R. A., & Trice, R. (2000). Poverty as we know it: Media portrayals of the poor. *Public Opinion Quarterly, 64,* 53–64. doi:10.1086/316759

Cohen, R. L. (1991). Membership, intergroup relations, and justice. In R. Vermunt & R. Steensma (Eds.), *Social justice in human relations: Vol. 1. Sociological and psychological origins of justice* (pp. 239–258). New York, NY: Plenum Press.

Conger, J. A. (1989). Leadership: The art of empowering others. *Academy of Management Executive, 3,* 17–24. doi:10.5465/AME.1989.4277145

Conger, J. A., & Kanugo, R. N. (1988). The empowerment process: Integrating theory and practice. *Academy of Management Review, 13,* 471–482. doi:10.2307/258093

Crabtree, R. D. (1998). Mutual empowerment in cross-cultural participatory development and service learning: Lessons in communication and social justice from projects in El Salvador and Nicaragua. *Journal of Applied Communication Research, 26,* 182–209. doi:10.1080/0090988980936501

Daniel, J. (1970). The poor: Aliens in an affluent society: Cross-cultural communication. *Today's Speech, 18,* 15–21. doi:10.1080/01463377009368921

de Certeau, M. (1984). *The practice of everyday life* (S. Rendall, Trans.). Berkeley: University of California Press.

de Goede, M. (1996). Ideology in the US welfare debate: Neo-liberal representations of poverty. *Discourse & Society, 7,* 317–357. doi:10.1177/0957926596007003003

DeNavas-Walt, C., Proctor, B. D., & Smith, J. C. (2010, September). *Income, poverty, and health insurance coverage in the United States: 2009.* Washington, DC: U.S. Government Printing Office. Retrieved from http://www.census.gov/prod/2010pubs/p60-238.pdf

Eisenberg, E. M. (1994). Dialogue as democratic discourse: Affirming Harrison. In S. A. Deetz (Ed.), *Communication yearbook* (Vol. 17, pp. 275–284). Thousand Oaks, CA: Sage.

Eyler, J., & Giles, D. E., Jr. (1999). *Where's the learning in service-learning?* San Francisco, CA: Jossey-Bass.
Eyler, J. S., Giles, D. E., Jr., Stenson, C. M., & Gray, C. J. (2001, August 31). *At a glance: What we know about the effects of service-learning on college students, faculty, institutions and communities, 1993–2000* (3rd ed.). Nashville, TN: Vanderbilt University. Retrieved from http://servicelearning.org/filemanager/download/aag.pdf
Fernandez, W., & Tandon, R. (Eds.). (1981). *Participatory research and evaluation: Experiments in research as a process of liberation.* New Delhi: Indian Social Institute.
Forester, J. (1989). *Planning in the face of power.* Berkeley: University of California Press.
Freire, P. (1970). *Pedagogy of the oppressed* (M. R. Ramos, Trans). New York, NY: Herder & Herder.
Frey, L. R. (1998). Communication and social justice research: Truth, justice, and the applied communication way. *Journal of Applied Communication Research, 26,* 155–164. doi:10.1080/00909889809365499
Frey, L. R., & Carragee, K. M. (2007). Introduction: Communication activism as engaged scholarship. In L. R. Frey & K. M. Carragee (Eds.), *Communication activism* (2 Vols. pp. 1–64). Cresskill, NJ: Hampton Press.
Frey, L. R., Pearce, W. B., Pollack, M. A., Artz, L., & Murphy, B. A. O. (1996). Looking for justice in all the wrong places: On a communication approach to social justice. *Communication Studies, 47,* 110–127. doi:10.1080/10510979609368467
Gilens, M. (1996). Race and poverty in America: Public misperceptions and the American news media. *Public Opinion Quarterly, 60,* 515–541. doi: 10.1086/297771
Gilligan, C. (1982). *In a different voice: Psychological theory and women's development.* Cambridge, MA: Harvard University Press.
Gould, C., Stern, D. C., & Adams, T. D. (1981). TV's distorted vision of poverty. *Communication Quarterly, 29,* 309–314. doi:10.1080/01463378109369420
Gring-Pemble, L. M. (2003). Legislating a "normal, classic family": The rhetorical construction of families in American welfare policy. *Political Communication, 20,* 473–498. doi:10.1080/10584600390244202
Gronemeyer, M. (1993). Helping. In W. Sachs (Ed.), *The development dictionary: A guide to knowledge as power* (pp. 53–69). Atlantic Heights, NJ: Zed Books.
Gronski, R., & Pigg, K. (2000). University and community collaboration: Experiential learning in human services. *American Behavioral Scientist, 43,* 781–792. doi:10.1177/00027640021955595
Guralink, D. B. (Ed.). (2008). *Webster's new world dictionary of the American language* (2nd ed.). Cleveland, OH: Prentice Hall Press.
Habermas, J. (1984). *Theory of communicative action* (T. McCarthy, Trans.). Boston, MA: Beacon Press.
Harter, L. M., Berquist, C., Titsworth, B. S., Novak, D., & Brokaw, T. (2005). The structuring of invisibility among the hidden homeless: The politics of space, stigma, and identity construction. *Journal of Applied Communication Research, 33,* 305–327. doi:10.1080/00909880500278079

Harter, L. M., Edwards, A., McClanahan, A., Hopson, M. C., & Carson-Stern, E. (2004). Organizing for survival and social change: The case of StreetWise. *Communication Studies, 55*, 407–424. doi:10/1080/10510970409388627

Heffernan, K. (2001). *Fundamentals of service-learning course construction*. Boston, MA: Campus Compact.

Hindman, E. B. (1998). "Spectacles of the poor": Conventions of alternative news. *Journalism & Mass Communication Quarterly, 75*, 177–193.

Hoover, T. S., & Webster, N. (2004). Modeling service learning for future leaders of youth organizations. *Journal of Leadership Education, 3*(3), 58–62. Retrieved from http://www.fhsu.edu/jole

Howley, K. (2003). A poverty of voices: Street papers as communicative democracy. *Journalism, 4*, 273–292. doi:10.1177/14648849030043002

Jenkins, H., III. (1988). *Star Trek* rerun, reread, rewritten: Fan writing as textual poaching. *Critical Studies in Mass Communication, 5*, 85–107. doi:10.1080/15295038809366691

Jeppesen, S. (2009). From the "war on poverty" to the "war on the poor": Knowledge, power, and subject positions in anti-poverty discourses. *Canadian Journal of Communication, 34*, 487–508. Retrieved from http://www.cjc-online.ca/index.php/journal

Jermier, J. M., Knights, D., & Nord, W. R. (Eds.). (1994). *Resistance and power in organizations*. New York, NY: Routledge.

Kingfisher, C. P. (1996). Women on welfare: Conversational sites of acquiescence and dissent. *Discourse & Society, 7*, 531–557. doi:10.1177/0957926596007004005

Knights, D., & Vurdubakis, T. (1994). Foucault, power, resistance and all that. In J. M. Jermier, D. Knights, & W. R. Nord (Eds.), *Resistance and power in organizations* (pp. 167–198). New York, NY: Routledge.

Kubisch, A. C., Brown, P., Chaskin, R., Hirota, J., Joseph, M., Richman, H., & Roberts, M. (1997). *Voices from the field: Learning from the early work of comprehensive community initiatives*. Washington, DC: Aspen Institute.

Marston, G. (2008). A war on the poor: Constructing welfare and work in the twenty-first century. *Critical Discourse Studies, 5*, 359–370. doi:10.1080/17405900802405312

McEachern, R. W. (2006). Incorporating reflection into business communication service-learning courses. *Business Communication Quarterly, 69*, 312–316. doi:10.1177/108056990606900309

Morgan, W., & Streb, M. J. (2003). First, do no harm: Student ownership and service-learning. *Metropolitan Universities, 14*(3), 36–52.

Mumby, D. K. (1997). The problem of hegemony: Rereading Gramsci for organizational communication studies. *Western Journal of Communication, 61*, 343–375. doi:10.1080/10570319709374585

Niederkohr, T. (1999, September 30). "Good" gifts by students. *The Post*. Retrieved from http://www.thepost.ohiou.edu

Nielsen, G. M. (2008). Conditional hospitality: Framing dialogue on poverty in Montréal newspapers. *Canadian Journal of Communication, 33*, 605–619. Retrieved from http://www.cjc-online.ca

Novak, D. R., & Harter, L. M. (2008). "Flipping the scripts" of poverty and panhandling: Organizing democracy by creating connections. *Journal of Applied Communication Research, 36*, 391–414. doi:10.1080/00909880802104890

Ohio Department of Health. (2003). *Leading causes of death: Number and average annual death rate per 100,000, Ohio and counties, 1992* [Table]. Columbus, OH: Author. Retrieved from http://www.odh.ohio.gov/ASSETS/C53E260C39A049 CCA5E9F1579D57EA14/dth1992.pdf

Ontario Coalition Against Poverty. (2007, September 17). *OCAP challenge to Toronto community housing is growing.* Retrieved from http://update.ocap.ca/node/479

Pacanowsky, M. (1988). Communication in the empowering organization. In J. A. Anderson (Ed.), *Communication yearbook* (Vol. 11, pp. 356–379). Newbury Park, CA: Sage.

Papa, M. J., Auwal, M. A., & Singhal, A. (1995). Dialectic of emancipation and control in organizing for social change: A multitheoretic study of the Grameen Bank in Bangladesh. *Communication Theory, 5*, 189–223. doi:10.1111/j.1468-2885.1995.tb00106.x

Papa, M. J., Auwal, M. A., & Singhal, A. (1997). Organizing for social change within concertive control systems: Member identification, empowerment, and the masking of discipline. *Communication Monographs, 64*, 219–249. doi:10.1080/03637759709376418

Papa, M. J., Singhal, A., Ghanekar, D., & Papa, W. H. (2000). Organizing for social change through cooperative action: The [dis]empowering dimensions of women's communication. *Communication Theory, 10*, 90–123. doi:10.1111/j.1468-2885.2000.tb00181.x

Papa, M. J., Singhal, A., & Papa, W. H. (2006). *Organizing for social change: A dialectic journey of theory and praxis.* Thousand Oaks, CA: Sage.

Papa, W. H., Papa, M. J., Kandath, K. P., Worrell, T., & Muthuswamy, N. (2005). Dialectic of unity and fragmentation in feeding the homeless: Promoting social justice through communication. *Atlantic Journal of Communication, 13*, 242–271. doi:10.1207/s15456889ajc1304_3

Rogers, E. M. (1995). *Diffusion of innovations.* New York, NY: Free Press.

Risopatron, F., & Spain, P. L. (1980). Reaching the poor: Human sexuality education in Costa Rica. *Journal of Communication, 30*(4), 81–89. doi:10.1111/j.1460-2466.1980.tb02019.x

Scheibel, J., Bowley, E., & Jones, S. (2005). *The promise of partnerships: Tapping into the college as a community asset.* Boston, MA: Campus Compact.

Schmitz, J., Rogers, E. M., Phillips, K., & Paschal, D. (1995). The public electronic network (PEN) and the homeless in Santa Monica. *Journal of Applied Communication Research, 23*, 26–43. doi:10.1080/00909889509365412

Seidman, A., & Tremper, C. (1994). *Legal issues for service-learning programs.* Washington, DC: Nonprofit Risk Management Center.

Shehabuddin, R. (1992). *Empowering rural women: The impact of Grameen Bank in Bangladesh.* Dhaka, Bangladesh: Grameen Bank.

Shen, F., & Edwards, H. H. (2005). Economic individualism, humanitarianism, and welfare reform: A value-based account of framing effects. *Journal of Communication, 55*, 795–809. doi:10.1111/j.1460-2466.2005.tb03023.x

Shoshani, O. (2005, August 4). *Poverty in America: Over 35 million living below the poverty line.* Retrieved from http://ezinearticles.com/?Poverty-in-America:-Over-35-Million-Living-Below-the-Poverty-Line&id=56904

Singhal, A., & Rogers, E. M. (2003). *Combating AIDS: Communication strategies in action*. Thousand Oaks, CA: Sage.

Skilton-Sylvester, E., & Erwin, E. K. (2000). Creating reciprocal learning relationships across socially-constructed borders. *Michigan Journal of Community Service Learning, 7*, 65–75. Retrieved from http://www.umich.edu/~mjcsl

Sotirovic, M. (2000). Effects of media use on audience framing and support for welfare. *Mass Communication and Society, 3*, 269–296. doi:10.1207/s15327825mcs0323_06

Sotirovic, M. (2001). Media use and perceptions of welfare. *Journal of Communication, 51*, 750–774. doi:10.1111/j.1460-2466.2001.tb02905.x

Stephens, L. F. (1972). Media exposure and modernization among the Appalachian poor. *Journalism Quarterly, 49*, 247–257.

Strand, K. J., Cutforth, N., Stoecker, R., Marullo, S., & Donohue, P. (2003). *Community-based research and higher education: Principles and practices*. San Francisco, CA: Jossey-Bass.

Terry, A. W., & Bohnenberger, J. E. (2003). Service learning: Fostering a cycle of caring in our gifted youth. *Journal of Secondary Gifted Education, 15*, 23–32. doi:10.4219/jsge-2003-437

Trethewey, A. (1997). Resistance, identity, and empowerment: A postmodern feminist analysis of clients in a human service organization. *Communication Monographs, 64*, 281–301. doi:10.1080/03637759709376425

Vogt, J. F., & Murrell, K. L. (1990). *Empowerment in organizations: How to spark exceptional performance*. San Diego, CA: University Associates.

Waldron, V. R., & Lavitt, M. R. (2000). "Welfare-to-work": Assessing communication competencies and client outcomes in a job training program. *Southern Communication Journal, 66*, 1–15. doi:10.1080/10417940009373182

Waldron, V. R., Lavitt, M., & McConnaughy, M. (2001). "Welfare-to-work": An analysis of the communication competencies taught in a job training program serving an urban poverty area. *Communication Education, 50*, 15–33. doi:10.1080/03634520109379229

Wallace, J. (2000). The problem of time: Enabling students to make long-term commitments to community-based learning. *Michigan Journal of Community Service Learning, 7*, 133–141. Retrieved from http://www.umich.edu/~mjcsl

Wilczenski, F. L., & Coomey, S. M. (2007). *A practical guide to service learning: Strategies for positive development in schools*. New York, NY: Springer.

World Bank. (2011). *Gross domestic product 2010* [Table]. Retrieved from http://siteresources.worldbank.org/DATASTATISTICS/Resources/GDP.pdf

Wright, J. (2003). *Administrator's guide to service learning*. Clemson, SC: National Dropout Prevention Center, Clemson University.

Yates, M., & Youniss, J. (1996). A developmental perspective on community service in adolescence. *Social Development, 5*, 85–111. doi:10.1111/j.1467-9507.1996.tb00073.x

Young, I. M. (1994). Punishment, treatment, empowerment: Three approaches to policy for pregnant addicts. *Feminist Studies, 20*, 33–57. doi:10.2307/3178429

Zoller, H. M. (2000). "A place you haven't visited before": Creating the conditions for community dialogue. *Southern Communication Journal, 65*, 191–207. doi:10.1080/10417940009373167

10

USING PARTICIPATORY RESEARCH TO ADDRESS SUBSTANCE ABUSE IN AN AMERICAN-INDIAN COMMUNITY

Lorenda Belone
University of New Mexico
John G. Oetzel
University of Waikato
Nina Wallerstein
Greg Tafoya
Rebecca Rae
University of New Mexico

Alvin Rafelito
Ira Burbank
Jennifer Henio-Charley
Yin-Mae Lee

Lula Kelhoyouma
Carolyn Finster
Phoebe G. Maria
Anderson Thomas

Ramah Navajo Advisory Council

Both the United States, in general, and New Mexico, in particular, present a picture of great disparities regarding alcohol-related (and other substance use) problems, with American Indians[1] suffering disproportionately from alcohol, illegal substance use, and suicide when compared to other ethnic groups (New Mexico Department of Health, 2009; Szlemko, Wood, & Thurman, 2006). The U.S. Department of Health and Human Services' (DHSS, n.d.-b) Indian Health Service (IHS), the federal health program for American Indians and Alaska Natives, estimated that, for the years 2000–2001, alcohol-related mortality for American Indians, compared with the general population, was eight times greater for those between the ages of 25 and 34, and 6.5 times greater for ages 35 to 44. Four of the 10 leading causes of death for American Indians at that time were alcohol-related chronic liver disease and cirrhosis (e.g., four times higher than the general population), homicide, and other injuries (DHSS, n.d.-b). In New Mexico, alcohol-related mortality affects American Indians disproportionately compared with non-Hispanic whites (96.1/100,000 vs. 41.5/100,000 for 2006–2008; New Mexico Department of Health, 2009). Overall in New Mexico, age-adjusted mortality rates for American-Indian males and females exceed those for non-Hispanic whites (DHSS, n.d.-b).

Research on early substance-use onset shows that American-Indian children begin using alcohol and other recreational drugs earlier than any other ethnic group (Beauvais, 1996; New Mexico Department of Health, Community Health Assessment Program, Epidemiology and Response Division, 2005). Early use of such drugs has been correlated with engaging in a number of high-risk behaviors, including driving under the influence, unprotected sexual activity, depression, delinquency, and suicide; disproportionately high mortality rates; and greater likelihood of using those drugs later in life (Hawkins, Cummins, & Marlatt, 2004). According to the IHS (as cited by Hawkins et al., 2004), 3 of the top-10 leading causes of death among American-Indian adolescents (accidents, suicide, and homicide) are associated with alcohol.

At the same time, there are a number of protective factors for health in American-Indian communities, such as strong community and cultural identities, strong families, and social capital (E. Duran & Duran, 1995; Wallerstein & Duran, 2006). These protective factors provided the basis for our communication and public health intervention project to prevent early onset of drinking alcohol in late elementary school and early adolescent youth that was implemented in the Ramah Navajo community in New Mexico. The project was a collaboration between Ramah Navajo community members and researchers from the University of New Mexico (UNM)[2] that was developed at the behest of the community to address this key health problem. In this chapter, we first describe some explanatory factors of substance abuse for American Indians, then discuss the nature of this communication activism intervention, provide an analysis of the partnership processes and some preliminary pilot outcomes, and conclude by discussing lessons learned about communication activism scholarship.

EXPLANATORY FACTORS OF SUBSTANCE ABUSE FOR AMERICAN INDIANS

Researchers have identified a number of explanatory factors of substance abuse for American Indians. In addition to poverty and discrimination, the role of culture, in general, and cultural conflict, in particular, are persistent themes in studies of the development of American-Indian children and adolescents. *Cultural conflict* refers to challenges that American Indians face interacting with mainstream U.S. Americans, as well as to internal struggles among American Indians as a result of external contact with others. Cultural conflict has been used to explain American-Indian academic problems, such as school dropout and low achievement (Bakes, 1993; Bowker, 1992), suicide (Bechtold, 1994; Lin, 1987), and substance abuse (Oetting & Beauvais, 1991; O'Nell & Mitchell, 1996). Most of those studies, however, are based on small samples and are exploratory in nature; systematic studies based on larger samples have yet to establish clear, replicable support for the influence of cultural conflict on these problems for American Indians (Oetting & Beauvais, 1991; Oetting, Edwards, & Beauvais, 1989).

Traditional norms within American-Indian communities surrounding proper childrearing also may complicate the role of culture in child development. Although varying by nation, parenting norms of noninterference and early independence of children (Ishisaka, 1978), laissez-faire childrearing practices (e.g., letting children learn from experience), and a lack of family sanctions for substance abuse (Oetting, Beauvais, & Edwards, 1988) may not curb early experimentation with alcohol and other recreational drugs in time, meaning that any lessons learned about those drugs may come too late (i.e., due to addiction to those drugs or because negative consequences have occurred). Some of these problematic parenting practices were a result of the boarding school catastrophes of the past 2 centuries, with American-Indian children who were taken away from their culture and families not learning to parent properly, and subsequent generations suffering for this loss (Whitbeck, Hoyt, McMorris, Chen, & Stubben, 2001).[3]

Although there are indications that cultural conflict plays a role in early onset of alcohol and other recreational drug use, there also is evidence that *cultural identification*, the strength of identity that a person has with his or her cultural group (Walters & Simoni, 2002; Whitbeck, Hoyt, McMorris, et al., 2001), may act as a buffer for health outcomes. Studies indicate that the effects of alcohol largely are indirect, with adolescents' cultural identification increasing their self-esteem, but not being directly related to their problem behaviors. Further cultural identification effects may be indirect through influences on prosocial behaviors (e.g., helping others), parenting (e.g., increasing parental warmth and supportiveness), and academic success

(Whitbeck, Hoyt, McMorris, et al., 2001; Whitbeck, Hoyt, Stubben, & LaFromboise, 2001).

COMMUNICATION ACTIVISM TO ADDRESS SUBSTANCE ABUSE PROBLEMS: FOUNDATIONAL PROGRAM

Although certainly understudied, communication researchers have examined a variety of communication/rhetorical patterns in American-Indian communities (e.g., Black, 2007; Bolls, Tan, & Austin, 1997; Bresnahan & Flowers, 2008; Carbaugh, 1999; Covarrubias, 2007; Cowden, 2008; Merskin, 1998; Morris & Wander, 1990; Rogers, 2009; Sunwolf, 1999). These studies identify American-Indian cultural communication patterns, often juxtaposed with those of the dominant culture and placed in a context of a lack of privilege and discriminatory practices. For example, Covarrubias (2007) interviewed American-Indian college students to examine mismatches between the communication style of those students and mainstream university education. The findings showed that although American-Indian college students preferred using silence in strategic and culturally supportive ways, compared with talking, to learn, that strategy did not serve them well in the university classroom, and that it was one of the reasons American-Indian students felt disconnected from the university.

Such research helps to understand how communication plays a role in creating culture and in contributing to negative social consequences, such as a lack of school achievement, but there are only a few studies of American-Indian communities and health outcomes, let alone substance use. A study conducted by Kalbfleisch (2009) identified strategies (e.g., providing information indirectly through storytelling and using examples) for effective communication with American Indians by health-care providers. Additionally, Oetzel, Duran, Jiang, and Lucero (2007), examining the relationship between social support and social undermining (negative communication) for mental health disorders in American-Indian women presenting for primary care, found that social undermining, in comparison with social support, within participants' social networks had a stronger impact on alcohol and recreational drug use, and mental disorders in this population.

In addition to the limited examination of communication and health outcomes in American-Indian communities, such research has been conducted from a third-person perspective (see Carragee & Frey, this volume; Frey & Carragee, 2007). In contrast, this study uses a first-person perspective to examine an intervention that was created in collaboration by the researchers and members of an American-Indian community (Ramah

Navajo) who had an active role in addressing a social problem that was important to them. The result was a culturally supported intervention (CSI) that is an example of communication activism scholarship.

CSIs represent a stream of research-based programs that, historically, have been conducted to address alcohol problems in tribal communities (B. Duran, Wallerstein, & Miller, 2008; Hall, 2001). In general, among tribal populations, CSIs often rely on spiritual–religious practices that are deeply embedded in the culture and may be readily adopted by members of tribal communities, although CSIs have not been well documented or evaluated (Miller & Meyers, 1999). Additionally, CSIs often integrate culturally supported indigenous theories on alcohol use that have emanated from community and tribal social service agencies in the field; these theories, and corresponding interventions, have been widely circulated at regional and national American-Indian conferences, and at other meetings. Despite their strengths within American-Indian communities, these theories and interventions have not been fully tested, especially with American-Indian children or youth, as contributing to a reduction in substance abuse and care of mental disorders.

An assumption of these indigenous approaches is that age-specific behavioral expectations and sanctions against deviant behavior (e.g., alcohol and other recreational drug use) have been weakened due to the dominance of external societal demands, discriminatory practices against American Indians, and the disruption of cross-generational teachings on traditional values and behavior (B. Duran, Duran, & Brave Heart, 1998; E. Duran & Duran, 1995). Additionally, some mainstream alcohol and other recreational drug-prevention approaches may be complicated by values embedded in American-Indian cultures; for example, individual refusal skills found in mainstream approaches may conflict with the high value placed in tribal cultures of fitting into one's peer group and not standing out (for an overview of a drug-resistance strategy project that takes into account the effects of culture and ethnicity, see Hecht & Miller-Day, 2009).

The public health and communication intervention implemented in the Ramah Navajo community was based on an empirically supported project, called "Bii-Zin-Da-De-Dah" (Listening to Each Other), which has been culturally embedded within the Anishinabe of Minnesota (Whitbeck, Hoyt, McMorris, et al., 2001; Whitbeck, Hoyt, Stubben, et al., 2001). Bii-Zin-Da-De-Dah is a psycho–cultural–educational intervention that seeks to reduce alcohol and other recreational drug problems through combining culturally supported approaches (e.g., cultural transmission, work with families and elders, and cultural sanctions for substance abuse) with dominant-culture, adolescent-oriented empirically supported interventions (ESIs; such as developing parenting skills and adolescents' communication refusal skills, and providing academic support to adolescents). Central to the notion of cultural adaptation of ESIs is that proven efficacious mainstream components are maintained, but additionally, consideration is given to specific cultural risk factors (e.g., discrimination and historical trauma) and cultural protective factors (e.g., enhancing cultural identification). Results from the Bii-Zin-Da-De-Dah prevention trial (a pretest–posttest design) suggested that the strongest effects were for program components that had extensive cultural adaptations; specifically, the sessions on family strengths, cultural values, traditional communicative practices, and traditional help-seeking practices (Whitbeck, 2001). Other sessions where the cultural context was less developed (e.g., managing anger and solving problems) showed less change in posttest results.

The results for the Bii-Zin-Da-De-Dah program showed significant effects for younger children (ages 10 and 11) who had not begun drinking (Whitbeck, 2001). Both boys and girls who were not drinking prior to participating in the prevention program had significantly lower levels of drinking onset 1 year after the program than did the same-aged children in the control group (who received no intervention). Specifically, among the 10-year-old boys, only 5% of the prevention program graduates started drinking in the following year compared with a 37% onset rate among the same-aged control group boys. The results were similar for the 11-year-old boys, with onset of drinking for 12% of the intervention group and 37% for the control group. For the 10-year-old girls, 13% of program graduates and 53% of the control group started drinking in the year following the intervention. As with the boys, the prevention program effects were smaller for the 11-year-old girls, with 28% of intervention program graduates starting to drink in the next year compared with 51% of the control group girls. There were no program effects for nondrinking youth who began the prevention program at a later age (ages 12–13), with older youth who received the prevention program just as likely to begin drinking 1 year later as those who did not receive the program. Finally, among children who had initiated drinking prior to the start of the program, regardless of their age, there was no program effect. Combined, these findings suggest the importance of targeting prevention programs at a young age (e.g., third and fourth graders), when fewer children have initiated substance use and when the cultural prevention messages appear to be most likely to have an impact (Whitbeck, 2001).

COMMUNICATION ACTIVISM TO ADDRESS SUBSTANCE ABUSE PROBLEMS: THE CURRENT INTERVENTION

The purpose of the Ramah Navajo Family Listening (RNFL) intervention research project was to develop, pilot, and prepare for implementation a cultural and intergenerational family intervention to reduce alcohol and other recreational drug initiation, use, and abuse among Ramah Navajo late elementary school youth. The RNFL project was designed in partnership with the Ramah Navajo and funded by the Native American Research Centers for Health (NARCH), which "develops opportunities for conducting research, research training and faculty development to meet the needs of American Indian/Alaska Native (AI/AN) communities" (DHHS, n.d.-a, para. 1). The collaborative development of this intervention is essential because of the history of mistrust by American-Indian people of white researchers. Historically, many outsiders, with little knowledge of American-Indian cultures, have brought interventions into tribal communities that have had little impact on improving the lives of American-Indian families, and, in fact, largely have created mistrust of researchers (Davis & Reid, 1999; Warne, 2006). Hence, it is critical to develop any intervention not only from insiders' perspective but also from the actual work of insiders.

This intervention research project directly addressed these and other issues by developing culturally specific prevention materials based on the wisdom and suggestions shared by members of the tribal community and elicited by trained facilitators from the community. This project constituted *community-based participatory research* (CBPR), which Minkler and Wallerstein (2008) defined as a collaborative approach that equitably involves partners in the research process and recognizes the unique strengths that each partner brings. CBPR begins with a research topic of importance to a community, with a key aim being the combining of knowledge and action for social change to, in this case, improve community health and to eliminate health disparities. The following sections describe the community in which the intervention occurred, discuss the coalition-building process used to develop the intervention, and detail the communication intervention.

The Ramah Navajo Community

The Ramah Navajo community is located in northwest New Mexico, near the Arizona border, about 2.5 hours west of Albuquerque; it encompasses about 146,953 acres, most of which is mountainous, high desert rangeland. The Ramah Navajo community is one of three noncontiguous satellite reservations from the main Navajo Reservation. Its land status is known as "checker-boarded" because it includes tribal land, Ramah Navajo Chapter land, individual American-Indian allotment land, privately owned land, and state land. Ramah officially was recognized as a Chapter of the Navajo Nation in the early 1930s, and the Ramah Navajo community has a council delegate that represents it during the annual Navajo Nation Council Legislation session. Local government is through the recognized Chapter and the elected officials of Chapter president, vice president, and secretary/treasurer, each of whom serve 4-year terms.

In 1970, under Public Law (PL) 93–638, the Ramah Navajo community exercised its right to self-determination and took control of allocated money for its education system. This initiative led to the development of the Ramah Navajo School Board, Inc. (RNSB) as a nonprofit organization to oversee the tribal school and to provide health care, job training, and social services to the community. School board members are elected and they appoint administrative staff. In 1978, the RNSB expanded its role and assumed control of its health clinic and health and human services department, by contracting with the IHS through PL 84–437, the Indian Health Care Improvement Act.

Tribal rolls estimate that there currently are 3,500 people in the Ramah Navajo community, with more than 400 students in Pine Hills Schools, Head Start through 12th grade, served by a full-time staff of 85. The following demographic characteristics were found according to a random community profile conducted by the Ramah Navajo community and by us in 2004: 64% of the population was employed, 59% earned less than $20,000 per year, 27% had less than a high school diploma, 25% had a high school diploma, 27% had completed some college, and 21% were college graduates (including graduate degrees). In terms of alcohol use, the 2003 Navajo Nation Middle and High School Youth Risk Behavior Survey (DHHS, 2003) found that 40% of middle school students and 69% of high school students had more than one drink of alcohol in their lifetime. For the past 30 days use, the percentages were 22% and 39% for middle school and high school students, respectively, compared with U.S. rates for high school students of 78% lifetime and 47% for the past 30 days. Furthermore, 36% of Navajo Nation middle school students and 67% of high school students had used marijuana during their lifetime (with 25% of middle schools students and 38% of high school students using it in the past 30 days), compared with U.S. rates for high school students of 42% lifetime and 24% for the past 30 days.

Building a Coalition

Building a coalition of internal and external partners is an important element in a CBPR approach. The RNSB participated in capacity development processes with Wallerstein and Belone (among others) of UNM through two prior research projects. The collaboration began through the Ramah Navajo's connection to the Albuquerque Area Indian Health Board (AAIHB). Wallerstein knew AAIHB's director, who connected Ramah Navajo community members and leaders to Wallerstein. Through these meetings, Wallerstein let these leaders and members know about an opportunity to participate in a capacity-building project, which they thought was a good idea. Ramah Navajo conducted an assessment of its capacities using the Centers for Disease Control and Prevention's (CDC) instrument that measures the performance of 10 essential public health services (English et al., 2004). Two priorities emerged from this assessment: (a) to deepen the tribe's understanding of community members' concerns and strengths in health, social services, education, and economic development; and (b) to enhance the health-education capacities of the tribe. These priorities provided the context for continuing intervention work that integrated the importance of culture and language to promote the health of tribal families and youth. Thus, UNM and the Ramah Navajo decided to collaborate on this family intervention project.

To develop this intergenerational family communication intervention, a coalition was established with Ramah Navajo that required gaining tribal approval from key leadership organizations (e.g., RNSB) through tribal resolutions and letters of support. A formal coalition was created, termed the "Ramah Navajo Advisory Council" (RNAC) that held monthly strategic planning meetings, with membership from tribal administrators, program directors, and program staff, as well as community members and the UNM research team. The original Anishinabe family intervention (Bii-Zin-Da-De-Dah) was coadapted by RNAC and UNM, which resulted in a curriculum manual specific to the cultural relevance of the Ramah Navajo community over a 3-year process. An example of this adaptation is the integration of stories, cultural symbols, and cultural traditions into the curriculum manual.

Monthly meetings of the RNAC concentrated on (a) reviewing the community health assessment results, (b) planning and conducting focus group research on the adapted family intervention, (c) adapting and revising the Anishinabe version of the curriculum, and (d) codeveloping process evaluations and outcome measures. The focus groups were conducted by RNAC members with elders (three groups, up to 6 hours each) at their request, and explored key cultural traditions and lessons to impart to the youth. The Navajo language transcription of the focus group discussions (conducted by the RNAC) created rich historical teachings to insert in the curriculum, but slowed the final production, with the piloting of the program beginning in fall 2008, after a 3-year start in fall 2005. The RNAC provided detailed oversight of the curriculum development, with members serving as cultural consultants to every aspect of the curriculum content, being trained as interviewers and conducting pretest–posttest interviews, facilitating the intervention, and coanalyzing the process and outcome evaluation data that were collected.

Reports written by the research team and RNAC were submitted to both the Navajo Nation Human Research Review Board and the RNSB, with the latter having ultimate approval of the final version of the cultural intervention curriculum. All research was approved by UNM's Institutional Review Board and by the Navajo Nation Human Research Review Board. Tribal approval and oversight create lengthy, but necessary, processes on American-Indian reservations to assure that ethical research practices are employed, that there is active tribal participation in research, and to minimize the potential for misunderstandings. Although these approval processes extended project time-lines and required substantial time involvement of the UNM research staff, this participatory research model greatly improved the chances of success and the sustainability of this intervention.

Intervention

Using the process just described, the RNAC created a detailed, 186-page family-strengthening curriculum consisting of 14 weekly sessions. The structure for each of the 14 sessions followed the following framework:

1. a family meal and prayer;
2. sharing of individual clans (i.e., extended relations that are traced matriarchally) by each participant (child and parent or caregiver, which is traditional in Navajo introductions);
3. sharing of "take-home practice" activities from the previous session;
4. an icebreaker activity;
5. facilitated experiential activities of the current session theme with a separate youth and adult groups;
6. rejoining of youth and adults for a reflection on the experience and activities of the current session through presentation and writing journals;
7. planning of community action project by each family;
8. session wrap-up, including handouts of the take-home practice activities and planning for the next session; and
9. journaling by facilitators.

The 14 sessions covered the following topics: (a) A welcoming dinner, (b) My family, (c) Ramah Navajo History, (d) Ramah Navajo Way of Life, (e) Our Ramah Navajo Vision, (f) Community Challenges, (g) Communication and Help Seeking, (h) Recognizing Types of Anger, (i) Managing Anger, (j) Problem Solving, (k) Being Different, (l) Positive Relationships, (m) Building Social Support, and (n) Making a Commitment.

Additionally, embedded in this curriculum are New Mexico state educational standards, and alcohol and other recreational drug-prevention messages, and other health-promotion messages (e.g., participating in community events, such as picking up trash), for individuals (both youth and adult), families, and the community, which, simultaneously, reinforce Ramah Navajo knowledge. Furthermore, each family engaged in a community action project that involved selecting something that would be beneficial to the community and that built on lessons learned in the curriculum (although this project was not directly evaluated; see later for details on the evaluation).

The theoretical underpinnings of the curriculum include family resiliency building (Benzies & Mychasiuk, 2009), cultural embeddedness (Dutta & Basnyat, 2008), and community empowerment within a public health-prevention framework (Wallerstein, 1999). *Empowerment* is a "a process ... by which people, organizations, and communities gain mastery over their affairs" (Rappaport, 1987, p. 122; see also Papa, Papa, & Buerkel, this volume), with *community empowerment* being a social action process by which individuals, groups, organizations, and communities gain mastery to change their social, economic, and political environments to improve equity and quality of life (Wallerstein, 1999). The public health framework also recognizes that disparities cannot be addressed successfully by single-level interventions but must be based on a socioecologic framework, engaging changes at individual, family, organization, and community levels to promote healthy communities (Stokols, 1996). The community action projects chosen by the families recognize the strength of psychological and family empowerment for community-level change as an important component of the intervention.

Implementation of the intervention required the development of a facilitator pool of six individuals from various tribal programs (e.g., behavioral health, health clinic, and scholarship, education, and training services) and the use of an elementary counselor from the local reservation school. A pool of facilitators ensured that there always were at least four facilitators present during each of the 14 sessions. Facilitator training, carried out by the UNM research team prior to each session, was critical not only in terms of delivering the program but also for maintaining a team structure, logistics, and planning.

Each session was led by two primary facilitators and two assistant facilitators, generally working as pairs, particularly when parent and youth groups were separated during a session. A Ramah Navajo tribal member or an individual who was working in the community served as one of the primary facilitators. The two lead facilitators guided participants through the curriculum activities, which required managing group discussion in an inclusive group learning atmosphere; the assistant facilitators helped the lead facilitators to manage time and capture discussion points on flipcharts. The facilitators and assistants kept all participants engaged in the material and active during discussions. The facilitators of the adult sessions required the additional skill of verbally translating the English-written curriculum into the Navajo language.

Evaluation Design

During fall 2008, the fourth year of this research project, the pilot test of the intervention was launched, consisting of 11 families (selected through network/snowball sampling and not based on any strict inclusion criteria), to assess the effectiveness of the curriculum through program operation (process evaluation) and participant pretest–posttest changes (outcome evaluation). All instruments were codeveloped by the researchers and the RNAC. The process evaluations, which were comprehensive and conducted on a weekly basis, included: (a) attendance sheets to assess dose (i.e., whether everyone got the full intervention); (b) logs completed by facilitators to document their fidelity to the curriculum objectives and the degree of activity completion, flow of delivery, and barriers experienced with regard to implementation; (c) researchers' observations of facilitators' confidence and their ability to complete the activities; and (d) debriefing of facilitators and researchers through collaborative discussion about what curriculum components worked and what needed to be changed in the curriculum manual. Facilitators completed process evaluation forms after each session using a 5-point Likert-type scale (1 = *Not at All*, 2 = *A Little*, 3 = *Somewhat*, 4 = *Considerable*, 5 = *Extensively*) to assess four areas:

1. cultural connections (e.g., "To what extent did you encourage the participants' exploration of their cultural values and traditions?"),
2. use of facilitation skills (e.g., "To what extent did you follow the structure of the session and maintain the agenda?"),
3. group process (e.g., "To what extent did participants verbalize their thoughts and opinions related to the topic presented?"), and
4. social analysis/critical thinking (e.g., "To what extent did you apply problem-solving strategies to a problem/issue raised during the session?").

The outcome evaluation consisted of a pretest–posttest, closed-ended questionnaire, as well as a qualitative set of 360-degree evaluation questions, asking family members to assess changes made by them and other family members after completing the sessions. The instrument assessed a number of variables (e.g., sense of community, coping behaviors, and social norms), but the focus here is on four key variables: (a) cultural identity, (b) family communication, (c) substance use/intention, and (d) general health. (The items and measures of internal consistency, where appropriate, are included in the Appendix.)

Our purpose was to determine if the intervention increased participants' cultural identity, family communication, and perception of general health, as well as lowered substance use intention by youths (and substance use by adults), from pretest to posttest. We examined substance-use intention because we anticipated low, if any, substance use by the children.

The measures were adapted from validated scales created by Whitbeck (2001; Whitbeck Hoyt, Stubben, et al., 2001). The RNAC reviewed each measure and made slight adaptations to items to assure cultural appropriateness. Measurements were collected from adults and youths by trained Ramah Navajo interviewers.

ANALYZING THE COMMUNICATION ACTIVISM INTERVENTION

The analysis of this communication activism intervention centers on three aspects: (a) group dynamics in CBPR, (b) addressing paradoxes and tensions involved in research partnerships, and (c) outcome evaluation. These three aspects are central to the key processes involved in creating the intervention and its effectiveness.

Group Dynamics in Community-Based Participatory Research

Wallerstein and Duran (2006) maintained that "CBPR is not simply a community outreach strategy but represents a systematic effort to incorporate community participation and decision making, local theories of etiology and change, and community practices into the research effort" (p. 313). Wallerstein et al. (2008) developed a model to advance understanding and investigations of how CBPR processes influence or predict outcomes (see Figure 10.1). The model identifies four CBPR characteristics and suggests relationships between each category. First, *contexts* shape the nature of the research and the partnership, and can determine whether and how a partnership is initiated. Second and third, *group dynamics*, consisting of three subdimensions (structural, individual, and relational dynamics), interact with contexts to produce the *intervention*. Fourth, *outcomes* (i.e., system and capacity outcomes, and improved health) result directly from the intervention research. Although CBPR partnership processes and practices are presented visually in this model as linear, they are, in fact, dynamic and changing, with embedded paradoxes and tensions that are driven by both external and internal context changes (e.g., loss of funding, new leadership, and differences in partners' interpretations of events; see discussion below).

Contexts

- Socio-economic, cultural, geographic, political-historical, environmental factors
- Policies/Trends, National/local governance & political climate
- Historic degree of collaboration and trust between university & community
- Community capacity, readiness & experience
- University capacity, readiness & reputation
- Perceived severity of health issues

Group Dynamics

Structural Dynamics:
- Diversity
- Complexity
- Formal Agreements
- Real power/resource sharing
- Alignment with CBPR principles
- Length of time in partnership

Individual Dynamics:
- Core values
- Motivations for participating
- Personal relationships
- Cultural identities/humility
- Individual beliefs, spirituality & meaning
- Bridge people on research team
- Community reputation of PI

Relational Dynamics:
- Safety
- Dialogue, listening & mutual learning
- Leadership & stewardship
- Influence & power dynamics
- Flexibility
- Self & collective reflection
- Participatory decision-making & negotiation
- Integration of local beliefs to group process
- Task roles and communication

Intervention

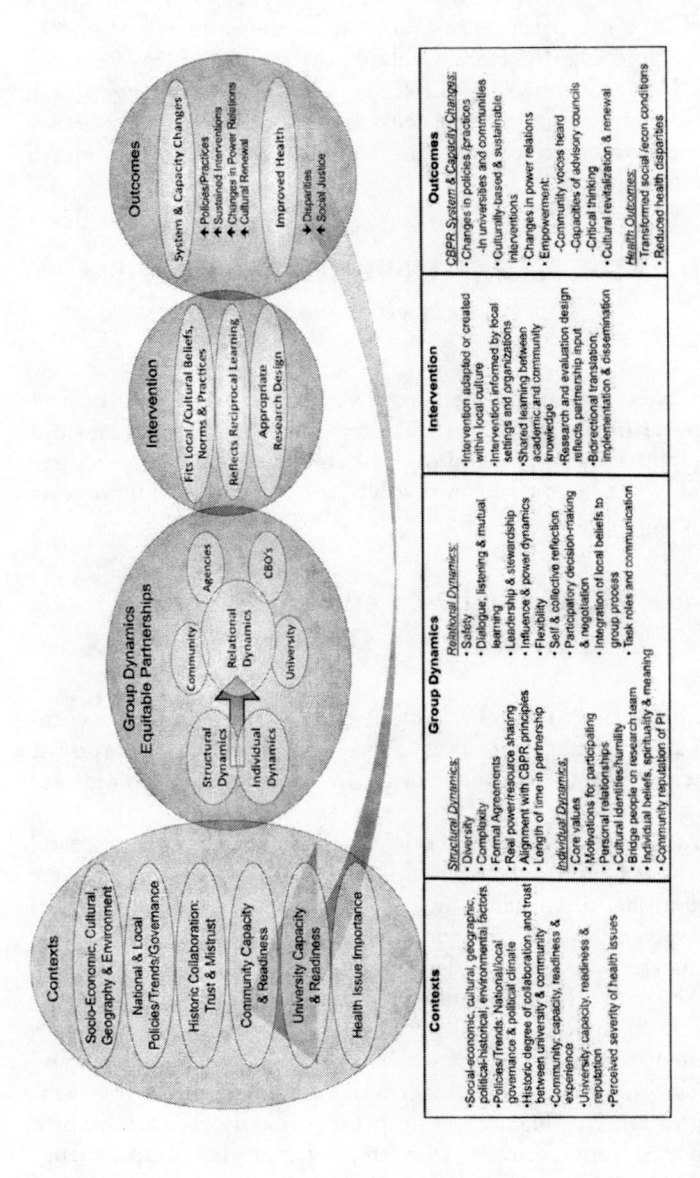

- Intervention adapted or created within local culture
- Intervention informed by local settings and organizations
- Shared learning between academic and community knowledge
- Research and evaluation design reflects partnership input
- Bidirectional translation, implementation & dissemination

Outcomes

CBPR System & Capacity Changes:
- Changes in policies/practices
  - In universities and communities
- Culturally-based & sustainable interventions
- Changes in power relations
- Empowerment:
  - Community voices heard
  - Capacities of advisory councils
  - Critical thinking
- Cultural revitalization & renewal

Health Outcomes:
- Transformed social/econ conditions
- Reduced health disparities

Note: CBOs means community-based organizations

Fig. 10.1. Community-based participatory research conceptual logic model.
Source: Adapted from Wallerstein, N., Oetzel, J., Duran, B., Tafoya, G., Belone, L., & Rae, R. (2008). What predicts outcomes in CBPR? In M. Minkler & N. Wallerstein (Eds.), *Community-based participatory research for health: From process to outcomes* (2nd ed, pp. 371–392). San Francisco, CA: Jossey-Bass, p 381. Reprinted with permission by John Wiley & Sons, Inc.

We center this analysis of the intervention on the group dynamics portion of the model because that is the process by which the intervention was created. Although the intervention is the communication activism directly, the process (i.e., group dynamics) creating this intervention is a key component. In fact, group dynamics are a central part of what makes CBPR work and they enable culturally supported and sustainable interventions (Wallerstein et al., 2008). One key communication theory focusing on group dynamics in culturally diverse groups is Oetzel's (2005) intercultural workgroup communication theory, which examines contextual factors that affect group communication and how group communication affects outcomes. A key concept in the theory is *effective communication*, which is operationalized as respectful, collaborative, and equal participatory communication.

In terms of contextual factors, intercultural workgroup communication theory posits that the more culturally heterogeneous a group is and the more negative contextual factors (e.g., history of conflict and inequality) that a culturally diverse group faces, the less likely that group will experience effective communication. These propositions are supported in the extant literature (see, e.g., Oetzel, 2005), but fortunately, they were not supported in this intervention because of the use of CBPR processes that created effective group communication.

Although, as mentioned previously, Wallerstein and Belone were involved in two prior research projects over the span of 6 years with the Ramah Navajo, the individuals from the community who served as RNAC members, as well as some of the researchers, were not all involved in those two earlier projects; consequently, in early RNAC meetings, negative historical factors raised by new community members had to be addressed. For example, community members recalled research conducted by other institutions prior to the UNM projects in which information was gathered from the community but the results never were given to them. In line with the CBPR model, the development of the present intervention could not move forward with the RNAC until the historical context of this community's involvement with researchers from other universities was acknowledged and some level of trust was established with this new working group. Trust was established by engaging in effective communication and by demonstrating our commitment to the community over time. Finally, although the partnership included people with different cultural backgrounds (e.g., white researchers and American-Indian researchers from different tribes), there was homophily in terms of their desire to work on the project and the manner in which it should be carried out (Lindamer et al., 2009).

In terms of the impact of group communication processes on group outcomes, Oetzel's (2005) theory proffers that the more groups use effective communication processes, the more likely they will achieve *task effectiveness* (i.e., the quality of group products) and *relational effectiveness* (i.e., the degree to which members can and want to work together interdependently in the future). The process evaluation and history of continued work between UNM and the Ramah Navajo indicates that our team has been successful in achieving relational effectiveness. A large reason for this effectiveness is the strong effort to use effective and appropriate channels and messages. For instance, the university research team recognized early on that communicating primarily through e-mail would not be sufficient because many RNAC members did not have e-mail addresses or access to the internet. Communication, therefore, was conducted through telephone calls, faxing, and once-a-month, face-to-face meetings in the community, with e-mails and telephone calls primarily used to remind RNAC members of upcoming meetings. The monthly meetings were planned around the schedules of RNAC members, choosing a time of day that best fit their schedules. This decision represented a significant commitment by our research team because the community is a 2-hour drive from the university. The impact of group communication on task effectiveness is discussed in the outcome evaluation section.

Addressing Paradoxes and Tensions Involved in Research Partnerships

CBPR processes, like all research processes, are marked by potential (ethical) paradoxes (McDermott, Oetzel, & White, 2008). A *paradox* exists when people's need to fulfill a goal requires them to act in ways contrary to that goal (e.g., people working to achieve a participatory goal ignoring the participation process to be more efficient; see, e.g., Stohl & Cheney, 2001; Wendt, 1998). McDermott et al. (2008) identified three ethical paradoxes in CBPR: power, participation, and practice.

First, although partnership is the basis of CBPR, which implies equality and equity among partners, the paradox of power recognizes tensions in negotiating this partnership. For example, community members and researchers need to recognize that the structure of a research and program development partnership usually does not start off with those involved in equal roles. McDermott et al. (2008) identified three specific tensions associated with the paradox of power: (a) the process is researcher initiated but must remain community driven (i.e., who starts the process), (b) researchers have more access to funding mechanisms than do community members and yet are sharing financial resources with the community, and (c) equal partners and community members need to protect their community (and, thus, potentially withhold information from researchers). This intervention was designed collaboratively based on priorities that emerged from the community assessment conducted with the Ramah Navajo; specifically, these priorities were based on understanding the importance of the community's culture and language in developing interventions to promote the health of tribal families, elders, and youth. For that reason, UNM and the Ramah Navajo jointly submitted a research plan to NARCH, which addressed the paradox of power with a community focus and the sharing of resources (primarily money). This solution was not perfect, as resources were not shared equally, but we did our best to allocate resources to the community.

Second, although participation in the CBPR process is intended to be empowering for those involved, the structure of the participation may hinder people from fully expressing their thoughts. For example, a discussion of key research ideas may result in community members being relatively silent because they believe that they are not knowledgeable. McDermott et al. (2008) identified three tensions associated with the paradox of participation: (a) competing needs to value but change the community, (b) researchers and community members deciding which community members get to participate (i.e., not everyone can be included in the partnership), and (c) balancing leadership with collaboration. This intervention was based on the findings of the community assessments and the community's need for a family intervention project; consequently, through the intervention, the community was valued. Furthermore, the intervention honored the community's request for a change within the community's fourth and fifth graders, and their families. However, despite the strengths of this intervention, we were not able to include every community member's perspective about the intervention nor were we able to include youth of older ages.

Third, given that researchers and community members may have different end goals and time-lines, problems in practices may arise. McDermott et al. (2008) identified three tensions associated with the paradox of practice: (a) focusing on long-term outcomes and meeting immediate needs of the community, (b) adhering to best research practices and addressing community needs (e.g., sometimes community members want an intervention without evaluating its effectiveness), and (c) being both supportive and critical of the research process. This intervention addressed these tensions by being a unique intergenerational alcohol- and recreational drug-prevention program, tailored to reinforce Navajo language use, in general, and Ramah Navajo values and way of life, in particular, to support healthier children and families, and to protect them from alcohol and recreational drug abuse, but based on an empirically supported project (Whitbeck, Hoyt, McMorris, et al., 2001). The process of creating the adapted intervention managed the paradox of practice by encouraging both collaboration and critique, and, thereby, emphasized directly the paradox to manage its associated tensions.

Outcome Evaluation

The effectiveness of the CBPR collaboration and the intervention itself can be evaluated in two ways. The first way is whether the curriculum manual (i.e., intervention) was of high quality. Although an independent evaluation of the intervention was not conducted, the intervention was based in both culturally and empirically supported evidence. Furthermore, the intervention was coconstructed collaboratively by the UNM team and the RNAC, making it effective (or perhaps sustainable) because it was created through high-quality interaction among members of this diverse team.

The second way is whether the intervention resulted in outcomes in the desired direction. In addition to reporting statistical significance, we provide effect sizes, as these are better indicators of the strength of the outcomes, given the small sample size. The children demonstrated an increase from pretest to posttest in both cultural identity, $t(6) = 1.27, p = .25, d = .77$, and family communication, $t(9) = 1.27, p = .42, d = .19$ (see Table 10.1 for means and standard deviations), but these effects were not statistically significant. The low Cronbach's α for the cultural identity measure led us to examine individual items, with one cultural identity item, "How much do you know about the Navajo culture?" showing a statistically significant increase from pretest to posttest, $t(7) = 2.38, p < .05, d = 1.05$. Additionally, children reported an increase in their general health, $t(9) = 1.86, p = .09, d = .29$. There were no significant differences in their actual substance use, but that likely is due to only one child reporting any substance use at the times of the pretest and

TABLE 10.1. Means and Standard Deviations of Measures

	Measure	Pretest M	Pretest SD	Posttest M	Posttest SD
Child	Cultural identity	2.05	.47	2.38	.38
	Knowledge of Navajo culture	.88	.35	1.50	.76
	Family communication	1.82	.79	1.98	.86
	Substance-use intention	2.33	1.51	3.00	1.55
	General health	3.10	1.10	3.50	1.65
Adults	Cultural identity	2.17	.61	2.16	.55
	Special things based on Navajo way of life	1.10	1.08	1.82	1.08
	Family communication	2.18	.67	2.11	.60
	Child's general health	4.09	1.04	4.45	.82

posttest (that child reported at both the pretest and posttest having a sip of alcohol, smoking a cigarette, and using an inhalant). As a result, we examined the single item measuring behavioral intention toward future substance use ("Drinking as a teen will cause problems"), which demonstrated a moderate increase, $t(5) = 1.35, p = .24, d = .44$. In summary, the intervention had effects in the expected direction for most of the variables, with, in particular, a large effect on cultural identity, a medium effect on intended substance use, and small effects on general health and family communication.

The adults failed to demonstrate an increase from pretest to posttest in cultural identity, $t(9) = .09, p = .93$, and family communication, $t(10) = 59, p = .57$. However, one cultural identity item, "In your own family, do you do special things ... based on the Navajo way of life?" did show a substantial increase from pretest to posttest, $t(10) = 2.06, p = .07, d = .59$. Additionally, parents reported that their children's general health had substantially increased, $t(10) = 1.79, p = .10, d = .38$. Substance use demonstrated no change, but this result largely is due to 7 of the 10 participants using no substances at the time of the pretest. In summary, the intervention had medium effects in the expected direction for one of the cultural identity items and for adults' perception of their children's general health, but not on the cultural identity and family communication variables overall.

The 360-degree evaluation produced short, open-ended responses about outcomes that participants perceived as a result of the intervention. The items were intended to provide supporting (or countering) evidence of the quantitative findings, especially regarding themes related to the quantitative measures for cultural identity, family communication, substance use, and general health. Two key findings emerged from this evaluation for both children and adults: improved family communication and enhanced understanding of Navajo culture. In terms of family communication, one parent reported that "there has been better communication between myself and my children ... [in terms of] listening to their concerns," with her child reporting that "I'm listening to mom more." Another mother offered, "We're concentrating on being more open with each other... being more open with my daughter by expressing feelings." Her daughter supported this perspective, saying, "I had fun with my mom. We got to do something together, especially with our clan system." In terms of cultural identity, one parent stated, "We're practicing saying our clans," and her child said, "I learned how to say my clan. ... She [her mother] encouraged me to learn my clan by saying it over." Another child explained that "I learned how to say my clan in Navajo and I didn't know my clan until I went to the listening project." These two themes were addressed by almost every participant in the program and, thus, provide supporting evidence for the positive outcomes of the intervention in these two areas. Substance use and general health were not directly addressed by the participants in this evaluation method.

Taken together, the quantitative and qualitative results demonstrate some initial support that the intervention has positive effects on cultural identity, family communication, substance-use intention (for children), and children's general health. This conclusion is offered with two caveats. The qualitative findings indicated stronger support for the benefits of the intervention on cultural identity and family communication than did the quantitative findings. Furthermore, although there was statistical significance for the two single items of cultural identity, the overall means indicated only "a little" interest in cultural identity. There are at least three potential reasons for these findings. First, the qualitative interviews followed the entire program and the recall about the benefits may have been more salient for participants than were the quantitative interviews conducted 3 months earlier. Additionally, participants may have demonstrated a recall bias about the benefits of the intervention to cultural identity and family communication. Second, the strength of children's cultural identity may be tempered by their age. The children were approximately 10 years old and, as a consequence, the importance of cultural identity may be relative given their other interests (e.g., playing with friends). However, recalling the importance of sharing clans was salient and easy for them to recall. Third, there may have been some measurement issues, as the cultural identity measure for children demonstrated low consistency, and the RNAC mentioned that rating scales can be problematic to use for some Navajos (usually elders and traditional Navajos) who distinguish more between the presence or absence of a phenomenon. Thus, a referent such as "a little" on a rating scale means that the phenomenon is there, but the referents "somewhat" and "extremely" are not important qualifiers. These measurement issues will have to be more carefully addressed in future evaluations of the intervention. Nonetheless, there was a significant increase from pretest to posttest on these items, meaning that the intervention did have a positive impact.

LESSONS LEARNED ABOUT COMMUNICATION ACTIVISM SCHOLARSHIP

The intervention involved two types of communication activism. The first type was the communication among the research team and the community members, using effective CBPR processes to negotiate issues of difference, such as cultural background and community versus researcher perspectives. The second type was the communication activism in the intervention itself, with the sessions centering on improving family communication, communication about culture, and communication through the community action projects for families to have a positive impact in the larger community. All of these are key protective factors for adolescent substance use in American-Indian communities.

In this manner, this project constitutes communication activism scholarship that involves engagement and advocacy with those who are underresourced and marginalized to address issues of social justice (Frey, Pearce, Pollock, Artz, & Murphy, 1996). The overall purpose of the current intervention was to address a key health issue in an American-Indian community, which has been historically underserved and underresourced. The CBPR process, in particular, was employed to address social justice issues for several reasons: (a) the partnership process helps to address issues of historical mistrust, (b) the CBPR process involves reciprocal learning that increases the capacity of community members and researchers, and (c) the CBPR process results in a culturally supported and sustainable intervention (Wallerstein et al., 2008). Thus, CBPR is an important method for creating and implementing communication activism scholarship, especially for populations in need of social justice.

A key component of any CBPR project is to critically reflect on what worked and did not work, and why. This project involved a great deal of process evaluation, in addition to outcome evaluation. Through these evaluations and reflections, we identify several lessons learned about CBPR and this particular communication activism intervention.

First, CBPR is key to working with American-Indian tribes and to addressing paradoxes and tensions associated with research partnerships (Fisher & Ball, 2003). CBPR does not impose academic knowledge on communities as some other approaches do but, rather, relies on sharing perspectives (both culturally and empirically supported perspectives). Such open sharing and recognizing of paradoxes and tensions is especially important when historical mistrust is a significant issue, as was true in this case. In working with American-Indian tribes, CBPR emphasizes place, setting, culture, and identity, building community confidence and trust through stated agreements that research processes and data belong to the community. These steps are necessary for researchers to be proven sufficiently trustworthy, and they are effective for developing culturally centered interventions. CBPR also directly addresses the paradoxes of power, participation, and practice through the valuing and respecting of indigenous knowledge and expertise.

Second, communication is central to effective CBPR. Scholars have identified the partnership (or research team), and the group dynamics that characterize it, as key to effective CBPR (e.g., Minkler & Wallerstein, 2008; Wallerstein, Duran, Minkler, & Foley, 2005). A critical element in partnerships between tribal communities and researchers is that the research team be culturally diverse. Although Oetzel (2005) noted that, all things being equal, culturally homogenous groups engage in more effective interaction processes than do culturally heterogeneous groups, our primarily American-Indian

UNM graduate research team worked very hard over time to engage in effective group interaction and had the advantage of being "Indian," although members were not from the Ramah Navajo community. We were concerned with respectful, collaborative, and equal participatory communication, seeking ways to effectively manage the paradoxes and tensions inherent in CBPR (McDermott et al., 2008). The bottom line is that effective CBPR demands competent management of group interaction processes.

Third, managing differences is a key focus of positive group interaction. Two differences in our partnership were community versus researcher perspectives and cultural differences. We managed community versus researcher perspectives very well through effective group interaction. Specifically, the research team listened carefully to community perspectives and focused on what the community wanted. Community members also "bought into" the importance of this research. As one advisory council member stated, "The capacity has been built within me to go back and start questioning things again and really looking at these issues and these policies," demonstrating the understanding that research could directly benefit the community.

With respect to cultural differences, a key starting place was that three members of the UNM research team were native graduate students who are from several southwest tribes. The composition of the team was perceived as positive by one council member, who said:

> The research team has representatives of the Native community. Having your research team include Native people, even though they're not from our community, it still was a big comfort. And, I think for us, it was bonding; that first connect with us being that they were Native.

Furthermore, the research team and community had value homophily in that they shared a desire to work together on children's substance use and to emphasize positive aspects of the community to address the issue (Lindamer et al., 2009). Other potential difficulties with cultural differences largely were averted because of the strong collective reflection by the research team and self-reflection by its members. We examined why we were doing this work, what privileges we have, and how we could ameliorate power differences. The Native researchers also had added pressures to be positive stewards, knowing that if they "screwed up," they were negatively impacting the (and their) American-Indian community, which can be a small place in New Mexico. Thus, our efforts to form a culturally diverse research team and to be self-reflective during the process provided strong pieces to managing potential difficulties during the partnership.

Finally, CBPR helps community researchers to create culturally appropriate interventions that are sustainable and empowering by building capacity in communities. CBPR is an improvement over other forms of research (e.g., community-placed research that is done in the community but is led and performed by researchers) because it increases community health through the contextual application of research findings to key health outcomes (including health disparities). CBPR also can lead to further collaboration between communities and researchers, and to generalizable processes for planning, diagnosing, and matching, adapting, and evaluating interventions with specific communities. Furthermore, CBPR results in enhanced skills for community members. In our case, a number of community members now feel competent creating curriculum, facilitating discussion groups, and conducting interviews to address their community's issues in the future. As one advisory council member noted, "You have to have education, but if you play the game right, you can go all the way to change policy to have better outcomes in your Native communities." The "game" to which this member referred is understanding the importance of research to achieve positive community outcomes.

Certainly, the process of creating and implementing this intervention was positive, with the community and university team both feeling pride in what was created and establishing long-term relationships. Additionally, community members believe that they have an intervention that will address cultural loss and substance use by their youth (given the results of the substance-use intention item). They also have stated a desire to sustain the project, which is a major milestone, as there are many curriculum manuals sitting on their shelves gathering dust because they were not applicable to their community. We have limited, although positive, evidence of the effectiveness of the intervention because the evaluation design is a short-term pilot study without a control group. The positive evidence of its impact includes adults and children reporting strong improvements in knowledge about their culture and improved family communication through the 360-degree evaluation. The quantitative results for the children demonstrated positive effects on all of the variables, including medium effects for substance-use intention and large effects for cultural identity. Furthermore, there were improvements in children's health, as reported by both parents and children. In the future, a more rigorous experimental design could provide stronger evidence of the effectiveness of the intervention. Moreover, a long-term analysis needs to determine whether this intervention addresses some of the important health disparities facing this community. Addressing health disparities is the key goal and, hopefully, the positive features of this intervention and the CBPR process will reduce these disparities.

CONCLUSION

We began this project as a collaboration between the Ramah Navajo community and the University of New Mexico research team to address a key health concern in the community: substance use by youth. Although there are many approaches to addressing substance use by youth, most are mainstream approaches rather than cultural-specific approaches. Thus, we culturally adapted a family-based intervention that had demonstrated evidence of success in American-Indian communities. The results of the pilot evaluation are very promising, with positive improvements in cultural identity and substance-use intention, although the long-term impact of the intervention remains to be seen and requires further evaluation. We will take heed of the lessons learned from this communication activism intervention as we continue its implementation.

APPENDIX
OUTCOME EVALUATION ITEMS AND MEASURES OF INTERNAL CONSISTENCY

Child Measures
Cultural Identity (pre α = .53, post α = .33)

(*Not at All* = 1, *A Little* = 2, *Somewhat* = 3, *Extremely* = 4)
1. How important is it to you to maintain your Navajo identity, values, and practices?
2. How much do you know about Navajo culture?
3. How interested are you in learning more about Navajo culture?
4. How different do you think Navajo culture is from white culture?
5. I am proud to be a Navajo.
6. Do you see yourself as Navajo?

Family Communication (pre α = .65, post α = .71)

1. Have you had arguments with your parents in the last 2 weeks? (5 = *We always got along very well*, 4 = *We usually got along very well but had some arguments*, 3 = *I had more than one argument with at least one parent*, 2 = *I had many arguments*, 1 = *I was always in arguments*)
2. Have you been able to talk about your feelings and problems with your parents in the last 2 weeks? (5 = *I can always talk about my feelings*, 4 = *I usually can talk about my feelings*, 3 =

About half the time I felt able to talk about my feelings, 2 = I usually was not able to talk about my feelings, 1 = I was never able to talk about my feelings)

3. Have you wanted to do the opposite of what your parents wanted in order to make them angry during the past 2 weeks? (5 = *I never wanted to do the opposite of what my parents wanted, 4 = Once or twice I wanted to do the opposite of what my parents wanted, 3 = About half the time I wanted to do the opposite, 2 = Most of the time I wanted to do the opposite, 1 = I always wanted to do the opposite)*

4. Have you been worried about things happening to your family without good reason in the last 2 weeks? (5 = *I have not worried without reason, 4 = Once or twice I worried, 3 = About half the time I worried, 2 = Most of the time I worried, 1 = I have worried the entire time)*

5. During the past 2 weeks, have you been thinking that you let your family down or have been unfair to them at any time? (5 = *I did not feel that I let them down at all, 4 = I usually did not feel that I let them down, 3 = About half the time I felt that I let them down, 2 = Most of the time I have felt that I let them down, 1 = I always felt that I let them down)*

6. During the last 2 weeks, have you been thinking that your family let you down or has been unfair to you? (5 = *I never felt that they let me down, 4 = I felt that they usually did not let me down, 3 = About half the time I felt they let me down, 2 = I usually have felt that they let me down, 1 = I am very mad that they let me down)*

Substance Use/Intention (Yes or No)

1. Had more than one or two sips of beer, wine, or hard liquor?
2. Use chewing tobacco or snuff (such as Redman, Levi Garrett, Beechnut, Skoal, Bandits, or Copenhagen)?
3. Smoked a cigarette, even just a puff?
4. Smoked marijuana?
5. Used an inhalant (e.g., glue, paint, poppers, rush, whippets, or w-ite-out)?
6. Used cocaine (powder or rock)?
7. Used any other illegal drug not listed?
8. If I drink as a teenager, it will cause me problems in the future (1 = *Never, 2 = A Little, 3 = Somewhat, 4 = A Lot)*

General Health

1. I am doing just as well as other kids my age (1 = *None of the Time*, 2 = *A Little of the Time*, 3 = *Some of the Time*, 4 = *A Lot of the Time*, 5 = *Most of the Time*, 6 = *All of the Time*)

Adult Measures
Cultural Identity (pre α = .73, post α = .69)

1. Some families have special activities or traditions that take place every year at particular times, such as feast days, religious activities, healing ceremonies, squaw dances, or honoring powwows. How many of these special activities or traditions did your family have when you were growing up that were based on Navajo culture?
2. In your family, do you do special things together or have special traditions that are based on the Navajo culture?
3. In your family, do you do special things together or have special traditions that are based on the Navajo way of life?
4. To what extent does your family follow the Navajo way of life?
5. How well do you speak the Navajo language? (1 = *I don't speak the Navajo language*, 2 = *I speak Navajo a little but not very well*, 3 = *I speak Navajo moderately well*, 4 = *I speak Navajo very well*)
6. It is important for my children and future generations to speak the Navajo language (1 = *Strongly Disagree*, 2 = *Disagree*, 3 = *Neither Agree nor Disagree*, 4 = *Agree*, 5 = *Strongly Agree*)
7. How many of your close friends are Navajo? (1 = *None*, 2 = *Some*, 3 = *Most of Them*, 4 = *All or Nearly All*)

Family Communication (pre α = .88, post α = .87)
(1 = *Never*, 2 = *A Little*, 3 = *Often*, 4 = *All of the Time*)

1. How often did you and your child talk about schoolwork?
2. How often did you and your child talk about other things that he/she did at school?
3. How often did you and your child talk about things that he/she did with friends?
4. How often did you and your child talk about how he/she was feeling?
5. How often did you and your child talk about sex and/or romantic relationships?

Substance Use

1. Do you currently drink alcohol? (0 = *Never or less than monthly*, 1 = *Monthly*, 2 = *2–4 times a month*, 3 = *2–3 times a week*, 4 = *4 or more times a week*)

2. How many drinks containing alcohol do you have on a typical day when you are drinking? (1 = *1–2 drinks*, 2 = *3–4 drinks*, 3 = *5–6 drinks*, 4 = *7–8 drinks*, 5 = *9 or more drinks*)
3. How often do you have 6 or more drinks on one occasion? (0 = *Never or less than monthly*, 1 = *Monthly*, 2 = *2–4 times a month*, 3 = *2–3 times a week*, 4 = *4 or more a week*)
4. How often during the last year have you found that you were not able to stop drinking once you had started? (0 = *Never or less than monthly*, 1 = *Monthly*, 2 = *2–4 times a month*, 3 = *2–3 times a week*, 4 = *4 or more a week*)

General Health

1. Rate your child's health (5 = *Excellent*, 4 = *Very Good*, 3 = *Good*, 2 = *Fair*, 1 = *Poor*)

ACKNOWLEDGMENTS

This research was supported by funding from the Native American Research Centers for Health (a joint program by the National Institutes on Health and the Indian Health Service), #U26IHS300009. Principal Investigator: Nina Wallerstein. Pilot Program Facilitators: Ira Burbank, Gloria Folger, Tamara Hutchinson, Lula Kelhoyouma, Yin-Mae Lee, Alvin Rafelito; Curriculum Development Team: Ira Burbank, Carolyn Finster, Jennifer Henio, Lula Kelhoyouma, Yin-Mae Lee, Freddie Lee, Phoebe Maria, Anderson Thomas, Focus Group Participants (Service Providers, Parents, Elders, and Youth); Community Contributors and Supporters: Nancy Henio, Katie Henio, Pearl Alonzo, Sam Alonzo, Gilbert Sage, Benny Coho, Bailey Henio, Chemico Eriacho, Tom Skeet, Mary Skeet, Mike Pino, Kelsey Beaver, Bessie Randolph, Albert Frank, Elmer Yazzie, Bob Murdoch, Bob Hymer, Michaelena Beaver, Vanessa Frank, Aaron Celorio, Ramona Yazzie, Gavin Rafelito, Brian Salvador, Daryl Lorenzo, Gracie Apachito; Curriculum Artwork: Nataani T. Platero; Support and Approval of Project: Ramah Navajo School Board, Pine Hill Health Center, Ramah Navajo Behavioral Health, Pine Hill Schools.

NOTES

1. We use the term *American Indians* rather than the term *Native Americans* as per the recommendation of the *American Indian and Alaska Native Mental Health Research: A Journal of the National Center*. We use other group identifiers (e.g., Alaska Natives) if they were employed in a research study.

2. Oetzel was a professor at UNM at the time that this research was conducted.
3. In the 19th and 20th centuries, many American-Indian children were removed from their homes to be educated in boarding schools and assimilated into the dominant European-American culture. Children were not allowed to speak their Native languages, had to cut their hair short, and had all American-Indian cultural aspects removed from their lives. This practice had significant negative effects on the physical and mental health of those children, and those negative effects have been found to persist in later generations that never directly experienced the boarding schools (and other atrocities committed against American Indians) through intergenerational, or historical, trauma (Whitebeck, Hoyt, Stubben, et al., 2001).

REFERENCES

Bakes, J. S. (1993). The American Indian high school dropout rate: A matter of style? *Journal of American Indian Education, 32,* 16–29. Retrieved from http://jaie.asu.edu

Beauvais, F. (1996). Trends in drug use among American Indian students and dropouts, 1975 to 1994. *American Journal of Public Health, 86,* 1594–1598. doi:10.2105/AJPH.86.11.1594

Bechtold, D. W. (1994). Indian adolescent suicide: Clinical and developmental considerations. *American Indian and Alaska Native Mental Health Research, 4*(Mono.), 71–80. Retrieved from http://aianp.uchsc.edu/ncaianmhr/journal

Benzies, K., & Mychasiuk, R. (2009). Fostering family resiliency: A review of the key protective factors. *Child & Family Social Work, 14,* 103–114. doi:10.1111/j.1365-2206.2008.00586.x

Black, J. E. (2007). Remembrances of removal: Native resistance to allotment and the unmasking of paternal benevolence. *Southern Communication Journal, 72,* 185–203. doi:10.1080/10417940701316690

Bolls, P. D., Tan, A., & Austin, E. (1997). An exploratory comparison of Native American and Caucasian students' attitudes toward teacher communication behavior and toward school. *Communication Education, 46,* 198–202. doi:10.1080/03634529709379091

Bowker, A. (1992). The American Indian female dropout. *Journal of American Indian Education, 31,* 3–21. Retrieved from http://jaie.asu.edu

Bresnahan, M. J., & Flowers, K. (2008). The effects of involvement in sports on attitudes toward Native American sport mascots. *Howard Journal of Communications, 19,* 165–181. doi:10.1080/17513050802567056

Carbaugh, D. (1999). "Just listen": "Listening" and landscape among the Blackfeet. *Western Journal of Communication, 63,* 250–270. doi:10.1080/10570319909374641

Covarrubias, P. (2007). (Un)biased in Western theory: Generative silence in American Indian communication. *Communication Monographs, 74,* 265–271. doi:10.1080/03637750701393071

Cowden, K. (2008). Communicating crisis: Lessons learned in conducting field research among Native American populations. *Journal of the Communication, Speech & Theatre Association of North Dakota, 21,* 33–39. Retrieved from http://www.cstand.org/?page=journal

Davis, S. M., & Reid, R. (1999). Practicing participatory research in American Indian communities. *American Journal of Clinical Nutrition, 69*(4, Suppl), S755–S759. Retrieved from http://www.ajcn.org

Duran B., Duran E., & Brave Heart, M. Y. H. (1998). Native Americans and the trauma of history. In R. Thornton (Ed.), *Studying Native America: Problems and prospects in Native American studies* (pp. 60–76). Madison: University of Wisconsin Press.

Duran, B., Wallerstein, N., & Miller, W. R. (2008). New approaches to alcohol interventions among American Indian and Latino communities: The experience of the Southwest Addictions Research Group. *Alcoholism Treatment Quarterly, 25*, 1–10. doi:1300/f020v25n04_01

Duran E., & Duran B. (1995). *Native American postcolonial psychology*. Albany: State University of New York Press.

Dutta, M. J., & Basnyat, I. (2008). The radio communication project in Nepal: A culture-centered approach to participation. *Health Education & Behavior, 35*, 442–454. doi:10.1177/1090198106287450

English, K. C., Wallerstein, N., Chino, M., Finster, C. E., Rafelito, A., Adeky, S., & Kennedy, M. (2004). Intermediate outcomes of a tribal community public health infrastructure assessment. *Ethnicity & Disease, 14*(3, Suppl.), S63–S71. Retrieved from http:/ishib.org/ed_index.asp

Fisher, P. A., & Ball, T. J. (2003). Tribal participatory research: Mechanisms of a collaborative model. *American Journal of Community Psychology, 32*, 207–216. doi:10.1023/b:ajcp.0000004742.39858.c5

Frey, L. R., & Carragee, K. M. (2007). Introduction: Communication activism as engaged scholarship. In L. R. Frey & K. M. Carragee (Eds.), *Communication activism* (2 Vols., pp. 1–64). Cresskill, NJ: Hampton Press.

Frey, L. R., Pearce, W. B., Pollock, M. A., Artz, L., & Murphy, B. A. O. (1996). Looking for justice in all the wrong places: On a communication approach to social justice. *Communication Studies, 47*, 110–127. doi:10.1080/10510979609368467

Hall, G. C. (2001). Psychotherapy research with ethnic minorities: Empirical, ethical, and conceptual issues. *Journal of Consulting and Clinical Psychology, 69*, 502–510. doi:10.1037//0022-006X.693.502

Hawkins, E. H., Cummins, L. H., & Marlatt, G. A. (2004). Preventing substance abuse in American Indian and Alaska Native youth: Promising strategies for healthier communities. *Psychological Bulletin, 130*, 304–323. doi:10.1037/0033-2909.130.2.304

Hecht, M. L., & Miller-Day, M. (2009). Drug resistance strategies project: Using narrative theory to enhance adolescents' communication competence. In L. R. Frey & K. N. Cissna (Eds.), *Routledge handbook of applied communication research* (pp. 535–557). New York, NY: Routledge.

Ishisaka, H. (1978). American Indians and foster care: Cultural factors and separation. *Child Welfare, 57*, 299–308.

Kalbfleisch, P. J. (2009). Effective health communication in Native populations in North America. *Journal of Language and Social Psychology, 28*, 158–173. doi:10.1177/0261927x08330607

Lin, R. (1987). A profile of reservation high school girls. *Journal of American Indian Education, 26*(2), 18–28. Retrieved from http://jaie.asu.edu

Lindamer, L. A., Lebowitz, B., Hough, R. L., Garcia, P., Aguirre, A., Halpain, M. C., ... Halstead, S. (2009). Establishing an implementation network: Lessons learned from community-based participatory research. *Implementation Science, 4*, Article 17. doi:10.1186/1748-5908-4-17

McDermott, V. M., Oetzel, J. G., & White, K. (2008). Ethical paradoxes in community-based participatory research. In H. M. Zoller & M. J. Dutta-Bergman (Eds.), *Emerging perspectives in health communication: Meaning, culture, and power* (pp. 182–202). New York, NY: Routledge.

Merskin, D. (1998). Sending up signals: A survey of Native American media use and representation in the mass media. *Howard Journal of Communications, 9*, 333–345. doi:10.1080/106461798246943

Miller, W. R., & Meyers, R. J. (with Hiller-Sturmhöfel, S.). (1999). The community-reinforcement approach. *Alcohol Research & Health, 23*, 116–121. Retrieved from http://www.niaaa.nih.gov/Publications/AlcoholResearch

Minkler, M., & Wallerstein, N. (2008). Introduction to CBR: New issues and emphases. In M. Minkler & N. Wallerstein (Eds.), *Community-based participatory research for health: From process to outcomes* (2nd ed., pp. 5–23). San Francisco, CA: Jossey-Bass.

Morris, R., & Wander, P. (1990). Native American rhetoric: Dancing in the shadows of the ghost dance. *Quarterly Journal of Speech, 76*, 164–191. doi:10.1080/00335639009383912

New Mexico Department of Health. (2009). *American Indian health disparities in New Mexico*. Retrieved from http://www.health.state.nm.us/DPP/2009AmericanIndianReportCard.pdf

New Mexico Department of Health, Community Health Assessment Program, Epidemiology and Response Division. (2005). *New Mexico American Indian health status report 2005*. Retrieved from http://www.health.state.nm.us/pdf/health_status_report_final.pdf

Oetting, E. R., & Beauvais, F. (1991). Orthogonal culture identification theory: The cultural identification of minority adolescents. *Substance Use & Misuse, 25*, 655–685. doi:10.3109/10826089109077265

Oetting, E. R., Beauvais, F., & Edwards, R. W. (1988). Alcohol and American Indian youth: Social and psychological correlates and prevention. *Journal of Drug Issues, 18*, 87–101.

Oetting, E. R., Edwards, R. W., & Beauvais, F. (1989). Drugs and Native-American youth. *Drugs & Society, 3*, 5–38. doi:10.1300/J023v03n01_01

Oetzel, J. G. (2005). Intercultural work group communication theory. In W. B. Gudykunst (Ed.), *Theorizing about intercultural communication* (pp. 351–371). Thousand Oaks, CA: Sage.

Oetzel, J., Duran, B., Jiang, Y., & Lucero, J. (2007). Alcohol and American Indian youth: Social and psychological correlates and prevention. *Journal of Health Communication, 12*, 187–206. doi:10.1080/10810730601152771

O'Nell, T. D., & Mitchell, C. M. (1996). Alcohol use among Native American adolescents: The role of culture in pathological drinking. *Social Science Medicine, 42*, 565–578. doi:10.1016/0277-9536(95)001573-3

Rappaport J. (1987). Terms of empowerment/exemplars of prevention: Toward a theory for community psychology. *American Journal of Community Psychology, 15*, 121–148. doi:10.1007/bf00919275

Rogers, R. A. (2009). "Your guess is as good as any": Indeterminacy, dialogue, and dissemination in interpretations of Native American rock art. *Journal of International and Intercultural Communication, 2*, 44–65. doi:10.1080/17513050802567056

Stohl, C., & Cheney, G. (2001). Participatory processes/paradoxical practices: Communication and the dilemmas of organizational democracy. *Management Communication Quarterly, 14*, 349–407. doi:10.1177/0893318901143001

Stokols, D. (1996). Translating social ecological theory into guidelines for community health promotion. *American Journal of Health Promotion, 10*, 282–298.

Sunwolf. (1999). The pedagogical and persuasive effects of Native American lesson stories, Sufi wisdom tales, and African dilemma tales. *Howard Journal of Communications, 10*, 47–71. doi:10.1080/106461799246898

Szlemko, W. J., Wood, J. W., & Thurman, P. J. (2006). Native Americans and alcohol: Past, present, and future. *Journal of General Psychology, 133*, 435–451. doi:10.3200/genp.133.4.435-451

U.S. Department of Health and Human Services, Indian Health Service. (n.d.-a). *Native American Research Centers for Health (NARCH) background.* Retrieved from http://www.ihs.gov/medicalprograms/research/narch.cfm

U.S. Department of Health and Human Services, Indian Health Service. (n.d.-b). *Regional differences in Indian health, 2000–2001.* Retrieved from http://permanent.access.gpo.gov/lps5091/2000-2001/2000-2001.pdf

U.S. Department of Health and Human Services, Indian Health Service. (2003). *2003 Navajo middle and high school youth risk behavior survey report.* Retrieved from http://www.yrbs.navajo.org

Wallerstein, N. (1999). Power between evaluator and community: Research relationships with New Mexico's healthier communities. *Social Science & Medicine, 49*, 39–53. doi:10.1016/s0277-9635(99)00073-8

Wallerstein, N. B., & Duran, B. (2006). Using community-based participatory research to address health disparities. *Society for Public Health Education, 7*, 312–323. doi:10.1177/1524839906289376

Wallerstein, N., Duran, B., Minkler, M., & Foley, K. (2005). Developing and maintaining partnerships with communities. In B. A. Israel, E. Eng, A. J. Schulz, & E. A. Parker (Eds.), *Methods in community-based participatory research for health* (pp. 31–51). San Francisco, CA: Jossey-Bass.

Wallerstein, N., Oetzel, J., Duran, B., Tafoya, G., Belone, L., & Rae, R. (2008). What predicts outcomes in CBPR? In M. Minkler & N. Wallerstein (Eds.), *Community-based participatory research for health: From process to outcomes* (2nd ed., pp. 371–392). San Francisco, CA: Jossey-Bass.

Walters, K. L., & Simoni, J. M. (2002). Reconceptualizing Native women's health: An "indigenist" stress-coping model. *American Journal of Public Health, 92*, 520–524. doi:10.2105/ajph.92.4.520

Warne, D. (2006). Research and educational approaches to reducing health disparities among American Indians and Alaska Natives. *Journal of Transcultural Nursing, 17*, 266–271. doi:10.1177/1043659606288381

Wendt, R. F. (1998). The sound of one hand clapping: Counterintuitive lessons extracted from paradoxes and double binds in participative organizations. *Management Communication Quarterly, 11*, 323–371. doi:10.1177/0893318998113001

Whitbeck, L. B. (2001, August). *Bii-zin-da-de-da: The listening to one another prevention program*. Workshop presented at the Second National Conference on Drug Abuse Prevention Research: A Progress Update, Washington, DC.

Whitbeck, L. B., Hoyt, D. R., McMorris, B. J., Chen, X., & Stubben, J. D. (2001). Perceived discrimination and early substance abuse among American Indian adolescents. *Journal of Health and Social Behavior, 42*, 405–424. Retrieved from http://www.jstor.org/action/showPublication?journalCode=jhealsocibeha

Whitbeck, L. B., Hoyt, D. R., Stubben, J. D., & LaFromboise, T. (2001). Traditional culture and academic success among American Indian children in the upper Midwest. *Journal of American Indian Education, 40*, 48–60. Retrieved from http://jaie.asu.edu

ABOUT THE EDITORS AND AUTHORS

ABOUT THE EDITORS

Lawrence R. Frey (PhD, University of Kansas, 1979) is a Professor in the Department of Communication at the University of Colorado Boulder. He teaches courses on communication research methods, applied communication, and group communication. His research seeks to understand how participation (especially by those who are marginalized, oppressed, and under-resourced) in collective communicative practices makes a difference in people's individual, relational, and communal lives, as well as how communication researchers can use their theories, methods, pedagogies, and other practices to promote social justice. He is the author or editor of 16 books, 3 special journal issues, and more than 80 published works. He is the recipient of 17 distinguished scholarship awards, including the 2011 Elizabeth G. Andersch Award (for excellence in teaching, scholarship, and mentoring) from Ohio University's School of Communication Studies; the Outstanding Scholarly Book Award (five times) from the National Communication Association's (NCA) Applied Communication Division; the Ernest Bormann Research Award (four times) from NCA's Group Communication Division; and NCA's Gerald M. Phillips Award for Distinguished Applied Communication Scholarship (lifetime achievement). He is a past president of the Central States Communication Association and a recipient of the Outstanding Young Teacher Award from that organization, as well as the

2003 Master Teacher Award from the Communication and Instruction Interest Group of the Western States Communication Association.

Kevin M. Carragee (PhD, University of Massachusetts at Amherst, 1985) is a Professor at Suffolk University, where he teaches courses in communication theory, mediated communication, and persuasion. His scholarship focuses on news and ideology, interaction between the news media and social movements, cultural studies, and forms of communication activism. He has edited 4 books and has published more than 25 journal articles and book chapters. His scholarship has appeared in leading journals in communication and journalism, including *Journal of Broadcasting and Electronic Media*, *Critical Studies in Media Communication*, *Journal of Communication*, *Journalism & Communication Monographs*, and *Political Communication*. He received a Fulbright Scholarship in 1993 for research and teaching in Poland. Since 1990, he has been a member of the Media Research and Action Project, a group that assists social movement organizations and community groups in framing their messages, influencing news coverage, and securing social and political reforms.

ABOUT THE AUTHORS

Harry Anastasiou (PhD, Union Institute and University, 2001) is a Professor of International Peace and Conflict Studies at Portland State University. His primary research interests and publications focus on international peace and conflict issues, nationalism and ethnic conflict, peacebuilding and the European Union, the Cyprus problem, and Greek–Turkish relations. In the 1990s, he played a leading role in Greek–Turkish citizen rapprochement in Cyprus. His recent publications include *The Broken Olive Branch: Nationalism, Ethnic Conflict and the Quest for Peace in Cyprus* (2 volumes).

Jennifer Asenas (PhD, The University of Texas at Austin, 2007) is an Assistant Professor of communication studies at California State University, Long Beach. Her primary research interests are narrative, race/ethnicity, and social change. She has published in *Queens: A Journal of Rhetoric and Power*; in the books *Critical Problems in Argumentation*, *Intercultural Communication: A Reader* (12th ed.), and *Thinking About Sex, Love, and Romance in the Mass Media: Media Literacy Applications*, and *War and Film in America: Historical and Critical Essays*; and has forthcoming essays in *Rhetoric Society Quarterly* and in the book *A First Amendment Profile of the Supreme Court*. In Austin, Texas, she was active in the Campaign to End the Death Penalty, and since her return to California, she has been involved with the Chico Peace and Justice Center and with the California State University Chico Campus Involvement and Awareness group, and served as a consultant for the Hope and Freedom Film Festival in Long Beach, California.

Lorenda Belone (PhD, University of New Mexico, 2010), a member of the Navajo Nation, is a research scientist with the University of New Mexico's Master of Public Health Program. She was a Robert Wood Johnson Dissertation Fellow, has worked on several National Institutes of Health (NIH) and Centers for Disease Control and Prevention capacity research projects with American-Indian communities of the southwest, and currently is principal investigator of an NIH grant.

Rick A. Buerkel (PhD, Kent State University, 1996) is an Instructor in the Department of Communication and Dramatic Arts at Central Michigan University. His research interests focus on virtual organizing, entertainment education, and environmental communication.

Benjamin J. Broome (PhD, University of Kansas, 1980) is a Professor in the Hugh Downs School of Human Communication at Arizona State University, where he teaches intercultural communication, conflict resolution, and group facilitation. His research interests focus on third-party facilitation and interactive design methodologies. Since serving as Senior Fulbright Scholar in Cyprus from 1994 to 1996, where he offered workshops, seminars, and training in intergroup relations, he has continued to work actively with a number of citizen peacebuilding groups in the eastern Mediterranean. He also has facilitated design workshops with several American-Indian tribes and with numerous government, corporate, and nonprofit organizations. His publications have appeared in leading national and international journals, and his scholarship has been recognized with several awards from the National Communication Association and the International Association of Conflict Management.

Ira Burbank (BA, Fort Lewis College, 1995), a member of the Ramah Navajo community, currently works as a substance abuse counselor/victim advocate with the Ramah Navajo Behavioral Health Department, Ramah Navajo School Board, Inc. in Pine Hill, New Mexico. He is married, father of three daughters, and a veteran of the U.S. Army with an honorable discharge.

Christopher Carey (PhD, Arizona State University, 2008; JD, Southern Illinois University, 1995) is a former Deputy District Attorney and currently an Associate Professor in Portland State University's Interdisciplinary Program—University Studies. His expertise extends to the application of international law, with an emphasis on human trafficking and working with groups to improve collaboration within the field of human rights. He served as the executive director of a U.S.-based international human rights organization that addressed human trafficking, safe migration, and gender-based violence through culturally grounded, rights-based solutions, and, during his tenure, opened offices in Bangladesh, India, Mexico, and Nepal. His work on human trafficking and intercultural communication was recognized by the California Judicial System when he testified as an expert witness. His pedagogical interests center on civic engagement and the scholarship of teaching and learning. He is author of several publications that explore topics ranging from human trafficking to communication activism.

Dana L. Cloud (PhD, University of Iowa, 1992) is an Associate Professor of communication studies at The University of Texas at Austin. She researches and teaches Marxist theory, feminist theory, social movements, public sphere theory, and the intersections among gender–race–class–sexuality in the discourses of contemporary capitalism. She is the author of the books *Control and Consolation in American Culture and Politics: Rhetorics of Therapy* and *We Are the Union: Democratic Unionism and Dissent at Boeing*, and coauthor of the book *Marxism and Communication Studies: The Point is to Change it*. Her research has appeared frequently in *Communication and Critical/Cultural Studies, Critical Studies in Media Communication, Quarterly Journal of Speech, Rhetoric & Public Affairs*, and the *Western Journal of Communication*, and in numerous edited books. A longtime activist, she is a member of the International Socialist Organization.

Jeanette L. Drake (PhD, Bowling Green State University, 2004) is an Associate Professor of communication at The University of Findlay. Her scholarship is informed by 14 years as a public relations practitioner and focuses on ethics, social justice, and environmental communication, with an emphasis on food. She is particularly interested in the influence of framing on public dialogue about health and the environment, and, subsequently, on public policy.

Kathleen Feyh (MA, University of Texas at Austin, 2001) is a doctoral candidate in the Department of Communication Studies at the University of Texas at Austin, where she studies globalization and Russian popular culture from a Marxist perspective. She also is a Visiting Instructor at Southwestern University, teaching courses on social movements, rhetorical criticism, race and ethnicity, and hip-hop cultures. Her scholarly work has appeared in *Journal of Communication Inquiry*, the book *Activism and Rhetoric: Theories and Contexts for Political Engagement*, and conference proceedings in both Russia and the United States. A former union organizer and longtime activist, she has been involved for a number of years in the Campaign to End the Death Penalty and in the International Socialist

Organization, and she is committed to rebuilding a fighting left in the United States.

Carolyn E. Finster (MSHA, University of Colorado Denver, 1989) is the Acting Director of Health and Human Services, Ramah Navajo School Board, Inc., and Clinic Administrator for the Pine Hill Health Center, New Mexico. Since 1994, she has worked in the Ramah Navajo community, overseeing departments of the Pine Hill Health Center, Behavioral Health Services, and Ramah Navajo Social Services, tribally operated programs that are contracted with the Indian Health Service and the Bureau of Indian Affairs. She takes an active role in working with the various programs, services, and activities, and she participates in statewide and national committees that seek to improve the health status of American Indians and Alaska Natives.

Christopher R. Groscurth (PhD, University of Georgia, 2008) is a senior culture transformation consultant with Trinity Health, a nonprofit Catholic health-care system, where he designs culture change interventions that promote quality and associate engagement, and that ensure services for underserved communities. His engaged research and consulting practice mobilize communication and culture to promote positive organizational change.

Maria Hadjipavlou (PhD, Boston University, 1987) is an Associate Professor in the Department of Social and Political Sciences at the University of Cyprus, where she teaches comparative politics, gender studies, conflict resolution, international peace and security, and the Cyprus conflict. Her research interests include conflict resolution and ethnonational conflicts; feminist theories; gender, conflict, and peace; memory; narratives; and reconciliation. Her latest book is *Women and Change in Cyprus: Feminisms and Gender in Conflict*, and her work appears in *Cyprus Review*; *Journal of Peace Research*; *Gender, Place and Culture*; *Innovation Journal*; and *Journal of Mediterranean Studies*; and in many edited books. She was a postdoctoral fellow at Harvard University and is a research associate of Harvard's Program in International Conflict Analysis and Resolution at the Center of International Affairs. She also was a visiting scholar at the School of International and Public Affairs, Columbia University, where she cofounded and is a research associate of the Center of International Conflict Resolution. She is a founding member of the nongovernmental organizations "The Peace Center" and "Hands Across the Divide," and she is a consultant and member of experts at the Council of Europe on issues of intercultural dialogue and equality between men and women.

Jennifer Henio-Charley, a member of the Ramah Navajo community, is a State of New Mexico certified and licensed Substance Abuse Counselor with the Ramah Navajo Behavioral Health Department, Ramah Navajo School Board, Inc., in Pine Hill, New Mexico. She is a wife and mother of three children.

Karen Jeffreys directed communication for the Rhode Island Coalition against Domestic Violence (RICADV) for 10 years. She now is Associate Director of the Rhode Island Coalition for the Homeless (RICH), where she coordinates statewide communication campaigns to end homelessness.

Bülent Kanol (PhD, University of Brighton, 2003; MBA, Emory University, as the first graduate CASP scholar of AMIDEAST, 1984) is the founding executive director of The Management Centre of the Mediterranean (MC). As executive director and a senior consultant of the MC, he has been involved in capacity building and organizational development of civil society organizations. He led the major CIVICUS Civil Society Index study in Cyprus and organized international conferences on "Increasing the Role of Civil Society through Participatory Democracy." He has been an active member of the peacebuilding and conflict resolution community in Cyprus, and has contributed a number of research publications in that area, including coauthorship of the Cumulative Impact Case Study, titled "The Impact of Peacebuilding Work on the Cyprus Conflict."

Lula Kelhoyouma (BA, Fort Lewis College, 1998), a member of the Ramah Navajo community, has experience in social work and an associate license in substance abuse, and currently works with the Ramah Navajo Behavioral Health Department, Ramah Navajo School Board, Inc., in Pine Hill, New Mexico. She is pursuing a license alcohol and drug abuse certification.

Yin-Mae Lee is a grassroots organizer and educator in the Ramah Navajo community, working with community families and programs to promote and strengthen Ramah Navajo lifeways, values, and traditions. She is a firm believer in lifelong learning, as reflected in her work with traditional weavers in the Ramah Navajo Weavers Association and with developing multigenerational continuing education and family/early education programs at the Ramah Navajo School Board, Inc., in Pine Hill, New Mexico.

Phoebe G. Maria (BA, University of New Mexico, 2004), a member of White Mountain Apache Tribe of Arizona who has lived in the Ramah Navajo community for 30 years, has an associate license in substance abuse and currently works as a Victim Advocate for the domestic violence program with the Ramah Navajo Behavioral Health Department, Ramah Navajo School Board, Inc., in Pine Hill, New Mexico.

About the Editors and Authors

Steve May (PhD, University of Utah, 1993) is an Associate Professor in the Department of Communication Studies at the University of North Carolina at Chapel Hill (UNC). His research focuses on work and identity as related to public–private, work–family, and labor–leisure boundaries. Most recently, he has studied challenges and opportunities for organizational ethics and corporate social responsibility, with particular attention to ethical practices of dialogic communication, transparency, participation, courage, and accountability. His books include *The Debate over Corporate Social Responsibility*, *Case Studies in Organizational Communication: Ethical Perspectives and Practices*, *Engaging Organizational Communication Theory and Research: Multiple Perspectives*, and *The Handbook of Communication Ethics*. He is a Leadership Fellow at the Institute for the Arts and the Humanities, and an Ethics Fellow at the Parr Center for Ethics. He recently was named a UNC Houle Engaged Scholar and a Page Legacy Scholar by Pennsylvania State University, and he serves as an ethics advisor for the Ethics at Work program at Duke University's Kenan Institute for Ethics. He is a past editor of *Management Communication Quarterly*.

Bryan McCann (PhD, The University of Texas at Austin, 2009) is an Assistant Professor in the Department of Communication at Wayne State University. His published work on the rhetorical dynamics of the criminal justice system has appeared in *Communication and Critical/ Cultural Studies* and *Western Journal of Communication*. He is a member of the Prison Communication, Activism, Research, and Education (PCARE) collective, and has been active in community organizing around the death penalty and labor issues.

John G. Oetzel (PhD, University of Iowa, 1995) is a Professor in the Department of Communication Management at the University of Waikato, New Zealand. He teaches courses in conflict, intercultural communication, and health communication, as well as quantitative research methods. His research program centers on understanding and improving problematic interaction between and among people with different group identities (particularly cultural identities). He is the author of the book *Intercultural Communication: A Layered Approach*, coauthor (with Stella Ting-Toomey) of *Managing Intercultural Communication Effectively*, and editor (with Stella Ting-Toomey) of *The Sage Handbook of Conflict Communication*, as well as the author of more than 60 journal articles and book chapters.

Michael J. Papa (PhD, Temple University, 1986) is a Professor in the Department of Communication and Dramatic Arts at Central Michigan University. His research interests focus on organizing for social change, innovation diffusion, and conflict management.

Wendy H. Papa (PhD Ohio University, 1994) is a Professor in the Department of Communication and Dramatic Arts at Central Michigan University. Her research interests focus on organizing for social change, communication pedagogy, and conflict management.

Rebecca Rae (dual MA, community & regional planning, and water resources, University of New Mexico, 2010) is research scientist in the Master in Public Health Program at the University of New Mexico. She has worked on several Native-American Research Center for Health (NARCH) research projects, in collaboration with a few southwest tribes. In addition to conducting community-based participatory research projects, she works as an evaluator for a national Native leadership program.

Alvin Rafelito (MHA, Webster University, 2004), a member of the Dine Nation (Navajo) who has worked extensively with American-Indian communities, is Program Director of the Scholarship, Employment and Training Services, Ramah Navajo School Board, Inc., in Pine Hill, New Mexico. He has worked with the National Indian Council on Aging on health-disparity issues for American-Indian and Alaska Native Elders, and on diabetes disparity through community and family gardens. He is a board member of Hunger Grow Away, Inc., a nonprofit organization working on eliminating hunger one family at a time through abundant harvest gardens. He is a member of the American Public Health Association and has presented on community-based participatory research methods in collaboration with the University of New Mexico's Masters in Public Health Program. He also is a trained community interviewer for the Albuquerque Area Southwest Tribal Epidemiology Center's Tribal Behavioral Risk Factor Surveillance System Project.

Charlotte Ryan is a Professor in the Department of Sociology at University of Massachusetts Lowell. As codirector of the Media Research Action Project, she collaborated with the Rhode Island Coalition against Domestic Violence for a decade. Currently, she supports Praxis Project's Communities Creating Healthy Environments, a multipronged challenge to structural racism.

Greg Tafoya (MPH, University of New Mexico, 2010), a member of Santa Clara Pueblo in New Mexico and also of Sauk and Fox descent, currently is a research scientist at the University of New Mexico. He is committed to serving communities through participatory approaches and public health research that benefits all partners involved.

Anderson Thomas (MA, Western New Mexico University, 2002; LMHC, State of New Mexico, 2005), a member of the Navajo Nation, has served, for the past 10 years, as a Behavioral Health Counselor for the Ramah Navajo community, and currently serves as Program Director for the Ramah Navajo Behavioral Health Department, Ramah Navajo School Board, Inc., in Pine Hill, New Mexico.

Nina Wallerstein (DrPH, University of California, Berkeley, 1988) is a Professor in the Department of Family and Community Medicine, currently directs the Center for Participatory Research, and was the founding director of the Master in Public Health Program at the University of New Mexico. For more than 30 years, she has been involved in empowerment and popular education, and in participatory research, with youth, women, tribes, and underserved communities in the United States and in Latin American. She is the author or editor of six health and adult education books, including *Community-Based Participatory Research for Health: From Process to Outcomes* (2nd ed., with Meredith Minkler), as well as the author of more than 100 journal articles and book chapters.

Linda S. Welker (PhD, Southern Illinois University, Carbondale, 1995) is Project Manager of the nonprofit organization Hope for Women and Children of Southern Sudan (HWCSS) and an Adjunct Professor in the School of Communications at Grand Valley State University. Her research interests include the performative construction of identity politics and power relations in marginalized, underserved, and oppressed communities, with a particular focus on genocide and other strategies of oppression and control. She has conducted research with Southern Sudanese refugee communities, Darfurian refugee communities, and Eastern European communities that suffered under communist oppression. Using community-based performance techniques, Welker also advocates for such groups through performance productions (e.g., *A Prayer for Sudan*, *Voices Unheard*, and *Divine Reverberations*).

INDEX

Academia/academic(s), 2, 72, 90, 113, 124, 168, 194, 233, 249, 252, 263, 271, 283, 327–328, 331, 353, 357, 373, 375, 377, 390, 403–405, 423
   and (communication) activism (research), 4, 26, 193–194, 210, 252, 314, 421
   collaboration with others, 113, 124, 182, 191, 193–194, 210–211
   engaged research in, 18, 26, 353, 357
   power/privilege, 191, 211, 271, 302
   and theorizing, 2–3, 182, 211
   and service-learning, 389–390, 392
Acquired Immune Deficiency Syndrome (AIDS), 108–109, 122, 129
   activism, 29(n)
Action research, 10, 30(n), 167, 190, 192, 301, 309, 329–330. *See also* Community-based participatory research (CBPR)
Action Research, 30(n)
Activism/activist(s), 3–9, 11, 13–15, 20–21, 25–26, 28–29(n), 111, 151, 182, 185, 188, 191–194, 196, 203, 206, 211, 224, 226, 228, 236, 250–251, 269–271, 273, 310, 317, 331, 354, 369, 373, 377, 383. *See also* Communication activism/activist(s); Communication activism for social justice research
   contexts/forms of, 11, 13–15, 21–22, 25–26, 28–30(n), 70, 72, 83–84, 86, 89, 91, 94, 96, 97(n), 106, 124, 128, 179–180, 184, 195–196, 265, 269, 326–328
   pedagogy/teaching, 10, 27, 265
   and (community-based) performance (CBP), 11–12, 142, 161, 168–169, 171
   and research, 3–5, 26–27, 130, 194
   scholar-activist, 11–12, 15, 18–21, 26, 28, 72, 167, 172, 181, 192, 203, 206, 210, 226, 229, 252, 264, 271, 281–283, 295, 297, 301, 308, 314–316, 330
Advertising/marketing/sales, 8, 150, 181, 188–189, 191, 227, 237, 245, 270, 327, 330–331, 342, 350, 359(a), 379
Aesthetic(s), 143–144, 160–161, 167, 306, 314
   theatre, 143, 154
Africa/African(s), 132(n), 140, 142, 144–145, 148–149, 151, 153, 155–156, 164, 166, 168–170, 172, 173(n). *See also* Sudan

studies, 193, 210
African American(s)/black(s), 193, 271, 292, 294, 299–300, 305, 369
  activism, 29(n), 193
  death penalty/prison statistics, 266–267
  National Association for the Advancement of Colored People (NAACP), 277
  Legal Defense and Educational Fund, 266
  perceptions/portrayals of, 159–160, 267, 276–277, 291–292
Agency/agent (social change), 115–117, 160, 172, 185, 191, 203, 231, 237, 269, 278, 302, 307, 348–349, 352, 354, 390
Agenda(s), 143, 173, 236, 238 251, 412
  activist, 154, 156, 167
  political/policy, 185, 203–204, 207
  -setting, 183, 204–208, 236, 238
Agriculture, 224–229, 231, 234, 237–238, 244–245, 247–248, 253–254. *See also* Food; Sustainability
  industry, 224–225, 229, 244–245, 248
  Ohio Department of Agriculture (ODA), 225, 233, 235–236, 239, 240(f), 242, 246–248, 253
Alaska Native(s), 370, 401, 407, 427(n)
American Indian and Alaska Native Mental Health Research: A Journal of the National Center, 427(n)
America/American(s), 2, 108, 113, 153, 166, 212(n), 226–227, 267. *See also* African/American(s)/black(s); American Indian(s)/Native American(s); United States (U.S.)
  activism in (North/South), 29(n)
  European-American, 299, 302
American Indian(s)/Native American(s), 16–17, 25, 369–370, 404–405
  activism, 29(n)
  "Bii-Zin-Da-De-Dah" project with, 405–406, 409
  children/youth, 402–403, 405–406, 410, 413, 417–423, 424(a), 426–427(a), 428(n)
    boarding schools, 403, 428(n)
    Navajo Nation Middle and High School Youth Risk Behavior Survey (2003), 408
  community/tribes, 402–405, 407–411, 415–416, 421–424
    action projects, 410–411, 420
    assessment, 409, 412, 416–417
  community-based participatory research (CBPR) with, 407–408, 415–418, 421–423
  culture/cultural, 403–407, 409, 411, 413, 415, 417–419, 421, 423, 424(a), 426(a), 428(n)
    communication, 404, 406, 409, 420
    culturally/empirically supported interventions (CSIs/ESIs), 405, 415, 418, 421–422, 424
    differences with (white) researchers, 25, 407, 421–423
    identities/identification, 402–403, 406, 412, 418–420, 423–424, 424(a), 426(a)
    traditions and values, 406, 409, 412
  discrimination against, 403–406
  family/families, 402–403, 405–407, 409–412, 417, 420, 424, 425–426(a)
    communication, 409, 412, 418–420, 423, 424(a), 426(a)
  health, 401–404, 407–409, 411–412, 421, 423–424, 428(n)
    Albuquerque Area Indian Health Board (AAIHB), 408
    American Indian and Alaska Native Mental Health Research: A Journal of the National Center, 427(n)
    Indian Health Care Improvement Act, 408
  intervention/prevention, 402, 405, 407, 410–411, 417
  substance use, 401–408, 410, 417, 421–424
  Native American Research Centers for Health (NARCH), 407, 417
  Navajo Nation, 407–408
    Human Research Review Board, 409–410

Index

Ramah Navaho
  Advisory Council (RNAC), 409–410, 412–413, 415–416, 418, 420, 422-423
  community, 402, 404–405, 407–411, 415–417, 422, 424
  Family Listening (RNFL) project, 17, 21, 24, 27, 406–413, 415–424
  School Board, Inc. (RSNB), 408–409
Animal(s), 24. *See also* Buckeye Egg Farm (BE); Concentrated animal feeding operations (CAFOs); Concerned Citizens of Central Ohio (CCCO); Farm(s)/farmer(s); Food activism/rights, 14, 25, 29(n), 231, 237, 239, 254
  Animal Welfare Act, 224
  care, 224–225, 227, 248, 254
  farmed, 224–227, 237, 244, 252–254
  Humane Society of the United States, 233, 237
  Mercy for Animals, 237, 254
  People for the Ethical Treatment of Animals (PETA), 233
Applied research, 5, 18–19
  Bureau of Applied Social Research, 5
  communication, 6–7, 9, 23, 26, 120, 293, 297, 390
  Journal of Applied Communication(s) Research, 6
  special issue on "Communication and Social Justice Research," 9
A Prayer for Sudan, 12, 140–142, 149–150, 156–158, 160–167, 169, 172–173, 173–174(n)
  TalkBack session for, 141, 151, 153, 155–157, 167, 171–172
Arab(s)/Arabic, 145, 148, 160, 163–166, 173(n)
  United Arab Emirates, 144–145
Asia/Asian(s), 172, 299, 307, 369–370.
  See also Bangladesh; India/Indian(s); Nepal/Nepalese
  Americans, 305
  activism in, 30(n)
  Asian-American, 30(n)
  Korea/Korean, 300, 316
  South(east), 106, 116, 119, 123, 125–126, 129–131
  Cambodia, 108
  Dalit class, 122, 132(n)
  human trafficking in, 11–12, 19, 25, 27, 108, 111, 123–125, 128
  Thailand, 12, 124
Bangladesh, 106, 111, 122–126, 127, 132(n), 368, 371, 373
  Grameen Bank, 368, 371, 373
Basic (pure) communication research, 6, 18–19
Brainstorming, 81, 198, 201, 375, 384
Buckeye Egg Farm (BE; formerly AgriGeneral; now Ohio Fresh Eggs), 14, 224–226, 232–233, 236–239, 240(f), 241, 243, 245–248, 247(f), 254–255
  Pohlmann, owner Anton, 232
Business/corporate/managerial, 8–9, 15–16, 18, 22, 108–109, 111, 123, 125, 129, 131, 132(n), 183–184, 187–188, 212(n), 225, 227, 232–233, 238–239, 245, 247–252, 255, 292, 310–313, 315–316, 326–327, 329–334, 337, 339, 341–345, 347–350, 353, 355–357, 358–360(a), 371, 373–374, 376, 379, 384.
  See also Economics
  activism, 29(n)
  agriculture/livestock, 23, 224–225, 227–229, 231, 233, 238–239, 241–248, 247(f), 255
  industry–government/state alliance, 228, 238, 241–243, 246, 247(f)
  ethics, 16, 325–327, 333, 348, 350
  public relations, 14, 226, 249
  small, 234, 368, 377, 384, 393
Campaign(s), 12, 14–15, 17, 21, 27, 181, 188, 195, 207, 233, 250, 275, 279–283, 326. *See also* Rhode Island Coalition Against Domestic Violence (RICADV); Social movement(s)
  against animal feeding operations, 232–233, 239, 249

against death penalty, 270–271, 274
Campaign to End the Death Penalty (CEDP), 269–274, 277, 279–280, 282–283, 285(n)
Capacity building, 12, 112–113, 118, 123, 181, 195–196, 202–203, 205–206, 212(n), 309, 312, 423
communication, 13, 195
Capital punishment, 2, 11, 13–14, 19, 263, 265–269, 274, 276, 278, 282–284. *See also* Death penalty
Capitalism, 212, 274, 350, 371, 379
Case study/studies, 9, 23, 107, 171, 229, 242, 248, 328–329, 340, 345, 350
Caucasian(s)/white(s), 13, 15, 17, 25, 111, 126, 142, 144–145, 160, 252, 266–267, 271, 292–294, 297, 299–300, 302–306, 308–310, 316, 369–370, 402, 407, 415, 424(a). *See also* Whiteness
Charity, 16, 282, 377, 382–384, 387, 391, 393. *See also* Social justice
Chicano/a(s)/Hispanic(s)/Latino/a(s), 2, 266, 299–300, 316, 369, 402
activism, 29(n)
studies, 194, 210
Children, 122, 153, 161, 165, 185, 285(n), 309, 369, 372, 385. *See also* Youth
activities/care/services for, 85, 110, 118, 122, 181, 369
American Indian/Native American, 402–403, 405–406, 410, 413, 416–420, 422–423, 424(a), 426–427(a), 428(n)
sexual workers/slavery/trafficking of, 12, 105, 107–108, 115–116, 159
Citizen(s)/citizenship, 2, 19–21, 28, 75, 81, 91–92, 121, 156, 163, 173(n), 191, 204, 224–226, 228–229, 232–234, 239, 241, 246, 247(t), 248, 250, 254, 270, 277, 282, 300, 307, 311, 313, 374. *See also* Concerned Citizens of Central Ohio (CCCO)
Civic(s), 2, 5, 20, 25, 251, 295, 327, 389–391
Civil
behavior/disobedience, 263, 269, 274, 280, 282, 285(n), 313, 331
society, 12, 72, 80, 92–93
Civil rights, 21, 112, 186, 326. *See also* Human rights
activism, 29(n)
Highlander Center, 192–193
movement, 111, 193
Class, 8, 142, 162, 184, 186, 190, 252, 267, 270, 272, 278, 297, 316, 342, 354, 369, 383
classism, 169, 298
Dalit, 122, 132(n)
Coalition(s), 179–180, 195, 210, 212(a), 237, 243, 251, 273, 407–409. *See also* Collaboration(s)/partnership(s); Rhode Island Coalition Against Domestic Violence (RICADV)
Collaboration(s)/partnership(s), 16–17, 121, 142, 182, 186, 192, 209, 239, 299, 310, 326, 328, 342, 353, 358–360(a), 368, 372, 374, 378, 384, 387–391, 412, 415, 417–418. *See also* Coalition(s)
and community-based participatory research (CBPR), 407, 413, 416, 418, 421, 423
against domestic violence (DV), 13, 19, 24, 196, 210
against human trafficking, 12, 109–110, 117, 119, 124–125, 129, 132
industry–government/state, 228, 238, 241–242
with Ramah Navajo, 17, 25, 402, 404, 407–409, 415–416, 422, 424
scholars, 19, 130, 185, 188, 190, 193–194, 209–211, 316, 357, 413, 416–417, 421–422
and service-learning, 389–391
Collective, 142–143, 348–349, 373, 384–385, 422
action/actors, 13, 21, 75, 90, 93–94, 182, 185–188, 193–194, 203, 205–209, 211–212(a), 230–231, 237, 239, 275–276
empowerment, 189, 191, 203, 205–206, 377
Colonialism/postcolonialism, 77–78, 115–116, 127, 130–131, 186

Index

Communication(s), 11, 15, 21–23, 85, 93, 109, 111–112, 115, 119, 149, 154, 161, 167, 187, 189–190, 196, 198, 202–203, 205, 212(n), 224, 232–233, 236–238, 242, 249, 264, 266, 273, 292, 294, 297, 300, 311–312, 314, 370, 378, 390, 394, 410, 420–422. *See also* Communication activism; Communication activism for social justice research; Message(s)
   American Indian/Native American, 404–405, 416, 418–420, 423, 424(a), 426(a)
   capacity (building), 13, 195–196, 202
   and conflict, 70, 72, 80–82, 85–86, 92, 94–96
   and countertrafficking, 109, 117, 132
   cultural/intercultural/multicultural/interracial, 111, 119, 122, 296–297, 300, 303–304, 311–312, 415
   and democracy, 189–190, 298, 380
   dialogue, 16, 94, 119, 328–330, 333–335, 337, 339, 344–345, 351, 356–357, 380
   discipline/areas, 3, 6–7, 19–20, 22, 26, 109, 189, 235, 296, 357, 368, 373, 376, 390
   empowerment, 367, 377–380
   equipment/systems, 183, 185–186, 190, 195–196, 198, 201–202, 207, 209
   family, 17, 412, 418–420, 423, 424(a), 426(a)
   group/interpersonal, 22, 190, 315, 373, 415–416
   interventions, 22–23, 226, 318, 402, 405, 407, 409
   knowledge/skills/training, 3, 7, 13, 15, 21–22, 95, 123, 158–159, 169–179, 192, 195, 197, 207, 209, 300, 309, 311–312, 315, 345, 372, 375, 383–384, 388, 390, 405, 415
   mass/media/technologies (new), 3, 8, 22, 188, 190, 274–275
   (and) organizations/organizational, 8–10, 14–15, 21–22, 122, 202, 250, 292, 295–296, 300–302, 308, 315, 317, 327, 329–330, 355, 373
   participatory, 13–14, 22, 125, 180–182, 189–193, 202–203, 207, 211–212(a), 212(n), 421–422
   research/scholars, 3, 5–12, 14–28, 30(n), 72–73, 141, 148, 158, 167, 172, 180–181, 185, 188, 191, 226, 231, 263, 265, 293, 295–298, 302, 308, 346, 357, 368, 370, 372, 404
   by Rhode Island Coalition Against Domestic Violence (RICADV), 180–181, 197, 200–202, 210
   and social change/justice, 6, 8, 18, 22, 26, 121, 301, 382–383
   and social movements, 14, 181, 188, 194, 209
   strategies, 14, 19, 24, 81–82, 94, 106, 180, 185–190, 195–198, 202, 208, 210–211, 211–212(a), 233, 235, 242, 246, 249, 265, 274, 277, 280–283, 295, 311, 315, 335, 371, 404
   theory/theorists, 22–23, 182, 190–191, 194, 265, 296–297, 373, 415
Communication activism/activist(s), 5–7, 18, 20–21, 24, 27, 72, 94, 96, 106, 132, 142, 158, 161, 167, 171–172, 174(n), 181, 185, 196, 209–211, 224, 229, 233, 239, 248–249, 252, 254–255, 265, 282, 293–294, 307, 312, 314, 329, 357, 368, 373, 377–378, 393–395, 402, 404, 406, 413, 415, 420–421, 424. *See also* Communication activism for social justice research
Communication activism for social justice research, 3, 5–13, 15–16, 18–22, 24–28, 93, 142, 158, 161, 167, 171–172, 189, 196, 226, 293, 297–298, 301, 309–310, 312–314, 317, 326, 329, 352–353, 358, 368, 382, 402
   Communication Activism: Vol. 1. Communication for Social Change, 11
   Communication Activism: Vol. 2. Media and Performance Activism, 11
   contexts/forms of, 10–16, 18–23, 25, 27–28, 72–73, 106, 132, 180–182, 265, 357

and critical whiteness studies (CWS), 297–299
ethics of, 311, 317
and intervention, 7–11, 13–17, 21–24, 27–28, 297, 299, 308, 310–311, 357, 405
lessons learned about, 11, 13, 17–28, 92–95, 126–131, 167–172, 209–210, 249–254, 281–283, 314–317, 351–357, 393–394, 420–424
research methods/theory, 22–24, 28, 182, 211, 246
Communism/communist(s), 274
activism, 29(n)
Community/communities, 13, 17, 20–21, 25, 89–90, 115, 125, 180–181, 188–191, 197, 199–201, 208, 227, 238, 248, 264, 270, 272–275, 277, 279, 284, 292, 295, 297–299, 301–303, 307, 311–315, 326, 329–332, 342, 344, 347–349, 357, 360(a), 367–369, 372, 374, 376, 381–383, 385, 389–392
Alinsky, community organizer Saul, 193
American Indian/Native American, 402–405, 407–411, 415–416, 421–424
anti-/countertrafficking, 110, 113, 115–117, 121, 124–125, 128–131
diverse/marginalized/poor, 190, 204–206, 212(n), 243, 292, 300, 302–303, 305, 307, 312–314, 316, 318, 371
and Fire Services, 299–300, 304–310, 312–313, 316
Greek-/Turkish-Cypriot, 70, 73, 75–77, 80, 82–84, 86–88, 93, 95, 97–98(n), 120
international, 70, 76, 84–86, 94, 96, 106, 115
learning, 182, 191, 193, 209, 212(a)
in Ohio, 232, 234–235, 252, 254–255, 368, 376, 378–379, 381–383, 393–394
outreach/relations, 197, 199, 300–301, 311, 315, 327, 341, 343, 358–359(a)
peacebuilding, 72, 89, 97(n)
rural, 223, 228, 235, 253
research/scholars, 3, 5–12, 14–28, 30(n), 72–73, 141, 148, 158, 167, 172, 180–181, 185, 188, 191, 226, 231, 263, 265, 293, 295–298, 302, 308, 346, 357, 368, 370, 372, 404
Community-based organizations (CBOs), 16, 114(f), 191–192, 195
Community-based performance (CBP), 12–13, 140–144, 146, 151, 158, 161–163, 167, 169, 171–172, 174(n)
class/course, 141, 144–146, 149, 151, 159–160, 174(n)
Community-based (participatory) research (CBPR), 5, 9–10, 17, 19–20, 23–24, 30(n), 130, 407–408, 413, 414(f), 415–418, 420–423
Compromise, 70, 75–76, 94, 132, 192, 224–225, 274, 359(a)
Concentrated animal feeding operations (CAFOs), 14, 223, 225–228, 232–236, 242–246, 248, 252–254. *See also* Animal(s); Buckeye Egg Farm (BE); Concerned Citizens of Central Ohio (CCCO); Farm(s)/farmer(s); Food
Concerned Citizens of Central Ohio (CCCO), 14, 21, 226, 229, 233–239, 241, 248, 250–253, 255. *See also* Animal(s); Buckeye Egg Farm (BE); Concentrated animal feeding operations (CAFOs); Farm(s)/farmer(s); Food
Beneath the Shell (newsletter), 235, 237–239, 252
Conflict, 94, 120, 125, 183, 191, 194, 205, 225, 232, 236, 239, 242, 279, 298, 305, 415
between scholars and activists/marginalized, 25–26, 271
communication research on, 72–73, 94–95
cultural/(inter)ethnic, 19, 72–73, 77, 89, 403
in Cyprus, 27, 69–70, 72–81, 84, 88–90, 96, 97(n)
management/resolution, 23, 72, 77–78, 88, 90, 92–94, 97, 97(n), 122, 339
dialogue, 89–90, 94–95, 120

protracted, 12, 72–73, 77–78, 92, 94–95, 120
  in Sudan, 13, 163–164, 168, 172, 173–174(n)
  transformation, 72, 89, 91–93, 97(n)
  Lederach's theory of, 90–91
Consensus, 94, 121, 188, 224, 311, 327, 332, 349
Constituency/constituencies, 91, 183–184, 186–187, 190–192, 195, 200, 203, 205–208, 329. *See also* Stakeholder(s)
Consulting, 11, 18–19, 72, 84, 92, 113, 115, 200, 209, 233, 235, 310, 332, 353, 409; *see also* Training/trainer(s)
  National Consultation on Better Legal Response to Human Trafficking, 118, 124–125, 131–132
Consumerism/customer(s), 237, 242, 253, 295, 305, 326–327, 342–344, 350–352, 359(a), 373, 375, 377–379, 384, 388, 390. *See also* Constituency/constituencies; Stakeholder(s)
  activism, 29(n)
Content analysis, 23, 231, 238
Countertrafficking, 12, 109, 117, 119, 122–123, 128–130. *See also* Human Trafficking
  community/network, 110, 116–117, 123–125
  field, 105–106, 109–110
  stakeholders, 110, 116–117, 124
Credibility, 152, 208, 232, 238, 252, 265, 272–274, 277–278, 310, 355
Crisis/crises, 139, 143, 172, 181, 208, 244–245, 248–249, 253
  economic, 325–326
  Hurricane Katrina, 291
Critical pedagogy, 16, 377, 387–388
Critical research, 8, 141, 296–297, 300, 329, 355–356, 372
  perspectives/theory, 8–10, 22–23, 233, 249–251
  whiteness (studies; CWS), 15, 293, 296–299, 301, 314, 317
Criticism/critic(s), 26, 185, 191, 193, 203, 228, 232, 239, 246, 295, 308, 329, 331
  rhetorical, 7, 9, 23, 296

Culture/cultural, 12, 15, 17, 19, 22–24, 147–149, 154, 158–159, 162–163, 167, 172, 180, 186–187, 192–193, 203, 207–210, 226, 230, 233, 239, 253, 292–294, 297, 302, 306, 311, 313, 315, 317, 330, 382–383, 403. *See also* Intercultural
  American Indian/Native American, 25, 403–407, 409, 411–413, 415, 417–419, 421–423, 424(a), 426(a), 428(n)
  communication, 111, 119, 122, 296–297, 300, 303–304, 311–312, 415
  conflict, 19, 72–73, 77, 89, 403
  cross-cultural, 144–145, 161, 168
  culturally supported interventions (CSIs), 405
  differences, 93, 308–309, 311, 313–314, 317, 422
  diversity, 12, 17, 292, 305, 314, 316, 415, 421–422
  identities/identification, 292, 316, 402–403, 406, 412, 418–420, 423–424, 424(a), 426(a)
  multicultural, 15, 300, 312, 316
  norms/other practices, 8, 187, 203–204, 302, 315, 390
  organizational/organizing, 183, 206, 325, 328, 330–333, 337, 347–349, 351, 355
  Others, 148, 169
  systems, 18, 183, 205
Cultural studies, 7–9, 189, 293
Cyprus, 20, 73, 78–80, 93
  bicommunal communication/movement in, 12, 22, 70, 72, 74, 78–91, 93–96, 97–98(n)
  buffer zone ("Green Line"), 11, 69–70, 71(f), 72–76, 80–83, 85–87, 89, 94–96, 97–98(n)
  events, 70, 72, 74–77, 80–93, 95–96, 97–98(n)
  conflict in, 69–70, 72–81, 84, 88–94, 96–97, 97(n)
  ethnocentric nationalism in, 73, 76–80, 84, 89, 94–95
  Greek Cypriots, 11–12, 22, 25, 27, 70, 72–86, 88–91, 93–96, 97(n), 120
    Clerides, leader Glafcos, 88

history of, 69–70, 73–74, 78–79
map of, 71(f)
  cities in, 69–70, 71(f), 73, 75–76, 86, 96
news media coverage of, 70, 77, 82–83, 90, 97(n)
peace
  activists/movement in, 70, 72, 80–84, 86–89, 91, 93–96, 97–98(n)
  building in, 11, 72–73, 80, 82–83, 85, 89–96, 97–98(n)
  and United Nations, 70, 74, 76, 86, 96
Republic of, 69, 74, 79
rhetoric in, 70, 75–76, 81, 83, 94–95
Turkish Cypriots, 11–12, 70, 72–86, 88–91, 93–96, 97(n)
  Denktash, leader Raulf, 88
Youth in, 76, 86–87, 96

Death, 1, 70, 140, 152–154, 164, 197, 224, 254–255, 270, 309, 370, 402. *See also* Death penalty
Death penalty, 14, 326. *See also* Capital punishment
  anti-death penalty movement, 15, 21
  Campaign to End the Death Penalty (CEDP), 269–274, 277, 279–280, 282–283, 285(n)
  death row, 2, 263, 265–267, 269–270, 274, 276, 278–279, 282–283, 370
  Death Row Inner-Communalist Vanguard Engagement (DRIVE), 269, 271–272, 279, 283
  Enmund v. Florida (1982), 269
  executions, 263–267, 270, 274, 276–279, 281–282, 284, 285(n)
    Graham, Gary (aka Shaka Sankofa), 264, 274, 285(n)
    Newton, Frances, 264, 286(n)
  McCleskey v. Kemp (1987), 266–267
    Baldus Study, 266–267
  poverty/race and, 14, 266–268
  Prejean, abolitionist Sister Helen, 264
Decision making, 93, 95, 113, 121–122, 131, 171, 186, 201, 204–205, 207–208, 235, 243, 246–248, 274, 326, 335–336, 338, 346, 348, 356–357, 391

collective/community/group, 3, 89, 92–94, 186, 206, 211(a), 283, 385
ethical, 16, 328, 330, 332–334, 336–338, 341–342, 345, 348–350, 352, 355
research (communication activism), 86, 283, 301, 317, 354–355, 413, 416
Deliberation, 82, 88, 94, 186, 328, 332, 339, 349, 351, 357
Democracy, 3, 8–9, 13–14, 24–25, 74, 93–94, 127, 180, 183, 185, 190, 203, 205, 207, 282, 372
  and communication, 189–190, 298, 380
Development, 111–112, 130, 142, 166, 204, 236, 337, 339, 344–345, 348, 351, 390, 403, 407, 409, 417
  business/economic, 367–368, 371–372, 376–377, 384, 393–395, 409
  capacity building, 112–113, 408
  communication, 112, 372
  developing/Third World, 112–113, 126
  international, 12, 110–117, 128–130
  participatory vs. top-down models of, 189–190
  sustainable, 113, 224–224
Dialectical perspective, 127–128
  and communication, 132
  activism (research), 210, 252
  tensions, 11, 16, 106, 119, 127–131, 210, 249, 252–253, 298, 328, 346–351, 354–356, 390
Dialogue, 15–16, 94, 119–121, 170, 193–194, 202, 212, 246, 272, 274, 292–294, 298, 306, 348–349, 351, 357, 381–382, 391. *See also* Ethics/morality
  between activists and scholars, 182, 194, 210
  bicommunal/intergroup, 11–12, 22, 72, 90, 95–96, 97(n)
  communication, 380
  activism, 94–95
  community/public, 11–13, 21, 117, 121, 124, 131 189, 229, 242, 245
  in conflict situations, 89–90, 94–95, 120, 125

and emancipation/empowerment, 162, 191, 193, 380
and ethics, 339–340, 342, 345
facilitating, 25, 72, 87, 98(n), 292, 317
and performance, 145, 156–157, 162–163, 167
theory, 12, 22, 89–90, 94, 119, 122, 293–295
Bakhtin, 15, 293–295
Bohm, 90
Foucault, 15, 293–295
transcendent/transformative, 12, 120, 125
Difference(s)/divergence(s) (between people/views), 13, 25, 73, 77–78, 82–83, 87, 93–94, 97(n), 111, 113, 116–117, 126, 129–131, 142, 144–145, 147–148, 157, 159–160, 164, 167, 169, 189, 192, 194, 235, 237–238, 244, 250, 252, 254, 264–265, 271, 273, 281–282, 284, 297, 300–301, 303–306, 308–309, 311–313, 340–341, 346–347, 371, 380, 383, 394, 424(a). *See also* Diversity; Ethnicity
performing, 13, 145, 159, 171
in research, 7, 9, 11, 18–21, 25, 182, 192, 210, 252, 282–283, 298, 310, 314–317, 350, 353–354, 413, 415, 417, 420, 422
Disability, 327, 374. *See also* Health
activism, 29(n)
-first language, 372, 395(n)
Discourse, 15, 109, 120, 163, 276–278, 292, 294–296, 306–307, 313, 315, 372
dominant, 97, 189, 276–277, 372
interventions into, 7–9, 301, 308, 315, 372
news media, 180, 183–184, 189
organizational, 292, 295, 300–302, 355
public, 159, 183, 204, 230–231, 265, 302–303, 371
whiteness, 298, 301
Discourse analysis, 15, 23, 301, 311
critical (CDA), 301–302
Discrimination, 2, 107, 163, 165, 243, 267, 300, 311, 331, 369, 403–406. *See also* Domination/subjugation; Exploitation; Marginalization/oppression
Disparity, 183, 187, 191–192, 203, 250, 267, 326, 401, 407, 411, 423. *See also* Equality; Fairness; Justice; Social Justice
Diversity/heterogeneity, 12, 14–15, 25, 87–88, 109, 113, 120–121, 143, 159, 211–212(a), 248, 252–253, 280, 282, 292, 300–306, 309–318, 328, 330–331, 341–342, 347, 358(a), 380, 390–391, 415, 421. *See also* Community/communities; Difference(s)/divergence(s); Ethnicity; Group(s)/team(s)
and research, 17, 265, 297, 316, 327, 418, 421–422
Documentary/documentaries/documentarian(s), 113, 144, 146, 153, 265, 280
theatre, 142–143
Domestic violence (DV), 11, 18–19, 21–22, 27, 180, 369. *See also* Rhode Island Coalition Against Domestic Violence (RICADV)
activism/activists/movement, 29(n), 179–182, 184–185, 196, 201–202, 204–205, 209
Blackstone Valley Advocacy Center (formerly Blackstone Shelter), 181, 197, 199–202, 208
Farrell, Rhode Island state legislator Michael, 13, 24, 179
case, 180–182, 199–203, 207–209, 212(n)
news media coverage/framing of, 13, 180–181, 184–185
Sisters Overcoming Abusive Relationships (SOAR), 180, 196, 207
survivors/victims, 184–186, 204, 207–209
Domination/subjugation, 9, 19–20, 22, 74, 76, 127, 130, 160, 162–165, 181, 189, 193, 195, 207, 226–227, 231, 242, 246, 251, 253, 271, 276–277, 295, 299, 350, 372, 405, 428(n). *See also*

Discrimination; Exploitation; Marginalization/oppression
matrix of, 141–142, 144, 166–167

Economics, 8–9, 18, 74, 77, 91, 107–109, 123, 126, 183, 186–187, 189, 203, 212(n), 225–226, 234, 239, 240(t), 243, 247(t), 266, 294, 299–300, 307, 315, 325–326, 329, 341, 344, 350, 352, 357, 368, 372–373, 376, 382–384, 389–390, 394–395, 409, 411. *See also* Business/corporate/managerial

Education, 14, 111–122, 120, 126, 145, 181, 184, 190, 192, 197, 201–202, 210, 212(a), 251–252, 267, 271, 293, 296, 300, 302, 307, 372, 374, 376, 387, 389, 394, 404–405, 408–411, 423, 428(n). *See also* Pedagogy; School(s)/schooling; Service-Learning; Teaching/teacher(s); University/universities/college(s)
  and activism, 4, 25, 27, 29(n), 210–211
  Freire, Brazilian philosopher/educator Paolo (critical pedagogy/liberation), 181, 189, 191–192, 377, 387, 393
  higher (institutions of), 2, 4, 165, 297
  learning, 27, 88, 106, 110, 120, 125, 128, 146–149, 153, 155, 160, 167–169, 190, 195, 199–200, 209–211, 224, 234–235, 243, 251, 272–273, 292, 299, 307–308, 313, 315, 368, 373, 377, 380, 383–384, 387–388, 393–395, 403–404, 411, 419, 424(a).
    community/group, 182, 191, 193, 209, 212(a), 385, 411
    social learning theory, 16, 23, 377, 388

Elite(s), 23, 92, 183, 232

Emergency response discourse/organization(s)/worker(s), 291–292, 299–302, 304–306, 309, 311. *See also* Firefighting/firefighter(s)

Employment/employee(s)/employer(s), 15–16, 19, 25, 27, 107, 110, 236, 251, 299–300, 303–304, 306, 309, 311–313, 317, 326–357, 358–359(a), 368, 375–376, 383–384, 393. *See also* Organization(s)/organizational; Superior(s)/subordinate(s); Work/worker(s)

Empowerment, 9, 12, 22, 24, 112, 162, 203, 271, 371–372, 382–383
  collective/participatory, 12–13, 115, 181, 189–191, 203, 205–207, 211, 211(a), 411
  communication, 162, 205, 367, 377–380
    activism for social justice research, 182, 209, 378
  disempowerment, 189, 202, 204–208, 210, 372
  education and, 181, 192, 251
  and (social justice) interventions/research, 16, 22, 28, 417, 422

Engaged research, 5, 7, 11, 15, 18–20, 28, 330, 346, 352–357
  communication, 7–8, 20, 357
    activism for social justice, 20, 158, 226, 329, 355, 382, 421
  critique of, 7–8, 15, 18, 26

Environment/environmental, 14, 77, 86, 95, 126, 129, 188, 192–193, 225, 227–228, 230–232, 238, 242, 244, 253–254, 327, 332, 341–342, 348, 350, 358(a), 383, 385, 411
  activism/movement, 21, 29(n), 239, 326
  justice, 231, 237, 243, 248
  Natural Resources Defense Council, 232
  Ohio Environmental Council, 233
  Ohio Environmental Protection Agency (OEPA), 232, 239, 240(f), 241–242, 244
  Sierra Club, 233, 237

Equality, 8–9, 15, 20, 27, 77, 93, 115, 120, 182–192, 194–195, 202–204, 207–209, 211–212(a), 229–230, 252, 265–266, 272, 283, 301–302, 306, 308, 326–327, 336, 338, 382–384, 394, 415–417, 422. *See also* Disparity; Fairness; Justice; Social Justice

Ethics/morality, 9, 15–16, 18–19, 24, 27, 115, 117, 130, 145, 152, 230, 244, 250–251, 253, 265, 267, 271, 274, 306, 310–311, 314, 317, 325, 385

of animal care/factory farms, 237, 248, 254
business/economic/organizational, 15–16, 326–330, 347–348, 350–351, 356–357
dialectical analysis/dilemmas/tensions, 16, 325, 328, 330, 346–351, 354–355
engagement, 16, 328–330, 348–349, 351, 353–354, 357
  accountability, 16, 328–330, 333–337, 339, 345–346, 351, 356, 358
  courage, 16, 326, 328–330, 333–334, 336–338, 340–341, 345–346, 351, 356, 358
  dialogic communication, 16, 328–330, 333–335, 337, 339, 344–346, 351, 356–358
  participation, 16, 328–330, 333–336, 338, 342–343, 345–346, 351–352, 354, 356–358
  transparency, 16, 328–330, 333–335, 337, 341, 345–346, 351, 356, 358
Ethics at Work Initiative at Southeastern Broadcasting Corporation (SBC), 16, 328, 330–346, 348–355, 357–358, 358–359(a)
research/theory, 34, 327–329, 348, 350, 385
  communication activism for social justice, 310–311, 317, 329, 357, 410, 416
  of speaking *with* rather than speaking *for* others, 265
Ethnic/Ethnicity, 12, 15, 78–80, 88, 159, 186, 252, 292, 300, 302, 305, 308–309, 311, 313, 316, 354, 370, 401–402, 405. *See also* Difference(s)/divergence(s); Diversity
  conflict, 19, 120
    in Cyprus, 69, 72–76, 78–80, 84–85, 88–90, 92–93
    in Sudan, 164, 166, 173(n)
  cross-ethnic performances, 13, 145, 159, 171
  ethnocentrism, 11, 73, 76–78, 80, 89, 169, 271

ethnocentric nationalism, in Cyprus, 73, 76–78, 79–80, 84, 89, 94–95
studies, 193–194, 210
Ethnography, 23, 130, 146–147, 174(n)
  autoethnography, 23
  critical, 10, 23, 30(n)
  performance, 10, 23, 30(n), 130, 141, 146–147, 163, 167, 169–170
Experiment(s), 23–24, 190–191
Europe/European(s), 29(n), 226, 279–280, 299, 302, 420(n)
  Council of Europe, 88
  European Union, 12, 95–96
Evaluation/assessment research, 16–17, 107, 121, 128, 188, 190–192, 195, 210, 299, 313, 316, 328, 331–339, 341, 351, 409, 411–413, 416–421, 423–424, 424(a)
Exploitation, 19, 107–108, 271, 292, 353. *See also* Discrimination; Domination/subjugation; Marginalization/oppression

Face, 123–124
  of power, 204–205, 208, 211, 379
  public, 277–278, 303, 311
Facilitation, 25, 73, 82, 87, 292, 309, 312, 331, 339, 354, 407, 409–412. *See also* Interventions; Training/trainer(s)
  and activism, 295, 310–311, 315, 317
  of communication, 12, 21, 25, 72, 82, 120, 125, 148, 156, 309, 316–317, 339–340, 358, 423
  of performance, 155, 161
Fairness, 2, 235, 243, 326–327, 330, 336, 338, 340, 356, 359–360(a), 371, 387, 425(a). *See also* Disparity; Equality; Justice; Social Justice
Family/families, 267, 278–279, 282–284, 285–286(n), 326, 330, 332, 369, 386, 411
  activism, 29(n), 281
  American Indian/Native American, 403, 406
    Ramah Navajo Family Listening (RNFL) project, 406–413, 415–424

communication, 17, 409, 412, 418–420, 423, 424–426(a)
and domestic violence (DV), 180, 200, 204
Farm(s)/farmer(s), 224–225, 227–229, 231, 233–234, 240(t), 242, 244–246, 247(t), 248, 252. *See also* Agriculture; Animal(s); Buckeye Egg Farm (BE); Concentrated animal feeding operations (CAFOs); Concerned Citizens of Central Ohio (CCCO); Food
factory (mega), 13–14, 18–19, 21–23, 25, 27, 225, 227–229, 231–237, 239, 240(t), 241–245, 247(t), 247–248, 254–255
family, 225–227, 234
Farm Aid, 237
Nelson, country singer Willie, 237
Farm Bureau (FB), 225, 228, 240(t), 241, 246–247
Ohio Farmers Union, 237
Feedback, 156, 301, 309, 311, 337, 340, 343–345, 359(a)
Feminism/feminist(s), 10, 16, 21–22, 329, 376–377, 384–386
activism, 30(n)
Firefighting/firefighter(s), 291–292, 300–301, 303–309, 316. *See also* Emergency response discourse/organization(s)/worker(s)
Fire Services (pseudonym), 292–293, 298–304, 306–317
Cooper, senior officer at (pseudonym), 303, 309–313, 316
First-person-perspective research, 7, 21, 23, 167, 372, 404. *See also* Third-person perspective research
Focus group(s), 16, 191, 331, 333, 375, 409
Food, 224–229, 231, 234, 254–255, 369, 374, 382, 386. *See also* Agriculture; Animal(s); Buckeye Egg Farm (BE); Concentrated animal feeding operations (CAFOs); Concerned Citizens of Central Ohio (CCCO); Farm(s)/farmer(s); Sustainability
activism, 29(n)
Poultry Association, 245–246

Foster, Kenneth, Jr., 14–15, 21, 27, 263–265, 268–270, 272, 275–278, 282, 284, 285–286(n)
accomplices, 268, 279
attorneys, 264, 270, 273, 278
family, 270, 273–274, 278, 285(n)
Sarandon, supporter actress Susan, 264
Save Kenneth Foster Campaign (SKFC), 21, 24, 264–265, 269, 273–284
Carver Library (Austin, TX), 264, 270
Juneteenth, 273, 276–277, 285(n)
The Kenneth Foster, Jr. Act, 284
Tutu, supporter Archbishop Desmond, 264
Frame/framing analysis, 13–14, 22, 196, 198, 225–226, 229–231, 233–235, 237–238, 243–244, 311, 389. *See also* Media; News media
of/by activism/activists, 187–188, 195–196, 212(a), 230–231, 236–237, 274, 317
of domestic violence (DV), 13, 180–181, 184
of (factory) farming (Buckeye Egg Farm), 231, 237–239, 240(t), 241–247, 247(t), 248
(news) media, 180, 184, 187, 195, 226, 230–231, 234–236, 238, 240(t), 241, 243, 248, 276
web of impediments, 246
Freedom, 77–78, 89, 91, 154, 164, 166, 205, 228, 240(t), 242, 246, 247(t), 252, 285(n), 384
Rides, 275
Funding, 113, 117–118, 124–125, 130–132, 151, 161, 190–192, 195–197, 228, 237, 299, 415–417
grants, 115, 128, 237
organizations, 106, 111, 116, 119, 123, 128–131, 133(n), 373, 407, 427(a)

Gay, lesbian, bisexual, and transgendered (GLBT), 2, 190, 205, 279, 297
activism, 30(n)
queer studies, 193–194, 210

Gender, 131, 162, 171, 292, 297, 315–316, 327, 342, 354
 activism, 30(n)
 bias/discrimination/marginalization, 107, 184, 186, 201
 studies, 193, 210
Genocide, 19, 152, 155–156, 172–173
 in Sudan, 11–12, 27, 139–140, 144, 147, 150
Global, 16, 21, 87, 107–108, 111, 127
 activism, 4, 16, 20–21, 297
 globalization, 11
 North, 14, 181–182, 189, 191, 193, 202–203, 205
 South, 13, 22, 181, 205, 212(n)
 participatory models, 181–182, 189–193, 202–203
Good Gifts, 16, 367–368, 373–376, 378, 383–387, 389, 391–394
 Students for Good Gifts (SGG), 376, 378–379, 386, 391
 Ten Thousand Villages, 16, 374, 376
Good Works, 16, 367–368, 373–376, 378–379, 381, 384–385, 390–391, 393–394
 Hannah House, 379, 386
 Cluggston, Ohio University communication major/intern Heather, 373–376, 378–381, 386, 391, 394
 Wasserman, founder/executive director Keith, 367–368, 373–376, 378, 381, 386, 391
Governance/government(s), 4, 14, 92, 107, 112, 123–125, 129, 161, 183–184, 187, 191, 204, 224, 226, 228, 230, 239, 241, 246, 279, 297, 299, 326–327, 330, 335, 342, 348, 360(a), 371–372, 391, 395
 Cyprus, 69, 73–75, 77, 95
 Navajo Nation, 407–408
 other countries, 127, 132, 192, 250
 (North) Sudan, 125, 163–164, 166–167, 173–175(n)
 United States (U.S.), 115–116, 129–130, 370
 Ohio, 246, 248

Grassroots
 activists/social movements, 14–15, 21, 90–91, 179, 189, 195, 199, 223, 226, 229, 233, 235, 254–255, 272–273
 campaigns/organizing, 13–15, 179, 181–182, 190, 232–233, 236, 264, 269, 274–275, 371–372
 Grassroots Policy Project, 203–204
 theatre, 142, 144
Great Britain/British/United Kingdom, 12, 79, 84, 96, 98(n), 127, 164, 194, 280
Greece/Greek(s), 3, 12, 69, 73, 78–79, 87, 186, 380
 Greek Cypriots, 11–12, 22, 25, 27, 70, 72–86, 88–91, 93–96, 97(n), 120
Group(s)/team(s), 2–3, 11–13, 21–23, 25, 78, 87–88, 93, 95–96, 112–113, 115, 124–125, 140, 149, 164–165, 174(n), 188, 192, 194, 196, 198, 209–210, 211(a), 231, 240(t), 246, 247(t), 250–251, 270–272, 277, 279, 282, 295, 298, 307, 309, 311–313, 316, 329–332, 337, 339–344, 347, 353, 356–357, 358(a), 360(a), 369–370, 376, 378, 382, 384–385, 394, 405–406, 410–412. *See also* Focus group(s); Organization(s)/organizational
 activist/social movement, 4–7, 12, 14, 21, 72, 82, 89, 92–94, 98(n), 107, 113, 124, 180, 190–192, 194–196, 198, 201–202, 208–209, 224, 234–238, 247(t), 248, 250, 252, 254–255, 275, 285(n)
 bicommunal/intergroup, 70, 72, 82–83, 87–88, 90, 95–96, 97(n), 315, 317–318
 communication, 10, 12, 22, 86, 88, 119, 190, 198, 280, 304, 309, 315, 373, 411, 416, 422–423
 (activism) research, 10, 22, 190, 313, 315, 317–318
 intercultural workgroup communication theory, 23, 415–416
 diverse, 12, 75, 78, 88–89, 93, 115, 307, 312, 369–370, 391, 401–403, 415, 421

empowerment, 162, 189, 209, 380
marginalized/oppressed, 10, 12–13, 15, 18, 20, 24, 28, 157, 163, 171, 186, 189–190, 203, 212(n), 271, 292, 353, 382–383, 393
performance, 142–143, 146–147, 149
research, 12, 17, 192, 409, 411, 416, 418, 420–424
community-based participatory research (CBPR), 413, 414(f), 415–416, 421
student, 86–88, 376, 385, 390

Health, 20, 109, 161, 240(t), 241, 247(t), 341, 358(a), 360(a), 394, 401, 403. *See also* Disability
activism, 29(n)
American Indian/Native American, 401–412, 317, 421–424, 428(n)
intervention/prevention with, 17, 21, 27, 402, 405–413, 415–424
care, 112, 118(f), 202, 269, 326, 369–370, 404, 408
Centers for Disease Control and Prevention (CDC), 409
Lufkin, Director of the Marion County, OH Health Department Lowell, 224
public, 17, 21, 24, 27, 108, 111, 113, 117, 227–229, 232, 235, 237, 248, 372, 409, 411
World Health Organization (WHO), 120–121
Healthy Cities/Healthy Communities project, 120–121
Hegemony, 142, 162, 164–166, 231, 250, 274, 294
Hispanic(s)/Latino/a(s), 2, 299–300, 316, 369, 402
activism, 29(n)
Latin America/American, 112, 192
studies, 210
History/histories, 3, 8, 108, 116, 130, 145, 152, 157, 186–187, 196, 200, 212(n), 225, 249, 255, 264, 292, 336, 357, 407, 410, 415–416
Austin (TX) History Center, 273
of Cyprus, 69–70, 73–74, 78–79
oral, 141, 146–147, 174(n), 196
(of) performance, 143, 157, 163
United States (U.S.), 21, 111
Homelessness, 16, 181, 297, 367, 371–372, 376, 381–384. *See also* Housing; Poverty/poor
activism, 29(n)
Homogeneity/homophily, 74, 78, 195, 252, 292, 316, 415, 421–422
Housing, 195, 234, 243, 369, 371. *See also* Homelessness; Poverty/poor
Human resources/social services, 113, 124, 202, 238, 310–312, 326, 331, 367, 382, 394, 405, 408–409
Human rights, 105, 110, 117, 128, 140, 147, 174(n). *See also* Civil rights
activism, 29(n)
Amnesty International, 144, 277, 279
Human Rights Watch, 141
Human Immunodeficiency Virus (HIV), 108, 117, 122, 129–130
Human trafficking (trafficking in persons; TIP), 11–12, 25, 27, 106–109, 113, 117, 124. *See also* Countertrafficking; The Daywalka Foundation (TDF)
Born into Brothels (Motion picture), 112
international development approaches to, 115–116, 128
Palermo Protocol about, 107
Rescue Foundation, 123
stakeholders, 106, 109–110, 113–117, 114(f), 117–119, 118(f), 121, 124
collaboration model, 113, 114(f), 119
engagement model, 117, 118(f), 119
statistics, 12, 106–108, 132(n)
trafficked persons/traffickers, 12, 107–108, 113, 118(f), 123
United States (U.S.) and, 12, 108, 112, 124, 129, 132, 132(n)

Identity/identities/identification, 26, 77, 93, 95, 112, 115–116, 123–124, 126, 129–131, 142, 162, 170, 192, 207, 231, 237, 252, 265, 292–297, 299, 315–316, 333, 346, 352, 423

Index

and collective action/social movements, 186, 192–193, 206, 231, 237
cultural/ethnic/racial, 78–79, 89, 112, 145, 162, 292, 294–295, 306, 314, 316, 402–404, 406, 413, 418–420, 423–424, 424(a), 426(a),
Cypriot (Greek and Turkish), 70, 73–74, 79–80, 93
Ideology, 8, 144, 162, 165–166, 169, 184, 204, 208, 225, 231, 244, 254, 279, 302–303, 307, 329
ideological criticism, 8
Immigration, 2, 113, 124, 130, 144, 188, 371
activism, 29–30(n)
India/Indian(s), 12, 105–106, 108, 110–111, 113, 115, 122–129, 131–132, 145, 160, 372, 379
cities/states in, 105–106, 108, 122–126, 131, 132(n)
Innovations. *See also* Concentrated animal feeding operations (CAFOs)
diffusion of, 23, 229, 242, 390
subterfuge of, 23, 238, 242–249
Institution(s)/institutional, 2, 20, 23, 74, 112–113, 119, 163–165, 183–188, 195, 203–205, 207, 209, 211, 236, 266, 279, 292–293, 295, 297, 299, 310–314, 326, 345, 349, 382–383, 389, 392, 415. *See also* Organization(s)/organizational
Intercultural, 95, 113, 308, 311
communication, 111, 119, 122, 296, 313
intercultural workgroup communication theory, 23, 415–416
International, 11, 21, 107–108, 125, 131, 174(n), 374
aid/development, 12, 110–116, 128–130, 173(n)
arena/community, 12, 106, 115, 129
organizations (IOs), 110–111, 114(f), 117, 122, 130, 212(n)
international nongovernmental organizations (INGOs), 114(f)
studies, 145
Interpersonal, 119, 124, 162, 166, 184–185, 304, 380, 385
communication, 21–22, 375
research, 10, 22, 190
Interpretive methods/theories, 10, 22–23, 141, 146, 372
Intervention(s), 11, 13–16, 21–25, 69, 75, 77, 79, 93, 97(n), 106–107, 117, 122–123, 129, 161, 173, 180, 190, 194, 208, 301–310, 313, 329–330, 354, 357, 372, 393. *See also* American Indian(s)/Native American(s); Facilitation
activist, 160, 163, 265, 292–293, 295, 299–301
communication, 292, 301, 308, 313, 315, 318, 407, 415
activism (research), 7–10, 21–22, 24, 28, 276, 293, 295–299, 308, 314–317, 372, 402, 404, 413, 420–421, 424
culturally supported (CSIs)/empirically supported (ESIs), 405, 415, 421–422, 424
(community) performance-based (CBP), 139, 141, 143, 162
social justice, 16, 22, 226, 297
Interview(s)/interviewee(s)/interviewer(s), 13, 15, 23, 115, 117, 121, 124–126, 130, 132(n), 147, 149, 161, 198, 212(n), 238, 267, 280, 300, 302–308, 311, 316–317, 332–333, 350–353, 392, 404, 409, 413, 420, 423. *See also* Focus group(s)

Journalism/journalist(s)/press, 180, 183–185, 187–188, 194, 197, 199, 200, 202, 207–209, 223, 225, 230, 232, 236–238, 244–245, 247–248, 263, 279–281, 283. *See also* Media; News media
Justice, 15, 19, 77, 80, 83, 112, 115, 141, 173(n), 181, 210, 231, 235, 237, 249, 252, 255, 265, 278–279, 282–283, 293, 297, 307–309, 315, 317, 348, 382–383, 389. *See also* Social justice
criminal system, 110, 116, 118, 123–124, 266–267, 270, 276–277, 281
environmental, 231, 237, 243, 248

Labor
activism/movement, 21, 30(n), 194, 326

conditions/practices (forced), 12, 106, 108, 110, 117, 327, 371
studies, 193, 210
Language(s), 111, 121, 123, 129, 131, 132(n), 143, 147, 160, 186, 190, 194, 210–211, 300, 302–303, 311, 313, 316, 343, 380, 388, 409, 417
  American Indian (Navajo), 411, 417, 426(a), 428(n)
  English, 13, 122, 125, 132(n), 148–149, 161, 171, 174(n), 201, 302, 313, 411
  other languages, 113–115, 124–125, 132(n), 148, 150, 154, 160, 164, 171, 201, 308
Leadership/leader(s), 24, 26, 72, 75, 81–82, 85–86, 88, 90–91, 95–96, 97(n), 108, 111, 121, 163, 186, 189, 192, 208, 237, 241, 247(t), 252, 292, 312, 326, 330, 332, 334–339, 342–343, 345, 347, 349, 351, 356, 360(a), 408–409, 413, 417
Legal/judicial, 2, 15, 17, 106–107, 109–111, 113, 116–118, 118(f), 119, 123–127, 129, 152, 166, 179–181, 199–201, 205, 208, 224–225, 228, 247(t), 264, 267–268, 270, 274–275, 281, 284, 285(n), 293, 299, 304, 311, 329, 339, 374
  activism, 29–30(n)
  Criminal Responsibility for Conduct of Another Act of the Texas Penal Code ("Law of Parties"), 268–269, 277, 284, 286(n)
  Public Law (PL) 93-638, 408
  Sharia (Islamic), 164, 166, 173(n)
Liberation, 192, 279, 380, 389
  theology, 189
Listening, 13, 24, 88, 95, 124, 139, 149, 152, 155, 159, 161, 169, 271, 298, 304–306, 308, 310, 332, 336, 359(a), 405
  Ramah Navajo Family Listening (RNFL) project, 406–413, 415–424
Lobbying, 14, 179, 198, 201, 237, 239, 246, 282. *See also* Petition(s)

Marginalization/oppression, 16, 23, 78, 82, 84, 147, 105, 116, 126, 128, 130, 143, 145, 153, 157, 160–166, 183–185, 188, 190–192, 195, 203–207, 209, 212(n), 246, 253–254, 271, 281, 292, 297, 302, 308, 312, 326–327, 354, 371–372, 380, 382–384, 387, 389–393. *See also* Discrimination; Dominance/subjugation; Exploitation
  and (communication) activism (research), 10, 12, 15, 18–20, 22, 24, 28, 171–172, 186, 226, 271–272, 302, 316, 326, 353, 382–383, 421
Media, 3, 8, 19, 75, 142, 168, 179, 181, 184–185, 188, 190, 195, 197, 200–201, 207–209, 230–231, 233, 235, 238, 274–275, 280–281, 288, 296–297. *See also* Frame/framing analysis; Journalism/journalist(s)/print; News media
  activism/advocacy, 6, 251, 255, 283
  arenas/institutions/organizations/systems, 15–16, 27, 180, 182–186, 189, 194, 246, 280, 327–328, 330, 341
  in Global North (and United States), 180–181, 185, 191
  caucuses, 198–199, 207
  and collective actors/social movements, 181–182, 185–192, 195, 206, 210, 274–275, 279–280
  coverage/portrayals, 22, 84, 87, 244, 284(n), 357, 370–371
  effects, 229, 231, 370
  mainstream/popular, 182, 194, 280, 296–297, 371
  Media Fellows, 195–196, 198
  Media Research Action Project (MRAP), 180–182, 185, 193–195, 198, 202, 209
  new, 188, 191, 212(n)
  practices/strategies, 3, 180, 186–188, 195, 280
  reform, 185, 187
  studies (communication research on), 3, 8, 10, 22, 296
Message(s), 14, 119, 195, 200, 235–236, 241, 246, 267, 277–278, 302, 336, 344, 353–354, 406, 410, 416. *See also* Communication(s)
  activist/social movement, 151, 185, 188, 195–196, 198–199, 207, 210, 275, 280

caucuses (framing), 196, 198, 208
(news) media/mediated, 3, 83, 183, 194
political, 83, 87, 198, 275
Mexico/Mexican(s), 111–112, 122, 276
Mexican-American activism, 30(n)

Narrative(s)/story/stories, 141–143, 145–150, 152, 154, 156–158, 161, 163, 165, 167–168, 172, 174(n), 237–238, 245, 250, 252, 254, 269, 276, 285(n), 293, 304–305, 308, 315, 380, 404
counternarratives, 163, 276–282
news media, 230, 237, 300, 371
Negotiation, 69, 74, 77, 90, 92, 96, 187, 189, 192, 254, 332, 339, 353, 373, 378, 391, 416, 420
Nepal/Nepalese, 12, 106, 108–111, 119, 122–124, 132(n)
cities/regions in, 106, 109–110, 119, 122–123
and human trafficking, 106, 108
Network(s), 330, 371, 394, 404, 412
activism, 4
of Campaign to End the Death Penalty (CEDP), 279–280
human trafficking, 107, 122–123
social, 20, 186, 204, 211, 278, 404
News media, 13, 22, 82, 147, 160, 179, 180, 183, 188, 230, 232, 234, 241, 246, 250, 263, 279, 371. *See also* Frame/framing analysis; Journalism/journalist(s)/press; Media
and activists/marginalized/social movements, 13–14, 179–183, 185–188, 192, 194–195, 198–202, 208, 230, 274–278, 279–282
context/systems, 13, 15–16, 27, 183–184, 187, 195, 198, 209, 275, 280, 328, 370
coverage/messages/narratives/reporting, 6, 14, 21, 70, 77, 83–84, 87, 90, 97(n), 147, 183, 194, 230–232, 236–237, 243–244, 278–281, 300, 329, 370–371
of *A Prayer for Sudan*, 172, 174(n)
of agriculture/animals/farming/food (Buckeye Egg Farm), 229, 231, 233–239, 240(t), 241, 243, 245, 247–248, 255
of domestic violence (DV), 180–181, 184, 201, 204
of Save Kenneth Foster Campaign (SKFC), 15, 279–281, 284(n)
editorials, 201, 245, 248, 252, 263, 277, 284(n)
mainstream, 77, 183, 185–188, 194, 202, 204, 371
newspapers/internet/radio/television, 14, 76, 83, 160, 174(n), 188, 199–201, 232, 234–239, 241, 243–245, 247(t), 247–248, 255, 263, 268, 277, 280, 330, 370–371, 379
practices, 13, 180, 183–185, 187–188, 202
Nongovernmental organization(s) (NGOs), 90, 98(n), 107–108, 110, 114(f), 118(f), 121–123, 128, 132, 160–161, 191. *See also* Nonprofit organization(s); Organization(s)/organizational
Nonprofit organization(s), 16, 18, 106, 132(n), 191, 195, 212(n), 226, 233, 327, 367, 408. *See also* Nongovernmental organization(s) (NGOs); Organization(s)/organizational
Norms, 9, 204, 382
cultural/social, 119, 131, 184, 187, 204, 302, 315, 403, 412
news media, 183–184, 187, 202
organizational, 315, 356

Observation, 115, 147, 155, 298–299, 302–305, 308–309, 314–318, 412
participant observation, 23, 147, 155, 304, 311
Oral history/histories, 141, 146–147, 174(n), 196
Organization(s)/organizational, 13–17, 21–22, 75, 112–113, 115, 119, 150–151, 161, 182–183, 233, 236, 325–329, 346–348, 350–351, 353–357, 367–368, 373–376, 378, 384, 390, 394, 408–409, 411, 414(f). *See also* Business/corporate; Employment/employee(s)/employer(s); Group(s)/team(s);

Organizing/mobilizing; Southeastern Broadcasting Corporation (SBC); Superior(s)/subordinate(s); Work/worker(s)
  activist/marginalized/social movement, 5–7, 10, 12–13, 15, 18, 20–21, 24, 27–28, 110, 112, 122, 141, 150–151, 180–181, 183, 185, 187–188, 191–192, 195, 202, 204, 206, 209, 211(a), 226, 231, 233, 237, 239, 275, 297, 371
  change, 15–16, 185, 251, 291–293, 308–310, 312, 314, 316–317, 329–331, 334, 337, 342, 344, 346, 356
  communication, 14–15, 122, 194, 202, 292, 295, 300–303, 327, 329, 349, 354–355, 358, 373, 379–381
    activism for social justice research, 295, 313, 315, 317–318, 326, 329, 356
    interventions, 15–16, 22, 25, 307, 358
  culture, 328, 330, 347–348, 355
  dialectical tensions in, 16, 328, 341, 346–351, 354–355
  emergency response (firefighting; Fire Services), 292–293, 298–304, 306–317
  ethics (engagement), 16, 327–331, 333, 345–351, 354–358
  and framing/lobbying/public relations, 230, 233, 242, 246, 249–250
  international, 110–111, 117, 130
  performance (appraisal), 16, 328, 335, 338, 345–346, 348–351, 354–355
  research/scholars, 8–10, 21, 189, 195, 296, 313, 327–329, 347–348, 353, 356–357, 379
Organizing/mobilizing, 15, 85, 93, 191, 195, 233, 263, 267, 281, 292, 377, 379, 382, 391. *See also* Institution(s)/institutional; Organization(s)/organizational
  campaigns/strategies, 14, 181, 192, 196, 206, 234–235, 239
    Save Kenneth Foster Campaign (SKFC), 21, 24, 264–265, 269, 273–284
  by collective actors/marginalized/social movements, 14, 16, 179, 181, 186, 192, 199, 201, 203–204, 206, 211–212(a), 212(n), 253, 271, 275, 280–282, 371–373, 376
  for social change, 368, 376, 394
  course, 376, 385, 389, 391–392
  theories of, 16, 181, 193, 379
    feminist, 384–386
Outreach, 14, 179, 181, 197–200, 300–302, 311, 413

Paradoxes, 11, 249, 300, 302, 305–306, 413, 416–417, 421–422
Participation/participatory, 125, 190–191, 198–199, 203–205, 229, 242–244, 265, 280, 282, 295, 301–302, 307, 313, 326, 372–373, 375–376, 381, 384–385, 390–393, 406, 409–410, 416. *See also* Ethics/morality
  and activism, 191–192, 274, 280
  communication, 125, 180, 190, 192–193, 211–212(a), 421–422
  and empowerment, 190–192, 203–204, 207
  perspectives (Global South) of, 13, 22, 181–182, 189–193, 202–203, 207, 211(a), 212(n)
  (community-based) performance (CBP)/theatre, 158, 162
  research, 10, 30(n), 190–192
    community-based participatory research (CBPR), 17, 23–24, 407–410, 413, 414(f), 415–417, 420–422
Peace
  activists in Cyprus, 70, 72, 80–84, 86–89, 91, 93–96, 97–98(n)
  -building/making, 385
  in Cyprus, 11, 72–73, 80, 82–83, 85, 89–96, 97–98(n)
  Lederach's theory of transformative peacebuilding, 12, 22, 90–91
  in Sudan, 141, 151, 164, 167, 174(n)
Pedagogy, 146, 296, 317. *See also* Education; Teaching/teacher(s)
  communication activism, 10, 27, 180

Index

Dewey, founder of pragmatism John, 146
Freire, Brazilian philosopher/educator Paolo (critical pedagogy/liberation), 181, 189, 191–192, 377, 387, 393
service-learning, 16, 110
Performance, 13, 110, 116, 128, 145–147, 149, 162–163, 278, 294, 409. *See also* Theatre
   of *A Prayer for Sudan*, 12–13, 141, 150–154, 156–164, 167, 169, 172
   TalkBack sessions, 141, 154–156
   activism, 4, 11–12, 142–144, 154, 161–162, 168, 170–172
   community-based (CBP), 12, 141–143, 154, 174(n)
   course, 13, 145, 168
   and embodiment, 142, 149, 158–159, 162, 167
   and empathic engagement, 158, 170–171
   (ethno-/ethnography/ethnographic) studies, 10, 23, 30(n), 130, 147, 163, 167, 169, 171, 296
Petition(s), 140–141, 151, 264, 271, 273, 277, 280. *See also* Lobbying
Philosophy/philosophical, 117, 127–128, 189, 253, 293, 317, 327–328, 350, 374–375, 382, 385
Politics/politician(s), 8–9, 13, 18, 20–22, 26–27, 70, 73, 75, 79, 81, 83–84, 86–88, 90–93, 95–96, 97–98(n), 108, 115, 131, 141–142, 151, 155, 172–173, 179, 181–183, 185–187, 189–192, 195–196, 198, 201, 203–204, 206–208, 226, 228–231, 238, 240(t), 241, 243, 246, 247(t), 252, 254, 265–266, 269–278, 281–284, 284(n), 286(n), 293, 298, 302, 305, 314, 329, 352, 357, 382, 387, 394, 411. *See also* Power
Perry, Texas Governor Rick, 14, 264, 270, 273–274, 276, 281, 284
political science, 22, 187, 189
Rice, Secretary of State Condoleezza, 141
of speaking, 271–272
Stabenow, Michigan Senator Deborah, 141

Voinovich, Ohio Governor George V., 239
Poverty/poor, 105, 107, 112, 184, 190, 212(n), 243, 368, 374, 376, 381–383, 387, 389–392, 394–395, 395(n), 403. *also* Good Gifts; Good Works; Homelessness; Housing; Wealth; Welfare
   activism, 29(n), 383
   communication (activism) research on, 16, 19, 22, 370–372
   and death penalty, 14, 266–268
   Ontario Coalition Against Poverty (OCAP), 371
   in United States, 2, 368–369, 394–395
   Ohio (Athens), 16, 25, 27, 243, 368–370, 378, 388, 394
Power, 2, 8, 14–17, 24, 77, 107–108, 111, 120, 124, 126, 131, 141–142, 162–166, 173(n), 182, 185–186, 203–207, 209, 224, 231, 243, 245–246, 249–251, 264, 266, 271, 273, 292–293, 296–299, 310, 315, 371, 378–380, 393. *See also* Empowerment; Politics/politician(s)
   Bakhtin's and Foucault's work on, 293–295
   of businesses/organizations, 326, 354–355, 357
   and collective actors/marginalized/social movements, 183, 187, 189–191, 206, 209, 387, 394
   in community-based participatory research (CBPR), 416–417, 421–422
   and (international) development, 111–112, 130
   disparities/inequalities, 189, 191–192, 202–204, 208, 229–230, 235
   domains of, 162–166
   and framing, 230–231, 238, 243–244
   Global North/South perspectives of, 202–203
   Lukes's perspective, 13, 203–204, 208
      added dimensions, 205–208, 211
      power lens, 205–206
   and (news) media, 184, 187, 229, 231
   in participatory communication models, 182, 191, 203, 207, 211–212(a)

political, 8, 183, 231, 243
research, 7–8, 18, 20, 111–112
of whiteness, 297–299, 302, 306, 313, 315
Praxis, 3, 24, 128, 143, 190, 193, 292, 295–297, 299
relational, 291, 314
Prison/prisoners, 79, 143, 265–266, 269, 276, 281–284, 285(n), 297, 326
activism, 30(n), 283
prison-industrial complex, 265, 282–283
Texas Board of Pardons and Paroles, 264, 270, 277
Privilege/privileging, 2, 9, 20, 27, 28(n), 112, 144, 168, 171, 180, 189, 230, 234, 239, 245, 251, 253, 271–272, 280–281, 292, 295–296, 298–299, 301–304, 306–309, 312–315, 342, 356, 358(a), 371–372, 404, 422. See also Whiteness
white, 15, 111, 126, 271, 292–293, 295–299, 301–302, 305, 307, 311, 313–316
Protest(s), 5, 74–76, 80, 87, 186, 199, 201, 206, 225–226, 233, 235–236, 238–239, 255, 263–264, 269, 271, 274, 276–280, 283, 284–285(n), 310, 326, 371
Psychology/psychological, 78, 88, 116, 119, 376, 390, 411
Public(s), 3, 5, 123–124, 202, 208, 132(n), 231–233, 234–237, 240(t), 242, 243–244, 246, 247(t), 250, 263, 270, 272–273, 275, 277, 279–281, 283, 291, 299, 301, 303, 307, 311, 326, 331, 342, 353, 356–357, 358(a), 360(a), 373, 391, 393
awareness/education/opinion/perceptions/support, 172, 183–184, 197, 201–202, 204, 225, 236, 241, 244, 246, 248, 250–251, 267, 274, 278–279, 291, 295, 370–371
communication, 11, 21, 83, 159, 161, 183, 185, 189, 202, 204, 229–231, 234–235, 238–239, 242, 245–246, 254, 265–266, 278–279, 302–303, 337, 351, 353, 371
policies, 13, 184, 225, 229, 234, 267, 282

service, 297
announcements, 180
organizations/employees, 291, 300, 313
Public relations, 8, 14, 183, 194, 226, 229–230, 233–235, 241, 246–247, 249–250
activism, 30(n)
education, 251–252
reclaiming for social justice, 249–252
research, 8, 231, 233, 249, 251
Queer studies, 193–194, 210
Race, 8–9, 15, 22, 162, 184, 186, 252, 272, 281, 291–295, 297–303, 305–309, 311, 313–316
and communication, 294–295, 297, 300, 304, 306, 309–310, 316, 327, 342, 354, 370
Congress of Racial Equality, 275
and death penalty, 14, 266–267, 277–278
identity/identities, 292, 294–296, 306, 314
interracial, 15, 282, 296, 304, 313
people of color, 14, 184, 190, 205, 266, 281, 300, 304, 312, 316
color-blindness, 302–303, 305–307
(anti)racism, 11, 169, 266–267, 275–276, 296–298, 300, 311
relations, 293–294, 296, 299, 309
Rapport, 158, 252, 304, 310. See also Trust
Reflection, 14, 143, 185, 190, 193, 201–202, 206, 210, 212(a), 292, 298, 301, 306, 308–309, 380, 382, 389, 391, 392, 410, 421–422. See also Service-learning
Reflexivity, 24, 185, 211–212(a), 280, 292, 298–299, 308, 317, 329, 352
Relational, 90, 127, 170–171, 270, 291, 293, 295, 304, 308–309, 314, 316, 328, 413, 415–416
Religion/spirituality, 73, 90, 105, 111–112, 115, 118(f), 120, 142, 162, 164–166, 173(n), 237, 239, 294, 297, 300, 302, 315, 368, 381, 405, 408, 428(a)
activism/activists, 30(n), 239

Index

(Judeo-)Christian, 117, 142, 144, 147, 156, 160, 164–166, 173(n), 254, 277
    Roman Catholic Church, 327
Islam/Muslim, 145, 155, 163–166, 173(n)
    Nation of Islam, 277
    National Islamic Front, 173(n)
Representation, 19, 90, 93, 95, 113, 142, 147, 190–191, 194, 251, 264–265, 271–272, 300, 302, 312, 327, 360(a)
    –objectification dialectic, 130–131
Research/researcher(s), 2, 5, 7–10, 14, 17–18, 22–24, 27, 72–73, 93–94, 97(n), 106, 112, 122–123, 125, 130, 149, 167, 174(n), 191–195, 202, 231, 233, 238, 249, 251, 283, 296–297, 299–302, 304, 308, 327, 329, 331, 348–350, 356, 402–403, 406–407. *See also* Communication activism for social justice research; Research method(s); Scholar(s)/scholarly
    (and) action, 9, 30(n), 167, 330
    and activism, 3–5, 14, 130, 180–182, 184–185, 188, 190, 194, 196, 203, 206, 209–210, 292–293, 295, 327, 329, 368, 377, 405
    communication, 3, 6–8, 10, 16, 18–19, 22–24, 26, 30, 180–181, 185, 188–191, 195, 231, 233, 249, 251–252, 265, 292–293, 297, 329, 368, 370–373, 404–405
    community (partnerships), 5, 11, 15, 18–21, 24, 130, 180–182, 209–210
    community-based participatory research (CBPR), 17, 23–24, 407–410, 413, 414(f), 415–417, 420–422
    engaged/public, 5, 7–8, 15, 18–20, 26
    evaluation/assessment, 16–17, 107, 121, 128, 188, 190–192, 195, 210, 299, 313, 316, 328, 331–339, 341, 351, 409, 411–413, 416–421, 423–424, 424(a)
    and intervention, 7–10, 16, 21–22, 24, 28, 297–301, 308, 314–315, 317–318, 329, 330, 372, 404–405, 413, 415, 420–423
    and performance, 141, 146–147, 150, 167–168, 172

phenomenological, 149, 158
quantitative and/vs. qualitative, 17, 26, 121, 328, 332, 419–420, 423
rhetorical, 5, 7
subjects, patronizing view, 24, 130
third-person-perspective *vs.* first-person-perspective, 7, 21, 372, 404
Research method(s), 9–11, 24, 35–36, 118, 121–122, 125, 147, 298. *See also* Research; Scholar(s)/scholarly
    action/collaborative/participatory, 5, 10, 17, 24–25, 30(n), 190, 192–193
    applied *vs.* basic, 6–7
    case study/studies, 9, 23, 107, 171, 229, 242, 248, 328–329, 340, 345, 350
    in communication activism for social justice research, 10, 19, 23–24, 27–28, 308, 317
    community-based participatory (CBPR), 17, 23–24, 407–410, 413, 414(f), 415–417, 420–422
    content analysis, 23, 231, 238
    critical, 317
    discourse analysis, 15, 23, 301, 311
        critical (CDA), 301–302
    ethnography, 23
        autoethnography, 23
        critical, 10, 23, 30(n)
        performance (studies), 10, 23, 30(n), 130, 147, 162, 167, 169, 171, 296
    evaluation/assessment, 16–17, 107, 121, 128, 188, 190–192, 195, 210, 299, 313, 316, 328, 331–339, 341, 351, 409, 411–413, 416–421, 423–424, 424(a)
    experimental, 23–24, 190–191
    feminist, 10, 30(n)
    fieldnotes, 147–150
    interviews, 13, 15, 23, 115, 117, 121, 124–126, 130, 132(n), 147, 149, 198, 212(n), 238, 267, 280, 300, 302–308, 311, 316–317, 332–333, 350–353, 392, 404, 409, 413, 420, 423
        focus group, 16, 191, 331, 333, 375, 409
    observation, 115, 147, 155, 298–299, 302–305, 308–309, 314–318, 412

participant observation, 23, 147, 155, 304, 311
oral history/histories, 141, 146–147, 174(n), 196
qualitative/naturalistic and/*vs.* quantitative, 10, 23–24, 121, 328, 332, 412
rhetorical (criticism), 7–9, 23–24
sampling, 333, 403, 412, 418
scales, 333, 412–413, 420
survey, 23, 121, 225, 248, 267, 306, 333, 375, 391, 408
textual analysis, 23, 297, 299, 301, 305
Resistance/dissent, 22, 77, 115–117, 144, 163, 165–166, 172, 173(n), 184–185, 201, 206, 211(a), 251, 269, 279, 281, 292, 294, 305–306, 308, 313, 326, 347, 356–357, 370, 379–380, 394, 405
Rhetoric/rhetorical, 8, 11, 19, 70, 75–76, 81, 83, 94–95, 109, 139, 143, 155, 164, 166, 168, 190, 203, 229, 232, 249, 254, 266, 275–276, 302, 404
  methods, 10, 24
    rhetorical criticism, 8–9, 23
  studies/theory, 5, 7–8, 296
Rhode Island Coalition Against Domestic Violence (RICADV), 13, 179–182, 184–185, 196–202, 207–210, 212(n). *See also* Domestic Violence (DV)
Risk, 116, 170, 172, 182, 196, 205, 207, 227–228, 244, 274, 291, 299, 311, 325–326, 330, 334, 336–340, 357, 371, 387, 389, 393, 402, 406
  at-risk youth, 12, 118–119, 122, 125–126
    Kalam: Margins Write—A poetry program for at-risk youth, 12, 105, 116, 118, 125–126, 128–129, 132(n)
    Navajo Nation Middle and High School Youth Risk Behavior Survey (2003), 408
  management, 310, 327, 393
Rural, 223, 226, 228–229, 235, 241, 243, 245, 252–254, 300, 368, 372, 394
  redlining, 242–243
  –urban dialectic, 252–253

Scholar(s)/scholarly, 2–4, 92, 111–112, 147, 152, 158, 193, 231, 233. *See also*
Research/researcher(s); Research methods
  and (collaboration with) activists, 14, 25, 130, 182, 184–185, 188, 190–191, 194, 203, 206, 209–211
  communication (media/performance), 3, 7–10, 18–23, 27–28, 72–73, 95, 111, 141, 158, 167, 181, 188, 190, 210, 224, 226
  activism, 7–9, 18–20, 22, 24–25, 27–28
  public relations, 233, 249, 251
  scholar-activists/citizens, 11–12, 15, 18–21, 26, 28, 72, 167, 172, 181, 192, 203, 206, 210, 226, 229, 252, 264, 271, 281–283, 295, 297, 301, 308, 314–316, 330
  scholarly practices, 2, 18, 182, 194, 296–298, 302, 308, 330
  social movement (resource mobilization), 191, 193–195, 206
  U.S. Fulbright, 72, 87
School(s)/schooling, 87, 109–110, 122–123, 125–126, 143, 151, 154, 160–161, 164, 166, 171, 209, 270, 299, 369, 372, 382, 392, 402–404, 407–408, 411, 426(a), 428(n). *See also* Education; Teaching/teacher(s); University/universities/college(s)
Science, 249, 350
  activism, 30(n)
September 11, 2001, 252, 291
Service-learning, 16, 395(n). *See also* Education; Pedagogy; Reflection; Teaching/teacher(s)
  Alliance for Service-Learning in Education Reform, 389
  benefits of, 377, 389–392
  courses (components of), 110, 368, 376, 389–390
  pitfalls of, 377, 392–393
Sex/sexuality, 2, 11, 108–109, 117, 130, 184, 186, 297, 354, 372, 402, 426(a)
  commercial industry/work, 106–110, 115, 117, 129
  sexism, 11
  slavery/trafficking, 106, 117, 129–130

Index

Silence/silenced, 76, 116, 157, 246, 272, 309, 326, 330, 371, 404
Skill(s)/competency/competencies, 13, 25, 28, 112–113, 145, 185–186, 188, 192, 204, 206, 210, 230, 242, 251, 267, 292, 305, 308–311, 317, 332, 339, 345, 354, 367–368, 377, 383–385, 405, 411–412, 422–423
  communication, 7, 15, 21–22, 169, 192, 195, 207, 209, 300, 311–312, 315, 345, 375, 383–384, 390, 405
Slavery, 106–107, 266, 285(n)
Social change, 3, 9–11, 16, 23, 25–26, 142, 167, 189, 191, 211–212(a), 274–275, 279, 295, 297, 299, 308, 310–311, 367–368, 376, 389–390, 392, 394, 407.
  See also Status quo
  and communication (activism), 121, 167
  Communication for Social Change Consortium, 212(n)
  Organizing for Social Change course, 376, 385, 389, 391–392
Social construction(ism), 22, 229, 279, 294
Social justice, 8–9, 11–16, 25–26, 111–112, 141, 150–151, 163, 168–169 180, 211, 224, 226, 231, 233, 255, 265, 292, 301, 307–308, 310, 314–316, 326, 328, 383, 389–391, 393, 421. *See also* Communication activism for social justice research; Disparity; Equality; Fairness; Justice
  for animals, 226–229
  and communication (activism research), 3, 5–11, 14, 16–24, 26–28, 298–299, 311, 315, 377, 382–384
  and community-based performance (CBP), 142–144, 162
  and critical whiteness studies (CWS), 297, 301
  and intervention, 9–10, 16, 226, 292, 297–299
  Journal of Applied Communication Research, special issue on, 9
  movements/organizations, 141, 150–151, 254
  reclaiming public relations for, 14, 226, 249–252

Social learning theory, 16, 23, 377, 388
Social movement(s), 6, 13, 21, 180, 210, 230, 235–236, 249, 250–252, 274–275, 280–281
  actors/campaigns/organizations, 20, 181–182, 183–184, 186–188, 192, 196, 204, 232, 235, 245, 248, 254–255, 264, 275
  communication (participatory) and, 14, 181, 207, 209
  Gamson, scholar William A., 193
  (in) Global North (Britain and United States), 14, 181–182, 189, 191–194, 203, 209, 212(n)
  messages/practices/strategies, 185, 187–188, 195–196, 198–199, 207–208, 210
  MOVE, 271, 278, 285(n)
  research/theory, 13, 189, 191, 193–194, 229
Social/human services, 113, 124, 195, 200, 202, 367, 382, 394, 405, 408–409
Social support, 140, 143, 151, 154, 207, 278, 335, 367–368, 385, 403–405, 410
Sociology/sociologist(s), 5, 13, 22, 189, 231, 390
Solidarity, 24, 28, 93, 145, 265, 271, 273, 275–276, 281–284, 387, 393–394
Southeastern Broadcasting Company (SBC; pseudonym), 330–357
  Ethics at Work initiative at, 330–346, 348–358
  appreciative inquiry, 340–341
  stakeholders, 334, 336, 340, 342–344, 351, 358(a)
Speaking/speaker(s), 3, 13, 15, 116, 124, 132(n), 140, 148, 153, 161, 164, 171, 174(n), 185–186, 192, 205, 207–208, 211, 226, 235, 272, 277–279, 282, 302, 306, 309, 380, 385, 426(a), 428(n)
  for others, critique of, 15, 24, 130, 249, 252–254, 265, 270–272, 274, 281–282, 316
  with others, 15, 24, 263, 265, 272–276
  out/up, 82–83, 200, 207, 254, 278–279, 282, 330, 336–337, 341, 354
Stability, 97(n), 126, 253, 347
  –change dialectic, 356, 390

Stakeholder(s), 9, 12, 21, 25, 292, 295, 301, 307, 311–313, 316, 326–327, 329–330, 346, 348, 353, 358. *See also* Constituency/constituencies; Consumerism/customer(s); Southeastern Broadcasting Corporation (SBC); The Daywalka Foundation (TDF) activism, 29(n)
Status quo, 142, 205–206, 232, 303, 390, 392. *See also* Social change
Strategy/strategies/strategizing, 165, 167, 211, 234, 237–238, 241–243, 264, 282, 311, 374–375, 379, 412–413
  activist/campaign/collective actor/organizing/social movement, 181, 185–188, 192, 195–196, 202–204, 206, 265, 271, 274, 277, 280–283
  American Indian/Native American, 404–405, 409
  business/organizational, 325, 343, 345–346, 349, 359(a)
  communication, 14, 19, 24, 81–82, 94, 106, 180, 185–190, 195–198, 202, 208, 210–211, 211–212(a), 233, 235, 242, 246, 249, 265, 274, 277, 280–283, 295, 311, 315, 335, 371, 404
  countertrafficking, 117, 125
  framing, 82, 230, 244
  peacebuilding, 81–82, 84–85, 89–94
  performance/theatre, 143–144
  public relations, 229–230, 249
Student(s), 12–13, 16, 23, 25, 27, 106, 110, 116, 122, 126, 139, 142, 144, 150–151, 172, 234, 249, 251, 263, 297–298, 367–368, 373, 375–379, 383, 385, 388–394. *See also* Youth
  activism (communication), 13, 20, 30(n), 158–160, 168, 170
  American Indian (Ramah Navajo), 406, 410, 424
  Cypriot, 12, 83, 87–88, 98(n)
  and performance (*A Prayer for Sudan*; community-based performance course), 25, 141, 144–150, 158–160, 168–169, 171, 174(n)
Student Nonviolent Coordinating Committee, 275

Subjectivity, 121, 293–294, 346, 348
Substance intention/use, 17, 401–406, 412–413, 418, 418(t), 419–424, 425–426(a)
  alcohol/other recreational drugs, 17, 19, 107, 201, 224, 401–405, 407–408, 410, 417, 419, 425–427(a)
Sudan/Sudanese, 140, 144
  A Prayer for Sudan, 12, 140–142, 149–150, 156–158, 160–167, 169, 172–173, 173–174(n)
    news coverage of, 172, 174(n)
  al-Bashir, Sudan President Omar Hassan Ahmad, 145, 155, 163, 173(n)
  conflict/genocide in, 11–13, 27, 140, 146–147, 149–150, 156, 163–164, 168, 173–174(n)
  Comprehensive Peace Agreement (CPA), 166–167, 174(n)
  Darfur, 155, 160
    Darfur Matters, 160
  Dinka (language/tribe), 140, 148, 150, 154, 165, 171
  enslavement, murder, and rape in, 140, 144–145, 152, 165, 169–170
  Jihad/Jihadists in, 153, 161, 163–165, 173(n)
  North (government), 155, 164–167, 174(n)
  refugees, 13, 25, 139–141, 144–145, 159, 161, 169
  South (Sudanese), 11–13, 140–141, 145–146, 149, 151–155, 161–166, 172–173, 173–174(n)
  Sudanese Anglican Christian community members, 144, 148, 170–171
  Sudanese People's Liberation Army/Movement (SPLA/M), 165, 167, 173–174(n)
  The Lost Boys of Sudan (DVD), 144, 146
Superior(s)/subordinate(s), 303, 336–337, 341, 353, 356. *See also* Organization(s)/organizational; Work/worker(s)

Survey (method), 23, 121, 225, 248, 267, 306, 333, 375, 391, 408
  Zogby International, 225
Sustainability, 9, 14, 78, 87–88, 96, 113, 179, 312–313, 316–318, 329, 332, 343, 359(a), 381, 383–385
  agriculture/food, 14, 224, 226, 228, 248, 254–255
  of collective actors, 13, 181, 185–186, 188, 192–193, 195, 206, 208–209, 211(a), 269
  communication, 86, 185, 207, 209, 248, 380
    activism for social justice research, 27–28
  development, 224–225
  of interventions, 12, 354, 385, 410, 415, 421–423
  of scholar–activist collaborations, 181–182, 193, 209–210, 354, 357, 418
Symbol(s), 19, 23, 25, 75, 86, 111, 189, 229–230, 244, 255, 291–292, 409
  metaphors, 127, 236, 295

TalkBack sessions, 154–155
  for *A Prayer for Sudan*, 141, 151, 153, 155–157, 167, 171–172
Technology/technologies, 123, 165–166, 173(n), 234, 274–275, 299
Teaching/teacher(s), 122, 148–149, 172, 208, 249, 252, 265, 285(n), 312, 314, 372, 386–388, 390, 405, 409. *See also* Education; School(s)/Schooling/Service-learning
  activism, 29(n)
  classes/courses/components, 139, 165, 312, 375
    English-as-a-second-language, 161
    (community-based) performance (CBP), 141, 144–146, 149, 151, 159–160, 174(n)
    public relations, 235, 249
    Organizing for Social Change, 376, 385, 389, 391–392
  classroom, 26, 140, 146–147, 149, 296–297, 317, 389, 392, 404

Textual analysis, 23, 297, 299, 301, 305
The Daywalka Foundation (TDF), 12, 21, 106, 110, 127, 130, 132–133(n). *See also* Human trafficking (trafficking in persons; TIP)
  board of/executive director, 106, 111, 119, 128, 132(n)
  focus on dialogue, 106, 117, 119–121, 124–125
  methodological approach, 121–122
  programs, 117–126
    criminal justice and prosecution capacity building, 123–124
    Kalam: Margins Write—A poetry program for at-risk youth, 12, 105, 116, 118, 125–126, 128–129, 132(n)
    National Consultation on Better Legal Response to Human Trafficking, 12, 118, 124–125, 131–132
    scholarship programs for at-risk youth, 119, 122
  stakeholders, 117–119, 121, 124
    engagement model, 118(f), 119
    theoretical influences on, 119–121
    Women's and Children's Security Resources Centers (WCSRC), 117–118, 122–123
Theatre, 142–144, 147, 154, 157. *See also* Performance
  and activism, 162
  applied, 143
  community-based participatory (CBP), 12, 141–144, 158, 162
  representational/traditional, 143, 147
  social, 139, 143, 154
Theory/theories/perspectives, 2–3, 8, 10, 13, 22–23, 89, 93, 112, 118–121, 180–182, 193, 198, 201, 226, 245, 274, 296, 298, 302, 317, 327, 331, 348, 356, 377, 410
  activism, 4
  charity, 16, 282, 377, 382–384, 387, 391, 393
  communication, 6, 181, 189–190, 207, 296, 298, 373, 415

and social justice (activism research), 5–10, 16–28, 179, 226, 297–299, 315, 317, 382–384, 421
community-based participatory research (CBPR) model, 407, 413, 414(f), 415–417, 421–423
community-based performance (CBP), 143, 146
conflict/peace, 89–92, 122
  enemy system theory, 78–79
  theory of parallel tracks, 92
  transformative peacebuilding theory, 12, 22, 90–91
critical pedagogy, 16, 377, 387
critical rhetoric, 8
critical theory, 8–9, 22–23, 251
critical whiteness studies (CWS), 15, 22, 296–299
cultural embeddedness, 405, 411
cultural studies, 7–9, 189, 293
development (communication), 12, 111–113, 114(f), 115–177
dialectical, 119, 127–131, 252–253, 346–351, 354–355, 357, 390
dialogue, 12–13, 15–16, 22, 89–90, 94, 119–121, 125, 145, 156, 162–163, 189, 191, 193, 293–295, 298, 328, 330, 357, 380, 391
ethics, 265, 310–311, 317, 327–329, 346–351, 357–358
  ethical (organizational) engagement model, 16, 328–330, 357
  social contract theory, 327–328
family resiliency building, 411
feminist, 16, 22, 329, 384–386
framing, 13, 22, 117, 187–188, 195, 225, 229–231, 243–244
innovations
  diffusion of innovations model, 23, 242, 390
  subterfuge of, 23, 238, 242–249
intercultural communication, 119
  contact hypothesis, 119
  intercultural work group communication theory, 23, 415–416
matrix of domination *vs.* matrix of performance resistance, 141–142, 144, 162–163, 166

media–movement interaction models, 185
participatory communication, 13–14, 22, 181–182, 189–193, 202–203, 207
power, 191–192, 203–208, 211, 229–230, 271, 292–295, 416–417
  empowerment, 9, 12–13, 16, 22, 24, 28, 112, 115, 162, 181, 189–191, 203, 205–207, 209–211, 271, 377–383, 411
racial subject, 293–295
social construction(ism), 22, 229–232, 294
social learning theory, 16, 23, 377, 388
speaking *with vs. for* others, 15, 24, 130, 252–254, 265, 270–272, 316
trickle-up, 182, 211
trafficking in persons (TIP) stakeholder models, 113, 114(f), 117, 118(f), 119
Third-person-perspective research, 7, 21, 372, 404. *See also* First-person-perspective research
Training/trainer(s), 15–16, 27, 95, 111, 115, 117, 121–125, 130, 163, 165, 180, 184–185, 192–195, 198, 202, 207, 235, 295, 298, 300, 303, 308–309, 311, 315, 317, 328, 332, 339, 344–345, 349, 351–352, 355, 372–375, 384, 386–388, 392, 407, 409, 411, 413. *See also* Consulting; Facilitation; Workshop(s);
  diversity, 292, 303, 309, 311–313, 315–316
  job, 367–368, 372, 377, 394, 408
Transcription/transcript(s), 147, 149, 169, 196, 304–305, 409
Trust, 74, 77, 117, 119, 125, 130, 170, 188, 192, 224, 292, 304, 306, 313, 355, 380. *See also* Rapport
  in communication activism for social justice research, 24–25, 283
  of scholars, 17, 25, 148, 354, 407, 415, 421
Turkey/Turkish, 70, 73–75, 79, 81–82, 95
Turkish Cypriots, 11–12, 70, 72–86, 88–91, 93–96, 97(n)

Index 469

United Nations (UN), 11–12, 70, 71(f), 73–76, 82, 83–86, 89, 92, 96, 98(n), 108, 141, 153, 155
  Boutros-Ghali, Secretary General Boutros, 75
  General Assembly, 98(n), 224
  International Day of Peace (Peace Day), 83–86, 89–90, 98(n)
  Palermo Protocol, 107, 123
  UN Day, 85–87, 98(n)
United States (U.S.), 1–2, 11–15, 21, 28, 72, 82, 84, 87, 93–94, 96, 110–112, 127, 141, 145, 156–157, 166, 171, 181, 185, 188, 191–192, 194, 225–226, 244, 250, 253, 264, 266–267, 276, 279–280, 282–283, 285(n), 291–293, 299–300, 325–328, 330, 367–370, 394
  activism/social movements, 182, 191–194, 202–203, 209
  agencies/institutions
    U.S. Agency for International Development, 96
    U.S. Census Bureau, 369
    U.S. Department of Health and Human Services (DHSS), 180, 196, 401
      Indian Health Service (HIS), 401–402, 408
    U.S. Department of State, 107–108, 110–111
    U.S. Foreign Service Institute, 111
    Hall, anthropologist Edward T., 112
    U.S. Library of Congress, 5
    U.S. National Intelligence, 172
    U.S. Senate, 239, 250
    U.S. Supreme Court, 266–267, 269
  and American Indians/Native Americans, 401, 403, 408
  Bush, President George W., 141, 155, 228, 268
  Carter, President Jimmy, 264
  confined animal feeding operations (CAFOs)/(factory) farms in, 226–228, 239, 245, 254
  poverty/poor/welfare in, 369–370, 372
  regions/states/cities, 14, 16–17, 19, 21, 25, 27, 141, 146, 179, 181, 196–201, 205, 223–228, 232–239, 240(t), 243–246, 248, 254–255, 263–264, 267–271, 273–274, 276–280, 282–284, 284–285(n), 367–376, 378–382, 388, 390, 393–394, 401–402, 407–411, 413, 415–418, 422, 424, 428(n)
  Sudanese refugees in, 13, 141, 146, 148–149, 153, 161, 170, 174(n)
  and (counter)trafficking, 12, 108, 124, 129, 132, 132(n)
universities/colleges, 2, 141, 150, 327
University/universities/college(s), 2, 5, 8, 13, 16–17, 25–26, 110, 124, 141, 166, 171, 234–235, 270, 284–285(n), 296–297, 303, 317, 367–368, 373, 375–376, 378–380, 383, 388, 391–392, 394, 402, 408–411, 415–418, 422, 428(n). *See also* School(s)/schooling
  and communication activism for social justice research, 20, 26
  institutional review boards (IRBs), 303, 410
  students, 13, 20, 23, 25, 86–87
  tenure, 26, 132(n), 299
Urban, 14, 108, 121, 252–254, 331
  –rural dialectic, 252–253

Value(s), 12, 16, 19–20, 93, 97(n), 115, 120, 183, 192, 206, 211–212(a), 227, 253, 283, 301–303, 315, 328, 330–336, 338–349, 351, 359(a), 405–406, 412, 417, 424(a)
Violence, 205, 207, 266, 292, 311. *See also* Domestic violence (DV)
  in Cyprus, 11–12, 70, 74, 79, 81, 89, 98(n)
  in Iraq, 1
  in (South) Sudan, 13, 141, 149, 165, 174(n)
Voice, 9, 126, 130–131, 154, 184, 202, 224, 243, 246, 251, 265, 271, 279, 282–283, 294, 345, 354, 356, 380, 389, 391
  citizen/marginalized/social movement, 185, 188, 237, 241, 250, 254, 371, 387
  "giving," critique of, 15, 24, 130, 271
  and performance (*A Prayer for Sudan*), 142–143, 157, 163

Volunteer(s)/volunteerism, 25, 161, 238, 312, 345, 368, 373–376, 378, 381, 383–390, 393

War(s), 90, 115, 157, 205, 285(n)
  in Afghanistan, 1
  in Cyprus, 69, 73–75, 81, 87
  in Iraq, 1, 15, 31–32, 250
  Persian Gulf, 250
  in Sudan, 140, 146, 149, 152, 163–164, 173–174(n)
  World War II, 8, 78, 111, 140
Wealth, 7, 228, 267, 300, 369, 372, 389, 393–394. *See also* Poverty/poor
Welfare, 195, 370, 374, 389. See also Poverty/poor
Whiteness, 15, 291–293, 296–299, 301–302, 314. *See also* Privilege/privileging
  critical, 297–299, 301, 314
    studies (CWS), 15, 22, 293–294, 296–299, 301, 314, 317
Women/girls, 2, 110, 144, 147–148, 184, 250, 252, 268, 282, 297, 299, 307, 326, 372, 375, 385, 388, 406
  activism/movement, 30(n), 184, 189, 196–197, 202
  and domestic violence (DV), 181, 184–185, 204
  and human trafficking, 105–110, 116, 119, 122, 132(n)
  and poverty, 370–371
  in Sudan/Sudanese, 140, 148, 152, 159–161, 166, 171, 174(n)
  Women's and Children's Resource Centers (WCRC), 118, 122–123
Work/worker(s), 9, 16, 20–21, 26, 83, 97(n), 106–111, 117, 122–123, 126, 154, 164–165, 171, 184–185, 190, 198, 200, 205, 209, 212(a), 234–236, 252, 267, 291–292, 297–298, 300, 303–306, 308–309, 313, 326–327, 330, 332, 349, 353, 357, 369–371, 373–374, 377, 379, 381, 383–388, 391–394. *See also* Employment/employee(s)/employer(s); Superior(s)/subordinate(s)
  activism, 30(n)
  Ethics at Work Initiative at Southeastern Broadcasting Corporation (SBC), 16, 328, 330–346, 348–355, 357–358, 358–359(a)
Workshop(s), 21, 72, 82, 88, 194–195, 312. *See also* Facilitation; Training/trainer(s)
World, 4–5, 9, 12, 19, 23, 26, 140, 150–151, 153, 157, 160–163, 169–170, 172, 173(n), 210, 227–228, 230, 250, 252–253, 255, 294, 298, 315, 317, 327, 332, 369, 374
  activism, 4
  developing/Third, 16, 112–113, 116, 126, 212(n), 374, 385, 387
  worldviews, 109, 116–117, 120–121, 124, 132, 160, 186, 206, 208, 211

Youth, 188. *See also* Children; Student(s)
  activism/movement, 30(n), 189
  American Indian (Ramah Navajo), 17, 402, 405–407, 409–411, 413, 417, 423–424
    Navajo Nation Middle and High School Youth Risk Behavior Survey (2003), 408
  at-risk/marginalized, 12, 105, 116, 118(f), 118–119, 122, 125–126
  in Cyprus, 76, 86–87, 96

CPSIA information can be obtained at www.ICGtesting.com
Printed in the USA
LVOW121151241011

251816LV00001B/12/P

9 781612 890623